ECONOMETRICS

SAMUEL CAMERON

The **McGraw·Hill** Companies

London	Boston	Burr Ridge, IL	Dubuque, IA	Madison, WI	New York
San Francisco	St. Louis	Bangkok	Bogotá	Caracas	Kuala Lumpur
Lisbon	Madrid	Mexico City	Milan	Montreal	New Delhi
Santiago	Seoul	Singapore	Sydney	Taipei	Toronto

Econometrics

Samuel Cameron

ISBN 10: 0-07-710428-5
ISBN 13: 978-0-07-710428-3

Published by McGraw-Hill Education
Shoppenhangers Road
Maidenhead
Berkshire
SL6 2QL
Telephone: 44 (0) 1628 502 500
Fax: 44 (0) 1628 770 224
Website: www.mcgraw-hill.co.uk

British Library Cataloguing in Publication Data
A catalogue record for this book is available from the British Library

Library of Congress Cataloging in Publication Data
The Library of Congress data for this book has been applied for from the Library of Congress

Acquisitions Editor: Kirsty Reade
Development Editor(s): Emily Jefferson and Catriona Watson
Marketing Director: Petra Skytte
Senior Production Editor: Eleanor Hayes

Text Design by SCW Ltd
Cover design by Fielding Design Ltd
Typeset by Keytec Typesetting Ltd
Printed and bound in Spain by Mateu Cromo Artes Graficas SA

Brief Table of Contents

Detailed Table of Contents

Preface

There are already a large number of textbooks in econometrics so some reasons are needed to justify another one. This book is based on my experience of teaching econometrics, and being asked for help from various people, with regression output to interpret and models to build, for over 20 years. This has led me to the conclusion that a new approach to the subject might be useful in dispelling the fear and confusion that surround this subject.

My particular interest in this book is the audience of (sometimes reluctant) undergraduate students for whom econometrics is compulsory and those (usually PhD students in economics) who have taken some econometrics in the past but are finding it very hard to relate this knowledge to their own research work or articles they need to read. The book should also be useful for those who have chosen undergraduate options particularly for forms of assessment based on collecting data and submitting written reports on the results.

I have been inspired by the basic fact that the people mentioned above do not seem to have been able to find what they want in the existing books. This has come as something of a surprise to me as for years I have been recommending books which seemed to me to contain all the relevant knowledge in a suitable format, but have increasingly been met with a negative reaction to these books.

The problem seems to be that the existing books do make perfect sense *if* you already have a good knowledge of the subject and a fairly solid background in statistics.

This book starts with the assumption that you know nothing about the subject but are at least interested in economics, or other social sciences, and may have some background in basic statistics. The approach I have taken differs in a number of ways from what is usually the case in econometrics texts. I now elaborate on these.

The emphasis in this book is on econometrics in terms of why it exists, and how it is used in daily practice, rather than just as a set body of rules which have to be learnt. This daily practice involves three things – doing econometrics 'as in collecting data and running regressions', writing these up into some kind of report and reading such reports written by others. I have attempted to make most chapters of this book an integrated treatment of all three aspects.

I have taken as the starting point the fact that most people's interest in this subject stems from a need to analyse data that requires them to have tools to do so. Many econometrics texts seem to start from the opposite point of view, which is that econometrics is a branch of statistics, which is of interest purely for its own sake and requires some data as a vehicle to use the tools. Following this principle, the idea of probability and hypothesis testing is introduced in the context of a discussion of types of data rather than as a separate area of formal study.

This text contains relatively little mathematics and also has fewer graphical illustrations than is conventional. Despite this, the book is not intended to be a 'watering down' of the subject, as it does address the fundamental issues encountered in applied econometric research. The reduction of graphical material is deliberate became I have found the use of two-dimensional diagrams to illustrate the concepts of econometrics tends to lead to later mistakes in thinking in the context of a multi-dimensional data matrix. It would be better, conceptually, if the whole subject was approached in terms of matrices but this does not seem feasible for a general audience. I only provide graphs of actual data-series occasionally since these do not provide that much insight into a regression model. The earlier chapters feature a number of time series where the pattern is fairly obvious without a graph and the end-of-chapter exercises invite students to draw graphs where appropriate.

The mathematical notation, which is used in this book, has been chosen with the student in mind. I have stuck to the English alphabet in describing parameters – hence we have b and b hat rather than the more usual beta and beta hat. There are various reasons for this. One is that the student is likely to be more used to this notation (in their micro-, macro-, and maths for economists courses) as a way of writing down models algebraically. A further reason for not using beta is that some software packages present beta coefficients as part of their default output (and some also use the b notation for regression parameters). Using the term beta for regression parameters, in the econometrics texts, leads to students getting confused when they move to computer output.

I have taken the step all through of using a 0 subscript for the intercept and subscripts from 1 to k for the parameters in an OLS regression. This is because numbering up from 1 starting with the intercept would lead the struggling reader to be more confused by finding variable X_1 attached to parameter b_2 and so on.

I have paid particular attention to the order of the material covered here. All econometrics texts cover much the same basic topics and this one is no exception. However, the material comes in a bewildering array of orders, in different books, which far exceeds the diversity found in a core micro- or macroeconomics text at the same level. Some books feature subjects at very different locations in the book. I have strived to produce an order that forms a coherent and stimulating flow for the intended readership. This means that some subjects are given a chapter to themselves when they do not really warrant this in terms of their conceptual importance. The chapter division and section divisions used are intended to help the continual reinforcement of the learning experience. Thus we have a whole chapter on dummy variables when this is something that could really be disposed of in a few pages if one has a strong grip on the subject. The dummy variables chapter, like most other chapters, is used not just to instruct in the topic of the chapter but also to help build the reader's confidence in seeing some sort of developing pattern to what they are learning. We thus have some repetition of how to interpret results as we go through the book.

This book adopts a direct conversational style in addressing the reader, often dealing with issues in terms of questions that might be asked by the puzzled reader. It also seeks to assist the reader by reminding them which earlier topics may be useful in assisting them on the current topic.

The use of illustrative material is different in this book. I have tried to strike a balance between providing a variety of topics (including sex and drugs and rock and roll) which show how widely econometrics can be applied and avoiding confusion by showing people too many different results.

In my experience students learn econometrics more efficiently when they see techniques being applied to data they have already seen rather than every new topic having an entirely new data set. In teaching econometrics to classes of 100+ (mostly reluctant) students I have resorted to the extreme strategy of using the same data set for the computer class exercises. This does seem to produce remarkable improvements in customer satisfaction among other things. It is much less interesting for the instructor and there may be some kind of trade-off between teacher boredom and student comprehension in this particular subject.

Such an extreme strategy, of using the same data all the way through, would not be acceptable in a book but I have taken the same sort of approach by using a limited set of data sets for the illustrative results based on analysis of data, which is available to the reader. For example, non-linear functional forms are illustrated by estimation on the same data that was used earlier to compute partial correlation coefficients, bivariate regression and multiple regressions. The same data set is later used to look at the results of proposed solutions to multicollinearity.

The illustrative results are also used to demonstrate to the novice econometrician that things do not always work out as perfectly as they should and we might even get some very strange looking results. This leads on to an emphasis on how much results do change when you change the specification. This is a very obvious point, and one that should be obvious from the existing texts, but my experience suggests it is only really grasped by repetition and more likely personal experience of doing regressions. To this end, I have provided end-of-chapter exercises which are integrated with the text. These often ask the reader to attempt different equations on data for which results have already been displayed in the text.

In the text I have given more background on the underlying rationale behind any equation than is normally given, as this lack of context often seems to add to confusion. I have largely resisted the temptation to quote results of estimated equations from published literature as people seem to find it hard to digest these shorn of the context in which they were originally presented.

As an alternative, I have developed a template (shown in Appendix 1) suitable for summarizing the essence of a published paper. Most chapters contain examples of how to write such summaries with additional background material on the articles chosen. To get the most out of this, the reader would really need to obtain copies of the source articles. However, this approach is easily configurable to the needs of a particular econometrics module. It would be possible to make the act of filling in the template, using different articles of the instructor's choosing, a part of the course assessment.

Guided Tour

Learning Objectives
Each chapter opens with a set of learning objectives identifying the key concepts that will be covered within the chapter

Introduction
This sets the scene for the reader and introduces them to the issues that will be addressed in the chapter

Figures and Tables
Each chapter provides a number of figures and tables to illustrate and summarize important concepts

Review Studies
Review studies allow the reader to understand the essence of a published paper and a template for these has been provided in Appendix 1

Conclusion
This briefly reviews and reinforces the main topics you will have covered in each chapter to ensure that you have acquired a solid understanding of key topics

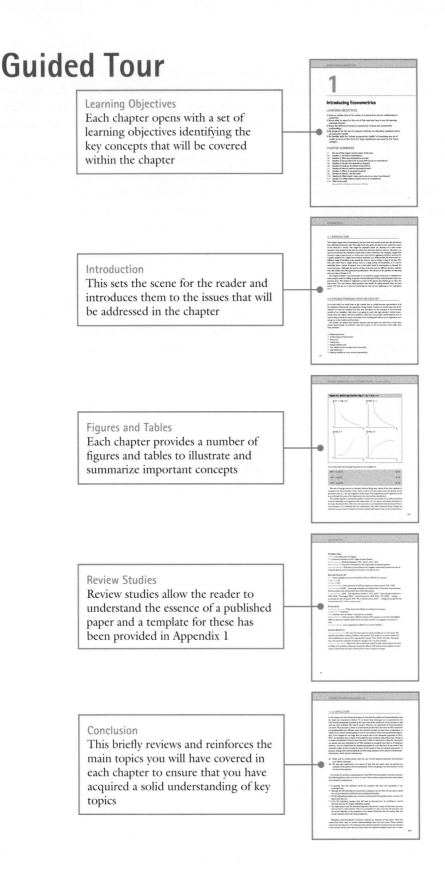

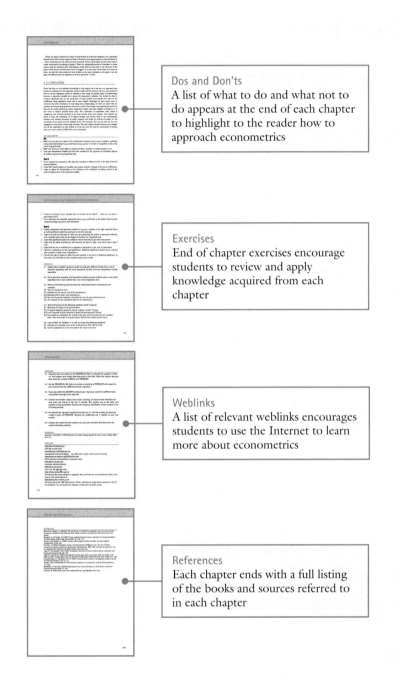

Dos and Don'ts
A list of what to do and what not to do appears at the end of each chapter to highlight to the reader how to approach econometrics

Exercises
End of chapter exercises encourage students to review and apply knowledge acquired from each chapter

Weblinks
A list of relevant weblinks encourages students to use the Internet to learn more about econometrics

References
Each chapter ends with a full listing of the books and sources referred to in each chapter

TECHNOLOGY TO ENHANCE LEARNING AND TEACHING

Visit www.mcgraw-hill.co.uk/textbooks/cameron today

Online Learning Centre (OLC)

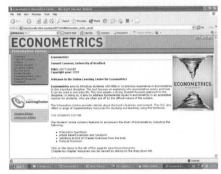

After completing each chapter, log on to the supporting Online Learning Centre website. Take advantage of the study tools offered to reinforce the material you have read in the text, and to develop your knowledge of econometrics in a fun and effective way.

Resources for students include:

✦ Commentaries on Existing Papers with Missing Words to be Completed by Students
✦ Self Assessment Quizzes on Selected Papers
✦ 'Guided' Student Homework Projects

Also available for lecturers:

✦ Lecturer's Manual
✦ Power Point Slides
✦ Links to Further Illustrative Journal Articles
✦ Multiple Choice Questions
✦ Marking Notes for 'Guided' Student Projects
✦ Specimen Exam Papers
✦ Mid-term Review Tests
✦ Answers to 'Guided' Student Homework Projects

FOR LECTURERS: PRIMIS CONTENT CENTRE

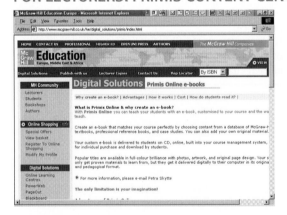

If you need to supplement your course with additional cases or content, create a personalized e-Book for your students. Visit www.primiscontentcenter.com or e-mail primis_euro@mcgraw-hill.com for more information.

STUDY SKILLS

We publish guides to help you study, research, pass exams and write essays, all the way through your university studies.

Visit www.openup.co.uk/ss/ to see the full selection and get £2 discount by entering promotional code study when buying online!

COMPUTING SKILLS

If you'd like to brush up on your Computing skills, we have a range of titles covering MS Office applications such as Word, Excel, PowerPoint, Access and more.

Get a £2 discount off these titles by entering the promotional code app when ordering online at www.mcgraw-hill.co.uk/app

Acknowledgements

Our thanks go to the following reviewers for their comments at various stages in the text's development:

Keshab Bhattarai, University of Hull
Peter Dawson, University of Bath
Ramesh Durbarry, University of Nottingham
Francesca Flamini, University of Glasgow
Richard Godfrey, University of Wales Institute
Christiaan Heij, Erasmus University
Hilary Ingham, University of Lancaster
Hugh Metcalf, University of Newcastle
Joanne McGarry, University of Birmingham
Jean-Yves Pitarakis, University of Southampton
Mike Pokorny, London Metropolitan University
Geoff Pugh, University of Staffordshire
Hedley Rees, University of Bristol
John Wildman, University of Newcastle
Ulrich Woitek, University of Munich

Thanks also go to the McGraw-Hill team – Kirsty Reade, Emily Jefferson, Catriona Watson and Eleanor Hayes.

1

Introducing Econometrics

LEARNING OBJECTIVES

▓ Have an outline idea of the nature of econometrics and its relationship to economics

▓ Know what to expect in the rest of this book and how to use the learning materials therein

▓ Know the difference between econometric method and econometric methodology

▓ Be prepared for the use of computer software in estimating equations based on economic models

▓ Be familiar with the 'instant econometrics toolkit' of examining any set of results in terms of the 'three S's' (sign, significance and size) for the 'focus' variables

CHAPTER SUMMARY

1.1 THE ROLE OF THIS CHAPTER AND THE NATURE OF THIS BOOK

This book has a strong pedagogic style geared towards undergraduate study. The writing is addressed to the reader and a question and answer format is used on many occasions. It is intended, however, that the book can be read through as a whole to give a general overview of the subject in terms of not just tricks and techniques, but also the meanings that economists attach to econometrics and the role that it plays in their subject. This should be particularly useful to the PhD student or beginning researcher who has had some econometrics training, in the past, but is not a specialist in the field. The book is a self-contained course, which is designed to be flexible in use. There are additional materials available on the book website particularly with respect to examination and self-assessment.

This chapter begins with a set of ten questions (Sections 1.2–1.11) about econometrics and my attempts to answer them. These questions and answers are designed to get across quickly an understanding of the nature of econometrics and how to go about studying it. A full understanding of how to 'do' econometrics and the acquisition of the tools required necessitates study of the remaining chapters. I will turn to the matter of how to read the chapters, and in which order, in Section 1.9 below. The question and answer format of this chapter is also useful for those who are impatient with introductions, as it should make it easier to find those bits of the introductory material in which they are most interested.

By the end of this chapter you should be aware that the study of econometrics involves three basic skills: reading econometric papers written by other people, using data to estimate equations using a computer, and being able to write reports or articles based on these computer estimates. This book attempts to develop all of these skills.

Most of the chapters begin with the explanation of a technical method and indicate how one would use it. Examples are then given of the method using actual data sets, which have been made available in the form of standard Excel files (*.XLS) on the website. A list of these data sets and a brief description of their contents is given in Appendix 2. The chapters then move on to further developments of the methods introduced and to problems that have to be borne in mind when using them.

Late in most chapters, there appears a pair of econometric papers by other authors. Use of these review study panels should also help you advance in being able to write up your own econometric work. Additional support for this will be given throughout the chapters and is reinforced by the appearance, at the end of the chapters, of a list of 'Dos and Don'ts' to remind you of the most important points.

There are a short number of exercises at the end of the chapters. These are integrated with the text in that they refer to the examples given in the chapter and, in some cases, they require re-estimation of the equations given in the chapter using the Excel files provided on the website. Some of the questions given are intended to provoke discussion rather than having 'correct' or definitive yes/no answers.

Before we move on to the first question, it may be helpful to instructors if the precise nature of the review study panels is made clear. I have decided not to include any actual results from the papers reviewed in the panels, thus the panels are purely summaries. They are something more than abstracts as they distil the contents of papers according to a strict set of categories. Actual results are not included for several reasons:

▶ A blank template is made available (in Appendix 1) if the instructor or student wishes to use different studies to those I have chosen.

▶ Assuming people do wish to use the studies I have chosen, the absence of the results will hopefully create an incentive to go and read the sources to check whether they agree with the summary I have given.

▶ The absence of tables of results to refer to is intended to highlight the clarity of the summaries. That is, the amount of information to be taken in is deliberately reduced so that the crucial elements involved in making a summary are highlighted. It is hoped that the reader will be encouraged to go and make some summaries of their own, in this style, even if it is felt that the studies I have used are sufficiently interesting and appropriate for the purposes of a particular course.

Ideally, a student should read the source articles in the review studies or use the blank template (in Appendix 1) to summarize ones given to them by their lecturer. A supplement to these studies is given on the website in the form of a set of one-page articles from the anthologies section of the *Atlantic Economic Journal*. The articles are reproduced along with a set of questions. This work is appropriate for those who have reached Chapter 7. One of the studies is reproduced at the end of Chapter 7.

1.2 QUESTION 1: SO WHAT IS ECONOMETRICS?

The short answer to this would be 'equations'. The slightly longer answer is 'equations derived from data'. Let us turn to the full answer.

The word 'econometrics' is a combined term for the application of measurement (metrics) to the concepts used in economics. There are parallels in, for example, biology, sociology and psychology to the fields of biometrics, sociometrics and psychometrics. When statistical methods began to be applied to history, particularly economic history, this was known as cliometrics.

These various types of '-etrics' do have some things in common. Unsurprisingly they all now involve the use of a computer to analyse data. However, they differ in a number of respects, such as:

(i) The names given to statistical concepts.
(ii) The popularity of particular techniques. In basic econometrics the technique used is that of ordinary least squares (OLS) regression. This is often known as 'regression analysis'. A regression is a statistical equation in which a variable on the left-hand side is 'regressed' on the variables on the right-hand side. The usual practice is to call the variables on the right-hand side 'independent' variables and the one on the left the 'dependent' variable.
(iii) The type of data used: the most obvious distinction here is between experimental and non-experimental data.
(iv) The conventions about rules for hypothesis testing: that is, scholars in different fields may differ on what margin of error is acceptable when coming to a conclusion.
(v) Methodology.

It will be useful at this point to go a little further into the third (type of data) and fifth (methodology) of these, beginning with the issue of methodology and then moving on to data. Following this, we have a preliminary discussion of testing.

METHOD VERSUS METHODOLOGY

It is important to make a distinction between methodology and method. The method of econometrics is to estimate OLS or more sophisticated equations but this is *not* the methodology. Methodology is the philosophy of how one goes about conducting a piece of research. Or, in simpler terms, methodology is a point of view on how things should be done within a field of scientific research.

In econometrics, the general methodology is one of deriving a hypothesis from a model then collecting data to test this on and looking at the results to see if the tests of the model support the most important hypotheses generated from it. This three-stage approach can be summarized as follows:

Hypothesis > Tests > Appraisal of results

This is a 'positivist' view of how scientific research is done. It may help to point out what the opposite approach would be. This would be the 'exploratory data analysis' methodology where we simply collect some data about the research topic and start to investigate it to see what useful information might be derived from it. This 'inductivist' (as opposed to the 'deductivism' of positivism) approach may share some methods with the positivist econometrics we are going to be dealing with, but the use and interpretation of the results is different.

The general positivist methodology under which econometrics developed was a distillation of the 'logical positivism' of the philosopher Karl Popper in a famous essay by Milton Friedman in 1953. There are two main ideas that we can pull out of this essay that will help to illuminate methodological debates in econometrics that are going on today, and will continue to go on. These are:

▲ The 'as if' postulate
▲ Falsification

The 'as if' postulate justifies the use of models that are deliberately unrealistic. Friedman said that we treat consumers and producers 'as if' they were maximizing utility or profits. Perhaps the most notable feature that separates most econometrics from other uses of statistics is the reliance on this 'as if' assumption. The interpretation of demand curves and supply of labour curves is based on the premise that the individuals in the data set are all maximizing their utility. They may make mistakes in trying to be efficient but the assumption is that, on average, the mistakes they make will cancel out.

The important point about the 'as if' assumption for understanding the uses made of econometrics is that it brings in the use of untested assumptions. So, when we come to testing hypotheses we are testing the predictions of the models. We are *not* testing the assumptions on which those predictions are based. Hence it is always possible that the results, which seem to confirm or reject our hypothesis, arose for some other reason than the inherent accuracy of the hypothesis.

It may be that some of the untested assumptions can never be tested, as it is impossible to formulate them in such a way that they can be tested. They may also be so fundamental to the core ideas of the discipline (in this case economics) that they are maintained in the face of all contradiction and thus there is no point in testing them (see Cross, 1982, for a discussion of these issues with respect to macroeconomics).

I have just expressed this in quite an extreme way in order to make a point. However, one can find relevant examples in the literature on demand for goods. Economists are very reluctant to leave prices out of an econometric demand equation, even if there is little evidence to support its presence, while marketing academics are prepared to drop the price variable, as their primary focus is on the role of advertising (see references in Cameron, 1998). What we are saying here is that researchers in different topic areas have different 'maintained hypotheses', which will be untested unless there is some major crisis in the discipline.

We now turn to falsification as this has further bearing on the matter of testing hypotheses. Popper argued that scientific research is not about proof or confirmation of one's hypotheses, rather it is about looking for evidence that rejects the hypotheses. His famous example is the proposition that 'all swans are white'. If we go out to look for all the swans in the world, and find some more white ones, then this does not mean we have proved the proposition. Instead, we should see the proposition as one that is not yet falsified. If we then find a black swan the proposition will be falsified and will have to be replaced with a reformulated proposition that is more qualified than the one we started with. For example, if the black swan was found in Sweden the hypothesis might be that 'all non-Swedish swans are white'.

One equivalent of a black swan in econometrics would be regular occurrences of 'wrong' looking demand curves. Let us say, for example, that we discover demand curves which seem to slope upwards in price and have negative income elasticity. This seems to contradict the underlying premises of economics and is therefore termed an anomaly. Revisions to theory may be able to deal with the anomaly. For example, the concepts of a Geffen good or a Veblen good in demand theory are able to generate upward-sloping demand curves.

The example given was an anomaly in the sense that something that should have happened did not, namely, an expected relationship was not found in the data but instead no relationship or the wrong one was found. A common anomaly in conducting research is the finding of no relationship whatsoever between the variables.

If a discipline was completely sealed off from the 'real' world then the 'unexpected relationship' anomaly could not be tested as there would never be any reason to include variables that are not expected to appear for theoretical reasons. However, unexplained relationships do come to be tested because when they have been observed, perhaps by journalists or workers in an industry, they present a challenge to the econometric researcher to see if they can be explained in some way if they are not simply rejected by the data.

In order to be able to talk about the notion of a proposition being 'rejected by the data' as I have just done, I need to give some outline idea of the method of testing that underlies the methodology of econometrics.

METHODS OF TESTING

Econometrics uses some of the same techniques as other disciplines, such as sociometrics, but is distinguished by the fact that its main technique is the OLS estimation of a multiple regression equation. This requires something more than just measurement. Specifically, it involves the testing of hypotheses about the relationship between the variables we have measured. Usually the testing takes place using an equation in which there is a focus variable that we think has some kind of connection with the dependent variable. Other variables will also appear as controls, as we shall see when we get into the examples in the main body of this book.

My approach to hypothesis testing in this book is to focus on the three S's:

▲Sign
▲Significance
▲Size

It is a good idea that you discipline yourself to immediately look at these three things every time you see some econometric results. Here is a brief explanation of what you need to do.

Sign

The most obvious example is a simple demand function where some measure of quantity is regressed on measures of price and income to obtain estimates of the impact of changes in these variables on quantity demanded. We would look at the signs of the variables. The usual expectations about demand curves is that the impact of price is negative and the impact of real income is positive. So the first thing we will do when we have to read a set of statistical results is check whether the table has negative signs in front of any of the figures reported. Computer packages (and people who write econometric reports and articles) will not put positive signs in front of the numbers which are positive so you should automatically assume that these are positive unless you see a negative in front of them.

Significance

The idea of statistical significance is introduced properly in the next chapter. However, an outline grasp of the idea is needed before we wrap up this brief explanation of what econometrics is. The use of the word 'significance' in econometrics derives from its use in the statistical theory of hypothesis testing. That is, a hypothesis – for example, that the growth of the money stock determines the rate of price inflation – cannot be found to be either absolutely true or untrue. It is true or false to some extent. The hypothesis has to be compared with the likelihood of some alternative happening. This requires an assumption about the distribution of chance events. Econometrics has historically tended to use a comparison of the results we find with chance outcomes assumed to follow the normal distribution, which shall be reviewed in the next chapter.

Size

As you will discover, size would usually be based on elasticities, e.g. is the effect of price on demand inelastic (less than one in absolute terms) or elastic (more than one in absolute terms)? Calculating elasticities from econometric work is a fairly simple matter until we get to the use of logit and probit models in Chapter 8.

Once we have established the sign and statistical significance of a parameter such as the impact of price on demand we will need to go further to check whether our result is of much interest.

If it turns out that our relationship is extremely small then it may be difficult to conclude that it is important. However, one always has to be cautious in making statements about what is small because this depends on the problem in which you are interested. If we are dealing with the income elasticity of demand for a product and it turns out that it is 0.00001, this seems to suggest such an enormous amount of income required to increase demand that it may as well be ignored. However, if we are dealing with an equation to predict something like car crashes, which may cause serious injuries and loss of life, then a relatively small elasticity in response to a policy such as increasing fines for speeding could be large enough to warrant interest. In this case, the econometric results would need to be an input into a wider cost–benefit analysis before we can reasonably decide if the size of the results is worthy of interest.

As indicated above, examination of the three S's might not need to be applied to every result in our results, or those of a published article, as there may be a large number of variables included which are not of direct interest to us. We may only want to look at the 'focus' variables; for example, we may only be interested in the price elasticity of cannabis not the impact of other variables on its consumption. Taking the idea of the focus variables and examining the three S's gives us what we might call an 'instant econometric toolkit' to apply to any set of results we see. That is, a page of numbers can quickly be interpreted into something of real world relevance. Of course, you will not be at the stage of being able to use such a toolkit fully until we have gone through many more chapters.

To sum up then, econometrics means measurement in economics but it is much more than just measurement. Its central theme is the testing of hypotheses about the size and direction of economic relationships. The discipline of econometrics is an attempt to use the theories of economics to generate testable hypotheses which are then tested in a way that will depend on the methodology the researcher uses. We will look at methodology in more depth when we come to the fourth question, which is: do users of econometrics disagree?

1.3 QUESTION 2: WHO USES ECONOMETRICS AND WHY?

Econometrics is used for three basic reasons:

(i)   Academic researchers will use it to attempt to support or refute theories and models in their discipline.

(ii) Businesses can use econometrics to prepare forecasts, for example of the response of the sales of their products to changes in price or the amount of advertising.

(iii) Governments can use econometrics to prepare forecasts to help them devise policies. For example, suppose it is proposed to introduce a national minimum wage (or increase the level of an existing one). This is often argued to be a factor leading to increased unemployment. Econometric equations could be used to work out if this is the case and the size of the impact if one does exist.

So, econometrics is carried out for any of the above three reasons. It is therefore used by full-time government policy advisers, businesses and consultants who work for these and academics who work for any of the above or who carry out research for its own sake.

1.4 QUESTION 3: DO YOU HAVE TO BE AN ECONOMETRICIAN TO DO ECONOMETRICS?

The simple answer to this would be 'no'. There is a large amount of econometrics carried out by people who would not call themselves econometricians and would not be called this by other people.

A more detailed answer requires some distinction to be made between theoretical and applied econometrics. Applied econometrics refers to the use of econometrics to do research on actual data; for example, in the next chapters we will be looking at the Belgian consumption function and a demand equation for cigarettes. Theoretical econometrics is concerned with mathematical proofs of the properties of estimators and tests. For example, there is more than one way we could arrive at a figure for the marginal propensity to consume using the Belgian statistics employed in later chapters. Econometric theory will tell us which of these alternatives is most likely to meet certain criteria under particular circumstances. As an applied econometrician, you are expected to have a basic level of knowledge on these kinds of issues. That is, you would know the assumptions required for OLS estimators to be BLUE and you would be expected to know, for example, why a heteroscedasticity test may be necessary under certain circumstances.

The typical applied econometrics user might then be compared to someone who is driving a car or flying a plane, with the computer package taking the place of these means of transportation. A driver or pilot will not know in detail how the plane or car works and would not know how to build one and may not be able to fix one if it broke completely. Likewise many users of econometrics will be able to get a piece of research to its destination successfully without ever having to develop new estimators or write original pieces of computer programming to get their results.

In summary, you need a good working knowledge of the subject to do useful econometrics, but you do not need the degree of in-depth theoretical knowledge you would require to be called an econometrician as such.

1.5 QUESTION 4: DO USERS OF ECONOMETRICS DISAGREE?

In terms of purely theoretical econometrics, it is difficult for there to be much disagreement because once a proof has been established it is likely to stay established. If someone comes along with a new proof then the formal rules of mathematics mean that agreement on the change should be fairly soon established.

We could follow the same kind of principle for applied econometrics as well. That is, once someone has established a result of some sort – take, for example, the Phillips curve in 1958 – we would expect that the result is either confirmed or denied in the body of replications that follow. That is, after many further studies have been made, the community of researchers could agree that there is, or is not, a statistical relationship in the data sets or even that there is some ambiguity about the findings.

Unfortunately, as we shall see in the next 14 chapters, things are never this simple. This takes us back to the issue of methodology to some extent. If econometrics has an agreed methodology, and all its users follow this, then we would expect there to be convergence to agreement on the evidence in the set of results. However, there are some obvious reasons why agreement is not guaranteed.

REASONS FOR DISAGREEMENT
Data problems
A considerable shadow of doubt can surround the reliability of any econometric equation. The most basic reason for this is that the raw material available to econometricians is itself never going to be perfect. This does mean that we will tend to have disagreements that come down to judgements about the validity of studies in terms of their underlying database. As an example, let us assume there are 50 studies of a subject and 37 of them find in favour of the accepted hypothesis, 8 reject it and 5 of them come to no conclusion. We might not be prepared to conclude that the hypothesis is convincingly upheld, as it might be that the 8 studies in which rejection is found are on newer data, which is deemed more appropriate for the hypothesis being tested. A common data problem is the extent of the difference between the data we have to use to measure a variable and the theoretical concept it is being used to represent. For example, any model in which risk is important faces the problem that there is no clearly defined way of measuring risk. One might then make subjective judgements about which measures are best and this can lead to disagreement.

Data mining
Even if all the data, in all the studies conducted, was regarded as equally suitable we may still have problems. Say we find that studies overwhelmingly find in favour of the hypothesis, does this mean we can be contented and safely move our resources to other areas of research where there are unsettled or new questions to deal with? Unfortunately, not all areas of science are open to the charge of data mining. I am leaving aside the problem of outright cheating in the form of 'making up' data, which has certainly brought shame on some natural science researchers. Data mining refers to the problem that the researcher may engage in processes of selection designed to produce a particular type of result. A methodology based on falsification is supposed to prevent this, as we are meant to be looking for types of evidence that might reject our hypotheses, not going out of our way to confirm it.

So we need to ask: why might the falsification principle break down in practice? This takes us into a 'sociology of science' view of methodology. Producing publishable (and PhD worthy) research is an input into the long-run utility function of the academic researcher. It brings prestige, income and other benefits. Whether or not a piece of work is deemed to be fit to be awarded a thesis, or published in a journal, is decided by other academics who are then the 'gatekeepers of science'. In the case of journals and books, the gatekeeping function is performed by refereeing the work submitted for publication. This can be rejected outright or sent back to the author(s) for revision until it is in a suitable form. Utility maximizing academics have an incentive to invest effort in increasing their chances of publication.

While referees may be judging work on the basis of its contribution to the advancement of the subject, they also seek to preserve the 'hard core' propositions of the discipline against ridicule or loss of credibility. This may lead to some conservatism in terms of selecting in favour of work that is confirmatory in approach rather than falsificationist. In the extreme case, this will induce researchers to engage in 'data mining' in the sense that they choose not to report contradictory findings and instead strive to get results which conform to those they are expected to find. This may come about due to changes in the variables used or the data or the techniques.

We could then end up with what might be called 'empiricism' as opposed to proper scientific testing. What I mean by this is that we end up with a growing collection of statistical findings that cannot lead to any growth in our knowledge of how the world works. Indeed the body of knowledge might be a systematically misleading image of the world it claims to represent, as there may be a vast horde of unreported results which are very different from those which get printed.

One thing which the gatekeepers of science could do to promote expansion of accurate knowledge in their subject is to insist on replication, which leads us to the next point – that unsystematic replication could be a cause of disagreement.

UNSYSTEMATIC REPLICATION

We have introduced the word replication above. It is now time to go into this idea in more depth. Mittelstaedt and Zorn (1984) give a classification of types of replication. The most basic type is what we might call the 'literal' replication where the study has to be exactly the same as the previous one. Taken to extremes this would mean exactly the same data using the same software on the same computer. This would be in the spirit of scientific replication where laboratory workers attempt to make sure that there are no variant factors that could account for differences in results between two laboratories.

The literal replication is simply a form of checking the accuracy of results. There seems to be comparatively little attention to this in econometrics given two apparent facts:

(i)   Economic journals still do not require authors to submit a copy of their database for the referees of the paper to check or otherwise interrogate.
(ii) One sees few literal replications being published nor does one find the publication of very short notes which just say 'we checked this in the following way and we found the same results'.

The literal type of replication has to be systematic. The other types of replication should really be done systematically in the sense that we vary one element of the research design at a time in order to find out which factors lie behind discrepant results. The types of replication we can have then involve:

▶ changes in the specification of the model which, at the simplest level, means using different variables to 'explain' the variable we are interested in;
▶ changes in the statistical techniques used;
▶ changes in the data set used.

An example of how unsystematic this might be is the following: say the first 20 studies on some new fashionable question are American (this would not be unusual as the world of econometric research is heavily dominated by the USA) and the next three studies use data from Australia, Austria and Germany. It would not be unusual that these follow-up studies may use a different set of variables. Or even that they use different definitions even where the same variables are used. They may also use a different functional form and different estimation techniques. With so many changes going on it is difficult to establish what exactly is responsible for discordant results.

Some people now advocate the use of meta-analysis to bring some discipline into the process of reviewing the outcomes of this uncoordinated growth of research findings. You may find it a little difficult to grasp this idea until you get to the end of the first six or seven chapters of this book, so you may like to come back to this when you have mastered the core content of regression analysis. The basic idea of this approach is that you treat the *findings of research as data to be subjected to further research*. Meta-analysis estimates an equation to try to explain the variations in some feature of the research. For example, if we were looking at the differences in the interest elasticity of the demand for money in developing countries, then a meta-analysis would include features of the studies – such as which kind of countries they were for, what time periods they covered, whether they were quarterly data or annual data – as factors that might 'explain' the different findings.

Meta-analysis can be useful in condensing the kind of results found into a useful format. It may even provide useful 'sociology of science' type information if the researchers see fit to look for it. For example, what do we read into findings that journals of different types (such as those specific to a certain school of thought or those deemed to be of the highest 'quality') systematically publish higher or lower estimates of the effect of minimum wage laws on unemployment? It might be seen as data mining.

To sum up this answer, then, we find that users of econometrics will show some disagreement because of unsystematic replication. Disagreement may be a good thing and total absence of it might lead us to suspect data mining.

1.6 QUESTION 5: COULD WE DO WITHOUT ECONOMETRICS?

Whether the answer to this is yes or no depends on what it is we are trying to do *with* econometrics and also perhaps *why* we are trying to do it.

Can we imagine a world where economists are free from the shackles of having to apply econometrics? And, if so, can we explain why it has taken such a strong hold in the profession?

Clearly, if we want to give people numbers (even though these numbers will only be the centre figure of a potentially very wide range) to use to make forecasts and decide policies then we cannot do without econometrics. At least, if we do, we would have to resort to some other form of statistical estimation and these can usually be incorporated in the body of econometrics. Having adopted a 'hard' science methodology, economists were naturally inclined to move into econometrics, as it is necessary for them to test their theoretical models.

However, if one adopts an extremely sceptical position that the use of numbers in this way is misguided and could be dangerously misleading then econometrics might be abandoned altogether. This position has been advocated, at times, in the field of Austrian economics and is also to be found among some heterodox economists and was strongly put forward by historians (see Fogel, 1967) when econometrics began to invade their field in the form of cliometrics. There are two factors, then, in favour of abandoning econometrics altogether:

(i) It might be a hindrance to the application of a scientific discipline. That is, the testing of hypotheses using data may draw attention away from more important issues and ultimately it may not lead to progress. Lack of progress may arise from the fact that the 'hard core' assumptions of the subject will never be surrendered as a result of empirical research. We then accept that there cannot be 'scientific' progress in the study of humans; rather, we decide to accept a certain body of theory as correct and get on with using it to give us insights into economic problems.

(ii) We might accept the principle of using econometrics to test hypotheses, make forecasts etc., but be unwilling to accept its reliability in practice. Put simply, the key difficulty is that human behaviour may be too unpredictable to be summed up in sets of equations.

There have been famous and successful economists who have probably never run a regression themselves and have had very little contact with econometrics. Likewise, there are many little-known economists in the same situation. Nevertheless, the propositions of the famous non-econometric economists (like Becker, Buchanan, Stigler and Tullock) have given rise to many attempts to test them using econometrics. Similarly, the less famous have to contend with the fact that econometrics may be very influential whether they like it or not.

The summary answer to this question is that we could do without econometrics but it reduces the number of things we can do. Further, the fact that so many other people are at least prepared to act 'as if' they believe in it means that we cannot really afford to ignore it. This is not a yes/no issue and in the end we should decide on the merits of the problem at hand whether the use of econometrics is appropriate.

1.7 QUESTION 6: HOW DID MODERN ECONOMETRICS START?

A brief journey into the history of econometrics will help us to understand the importance of the desire to produce 'scientific economics' to the development of econometrics in its current form.

I will take the unusual step of beginning the history at the end. Econometrics today is found in all fields of economics. Whether an economist works on international trade or the environment or the provision of subsidies to education they will be expected (even if not expected to practise the art themselves) to understand a literature in which the key propositions are tested using statistical methods. Consequently, there are few journals in which you will not find frequent use of econometric methods.

As noted by Leamer (1994) there is something of a paradox in terms of how much faith is placed in econometrics. That is, it may be very popular but at times it seems that no one takes it seriously. This is because of suspicions of data mining, which are not helped by the lack of systematic replication. In the extreme case you will hear people say that 'a good econometrician can prove anything'.

The history of econometrics shows us moving to this point. We are now extremely well endowed with technology and large data sets, so the focus of improvement has moved to the methodological debate. This tends to be most focused on the area of time-series econometrics where the main arguments have been about David Hendry's 'general to specific methodology'. Some early critics felt that this was just data mining in disguise but this criticism has gone away. It is not until we get to Chapter 14 that we encounter modern time-series analysis.

THE ERAS OF ECONOMETRICS

It probably seems to the outsider that economics would lend itself naturally to the development of a sub-discipline like econometrics but the major obstacles have been resource scarcity. We can therefore distinguish a number of eras within the development of econometrics that have been delineated by changes in the technology available to do research. At all times, there have been methodological ideas being developed but these are unlikely to come to the fore until the technology to implement them easily has arrived.

The prehistoric era

The prehistoric era refers to the period before there was widespread availability of any kind of computers. This meant that calculations had to be done by hand or on a primitive calculator. The number of calculations required to estimate an equation multiplies when you bring more variables and larger numbers of observations into the process. Even more calculations would be required to perform tests using the equations that had been estimated. Thus the prehistoric era of econometrics was one in which there were relatively few people estimating equations and they used some very simple models which were not subject to very much testing. Certainly, the period up to 1945 falls into this era. Most econometrics at the time seemed to be on demand functions for agricultural products. Nevertheless, as we shall see in Chapter 13, some quite sophisticated ideas on method were introduced at this time. These ideas, on using models with more than one equation, began to be developed fully after the war but calculations were still laborious and much econometric research still consisted of graphs and tables without any estimation or testing. A defining feature of the prehistoric era is that few people, on an economics degree, would have been able to do courses on econometrics.

The early modern era

We can regard this era as having fully arrived by the early 1970s, largely due to the spread of access to mainframe computers and the arrival of packages like the now defunct (and unfortunately named) RAPE (regression analysis package for economists) and TSP (time-series processor). Courses and textbooks in econometrics had also arrived. Undergraduate textbooks at this time were more heavily focused on the theoretical statistical proofs, at the expense of how to actually do econometrics, than is now the case. It was not uncommon for people to be taught econometrics without gaining much 'hands on experience' using data or a computer.

Mainframe computers required the user to type their data and instructions on to a large collection of punched cards which they had to hand in to be fed into the machine. Packages like TSP could not handle large data sets. If a very large data set (i.e. one of thousands of observations and dozens of variables) was being used it had to be stored on a reel-to-reel magnetic tape which would only be loaded into the computer system when the operator found it had moved up a queue for resources. This meant one might have to wait a day for a regression and find that it was useless because of a typing error on the punch cards. The lack of software also meant that large data sets would tend to be used on software developed for other subjects like biology (BMDP) or sociology (SPSS).

Despite the (by modern standards) limitations, this era displayed a rapid growth of the use of econometrics. By the late 1970s all the specialist fields of economics, like labour or industrial or public finance, were being invaded by econometric studies. There was a vast legacy of economic propositions waiting to be tested, such as Wagner's Law (on which, see Chapter 14), the Fisher hypothesis (see Chapter 14), the quantity theory of money, purchasing power parity (see Chapter 9), the relationships between advertising, concentration and profitability in industry (see Chapter 13) and Becker's propositions from the economic theory of crime and punishment (see Chapters 5 and 11). Econometrics thus became a regular part of economics and one that met with little criticism in the mainstream.

The modern era

Let us say the modern era arrived with:

- the expansion of mainframe access;
- the arrival of the personal computer (PC);
- the increase in software availability;
- the spread of econometrics courses;
- the increased number and 'friendliness' of econometrics textbooks.

This, roughly speaking, takes us through the 1980s and up to the mid-1990s. Econometrics now takes over the subject of economics to a large extent. The change in technology means that it is cheap and easy to do econometrics. Furthermore, it is even possible to use econometrics when you have relatively little knowledge of the underlying statistical foundations. Econometric research becomes a fairly obvious way to get a PhD thesis as one can satisfy the 'originality' requirement more easily than with theoretical work.

The new 'instant econometrics' era

The typical PC in the 1990s was not especially quick as it had a fairly slow central processing unit (CPU), little random-access memory (RAM), and one would have had to fit an extra 'maths chip' to speed up processing. Results of small equations would arrive more or less instantly but larger work using more sophisticated methods could take over 30 minutes and if the model was particularly large a mainframe would still be used. As increasingly powerful computers became available at a lower price we entered the era of 'instant econometrics'. For example, the logit and probit equations shown later in this book have over 13 000 people in them and 7 variables and yet were produced in seconds using a cheap laptop using Windows XP.

There are two more factors which made econometrics much more instant:

(i) Software has become more user-friendly. For some time econometric software still ran in DOS even though the Windows operating system had become widely available. But now the major econometric software runs in Windows and has Windows-style interfaces.

(ii) The much more rapid availability of data and dissemination of results via the Internet and CD copying of large amounts of information. This can make co-authoring of papers remarkably easy compared to even 10 years ago. It would be quite feasible to run regressions while online and send the findings to a co-author for feedback to run revised regressions during a web relay chat.

1.8 QUESTION 7: WHERE IS ECONOMETRICS GOING?

Econometrics today is unquestionably radically different from what it was in the 1960s or even the 1970s and 1980s for fairly obvious reasons. All of these come down to progress in computing. Three major factors are advances in:

▶ rapidly increased speed of computation;
▶ increased ease of communication of data and results;
▶ drastically reduced costs of both of the above.

At first sight all of these seem to be good things that should lead to economics being more scientific. The facility to conduct econometric research is now available to a wider range of people than ever before, thanks to the above factors. In addition, the sophistication of what is available in terms of estimation methods, pre-packaged in econometric software, has grown enormously.

However, there are certain limitations on the growth of scientific economics which do not go away. These are:

▶ The processing capacity of the human mind is not advancing in the same way and results still need to be appraised and interpreted even if there is some scope for delegating this work to artificial intelligence systems.
▶ Philosophical and methodological problems are not going to go away. Quicker, cheaper ways of processing large amounts of data are not able to resolve fundamental disputes. They cannot do anything to convince those who doubt the validity of the application of statistics to human behaviour.
▶ Quality of data. While there is more data available, especially large data sets, the quality of data is not necessarily growing. It may have declined in some areas due to pressures on government expenditure in these areas. There is also the problem that the large amount of available data sets encourages users to use these in preference to the deliberate construction of more appropriate data.

1.9 QUESTION 8: HOW DO I USE THIS BOOK?

Econometrics books are commonly described as being 'like cookbooks'. This is more a description of how such books are used than of how the writers intended them to be used. That is, people do not usually read a cookbook (or for that matter, a technical manual for a car or a piece of computer software) all the way through in order to learn the theory, practice and philosophy of cooking. Rather, they tend to dip into such a book to find out how to perform a specific task such as baking a cake or fixing a cake that has begun to sag in the middle.

In the case of econometrics, the most basic 'recipe' is how to estimate a single-equation OLS model whether it is for a consumption function or Phillips curve in macroeconomics, or supply and demand functions in microeconomics. The first part of this book (up to and including Chapter 8) seeks to impart the basic variations in this recipe.

The second part concerns some more complicated recipes and 'corrections' or 'fixes' for what might go wrong in the basic case. For example, one might be working on a model and find oneself questioned as to whether it suffers from serious multicollinearity, which would lead one to consult that section of the book (in our case the whole of Chapter 10), or heteroscedasticity, which would lead to consultation of Chapters 9 and 11.

In order to make this book more usable as a cookbook I have attempted to make the sections self-contained to a high degree. This does entail some repetition for those who may be reading the book all the way through in a sequence.

The overall intention is to provide more than just a cookbook – i.e. it contains not just recipes but instruction in the 'art' and 'philosophy' of econometrics. It is a feature of this book that it tries to give emphasis to each of these elements.

There are many excellent textbooks on econometrics *per se*, but many of them are sadly out of print. Modern texts contain reference to and discussion of computer printout of the results of estimating a multiple regression equation by the OLS technique and in some cases more advanced techniques are also depicted in this manner.

As indicated above, the book falls roughly into two parts. Chapters 1–8 cover the basic model and simple extensions, which broaden its applicability. Chapters 9–14 offer advice and solutions on what to do when the basic model is inadequate.

Throughout the book a similar style is adopted in each chapter. Each chapter begins with a short introduction and has around 8–12 sections which are broken into short sub-sections where necessary. Footnotes are avoided.

The style of the chapters is to concentrate on the simplest cases of each topic at the beginning and only to introduce complications when the simplest case has been illustrated through the use of actual data and the review studies.

I return to the same data sets throughout the book and give some rationale for the models that lie behind the reported results.

ROUTE MAPS

One can use this book in different ways. If it is being used as a cookbook to get quick advice on a particular problem, then this should be readily found by using the list of chapter sub-headings given at the front and/or the index at the back of the book. The self-contained nature of individual sections means that any necessary linkages to other parts of the book will be explicitly referenced.

One could read the whole book from beginning to end in sequence as a means of either refreshing prior knowledge of the subject or getting an initial glimpse of the field before more detailed study of specific elements.

You may be reading the book in sections as part of a conventional course of instruction including lectures and data exercises. Given that not all courses in econometrics are identical (although they do all cover a large number of the same 'core' topics), it is unlikely that any textbook will follow precisely such a course of instruction. Indeed books differ quite radically in where a topic occurs and how much space is given to it, thus reflecting the very different focus of attention in the courses presented by the people who wrote the books.

It should be possible to reconfigure the sequence in this book to suit other courses. The logic of the current sequence is that we begin with the simple linear model and then extend it using transformations, dummies and trends. The chapter on logit and probit models is included because so many research studies now draw on these methods, but there is still some tendency to report them as if they were the same as OLS regression equations.

I have taken the step of grouping diagnostic tests of the basic OLS equation into one chapter – Chapter 9. How to deal with the problems in terms of using GLS/IV methods is given over to separate chapters. The rationale behind this is that it is a logical structure for a person new to the subject. That is, in the first part we build up skills in using OLS regression based on an unquestioning acceptance of the classical assumptions. Then we test these assumptions. These days quite a lot of software automatically throws up a battery of tests of specification (or they are only another menu or command away) so the beginner is likely to experience the tests as a collective experience when they do get to software.

It might turn out that a regression passes all the diagnostic tests and therefore we can use OLS without needing to worry about the chapters that follow in the rest of the book.

Multicollinearity and the identification problems have been given separate chapters for specific reasons. Multicollinearity is a problem for which technical 'solutions' are very questionable, meaning this needs to be highlighted. Identification is always stated in textbooks to be logically prior to estimation in multiple equation systems, yet it is often presented after the estimation issues. Putting it in a separate chapter serves the purpose of making clear that it is a distinct problem from the estimation method.

SOME ALTERNATIVE ROUTES
Full course
Make some or all of Chapters 4, 8 and 9 option 1 apart from Sections 9.6 and 9.7. Cover Chapter 10 directly after Chapter 7.

Basic one-semester course
In a very basic course only Chapters 1–8 might be covered, with Chapter 8 being optional and Chapter 4 also possibly being omitted, particularly if the students do not do any independent work involving data collection.

WEBSITE
The website contains the data sets used in this book in the form of Excel files which you can download to do some of the exercises and otherwise experiment on. It also contains additional examination and self-assessment materials, including the one-page articles with attached questions which were discussed above.

1.10 QUESTION 9: WHAT SHOULD I KNOW, AND BE ABLE TO DO, WHEN I HAVE FINISHED?

There are a number of key skills you should have developed by the time you have completed this book.

The most basic skill is that you should be able to use a computer to estimate an equation on which you can conduct hypothesis tests and produce interpretations of the results. Clearly one can reach different levels of this – the most basic is to be only able to deal with the material up to Chapter 5.

Even if one has mastered the art of performing and interpreting all the techniques discussed in the following chapters, this is not the whole of econometrics; you also need to be able to know how to present your work and how to interpret the work presented by others.

HOW TO READ ECONOMETRICS

The skill of reading an econometrics article is to be developed by using the review studies which appear in many chapters. These studies appear in pairs in isolated panels towards the end of the chapters. Each panel shows a research study summarized in a template – the blank version of which is given in Appendix 1 or at www.mcgraw-hill.co.uk/textbooks/cameron. You may find it instructive to try to condense other articles, of your own choosing, into this format.

Reading an econometrics article is not the same as reading a book or a newspaper article because you need to have a critical awareness of such things as the quality of the data and the steps the authors took to arrive at their results. You also need to keep in mind the things the authors may have overlooked – tests they did not perform and econometric problems they seem to have ignored.

HOW TO WRITE ECONOMETRICS

There are really three types of paper one could be writing:

(i) An original research paper reporting work undertaken.
(ii) A literature review that summarizes the existing body of work on the subject.
(iii) A meta-analysis.

I will concentrate on the first of these and then move to the other two. Writing up an econometric paper is a different skill from performing the econometric analysis. There is no reason why a person should be equally good at these tasks, and such differences in ability could be one reason why so many papers in econometrics are co-authored.

The template used in the review studies in this book gives an outline of the kind of things that need to go into a report. We need to distinguish between a purely technical report, such as for a consultancy contract, and an article for a journal. Very often, articles for the leading journals attempt to be more than just a report. That is, they seek to be eye-catching, original or provocative in some way. This is reflected in the titles of the papers. If you skip to Section 5.7 of Chapter 5 and look at the review study by McCormick and Tollison (1984) it is called 'Crime on the Court' rather than, say, 'An empirical study of the effect of the number of referees on the number of fouls in college basketball'.

This rhetorical element in academic work makes it somewhat harder to reduce the task of writing an econometric article to a set formula. Despite this, however, we might attempt to set the presentation of a written piece into the following sections:

SUGGESTED STRUCTURE OF AN ECONOMETRICS REPORT

▲**Introduction**. What is the reason for the study being done in the first place? A brief summary of the key findings. Did the evidence support the major hypotheses? If so, are there any reservations about this support?

▲**Brief literature review**. If the study is an original sole piece of research, the literature review will be brief and selective. If you are fortunate there may be a well-known literature review that you can refer to and give the highlights of. If there are no substantial reviews of the literature on the topic, then you could concentrate on the major work in some detail and then briefly summarize the later findings. The link to previous work should be indicated – is this a replication or does it add some new element?

▲**Model**. Development of the model leading to expectations about the sign, and if possible, size of the relationships.

▲**Data sources**. Indicate where data was obtained, how it was manipulated and any alternatives that may have been tried.

▲**Estimation and results**. Usually results will be presented in tables. It is not feasible to present every equation that was tried but ideally there should be some discussion of the sensitivity of the results to different specifications.

▲**Discussion of results**. This should indicate whether the results conformed to expectations, and if they did not, should attempt to explain why this has happened. Further calculations might be made to show the importance of the findings. Suggestions for further research should be made.

▲**Conclusion**.

Appendices should indicate the precise data sources used and may provide further statistical results or elements of the theoretical model that were omitted from the main text.

You should also be able to write an abstract of 100 words or less which summarizes the piece.

1.11 QUESTION 10: WHAT SOFTWARE SHOULD I USE TO DO ECONOMETRICS?

If everyone used exactly the same econometric package, the production of this book would be much easier because every chapter could be illustrated using the standard package. Unfortunately, this is far from the case. There are a large number of rival packages, meaning it is not easy to give specific instructions on how each technique is dealt with on a computer.

If all packages were available to all persons things would be a little easier as one could probably then be sure that all techniques and tests are available to all readers. Unfortunately, the major econometrics packages tend to be rather expensive for site licences hence many university departments will only have one or two of the leading specialist packages for econometrics. On the other hand, you will find that many software packages offer cut-down versions for students at a greatly reduced price which can be downloaded for a limited period demo. It might be worth trying software, as in all fields of computer usage relatively minor stylistic differences in presentation can make a huge difference to how quickly someone learns.

You can find information on the leading software packages at the following website:

http://www.oswego.edu/~economic/econsoftware.htm. You can find reviews of the latest releases of the software at http://www.economics.ltsn.ac.uk/cheer and there is a list of reviews published in academic journals at http://www.tspintl.com/products/tsp/reviews.htm.

Table 1.1 gives some background information on this software.

Table 1.1 Available software that is commonly found

Name	Specialist econometrics	Area of specialism
Easyreg	Yes	General
Eviews	Yes	General – was formerly TSP – is also for Mac computers
Excel	No	
GiveWin/PcGive/PCFIML	Yes	Time-series
Limdep	No	Large data sets
Lotus	No	Database
Microfit	Yes	Time series
Oxmetrics	Yes	Time series – financial analysis
RATS and CATS	Yes	Time series
Shazam	Yes	General
SPSS	No	Large data sets
SST	Yes	Large data sets
TSP (International)	Yes	Time-series

How do packages that could be used differ? The main things that differ are the size of data set that can be handled and the tests and methods available.

In the above list, Excel, Lotus and SPSS are not expressly designed for economists. They are general packages that one can be almost guaranteed to have access to in any university. Also, in the UK, students and staff can purchase SPSS for a nominal fee under the CHEST (Combined Higher Education Software Team) agreement.

So far, I have not dealt with the simple question of the reliability and accuracy of the packages. Certainly, in the case of basic OLS regression this is not an important question. A number of more complicated methods are also standardized to the point where one might get the same results whichever package you use. For example, the logit equations shown in Chapter 8 were estimated by both SPSS and Limdep and the results were identical to several decimal places.

Where there might be differences is where data are not 'well behaved' and/or complicated procedures have to be used.

1.12 WHAT COMES NEXT?

This chapter introduced the general idea of what econometrics is, and indicated how it is used in research. This was done in the form of answers to ten questions.

In these answers, we have encountered the distinction between theoretical and applied econometrics. It should be clear that the primary focus of the current text is on applied econometrics. That is, we are learning how to estimate parameters and test hypotheses and how to critically appraise similar work by other people. This inevitably means that the issue of data is central to the chapters that follow. We do, however, also have to know the relevant statistical theory that underlies the analysis of data. This is outlined in Chapter 2 but the more technical aspects are relegated to a number of appendices.

What comes after Chapter 2 are the relevant techniques to put you in full command of the 'instant econometrics toolkit' of seeking out the focus variables in any equation and examining the three S's (sign, significance and size). This process should largely be completed by the end of Chapter 8. From Chapter 9 onwards, we will be looking at how reliable results are and methods of 'correcting' deficiencies in models that may be suspected of inadequacy.

DOS AND DON'TS

Do

✓ Make sure you look at the three S's – sign, size and significance – every time you are presented with a set of econometric results.

✓ Adopt a critical attitude to all the results you are presented with – in particular make sure you can tell how the variables used were defined.

✓ Be wary of the pitfalls of 'instant econometrics' – results do not speak for themselves and you need time to think about what they mean.

Don't

✗ Forget that econometrics follows a particular methodology of hypothesis > test > result and therefore it requires attention to the theory underlying the results. It is not supposed to be just 'number crunching'.

✗ Imagine that you have done something wrong when you come to work on your own data and it 'doesn't work' in the way that the published studies do. Of course, you need to check your work but it may be that the data and model you are using simply do not support the hypothesis that others have found in favour of.

EXERCISES

1.1 Which of the following do you feel is the most accurate description of econometrics:

(i) It is the use of computers to prove that you are right and someone else is wrong.

(ii) It is the use of computers to prove at all costs that the established body of economic theory is correct.

(iii) It is the use of statistical methods to test predictions derived from economic theory.

(iv) It is the collection of data.

1.2 See if you can gain access to some of the packages listed in Table 1.1 and try to load one of the data sets given on the website or any other Excel files that have been given to you. Having loaded such a file, see if you can find the command for 'regression' or 'linear regression' on the package.

1.3 Find a report in the recent news media (i.e. on the Internet, in newspapers/magazines or on television/radio) which makes statistical claims of a causal nature (for example, that

passive smoking does or does not cause cancer or that too much computing is bad for your health). Critically examine the report you have found to see how much information is given about the size, strength and significance of the results.

1.4 What are the essential differences between the following pairs of ideas:
(i) statistical significance and economic significance;
(ii) method and methodology;
(iii) evidence and proof;
(iv) a hypothesis and a model.

REFERENCES

Note: References are given at the end of each chapter in all cases. In the subsequent chapters, the references will all have been cited in the text, however in this particular case some of the items cited are further reading, which you may find useful. You may wish to re-read some of these works regularly as you progress through the subject.

Blaug, M. (1992) *The Methodology of Economics or How Economists Explain*, 2nd edn, Cambridge University Press, Cambridge.

Cross, R. (1982) The Duhem-Quine thesis, Lakatos and the appraisal of theories in macroeconomics, *Economic Journal*, **92** (366), 320–340.

Darnell, A. (1989) General to specific modelling: A methodological perspective, *British Review of Economic Issues*, **11** (25), 53–88.

Fogel, R.W. (1967) The specification problem in economic history, *Journal of Economic History*, **27**, 283–308, repr. in P. Temin (ed.), *New Economic History*, Penguin, 1973.

Hausman, D. (1989) Economic methodology in a nutshell, *Journal of Economic Perspectives*, **3** (2) Spring, 115–128.

Hendry, D.F. (1983) Econometric modelling: The consumption function in retrospect, *Scottish Journal of Political Economy*, **30**, 193–220.

Leamer, E. (1994) *Sturdy Econometrics*, Edward Elgar, Hampshire.

McCloskey, D. (1985) *The Rhetoric of Economics*, University of Wisconsin Press, Ch. 9.

Mittelstaedt, R.A. and Zorn, T.S. (1984) Econometric replications: Lessons from the experimental sciences, *Quarterly Journal of Economics and Business*, **23** (1), 9–15.

Pagan, A. (1987) Three econometric methodologies: A critical appraisal, *Journal of Economic Surveys*, **1** (1), 3–24.

Stanley, T.D. (2001). Wheat from chaff: Meta-analysis as quantitative literature review, *Journal of Economic Perspectives*, **15** (3), 131–150; and follow-up discussion in *Journal of Economic Perspectives*, Summer 2002, 225–229.

WEBLINKS

http://www.oswego.edu/~economic/econsoftware.htm
Guide to econometrics software.

http://www.economics.ltsn.ac.uk/cheer
Reviews of software, classroom ideas and exercises.

http://www.tspintl.com/products/tsp/reviews.htm
Index of reviews of econometric software in academic journals.

http://www.oswego.edu/~economic/journals.htm
A–Z listing of economics journals with weblinks to their sites which will give you access to the contents list.

http://ideas.repec.org/
IDEAS website. This site gives access to journals but also huge numbers of working papers, many

of which can be downloaded (free) in full. At the time of writing over 120 000 items of research can be downloaded free in full text.

http://www.sscnet.ucla.edu/ssc/labs/cameron/e143f98/regex94.htm

This is a list of suitable econometric articles for students to read given in T.A. Cameron's Econometrics 143 course.

2

Statistical Testing and Modelling: The Basics

LEARNING OBJECTIVES

■ Understand the different sources of data – cross–section, time–series and panel
■ Understand the different levels of measurement – categorical, ordinal and ratio
■ Be aware of the concept of probability and its use in econometrics
■ Be familiar with the important probability distributions, especially the normal
■ Know how to write down and carry out hypothesis tests
■ Understand the concepts of covariance and correlation

CHAPTER SUMMARY

2.1 TYPES OF DATA

The purpose of this book is to teach the theories and techniques used to impose models on a body of data using a computer package. It also aims to convey some idea of how to write and read reports based on statistical research. Before we can start we need some data to analyse. I postpone discussion of how to handle data until Chapter 4, as it is better if we have some idea of the fundamental ideas that lie behind data analysis before we rush into the estimation of equations. The word 'data' is the plural of the Latin word *datum*, which roughly means 'fact'. So data is a collection of facts. As the word is a plural the correct usage is to say 'these data' rather than 'this data'. One of the questions you should immediately ask when reading a piece of research is: 'What type of data has been used?'

Econometrics is based on applying concepts from probability to the analysis of data. Technical details about the concept of probability are to be found in appendices at the back of the book.

The type of data is a very important factor. It should influence the form of statistical test/ model being used and it will also influence the results produced by econometric software. There are two ways in which we can refer to the type of data that we have collected or been given. One is by reference to where it comes from and the other by the way in which it is measured – more specifically, the type of units in which it can be measured.

SOURCE VARIATION

Where does data come from? Ultimately, in social science it comes from recording the behaviour of individual households, businesses, governments and so on. On occasions we may also require measurement of non-human elements such as rain, temperature or chemical discharges. In this book we adopt the convention of calling a piece of data by the symbols X or Y and treating each **series** of X or Y as a **variable**. We commonly refer to the set of such variables we have stored on our computer as a **data set.** A data set is then a collection of variables (such as weather, unemployment rates, sales, exchange rates etc.) for a defined group of persons, times or places, which we refer to as **observations.** If we had a data set showing the age and income of the head of household in each house in a particular street, then each row element in the data set is the **observation**. For example, if the data is entered consecutively in terms of door numbers then the seventh line of the spreadsheet will show the observation of the income of the head of household living at number 7. This is illustrated for some imaginary survey data in Table 2.1.

So the observation unit here is the head of household. In other cases, it will be years or countries or states/districts/counties etc. within a country. There are three variables – house number, age of head of household and income of head of household. Each variable can be called a series and the three series together form the data set.

The total collection of all the possible such units of observation for a particular study is called the **population**. This is a technical term in statistics not to be confused with just the everyday meaning of the number of people living in an area. If we are studying, for example, the degree to which motorists comply with compulsory seat belt regulations, in a country, then the relevant population is all the vehicles in that country. Regression analysis, which is the main subject of this book, is usually based on a **sample** from the population (see Section 2.2 below).

Populations and their samples fall into the following groups:

Table 2.1 Example of (imaginary) data from a survey in one street

House number	Age of head of household (to nearest year)	Income of head (£ per year before tax)
1	43	15 250
2	29	23 675
3	55	29 725
4	48	42 675
5	44	37 580
6	38	32 500
7	59	72 700

(i) **Cross-section data:** where all the observations have been drawn from the same point (or period) in time. For example, the imaginary data we have just looked at is a cross-section. Likewise, a study, which uses data from the states of the USA would be called a cross-section study. In this case, the observation subscript, i, will refer to each individual or country. For example, let us call the Age variable X_2, when we add the subscript it is X_{2i} where i will be the numbers from 1 to n where n is the total sample size. Here $n = 7$, so if the i subscript were 7 then the value of X_2 would be 59 as we are referring to the 7th individual. If the i subscript was 4 then the value of X_2 would be 48.

(ii) **Time series:** where all the observations are drawn from a historical sequence of data such as the consumption and gross domestic product (GDP) figures for a country from 1960–99. In this case, the observation subscript refers to the year, for example, $._i = 1960, 1961$ and so on up to 1999 in this case. Later in this chapter (in Section 2.7) you will find some correlations computed from time-series data for 1960–88 and there are examples of time-series regressions in Chapters 3, 5 and 6. More detailed analysis of time series is covered in Chapter 14.

(iii) **Pooled cross-section/time-series data.** It is possible to combine these two types of data. For example, Brainerd (2001), in an economic model of suicide in the former Soviet Union, combines time series from 1988–98 for 22 transition economies. This produces a pooled cross-section time series of 242 observations. Pooling involves stacking these two types of data vertically in a database. Techniques for analysing pooled data are discussed further in Chapter 7 after we fully develop the classical linear regression model (CLRM). In the pooled cross-section time series a variable such as X_2 would have two subscripts. So we might write X_{2ij} to describe the variable where i may represent the cross-section and j the time-series element. For example, if we came back in 5 years' time to the sample in Table 2.1 and collected the data again, then if i was 4 and j was 2 we would be referring to data for the household that lived at number 4 in the second sample taken 5 years after the first one.

(iv) **Panel data.** Strictly speaking, a panel is a pooled cross-section where exactly the same observations have been used in each cross-section. A good example of this is the National Child Development Survey (NCDS) in the UK, which interviews those born in the same period in 1958 at intervals of 7 years. Panel data would follow the same subscripting methods as pooled cross-section time-series data.

A cross-section/time-series study, such as that of Brainerd mentioned above, might sometimes be termed a 'panel' as it has the same group of economies. However, the population in each year might not be exactly the same in each country. The most usual use of the term 'panel' is where we have a longitudinal survey of individual households or firms. This can be approached by the techniques in Chapter 7, although more sophisticated methods have been developed due to the increased popularity and availability of panel data.

You will find that all of these types of data are used in research studies but some topic areas show a dominance of one particular type of data. Studies in the core areas of macroeconomics tend to use time-series data. A common argument has been that the use of these different data sets will bring us different types of estimates of key concepts, such as elasticities due to the information in the data. The usual claim was that time-series data show short-run effects while cross-sections show long-run effects. A pooled cross-section/time series will show effects that are somewhere in between the long run and the short run.

LEVEL OF MEASUREMENT

Now we come to discuss the way in which data has been measured. We can rank types of data in terms of how much information the number attached to a given observation contains. It would be impossible to call something data if it contained no information whatsoever.

However, we can have data that contains very little information. Take the case of a train or bus. If we are given the number of the bus or train (such as 679) where this denotes the route on which the journey goes, this only tells us that each vehicle takes a different route from another bus, such as a 675. It does not tell us anything else about the vehicle or the journey. There is nothing to stop us dividing 679/675 to get the number 1.0059259259259259259259259259259259 as the ratio between the two buses. But this will be useless information – it is not the ratio of the weights, heights, miles travelled or anything else of relevance about the buses that go on these routes.

This (the bus route numbers) is categorical data, which is the least informative type of data. All it tells us is that there is some kind of difference between the items in our sample. The simplest type of categorical data is where there are only two sets of labels or two different types of item. In econometric applications, common examples of this are whether someone is, or is not, female or white, whether they own their own home or have a university degree. Econometricians code this type of data as a binary variable where 0 is the absence of the category. We have just encountered the concept of a **dummy variable**, which will be fully explored in Chapter 7.

You might find yourself with a data set that consists mainly, or even entirely, of categorical data. This may well be the case if you are using a questionnaire survey, which was not originally designed for the purpose of testing the propositions of economics. Given the limited information content you could be forgiven for thinking that econometric work will not be carried out on a data set that is mainly comprised of categorical variables. However, this is not true. When we get to Chapter 8, we will discover the increasingly popular logit and probit models, in which we model the prediction of categorical events.

Categorical data can be more informative if it has some degree of ordering. Let us imagine that, instead of the computer codings representing buses or trains, there are five different types of low-fat sandwich spread and supermarket shoppers have to choose which one they prefer. These could be ranked in terms of which gives the consumer the best utility levels from 1 to 5. This would be a subjective measure. This type of data could be, and often is, coded in a database as literally 1, 2, 3, 4, 5, but given that this is a ranking it would be a mistake to treat 5 as if it is 5 times the utility of category 1, 2.5 times category 2 and so on, as preferences do not convey cardinal utility.

If we had the data on the rankings which the consumers give to each sandwich spread then we have **ordinal** data. For example, the first consumer might place the spreads in the following order:

$$S_3 > S_5 > S_2 > S_1 > S_4 \qquad\qquad (2.1)$$

showing that they prefer spread 3 to spread 5 and so on. The usual assumptions of microeconomic theory are that we cannot measure utility directly, therefore the ranked/ordinal data is the only type that would be valid.

There is more information in this ordinal data than there is in the categorical data of the earlier bus number example. It would be a mistake to treat it as if it was the same as **ratio** or **continuous** data. Ratio data is measured in scalar units such as kilograms of weight or metres of height. In the sandwich spread example of Equation (2.1), we could directly measure the amount of fat or percentage of fat in each spread, which would then be ratio/continuous data. Look at Table 2.2, which shows some more imaginary data for the sandwich spreads combined with the data in Equation (2.1).

Table 2.2 (Imaginary) Data for low–fat sandwich spreads

Spread	Percentage fat	Consumer ranking
1	23	4
2	12	3
3	6	1
4	7	5
5	2	2

I have adopted a simplifying assumption that all consumers agree on the rankings given in Equation (2.1) in order to produce this table. At the moment we are not interested in things like the relationship between fat content and price or between the consumer rankings and fat content. These are the sorts of issues we can deal with when we have made some progress in the study of econometrics.

As fat content is measured in continuous terms we can say that spread 3 has 3 times as much fat as spread 5. From the consumer preferences, we can see that spread 3 is more popular than spread 5, but because this data is ordinal we cannot say by how much spread 3 is preferred.

Most important macroeconomic variables have scalar measurement as ratio variables. If we have a series for inflation rates, unemployment rates or national output and we divide any observation (for example, the value for 2001) by another (for example, the value for 1980), then the ratio of the two figures can be interpreted literally. That is, if it was 1.25, then the first observation is one-quarter larger than the former.

The CLRM (classical linear regression model) does *not* have to have all the variables in continuous form. It is okay for the right-hand side variables to be in categorical form once they are suitably coded. But the model which is explained in Chapter 3 and used throughout the text (with the exception of Chapter 8) is only strictly valid when its dependent variable is a continuous/ratio variable.

Continuous variables do not have to be positive. Once we start to use variables like growth rates, or other measures of change, in a regression equation we can have negative values for certain observations. This does not cause any problems for regression analysis in theoretical terms but in Chapter 6 it will give us the practical difficulty that you cannot take the logarithm, or square root, of a negative number.

2.2 SAMPLING

The body of statistical theory on which econometrics is based is premised on the assumption that we are not usually working with the total population but only a part of it. The technical term for a selection from the population is a **sample**. We should ask ourselves how any sample was taken. A sample is used mainly because of cost barriers to obtaining data for the relevant population in any study. There are two ideas most people are familiar with about what constitutes 'good' sampling. These are:

▶ that the sample should be random;
▶ that the sample should be of a reasonable size.

RANDOMNESS

Randomness is an inherently statistical concept. The idea of a **random variable** (let us call it X) is that it is free to take on a range of values without being determined by the influence of other variables. A **random sample** refers to the process by which variables are measured. If a sample is random we are taking a fraction of the population in order to measure X in such a way that there are no other variables influencing those **observations** selected from the sample.

There are two main ways in which a sample would depart from randomness. The first is when there is 'self-selection'. Take the case where our data comes from people who call a telephone help line for such things as intended suicide, domestic violence, debt problems or financial advice. These people may not be a representative sample of the population as they have selected themselves into the sample due to the fact that their need for the telephone advice may be greater than that for the general population. The other form of non-randomness is where the researcher has engaged in some kind of sample selection bias. A simple case would be where a street interviewer deliberately picks people whose appearance they like in preference to other individuals who might be sampled. Another good example of this is the use of an Internet distributed questionnaire. This will exclude people who are not Internet users. But, on top of this, it will tend to exclude those who are time constrained, disinclined or absent-minded and hence do not respond. There are elements of self-selection in these latter factors.

Randomness would seem to be a good thing if we want to accurately measure the value of certain statistics such as people's heights or weights or how much money they spend on different items.

However, it is not necessarily a good thing for a social scientist, or a market research company, to attempt to collect a truly random sample. The reason for this is that they are generally more interested in hypothesis testing rather than measuring the general characteristics of populations accurately. That is, they are trying to use data collected by themselves, and others including governments, 'as if' it was the result of a controlled experiment. The truly random sample may contain too many factors that confuse the relationships between the **focus variables.** The technique of multiple regression, which is the bulk of the knowledge imparted in this book, is a method for 'artificially' holding constant the influence of other variables in non-experimental data. As you shall see, however, regression results are prone to variation, debate and unreliability particularly with respect to the quality of the data and models used. Economists have, in recent times, shown more awareness of the idea that it is desirable to obtain data sources that already factor out some of the key variables that are not the focus of our main hypotheses.

The influence of IQ on earnings is a good illustration of this (see Section 7.6 in Chapter 7). Economists are mainly interested in acquired skills and market factors as determinants of earnings but are often handicapped by having to use data which lacks any good 'controls' for underlying intelligence. You can see an attempt to deal with this by deliberate non-random sampling of the population in Chapter 7. Market researchers also use deliberate non-random-ness, and others, due to the self-selection problem. An example of this is 'quota sampling', where interviewers are instructed to collect specific quantities of completed schedules from certain sorts of individuals (such as single males or females between a certain age) rather than simply accepting those who present themselves 'at random' as willing interview subjects.

Randomness is a very important concept that will be developed further below and its major role in econometrics in terms of the disturbance term will be explored in Chapter 3.

SAMPLE SIZE

Why is a bigger sample good? The answer relates again to the desire for representativeness when we cannot get the whole population. If a marketing firm wanted to know the average rate of spending on holidays in a particular suburb, it is unlikely to trust a very small sample. Interviewing only one household would be the extreme case of a small sample. Three would seem to be better than two and four better than three and so on.

But why do we think this? The problem of using a sample of one is that it might come from an extreme of the **distribution** of values in the population. The holiday firm might have asked someone who spends a lot more than everyone else on holidays. If they ask two or more they can calculate average holiday spending from the familiar formula for the arithmetic **mean:**

$$\bar{H} = \sum_{i}^{n} H_i \qquad\qquad (2.2)$$

where the Σ operator means 'add up all the observations from i to n where n is the size of the sample and H is the symbol chosen to represent holiday spending'. If we use i equal to 1, then we would be using the whole sample. If i was 10, then we would be ignoring the first 9 observations. We hope that by using larger samples the extreme observations cases (which are not representative) will be dominated in the average calculation by the more representative cases.

You should note that Equation (2.2) is not the average of holiday spending. It is an estimate of the population mean derived from a sample of the population. If our samples are truly representative, then if we keep taking samples (which is called repeated sampling) we would expect to find that means of the samples will be equal to the 'true' mean in the population. This can be written as:

$$E(\hat{H}) = E(\bar{H}) \tag{2.3}$$

where the ^ symbol tells us that the item underneath it is an **estimate.** This symbol will be used regularly throughout this book and you should make sure that you remember what it means. An estimate is used because we do not know the true value and are using sampling to make an **inference** about what the true value might be. The symbol E outside the bracket represents 'expectation'. The expectation is the value that is most likely to occur in repeated sampling.

The concept of **statistical inference** is that we draw conclusions from an estimate made using a sample: we infer properties of the population from the sample. This means that we will often be making assumptions about the properties of the sample data. The beginner would be inclined to believe that the more observations we have the better, as more accurate estimates of the pattern of a variable and more reliable estimates of the parameters of a function will be obtained. Two observations need to be made about this:

(i) Accuracy of estimates does not rise in direct proportion to the increase in the sample size. The availability of surveys with 30 000 observations may look very impressive but they are not 30 times more reliable than an otherwise identical survey of 1000 other things being equal. If you like to use the terms familiar from economics, you might say that there are diminishing returns to increasing the sample size in terms of the improvements in accuracy.

(ii) Data is information. If it is to be used to test hypotheses, in the absence of scientifically controlled experiments, then the information has to vary enough for us to be able to observe the relationships between variables. Suppose we want to estimate a function to explain how the demand for cash balances (money) depends on the level of income and the rate of interest and we are faced with two otherwise identical studies apart from the fact that one has 28 annual observations and the other has 112 quarterly observations. Should we jump to the conclusion that the larger sample gives us more reliable statistical results? No, we should not necessarily do so. This is because there may not be enough 'span' in the data, i.e. the relevant variables do not vary enough. In an economy where the government has fixed interest rates, and for religious reasons the interest rate could possibly be zero, and the inflation rate is relatively unvarying over the period, then we may simply be unable to **identify** the link between real interest rates and money demand.

The broader issue of identification of relationships will be covered when we get to Chapter 12. There is sometimes a further problem in time-series data of using series of a span shorter than one year, which is the simple absence of some of the information. Some governments only collect annual data on some macroeconomic and financial variables. This has never stopped economists going on to perform quarterly or monthly studies. This is because they resort to **interpolation** to generate the missing data. Interpolation involves using some rules based on assumptions about the patterns in the data points we do have to produce estimates of the missing values. The simplest method is just to equally divide the change between two observations across the number of missing observations.

There are more sophisticated methods than this for interpolating and for producing missing variables in general but it is questionable whether a study in which the sample size has been quadrupled yet most of the variables are interpolated is a significant improvement. It is also necessary to state the rather obvious point that 'more garbage' is still garbage. If a particular source of data is so poorly measured that the measurement error dominates the other information in the data, then there is no advantage to be gained from increasing the sample size.

2.3 THE USES OF THE CONCEPT OF PROBABILITY

By far the most important idea which you should strive to master at this stage is that of probability. Data in non-experimental subjects, such as economics and other social sciences, is a long way from accurate and reliable. Often it has not been explicitly designed for the study it is being used for. It is therefore necessary that statistical analysis of such data is founded on probability theory. This leads to the need for us to make assumptions before we can draw any conclusions from our research. The basic assumptions are found in the CLRM and will be examined in Chapter 3. Economic theories are already premised on a set of assumptions before they reach the stage of being tested on data. One should avoid confusing the role of these assumptions with the statistical assumptions made. The statistical tests of econometrics are *not* typically used to test the assumptions of economic theory. Instead they tend to take these as given and test the implications or **predictions** of the theories. Assumptions are made about the process underlying an individual data series and about the way in which such series relate to each other. Given that any statistical testing rests on some assumptions being taken for granted, it would be misleading for us ever to claim that we have 'proved' a proposition.

Take the following propositions, which are often made:

▶ A devaluation of exchange rates will cause the balance of payments to alter.
▶ Longer sentences will deter criminals.
▶ Economic growth is increased by the amount of scientific research in a country.
▶ Higher unemployment benefits lead to higher unemployment rates.
▶ Television violence leads to more actual violence on the streets.
▶ Advertising increases the sales of products.

There are three broad sets of reasons why these propositions could never really be proven conclusively.

(i) The direction of causality (see Appendix 3) may be difficult to establish. Take the last proposition above. We can easily see that there is a two-way relationship in that nations with higher economic growth have more resources to do scientific research. The regression model can be developed to attempt to deal with this problem and this is presented in Chapters 12 and 13. It will be ignored until we get to those chapters.

(ii) The influence of **covariates**. All the above have been presented in terms of a bivariate relationship where one is trying to argue that 'X causes Y'. There is always the risk that any relationship which we discover between two variables is actually due to other variables which we did not know about or were unable to measure. This is shown in Figure 2.1, where the arrows represent the influence of X and four other variables (M, N, O, P) on Y. If we ignore the other four variables then we may incorrectly attribute some of their influence to the influence of X on Y. For future reference it should be noted that this mistake will not be made if there is a total absence of multicollinearity (see Chapter 10).

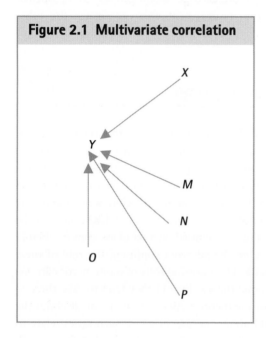

Figure 2.1 Multivariate correlation

The technique of multiple regression, as developed throughout this book, is designed for this problem. If we take one of the relationships posited above as being the main interest of a researcher we can call the supposed causal variable, such as longer prison sentences, the **focus** variable. Other variables that we include to make sure this relationship is not a false or illusory one may be termed **control** variables. In the case of criminal behaviour, we might wish to include such things as measures of the value of property available for theft and the risk of being caught by the police and arrested as controls. This specific topic will be examined in the review studies in Chapter 11.

(iii) Statistical tests are, as mentioned above, based on assumptions imposed on data, which is not strictly scientifically controlled nor indeed accurate. Economists tend to impose notions of causality on data. Theory tells them that price influences demand but any statistical evidence on this does not necessarily show that there is causation rather than just mere association. Although we may be sceptical about causality ever being demonstrated, it is nevertheless the case that econometrics is largely premised on it (see Appendix 3 for a discussion on causality).

The main technical ideas about probability and sampling are discussed in Appendix 5. We now enter a more general discussion about the idea of probability.

THE IDEA OF PROBABILITY

Every person deals every day with problems involving uncertainty or risk and has therefore a regular relationship with the problems of taking into account the nature of probability. For example, do they need to take precautions against the possibility that it may rain or be extremely hot? A common example is attempting to deal with whether some event is a coincidence. For example, newspapers may give great attention to the claims made that a noted psychic has dreamt the details of a plane crash in advance of its occurrence, or has found the name of a murderer in a vision. Sceptics rejecting the idea of any paranormal prevision are implicitly testing a hypothesis based on some notion of the probability of two separate events being causally linked.

One difficulty in this example is defining the **sample space**. This refers to the categories of possible events that could occur. The sample space is easy to define in the controlled situations of throwing a die or tossing a coin. That is, the former has six events and the latter two. These are univariate sample spaces. These are shown below for the case where we only make *one* throw of the die or coin.

Sample space for *one* throw of a coin: H   T

Sample space for *one* throw of a die: 1   2   3   4   5   6

All the hypotheses given above, and the psychic example, are bivariate sample spaces because we are concerned with joint events. We can produce a simple controlled bivariate event space by tossing a coin and throwing a die at the same time. This joint distribution will have 12 possible values. The dimensions of the sample space expand as we expand the number of 'trials', as we shall see below. A trial would be an individual instance of coin tossing or die throwing. Here are the sample spaces for *two* trials.

Sample space for *two* throws of a coin: HH   TT   HT   TH

Sample space for *two* throws of a die: 11   12   13   14   15   16   21   22   23   24
25   26   31   32   33   34   35   36   41   42
43   44   45   46   51   52   53   54   55   56
61   62   63   64   65   66

There are 4 possible outcomes for the coin and 36 for the die.

Having discussed the general idea of probability and how it features in events, it is time to move on to look at its application in hypothesis testing.

2.4 HYPOTHESIS TESTING AND PROBABILITY DISTRIBUTIONS

The core idea of hypothesis testing is to compare an expected value with a calculated value on the basis of a prior decision about the chance of different values coming about. Some assumption about the distribution of events is needed in order to test a hypothesis. Take the 'psychic' example; there are numerous studies of applied 'psi' based on testing whether an individual's psi hits are based on chance. A 'psi' hit is when a person correctly knows, for example, which of two cards is being selected by someone in another room. We would not expect the value of correct predictions to be zero even if the person has no psychic ability, so we need to calibrate the observed number of hits against some critical value of expected outcomes. This requires an assumption about the probability distribution of the events in the relevant sample space. You should note that in this case, as in all cases, performing below expectations is an important feature of the results from the data. That is, if a person was failing to make as many correct 'guesses' as we would anticipate of which card is being held up. This is called 'negative psi' and is an example of the other 'tail' of the hypothesis test. When we are interested in both possibilities (outcomes above and below the expected) then we have the **two-tailed hypothesis test** that econometrics, and more general statistical packages, will assume you are interested in when they report test statistics.

BINOMIAL DISTRIBUTION

It is time that we looked at the specific formulae for some probability distributions. In the case of tossing a 'fair' coin it is obvious that the suitable comparison with the actual outcomes is a **binomial distribution** based on a central tendency of half the outcomes being tails and half heads. For a small numbers of trials, we can calculate probabilities and confidence intervals by hand (or using binomial tables). When there are large numbers of trials it is possible in the normal distribution (shown below) to construct binomial tests. The formula for the likelihood of observing any given number of objects, from a sample of n trials, in one category (e.g. heads $= x$) and in the other category (e.g tails $= n - x$) is

$$p(x) = \binom{n}{x} P^x Q^{n-x} \tag{2.4}$$

where $\binom{n}{x} = n$ factorial/(x factorial) $\cdot$ ($n - x$, factorial); p is the probability; P is the number of cases in the x category; and Q is the number of cases in the other category. In the fair coin case we expect half of the trials to fall in each category (that is, heads or tails).

Suppose we threw a coin 6 times and it turned out that we got 4 heads. Is this so unlikely (improbable) that we might think this is not a 'fair' coin? That is, that it is heavier on one side or there is some deviation in the action of the tosser or there is an extraneous factor at work, such as wind in the case of tossing outdoors. We calculate from Equation (2.1) that the probability of getting 4 heads with a 50/50 probability is:

$$p(4) = [6 \cdot 5 \cdot 4 \cdot 3 \cdot 2 \cdot 1/(4 \cdot 3 \cdot 2 \cdot 1) \cdot (2 \cdot 1)] \cdot (1/2)^4 (1/2)^2$$

which equals 15/64 $= 0.2344$ (rounded). Given the symmetry of outcomes this will also be the probability of getting 2 tails. The sample space here consists of 7 possible outcomes. Using *H* for head and *T* for tail we get these as:

6 *H* 0 *T*, 5 *H* 1 *T*, 4 *H* 2 *T*, 3 *H* 3 *T*, 2 *H* 4 *T*, 1 *H* 5 *T*, 0 *H* 6 *T*.

This is a collapsed sample space as we have decided that the order in which the events occur is not important. That is, we only care about the number of heads and tails in a set of trials not the sequence in which they occur.

If we do our calculations correctly, then the probabilities of each of these should add up to 1 as the sum of all the possible outcomes must exhaust the sample space. The figures are then in the above order:

0.0156, 0.0938, 0.2344, 0.3124, 0.2344, 0.0938, 0.0156

This is only symmetrical about the modal (most likely) outcome (i.e. 3*H*, 3*T*) because the probabilities of heads and tails are treated as equal. If the probabilities are not 0.5, 0.5 then the distribution of outcomes will be skewed. The above calculations are for the probability of individual values arising. In most situations we are more interested in the range in which a value will lie. For example, how likely is the number of heads to lie between 4 and 6: that is, what is the chance of getting more than three heads? One reason we may want this kind of information is in the hope of making money by making bets with people who do not fully understand probability distributions. We can readily see that the probability of getting more than three heads is 0.3438 as it is just the sum of the three probabilities in the right-hand 'tail' of the distribution.

We have just dealt with the elements needed to use the important statistical concept of a **confidence interval.** The confidence interval is usually expressed in the opposite form from the way in which we have just introduced it. We have a statement such as 'the 95 per cent confidence interval for X lies between −23 and 69', which means that if we could keep repeating the drawing of our sample, we would find that, on average, 95 per cent of the values of X are to be found between the minimum of −23 and the maximum of 69. This kind of statement is a two-sided confidence interval. The coin example above dealt with one side of the distribution. To avoid confusion, we should note here that the words 'side' and 'tail' may be used interchangeably in the reporting of statistical tests. Effectively, we know that repeated samples (or trials) of sets of six throws would show 34.38 per cent of the sets having the number of heads greater than three.

In cases involving human choices, things are much more complex and it is not immediately clear what distributions should be used. Within any field of applied statistics this leads to the adoption of what seems 'reasonable' on the basis of a number of assumptions. The most usually adopted assumption about probability distributions is that of the so-called 'normal' distribution, which is discussed below. This is the crucial distribution in basic econometrics as you shall see in Chapter 3. The normal distribution can be used to test hypotheses from binomial distributions as the binomial distribution approaches the shape of the normal distribution as sample size increases. This happens more rapidly the closer is the probability of an individual result (head or tail) to 0.5. Where it is 0.5, the normal distribution can be used if $n > 25$.

THE CHI-SQUARED (χ^2) DISTRIBUTION

Let us move away from coin tossing to a more typical example from economics, such as the argument given above that unemployment benefits might **cause** unemployment to rise. Say we look at years when unemployment benefit rose or fell and tabulate whether unemployment rates rose or fell in the same years. This could be presented as shown in Table 2.3.

Table 2.3 Imaginary tabulation of unemployment rate changes against benefit changes		
Benefits go:	Unemployment rates go:	
	Up	Down
Up	6	9
Down	7	11

This is known in statistics as a **2×2 contingency table** and it may be described in a statistical package as a **crosstabulation.** If we originally had the actual values for benefit rates and unemployment rates, then we have thrown away some information from the continuous data by turning it into this up/down categorical data. This is just being done here for purposes of simplification. You should not normally turn data into a less informative format without some good reason for it. There are 33 data points in this sample. Could the pattern we see in Table 2.3 have come about by chance? For this particular case we must resort to a **Chi-squared (χ^2) distribution** in order to do a Chi-squared test. This is a bivariate test as it involves two variables. The worked example for the binomial distribution was a univariate test as it only involved one variable. The Chi-squared distribution can be used to perform univariate tests but we shall pass on to the bivariate case.

This and the other important distributions are presented in tables of critical values which would occur with a certain probability. These critical values depend in this case on the **significance level** we have chosen and the **degrees of freedom**. The test is calculated using the following formula:

$$\chi^2 = \Sigma(O_{ij}) - E_{ij})^2 / E_{ij} \qquad (2.5)$$

where E is the expected outcome and O is the observed outcome. The i and j subscripts represent the row and column of the cells in the table. O is simply taken from the data of the problem. The precise figures for E depend on the hypothesis being tested.

The **degrees of freedom** will be $(k-1)\cdot(m-1)$ where k and m are the number of rows and columns. For our example, there is only one degree of freedom. This means the table of critical values in Appendix 4 should be looked up for one degree of freedom and a significance level such as 5 per cent (0.05) to test the null hypothesis of no association between unemployment benefits and unemployment rates. This critical value is 3.84. So, if we can get a value of χ^2 from Equation (2.5), which is bigger than this, then we can reject the null of no association at the 5 per cent level. But, we still have to explain how the E values are determined in the formula. This requires us to sum across the rows and columns (see Table 2.4) giving us the information that:

- Benefits go up in 15 years but down in 18 years.
- Unemployment rates go up in 13 years and down in 20 years.
- The expected frequencies in any cell are worked out by multiplying the row total by the column total and then dividing by the sample size ($n = 31$ in this case).

Table 2.4 Expected frequencies in each cell for Table 2.3		
Benefits go:	**Unemployment rates go:**	
	Up	**Down**
Up	(13.15)/33 = 5.91	20.15/33 = 9.09
Down	(13.18)/33 = 7.09	20.18/33 = 10.91

So the calculation is

$$(6 - 5.91)^2/5.91 + (9 - 9.09)^2/9.09 + (7 - 7.09)^2/7.09 + (11 - 10.91)^2/10.91$$

$$= 0.0081/5.91 + 0.0081/9.09 + 0.0081/7.09 + 0.0081/10.91$$

$$= 0.0041 \text{ approx.}$$

which is not statistically significant at the 5 per cent level, leading to the suggestion that there is no association between these two events.

The **Chi-squared (χ^2)** test is a 'goodness of fit' statistic in the sense that it is computing how well observed data fit to a hypothetical distribution. For future reference you should note that, although it dealt with the relationship between two variables, which may be linked, it did not estimate any parameters to show the strength of the relationship between these two variables. In econometrics our major interest is on the parametric relationship between variables. This is developed when we come to Chapter 3. You may be wondering why a 5 per cent significance level was chosen in this case and not some other figure. You may even be unclear about the precise role of a significance level. These issues are dealt with in Section 2.6 below.

THE NORMAL DISTRIBUTION

This is the most important distribution for the purpose of this book. It is useful to begin our discussion of the normal distribution by reviewing the idea of the **central tendency** of a variable. We have already considered the idea of an arithmetic mean when talking about the issue of sampling earlier in this chapter. If we repeatedly take samples of a random variable (X) then its distribution will tend towards the arithmetic mean as its most likely outcome. The central tendency is the most likely outcome value. For a die, the central tendency turns out to be 3.5. That is, the expected value is $(1 + 2 + 3 + 4 + 5 + 6)/6$. This value can never occur in reality as dice have a limited integer sample space. They can only generate six possible outcomes one unit apart. Now we have some grasp of the idea of probability and central tendency, it is time to look at the matter of how and why we choose to work with particular **probability density functions**.

The answer to the 'why?' question is because we want to do hypothesis testing. The so-called 'normal distribution', which is applicable for continuous variables, makes hypothesis testing quite easy. This so-called 'bell shaped' curve has had many applications throughout history, most notably attempts to argue that it is a good representation of the spread of human intelligence (and many other things) throughout the population. There are some important real world phenomena that do not seem to approximate the normal distribution, most strikingly the distribution of income and wealth. In many cases it is possible to transform the distribution into a normal one by using logarithms and thus imposing a **log-normal distribution.** The importance of the normal distribution for this book is not whether it actually describes the variables we are going to be analysing – its main significance lies in the fact that we are going to use it to represent the disturbance or error term (u) in the regression equation.

An example of a normally distributed variable for a single variable such as height or weight in a sample is shown in Figure 2.2.

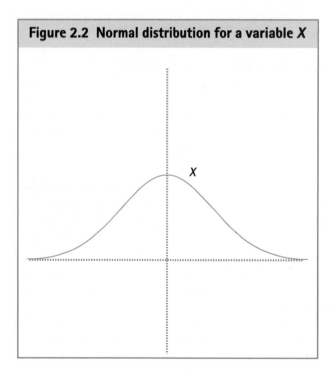

Figure 2.2 Normal distribution for a variable X

The first major feature of the normal distribution is that it is symmetrical. The highest point on the curve represents the value of X that is most likely to occur in repeated sampling. As a point this is infinitely small, so we can only feasibly represent probabilities by areas on the graph. A region of probability can be formulated in terms of lying between two numerical values of X, or in terms of being greater or less than X. Due to the symmetry of this distribution we have the implication that there is a 50 per cent chance ($p = 0.5$) of X being greater than the central value and a 50 per cent chance ($p = 0.5$) of X being less than the central value. This adds up to 1 and thus exhausts the sample space.

Let us suppose we want probability of a value lying between one unit below the central value and one unit above (for example, if we were estimating weight this might be one kilogram above and one kilogram below). We need to work out in Figure 2.2 what the relevant areas are.

Now we seem to have a problem that we did not have in the die example. There it was obvious what the size of this area would be. Here it is not. To overcome this difficulty we need an estimate of the size of these areas which requires evaluation of the following, rather difficult looking, formula called the **normal probability density function:**

$$f(x) = 1/\sqrt{2\Pi}\sigma \cdot e^{-(x^2)/2\sigma^2} \qquad (2.6)$$

The terms of Equation 2.6 are: $\Pi = 3.14159$; $e = 2.71828$ (this is the base of natural logarithms which we will use in Chapter 6); $\sigma =$ standard deviation of X.

Fortunately we do not need to calculate this formula every time we want to explore the confidence interval for an estimate. To get the two-sided 95 per cent confidence interval from a normal distribution curve, we find the points where 2.5 per cent of the values are expected to lie at each tail of the distribution – that is, 2.5 per cent are below the lowest point and 2.5 per cent are above the highest point – then we have found the values that enclose the 95 per cent confidence variable.

The relevant numerical values from a **standardized normal distribution** have been tabulated and are shown in Appendix 4. This is called a 'z' distribution and gives rise to 'z' tests, which are members of the family of **significance tests**. The process of standardizing data/variables involves transforming them to have certain properties. In this case we subtract the hypothesized value of the variable and divide by the standard error of the estimate of the mean. That is:

$$Z_i = (X_i - X^0)/\tilde{\sigma}_x \qquad (2.7)$$

where X^0 is the hypothesized value of the mean of X.

The transformed variable (z) has a mean of zero. A significance test is an alternative to the confidence interval in terms of representing the likelihood that certain ranges of values will occur. As you proceed through the study of econometrics, you will find that economists use significance tests the vast majority of the time rather than confidence intervals. We have already encountered the idea of a significance test in this chapter when looking at the application of the binomial distribution to coin tossing and the use of the Chi-squared test to look at the association of imaginary data for changes in unemployment rates and unemployment benefits.

Calculating a test statistic and comparing it with a critical value is how we carry out the significance test. Suppose we have a sample of 2000 males and we wish to test the hypothesis that they are taller than 5 ft 9 in (69 in.). This is a one-tailed test (see Section 2.5 for a full discussion of hypothesis testing), as we are only concerned with values lying above the mean not those below it. If you look down and across the normal distribution table, to find a 'z' of 1.96 you will see that the probability 0.025 occurs in the table. This indicates that 1.96 is the critical 'Z' value at the 2.5 per cent significance level. If the computed 'z' from our data is greater than 1.96 then we reject the null, that is, we conclude that individuals are greater than 69 in. tall, with there being less than a 5 in 200 chance that this is an 'accident' of sampling.

But where do we get this 'z' value from? The correct approach is to compute, as explained above:

[Mean of X – hypothesized value of X (69 in this case)]/standard error of the mean.　**(2.8)**

where the estimated standard error is:

$$\tilde{\sigma}_x = \left(\sqrt{1} \sum x_i^2/n - 1 \right)/\sqrt{n} \qquad\qquad \textbf{(2.9)}$$

where x is the deviation of X from the mean of X.

This is the standard error of the estimate of the mean, which must not be confused with the standard deviation of the data. For the example given, we would come to the conclusion that the average height of males in the sample is significantly different from 69 in. We would not have to do this test if we had the whole population. In that case we would be able to say that the average is greater than 69 in. if this is so in the population average. For example, even if the population average was only 69.000000035 we could still conclusively state the average was greater than 69. On the other hand, if the *sample average* was only 69.000000035, we would have to have a very limited range of variation in the sample (and/or a very large sample) according to Equation (2.9) in order to conclude that that average height was greater than 69 in.

The example just given is a univariate test. That is, a test on a single variable – height – in one sample. The aim of this book is to develop multivariate tests based on the assumptions of the normal distribution. The simplest type of multivariate test is the bivariate test that involves two variables, as in the Chi-squared test example given earlier. One form of bivariate test, developed from the assumption of normal populations (with normal samples taken from them), is to test the hypothesis that the means of two samples are identical. We might, for instance, have a sample of 2000 male heights from the rural population of a country and 2000 (it would not matter if it was some other number unless it was extremely small) from the urban population of a country. There are formulae for this test and statistical packages, such as SPSS, include it as an option. I will not develop this here as by the time you have completed Chapter 7 you will be in possession of a simple way to do such a test. That is, run a regression of the variable in question for the combined samples (this is called 'pooling') on an intercept/constant term and a dummy variable which is 0 for one of the two samples and 1 for the other one.

THE STUDENT 't' DISTRIBUTION

You are not going to see much mention of the 'z' test of significance in economics. Rather, computer packages and journal articles are filled with 't' tests based on 't' statistics. Originally these were called Student 't' tests but the 'Student' prefix has now been dropped.

The Student 't' distribution gets its name from the work of an analyst who conducted statistical trials at the breweries of the Guinness company. He wrote under the name of Student and hence the distribution he developed acquired this name. The 't' distribution will approximate the normal distribution as degrees of freedom approach infinity. For practical purposes, this means degrees of freedom of 120 or more, as you can see if you read down the values for the critical 't' shown in Appendix 4. The 't' values are very close to the 'z' values for degrees of freedom of 120 and above. The bottom line on a 't' table, which is that for infinite degrees of freedom, is identical to the 'z' value.

To make clear the difference between using a 't' test and a 'z' test, let us go back to the example of testing that mean height was greater than 69 in. in a sample with an estimated mean of 72 in. Let us suppose that the standard error of the mean was 1.8. The significance test value is then $1.67 = (72 - 69)/1.8$. If there were 2000 observations, then the degrees of freedom are effectively infinite, therefore the 5 per cent critical value for this one-tailed test is 1.645 and so we reject the null in favour of the alternate hypothesis that average height is more than 69 in. Let us suppose instead that the sample had only been for 21 males, giving us 20 degrees of freedom. Looking up the 't'-table, we find the critical value to be 1.725. As this exceeds the actual 't' ratio of 1.67 we must accept the null that average male heights are not in excess of 69 in. Using the standard normal distribution would have given us the wrong answer. It would always make us more likely to reject the null than we should be at a given significance level.

The 't' distribution is by far the most important for the basic study of econometrics. However, there are some other distributions, which you need to be familiar with, in particular the 'F' distribution. This gives rise to 'F' tests. We shall see, in Chapter 11, that it is possible to perform 't' and 'F' tests on the same econometric model and get apparently contradictory results.

THE 'F' DISTRIBUTION

The distribution is derived for the purposes of testing hypotheses about the relative magnitude of two variances. The calculation of an 'F' value is:

$$F(x_1, x_2) = \sigma x_1^2 / \sigma x_2^2 \qquad (2.10)$$

The expression shown is the ratio of the two variances for variables X_1 and X_2. F will be 1 if they are identical. It may be easier for you if you remember that we will put the larger of the two variances on the top line and use a one-tailed test on the hypothesis that the 'F' value is 1.

The 'F' distribution will have a mean of 1. Unlike the normal distribution this is not a symmetrical distribution, as can be seen in Figure 2.3. It is skewed – it leans towards the left

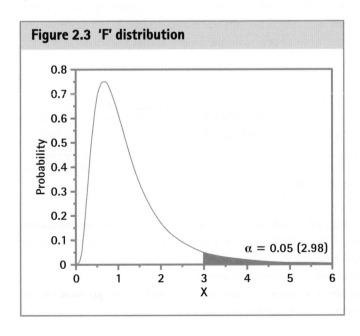

Figure 2.3 'F' distribution

thus showing a long tail to the right. Like the 't' and 'z' tests, the 'F' test is based on the assumption of a normally distributed pair of variables. It extends this by testing whether they have different variances.

You may be wondering why any economist, or other social scientist, would want to test whether the ratio of two variances is equal. This might be of interest for its own sake. You might have a hypothesis that predicts unequal variances. For example, you might have data for share prices in the stock markets of two countries, which are very similar except that one market is thought to be more efficient than the other in dealing with price relevant information. This hypothesis would say that share prices are more 'volatile' in the country with the less efficient market. Volatility would be measured by the variance of share prices. Most of the time the 'F' test is used to perform hypothesis tests about regression equations, as demonstrated in Chapter 5.

2.5 HYPOTHESIS TESTING: HOW TO WRITE IT DOWN PROPERLY

The above discussion has introduced the idea of confidence intervals and significance tests as a means of testing hypotheses. Once you begin to study closely the use of statistics by economists, you will see that they are not that keen to use confidence intervals as a way of presenting their work. Significance tests are the major means by which economists seek to demonstrate the correctness or superiority of their research. The form of presentation for a hypothesis test (in the case where we are dealing with a single isolated proposition), which is most commonly used in econometrics, is shown below:

$$H_0: \ b = 0$$
$$H_1: \ b \neq 0$$

(2.11)

where b is a parameter; for example it could be the price elasticity of demand for a good.

H_0 is the **null hypothesis** which will be written in the form of an equals sign or a greater than or equal to or less than equal sign. H_1 is the **alternate hypothesis**. The hypothesis test must be thought of as taking the form above with the only allowed variations being the following:

▶ Different values from 0 may be used in H_0.
▶ A greater than ($>$) or less than ($<$) sign may take the place of the 'not equal to' in H_1. These are one-tailed tests as opposed to the two-tailed test of Equation (2.5). We cannot have an equals sign in H_1.
▶ H_0 and H_1 may involve multiple items: for example, the sum of two or more parameters might be equal to 0 or some other number in H_0.

The final key ingredients of a correctly formulated hypothesis test are the degrees of freedom and the significance level. Once we have selected a set of data and a model to be applied to it we have no choice over the degrees of freedom. The only way to have more degrees of freedom is to get more data or have a 'smaller' model by imposing **restrictions** that will exclude variables if the restriction is that the parameter equals zero or will reduce the number of parameters if the restriction is on the sum, ratio or product of parameters.

Other things being equal, a larger sample size means that any statistical estimate can be tested with a greater number of degrees of freedom. It is very important that you check at all future stages of your study of econometrics that you are completely sure on how to work out the correct degrees of freedom for any test. One degree of freedom was lost, in the case above of testing the mean, because one estimate was made; that is, the mean of the sample was estimated. When more values are estimated, as we do later, we will lose a degree of freedom for each estimate. So, the general formula for estimating degrees of freedom is $n - k$ where k is the number of **parameters** being estimated.

2.6 HOW DO WE DECIDE ON THE SIGNIFICANCE LEVEL?

Any subject relying on hypothesis testing requires its researchers to make decisions about what the significance level for a particular piece of work should be. It is unlikely that we would call 'good science' the situation where an individual simply decides, for no apparent reason, to use a particular significance level. So there ought to be some criteria for picking a particular significance level. It would be wonderful if every important hypothesis in the world could be accepted or rejected at some fantastically high level of certainty, for example, a low 'p' value such as $p = 0.000001$, that is, there is only a one in a million chance that a result came about by chance (assuming the distributional assumptions are valid). This kind of certainty is not going to occur, not least because of the problem of choosing between Type I and Type II errors, which we now encounter in the context of the **loss function** for errors in hypothesis testing. The literature of applied econometrics is almost entirely couched in terms of the Type I error. You could pick hundreds of journal articles from the library at random and never see the Type II error being considered. The Type I error is unlikely to be mentioned directly because it is implicitly assumed to be the only error in which economists are interested.

The essence of the Type I/Type II distinction is simply that between a 'false positive' and a 'false negative'. People who were in no way statisticians have long noticed the consequences of ignoring this. Matters of life and death have a habit of bringing it to our attention, most notably where capital punishment is being contemplated. It can even be seen in the following comment around 1692 relating to the infamous Salem witch trials:

> it were better that ten suspected witches escape than that one innocent person be condemned. . . . I had rather judge a witch to be an honest woman than judge an honest woman to be a witch (Pickering, 1996, p. 425).

The writer is displaying a clear preference for an asymmetric treatment of errors where the false positive in the hypothesis (i.e. wrongly finding for H_1) is giving less weight than the false null (wrongly finding for H_0) in the following test:

H_0: This person is not a witch

H_1: This person is a witch

The false negative, as the hypothesis has been set up here, is the Type I error. This is the type normally set in statistical work by economists, as will be amply displayed in the illustrations used in the later chapters of this book. In theory the anxieties of Increase Mathers could be formulated in a loss function, indeed he has already given the orders of magnitude for such a function. The abstract form of such a function is:

$$E(UL) = p_1 U(\text{Type I error}) + p_2 U(\text{Type II error}) \qquad (2.12)$$

where E stands for expectation, p_1 is the probability of a Type I error and p_2 stands for the probability of a Type II error. U represents the utility function of the decision maker. This is basically the standard Von Neumann–Morgenstern utility function of the core economic analysis of risky decision making. It is easy to think of important everyday examples of this kind of problem in the modern economic world. For example, in the field of medical testing, such as smear tests for cancer or detection of HIV-AIDS, there is always the risk of false rejection of the null of no infection (Type II error) which cannot be treated as costless as the error will have consequences such as loss of earnings and loss of utility from treatment for the wrong diagnosis. Similar considerations apply to macroeconomic forecasting where the government may be wrongly advised of the impact of a variable on growth where the costs would be felt in either inflation or unemployment.

The choice variables are the two levels of 'p'. There will have to be a trade-off between the 'p' values. The only way to decrease both 'p's simultaneously is by increasing the sample size. In an ideal world, the researcher might establish the desirable values of 'p' and the sample size when they are designing their research plan prior to actually obtaining data. Econometrics does not inhabit this ideal world. Instead it dwells in one where, most of the time, researchers start with a fixed sample size and proceed to ignore the Type II error in preference to focusing on the reduction of Type I error by imposition of a strict level on the value of 'p' used in significance testing using the critical 't' values. This level is not even arrived at by minimizing a loss function in which the researcher has purposefully ignored the p_2 value from Equation 2.6. Rather, economists, and a very large percentage of statistical research in other social science disciplines, simply operates on the basis of rules of thumb arrived at by convention. That is, we choose a critical significance level, on which to base our conclusions, by simply following those who have previously worked in the topic area. Put crudely, the general impression from the economics literature is that a hypothesis for which the null is rejected at the 5 per cent level has done quite well, while one that has done so at 1 per cent or better is doing extremely well. Rejection in the vicinity of the 10 per cent level is the borderline where economists become uncomfortable. You will see guarded support for a hypothesis which is just making this level, and perhaps more enthusiastic support the closer to the core propositions of economics is the test proposition. It should, of course, be reiterated at this point that economists are not going to overthrow a central feature of their models just because of acceptance of the null. Even if the null is accepted at a high level of the null it could be that this is just a property of a particular specification and data set so that we would await substantial exploration and replication before we would drastically change theoretical models in response to null results.

So why do economists refrain from developing an explicit loss function to determine and thereby generally ignore the Type II error issue? The following possibilities suggest themselves:

▶ They are lazy.
▶ It doesn't matter as the costs of their errors are minimal.

- They do not feel competent to evaluate the social welfare function implicit in formulating a loss function and so go with only Type I because:
- They frame their hypotheses in such a way that they are primarily seeking support/confirmation for the existence of a relationship between two variables – e.g. interest rates influence money demand, money supply influences inflation etc. – so, although we can never have proof in an absolute sense, there is an attempt to increase the likelihood of Type I error because it is seen as more important.

2.7 COVARIANCE AND CORRELATION COEFFICIENTS

In Section 2.3 above we gave a number of examples of situations where there might be a relationship between two variables and we also voiced the criticism that it might be difficult to be sure if a claim that 'X caused Y' is reasonable. We can describe the relationship between two variables in terms of their **covariance**. That is, we are interested in whether they co-vary in the sense that they share variation. Look at the Venn diagrams in Figures 2.4 and 2.5.

Each shape is a summary of the amount of variation in the variable. In Figure 2.4 the two shapes do not intersect and hence we would say there is zero covariance between the two. In Figure 2.5 there is an area of overlap that seems large in comparison with the size of the two

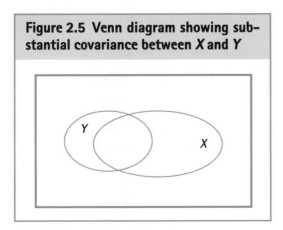

Figure 2.4 Venn diagram showing zero covariance between X and Y

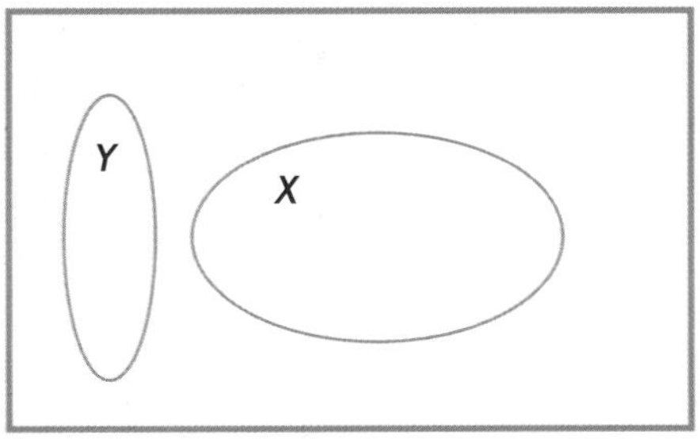

Figure 2.5 Venn diagram showing substantial covariance between X and Y

shapes. Given this, we might roughly conclude that there is a large amount of covariation in this case.

The formula for covariance is contained in the top line of Equation (2.13) below. The main problem with a numerical measure of covariation is that its size will vary dependent on the units of measurement.

It needs to be standardized. The most obvious method of standardization is to transform a variable so that it lies between 0 and 1. If we adopt the assumption of two normally distributed variables then we can compute a correlation coefficient, which is derived from the following formula:

$$r = \left\{ \sum_{i=1}^{n} x_i y_i / (n-1) \right\} / \sqrt{(\text{var}(X).\text{var}(Y))} \qquad (2.13)$$

where x and y denote, respectively, the deviation between X and Y and their respective means.

The top line of this formula is the estimated **covariance** between Y and X, which will prove to be a useful concept in Chapter 3. It can be either positive or negative and it has no limitations, i.e. can range from plus to minus infinity. If it is zero then there is no association whatsoever between X and Y so 'r' will equal 0. The bottom line serves the function of making 'r' bounded between 1 and −1. The bigger is 'r', the greater is the degree of association between X and Y. One should be cautious in being over-enthusiastic about moderately large 'r' as the percentage of variation that the two variables share in common is, in fact, measured by 'r' squared rather than 'r' itself. Further, 'r' is only a descriptive statistic so you cannot perform a hypothesis test simply by looking at its value. The appropriate hypothesis test is:

$$H_0: \quad r = 0$$
$$H_1: \quad r \neq 0 \qquad (2.14)$$

This test is performed by using the significance test called a 'z' test which we looked at earlier in this chapter. For the correlation coefficient $Z = \frac{1}{2}\log_e(1+r)/(1-r)$ should be compared with its standard error, which is

$$1/\sqrt{(n-3)} \qquad (2.15)$$

This ratio must be compared with figures in Appendix 4 for areas under the normal distribution. A calculation is given below to illustrate how this is done.

The statistic, 'r', is known by various names. It is most correctly called a **zero-order (or simple) correlation coefficient**. Such coefficients are also sometimes known as Pearsonian correlation coefficients (after nineteenth-century scientist Karl Pearson). On occasions, you may see references to 'correlation coefficients' which may be taken to be this formula. The term correlation is used because we are dealing with a measure of how two variables relate to each other, i.e. how they co-relate.

The reason for mentioning the qualifying phrase 'zero order' is that such a measure does not take account of the possible intervening influence of variables other than X and Y. That is, the influence of such variables is assumed to be zero. If we start to take account of these by modifying the formula then we produce 'higher order correlation coefficients'. I will not pursue this because the present work is more concerned with how we deal with such things in a regression equation, as you shall see in Chapter 3.

The value of 'r' can be easily obtained on most econometrics and spreadsheet packages. In software, dedicated specifically to econometrics, the most useful means of obtaining it is usually in the form of a **partial correlation matrix** such as that shown in Table 2.5.

Table 2.5 Zero-order partial correlation matrix for Turkish data on cigarette smoking, GNP and relative prices

Data for Turkish smoking 1960–1988 (annual)				
	CCA	GNP	RPC	TER
CCA	1			
GNP	0.61666	1		
RPC	0.23274	0.83540	1	
TER	0.57221	0.92383	0.77482	1

Note: CCA is per capita (based on adults) consumption of cigarettes; *GNP* is real gross national product per capita; *TER* is the rate of take-up of tertiary education and *RPC* is the relative price (price of cigarettes divided by the retail price index).
Source: Data is presented in Tansel (1993) and also in the Excel file TURKCIG.XLS on the website.

This is based on the same data that will be used to show the differences between bivariate and multiple regression in Sections 3.8 and 3.9 in Chapter 3. You can see that it has a row of ones running down the main diagonal as the correlation between a variable and itself is 1, by definition. The other elements in the matrix show the 'r' value between the two pairs of variables in the matrix. It follows that the top half of the matrix above the diagonal would reproduce an exact mirror image of the estimates of 'r' in the bottom half. These are not normally shown as there is no real need to have the same information twice on a table.

Examination of such a matrix is a useful first look at the data before we proceed to full-scale multiple regression equations. You will find, in Chapter 10, that we return to the simple correlation coefficient as a source of guidance in assessing the seriousness of the problem of multicollinearity.

If you look at the pattern of 'r' in Table 2.5 it seems that there is only one pair of variables that are quite weakly correlated. That is, the relationship between income and prices is only of the order of 0.23 *0.23, that is about 5.3 per cent shared variation. You may also note that all of the 'r' values are positive, implying that movements of all the variables tend to be in the same direction as each other.

So far we have only used the matrix of 'r' for descriptive purposes. It can be hypothesis tested on the assumption that the variables follow normal distributions, as implied above. To illustrate this, let us apply the formula in Equation (2.9) to the weakest correlation in the above table, that is, the 0.23274 between demand and relative prices. The log of the ratio $(1.23274 / 0.76276) = 0.48$ (rounded). The standard error is $1 / \sqrt{28} = 0.18899$ (rounded). If we divide the latter into the former we get 2.54 (rounded). Consulting the table in Appendix 4 shows that we can reject the null hypothesis at the 5 per cent level as the 'z' value corresponding to 0.05 is much less than 2.54.

The 'r' value is based on the assumption that we are dealing with continuous/ratio data measured on an interval scale. We should not leave this chapter with the idea that you cannot have correlation coefficients derived from data that contains less information. The example given in the Chi-squared table above could be used to construct a correlation coefficient. This is called a **contingency coefficient** and is computed as follows:

$$C = \sqrt{\chi^2/(n + \chi^2)} \tag{2.16}$$

where n is the sample size. This measure has the property of being zero when there is no association but it cannot reach one when there is a perfect fit. How large it can be depends on the size of the contingency table (in terms of rows and columns).

The contingency coefficient is a correlation coefficient for data of a very low information content. The **Spearman's rank correlation coefficient** can be used on data that is more informative, the level being ordinal. That is, we have information on the position of each observation in the data for the Y variable in the order of magnitude of Ys and we have the corresponding information for Xs. The formula is given in Equation (2.11), which is what Equation (2.7) simplifies to if we replace the original X and Y data with their ranks.

$$r_s = 1 - (6\Sigma d^2)/(n^2 - n) \tag{2.17}$$

where d is the difference between ranks, e.g. if the fifth observation appears as the fourth item in the order of the Y series from top to bottom and the eighth item in the X series from top to bottom then d will equal minus 4. The fact that d is squared in the formula means that differences of the same size in either direction are treated equally. This has the classic correlation coefficient properties of being one when there is a perfect fit (but note that a perfect fit in ranks does not necessarily mean that there would be a perfect fit if we had the underlying ratio/continuous data measured in scalar units) as all d's will be zero and it will tend to zero when there is no fit whatsoever between the series. Not all econometrics packages make this statistic available, although you can compute it by simply using the routine, which computes 'r' on the ranked data instead of the original data. That is, you use the ranks in the calculation in the form of 1 for the largest value, 2 for the second largest and so on.

I will not go into the issue of how to test this coefficient or how to deal with the problem of 'tied ranks'. You can read about this in any non-parametric statistics textbook. This test will not be as reliable as the Pearsonian test in circumstances where the underlying assumptions of normality and scalar measurement are met and hence it should only be used when there is doubt about these. In any case, the interest of the rest of this book is in developing multiple regression. Hence you should only regard the above discussion of correlation as a means of getting you started thinking along the necessary lines to understand multiple regression.

2.8 CONCLUSION

This chapter has covered the preliminary concepts that are necessary to the understanding of the multiple regression model that forms the backbone of the rest of this book. The important concepts of probability distributions and hypothesis testing have been introduced. Hypothesis testing will be further developed in Chapters 3 and 5 and will be regularly revisited in the remaining chapters. This chapter ended with the computation of measures of association (correlation) between two variables. The next chapter progresses to the estimation of measures of the intercept and slopes of straight line relationships between a **dependent variable**, which appears on the left-hand side of a **regression equation**, and the **independent variables**, which are on the right-hand side. The data which we have just used, from Turkey over the period 1960–88, to compute (zero order) correlation coefficients, r, will be used again in Chapter 3 to compute bivariate and multiple regression equations.

DOS AND DON'TS

Do

✓ Make sure you understand the concept of probability and are familiar with the idea and uses of a normal distribution.

✓ Make sure you understand hypothesis testing and each of its key elements: degrees of freedom, significance level and critical value.

✓ Stay aware of the fact that social scientists do not usually work out the optimal significance level to use for a test. The most common approach is to rely on a 5 per cent level.

Don't

✗ Fall into a confused use of the word significance. Statistical significance should not be confused with economic or other forms of significance. You can have a statistically significant relationship that is very small numerically.

✗ Forget that the tables and tests you will encounter are tests for Type I error.

✗ Confuse correlation with regression. Correlation has just been covered in Section 2.7. Regression is covered in the next chapter. In everyday speech we tend to lapse into using the word correlation when we mean regression.

EXERCISES

2.1 What is the difference between the meaning of the terms:
(i) variable and observation;
(ii) population and sample;
(iii) cross-section and time-series data;
(iv) categorical and continuous data.

2.2 Say whether the following are true, false or indeterminate:
(i) a 't' test is the same as an 'F' test;
(ii) a 't' test is the same as a 'z' test;
(iii) an 'F' test can be used to test the hypothesis that two variances are equal;
(iv) no one knows how to arrive at the correct significance level for testing hypotheses.

2.3 Explain the relationship between the confidence interval and the 'point' estimate.

2.4 Should you be more interested in the point estimate or the confidence interval for a set of results?

2.5 Use the following data sets (see website) to calculate partial correlation coefficients for the variables indicated and comment on your results:

(i) THEATRE.XLS – television hours watched and estimated family income;

(ii) THEATRE.XLS – radio hours watched and estimated family income;

(iii) THEATRE.XLS – TV hours watched and radio hours watched;

(iv) AUSCIN.XLS – population and cinema attendance.

Note: The data used in the THEATRE.XLS file is explained in some detail in Chapter 4. The data in AUSCIN.XLS is reproduced and discussed in Chapter 14.

REFERENCES

Brainerd, E. (2001) Economic reform and mortality in the Former Soviet Union: A study of the suicide epidemic in the 1990s, 12A Discussion Papers, No. 243, January, Bonn.

Pickering, D. (1996) *Cassell's Dictionary of Witchcraft*, Cassell, London.

Tansel, A. (1993) Cigarette demand, health scares and education in Turkey, *Applied Economics,* **25**, 521-529.

FURTHER READING

If you need to review the statistical background further, consult:

Sanders, D.H., Smidt, R.K., Adatia, A. and Larson, G. (2001) *Statistics: A First Course,* McGraw-Hill-Ryerson, New York.

WEBLINKS

http://www.itl.nist.gov/div898/handbook/eda/section3/eda36.htm

This is an Exploratory Data Analysis Handbook for Engineering Statistics. It gives 't' and 'F' tables and good explanations of how to use them among other material useful for econometrics.

http://www-gap.dcs.st-and.ac.uk/~history/Curves/Curves.html

This is an interactive website which allows you to play with famous curves (i.e. distributions). The normal distribution is listed as the 'Frequency Curve'.

http://www.radstats.org.uk/

This gives access to articles critical of the use made of data and statistical analysis.

http://www.mala.bc.ca/~johnstoi/darwin/sect4.htm

This page provides a brief history of the concept of probability.

3

The Classical Linear Regression Model Introduced

LEARNING OBJECTIVES

- Be able to perform and interpret basic bivariate and multiple regression
- Understand the role of the disturbance term and know the classical assumptions made about it
- Be aware of what is meant by OLS being BLUE
- Know how to interpret the R squared statistic
- Understand the derivation of the OLS estimators
- Begin to understand how to summarize an academic article which uses econometrics

CHAPTER SUMMARY

3.1 BIVARIATE REGRESSION

Now that we have introduced the idea of econometrics as a subject field and its statistical foundations, we are ready to move onto elementary econometric models. The simplest type of model may be termed a bivariate regression. Later we will move on to the more complicated **multiple regression equations**. The bivariate model has only one variable on each side of an equation, while the multiple regression equation has one variable on the left-hand side and two or more variables on the right-hand side. This difference is illustrated below:

$$Y_i = b_0 + b_1 X_i + u_i \qquad \text{Bivariate regression} \tag{3.1a}$$

$$Y_i = b_0 + b_1 X_i + b_2 X_2 + u_i \qquad \text{Multivariate regression} \tag{3.1b}$$

The full meaning of the parts of these equations will be explained as we progress throughout the book. We begin with a bivariate model because it is easier to explain than the multivariate model. A bivariate model is not likely to be used very often in practice.

It is common to refer to the variable on the left-hand side of such an equation as the **dependent variable** (Y) and those on the right-hand side as **independent variables** (these will be denoted by X throughout this book). This form of words seems to imply some notion of **causality** (see Appendix 3 for more discussion on this) which was not present in the bivariate correlation, using 'r' and the Spearman rank correlation coefficient introduced at the end of Chapter 2.

We have a model where the value of Y 'depends' on the value of the X variables. The idea of which variable belongs on the left, and which belongs on the right should come from some prior theory. For example, in economics, the normal approach in modelling demand supposes that quantity demanded depends on price. Thus we have an equation such as

$$Quantity\ of\ Lipstick\ Demanded_i = b_0 + b_1 \quad (Price\ of\ Lipstick)_i + u_i \tag{3.2}$$

where the b's are **parameters**. The variable u is an extremely important concept which tends to be called the **error term** or **disturbance term.**

Throughout the text, we shall adopt the convention of treating the parameter which is not multiplied by a variable as b_0 and those which are as b_1, b_2 and so forth. The parameter b_0 is implicitly multiplied by the value 1. There is then a variable consisting of the number 1 for all observations. You will not be required to enter a row of ones into a spreadsheet on a computer package. The package will automatically do this for you when you ask for a regression with a 'constant term'. In many cases, the package will automatically assume that you want a constant term and include one for you.

The estimated value of b_0 will be an estimate of the intercept of the plotted line of Quantity of Lipstick against the Price of Lipstick. This is shown in Figure 3.1.

The intercept tends to be called the 'constant term' or 'regression constant' in articles and computer packages. The slope of the line in Figure 3.1 will be b_1 and so the value of this is often called the 'slope coefficient'.

We have just written out the full names of variables. In future we will usually follow the practice of most economists of using symbols in the theoretical equation and mnemonics in the estimated equations. For example, a typical economist might call these variables *QTLIP* and *PRICELIP* to remind them what the variables are rather than using the full names. Certainly,

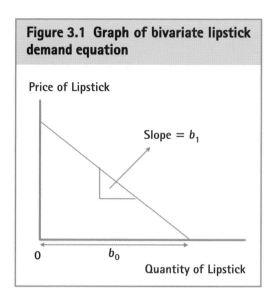

Figure 3.1 Graph of bivariate lipstick demand equation

Price of Lipstick

Slope = b_1

0   b_0

Quantity of Lipstick

if you trawl through the journal literature you will find equations with dozens of variables in them, many of which have names that make it virtually impossible to recognize what they represent. This tendency may be due to simply pasting across names from computer packages, which require variables to be kept below 8 characters.

Throughout this text, we will adopt the convention of using lower case i to represent the observation subscript. Sometimes there is a tendency to use lower case t, particularly in the case of time series, but we shall avoid this except for specific examples involving time series.

The above equation (3.2) is based on an economic hypothesis that *the price of lipstick determines the demand for lipstick and not the other way round*. You could argue that the quantity of lipstick will influence the price through its interaction with supply. This involves us having a two-equation model, which we postpone until Chapters 12 and 13.

We treat equations like Equation (3.2) as being an equilibrium schedule in terms of representing the choices of a utility-maximizing consumer, which varies in response to an exogenously fixed price. The u term, which will occupy much of our attention in this chapter, is in the equation in order to deal with any tendency for the equation to deviate from its equilibrium, although it also represents other data and **specification** problems in the equation.

From basic microeconomics, we know that a hypothesis of a negative price-quantity relationship applies so long as we rule out the case of a 'Giffen good'. That is, the demand curve slopes downward. This hypothesis should be written in the following form following the instructions in Chapter 2:

$$H_0: \quad b_1 \geqslant 0$$
$$H_1: \quad b_2 < 0$$

(3.3)

This would be a one-tailed hypothesis test. In Equation (3.2), the Quantity of Lipstick Demanded is the dependent variable while the Price of Lipstick is the independent variable. This is a linear equation – a graph of the equation for lipstick sold on the X-axis against its price on the Y-axis would be a straight line.

3.2 THE ROLE OF THE DISTURBANCE TERM

Understanding the nature and purpose of the disturbance term is the most important ingredient of this chapter. It is vital that you spend time in trying to understand it before you proceed to the remaining chapters. The right-hand side of Equations (3.1) and (3.2) are made up of two distinct parts. The variable u at the end is the disturbance term and is *not* part of the theoretical model. It is assumed to be a random variable. The price term and the parameters are assumed *not* to have a random element. The price variable is something which we will either go and collect or have given to us. The b_0 and b_1 parameters are fixed also, in that we assume that they do not vary over the sample: for example, if the sample covered the period from 1979–2002 we would assume that the slope of the demand curve is the same in each of these years. For this reason, we do not have an i subscript on the parameters. So, the disturbance term is an addition to the theoretical model (although we can have theoretical models that contain random elements, these are not part of elementary economics). It allows for the fact that the demand function in our example may be shifting about due to forces other than those included in the model.

You should note that the statistical assumptions about the right-hand side (normally written as X) variables and the left-hand side variable (normally written as Y) are different. We assume the X's to be measured without error, which means we can treat them 'as if' the researcher decided to choose different levels of X in order to see how people would behave in their choice of Y. We are treating the Y data 'as if' it was generated by a controlled experiment in which we varied the values of X. Any measurement errors are embodied in the u term. Y is written down as the sum of the u term and the 'exact' equation from simple microeconomic theory. This must mean that Y has the same statistical properties as the disturbance term.

So, Y is a variable that embodies any assumptions we make about the disturbance term. It is essential that we do make assumptions about the disturbance term. If we do not, it is impossible to do any statistical testing of the parameters of the regression equation.

Before we turn to the **classical** assumptions about the disturbance term, we must explain more clearly exactly what the disturbance term is doing in the equation. The form of the equation, i.e. the shape of the relationship and the variables it includes, is referred to as the **specification** of the regression equation. Given the limitations of our knowledge and the data that we use, no specification will ever be 100 per cent correct. The u term is then an 'imaginary' variable in which all these **specification errors** are captured. The main types of error that are captured in the u term are as follows:

▶ Omitted variables – for example, in Equation (3.2) the demand for lipstick might be dependent on other variables such as income, the strength of feminist thinking and the age of individuals in the sample.

▶ Wrong choice of functional form. If it turns out that the linear relationship is not appropriate then this will be reflected in the error term. Adjustments to the model to allow for non-linear functional forms are introduced in Chapter 7.

▶ Differences between the theoretical concepts and the variables, in the data, that are used to represent them. For example, some versions of the consumption function depend on permanent income rather than measured income. If we simply use measured income then we have 'errors in variables', a term referring to the right-hand side being measured with error contrary to the assumptions used in the model.

▶ Errors in the collection of the data. Even if the variables collected do correctly represent the variables used in economic theory, they may suffer from inaccuracies owing to the limitations of data collection methods. For example, an interview study of households will be relying on the memories of the household members to give figures for earnings, expenditure etc.

▶ The parameters may shift. People's tastes may be changing in the real world contrary to the assumptions of simple economic models.

Analysis of the estimates of the u term could be useful in diagnosis of the performance of the model. We cannot analyse the disturbance terms themselves as these are not actually known. They are assumed to exist, and to follow the assumptions we are about to give. Analysis of the errors in the model is based on the estimates of the u term known as **residuals.** In many cases they are denoted by e, not to be confused with the similar looking e which is the traditional mathematical symbol for the number used as the base of natural or Napierian logarithms, which we shall find to be useful in Chapter 7. These regression residuals are important as they form the basis of the popular descriptive statistic – the **R squared (R^2)** and the standard errors of the parameter estimates, which we use to construct the hypothesis tests on the parameters.

The residuals are obtained by working out the predicted values of Y from the estimated values of the b's and subtracting this from the actual Y. Before we come to the formulae used to produce these estimates, we will need to discuss the **classical assumptions** about the u term.

3.3 CLASSICAL ASSUMPTIONS OF THE DISTURBANCE TERM

The **classical linear regression model** (CLRM) has two components: a linear regression equation which is estimated by the technique of ordinary least squares (OLS) plus a list of assumptions about the stochastic variable u. Our bivariate estimating equation in the lipstick example above written in algebraic form is just Equation (3.2) again:

$$Y_i = b_0 + b_1 X_i + u_i \tag{3.4}$$

When the equation is estimated from some data, we write the estimated equation as:

$$\hat{Y}_i = \hat{b}_0 + \hat{b}_1 X_i \tag{3.5}$$

where the ^ on top of variables and parameters, as explained in Chapter 2, represent estimated values. This symbol is described as 'hat', so you will hear econometricians speak about 'b hat' or 'beta hat'.

Unless the fit of the model is perfect, which is very unlikely, then Y (which is from the data) in Equation (3.4) will not be the same as predicted Y in Equation (3.5). The difference between them will provide us with an estimate of u which is the regression residual. Hence, we can write an equation for the residuals as:

$$\hat{u}_i = Y_i - \hat{Y}_i = Y - \hat{b}_0 + \hat{b}_1 X_i \tag{3.6}$$

The following assumptions about the u term are made in the classical model:

(i) u is a continuous random variable.
(ii) It has a normal distribution.
(iii) It has a mean of zero.
(iv) It has zero covariance with the right-hand side variables (X's).
(v)   It has a constant variance (homoscedasticity) across the sample.
(vi) The covariance of u for any observation i with any other observation later or earlier in the sample is zero. This assumption cannot really be summed up easily in one word and is usually described as 'absence of serial correlation'. The full definition and tests for serial correlation are given in Chapter 9.

The regression residual need not have these properties, although the use of OLS, with a constant term included, will force them to have a mean that is very close to zero.

The relevance of some of these assumptions will become clearer when you read later chapters, in particular Chapter 9 and more specifically Chapter 13 for Assumption 4, Chapter 11 for Assumption 5 and Chapter 9 for Assumption 6. I do not propose to discuss these further at this point. However, it will be helpful if we spend a little time on justifying the first three assumptions.

The justification for Assumptions 1–3 is that it is reasonable to suppose that the errors in the model come from a large number of small, independent causes. Given such an argument, we might feel justified in claiming that the errors should be symmetrical since positive errors will be as likely as negative errors of the same size.

However, we cannot know, for certain, that a disturbance term would have zero mean and a normal distribution. This is still an assumption imposed on the data for hypothesis testing purposes. The normal distribution is a very convenient one for hypothesis testing. Assuming that the disturbance term is normal we shall be led to the conclusion that the estimators of b_0 and b_1 must also follow a normal distribution. This means that we only need the estimated standard errors of the b estimates and the residuals in order to conduct hypothesis tests (using 't' and 'F' ratios) about the b's.

3.4 OLS ESTIMATORS: WHAT MAKES THEM BLUE AND WHERE DO THEY COME FROM?

By now, you should be familiar with the term OLS used as an abbreviation for the term 'ordinary least squares' but we have yet to fully discover what OLS is. OLS is a set of formulae that produces an **estimator** for the parameters of our model. In other words, it is a set of mathematical rules that tell us how to produce the values which correspond to the b hats.

It is only one possible estimator. Indeed, an alternative is simply to make up what you think is a plausible value. If I were to guess that the marginal propensity to consume in the USA is 0.6 then that is an estimate derived from some form of estimator in my mind. We would expect that using a computer package to analyse data from the real world can improve on my guess. OLS is one algorithm, or set of calculations, that is programmed into computer packages to produce an estimator. Given that there are alternatives, we need to spend some time discovering why OLS might be thought to be a good estimator. It turns out that this is judged in terms of the fact that it can be shown to be **BLUE** under the classical assumptions, which have just been described above. BLUE is another acronym, or abbreviation, which stands for Best Linear Unbiased Estimator.

This covers four criteria for what makes an estimator a good estimator. I shall deal with these in reverse order

E is for estimator

It is desirable that a formula is used to estimate something; in this case the regression parameter can be shown to be an estimator of it. As the formula for OLS estimation of b_1 shown in Equation (3.9) below contains data from both the X and Y data series then it should be an estimator of b_1.

U is for unbiased

An estimator is biased if it has a tendency to produce estimated values for the b's that are systematically higher, or lower, than the true value. It is easy to see why we would want unbiased estimators. If we used a regression equation for forecasting for business purposes then we would potentially lose profits from using a biased estimator instead of an unbiased estimator. Say we own a restaurant and our model systematically over-estimates the price elasticity of demand, then we may well end up setting prices that are not optimal. If we are using a regression equation to test hypotheses from a particular model or theory then bias runs the risk of working for or against the null. In this case it is important to know whether the bias is upward or downward in conjunction with whether the alternate hypothesis for the parameter is greater than or less than zero.

To make this clearer, let us imagine that we have a piece of work where we know that the income coefficient in a demand equation is biased downwards and another where the price coefficient is biased downwards. Assuming the product is a normal good, then a finding of a statistically significant negative coefficient on price is questionable as it is possible that this negative result is due to the bias and not the 'true' relationship in the two variables. If we find a positive income coefficient, which is statistically significant, this will not be open to doubt on grounds of the negative bias as this simply means that the true income coefficient is higher than we think. Working out the likely direction of bias that may be in an estimated equation is not easy and there are some situations where bias can be shown to exist but its direction is not known.

The strict definition of an unbiased estimator is that its expectation $(E(\hat{b}))$ will be equal to its true value (b). In practical terms this is equivalent to the situation where we could draw repeated samples to estimate b and find that the average of these estimates equals the 'true' value. In real life, we can never know what the true value of a parameter is. However, it can be shown that, if the classical assumptions hold, then the OLS estimator will have the expectation of being equal to it.

L is for linear

An estimator is described as linear if its calculations can be shown to be based on some form of 'adding up' the data used. It can be proven that this is the case for the formula in Equation (3.9) below. There is no obvious reason why we might think linearity is a 'good thing' but it has the virtue of being, mathematically, much easier to work with than the alternatives.

B is for best

The use of the term 'best' is not immediately obvious here. It refers to the variance of the estimators. We have argued that they should have an unbiased mean which is expected to equal the 'true' value of the parameter. However, two estimators could have the same mean and very different variances as shown in Figure 3.2, which shows three estimators which give the same point estimate but with differing variances. If the narrowest of these distributions is the smallest variance estimator that could be obtained then it has the property of being 'best', as this word means minimum variance. Put loosely, we would regard minimum variance as a good thing because it signifies greater accuracy and thus makes us less likely to come to the wrong conclusions from hypothesis testing.

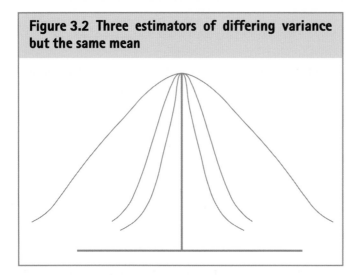

Figure 3.2 Three estimators of differing variance but the same mean

The crucial assumptions which are needed in order to ensure that estimators have the Best property are Assumptions 5 and 6 in the above list. Their role will be explained in Chapters 11 and 14.

In typical situations of hypothesis testing, we would like our estimators to be both best and unbiased. Chapters 11, 13 and 14 develop modifications to 'improve' OLS estimators in circumstances where one of these properties has been lost. In a situation where we are unable to totally eliminate both problems, we might be faced with the choice of finding estimators that trade off the amount of bias against the amount of deviation from the minimum possible variance of estimators. We will simply ignore this possibility in this book and will proceed on the basis of the assumption that the BLUE formula is a set of rules we will try to follow.

DERIVATION OF OLS ESTIMATORS

To simplify matters, the derivation of the OLS estimators is only given in terms of a bivariate model, that is for Equation (3.4) above. If we plotted the data for Y and X on a graph and drew the best fitting straight line we could through the points this would be a linear estimator. See Figure 3.3. From this graph we can work out the values of b_1 and b_0 by measuring the slope and the cut point on the axis. Let us imagine that every student in a class did this. It is unlikely that they will all produce the same estimates as each other as people's eyesight and drawing abilities differ. Maybe the teacher would like to offer a prize for who produced the best estimates. How would she or he do this? The first obvious criterion for judging the attempts is how well does the equation fit. So we need a measure of **goodness of fit.** Measures of fit need to be derived from the residuals of the line, which will be the gaps between the freehand line and the actual data as shown in Figure 3.3.

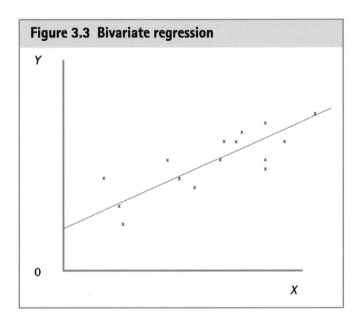

Figure 3.3 Bivariate regression

These residuals will all be zero if the line is a perfect fit. It would be a miracle if a perfect fit ever happened. We will end up with a **sum of residuals** that is:

$$\sum_{i}^{n} \hat{u}_i \tag{3.7}$$

of zero, or near zero, when there is not a perfect fit but we have obtained the best fit possible from drawing a straight line through the data. The positive and negative errors will cancel each other out. We may feel uncomfortable calling an equation a 'good' fit (sum of residuals near zero) when the line goes nowhere near any of the individual data points, which may be a long way above and below it. There are two basic methods of removing this problem.

(i) Either we can use the sum of absolute residuals:

$$\sum_{i} |\hat{u}_i| \tag{3.8}$$

(i.e. we simply ignore the negative sign in front of a negative number) as a measure of fit.

(ii) Or we can use the **sum of squared residuals**:

$$\sum_i \hat{u}_i^2 \tag{3.9}$$

We could use the first of these methods and if we continue with it we would end up with LAR (least absolute residual) estimators rather than OLS. Econometrics has developed on the basis of usage of the second approach, which means we judge fit by the sum of squared residuals. We would give the prize to the student who has produced the line that has the smallest sum of squared residuals according to the formula in Equation (3.9). We should pause to note at this point that the residual sum of squares is another name used for the sum of squared residuals and that both give rise to the abbreviations SSR and RSS on econometrics packages.

If a perfect fit has been produced the sum of squared residuals will, like the sum of residuals, be zero, but this would be a near miracle for any real world data. For a given set of data, and relationship, the lower the sum of squared residuals the better the fit. As drawing is imperfect, it is most unlikely that the graph will have **minimized the sum of squared residuals.** One way of checking that we have not got a minimum would be to slightly vary the parameter estimates by a small amount, in each direction, and see if it is possible to find a pair of estimates that gives a smaller sum of squared residuals. With modern high speed computing, it would be possible to simply pick any pair of b's as starting values and let an algorithm search for reductions in the SSR by incrementing and recalculation of the SSR each time we do this and then pick the 'best fitting' pair of b_0 and b_1.

The OLS method provides a solution to this problem that should produce b's that minimize the SSR 'in one go' without resort to this trial and error approach. The SSR can be minimized by using calculus. We rearrange the model to get:

$$SSR = \sum_{i=1}^{n} (Y_i - \hat{b}_0 - \hat{b}_1 X_i)^2 \tag{3.10}$$

which we can then differentiate with respect to the b's to get (now dropping the summation information as it is always i to n):

$$\delta SSR / \delta \hat{b}_0 = -2 \left(\sum Y_i - n\hat{b}_0 - \hat{b}_1 \sum X_i \right) = 0 \tag{3.11a}$$

$$\delta SSR / \delta \hat{b}_1 = -2 \left(\sum X_i Y_i - \hat{b}_0 \sum X_i - \hat{b}_1 \sum X_i^2 \right) = 0 \tag{3.11b}$$

These are set equal to zero as this is the condition for a maximum. We can also rearrange the equations to get the rather confusingly named **normal equations.** This name has nothing to do with the normal distribution. An alternative way to arrive at the normal equations is to simply sum the equation over the sample to get Equation (3.12a) and multiply Equation (3.3) through by X_i and then sum over the sample to get (3.12b).

$$\sum Y_i = nb_0 + \hat{b}_1 \sum X_i + \sum u_i \tag{3.12a}$$

$$\sum X_i Y_i = \hat{b}_0 \sum X_i + \sum X_i^2 + \sum u_i X_i \tag{3.12b}$$

The final terms in these equations will drop out due to the assumptions of the CLRM, that is, the sum of residuals is zero as the expected residual is zero and the covariance of X with u must be zero.

This is a set of two equations in two unknowns, b_0 and b_1, which is in principle solvable. If you divide the first (3.12a) of these normal equations by the sample size (n) to get:

$$\bar{Y} = \hat{b}_0 + \hat{b}_1 \bar{X} \tag{3.13}$$

you will discover one property of a regression with an intercept (b_0) included. That is, it goes through the means of the data – no matter what the distributions of the values of X and Y may be, we are absolutely guaranteed that the regression line will go through the point represented by the mean of X and the mean of Y. This property remains even when we add more variables to give us a multiple regression. It is because of this property that regression with an intercept is known as 'regression through the mean'. It is possible to derive the OLS estimator directly from (3.12b) if we 'normalize' the data to have a mean of zero. That is, we subtract the mean of Y from Y and the mean of X from X so that we now use the lower case italicized X and Y to represent mean deviations. This will make the intercept vanish as the regression is now through the origin. This makes the second normal equation (3.12b) become:

$$\sum x_i y_i = \hat{b}_1 \sum x_i^2 \tag{3.14}$$

as the 'normalization of X and Y to have means of zero (now they are the mean deviations x and y) cause the other variables to drop out. This gives us the estimator formula for the slope parameter (b_1):

$$\hat{b}_1 = \sum x_i y_i / \sum x_i^2 \tag{3.15}$$

This is the key result in simple bivariate regression and it is the same answer you would obtain by rearranging the normal equations, which demonstrates that it does have the property of minimizing the sum of squared residuals and is therefore the OLS estimator.

You should note that this has the same top line as the formula in Equation (2.13), for bivariate correlation in the last chapter. This line is the covariance between Y and X. The bottom line differs between this **regression coefficient** and the **correlation coefficient.** The correlation coefficient is limited to the range of values from -1 to $+1$. The regression coefficient does not have this property due to the change in the bottom line. The top line of Equation (3.15) can be either positive or negative and it has no limitations, i.e. it can range from plus to minus infinity. The bottom line will, by definition, be positive. We reach the conclusion that b_1, the slope parameter, will be positive if there is a positive relationship between Y and X and negative if Y and X have a negative relationship. As simple as this sounds, it is something you may lose sight of once you get to see the confusing array of output from a regression package.

It is good practice in econometrics to state the expectations of the b's which our theories have given us *prior* to actually examining the estimates. That is, we should make explicit our hypotheses before we explore the data. For the lipstick demand curve example given in

Equation (3.2) of this book we have the expectation as explained above that $b_1 < 0$. For a consumption function the expectation would be b_1, the slope parameter, to be greater than 0. It is advisable when you see regression output, whether it is 'raw' as in fresh from a computer package or 'processed' into a neat table in a written report, to search first for the signs and see if they concur with expectations.

I have avoided stating the formula for the b_0 parameter or indeed any expectations about it. We can derive its formula explicitly from the set of equations above, although there is a shortcut to be had from the fact that OLS regression goes through the mean. We have two equations in two unknowns. Once the b_1 value has been estimated there is only one unknown, b_0. This can be obtained by this formula:

$$\hat{b}_0 = \bar{Y} - \hat{b}_1 . \bar{X} \tag{3.16}$$

What about the expectation of b_0? You might jump to the conclusion that it should be greater than 0 (positive) because most of the time the Y variable is a real number, such as quantity of a good or total expenditure. As b_0 is the value of Y when X has no impact on it, then it might seem strange to allow a real number to have a mean of zero.

Unfortunately this is not correct. The function of the intercept is to ensure that the mean of the disturbance term is zero. Indeed, if you ran a regression with only an intercept and no 'explanatory' (independent) variables, the value of the estimated intercept would be the mean of the dependent variable. The intercept should not be taken literally, as being the value Y_i would take if all the other variables were zero. Its value will reflect specification errors in the model such as non-linearity (see Chapter 6). A negative value of the intercept cannot be ruled out as a reasonable result. So, it might be best to have no specific expectation about the b_0 parameter. Some computer packages will automatically include an intercept and some will not. The estimated intercept will be provided with a 't' test for the hypothesis that it is different from zero. You should not be too keen to react to this test. In particular, if it suggests that the intercept was not significant then you should not jump to the conclusion that it is a good idea to drop the intercept from your model. The reasons for this are explained later.

3.5 HYPOTHESIS TESTING IN THE CLRM

Having estimated parameters and checked their signs we should go on from this to formally test our hypotheses but this will require the formulae for the standard errors of the b hats. Without these we cannot apply the 't' distribution introduced in Chapter 2. We have the formula for the estimates of b_1 from Equation (3.15). That formula is for the mean of this parameter estimate. To get its standard error we simply expand the formula (see Appendix 6) and we obtain:

$$\text{s.e.}(\hat{b}_1) = \sigma / \sqrt{\sum x_i^2} \tag{3.17}$$

The bottom line is calculated from the data for the X variable. It has already appeared as the bottom line of the formula for the estimator of b_1. The top line is the variance of the error term (it is not subscripted because of the assumption of homoscedasticity in the CLRM). However, the value of the top line is not known. It has to be estimated. We do this using the regression residuals in the following formula:

$$\hat{\sigma} = \sqrt{\left[\sum \hat{u}_i^2/(n-k)\right]} \qquad\qquad (3.18)$$

The division is by the degrees of freedom, $n-k$, rather than n in order to remove bias from the estimate of the standard error of the residual. The degrees of freedom in a regression equation are $n-k$, where k is the number of parameters being estimated, which must include the intercept/constant term (b_0) even though it is not attached to any actual data. In the case of the bivariate regression k must equal 2, that is, the intercept/constant term and the slope parameter (b_1).

You will not need to do any of these calculations as the computer package reports these standard errors alongside (or below) the coefficients. Most articles will report these in brackets below the coefficients except in cases where the authors simply report a 't' test or use an asterisk system to present levels of significance. Examples of the basic hypothesis tests that computer packages provide as default are provided in Section 3.8 below and also throughout many other chapters in this book. The default tests provided by a computer program relate to the form of the hypothesis as in Equation (3.2) above or its two-sided alternative (i.e. that the 'slope' coefficient b_1 is not equal to zero). This means we get given a 't' statistic in computer output, which is simply the regression coefficient divided by its standard error. To use this, we have effectively three options in most cases:

▶ Look up the critical 't' value, for the appropriate significance level and degrees of freedom in Appendix 4. If the 't' statistic exceeds this then we reject the null and accept the alternative.

▶ Compare the 'critical significance level' ('Prob value' or 'p' value in some regression packages) with our chosen level of significance. If this value is *below* the chosen significance level then we reject the null and accept the alternative. This method is the same as the first method (use of a 't' test) except that it has been done in the reverse manner. That is, the computer package has been instructed to give you the precise value of the significance level at which you would just switch from accepting a null to rejecting it. An example of this approach can be found in Chapter 5.

▶ Use a confidence interval as a hypothesis test. The idea of constructing confidence intervals was introduced in Chapter 2, when we looked at the probability distribution of throwing a fair die. In the case of hypothesis testing for regression coefficient we express the test the other way round from significance testing. That is, a 5 per cent significance test equates to a 95 per cent confidence interval. We can construct the two-sided confidence interval around the mean of a coefficient by using this formula (shown for the case of b_1):

$$\hat{b}_1 + \text{s.e.}_{(b_1)} \times \text{critical 't' value at the 5\% level} \qquad\qquad (3.19)$$

If the interval does not include zero, we may conclude that the coefficient is significantly different from zero at the 5 per cent level. This was a two-sided confidence interval, at the 95 per cent level, i.e. it includes 47.5 per cent of the values expected to lie on either side of the estimate. You can make it a one-sided confidence interval by simply adding or subtracting (but not both), and using the relevant 't'; i.e. for a one-sided 95 per cent confidence interval you would use the critical 't' ratio from a 10 per cent column in a two-sided 't' table.

Please note that I have listed these as three different methods but they are really just versions of the same test. You should **always** get the same answer for the same hypothesis test whichever one of these you use.

3.6 A NOTE ON THE R SQUARED STATISTIC

When we generate estimates that minimize the sum of squared residuals we will be maximizing the fit of the equation. This means that OLS automatically chooses a pair of b_0 and b_1 in a bivariate regression which produces the largest possible value on the goodness of fit statistic for the set of data and variables we are working with. It will also choose the set of estimates that produces the best possible fit in a multiple regression. In OLS regressions, goodness of fit is almost universally based on one summary statistic called the 'R squared', which is written as R^2. We will consider why it might be called R squared after we look at its formula.

You might ask why we need a measure of fit when we have already decided to use the sum of squared residuals. That measure has the limitation of being dependent on the units of measurement in the variables; if we were to change a variable from being in cents to being in dollars this would shift the SSR proportionately. The SSR also depends on the size of the sample. We could address the latter shortcoming by dividing by the sample size, but there is a better approach which solves both problems (unit and size dependency) at once. That is, we could benchmark the performance of our model against the worst possible result it could ever potentially produce. The worst possible performance of the model is for it to do no better than simply predicting Y by using its mean. If this happened then the b_1 parameter would effectively be zero, so the residuals would be equal to the sum of squared deviations of Y about its mean. So if we divide this into the sum of squared residuals then we have a statistic that is only able, under classical assumptions, to lie between 1 and 0. If it is 1, the model is useless in statistical terms as it fails to explain any of the variation in Y around its mean. If it is 0, the model is a perfect fit to the observed data on Y and the fitted line would go exactly through every point on a scatter diagram of Y against X.

However, this is not the statistic that we use; instead, we subtract the above formula from 0 to give us:

$$R^2 = 1 - \left[\sum \hat{u}^2 / \sum y^2 \right] \tag{3.20}$$

which will now lie between 0 for a useless fit and 1 for a perfect fit. If we multiply the number by 100 it gives us the percentage of the variation in Y, around its mean that is explained by the movements in X.

An alternate explanation of the R squared is that it is the square of the simple correlation, as defined in Section 2.7 of Chapter 2, between Y and the Y values predicted from the regression, thus possibly explaining why it is called R squared. R squared is not the only measure of fit and there are modifications to it, which are quite commonly used. This will be taken up in Chapter 5 (Section 5.4).

3.7 WHAT IS THE GAUSS–MARKOV THEOREM?

The Gauss–Markov theorem is the name given to the proof that the OLS estimator given in Equation (3.9) can be shown to be BLUE (best linear unbiased) under the classical assumptions. The assumption of normality of the disturbance term is *not* necessary for this proof. This assumption is used in order that we can do hypothesis tests, on the regression parameters, using the 't' distribution.

In the proof of linearity we must first define a weight term w_i which is equal to $x_i/\sum x_i^2$. After expansion of the formula for the estimators from Equation (3.9) it can be rearranged to:

$$\hat{b}_1 = \sum w_i Y_i \qquad (3.21)$$

The estimator is a linear function of Y, the error term and the 'true' parameters. The full proof that the estimator is unbiased is as follows:

$$\hat{b}_1 = \sum w_i Y_i = \sum w_i(b_0 + b_1 X_i + u_i)$$

$$= \sum w_i \cdot b_0 + \sum w_i b_i X_i + \sum w_i u_i \qquad (3.22)$$

As $\sum w_i = 0$ the first term drops out. The third term drops out because of the classical assumption that the error term is not correlated with the independent variables. It only remains to establish that the middle term is equal to b_1. This is so because we can take b_1 outside the $\sum$ operator and $\sum w_i X_i$ will be equal to 1 by definition.

The proof that the estimators are 'best', i.e. have minimum variance, requires us to show that they are smaller than the variance of any other possible estimator. The variance of any linear estimator of the slope (b^*) can be written as follows, once we define a new set of weights k which are not necessarily equal to the previous set (w) and recall that σ^2 is the variance of the disturbance term. We then have:

$$b_1{}^* = \sum k_i Y_i$$

$$E(b_1{}^*) = b_0 \sum k_i + b_1 \sum k_i X_i$$

$$E(b_1{}^*) = VAR \sum k_i Y_i = \sum k_i VAR\, Y = \sigma^2 \sum K_i^2$$

$$= \sigma^2 \sum \left(k_i - x/\sum x_i^2 + x_i/\sum x_i^2\right)^2$$

$$= \sigma^2 \sum \left(k_i - x/\sum x_i^2\right)^2 + \sigma^2 \sum x_i/\left(\sum x_i^2\right) + 2\sigma^2 \sum \left(k_i - x/\sum x_i^2\right)$$

$$= \sigma^2 \sum \left(k_i - x/\sum x_i^2\right)^2 + \sigma^2/\left(\sum x_i^2\right) \qquad (3.23)$$

The last term of the last line is a constant, so the minimization of the variance of the estimator depends only on the first term. If the k weights are set equal to the w weights, which are OLS weights, then the variance is minimized. Any other weight results in a larger variance.

The existence of the Gauss–Markov theorem should not blind us to two sets of assumptions that we have made:

(i) It is desirable for estimators to be BLUE.
(ii) That the classical assumptions hold.

When we get to Chapter 10, we will consider tests for the acceptability of the classical assumptions. If these tests indicate a violation of the classical assumptions then the estimators can no longer be BLUE and we need to develop techniques to deal with this.

3.8 EXAMPLES OF BIVARIATE REGRESSION

We have now covered enough theoretical background on the CLRM to enable us to look at some simple bivariate regressions. Rather than pursue the lipstick example, with which we began this chapter, we look first at a simple time-series consumption function using data from Belgium for the years 1960–1990. The results are shown in Table 3.1, which has been tidied up from the computer output into the form that you might find in a journal article. The model has also been re-estimated with the intercept excluded in the second column for purposes of illustrating the role of the intercept.

The equations estimated in Table 3.1 are as follows:

$$C_i = b_0 + b_1 Y_i + u_i \tag{3.24}$$

$$C_i = b_1 Y_i + u_i \tag{3.25}$$

where C is real consumption expenditure and Y is real GDP. The parameter b_1 is the 'true' value of the marginal propensity to consume. The u term is the classical disturbance term which we assume to have the properties listed above so that we can perform hypothesis tests using 't'

Table 3.1 Estimates of the Belgian consumption function: With and without intercept

Dependent variable:	Real consumption	Real consumption
Independent variables		
Intercept	0.717	
	(1.42)	
Real GDP	0.61	0.624
	(47.11)	(221.656)
R squared	0.987	0.986
N	31	31

Notes: Figures in parentheses are the 't' ratios for the null of a zero coefficient.
Data is annual for the years 1960–90.

tables. The i subscript in this case represents the 31 years from 1960 to 1990. As we have just written down two equations, we will get two different estimates of the marginal propensity to consume when we run the regressions. The second equation can be described as a version of the first one after a **restriction** has been imposed on it. The restriction can be written down in the form $b_0 = 0$, which is a hypothesis that can be tested using the 't' ratio on b_0 once we have estimated Equation (3.24).

The coefficient on real GDP is our estimate of the marginal propensity to consume, which conforms to our expectations of being between 0 and 1. The default 't' tests provided by the computer are very large for this, indicating that it will reject the null at a high (i.e. numerically low) level of significance. The default 't' test is for the null of a zero coefficient. If we wish instead to test that the marginal propensity to consume is less than 1 we would need to subtract the estimate from 1 and divide this by the standard error. Taking the first set of results, this means we need to divide 0.39 by the standard error. Table 3.1 does not give this standard error so we need to work backwards to get it. So we do the test as follows:

> **Step 1.** Divide 0.61 by the 't' ratio (47.11) = 0.0129 = standard error.
> **Step 2.** Compute (1 − 0.39)/0.0129 = 30.23 = the relevant 't' ratio.

This should be compared with the critical 't' value on a one-tailed significance test, as we are interested in the marginal propensity to consume being less than one. Given that 30.23 is extremely large for a 't' value, the null will be rejected at a high level of statistical significance.

In order to have a more detailed look at bivariate regression, we return to the subject of cigarette smoking. Some results using the same data from Turkey, used to compute partial

Table 3.2 Bivariate and multiple regression: Cigarette smoking in Turkey, 1960–1988

Dependent variable: Tobacco consumption per adult (CCA)				
Equation	1	2	3	4
Independent variables				
Constant	1.58	1.99	1.83	1.67
	(10.02)	(11.11)	(16.74)	(10.84)
GNP	0.152E−3			0.336E−3
	(4.07)			(3.8)
RPC		−0.423		0.105
		(1.24)		(4.31)
TER		6.225		0.3995
		(3.62)		(0.12)
R^2	0.38	0.054	0.327	0.645
N	29	29	29	29

1. Figures in parentheses are absolute 't' ratios.
2. The variable names are as used in Tansel (1993), from which this data is taken. *GNP* = national income per adult, *RPC* = relative price of cigarettes, *TER* = the tertiary education enrolment rate.
3. E followed by a minus sign and a number means that you need to alter the number shown by shifting the decimal point to the left by the number of places shown.

correlations in Table 2.2, are shown in Table 3.2. For the moment we will focus only on the first three columns of this table as the last column is a multiple regression, which will be discussed after the next section of this chapter. You will see that this shows three bivariate regressions that represent the following equations:

$$CCA = b_0 + b_1 GNP + u \qquad (3.26)$$

$$CCA = b_2 + b_3 TER + v \qquad (3.27)$$

$$CCA = b_4 + b_5 RPC + w \qquad (3.28)$$

where CCA is per capita (based on adults) consumption of cigarettes, GNP is real gross national product per capital, TER is the rate of take-up of tertiary education and RPC is the relative price (price of cigarettes divided by the retail price index). I have taken the step of dropping the observation subscripts here and will continue to do this except in cases where it is strictly necessary to show them to make a point. I have named the disturbance terms u, v, w to avoid any confusion that two or more equations share a common disturbance term. I have also subscripted the parameters consecutively so as to avoid confusion over the fact that each of the slope and intercept parameters here are different. Theory and intuition would lead us to expect the following results:

$$b_0? \qquad b_1 > 0, \ b_3 < 0, \ b_5 < 0 \qquad (3.29)$$

We can write this out in full hypothesis testing format as three tests in which the above appear as the H_1 statements.

$$H_0: \ b_1 \leq 0, \qquad H_1: \ b_1 > 0, \qquad (3.30)$$

$$H_0: \ b_3 \geq 0, \qquad H_1: \ b_3 < 0, \qquad (3.31)$$

$$H_0: \ b_5 \geq 0, \qquad H_1: \ b_5 < 0, \qquad (3.32)$$

The expectations for b_1 and b_5 are derived from economic theory, as is the expectation for b_3 which is less than 0 on the grounds that as the education level rises, the community will become more responsive to information about the dangers of smoking.

I will only deal with the basics of interpreting these equations. Further treatment will come in Chapter 5. The first thing to note is that one of the expectations is satisfied and two are contradicted. The third equation shows that the relationship between tertiary education and smoking is positive, suggesting that more education means more smoking. The figures in brackets below the coefficients are the default 't' ratios for the null hypothesis of a zero value on each parameter. The degrees of freedom in each case will be $29 - 2 = 27$, as the sample is of annual data from 1960–88. A degree of freedom is lost for the intercept and another by estimating the slope parameter. This means that the critical value for a two-tailed test at the 5 per cent significance level is 2.052 and the one-tailed level is 1.703. Using this criterion we find that the null is accepted for the RPC coefficient but is rejected for the coefficient values given for GNP and TER. The usual journal article expresses this kind of result in the following way: 'we have found that income and education are statistically significant but that price is not.'

You should not be surprised by these results for the sign and significance because they must be exactly the same as those found from the partial correlation matrix shown in Table 2.2. It should also be the case that the R^2 from the three bivariate regressions in Table 3.2 are equal to the square of the corresponding r's in Table 2.2 in Chapter 2. You can easily check that this is indeed the case.

So far, in our progress from correlation to regression we have not discovered anything new in terms of the direction of the relationships, in this data, and their statistical significance. We have, however, encountered some new information in the form of the estimated values for the intercept and slope parameters. The slope estimates are positive and highly statistically significant in the cases of *GNP* and *TER* – that is, they have extremely large 't' ratios. The slope estimates are very different in all three cases. The *GNP* coefficient is much smaller than the *TER* coefficient: 0.000152 compared with 6.225. However, we should not be tempted to read anything into such a comparison as the size of coefficients produced from the formula shown in Equation (3.9) is dependent on the units of measurement of the original variables. To take a simple example, if we were to switch from measuring consumption per capita to consumption per 100 000 people then all the coefficients would change by a factor of 100 000. In this model, *TER* is in much smaller units than *GNP* per capita. We will postpone further discussion of this matter of size of units of measurement until Chapter 5.

Unlike our Belgian consumption function, which gave us the kind of results we would expect, we now seem to have just found that price does not matter for the demand for cigarettes. Does this kind of statistical finding wreck the whole of economic theory as we know it? Of course not, for at least the following reasons:

▶ One set of results from one sample can never be conclusive. It is possible that replications using other sets of data will find different results.

▶ The data may be inadequate in various ways. There may be too much inaccuracy in the measurement of prices or there might be too little variation in relative prices for us to adequately trace out a downward sloping demand curve if one does exist.

▶ Cigarettes might be a 'special case' to which the theory of demand does not apply as goods are addictive, although it should be noted that the theory of rational addiction (see Becker *et al.*, 1994) is often used to argue that addictive goods are very price responsive.

▶ The model is too simple. It assumes a linear relationship when this might not be the case (see Chapter 6).

▶ The model is too simple. It only has a single equation to represent demand. It takes no account of supply behaviour (see Chapters 12 and 13).

▶ Bivariate regressions are inadequate, as each of the three estimates suffers from **omitted variable bias**. The simple solution to this problem would seem to be to put all three variables in the regression instead of using them 'one at a time' in bivariate regressions. This is what we are going to do next.

3.9. FROM BIVARIATE TO MULTIPLE REGRESSION

We now take up the last of these points. The important thing to note here is that you cannot establish unbiased estimates of the parameters of a multiple regression equation simply by running a set of bivariate regressions for each variable. There is only one (extremely unlikely situation) where you can do this, which is when the right-hand side variables are totally uncorrelated. That is, in the present case where the zero partial order correlations between *RPC*, *GNP* and *TER* are zero. This property is referred to as orthogonality or mutually uncorrelated variables (strictly it should be the case that there is no higher-order correlation either). We have already seen from Table 2.2 that this is far from being the case.

When there is more than one independent variable this means that new equations must be added, for each variable, in order to derive a set of OLS estimators that takes account of the variation of each of the *X*'s and their covariation with each other and with *Y*. I will not work through the derivation of the normal equations again but instead you should note that in matrix notation (see Appendix 6 for the derivation) the estimators for the *b*'s will become

$$b' = (X'X)^{-1}X'Y \tag{3.33}$$

where **X** is a matrix of the independent variables which includes the row of 1's for the intercept and **Y** is a column vector of the dependent variable with **b**' being the column vector or coefficients.

Given that the 'true' model will generally involve more than one variable, it follows that the omitted variables will mean there may be bias in the estimation of the coefficients using bivariate regression. There will be bias in the estimation of the intercept if the data has the property of orthogonality. If it has not then there will be omitted variable bias in the estimation of the slope coefficients. Obviously if you include all the 'correct' variables then this bias will be eliminated (assuming they are measured correctly). However, it is usually the case that we are not entirely clear of the correct specification and some variables could be called 'doubtful' variables which may or may not belong in the equation. We might then run into the problem of 'overspecifying' an equation by including 'too many' variables. This takes you into the opposite **specification error** to omitted variables which is '**wrongful inclusion of irrelevant variables**'.

Looking at the typical article that uses applied econometrics, you are likely to come to the conclusion that the preference in the profession is to take the risk of erring on the side of overspecification. The studies reviewed later in this chapter (see Section 3.10) and in the other chapters from Chapter 5 onwards are indicative of this as they include several variables which are loosely related to the underlying economic concepts. Econometrics textbooks have traditionally given a justification for this asymmetry in handling variable specification errors, on the grounds that omitted variables will be a source of bias while wrongly included variables will tend to increase the variance of the estimated parameters of the model. This will, in theory, tend to reduce the likelihood of rejecting the null for the 'correctly' included variables in the model.

One form of omitted variable bias, which you should definitely avoid, is the failure to include an intercept. You will recall that the consumption function in Table 3.1 has been estimated with and without an intercept. The marginal propensity to consume rises slightly when we drop the intercept and the 't' ratio increases enormously. This small change is quite a drastic change in the model. When there is no intercept the residuals will not automatically sum to (virtually) zero as the regression is no longer a 'regression through the mean' but is now a regression 'through the origin'. The R squared formula is no longer valid as the usual formula assumes that we have included an intercept. If we deny ourselves the use of an intercept, then we introduce bias to our attempt to produce the best fitting straight line. Figure 3.4 illustrates this for the bivariate case.

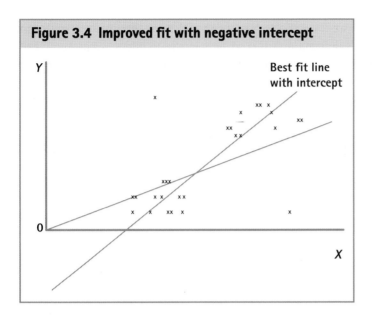

Figure 3.4 Improved fit with negative intercept

This illustrates the fact that the movement of the line away from the origin allows us to obtain a better fit to the scatter of data points and this correspondingly produces a very different 'slope' coefficient. Figure 3.4 shows a scatter of data points, which is broadly upward sloping. If they were downward sloping then it would be quite hard to make sense of a regression that dropped the use of an intercept term.

It is time to look at the differences between the bivariate and multiple regressions for smoking, in Turkey, as shown in Table 3.2. This shows some drastic changes from the bivariate regressions. The income variable still has the correct sign and the education variable still has the wrong sign, but the price variable now has the correct (negative) sign. The R squared rises substantially over the bivariate R squareds and indicates that 64.5 per cent of the variation of cigarette consumption, around its mean, can be accounted for by a linear combination of the three variables chosen as arguments in the demand function. This still leaves 35.5 per cent of the variation unaccounted for but without further exploration it is hard to tell whether this is due mainly to omitted variables or to measurement errors in the data.

There is no automatic relationship between the R squared for the first three columns and those in the final column for the multiple regression using all three variables. The value in the final column could not possibly be less than the largest of the three values in the rest of the table. Beyond this, how large the value is depends on the pattern of covariation in the matrix of data defined by Y and all the X's.

Things are starting to look better from the viewpoint of simple microeconomic theory now we have used a multiple regression. To see how much better this really is, one has to use the 't' ratios to test the hypotheses involved. There are no new rules to learn about hypothesis testing when we switch to multiple regression other than to make sure that you adjust the degrees of freedom by deducting a degree of freedom for every parameter estimated. The degrees of freedom now become $29 - 4 = 25$. Sticking with the 5 per cent significance level that most economists are comfortable with, we get a critical value of 2.06 for a two-tailed test and 1.708 at the one-tailed. The absolute values of the 't' ratios for the income and price coefficients easily exceed this and so we can reject the separate nulls of no influence of price and income on the demand for cigarettes. Before we leave this section we should stress that the meaning of the individual coefficients is slightly different now that we have moved to multiple regression. Each coefficient shows the estimated impact of a one-unit change in the attached variable on the dependent variable in its units of measurement *holding the impact of the other variables constant*.

We have just found two reasons why economists should like using multiple linear regression equations:

(i) They produce marginal impacts in the form of the coefficients.
(ii) They impose the *ceteris paribus* assumption provided that you can measure all those variables that need to be held constant.

3.10 REVIEW STUDIES

The two papers considered here are broadly focused on the same theme. That is, they ask the question: can an economy suffer from having 'too many lawyers' to the extent that it suffers a lower rate of economic growth than it otherwise would? Both papers use elementary single-equation multiple linear regression to estimate the determinants of the growth rate of real per capita national income (GNP in the Datta and Nugent paper published in 1986 and GDP in the Murphy *et al.* paper published in 1991). The approach of both papers is the simple one of collecting data for a number of countries and using a measure of extent of 'lawyerification' in the economy plus other independent variables as 'controls' for the presence of influences other than lawyers.

The papers are different in a number of ways in terms of their implementation. The sample countries differ (52 in the Datta and Nugent paper and 91 in Murphy *et al.*), the definitions of variables differ, the sources of data differ and the sample periods differ, being 1960–80 and 1970–85 respectively. The lawyer variable differs, in that Datta and Nugent use the number of lawyers as a percentage of the labour force, while Murphy *et al.* use the share of law students in total student enrolment. In addition to this, the papers also differ in terms of not using the same set of control variables, as you can see from consulting the lists in the panels.

A degree of discrepancy in data and variables between studies testing roughly the same hypotheses is not uncommon. The quite wide discrepancy in the present case is probably due to the fact that we are here looking at an area where the economic theory is not clear-cut in giving us a model specification (for more discussion of this aspect of specification of an equation see Salai-Martin (1997), which deals with the Barro growth equation on which Murphy *et al.* base their paper). If you were to look at studies in the more mainstream areas of economics like demand for money, consumption functions, Phillips curves and so on, the discrepancies would be much less than found here. Still, both studies come to the same conclusion: that an increased share of legal activity in the economy is detrimental to economic growth. This is decided purely on the basis of finding a negative sign on the lawyerification variable and the size of its 't' ratio. Datta and Nugent present three regressions with varying sets of right-hand side variables in which the 't' ratio on the *PLAW* variable ranges from 1.98 to 2.13 with the degrees of freedom being between 47 and 50. Murphy *et al.* present two sets of results with the comparable variable being insignificant in their full sample (which has 39 more countries) but the 't' ratio on their sample of 55 countries with $\geq 10\,000$ students is 1.95. The degrees of freedom are 47, in this case giving a critical value for a one-tailed test of between 1.679 and 1.684.

Murphy *et al.*'s coefficient on the lawyerification variable is much smaller than Datta and Nugent's which is between 3.68 and 4.36, while Murphy *et al.*'s is −0.024 (but not significant in the whole sample) and over 3 times larger in the cut down sample − −0.078. These look very different but it is not meaningful to attempt to compare them because the units of measurement are very different. The means for the lawyerification variable in Murphy *et al.* are 8.89 in the full sample, and 7.28 in the reduced sample. In the Datta and Nugent study, the mean is only 0.16. Given that the units of the dependent variable are roughly similar in these two studies (output growth rates) we could make a more appropriate approximate comparison by rescaling in the proportions of $7.28 / 0.16 = 45.5$ and focusing on the reduced sample where the lawyer variable is significant. If we scale Murphy *et al.*'s coefficient up by this ratio then it becomes 3.459, which is very close to the Datta and Nugent range.

The calculation we have just done was made possible because the articles gave the means of the data. In most circumstances, comparisons between different regression equations in terms of looking at the numerical strength of relationships will be done using elasticities. The calculation of these from a linear regression is explained in Chapter 5 at Section 5.2, and for non-linear equations at various points throughout Chapter 6.

The Basic Facts

Authors: S.K. Datta and J.B. Nugent

Title: Adversary Activities and Per Capita Income Growth

Where Published: *World Development*, 1986, **14**(12), 1457–1461.

Reason for Study: To test the 'transactions costs' hypothesis of economic growth.

Conclusion Reached: That there is some evidence of a negative relationship between the rate of economic growth and the prevalence of lawyers in the labour force.

How Did They Do It?

Data: Various published sources of data from 1960 to 1980 for 52 countries.

Sample Size: 52

Technique: OLS

Dependent Variable: Rate of growth of GNP per capita (at constant prices) 1960–1980

Focus Variables: $PLAW$ = percentage of lawyers in the labour force. Data taken from American Bar Foundation International Directory of Bar Associations.

Control Variables: $LIFE$ = Life expectancy at birth in 1970; $INVS$ = Share of real investment in GDP (1960–70 average); $EXPS$ = share of exports in GDP (1960–70); $REXP$ = average annual growth rate of exports 1960–80 at constant prices; $RINV$ = average annual growth rate of investment 1960–80 in constant prices.

Presentation

How Results Are Listed: Table shows all coefficients including the intercept.

Goodness of Fit: R squared

Tests: Absolute value of default 't' tests shown in brackets

Diagnosis/Stability: There are three different versions of the equation in the table with slightly different choices of variables which shows the lawyer variable to be significant whichever is used.

Anomalous Results: some insignificant coefficients on control variables.

Student Reflection

Things to Look Out For: The use of constant prices to ensure variables are in 'real' terms. The variables come from a variety of different time periods. The sample of countries is limited by data availability so it may not be a representative sample of the world's countries. This paper does not assess the sensitivity of results to changes in the countries included.

Problems in Replication: Most of the data in this study should be quite easily obtained but there are likely to be problems obtaining consistently defined GNP measures and satisfactory lawyer number measures for the same countries if you want to update the sample.

The Basic Facts

Authors: Kevin M. Murphy, Andrea Shleifer and Robert W. Vishny
Title: The Allocation of Talent: Implications for Economic Growth
Where Published: *Quarterly Journal of Economics*, May 1991, **106**(2), 503–530.
Reason for Study: To test the hypothesis that high returns to rent-seeking lures talented people away from productive activities into rent-seeking which damages growth.
Conclusion Reached: 'countries with a higher proportion of engineering college majors grow faster; whereas countries with a higher proportion of law concentrators grow more slowly' (p. 503).

How Did They Do It?

Data: Barro (1991) augmentation of the Summers and Heston income data set augmented by further variables.
Sample Size: 91 (55 in subsample regression which includes only countries with more than 10 000 students).
Technique: OLS.
Dependent Variable: Growth rate of real GDP per capita 1970–85
Focus Variables: Percentage of college enrolments who are lawyers; percentage of college enrolments who are engineers.
Control Variables: Real GDP per capita in 1960; investment; primary school enrolment; Government consumption; an index for revolutions and coups.

Presentation

How Results Are Listed: Table showing all coefficients including the intercept (Constant)
Goodness of Fit: R squared.
Tests: Standard errors shown in brackets.
Diagnosis/Stability: None in particular, although Table III presents a very 'reduced' version of the full model.
Anomalous Results: both engineering and law student variables are negative and insignificant in the full sample regression.

Student Reflection

Things to Look Out For: The use of constant prices to ensure variables are in 'real' terms. The variables come from a variety of different time periods. The sample of countries is limited by data availability so it may not be a representative sample of the world's countries. This paper does collect data for a larger number of countries than that of Datta and Nugent and it does assess sensitivity of results to changes in the countries included to a limited degree by looking at the subsample.
Problems in Replication: Most of the data in this study should be quite easily obtained but there are likely to be problems obtaining consistently defined GDP measures and satisfactory lawyer number measures for the same countries if you want to update the sample.

Reading these studies it is hard to escape the observation that economists *do* impute causality to statistical relationships. Although the authors of both these papers express reservations about their results, for example Datta and Nugent state that 'we would be surprised if someone could not come up with a specification and/or sample which might even support the opposite conclusion' (p. 1459), they still proceed on the basis that there is some evidence that 'too many lawyers' have cost the world in terms of lost economic growth. Indeed, it is the provocative nature of this conclusion that probably resulted in the papers being published. Economists outside the USA have shown little interest in this particular proposition. Many subsequent studies of economic growth were published which made no attempt to incorporate the insights of these papers. Not surprisingly, there has been further exploration of the 'rent-seeking lawyers damage growth' thesis, particularly from those in the law profession (see, for example, the issue of the journal *Law and Social Inquiry* published in 1993).

You have just read the first set of review studies in this book. There will be many others from Chapter 5 onwards. The review panels divide the variables chosen to be the 'independent variables' into a 'focus' (usually just one variable) group and a 'control' group. Not all economic studies fit this pattern but it is a useful way of summarizing quite a lot of them. Many papers in journals are based around a central proposition about an important or controversial relationship between two variables (the focus) variables being put into the regression mainly to take account of any omitted variable bias.

3.11 CONCLUSION

In this chapter we reached the stage of being able to understand elementary multiple regression. In it we were able to interpret an equation for the consumption function and another for the demand for cigarettes and to conduct hypothesis tests on its regression coefficients. We also developed the concept of an R squared. The techniques developed in this chapter enabled us to look at a review summary of two articles from economic journals on the subject of the impact of the volume of legal activity on the rate of economic growth. There is more to learn about hypothesis testing, coefficient interpretation and R squared before we move on to the useful extensions of the CLRM in Chapters 6 and 7. This material is covered in Chapter 5. You may wish to skip straight to Chapter 5 if you are not, at this moment, involved in estimating your own model on data that you are collecting or that has been given to you. If you are required to estimate models of your own at a later date then you should find Chapter 4 to be a self-contained guide, which will prove useful after completing the rest of the book to the level you are aspiring.

DOS AND DON'TS

Do

✓ Try to formulate expectations about the signs of your coefficients prior to estimation.

✓ Make sure you understand the nature and role of the disturbance term in the equation as it will prove to be important in the remainder of this book.

✓ Provide accurate information on how your data is defined and constructed. The information should be provided in such a way that someone else could replicate your study.

Include an intercept, if your package does not include one by default – unless you are given a good reason not to.

Try to implement all reasonable hypothesis tests on your coefficients as the default tests from the computer package may not be that informative.

Don't

Confuse independent and dependent variables. If you put a variable on the right-hand side this is an entirely different model from putting it on the left-hand side.

Forget to include the intercept in k when you are subtracting the number of parameter estimates from n (sample size) to give you the degrees of freedom for a hypothesis test.

Forget that significance tests and confidence interval tests have to give the same answer.

Forget that the tables and tests you will encounter are tests for Type I error which ignore Type II error.

Forget that the size of coefficients in a regression is dependent on the units of observation.

Fall into a confused use of the word significance. Statistical significance should not be confused with economic or other forms of significance.

Fall into the trap of relying on either the point estimate or the level of statistical significance to tell a story. You need both to make complete sense of your results.

EXERCISES

3.1 Explain why a multiple regression would normally give different results from a set of bivariate regressions with the same dependent variable and each independent variable separately.

3.2 Try to give three examples, from theoretical models you have studied, where a one–tailed hypothesis test is more suitable than a two–tailed hypothesis test.

3.3 Which of the following best describes the relationship between disturbances and residuals:

(i) They are exactly the same.

(ii) Residuals are the square root of the disturbances.

(iii) Residuals will be larger than disturbances.

(iv) The sum of squared residuals is less than the sum of squared disturbances.

(v) The residuals are the estimated values of the disturbances.

3.4 Give brief answers to the following questions about R squared:

(i) What does the figure for R squared show?

(ii) 'R squared adjusted' should be used to evaluate a model'. Discuss.

(iii) Is an R squared of 0.85 indicative of good forecasting power? Discuss.

(iv) Two models are estimated. The second is the same as the first but has two variables fewer. Does a decrease in R squared prove that the first model was the best?

3.5 Look at Table 3.2, Equation 4, in order to answer the following questions:

(i) Calculate the standard errors of the coefficients for *RPC*, *GDP* and *TER*.

(ii) Test the hypothesis of a zero intercept at the 10 per cent level.

(iii) Test the null hypothesis of a zero price (*RPC*) coefficient at the 10 per cent level.

(iv) Test the null hypothesis of a zero income coefficient at the 10 per cent level.

(v) Test the hypothesis that the coefficient on *TER* is different from zero at the 10 per cent level.

3.6 Are the following remarks about the disturbance or error term (*u*) false, true or indeterminate?

(i)   The *u* term is not needed in order to produce OLS estimates.

(ii) The inclusion of a *u* term means you do not have to worry about any mistakes in the specification of your model.

(iii) The value of the R squared has got nothing to do with the value of the estimated disturbance terms (residuals).

(iv) The classical assumptions about the *u* term are made for the purpose of hypothesis testing.

REFERENCES

Becker, G.S., Grossman, M. and Murphy, K. (1994) An empirical analysis of cigarette addiction, *American Economic Review*, **84**(3), 396–418.

Datta, S.K. and Nugent, J.B. (1986) Adversary activities and per capita income, *World Development*, **14**(12), 1457–1461.

Murphy, K.M, Shleifer, A. and Vishny, R.M. (1991) The allocation of talent: Implications for economic growth, *Quarterly Journal of Economics*, May, **106**(2), 503–530.

Salai-Martin, X. (1997) I just ran two million regressions, *American Economic Review*, **87**(2), May, 178–183.

Tansel, A. (1993) Cigarette demand, health scares and education in Turkey, *Applied Economics*, **25**, 521–529.

WEBLINKS

http://www.sscnet.ucla.edu/ssc/labs/cameron/e143f98/regex94.htm

This is a list of suitable econometric articles for students to read given in T.A. Cameron's Econometrics 143 course. You would find it useful to summarize such papers in the review template used in this book (Appendix 1).

http://www.itl.nist.gov/div898/handbook/eda/section3/eda36.htm

This is an Exploratory Data Analysis Handbook for Engineering Statistics. It gives 't' and 'F' tables and good explanations of how to use them among other material useful for econometrics.

http://edf5400-01.su03.fsu.edu/Guide7.html

An introduction to basic regression using the example of height and nutrition rather than an economics example.

Preparing and Using Data

LEARNING OBJECTIVES

▪ Be aware of the different types of error which may be present in a data set that one has been given or one has collected
▪ Be aware of the need to allow for missing variables
▪ Understand the idea of a proxy variable
▪ Be conscious of the need to explore a data set rather than simply imposing a model on it
▪ Be able to construct new variables from those which are in a data set you have been given
▪ Reinforce knowledge of how to assess a regression equation in terms of the sign, significance and size of the relationships in it

CHAPTER SUMMARY

4.1 INTRODUCTION

This chapter begins with the assumption that you have been handed some data that has already been collected by someone else. You might have been given this data by your instructor as part of the work for a course. You might be employed under the direction of a more senior researcher who already has the data set, which you have been hired to work on. However, it is also not uncommon for researchers to give data to other researchers. For example, I might have obtained a large sample survey, or constructed a data set from aggregate published statistics, for a specific purpose but I might know another researcher, in a different field, for whom there is a sufficient range of variables in my sample for them to wish to obtain a copy of my data. The data may come from a single source, such as a large survey of households, or it may be assembled from a variety of sources, as in a time-series study of consumption or demand for money functions. Although the sources of time-series data may be different between variables they will usually come from government publications. We will turn to the question of collecting your own data in Section 4.10.

The chapter involves a case study based on an interview sample carried out to establish how much people would be willing to pay for a local public good if they could determine their own purchase price. The chapter is organized in terms of the process that should go on when the data arrives. The next section raises questions you should be asking yourself when the data arrives. We then go on to issues of examining the data set and beginning to run regressions on it.

4.2 POSSIBLE PROBLEMS WITH THE DATA SET

In an ideal world, we would hope to get a sample that is a totally accurate representation of all the variables of interest for the population being studied. Further, we would hope that all the variables we need are included and that they correspond to the concepts in the theoretical models of our discipline. Real data is not going to reach this high standard. Indeed econometrics does not require data to be perfect in order for us to produce useful research, but we need to keep in mind the nature of the data we are working with before we run regressions on it and go on to draw inferences from these.

You should not assume that because someone else has given you data that it is free from serious shortcomings. In particular, data that is given to you by someone could suffer from these problems:

▶ Measurement error
▶ Limited range of measurement
▶ Entry error
▶ Coding error
▶ Sample selection bias
▶ Poor relation to the concepts used in your study
▶ Information loss
▶ Missing variables (or more correctly observations)

All of these problems could be features of the original data sources from which the data was collected, in which case it is going to be difficult to remove them. If the problems have arisen in the collection and coding by the persons who constructed the data set, then it should be possible to correct them by going back to the original sources.

We now briefly explain what each of these problems entails. How to spot these problems, where possible, is dealt with in Section 4.4. Measurement error will arise because of the limitations of data collection. A factory, or a household, may return incorrect figures in their responses to requests for information. They may do this by mistake, through lapse of memory or they may in fact be lying, exaggerating or concealing certain data. For example, if a survey question is on a sensitive issue someone may lie because of guilt, embarrassment or even because a partner or relative is in the room while they are being interviewed.

The range of measurement may be limited because of the way in which information was collected. This might be done in surveys in an attempt to trade off response rates (the fraction of the sample from which a response is obtained) against the level of detail in the answers. Good examples of this are for attempts to measure age or income earned as these questions may, in certain contexts, lead to a non-response to the question (and hence a 'missing variable', see below) or, in the extreme case, non-response to all questions thus lowering the response rate. There may also be measurement error as a result of asking the 'wrong' question or asking the right question in the wrong way. Different answers can arise from surveys depending on such slight changes as the size or colour of the paper or whether a question is asked in a negative or positive manner. For example, we could ask people what is stopping them increasing the level of an activity or we might ask instead what would be needed in order to make them do more of the activity. The concept being addressed is the same in both cases but the answers could give different sorts of results when the answers are coded and used as variables in a regression model.

The scale may also influence the answers to questions if a scale is offered. If we take the simple example of student appraisal of a university course, it is common to make statements of the type:

'I found the lectures stimulating'

with a request to tick a number code with 'neutral' as the mid-point. In a 5-point scale this would be 3 with 4 as agree, 5 as strongly agree, 1 as strongly disagree, 2 as disagree.

There is no specific reason to prefer a 5-point scale as attitudes, and many other variables commonly found in modern econometrics, do not have 'natural' units. The student opinion survey is an ordinal variable as discussed in Chapter 2. We could use a 3-point scale with 'agree' and 'disagree' as the 3 and 1 values respectively. Or indeed a 7-point scale with the two new points being 'very strongly agree' and 'very strongly disagree'. It would be obvious to anyone that these answers will give different means, due to the use of a different scaling choice. Even if we take account of this by 'normalizing' (subtracting the means to give a z-variable with zero mean) the variables may have different standard deviations.

Entry error and coding error are additional sources of error which are fairly self-explanatory. Entry error will occur when those recording the information have typed in or written down incorrect figures. A coding error will be a special type of entry error where the information gathered has been given the wrong coding. For example, a database may contain information on whether people are of white, black, Asian, Hispanic or other ethnic origin which could have a coding of 1, 2, 3, 4, 5 respectively. The information may have been collected properly but the wrong code entered. This kind of error will be difficult to detect and correct. Entry errors from published aggregate statistics, rather than surveys of individuals, will be easier to correct as we can simply go back to the published source from which the data was taken.

A sample obtained from someone else may be subject to information loss in the sense that a 'cut-down' version of the source sample may be used. For example, the original sample might have included full details on age and income of respondents but these may have been converted into a series of dummy variables for ranges. If this loss is felt to be a problem, then one can go back to the original source provided it has not been lost or destroyed.

As discussed in Chapter 2, there may be sample selection bias. This can arise in surveys of individual firms or persons as well as in aggregate data. Aggregate data on industrial statistics such as profit rates, concentration ratios or employment may be biased if firms' participation is dependent on their size. This can arise due to differences in the likelihood of responding or it may simply be due to the collecting organization deciding not to collect from respondents above or below a certain size.

The issue of the relationship between concepts and variables used was also mentioned in previous chapters. This is another type of measurement error. That is, suppose we have a conceptual idea of a variable in a model such as human capital which we term HK (examples of human capital earnings functions are given in Chapter 7). Direct measures of HK are unlikely to be available so instead we use variables which bear some relationship to HK. If there were three available we might write this as:

$$X_1 = HK + \Psi_1 \qquad (4.1)$$

$$X_2 = HK + \Psi_2 \qquad (4.2)$$

$$X_3 = HK + \Psi_3 \qquad (4.3)$$

where X are variables and Ψ is a term representing the measurement error involved in using the X's instead of the unobservable HK. It is common in econometrics to use the term '**proxy variables**' for the X's in this type of situation because the X variable is a proxy for HK. However, many articles use variables which are really proxies as if they were measures of the concept itself. Errors in the relationship between the proxy and the concept are an additional source of measurement error, i.e. there may still be measurement error in the recording of the proxy itself. For example, in the present case X_1, X_2 and X_3 might be dummies for the level of education that a person has attained at the end of their schooling. These dummies could be wrongly measured in the source data for the reasons given above.

The use of proxy variables does not necessarily mean that the estimates of econometric equations will be questionable. The reliability of the proxies depends on how good they are in terms of their connection with the variable being proxied. If the proxies are poor then we may come to an incorrect conclusion if we rely on them. This could involve falling into either Type I or Type II errors; that is, we might reject a null because of statistically significant relationships with the proxy (which do not exist in the conceptual variable) or we might accept a null because of the absence of statistically significant relationships (when such relationships do exist with the conceptual variable).

Having considered the above issues, you might come to the conclusion that the data provided is not very suitable for the topic being researched. This is not a problem if you are only using the data as an exercise in learning to do econometrics. If you are doing 'serious' research then you might like to abandon the data and look for a more suitable source or even go out and collect 'primary' data yourself.

4.3 HOW WILL MY DATA ARRIVE AND WHAT DO I DO WITH IT?

These days the most likely ways for your data to arrive is on a CD-ROM, other disc or memory media, or as a download from a web page. It may be given to you in printed form. If the data is in printed form then you will need to manually enter it into the format of the package you intend to use unless you resort to scanning the page back into a text file on a word processor and attempting to enter the resulting text as an ASCII file (see below).

If it is in a file then it has to be held in some kind of format, which may or may not be compatible with the regression package you are using. Unfortunately, econometrics and other data analysis software tend to be limited in the number of other formats they can handle. The sellers of software tend to prefer that the data is stored in the 'proprietary' format of their own package. If the data is in the appropriate format, then the package you feed it into knows that each number in the file belongs in the correct cell, i.e. it goes to the right observation-variable combination. It is possible for you to be given a file in a format that will not load into the program you are using, or will load incorrectly. The data will go to the wrong places in the file space used by your econometrics program. The data may load correctly into your package in a usable form but you may lose descriptive information, such as the names, definitions and coding rules in the data set in the process.

The formatting used by different packages tells the computer how to arrange the data when it is loaded in. If you have been given data in the same format as the package you are using you should, in theory, have no problem loading the data. If this is not the case, then you need to use some kind of 'interchange' format which can be one of those annoying things that don't work in the way you hoped and can provide a deeply unpleasant hold up in your work. The main contenders for interchange formats stem from two sources: widely used spreadsheet/database packages and established standards of storing data information that are not. We begin with the second of these.

(i) Raw ASCII

It would seem the best way to guarantee that data can be loaded is to use no formatting at all. This is what happens with 'raw' ASCII files. These are simply text files which contain just a string of data with no embedded characters in between each number. The string could be organized in two basic ways: by variable or by observation. Say we had 2000 observations on 10 variables then the ASCII file, usually stored with the suffix *.DAT would be just a plain list of 20 000 numbers, with the first 10 being the values of the first observation for each variable, the second 10 being for the second observations and so on, *or* the data would be arranged so that the first 1000 numbers were all the values for the first variable and so on.

Please note that popular word processors like the variants of (Microsoft) Word do *not* necessarily store data in this way. They also use a proprietary format, which stores information about page layout including the use of fonts, and this information could cause problems to any statistics package which tries to load data from the saved word processor file. So you may not be able to use data from a typical word processor file as input to regression running software even though the data may look like you can when displayed on the word processor on your PC screen. The preparation of an ASCII file from a word processor would then have to be done by saving the word processor file as a text file (i.e one with the suffix *.TXT) or by using a text editor instead (such as TextPad available free from **www.textpad. com**) in the first place.

Once you have established that you have an ASCII file (and not a text file with formatting) and it is named with the appropriate suffix you should be able to load it provided you have established 'which way round' it is organized, i.e. by string of observations or string of variables.

(ii) Excel files

Most packages will now handle standard Excel files (suffix *.XLS), which is a relatively unproblematic format. You do not actually have to have a copy of Excel on your machine to examine data in Excel format. You can download an Excel reader free from **www.microsoft. com**, which does not allow editing but it can be used for the pasting technique described below to transfer data to another package. The main problem that could arise with your variables is – if it so happened that the scale in the original data set had been set wrongly, for example if a scalar variable such as the rate of inflation had been categorized as an ordinal variable in Excel – you may then encounter problems when you import the data to another package.

(iii) Excel CSV files

Excel provides another format which is an alternative to ASCII. This is the CSV (comma separated variable) format. The free econometric software provided by Herman Biehrens (at **http://econ.la.psu.edu/~hbierens/EASYREG.HTM**) will accept input only from CSV or its own format.

(iv) Lotus 1-2-3 file

Lotus 1-2-3 has been an established spreadsheet package for many years and, as such, is a file format that most people will have access to whether free-standing or as part of the Lotus SmartSuite package. Some regression packages will accept Lotus 1-2-3 files.

(v) SPSS portable files

SPSS files cannot genuinely be described as a data interchange format as they are a proprietary format specific to SPSS which other packages do not use. However, it is worth mentioning here as it is a format in which agencies, for example the ESRC Survey Archive (see **www.esrc. gov.uk**) will supply data. Although not a standard format, it is one which should be available in almost any academic institution, which cannot be said of specialist econometrics software. It has the advantage of being small compared to say an Excel file. It can also contain useful information about the variables as well as their names. This type of file (suffix *.POR) was devised to interface between users of different versions of the SPSS package (now up to version 11) as these are not backward compatible.

None of the above formats can be guaranteed to be acceptable on every package you might find. The SPSS portable file will only be acceptable to SPSS. If the supplied data is in a format not compatible with your package then it may be possible to use another package such as Lotus 1-2-3, Excel or SPSS as an intermediate stage to convert the data into a usable format. If you were given an SPSS portable file you could use SPSS to re-save it in Lotus, Excel or as ASCII formats in order to pass it on to your first choice package.

PASTING

There is a quick approach that you can use on many packages which have some form of spreadsheet presentation running under one of the versions of Windows. To do this:

(i)   Open the data file in the spreadsheet of a package which supports the format.
(ii) Use your mouse to highlight all the cells of data and then use the copy command.
(iii) Switch to the program you wish to transfer the data to and make sure your cursor is in the first row first column and use the paste command.
(iv) You may now want to enter the names manually in the 'new' spreadsheet if it was not possible to transfer those by copy and paste.
(v)   Save the file in the format of the package you have moved it into for future use.

CHECKING WHAT THE DATA IS

Having processed some data into your package you could go ahead and run regressions using the variables imported. It is probably better that you do not do this but instead spend some time exploring the data set you have just imported. With a small data set it would be easy to cast your eye over the whole matrix of data in order to get some sense of its properties, but this is obviously not possible in a situation where you might have say 200 variables and 20 000 observations, as could easily be the case in a government survey. Suggestions as to how to explore this kind of sample are given in Section 4.4.

WHAT'S IN A NAME?

Having checked that the data corresponds to its expected arrangement – that is, the dimension of the matrix in terms of numbers of observations $\times$ number of variables is what it was supposed to be – the most logical thing to do next is look at the names of the variables. Since this chapter assumes you are being handed data to work on it is reasonable to assume that it will have mnemonics as variable names rather than the variables being labelled X_1, X_2... etc. or var0001, var0002 etc. as some spreadsheet entries would have it. You may lose variable names from an original spreadsheet in the process of transforming them to your package and thus might need to 'manually' rename the variables.

A variable name may well not make it entirely clear what exactly the variable is. For one thing, names tend to be short and abbreviated. Many economists have used the variable name *sex* to describe a 0–1 dummy for whether a person is male or female. It might be easier to guess what this variable is if the variable was instead called *gender* but we might still wonder which gender was the zero and which gender was the one. Clearly, if the dummy is male for 1 and named as *male* it will be much easier to understand. Not all variables are easily understood from a short name; for example, if a variable was measuring the number of years a woman had spent out of the labour force after her first child then one has difficulty using a name which conveys this, especially when there is a limit of eight letters on it.

Some packages provide help in this respect by storing a description of the variable in another field in the database. This can contain information such as the units of measurement (e.g. metres, kilograms, dollars etc.) or the coding being used (e.g. if the variable is a measure of how happy someone is it might be recorded as 1 = very unhappy, 2 = slightly unhappy, 3 = neutral, 4 = quite happy, 5 = very happy). The field should give the codings used for missing observations and estimates (see below).

SAVING YOUR DATA

Once you have managed to import a data set, which you have been given, you could conduct your analysis and exit the program; your next usage would then involve importing the source data again. The alternative is to save the data in the specific format of the package you have been using. You should be careful when saving your data as when a package operates in 'Windows' style the 'Save' command will overwrite the existing file which you opened with the version you are using. This could mean you accidentally overwrite a full sample with a reduced version of the sample; for example, your sample may have covered persons of all ages and you may have decided to work with only those above or below certain ages. This type of save command will automatically add any new variables you have created (such as dummies or transformations) on to the file. If you are in any doubt about the risk of overwriting a file you can take the precaution of using a 'Save as' command to create a different version of the sample file. Where the Windows style 'Save' commands are not used, you may need to ensure that you do not exit without saving an updated version of your file, if you have added new variables which you wish to keep.

If you are using a large survey you may find it too cumbersome to add all the new variables that you have created from the source variables to a revised version to be saved. You might want to use some kind of batch file (see below) to create the additional variables each time you start.

4.4 DESCRIPTIVE EXPLORATION OF YOUR DATA

The data may already have been processed in the sense that prior users have recoded variables, eliminated observations and carried out transformations (such as dividing one variable by another). Alternately it may be 'raw' in the sense that the data is in the format in which it was originally available to the user. For a survey, this would involve the answers to each question being given as they were on the questionnaires. If the data has been in the hands of economists it is unlikely to contain string or alphanumeric data other than perhaps identifiers, e.g. the name of countries might be included in an observation field.

It may not be necessary to use the computer to retrieve variable definition information as large-scale recurrent surveys (such as household income and expenditure and labour force surveys carried out by governments) may provide a printed codebook and interview schedule and/or give these in the form of Adobe Acrobat (*.pdf) files provided with the data.

MISSING OBSERVATIONS

A data set is essentially a matrix of rows of observations and columns of variables. There is no guarantee that this matrix will not have 'empty' elements in the form of missing data, e.g in a survey people might not answer a question because they were embarrassed, the interviewer may have forgotten to record the answer or it was decided that the answer given was not usable (for example, if someone put down their age as 299 years old). In aggregate data, some observations may simply not be available because they were not collected, published or otherwise made available.

Missing observations is the extreme case of missing information. In surveys we can find the lesser information loss of incomplete or partial answers to a question in which there are also full answers. For example, where people are asked how often they have performed an activity the answers may be a mixture of exact answers and answers given in a range, such as 10–20 where the range is one nominated by the respondent and not a band given in the questionnaire. One could replace these with the mid-point of the range as a compromise, but if they are excluded altogether, then you are treating them as missing observations.

If you do have missing observations, then decisions have to be made about coding them and dealing with them. One thing that should not have been done is to code them as zero as this will confuse them with actual zeros. Some file formats will treat blanks as zeros and so missing observations should not have been coded as blanks either.

The missing observation then has to be given a specific numerical code, usually one which is unlikely to occur in any of the actual variables such as −999. Individual packages may use specific code numbers for missing variables. This means that a single command can be used to tell the package to exclude missing variables. Unless specific provision is made for a separate code, then variables which are irrelevant for certain observations will also be coded as missing.

When we do have a missing variable, we face the problem of a reduction in the size of our usable sample. That is, we will delete the whole observation even if none of the other variables has any missing data. This will cause sample size to change in two situations:

(i) When we compute descriptive statistics individually for a variable as opposed to computing descriptive statistics from the sample used for regression analysis.

(ii) When we modify our specified model by adding or dropping variables during a specification search, i.e. if we add a variable which has missing observations then the sample size will go down unless its set of missing elements coincides exactly with the total set of missing observations in the current model specification.

Missing data causes problems for our analysis of two types. One is the reduction in the sample size. This may not be a worry in a large survey but can be a great worry in a cross-section analysis of countries. An example of this is the data set used in Chapter 9 to estimate a growth equation. Table 9.1 begins with a sample of well over 100 countries, which rapidly falls to around 40 or 50 once we begin to attempt to construct a multiple regression model.

Aside from the loss of degrees of freedom, there is a potential difficulty that the properties of the reduced sample are now vastly different from the sample originally chosen. For example, if we did have a cross-section of countries, and all the developing countries were excluded because they had missing data on a variable (or variables) in the model, then the resulting parameter estimates may differ markedly from what would have been found in the full sample. The last mentioned case is really an example of a selectivity bias. In a survey of individuals this may arise due to differential rates of non-response to certain questions which are correlated with properties of the sample, for example people may be more or less likely to answer a question depending on their age, their income, gender or other variables.

Given the above it is desirable that you examine your data to look for the incidence of missing variables. Having established the degree of their presence you need to make some decision about how to deal with the problems of potential bias which may arise. The only thing we can do is to seek a replacement for the missing information from some other source. The possibilities are:

▶ Reject the problematic variable and use a different one, which has less missing information, instead as a proxy. This option may not be viable in some studies.

▶ Use proxy information which has been explicitly provided in the data set. In a household survey this could involve drawing on a proxy interview schedule, such as where another member of a household has been asked to give information on behalf of someone who was not present at the time the data was collected.

▶ Replace the missing observation with the mean from the rest of the sample. This option has been available on some general statistical packages, although it is *not* an approach which would meet with the approval of econometricians.

▶ Replace the missing value with an *ad hoc* estimate. The same comments as made for the last suggestion apply here. For example, the missing value could be generated by using predicted values from a regression of the values of the variable, which are available, on some combination of other variables in the data set. A common example of an *ad hoc* estimate is the use of interpolation in time-series data to create monthly or quarterly observations when data is only available on a less frequent basis. The simplest method of simply splitting the difference between two periods across the periods in between can be fairly called an *ad hoc* method. More sophisticated methods of interpolation might be classified in the next suggestion.

▶ Replace the missing value with a theoretically based estimate. This is an extension of the previous suggestion. For example, the missing value could be generated by using predicted values from a regression of the values of the variable, which are available, on some combination of other variables in the data set which are suggested by a theoretical model of the determination of the variable with which we are concerned.

The last mentioned case is related to the instrumental variables technique which is explained in Chapter 13. In that case, we would use the predicted value for all the observations instead of just the missing observations.

So, we have broadly two choices when faced with missing variables, which is to simply delete the observations concerned or substitute some other value. The one thing we should not do is allow missing variables to be included in our analysis either as zeros or as a code value. A more subtle case arises where we have 'don't knows' included in the data set we have been given.

DON'T KNOW ANSWERS

'Don't know' responses can arise because the respondent in a survey genuinely does not know or it may be that the person responsible for the survey fills in a don't know response. A don't know is obviously not quite the same as a blank. Don't knows may also vary across surveys aimed at the same research topics in that an interviewer could take different strategies in collecting information:

▶ Accept don't know answers when they are offered them by the respondent.

▶ Prompt the respondent to give a don't know answer if they seem to be in doubt about the correct answer.

▶ Prompt the respondent to settle on the most likely answer if they are in doubt or instead prompt them to offer a range if the question is of a numerical type.

Dealing with the don't know involves the same issues as dealing with the missing variable problem. Clearly it should not be a literal blank and it should not be replaced with some kind of proxy value without a justification being given for this.

Spreadsheet packages may not allow you to enter a literal blank once a file has been defined as they may, by default, treat any non-entry as a missing variable and automatically give it their internal coding for a blank.

LOOKING FOR ERRORS AND ANOMALIES

Once we have found out how missing observations have been coded and decided how to deal with them, we need to go on to check our data for basic errors in the variables and for any kind of anomalies that may cast doubt on the usefulness of the sample. The easiest way to begin this is by computing some descriptive statistics. The basic level of variable description usually found is to give the sample (arithmetic) means, standard deviations and minimum and maximum values for the variables. Of these statistics, only the minimum and maximum values may give a clue to the presence of errors in that they could show numbers that might not possibly occur, such as negative height or age, or values above what is feasible. At most, this can only find two errors and so you will need some more detailed exploration of the distributions of the variables. The most complete approach is to get the package to display the frequency distributions of the variables. This will alert you to extreme forms of error, that is 'impossible' values as we have just described. However, descriptive statistics on the variables will never be able to help you find less drastic errors; for example, if someone has under-stated their income by 25 per cent, there is no way of working this out from looking at the figures.

Measurement errors, and biases, may show their influence in the form of outliers in the distribution for variables or even as outliers in regression residuals (see Chapter 9, Section 9.2). An outlying observation for a variable is one which is not impossible but is much larger or smaller than the general clustering of the observation. Unfortunately it is difficult to tell whether the outlying observation is a mistake of some sort or is merely a case of a larger or smaller than usual observation. For example, someone with modest income may genuinely be spending ten times what they earn if they have managed to establish a source of credit (or indeed are failing to repay what they owe and engaging in fraud) or it may be a measurement error. The most one could do in this situation is to examine the overall set of variables for the observation suspected of measurement error. We could look at the whole set of responses for the suspect observation *including ones we do not intend to use for the variables in our model*. If we find that an individual observation has several anomalous responses and even many missing variables we might wish to discard this observation altogether. In the case of a self-completion questionnaire we would probably come to the conclusion that someone has failed to under-stand the questions properly or is not taking the exercise seriously. In the case of aggregate data from published government sources, such as that used for growth models, consumption functions etc., then any such 'rogue' observations are likely to be data entry errors or errors in the publication from which data was taken. In principle, we should be able to go back and check the original sources to eradicate the errors.

The occasional large measurement error is not necessarily a problem for the use of econometric models as it is taken account of by the treatment of the disturbance term (u_t) in the classical linear regression model. To be more precise, it is not necessarily a problem so long as it is genuinely random. If it is systematically related to variables in the model then it gives rise to potentially large biases in the estimates of the model parameters in the form of regression coefficients. Large unsystematic errors in the dependent variable will give rise to a larger variance of the error term and should typically lead to a lower R squared.

You might go on to compare the sample with equivalent data for a larger sample from the population as a whole to give some insight on the representativeness of your data. This may suggest whether some sample selection bias has been taking place. There are, of course, limits on the extent to which you can do this. In individual data, on firms or households, it will usually be possible to compare with the age or marital status of the population. However, this is not the case for such things as happiness or feelings of health. For aggregate published data, there will be no larger population with which to do a comparison.

4.5 RUNNING A REGRESSION

It is possible to run a basic regression equation in spreadsheet/database programs such as Lotus 1-2-3 or Excel. If you feel comfortable with these programs you may want to start by running regressions using the help information given in these packages. Add-on packages for the use of Excel to do regressions are also available such as 'Analyse-it'. This can be found on the provider's website (**www.analyse-it.com**) where a 30-day trial download is available. A one-year student site licence is currently about UK£17.00 or US$25.00. Eventually you would find the facilities in these packages limiting; although it is still relatively easy to do some of the things in Chapters 5–7, you will be rather short of diagnostic statistics (see Chapter 9). It will also be much quicker to carry out some operations on a specialist package. When you come to use a specialist package there are broadly two ways in which you can do so: a menu-driven mode of operation or the batch mode.

Historically econometrics packages did not develop as menu-driven, although menus have gradually been added. There are degrees to which software can be menu-driven. In full-scale Windows-style menuing, it would be possible to carry out all your statistical analysis purely by using a mouse without having to type anything at all from the keyboard. This (full) menu option is easier to use for the beginner. Having loaded a data set from the file menu you can then progress to the regression menu. The first menu choice will be deciding which of the variables are dependent and which are independent. In the full menu set up you can simply drag these variables into their relative boxes using the mouse and then click 'OK'. You will then find a set of results appearing in a different window and these results can be saved in a file.

If the first regression you ever run turns out to be seriously faulty this is not a great problem as you can easily go back to the menu and change it. Using the menu system, it is very easy to add and drop variables as a means of exploring the stability of your model. One thing you should consider on your first regression is whether or not your program includes or excludes a constant term (intercept) by default. The normal rule in econometrics is to *always include an intercept* unless there is some very good reason not to. If the package does not include an intercept automatically then you must create one and add it to the list of independent variables. The other thing you may wish to consider before you allow a regression command to be run is what kind of output you want. This involves two questions:

(i) What do you want the regression output to look like?

It would be nice if you could order regression software to produce neat and impressive tables of results in exactly the form you desired. Unfortunately, there is often relatively little control over the type of table that appears; however, you should be able to copy and paste the output over to a word processor for further formatting. While the layout of the results may be quite inflexible in terms of visual style, there should be some control over the numerical presentation of the coefficients and 't' ratios. The default style of presentation tends to be to use scientific notation where a small number such as 0.00000036 is written as 3.6 E–7 and a large number such as 43 000 000 as 4.3E7. The one thing you may need to be wary of is programs with a default setting of rounding very small numbers to 0. You cannot have coefficients, standard errors or 't' ratios that are zero, so a figure of zero means you need to change the display defaults in order to obtain the actual number.

(ii) What do you want the regression output to contain?

The usual core regression output is coefficients, standard errors, 't' ratios and the R squared. Often, other information such as the R squared adjusted, the 'F' for the equation, and the critical significance may also be provided as default output. You may be able to suppress some of the regression output and you will be able to ask for additional output such as descriptive statistics, correlation matrices, the variance-covariance matrix elasticities and the diagnostic statistics in Chapter 9.

WHAT IS THE BATCH METHOD AND WHY WOULD YOU USE IT?

If you are not using a menu-driven method you would be typing out commands to give instructions to the software. This must follow the **syntax** of the package, for example you might need to type

OLS CONS INT INC;

to run a consumption function where *CONS* is consumption, *INC* is income and *INT* is the constant term (1 for each observation), which has to be explicitly entered here. The semi-colon (;) here is a message to the software that this is the end of the command line. Some kind of 'switch' may be used to give additional instructions to produce more than the default output. This will follow the main command with a / or a bracket to signal the start of the extra commands. The command may be prefaced with another command to select the sample to be used if the regression is not to be run on the full sample.

Rather than sitting and typing out a sequence of such commands within a regression package, you could use a word processor to write a list of commands, which could include transformations of the variables and sample selection commands. Feeding such a list into the package is a simple form of computer programming and is the **batch method.** This may save you a lot of time as you can, of course, use old commands with slight changes to run entirely different regressions by changing the sample used or the set of variables included. A batch approach is also useful as a way of making sure you keep a record of what you did in the past while exploring your data. The menu-driven approach may also be able to provide this service if the package has the facility of giving you a log of the session. It is desirable that some such log or batch file is kept of the transformations that have been performed on the original data set, in case mistakes have been made in creating new variables out of the original data. The instructions that come with software may not use the term 'batch method'; for example, SPSS is heavily menu-driven but it does come with a 'syntax' file method which can save you a lot of time if you use the package frequently.

4.6 INTERPRETING YOUR RESULTS

Regression output has to be interpreted before it is of any use. You should by now be aware that this requires concentration on the three S's:

▶ Size
▶ Sign
▶ Significance

The need to focus on these will be reinforced from Chapter 5 onwards but we also look at them in the case study in Section 4.9 below. The use of an 'F' test falls under the third S. The R squared does not fall under any of the S's as it is not a significance test. Every computer package is going to automatically provide information on the sign and the size of the coefficients; however, this measure of size is not usually a useful measure of the size of the relationship between the dependent and independent variables because of the units of measurement problem. Hence we might want to use elasticities.

In the example regression shown below (Section 4.9) most of the coefficients can easily be interpreted in terms of size but this is just good fortune due to the nature of many of the variables.

4.7 ADDITIONAL TREATMENT OF YOUR REGRESSION OUTPUT

The package you use will give you coefficients, standard errors, default 't' ratios, R squared and an F for the equation. It may also provide other diagnostic statistics (see Chapter 10) and possibly some descriptive statistics (means, standard deviations, correlation matrixes). Packages vary in terms of which of the above are default and which have to be requested.

Just because statistics come out of the machine does not mean that they are either:

(a) necessarily useful for your study;
(b) or even applicable to the model you have used.

The essential lesson of these points is that the computer package is incapable of reading the mind of its user nor is it an 'artificial intelligence' system that automatically knows how valid the model the user has applied is for the data they are using. It is set up to provide what most people are likely to need in most situations *not* what everybody will need in every situation.

You might need to do further tests on the regression output. Packages will include some of these as options, which will be explained in the menus or manuals. Even if an option is not available you may be able to construct it yourself by saving the regression output and entering new commands. For example, you may want to analyse the pattern of residuals, as is explored in Chapter 9. Or, you may want to assess the predictive power of your model. If you do not have prior knowledge, which suggests a point where you should divide the sample into a sample for estimation and a 'holdout' sample for prediction purposes, then you could just divide it down the middle.

4.8 TURNING YOUR REGRESSION OUTPUT INTO A PRESENTATION OR ARTICLE

You are likely to be writing your article or report on a word processor into which you may want to import your regression report. The easiest or laziest way to do this would be to simply copy and paste the tables of output from the regression package across to the word processor file. One disadvantage of this for the reader is that there may be fairly irrelevant output which is not discussed in the text. Although this does not do any harm it may rob your presentation of its clarity. By the term 'fairly irrelevant output', I have in mind descriptive or test statistics that you do not make use of but (as will be seen in the studies reviewed in Chapter 7) some people go so far as to exclude the results for some coefficients from their results table in order to provide a clearer presentation of the results for their 'focus' variables. Apart from deleting any superfluous output, the following factors need to be considered in copying across your output to a word processor file:

(i) Variable names
If you pasted a table straight across from your output you may well end up with fairly incomprehensible names. This does not seem to bother those involved in the 'hard core' of mainstream economics. This may be because areas in the core of economics have a fairly small well-defined set of variables which are well known to everyone. However, in subjects outside economics and in more eclectic applied economics fields there tends to be more emphasis on having meaningful variable names in the tables you present. For example, it may be preferable to actually use the words 'Length of time out of work' rather than shorthand like 'YRSNOJOB'.

(ii) Coefficients
When you run a regression, you may see very large or very small numbers appear as coefficients. The precision of modern computers is such that estimates can be produced to a very large number of decimal places. This can be extremely annoying and time consuming to deal with when we come to actually look at our results. Accordingly, most computer packages make some kind of decision (default) to reduce the visual clutter. Scientific notation is a universal example of this – that is, instead of giving the number 0.00000367 you may find it reported as 3.67 E–6. Not so common is rounding down by virtue of not reporting digits after a certain point. This could lead to the paradoxical appearance of a coefficient that is zero yet is statistically significant because the value of the point estimate is too small to appear after rounding. Clearly, you

should not be reporting a coefficient of zero so you would need to change the defaults on any package which does this to get the true value.

You might wish to give elasticities, evaluated at the means, alongside the coefficients if the units of measurement of the coefficients are such that they are not easily interpreted.

(iii) Significance

There are a number of ways of reporting the statistical significance of results. All packages assume by default that you want to test the separate individual null hypotheses zero for each slope coefficient against a two-sided alternative. This means they will give you a 't' statistic which you may reproduce in your table. Such 't' statistics will be identical to the number obtained when you divide the coefficients by their respective standard errors. In general, a 't' statistic above two in absolute value is going to be significant at the 5 per cent level unless you have a sufficiently small sample. If you present 't' ratios in your tables the reader has the option of looking these up in a set of 't' tables or you may choose to report these in the text. An alternative, which is popular in some journals, is to use the 'asterisk' system of giving symbols such as *, **, *** alongside the coefficients to denote different levels of significance – commonly 1, 5 and 10 per cent levels.

There are thus three items related to statistical significance – asterisks, standard errors and 't' ratios – which you will often find included in published tables. It is not really desirable that you should give only the asterisks as this denies the reader the opportunity to conduct alternative hypothesis tests on the results. It would also mean that they could not construct confidence intervals (which are virtually never found in results tables in econometric work). Hence the standard error and/or the default 't' ratio needs to be given. If only one of these is given it is possible to work out the other by dividing it into the coefficient. The provision of the actual standard errors and/or 't' ratios makes it possible for the reader to conduct different hypothesis tests to the default two-sided null of zero, if they so wish. That is, they can test whether the coefficient differs from some other value (for example, whether the price elasticity of demand is different from unity).

It is common to take the 'F for the equation' from the package output and reproduce it near the bottom of your table. Most packages automatically give the degrees of freedom for this and you should put these in brackets after the symbol F, e.g. $F(3,42)$ for the convenience of the reader. If the package does not give them automatically you should work out the degrees of freedom for yourself and include them in the table.

(iv) Goodness of fit

As we have already indicated, in earlier chapters, the only goodness of fit statistic usually reported for OLS regression is the R squared statistic, with the adjusted version of this also often being reported. It is convenient to present this near the bottom of the table, that is, after the coefficients and significance indicators. The normal practice is to report it as it comes out of the package, namely as a fraction of 1 rather than multiplied by 100 to get a percentage.

(v) Sample size

You will find articles that do not report the sample size in the regression results table, although they may give it in another table (such as for descriptive statistics or variable definitions) or in the text. The sample size will be fairly irrelevant if it is very large relative to the number of variables as it will become, for practical purposes, infinity – meaning we can use 'z' values rather than 't' variables for constructing confidence intervals and conducting significance tests. For degrees of freedom of over 120 the sample values on test statistics will approximate those for an infinite sample/infinite degrees of freedom.

Nevertheless, it is good practice to make a habit of including the sample size at the foot of a table so that the reader knows it. They may also need it if they wish to conduct further significance tests when the degrees of freedom are not large enough to approximate infinity.

4.9 CASE STUDY: THE WILLINGNESS TO PAY STUDY

BACKGROUND

The data explored in this section comes from a survey based on interviews conducted in the street in two UK cities in July–August 2003. The main objective of the study was to look at the prospects of funding non-profit theatres out of increased revenue from allowing people who would not have attended to pay the prices they would like to pay instead of the standard price. The questionnaire is reproduced as an appendix to this chapter. Questions were asked to elicit information about age, price perceptions, gross income, marital status and so forth. Many of the answers were given as a range in order to assist people's willingness to comply in a reasonably accurate manner. In all there were 210 responses from the two cities (106 from Harrogate and 104 from Leeds). Not all questions were answered or filled in, therefore there are a number of missing variables, meaning any regression we estimate will have fewer than 210 observations.

Table 4.1 shows a list of the variables originally entered from the questionnaires. The second column is the total number of valid cases. This plus the excluded cases will add up to 210. The valid cases are those for which the variable information is not missing. On the spreadsheet (THEATRE.XLS) for this data you will find that a decimal point on its own is used to represent a missing observation. Some of the missing observations are due to the fact that a person did not answer the question or the person interviewing them did not fill it in. In other cases the missing variable might have been entered as a zero but was not. Take the specific case of the questions on whether people would be unwilling to attend local non-profit theatres at any price. If they answer 'Yes' to this then the amount they are willing to pay to attend is zero. It was decided not to enter a zero here but instead a missing value for the variable *WILLPAY*. This can, of course, be changed at a later stage if it becomes necessary for statistical analysis that these are zeros.

You can see that the variables have been entered using short (8 letters or less) names that do not always give a clear indication of what the variable represents or how it has been measured. If you access the file THEATRE.XLS you will discover that this file does not contain any additional information to help us understand the variables. Some of this information has therefore been provided in Table 4.1. Each variable is derived from one of the questions given in the interview schedule.

This particular data set was entered without additional descriptive information to indicate what the values for each variable mean. Thus one has to resort to the questionnaire to work out the units of measurement in each variable. Some assistance on this has been given in Table 4.1 by putting the question relevant to the variable in the last column. The first two variables do not have a question because the identifier of whether it was Leeds or Harrogate was simply

Table 4.1 List of variables in the theatre survey

Variable	Units	Question
LEEDS	0–1	None
ATTLEEDS	0+	1(a)
ATTHARRO	0+	1(b)
AWARE	1–3	2
ATTSPDG	£	3(b)
TVHRS	Hours	4
RADIOHRS	Hours	4
ALONE	0–1	5(1)
WITHPTNR	0–1	5(2)
FAMILY	0–1	5(3)
FRIENDS	0–1	5(4)
NUMPARTY	0–1	6
WORK	0–1	7(1)
HOME	0–1	7(2)
WALK	0–1	7(3)
BUS	0–1	7(4)
TRAIN	0–1	7(5)
CAR	0–1	7(6)
LENGTH	Minutes	8
SPENDFD	£	9
SPENDBS	£	9
RSNPRICE	£	10
MAXPRICE	£	11
FEMALE	0–1	12
AGE	Years (Mid-point of range)	13
MARRIED	0–1	14(1)
COHAB	0–1	14(2)
SINGLE	0–1	14(3)
CHILDREN	0–1	15
KIDL5	0–1	16
KIDL16 208	0–1	17
GROSSINC	£	18
SENSLOSS	1–4	19
WILLPAY	£	20
NEVERCOM	0–1	21
VOLUNPAY	0–1	22
VOLOTHER	0–1	22
EDUC	1–7	23
OCCUPAT	1–9	24
HOUSING	1–3	25

Table 4.1 (continued)		
Variable	Units	Question
PARTNOW	0 – 1	26
PARTAGED	Years	26
R1	0 – 1	27
R2	0 – 1	27
R3	0 – 1	27
R4	0 – 1	27
R5	0 – 1	27
TALKRAD	0 – 1	27
CLASSICF	0 – 1	27
LOCRAD	0 – 1	27
NATPOP	0 – 1	27
OTHRAD	0 – 1	27
CHANGEPR	0 – 1	28
WELLKNOW	0 – 1	28
FACIL	0 – 1	28
ATMOS	0 – 1	28
LOYALTY	0 – 1	29
NOMRPRIC	£	30
JOBLIM	0 – 1	31
WISHMGEN	0 – 1	32
WISHMNPT	0 – 1	32
JAZZA	0 – 1	3
CLASSICA	0 – 1	3
OTHERTH	0 – 1	3
CINEMA	0 – 1	3
ARTGALL	0 – 1	3
COMEDY	0 – 1	3
OPERA	0 – 1	3
BALLET	0 – 1	3
MUSICALS	0 – 1	3
ROCK	0 – 1	3
EASY	0 – 1	3
OTHERMS	0 – 1	14(4)

done using different coloured paper, while the *ID* variable is the number of the inteview in the sequence of interviews on a particular site. This was written on the schedule. The scales show the minimum and maximum. There are a few complications to note here:

▶ Some questions have been turned into a single variable using the scale on the question, e.g. the variable *OCCUPAT* uses the 7 codings on Question 24.
▶ Other questions have been turned into a number of categorical (dummy variables) where 1

indicates a response and 0 a non-response. For example, Question 27 has been turned into a set of radio station variables.

▶ Some variables which ask for a number are given in the units (e.g. hours of radio listening as in *RADIOHRS*) appropriate to them while others have been taken from a range. For money and age scales the approximate mid-point has been entered. In the case of Question 26 the lower figure in the range has been entered.

▶ The *GROSSINC* variable which is derived from Question 18 was generated by giving people a visual analogue scale to look at and point to the position on the range that seemed closest to their situation.

SOME SUMMARY RESULTS FROM THE DATA SET

As a first look at the properties of the data set, Table 4.2 shows the basic descriptive statistics.

Table 4.2 Descriptive statistics from the theatre survey					
	N	Min	Max	Mean	Std. Deviation
LEEDS	210	0	1	0.50	0.501
ATTLEEDS	210	0	4	0.35	0.769
ATTHARRO	210	0	7	0.30	0.940
AWARE	206	0	3	1.7913	0.83819
ATTSPDG	205	0	50	95.810	111.3556
TVHRS	210	0	78	18.624	14.9081
RADIOHRS	210	0	68	14.760	16.9486
ALONE	209	0	1	0.0957	0.2949
WITHPTNR	209	0	1	0.3636	0.48220
FAMILY	209	0	1	0.1627	0.36996
FRIENDS	209	0	1	0.5215	0.50074
NUMPARTY	207	1	20	3.7778	2.79326
WORK	88	0	1	0.0795	0.27214
HOME	98	0	1	0.6939	0.46325
WALK	209	0	1	0.1531	0.36096
BUS	210	0	1	0.3571	0.48030
TRAIN	210	0	1	0.1286	0.33552
CAR	210	0	1	0.6190	0.48678
LENGTH	204	0	90	22.8456	13.15161
SPENDFD	209	0	100	10.5861	14.47867
SPENDBS	209	0	20	0.7057	3.17907
RSNPRICE	210	0	25	12.1214	5.11853
MAXPRICE	208	5	100	25.4952	14.07082
FEMALE	210	0	1	0.5524	0.49844
AGE	209	0	65	38.4211	17.51029
MARRIED	209	0	1	0.3397	0.47475
COHAB	210	0	1	0.1619	0.36924
SINGLE	210	0	1	0.4095	0.49292
CHILDREN	210	0	1	0.4238	0.49534

Table 4.2 (continued)					
	N	Min	Max	Mean	Std. Deviation
KIDL5	207	0	1	0.0918	0.28943
KIDL16	208	0	1	0.1346	0.34214
GROSSINC	204	4000	825000	42153.1863	90496.63945
SENSLOSS	208	1	4	2.4135	1.11304
WILLPAY	189	0	60	14.4471	10.04338
NEVERCOM	209	0	1	0.1053	0.30763
VOLUNPAY	209	0	1	0.0670	0.25060
VOLOTHER	209	0	3	0.3254	0.46963
EDUC	208	1	7	2.7692	1.58331
OCCUPAT	209	1	9	3.2392	2.40396
HOUSING	210	1	3	1.5048	0.60498
PARTNOW	210	0	1	0.1333	0.34075
PARTAGED	210	0	64	8.1095	13.16776
R1	210	0	1	0.2952	0.45724
R2	210	0	1	0.1857	0.38981
R3	210	0	1	0.0286	0.167
R4	210	0	1	0.1143	0.31892
R5	210	0	1	0.0429	0.20302
TALKRAD	208	0	1	0.0096	0.09782
CLASSICF	210	0	1	0.0762	0.26594
LOCRAD	209	0	1	0.3095	0.4634
NATPOP	209	0	1	0.0286	0.167
OTHRAD	210	0	1	0.0238	0.15282
CHANGEPR	208	0	1	0.2740	0.44710
WELLKNOW	210	0	1	0.4571	0.83039
FACIL	210	0	1	0.1190	0.32462
ATMOS	210	0	1	0.2381	0.42694
LOYALTY	209	0	5	2.3684	1.10643
NOMRPRIC	206	0	7	11.3568	6.61448
JOBLIM	210	0	1	0.3619	0.48170
WISHMGEN	210	0	1	0.7238	0.44818
WISHMNPT	209	0	1	0.2297	0.42163
JAZZA	210	0	12	0.2333	1.10581
CLASSICA	210	0	45	0.3667	3.16286
OTHERTH	210	0	10	0.4667	1.36649
CINEMA	210	0	50	4.9952	7.66992
ARTGALL	210	0	50	1.1286	4.28278
COMEDY	210	0	15	0.3095	1.25061
OPERA	209	0	2	0.0383	0.23711
BALLET	208	0	12	0.0865	0.85251
MUSICALS	210	0	20	0.5333	1.96411
ROCK	209	0	50	1.3493	6.68577
EASY	210	0	6	0.0667	0.52254
OTHERMS	208	0	1	0.1106	0.31436

The means and standard deviations are calculated only for the valid observations, the number of which is given again in the second column of the table. The mean figures for the categorical (0–1) variables when multiplied by 100 will be the percentage of people in the category for which the variable is 1. For example, the percentage who are female is 55.24 per cent. The mean and standard deviation of the variables which are on an arbitrary categorical scale will be meaningless. For example, it is not possible to draw any meaningful conclusion from the mean and standard deviations of *OCCUPAT*, the occupation coding variable. This is not entirely true of the variables that are on an arbitrary ordinal scale. For example, if we were to split the sample into its two distinct geographical areas and find that *LOYALTY* or *SENSLOSS* was higher in one than the other, then this does suggest that there is a difference in the strength of these feelings between the two areas. One could go on to test this using an appropriate significance test.

The chief interest in this research was to look at willingness to pay for a ticket at the local theatre. The effect of letting people have 'pay what you like nights' on revenue depends on the prices they are willing to pay and the normal price that is charged. One could envisage a situation where the scheme backfires because people who would have come anyway simply shift their night of attendance and pay a lower price. Table 4.3 shows the difference between what people say they would pay and what they consider to be the normal price at the venue which is closest to their residential area.

Table 4.3 Difference between 'willingness to pay' price and the perceived 'normal price' of local theatre events

	Difference (£)	Frequency	Percentage	Valid percentage	Cumulative percentage
Valid	−22.50	1	0.5	0.5	0.5
	−15.00	2	1.0	1.0	1.6
	−12.00	1	0.5	0.5	2.1
	−10.00	6	2.9	3.1	5.2
	−9.50	2	1.0	1.0	6.3
	−7.50	3	1.4	1.6	7.9
	−7.00	1	0.5	0.5	8.4
	−6.00	1	0.5	0.5	8.9
	−5.00	20	9.5	10.5	19.4
	−4.50	1	0.5	0.5	19.9
	−4.00	1	0.5	0.5	20.4
	−3.00	2	1.0	1.0	21.5
	−2.50	11	5.2	5.8	27.2
	−2.00	5	2.4	2.6	29.8
	−1.50	2	1.0	1.0	30.9
	−1.00	5	2.4	2.6	33.5
	−0.50	1	0.5	0.5	34.0
	0.00	31	14.8	16.2	50.3
	0.50	2	1.0	1.0	51.3
	1.00	1	0.5	0.5	51.8

Table 4.3 (continued)				
Difference (£)	Frequency	Percentage	Valid percentage	Cumulative percentage
1.50	1	0.5	0.5	52.4
2.00	11	5.2	5.8	58.1
2.50	9	4.3	4.7	62.8
3.00	6	2.9	3.1	66.0
3.50	1	0.5	0.5	66.5
4.00	3	1.4	1.6	68.1
4.50	1	0.5	0.5	68.6
5.00	19	9.0	9.9	78.5
6.00	1	0.5	0.5	79.1
6.50	1	0.5	0.5	79.6
7.00	2	1.0	1.0	80.6
7.50	1	0.5	0.5	81.2
8.00	2	1.0	1.0	82.2
8.50	1	0.5	0.5	82.7
10.00	10	4.8	5.2	88.0
12.50	1	0.5	0.5	88.5
13.00	1	0.5	0.5	89.0
14.00	1	0.5	0.5	89.5
15.00	4	1.9	2.1	91.6
17.50	1	0.5	0.5	92.1
20.00	4	1.9	2.1	94.2
21.00	1	0.5	0.5	94.8
22.00	1	0.5	0.5	95.3
25.00	1	0.5	0.5	95.8
25.50	1	0.5	0.5	96.3
30.00	3	1.4	1.6	97.9
37.00	1	0.5	0.5	98.4
37.50	1	0.5	0.5	99.0
40.00	1	0.5	0.5	99.5
50.00	1	0.5	0.5	100.0

There are 19 missing observations here, leaving us with a sample of 191. The negative figures show those who will pay less than what they think is the normal price and vice versa. The modal response is to give the same value as the normal price and the willingness to pay price with 31 people (16.2 per cent of the usable sample) giving this response. The over and under paying decisions are widely split around the zero point. It is of interest to multiply the price gaps by the number of people at each price gap to see if the over-paying exceeds the under-paying. On the basis of the above table the net revenue gap is in fact £525, suggesting that extra revenue can be gained.

Clearly, the amount people are willing to pay is likely to be a function of various social, taste and economic factors. We now move on to a simple regression equation to explore this.

A SPECIMEN REGRESSION FROM THE DATA SET

Table 4.4 shows a specimen OLS regression equation. The sample is 195 because those who were unwilling to ever attend performances at their local non-profit theatre were excluded rather than entered as zero observations.

Table 4.4 Estimates of an equation for attendance at cultural events	
Dependent variable: Total attendance at cultural events in the last year ($TOTGOUT$)	
Intercept	19.63
	(6.12)
$TVANDRAD$	−0.094
	(2.27)
$NUMPARTY$	0.0048
	(0.014)
$SURPLUS$	0.014
	(0.21)
AGE	−0.167
	(3.03)
$GROSSINC$	−0.00084
(in thousand pounds)	(0.08)
R^2	0.084
$F(5,189)$	3.48
N	195

Note: Absolute 't' ratios in parentheses under coefficients, degrees of freedom in parentheses for 't' ratios.

The estimating equation was as follows:

$$TOTGOOUT = b_0 + b_1 TVANDRAD + b_2 NUMPARTY + b_3 SURPLUS$$
$$+ b_4 AGE + b_5 GROSSINC + u \tag{4.4}$$

where three variables ($GROSSINC$, $NUMPARTY$, AGE) are taken directly from the original sample. The other two ($TVANDRAD$ and $SURPLUS$) have been constructed from the sample provided. $TVANDRAD$ is made simply by adding hours of television watched ($TVHRS$) and hours of radio listened to ($RADHRS$) together. The $SURPLUS$ variable is constructed by computing the difference between two price variables unrelated to local theatre attendance. It is the difference between the maximum price individuals would pay ($MAXPRICE$) to see a performer they greatly admired and what they consider to be a 'reasonable price for a night out' ($RSNPRICE$).

Figuring out the expected signs for the coefficients is fairly straightforward as most of the variables in the equation can be related to substitution effects on the demand for going out to live entertainment. We are limited by not using techniques which are to be covered in later chapters.

Notwithstanding the above, we might postulate that $b_1 < 0$, $b_2 > 0$, $b_3 > 0$, $b_4 < 0$, $b_5 > 0$. The argument for the sign of b_1 is that time spent in these activities is a substitute for live events and will therefore reduce willingness to go to any cultural event. The argument for the sign of b_2 is that those who go out in large parties may be willing to pay more for any given cultural event. The argument for the sign of b_5 is that it is a normal good. The argument for the coefficient on AGE is based on prior evidence that people become less keen to attend art and entertainment. The $SURPLUS$ variable is a measure of the potential utility gained from arts and entertainment and might then be expected to have a positive coefficient.

Let us apply the rule of three S's to this equation. For the five variables, we have broadly the expected signs although the income coefficient is unexpectedly negative. The intercept is positive. Only two of the variables are statistically significant to any reasonable degree. These are hours of television watched and radio listened to, which has a negative coefficient, and years of age, which has a negative coefficient. Given the nature of the units of measurement, these are quite easy to interpret in terms of size of relationships without resorting to elasticities or any other form of adjustment. The age coefficient says that, other things being equal, a person who is one year older will, on average, be expected to make 0.167 less visits to cultural performances per year. It is worth bearing in mind that the sample only contains people of 15 and over. As the model is linear it suggests that the passage of 10 years, from any starting age, results in 1.67 fewer attendances per year. Another way of putting this is that every 6 years approximately an attendance is lost. The $TVANDRAD$ coefficient suggests that a person who spends 10 hours more consuming TV and radio programmes will visit 0.94 fewer events per year on average. Or, using the 'how many does it take to lose a visit per year' calculation, we have a value of around 10 hours and 38 minutes of additional television watching and radio listening.

The R squared value of 0.084 is low in that only 8.4 per cent of the variation of willingness to pay around its mean has been accounted for by the linear combination of five variables included in the equation.

Now that we have looked at a simple regression from a provided data set there are various things we should remind ourselves of:

▶ The sample was taken from only two cities in the same geographical area. This may have the advantage of holding constant certain factors that might vary across a more widespread sample.
▶ The questions in the sample survey relate mainly to the last 12 months.
▶ Some variables were collected in ranges. It is not possible to conduct OLS regression estimation using ranges, therefore the mid-points of the ranges were used.
▶ There were missing observations for some variables which resulted in those observations being dropped from the sample for estimation.
▶ The model used is a fairly *ad hoc* one, which is just for illustrative purposes. There may well be a more suitable list of independent variables, available in the sample, than the one used here.
▶ The model used only the simplest techniques available in OLS regression. Extensions to these, covered from Chapter 6 onwards, may result in a superior model.

4.10 COLLECTING DATA: SOME FURTHER REFLECTIONS

This chapter has been mainly based on a case study involving the idea that you have been given some data to use. The particular data set was one constructed by the author and the originating questionnaire instrument is included as the appendix. In reality you might be given a set of data with less contact to the original source. Nonetheless, the same principles given above should apply.

Let us now suppose you are setting out to collect and assemble your own data set. How might this be done? There are a number of ways, some of which are really compiling your own version of some existing data:

▶ Go to published aggregate statistics such as those published by the OECD, Eurostat or central banks, and governments, within individual countries. From these you can model consumption functions, Phillips curves, demand for money functions or even whole macroeconomic models.

▶ Go to existing survey data. You can, for example, browse the collection of survey holdings at the University of Exeter by visiting the website **www.esrc.gov.uk**. This contains deposits of surveys carried out by other researchers on a wide range of subjects, including historical material, and for countries other than the UK. The data set used for illustration in Chapter 8 was compiled from this source. There are other sources of survey information such as those collected regularly by the Gallup organization. Some surveys may be quite expensive to access as they are produced by profit-making organizations.

▶ You could construct your own data completely without reliance on previous collection by others. This could be just by doing a survey or it could be based on experiments (such as game playing in a computer laboratory) or something more unusual such as turning observations of 'qualitative' data, such as text in an advertisement (see Cameron and Collins, 1997) or the events taking place in a video recording, into numerical data. Even when constructing one's own original data, it would still be expected that you are following methods which have been accepted as 'good' within the research community.

The most important thing in any of these approaches is that you ask critical questions about the relationship between the variables you are collecting and the underlying concepts, which they are meant to represent. It is much better to do this at the outset, than to be faced with problems which require you to go back and re-investigate your data set.

SURVEYS: TAKING A CRITICAL APPROACH

The nature of the critical questions is going to differ by source of data. If you are using surveys, then some care needs to be taken over whether the questions are going to produce an accurate estimate of the information sought. There is no point asking complex, elaborate hypothetical questions which the respondents may find totally meaningless to the extent that their answers are more or less random or simply 'don't know'. Likewise, a range question may be of little use if it is too wide. For example, if we are asking about weekly rental rates in student accommodation and we give too wide a range, we will end up with data in which there is little variation.

The classic solution to these kinds of difficulties is to have a 'pilot' study in which the answers are looked at, in detail, before investing large amounts of time and money in doing the full survey. As well as the pilot survey, you could attempt some detailed discussion with a sample of respondents to find out how they interpreted the questions.

The main focus in appraising a survey instrument should be always to ask:

▷ Could this question be put in a better way?
▷ Is the scale appropriate in terms of trading off accuracy of replies, response rates and relationship to the concept being measured?

A good example of the latter point is with age and income measures. People will almost always know their ages accurately but may feel unwilling to reveal it if asked directly. Hence a banding such as 20–24, 25–29 may produce better results. This may be why one so often sees this in market research surveys, including the documents included when you purchase a new electronics product. A similar kind of reluctance or embarrassment may apply in the case of income. There is a further issue in this case of memory. People may not be very good at recalling their exact income or wealth as there are many factors which might be forgotten, such as unexpected absences or windfall payments.

PUBLISHED AGGREGATE DATA: TAKING A CRITICAL APPROACH

Unfortunately the spread of the Internet has had a bad effect on the degree of critical perspective shown to aggregate published data. This seems to be spreading to academics as well as students. As it is likely that people are moving towards total dependence on Internet sources of aggregate data, it is a good idea if we point out some common failings which you might fall into through relying solely on the Internet:

▷ Believing that there is no data at all for a variable because it is not on the Internet.
▷ Believing that data for a variable does not exist before a certain time period because it is not on the Internet.
▷ Taking data from a secondary source because it was easy to find. This can, and has, led to mistakes being passed on repeatedly from someone's mistake in using the source data. For example, government statistics may have been modified wrongly and quoted on a web page which then becomes the standard source.
▷ Lack of attention to the units of measurement. There is no good reason why this should happen but people seem to be more careless about this point. One factor may be that the explanatory notes for data would typically be harder for the user to avoid in an older printed source.

THREE SIMPLE QUESTIONS YOU SHOULD ASK OF ALL DATA

▲ Where did these data come from?
▲ How exactly were they calculated?
▲ What do they really mean?

If you cannot find the answer to these questions from the source you are using, then you need to go a stage further back to the source from which they come. If this does not give you full details then it may be necessary to contact the providers of the data. Aside from careless reliance on Internet provision, there are other pitfalls in the use of aggregate published data.

(i) Ignoring deseasonalization

Series of shorter periods, less than one year, will sometimes be presented in a deseasonalized form, by governments and international bodies which collate national data. You should *not* confuse this with the 'data' for the same variable. A quarterly deseasonalized series for expenditure on consumer expenditure, for example, will have had adjustments made to it to take out the estimated impact of seasonal factors. The types of factors involved, and a simple method of dealing with them, are given later in Section 7.4 of Chapter 7. For the moment, we can state the principles that you should not mix raw and deseasonalized data series in the same equation. In general, in econometrics we prefer to avoid deseasonalized data and therefore use raw data. Any seasonal adjustments would be made in the specification of our model.

(ii) No, or faulty, index number splicing

It is not the place of this text to go into the theory of index numbers as it is assumed you are already familiar with this to a sufficient degree. Nonetheless, you need to be careful in collecting index number data not to make mistakes. The first thing to check is that the numbers in the series have a ratio interpretation. If the index number variable has only ordinal measurement then any series which it is adjusted by will then only have ordinal meaning.

The most common problem with index numbers is the shifting of the base year. You cannot simply join together two or more series, for the same variable, which have a different base year. This will totally distort the ratio proportions between years in the series. Thus you must re-base all items to the same base in order to splice series together. The quick and 'dirty' way to do this is to find an overlap year and simply alter the series by this proportion. If there is more than one overlap year you could use the average or run a regression on the overlapping series to get the adjustment factor. These methods would be called 'dirty', in the sense that they are inaccurate, if the weights used in the construction of the indices have also changed over the years. Ideally, adjusting the complete series to be consistent would require that we not only move to a common base year but also move to a common set of weights. It is now quite common to find academic work which does not do this.

(iii) Confusion of value and volume data

Suppose you need to find a series for exports or imports. What exactly is this? A little thought makes it obvious that you cannot simply add up different types of exports or imports as they are in different units. It makes no sense to add tons of feathers to inches of sticky tape. The only method of adding up is to use prices, and therefore we get a value measure of exports or imports. To get a volume measure (i.e. a series for the quantity of exports or imports) we have to divide the volume measure by an index number for the relevant set of prices.

(iv) Confusion over real and nominal data

This is similar to the last case. If we are looking at national income statistics, we have a number of choices: GNP or GDP and, within this, usually the choice of data at current (or market) prices versus data at constant prices.

Data at constant prices is 'real' income in the sense that the effect of inflation (changes in the value of money) is taken out by valuing all years at the same set of prices. This set of prices is a base year. We are not dealing with an index because the base year is not set to 100. However, the series is in units, which have no meaning in themselves. This is not a problem for regression as what we need is meaningful ratios in the data. This is then a volume measure of national income.

National income in current (market) prices gives the value of the national income in a particular year. It is nominal data which requires division by a price index series (RPI in the UK and CPI in the USA) in order to convert it into a series for real income.

You can use either of the methods above to obtain real income if that is the variable you are looking for.

4.11 CONCLUSION

Chapters 1–3 of this book dealt with the philosophy, theory and methods of econometrics. This chapter addressed the issue of how to actually 'do' econometrics when someone has already given you the data. One should approach the data set with an inquiring, or even critical, mind as no data set is ever perfect. Lack of attention to the properties of a data set may result in time wasted conducting meaningless or near-meaningless research. In particular, you should be focusing on the validity of the variables as measures of the concepts underlying the model and the potential for bias due to measurement error.

By now you should be aware of the need to develop some kind of theoretical model before estimating equations and the process of turning your estimated equations into the type of results table that could be incorporated in a class project or even an academic article or book, or a consultancy report. However, when first receiving a data set you may wish to run several regressions as an exploratory avenue. Only one regression has been provided in this chapter in order not to clutter the presentation. This data set was compiled in such a way that range values, in a questionnaire, were already converted to mid-points. For the regression to be run some new variables had to be constructed from those provided.

DOS AND DON'TS

Do

Save your files in multiple copies.

Keep a copy of the original source if you have done a format conversion or created an edited version.

Check exactly how the sample you have been given was collected or produced from a larger data set.

Check what the variables actually measure and how they have been coded.

Don't

Forget to take account of scientific notation when converting your regression package output into a results table.

Run a regression which includes variables which are purely categorical.

Forget to take account of the units of measurement when you are calculating the size of the relationship between two variables.

EXERCISES

4.1 Using the data set provided (in the THEATRE.XLS file) re-estimate the equation in Table 4.4. and compare your results with those given in the table. Note: this requires that you first create the variables *SURPLUS* and *TVANDRAD*.

4.2 Use the THEATRE.XLS file data to calculate an elasticity of TOTGOOUT with respect to gross income from the coefficients of your regression.

4.3 If you now added the *OCCUPAT* variable to your regression, would its coefficient have any sensible meaning? If not, why not?

4.4 Create a new variable, using a name of your choosing, to measure total attendance at rock music and cinema in the last 12 months. This requires you to add these two variables on the spreadsheet. Examine the frequency distribution of this variable to see if it looks plausible.

4.5 Re-estimate the regression equation from Exercise 4.1 with the variable you have just created in place of TOTGOOUT. Interpret the coefficients and 't' statistic on your new variable.

4.6 Compare the results from the equation you have just estimated with those from the original estimating equation.

REFERENCE

Cameron, S. and Collins, A. (1997) Estimates of a hedonic ageing equation for partner search, *Kyklos*, **50**(1), 409–418.

WEBLINKS

http://www.fedstats.gov/
USA data at state level.
http://ifs.apdi.net/imf/about.asp
International Financial Statistics – you will need to create a trial account to access.
http://www.oecdwash.org/DATA/online.htm
OECD collection of international comparative data.
http://www.abs.gov.au/
Australian national statistics.
http:/www.ons.gov.uk
Source for UK aggregate data.
http: //www.homeoffice.gov.uk
This site provides many examples of aggregate data, and interview and questionnaire data, in the area of crime and punishment.
http://www.data-archive.ac.uk
This is the site of the ESRC Data Archive. This is a collection of social science data sets in the UK and elsewhere. You can browse the catalogue of data sets and obtain access.

APPENDIX: QUESTIONNAIRE USED IN THIS CHAPTER

DRAFT QUESTIONNAIRE

1. Level of attendance in the last 12 months at the non-profit theatre: (a) in this area (b) in the 'other' area
   Number of times: (a)
   (b)

2. How aware have you been of the programme in production during this time?
   Not at all (1)   Moderately (2)   Fairly closely (3)

3. Attendance at other forms of art/entertainment in the last 12 months (number of times approximately):

   Jazz
   Classical music
   Other theatre
   Cinema
   Art gallery
   Rock music
   Easy listening
   Comedy
   Opera
   Ballet
   Musicals

3. Approximate spending on the above in the last 12 months (£):

4. How many hours on average per week do you consume of:
   television
   radio

5. Do you usually attend events:
   alone (1)   with partner (2)   with family (i.e. partner +) (3)   with friends (4)

6. What is the usual size of your party (including yourself)?

7. How do you usually get to evenings out
   from work (1)
   from home (2)
   walk (3)   bus (4)   train (5)   car (6)

8. How long is your door-to-door journey time by your chosen mode to this venue (in minutes)?

9. Approximately what do you normally spend on the following when you attend this venue (£)
   meal/drinks:
   babysitters:

10. What would you normally consider a reasonable ticket price for an evening out (excluding cinema)

    $< 55-10$ $10-15$ $15-20$ $20-25$ $25+$

11. What is the absolute maximum you would pay for an evening out in £ to see a performer/event you were extremely interested in?

12. Are you:

    male (1)   female (2)

13. Your age is:

    < 15 $15-19$ $20-24$ $25-34$ $35-44$ $45-54$ $55-64$ $65+$

14. Married (1)   cohabitating (2)   single (3)   other (4)

15. Children   yes/no

16. Children under 5   yes/no

17. Children under 16   yes/no

18. Could you please give an estimate of your (gross) annual income or family income if more relevant:

19. How would you rate your sense of loss if this theatre was closed?

    not bothered (1)   mild loss (2)   fairly bothered (3)   a great loss (4)

20. How much are you willing to pay tonight for an event if you felt interested and all other obstacles, to attendance, were removed (units of 50p intervals)?

21. Do you feel you would never want to come at any price: Yes   No

22. Have you ever done voluntary unpaid labour:

    at theatre/arts?
    other community activities?

23. What is your level of education currently:

    left school at 16 (1)   O (2)   A (3)   Degree (4)   Masters (5)   PhD (6)
    vocational qualification (e.g. nursing) (7)

24. Occupation:

    none presently (1)
    manual labour (2)
    skilled labour (3)
    self employed – trade (4)
    self employed – white collar (5)
    administrator (6)
    educator (7)
    senior level manager (8)
    other level manager (9)

25. Housing status: owner occupier (1)   renter (2)   other (3)

26. Have you participated, to a substantial degree, in arts yourself as a performer now?
    and/or
    when aged
    < 15   15–19   20–24   25–34   35–44   45–54   55–64   65+

27. Main radio station listened to:
    R1
    R2
    R3
    R4
    R5
    a talk radio station
    classic fm
    national music station-pop/rock/gold
    local radio
    other

28. Which of the following are most likely to increase your attendance at the normal ticket prices?
    change in programme (1)
    presence of well-known actors (2)
    greater bar/food facilities in theatre/vicinity (3)
    other things going on around the theatre (4)
    (pre-show music, displays of visual art etc.).

29. What best describes your sense of loyalty to this theatre as part of the local community?
    little sense (1)   some feeling (2)   moderate feeling (3)
    fairly committed (4)   passionate commitment (5)

30. What do you think the normal price is for a ticket at this theatre (units of 50p)?

31. Do you feel that the demands of your present job limit your capacity to go out in the evening (whether by stress/tiredness or time limitations)?   Yes/No

32. Do you ever wish you went out in the evening more often than you do:
    (a) in general (1)
    (b) to local non-profit theatre (2).

What Do All these Tests and Statistics Mean?

LEARNING OBJECTIVES

■ Be able to interpret OLS coefficients, and construct elasticities, in a linear model
■ Be able to use the 'F' test in three ways in a linear regression – as a structural stability test, as a variable addition/deletion test and as a test of the hypothesis that R squared is greater than 0
■ Know how R squared can be 'adjusted' and the limitations of doing this
■ Understand how to construct a forecast from a linear regression model and be able to use forecast evaluation statistics

CHAPTER SUMMARY

5.1 INTRODUCTION: TYPICAL TEST STATISTICS IN COMPUTER OUTPUT

By this stage, you should be familiar with single equation multiple regression equations estimated by ordinary least squares (OLS). We continue with the assumption that the model is strictly linear (i.e. a two-variable relationship will be a straight line if plotted on a graph). Once you have estimated such an equation, you will usually be presented with a display which contains, at a minimum, estimated coefficients, standard errors of these, an 'F' ratio, sum of squared residuals and an R squared. You may also be given a 'critical significance level', an R squared adjusted, sum of residuals and other statistics that do not concern us at the moment.

A specimen output is shown in Table 5.1, which is an exact copy of a regression estimated in a version of SST (Statistical Software Tools). The data used here is a cross-section of American states (including Hawaii) in 1980.

Table 5.1 Ordinary least squares estimation of a burglary equation
Dependent variable: *PCBUR*

Independent variable	Estimated coefficient	Standard error	t-statistic
INT	15.10120	10.13702	1.48971
CRROB	−0.11814	9.88712e0−002	−1.19485
CRBUR	−0.34167	0.26948	−1.26789
CRTHF	6.35066e−002	0.19346	0.32827
UR	−0.18846	0.40588	−0.46434
PINC	9.34656e−004	6.92072e−004	1.35052
POV	−9.20597e−002	0.37353	−0.24646
PCBLK	11.41881	7.53019	1.51640
Number of Observations		51	
R-squared		0.36813	
Corrected R-squared		0.26527	
Sum of Squared Residuals		8.39292e+002	
Standard Error of the Regression		4.41797	
Durbin–Watson Statistic		1.99202	
Mean of Dependent Variable		14.88223	

The estimating equation is:

$$PCBUR = b_0 + b_1\, CRROB + b_2\, CRBUR + b_3\, CRTHF + b_4\, UR$$
$$+ b_5\, PINC + b_6\, POV + b_7\, PCBLK + u \tag{5.1}$$

The equation has per capita burglary rates (*PCBUR*) as the dependent variable and the independent variables are clearance rates (that is, the fraction of crimes 'solved' or written off by the police) for burglary, robbery and theft (*CRBUR*, *CRROB*, *CRTHF*), unemployment rates (*UR*), percentage of households in poverty (*POV*) and percentage of the population classified as black (*PCBLK*). The clearance rates here have been converted to percentages by multiplying by 100 and the crime rate has been converted to per 100 000 population. You can find this data on the website in an Excel file called USADAT.XLS.

If you wish to replicate Table 5.1, you will need to create the variables *PCBUR* and *PCBLK* by dividing the *burg* and *black* variables by the *pop* variable. I have replicated this regression using SPSS, on the same data set, and obtained results which differed in all cases, in terms of the coefficients and the 't' ratios. This was sometimes by as much as 10 per cent but it would not have made any appreciable difference to hypothesis testing.

The 't' ratios shown here are the values of the coefficients divided by the corresponding standard errors, which are in the middle column of figures. These are based on the assumption that you want initially to test the null hypothesis of a zero coefficient. We can refer to this as the default 't' statistic, as it is the one every computer package will give us without asking for it. Almost all published articles, by economists, will give this 't' statistic. If they do not, they will tend to give the standard error in brackets below the coefficient. In cases where the standard error or 't' statistic is not shown, it will be impossible for a reader to carry out any hypothesis tests, on the individual coefficients, whatsoever. It is thus highly desirable that you do present either, or both, of these in your written reports. Where the 't' or standard error are not given they may be replaced by the 'asterisk' system of giving a number of * beside the coefficients to represent the critical significance level (usually out of 10, 5, 1 and 0.1 per cent) at which the null is rejected. The 'Corrected R squared' is a reformulation of the R squared which we discuss later in this chapter (Section 5.4).

The mean of the dependent variable is shown here but the means of the independent variables have not been provided. They are readily available on any package, however; all you need to do is ask for basic descriptive statistics. You will find considerable variation in practice over descriptive statistics in published work. Sometimes means and standard deviations of all the variables are given and sometimes they are not. If they are not given, it often makes it impossible for the reader to make further interpretative calculations using the equations such as elasticities. and predictions (both of which are discussed later in this chapter, in Sections 5.2 and 5.6 respectively).

The standard error of the regression is a formula which is closely related to the R squared. It is given by the following formula:

$$\sqrt{\left(\sum_i \hat{u}_1^2\right)/n - k} \tag{5.2}$$

which is the square root of the sum of squared residuals after it has been divided by the number of degrees of freedom in the regression where k stands for the number of parameters estimated (including the intercept).

The sum of squared residuals is 839.92, as we move the decimal point two places to the right because of the use of scientific notation in the results readout. We cannot say if this is telling us anything about how well this set of variables predicts the behaviour of the burglary rate, as it is dependent on units of measurement. Likewise, the standard error of the regression is not informative about goodness of fit, so people will use the R squared statistics to judge goodness of fit. In the present case, R squared is 0.36813, which says that 36.813 per cent of the variation in the dependent variable (burglary rates), *around its mean*, is accounted for by the independent variables. Obviously, 62.187 per cent of the variation is not accounted for and can be attributed to omitted variables, errors in the data and other errors in the specification of the model.

The Durbin–Watson test relates to one of the assumptions of the CLRM (that the u terms are not covariant with u's in other periods) and will be covered in Chapter 9. It is given automatically in many packages, although there are some situations, such as that in Table 5.1, in which it will be a meaningless statistic for the type of data involved (see Chapter 9). This output did not report the so-called 'F ratio for the equation' with its degrees of freedom for the default hypothesis test assumed by the package. This, and the alternative 'F' tests you might want are explained at Section 5.3 of this chapter.

Any package will provide you with a number of results that do not greatly interest you as well as those you do want. This particular table did not provide the sum of residuals, which you may well find on the package you are using. This should be a *very* small number given that we saw in Chapter 3 that the OLS technique constrains the sum of residuals to be zero. They will not be exactly zero due to small rounding errors on the computer. Therefore, any figures you see given for the sum of residuals are likely to be followed by E with a minus and a number of trailing digits.

This results table does not show the degrees of freedom for the 't' test and it shows the number of observations written in words rather than simply giving a figure for n (sample size). The degrees of freedom for the 't' tests will be $n - 8$, in this case being 43. The critical value for 't' at 43 degrees of freedom at the 5 per cent level on a two-tailed test is between 2.021 and 2.014. On a one-tailed test, the critical value is between 1.684 and 1.679.

The model estimated in Table 5.1 could be related to the rational choice theory of criminal activity put forward by Becker in 1968 and the subject of econometric work by numerous economists, including the published studies of basketball and 'skyjacking' reviewed in this chapter (see Section 5.7). Most economists expect that there will be substitution effects from the risk of punishment for a crime and hence the parameter on $CRBUR$ should be negative. $CRTHF$ and $CRROB$ represent the prices of crimes, which will be either substitutes or complements, and hence their coefficients will be indeterminate. The remaining variables are, in the case of UR and $PCBLK$, expected to have positive coefficients as they proxy labour market conditions. The $PINC$ variable is problematic: most writers suggest that it should have a positive coefficient if it is understood to be a measure of the expected rate of return for a burglary. However, it could represent the opposite in that higher wealth means that people have, on average, less incentive to steal. The model does not include variables for the length of the prison sentence for burglary.

We can summarize the above discussion in a list of expectations:

$$b_0? \quad b_1? \quad b_2 < 0 \quad b_3? \quad b_4 > 0 \quad b_5? \quad b_6 > 0 \quad b_7 > 0 \qquad \text{(5.3)}$$

Some of the coefficients in this table are very small numbers. In particular, the $PINC$ coefficient rounds to 0.000935. Such small coefficients may represent a small relationship between the two variables but quite often, as in this case, it will represent the fact that the left- and right-hand side variables are measured in very different units. $PCBUR$ is measured in the range of quite small fractions of 1, while $PINC$ is in the order of thousands of dollars.

There is some element of doubt as to whether these coefficients should be the subject of two-tailed or one-tailed tests. Looking at these results, we can see that this is not a problem as the 't' ratios are all extremely weak in terms of statistical significance. The largest 't' ratio is only

1.5164 (on the *PCBLK* variable). This is of the correct sign but it falls below the 5 per cent level on a one-tailed test. In summary then, this is a regression, which performs poorly in terms of supporting the usual theoretical model, as it is not possible to convincingly reject the null for any of the coefficients. In a typical article by economists, this is likely to be expressed in the more loose form: 'these variables are not significant'.

5.2 TELLING THE STORY OF THE REGRESSION COEFFICIENTS: THE USE OF ELASTICITIES

Let us now focus on the items in the regression output that do interest us, and which we already have some experience of from Chapter 3. The first thing we should look at is the regression coefficients themselves. You will notice that the package producing Table 5.1 has given the full set of information for the constant (intercept term). Some published work does drop this term in reporting the results (for example, studies from the world's leading economic journal examined in Chapter 7) which may seem to be of little interest given that we do not have any particular interest in hypotheses about this coefficient. However, its absence means that we are unable to construct predictions based on assumptions about changes in the level of the independent variables.

Let us turn now to the coefficients for the so-called 'explanatory variables'. We shall apply the method of checking the three S's.

SIGN

Do we have the correct signs? In Table 5.1 *CRBUR*, *POV* and *UR* seem to have the 'correct' signs: that is, they are negative as the theory most people would put forward would suggest. The other variables either have the wrong sign on their coefficients or are cases where the prediction is ambiguous (that is, we cannot readily tell whether the sign is negative or positive).

SIZE AND SIGNIFICANCE

Unfortunately, regression coefficients by themselves do not tell us very much. There are two reasons for this:

▶ They are not the 'true' values. They are just the most likely values to occur. You need a hypothesis test in order to establish the distance of this central value from zero. You will be hoping to find a coefficient that is statistically significant and of the correct sign except, of course, in the case where you are engaged in 'confrontational' hypothesis testing where you include a variable to demonstrate that it is not influential.
▶ Even if such a hypothesis test brings us the result we are looking for, we still face the problem that the numerical value of the coefficient may not mean very much. To put it bluntly, we could quite easily produce a regression in which there is a very economically significant relationship between the dependent and independent variable (i.e. small changes in the latter produce large changes in the former) but a very small coefficient and vice versa. This can happen because the estimators produced by OLS are dependent on the units of measurement in the variables we have chosen to enter into the estimation routine. The coefficient of a

regression only tells us the estimated impact of a one-unit increase in an independent variable (in the units in which it is measured) on the dependent variable in the units in which it is measured.

If we are going to present our work to others to convince them of the importance of the relationships we have identified then we are going to need some measures that do not depend on units of measurement, as well as convincing hypothesis tests. To obtain such 'unit free' estimators there are three approaches you could use:

(i) Make sure the variables are in units, which can provide meaningful measures of impact before you do the estimation. There are a few cases where this is easy. Take the simple consumption function as shown in Table 3.1. If we regress per capita consumption on per capita income, then the resulting coefficient will be the estimated marginal propensity to consume.

(ii) Use beta coefficients as alternatives to regression coefficients. These are not popular with economists, although they are found in other social sciences particularly those that use 'Path Analysis', which is a multiple equation system (related to those we discuss in Chapters 12 and 13). Beta coefficients are routinely printed alongside the regression coefficients (betas) in the SPSS program. A beta coefficient is obtained by multiplying the coefficient by the ratio of the standard error of the independent variable to that of the dependent variable. This takes a value between -1 and $+1$ and can be used to rank strength of relationships; that is, if we had six independent variables and the beta coefficient or the third was twice that of the fourth and four times that of the fifth we would know that their impact goes in this order. However, we could not say the relationship is two times as much or four times as much.

(iii) Use elasticities. This is by far the most popular approach among economists for summarizing the numerical strength of individual relationships estimated from a regression.

The notion of elasticity is familiar to anyone who has ever studied economics but the idea of elasticity itself is merely a form of measurement, which has no economic content as such. The elasticity is a unit-free form of measurement because we divide the percentage change in one variable by the percentage change in another variable. We usually make the presumption that the variable on the top line is the dependent variable and that on the bottom is an independent variable. There are three elasticities for the equation estimated in Chapter 3 and shown in Table 3.4. The elasticity of demand with respect to prices (price elasticity), the elasticity of demand with respect to income (income elasticity) and the elasticity of demand with respect to the take-up of tertiary education (education elasticity). By the same reasoning, there are seven elasticities for the supply of burglary in the equation in Table 5.1.

The formula for point elasticity can be written as follows:

Elasticity of Y with respect to $X = \delta Y / \delta X.(X/Y)$ (5.4)

which simplifies to the regression coefficient ($\hat{b}$) multiplied by X/Y. The regression coefficient, in a linear equation, will be the partial derivative of Y with respect to X. Y and X values will vary as we move along the fitted regression line although, until we reach Chapter 6, the estimated b value does not change as the levels of X and Y vary.

We have seven point elasticities in the present model:

$$\delta PCBUR / \delta UR.(UR / PCBUR) \tag{5.5a}$$

$$\delta PCBUR / \delta PCBLK.(PCBLK / PCBUR) \tag{5.5b}$$

$$\delta PCBUR / \delta CRBUR(CRBUR / PCBUR) \tag{5.5c}$$

$$\delta PCBUR / \delta XCRROB(CRROB / PCBUR) \tag{5.5d}$$

$$\delta PCBUR / CRTHF.(CRTHF / PCBUR) \tag{5.5e}$$

$$\delta PCBUR / \delta PINC.(PINC / PCBUR) \tag{5.5f}$$

$$\delta PCBUR / \delta POV.(POV / PCBUR) \tag{5.5g}$$

To calculate an elasticity, then, we have to set values of X and Y. We could choose any X and Y, although it would not really make sense to calculate an elasticity that does not lie on the estimated function. As well as this, we might want an elasticity that sums up in one figure the size of the relationship between two variables. The obvious candidate for this is to evaluate the elasticity at the means of the sample data. If you see an article in which an elasticity is produced from a linear equation then it has been calculated in this way. It may be described as an 'elasticity at the means'. There have been some econometrics packages (such as SHAZAM), which give the elasticity at the means in the tabulated output. If your package does not give the means of all variables (Table 5.1 only gives the mean of the dependent variable not the independent variables), then you can usually obtain the means of data as one of the options for descriptive statistics on a regression command.

As an illustration of the calculation, I have gone back to the data set used in Table 5.1 and obtained the mean of $CRBUR$ as 15.53137. Using this and the figures in the table gives a burglary own clear-up rate elasticity of

$$-0.34167 \times (15.53137 / 14.88223) = 0.3565731$$

At this stage we perhaps should point out some important facts, in case there is any confusion:

▶ It is just a coincidence that the elasticity is similar to the point estimate; a coincidence which is due to the units of measurement of the Y and X variables being on a similar scale in this case. You will see examples in Chapter 7 where the elasticity is quite different from the point estimate.

▶ Don't become too impressed by the false impression of accuracy given by the large number of decimal places to which the calculations are taken. I have simply used the full estimate reported by a computer package to the number of decimal places it uses as a default.

▶ The simple method of multiplying regression coefficients by the ratios of the means of two variables is only applicable to the linear estimating equation. The correct formulae for other functional forms are to be found in Chapter 7.

5.3 THE CONSTRUCTION AND USE OF 'F' TESTS IN REGRESSION

As we saw in Chapter 2, the 'F' test is formed by calculating the ratio of two variances, v_1 and v_2, where v_1 is greater than v_2 and comparing this with the critical value for degrees of freedom corresponding to the ratio v_1/v_2. The degrees of freedom will depend on the sample size and the number of regression coefficients estimated. In analysis of regression, we use the 'F' ratio to carry out tests that involve more than one parameter. The 't' test is limited to being able to test only hypotheses concerning one parameter at a time. There are circumstances where we want to test several hypotheses simultaneously. One example is where we are concerned with sums of parameters, as in the case of a production function where we want to test the hypothesis of returns to scale. To deal with this and more complicated cases of multiple hypothesis testing we have to use the 'F' test. Any 'F' test for a regression is based on the notion of there being two regressions, which give us the two different variances to be compared. One regression is called the **restricted regression** while the other is called the **unrestricted regression.** The difference between the two is due to our choice of **restrictions**. We have already been making restrictions when we did 't' tests. The default two-tailed 't' test is based on imposing the restriction that a parameter equals zero. Any restriction imposed on an equation must lead to a rise in the sum of squared residuals compared with the original unrestricted model. Thus, the restricted model must have a higher variance of its residuals than the unrestricted model. If the ratio of the two is not significantly different from 1, then it appears that the model has not been seriously affected by the restrictions in terms of its goodness of fit/ability to 'explain' the dependent variable. The general formula for F in regressions is:

$$F = \frac{(S_r - S)/g}{S/(n-k)}$$

(5.6)

where g and $n-k$ are the degrees of freedom we use to look up the critical value of the 'F' ratio in Appendix 4. S_r is the residual sum of squares from the restricted regression and S is the residual sum of squares in the unrestricted regression. n is the sample size, k the number of parameters estimated in the unrestricted regression and g the number of restrictions imposed in moving from the unrestricted form to the restricted form. The number of restrictions in a 't' test is only one. There is no need for an 'F' test and if we did an 'F' test for such a case we would always find that the square of the calculated 'F' ratio is exactly equal to the corresponding 't' ratio. We would always find exactly the same result doing the hypothesis test using the 'F' ratio as we would using the 't' ratio.

'F' FOR THE EQUATION

The specimen computer package table shown in Table 6.2 in the next chapter shows an 'F' statistic of 0.57685[0.457], while that of the regression in Table 6.4 gives a figure of 460.9527[0.000] for the same statistic without telling us what it is supposed to be testing. This is because all packages, which give an 'F for the equation' assume a default hypothesis of the following form:

$$H_0: b_1 = b_2 = b_3 = \ldots b_g = 0$$

(5.7)

against the alternative that these coefficients are not all simultaneously zero.

The g here represents the total number of parameters, other than the intercept, which have been estimated. Many published studies also report this statistic without further information, although some will call it 'F for the equation'. This tests the hypothesis that all parameters on the explanatory variables are simultaneously zero. This null hypothesis is stating that the regression has no explanatory power whatsoever. The restricted equation is simply a regression of Υ on the intercept. In this case, g will equal $k - 1$ where k is the number of parameters *but* not in any other case. For this case, S_r will be the sum of squared deviation of Υ from its mean. This means that this F test can be calculated from the R squared of the unrestricted regression as follows:

$$\{R^2/(1 - R^2)\}.\{(n - k)/(k - 1)\} \tag{5.8}$$

This formula cannot be used for any other null hypotheses about multiple restrictions.

The larger is the goodness of fit (R^2), other things being equal, then the more likely is the null to be rejected. This does not guarantee that a large R^2 will reject the null as small degrees of freedom for the model could lead to the acceptance of the null. The degrees of freedom for the example given in Table 6.1 will be (7,43). The computer output in Table 6.1 did not actually give the F for the equation but using the formula above, it is:

$$(0.36813/0.63157).(43/7) = 3.58055.$$

The critical value at (7,43) d.f. is between 2.20 and 2.25 at the 5 per cent level, and therefore we can reject the null that the coefficients in the equation are jointly insignificant. You are unlikely to ever have to do this calculation as most articles will inevitably give you the 'F' statistic, as will computer packages. Computer packages will also tend to report the critical significance level, meaning you will not need to look up the 'F' tables for this particular hypothesis test.

Finding that the 'F for the equation' is highly significant is not necessarily a good reason to get excited because it is not demonstrating that the model is particularly useful or powerful. Our focus should always be on the plausibility and significance of the individual coefficients as this is what distinguishes a subject (whether it be econometrics, psychometrics or biometrics) application of statistical methods from purely automated line fitting. It is even possible that we could have an equation in which none of the coefficients is statistically significant yet the 'F' for the equation strongly rejects the null. The results in Table 5.1 are tending towards this situation. The extreme case of this is symptomatic of multicollinearity, which will be explored in Chapter 10.

On the other hand, finding 'F for the equation' to be insignificant at say the 5 per cent level would worry most economists, as it implies the so-called 'explanatory' (i.e. independent) variables in our model are not doing any 'explaining' at all. However, we should note that the acceptance of the null from an insignificant 'F for the equation' does not conflict with findings of statistical significance for the findings on some of the individual coefficients in the model. This could, for example, come about if we had included a large number of irrelevant variables, which bring down the degrees of freedom.

The use of 'F for the equation', that we have just encountered, is effectively **a test of the null hypothesis that R^2 is zero against the one-sided alternative that it is positive.**

'F' TEST FOR EXCLUSION/INCLUSION OF TWO OR MORE VARIABLES

Let us say that we have instead the following null:

$$H_0: b_2 = b_3 = 0 \tag{5.9}$$

in a model such as :

$$Y = b_0 + b_1 X_1 + b_2 X_2 + b_3 X_3 + u \tag{5.10}$$

When we substitute the restriction in (5.9) into equation (5.10) we get equation (5.11):

$$Y = b_0 + b_1 X_1 + u \tag{5.11}$$

We use formula (5.6) for this case, once we have estimated the regression on X_1 only, and the regression on the unrestricted regression and retrieved the sum of squared residuals from the output. Most articles will not reproduce the sum of squared residuals in the output. If you are not given the residual sum of squares but are given the R squared for regressions in which some are 'nested' within another (i.e. you can get from the more general equation to the other ones by simply deleting some variables), then you can test the significance of the exclusion of variables using the formula below, which is equivalent to Equation (5.2) for this case:

$$\{(R_2{}^2 - R_1{}^2)/(1 - R_1{}^2)\}.\{(n - k)/g\} \tag{5.12}$$

where the 1 subscript refers to the smaller R squared (i.e. for the restricted equation) and the 2 subscript to the larger R squared (i.e. for the unrestricted equation). You should make sure you are using R^2 and not adjusted R^2 which is reported in some articles rather than the unadjusted. You would need to convert adjusted back to unadjusted if only the former was given.

We have just looked at a test of the null hypothesis that the change in R^2 is zero against the one-sided alternative that it is positive. Most packages provide options for this test in terms of 'variable addition' or 'variable deletion' tests once you have instructed the package which variables are to be deleted or added. A specimen of this kind of output, from Microfit, is shown in Table 7.2 in Chapter 7, which shows the use of forecast dummy variables. This test is equivalent to testing that the change in R^2 between the larger and smaller models is greater than zero. In packages aimed at the general social scientist (such as SPSS) you may find the program offers the option of doing the test described in this way.

For the moment, let us illustrate the variable deletion/addition 'F' test using the burglary equation from Table 5.1. I re-estimated this equation with the three punishment variables (*CRBUR, CRTHF, CRROB*) excluded, which gave an R squared of 0.18969 and a sum of squared residuals of 1076.31. Following the formula in Equation (6.2) we get:

$$[(1076.31 - 839.292)/3]/(10761.31/43) = (\text{rounded}) \ 3.1564$$

You should get the same answer using the formula in Equation (6.7), that is:

$$[(0.36813 - 0.18969)/(1 - 0.18969)] \times 43/3.$$

As the degrees of freedom are 3,43, the null hypothesis will be rejected at the 5 per cent level because the critical value is between 2.84 and 2.76 and these are the boundaries given by (3,40) and (3,60) degrees of freedom. You can easily check that the null will be accepted at the 1 per cent level by looking up the 'F' tables.

This result implies that the inclusion of these variables has made a significant difference to the extent to which the model 'explains' the burglary rate. You might notice a possible contradiction here. The individual 't' ratios for these three variables are not significant *but* the test on all three simultaneously *is* significant.

Why would we want to do this kind of 'F' test? There are two ways of looking at this: in terms of model reduction or model expansion. The reduction idea uses tests to get down to the most efficient model by deleting unnecessary variables that might have been included. This is the idea behind the 'general to specific' modelling strategy pioneered by the Scottish econometrician David Hendry. His work was directed against a tendency which had sprung up in applied econometrics to go from the 'specific to the general'. That is, write down what seems like a reasonable model then keep adding bits to it to see if you can make it better. Once this process has been finished an 'F' test for variable addition might be used to check whether the collection of 'add ons' has made a statistically significant contribution as a block or group. One might view the 'F' test on the results from Table 6.1 as a test that punishment variables matter as we have deleted them all from the model. In a similar vein we could construct a basic economic model of demand and then add 'sociological' taste variables to it and use an 'F' test on the block of these to see if they merit inclusion on purely goodness of fit grounds.

AN 'F' TEST FOR THE RESTRICTION THAT THE PARAMETERS ARE EQUAL ACROSS TWO SAMPLES

We have just looked at two variations on the use of the 'F' ratio to test hypotheses about multiple parameter restrictions in regression. The first of these was a special case of the second, where the alternative hypothesis involved deleting all explanatory variables from the model. In the first case, we did not literally have to run two regressions as we could use the R squared from the unrestricted regression. We now look at a test, often called the 'Chow test' (after the American economist Gregory Chow), which requires you to **run two *separate* regressions on different parts of the sample for exactly the same equation, as well as the full sample regression**. Having said this, it should be pointed out that the process can be simplified to one of running just two regressions once we have learnt the technique of dummy variables (see Section 7.5 in Chapter 7).

Here we modify formula (5.5) as follows:

(a) You must run *three* regressions – one for each sample and one for the two samples combined.

(b) The sum of the squared residuals from the whole sample regression is to be used as S_r (the restricted sum of squared residuals); you must add the sum of squared residuals from the other two regressions together to get S (the unrestricted sum of squared residuals).

(c) g in this case should be the total number of parameters in the equation including the intercept, that is, k.

(d) $n - k$ should be replaced by $n - 2k$ where n is the number of observations in the whole sample.

Why would we go to the bother of doing a test like this?

▶ It might be considered a good idea to test whether the sample has constant parameters. In the absence of a prior hypothesis about how the parameters might be shifting, we could simply divide the sample in two – if it is a time series we might as well divide it into a first and second half. This is the use of the 'F' ratio as a stability test. If the null were rejected then we would be concluding the parameters are not stable, as they have shifted from one part of the sample to the other.

▶ We might have a sample which is constructed by **pooling** a number of samples which might give us prior reason to suspect that parameters are not equal across all samples. For example, we might have pooled a sample of men and women, in which case the 'F' test is a test as to whether the functional forms for men and women are completely identical. Note that because this is a ratio test, it can only be used to test the pooling of two samples at a time. The stability test is also only concerned with the overall effect of the parameters *not* instability for each individual parameter. Given this, it seems better to use the form of the 'F' test, using slope and shift dummies, that is presented in Chapter 8.

EXAMPLE OF HOW TO DO A CHOW TEST

Here is an example of how to do a Chow test using a simple equation to explain the rates of death from motor vehicle accidents, in the USA, using a cross-section of data from 1980. If you wish to replicate this, the data is in the Excel file USADAT.XLS. The variable *DEAD* does not appear in this data set. You would need to create it by dividing *vad* (Vehicle Accident Deaths) by *mvr* (motor vehicle registrations). The three variables used are:

DEAD = deaths in motor accidents per registered driver

AVSPD = average driving speed in miles per hour

PINC = median per capita income.

The results are shown in Table 5.2. I have divided the full sample of 42 observations (42 states for which data were available) into sub-samples of 19 and 23. This was done purely arbitrarily as a stability test (the sample of 19 is the first 19 observations on the data file and that of 23 is the second 23) *not* based on any prior hypothesis about what might cause the parameters to differ between sections of the sample.

Before we do the 'F' (Chow) test for stability, a little bit of economic theory might be called on to justify such an equation. Vehicle deaths would be regarded here as a choice variable resulting from the private decisions of drivers about risk taking. The speed of driving might also be seen as a choice and therefore might strictly speaking be seen as endogenous (but we do not deal with this type of problem until Chapters 12 and 13). Faster driving by other motorists would lead us to expect a higher risk, therefore predicting a positive coefficient on the *AVSPD* variable. There is quite a large literature on this subject, in which some economists (see, e.g., Lave, 1985) have argued that speed, as such, is not the crucial factor (at least not within the range normally observed on highways), rather it is the variation in driver speed which causes accidents because it represents the number of opportunities where there is an accident risk.

The other variable here, per capita income, measures roughly the value of time to a driver, in that higher wage rates mean a greater opportunity cost of consumption and production opportunities foregone. The coefficients in this regression show, for *AVSPD* the impact of drivers driving, on average, one mile per hour faster on deaths per registered driver; and for *PINC*, the effect of a one-dollar increase in median income on the number of deaths per registered driver. The coefficients are extremely small because of the units of measurement chosen.

The sum of the sum of squared residuals from the split samples is 0.115562. The top line of the formula 6.2 $[(S_r - S)/g]$ becomes $(0.088208/4) = 0.022052$. The bottom line $[S/(n - k)]$ is 0.115562/34 which equals 0.003399. Therefore, the 'F' value is:

$$[(0.088208/4)]/0.115562/34 = 6.4878.$$

The degrees of freedom, at which we should look up the critical value, are 4 and 34. At the 5 per cent level this gives a value somewhere between 2.34 and 2.42. We would then reject the null at the 5 per cent level in favour of the alternate hypothesis that the equation is 'structurally unstable', in the sense that its parameters have shifted between one part of the sample and the other.

Table 5.2 OLS equations for the motor vehicle death rate in the USA in 1980

Equation Dependent variable:	(1) *DEAD*	(2) *DEAD*	(3) *DEAD*
Intercept	−0.83593	7.64293E−002	−1.30151
	0.49540	0.47222	0.53941
AVSPD	2.38871E−002	8.47768E−003	3.19664E−002
	8.77144E−003	1.06294E−005	9.14286E−006
PINC	−1.34079E−005	−2.48367E−005	−5.77049E−006
	9.07173E−006	1.06294E−005	9.14286E−006
R squared	0.20377	0.33281	0.35993
SSR	0.22310	2.59454E−002	8.96172E−002
N	42	19	23

Note: The figures below the coefficients are the standard errors.

5.4 ADJUSTING THE R SQUARED: HOW AND WHY?

In Chapter 3 we met the R squared statistic as a summary of the goodness of fit of a model. As such, it is a summary of the 'within sample' variation in Y 'explained' by the linear combination of X's. It is *not* a hypothesis test nor does it necessarily indicate the forecasting power of a model that is examined later in this chapter. Some version of the R squared is reported in almost every published study using a multiple regression equation. There seems to be no hard and fast rule whether a paper will present the R squared or the adjusted R squared, or indeed, both.

In the eyes of the average researcher it seems that a large R squared seems to be a good thing, and a small one a bad thing. However, many factors should lead us not to jump to such a hasty conclusion. Before I deal with these, let us look at the adjusted or 'corrected' R squared, which was included in Table 5.1. You may see it written in words as 'R bar squared' to represent the fact that it is normally written exactly as its unadjusted counterpart but with a bar on the top of it. This makes it look exactly like it is the arithmetic mean but you should not be confused by this. The use of a bar is just a convention, which economists have adopted to distinguish the adjusted R squared from the unadjusted R squared.

The form of adjustment, or correction, is performed to take account of the fact that when we add variables to a regression equation we lose degrees of freedom. The formula is often described as incorporating a 'penalty' for the loss of degrees of freedom. The formula is as follows:

$$\bar{R}^2 = 1 - \{[(n-1)/n-k)].(1-R^2)\} \tag{5.13}$$

The unadjusted R squared has the properties that it will tend towards one as we add variables or decrease the sample size. It is impossible for the R squared to fall when we add more variables as each new parameter being estimated will reduce the size of the sum of squared residuals. The formula for adjusted R squared does not have this property. When we add variables to a model, this statistic can either rise, fall or stay the same. If we are adding variables one at a time, then the R squared adjusted will rise so long as the 't' value on entry is greater than 1 in absolute value. It may be noted that given the conventions we use, in social sciences in general, that this means that adding 'statistically insignificant variables' can increase the R squared adjusted.

So, this is how you adjust R squared and almost any computer package will give you this statistic alongside the 'raw' or unadjusted R squared. Why would you prefer this statistic to the corresponding unadjusted measure of goodness of fit? Writers of econometrics textbooks have taken the view that it is a means of preventing you from falling into bad habits. Specifically from committing the crime of 'data mining'. For example, Hebden (1981, p. 112) says that it 'prevents the researcher from thinking he is doing better just by putting in more variables', while Gujarati (1988, p. 135, quoting from Theil, 1978) says 'R squared tends to give an overly optimistic view of the fit of the regression'.

These remarks are written from the perspective that inexperienced researchers or those with a sketchy statistical knowledge might become seduced into 'playing a game' of trying to maximize R squared simply by desperately searching for variables to put in. If they are doing this but are directed towards the target of a maximum adjusted R squared instead, then the game becomes one of searching for variables which enter with an absolute 't' of 1. This does not seem a great improvement. The best thing would be if you are encouraged to remember that your statistical model should be based on a well-specified theoretical model. It should not be an exercise in 'fitting up' the data. This leads us to the warning of the next section.

5.5 BE CAREFUL WITH ALL R SQUAREDS

It is clear that you should not imagine that guiding your efforts by the criterion of size of R squared adjusted is any better than that of R squared unadjusted. You should be careful in your handling of all R squareds. It is tempting to think that since it is a 'goodness of fit' statistic, and a good fit is a desirable thing, that a large value of R squared shows high quality research and a low value shows low quality research. However, this is something that you should *not* think.

The R squared is not a hypothesis test. It is a descriptive statistic that derives from the sum of squared residuals and as such it will be maximized automatically by OLS for a given sample and specification of variables and functional form. Although you will read people remarking on the fact that their R squared is quite good or fairly good and so on, this is not particularly meaningful in the absence of some hypothesis about how large it might have been expected to be. There are a number of factors which influence the size of R squared, some of which can be deliberately varied and which are not a reflection of the success of researchers in producing a 'good' model. The following list of these makes many references to topics that are only introduced in the later chapters of the book. You may wish to come back to this list when you have finished the book.

(i) The type of data matters. We discussed the different types of data in Chapter 2. Only in the case where the dependent variable is ratio/continuous in nature, measured in scalar units, and there is an intercept will the R squared formula have any sensible meaning. Beyond this, the source of the data matters. Given exactly the same underlying model, we would normally find that the size of the R squared tends to be largest in aggregate time-series data. R squareds of near 1 are not at all rare in such studies, especially of standard macroeconomic functions like the consumption function (as you can see in Tables 3.1 and 7.8) and the demand for money. The next largest R squareds tend to occur in aggregate cross-section data. Typical values for studies across regions or nations might be in the 0.4–0.7 zone. The lowest values will tend to be found in disaggregated individual level samples such as those from large interview studies. If you were asked to review the literature in a subject area, it would be a big mistake to give more prominence to the time-series studies than the cross-section studies just because they had larger R squareds.

(ii) Basic errors of measurement in the data may lead to a low R squared. The simplest case to imagine is a high variance in the dependent variable due to errors of measurement which will make it harder to predict and thus have a lower R squared than otherwise. If we were comparing identical models estimated in two different countries, by two different researchers, there is no reason to suppose that one researcher is better than the other because of an R squared difference due to measurement error.

(iii) Too little variation in the data may lead to a low R squared. This might seem like the opposite problem to the last problem. Let us think of a specific example. Say you were estimating an equation to explain the charitable donations of the same group of suburban dwellers, with identical tastes and similar incomes over a period of time. Donations may simply not change enough for any kind of meaningful regression model to be estimated and hence a low R squared would be obtained. The low value here may be telling us that we need to go and get a more appropriate set of data rather than abandoning the specified equation as a failure. In this case, there is very little variation around the mean of the dependent variable and you are likely to get a large 't' ratio on the intercept and a very low R squared.

(iv) The R squared for equations where the dependent variable is measured on a different scale of units (such as logarithmically; see Chapter 6) are not comparable. There is an even more serious problem when weights are used (for example, to deal with heteroscedasticity; see Chapter 11), in conjunction with a logarithmic dependent variable as the R squared can be varied by changing the weight.

(v) There are circumstances where the conventional R squared and adjusted formulae are inappropriate, such as when there is no intercept in the regression or the equation forms part of a system of equations (see Chapter 15).

(vi) The specification of the dependent variable matters. There is often more than one way we could define the dependent variable of an equation. For example, we might or might not divide it by some measure of population size. In the macroeconomic literature there are parallel literatures on the savings ratio and the consumption function, even though these are linked through the underlying $C + S = Y$ identity. Consumption function studies are in levels such as the results you have seen in Table 3.1. Switching to a ratio dependent variable (C/Y) would imply an underlying consumption function in levels that is non-linear. Leaving this issue aside, we may note that an equation to explain C/Y is the same model as an equation to explain S/Y and an equation to explain S in terms of Y is the same model as an equation to explain C in terms of Y. This is because of the national income identity. The R squared will not be the same because C is a much bigger fraction of Y than S is. In the case of the Belgian consumption function (with intercept) shown in Chapter 3, Table 3.1, the R squared falls to 0.96997 (the re-estimated equation is not reproduced here) if we use S instead of C as the dependent variable. This is not a big change in the present case but other data and model set-ups may produce more dramatic differences with such changes in the choice of dependent variable.

(vii) A high R squared may be due to the inclusion of variables that could well be argued to be not worthy of being termed 'explanatory'. One example of this is a model with seasonal dummy variables in it (see Section 7.4 in Chapter 7). If it turns out that a large part of the R squared is due to these seasonal adjustments then we are, in effect, 'explaining' the dependent variable by the simple fact that the dependent variable has quite different averages across the season. This would be exposed if the sample was divided up and separate equations were estimated for each season, as the R squared would then fall drastically if the more 'genuine' explanatory variables, grounded in some kind of theory, are not very influential. The point I am making here applies to all types of dummy variables being used to combine different samples. For example, if we had 20 country cross-section demand equations with 19 dummy variables to represent the countries and these 19 variables are largely the source of the size of the R squared then the 'explanatory' power of a model is somewhat dubious.

(viii) Correlated measurement errors may produce a spuriously high R squared. This may be illustrated in the case where the right-hand side variables contain the dependent variable. For example, the crime model in Table 5.1 has an 'explanatory' variable ($CLBUR$) which has the top line of the dependent variable as its bottom line. This makes the errors in the variable correlated with the u term in the equation thus breaking one of the classical assumptions. This may force up the R squared artificially although it has the far more important problem of causing bias in the parameter estimates. Chapter 13 discusses how we deal with this problem.

(ix) It is possible to get a very high R squared when there is no relationship whatsoever, in time-series data, in the case of a 'spurious regression' caused by 'non-stationary' data, as will be explained in Chapter 14.

5.6 BASIC ECONOMETRIC FORECASTING

Most packages will allow for forecasting or prediction and some measures of how accurate this has been. As indicated in Chapter 1, prediction is a major use of the CLRM. It can be used by businesses in an attempt to work out strategies to increase their profits. Governments use it to attempt to figure out policies to control the economy.

It is very simple to extend an OLS regression equation into a forecasting model. We first make the highly restrictive assumption that the parameters in the prediction sample will be the same as in the estimation sample. Say we are advising a government by forecasting the future rate of unemployment (UR) in the economy from an equation of the form:

$$UR = b_0 + b_1.X_1 + b_2.X_2 + b_3.X_3 + b_4.X_4 + u \qquad (5.14)$$

where X are explanatory variables and u is a classical disturbance term. You should be aware that, in reality, a government is unlikely to use a single equation model to inform its decisions. It is more likely to use models using many dozens of equations which draw on the techniques developed in Chapters 12 and 13.

Let us assume Equation (5.9) has been estimated on annual data for the years 1980–2002 and is to be used to forecast the years 2003–2010. The model will yield numerical estimates of each b, which can be tested against their null hypotheses with 18 degrees of freedom using the 't' test. To predict the unemployment rates we simply take the value for b_0 and add to it the products of each b by the value of the appropriate X for the year in question. Clearly, these forecasts will not be 100 per cent accurate and will over- or under-predict the value of UR in each year. The **differences** are called forecast errors and should not be confused with the residuals found in 'within sample' estimation. Forecast errors may reflect measurement error in the 'out of sample' data but could also be signs of a shift in the parameters of the specified equation or the importance of an omitted variable. As an example of the latter, suppose employer confidence is an important factor in determining labour demand but no measure of this appeared in the variables X_1, X_2, X_3, X_4, then movements in this would produce fluctuations in UR that the model could not track.

You may have noticed an obvious problem that was overlooked in the above discussion – where can we possibly get data from for future events that have not happened yet? The simple answer is, of course, that we cannot get this data. These data will themselves have to be forecasted either by some form of guessing, expert opinion or the use of data forecasted from other econometric equations.

Most interest in prediction in academic circles is concerned with forecasting in the literal sense of trying to predict the future, but this is not the only way to use a regression equation for prediction. We can 'hold out' part of a cross-section sample and use the retained portion to estimate the parameters which are then used to see how well the fitted model explains the 'hold out' sample. This is a very simple thing to do on a computer package. There are several reasons why we might want to do this:

▶ It might be seen as good scientific method in protecting us from accusations of data mining. That is, it is an antidote to the 'data mining' strategy of sifting through a collection of variables until you get a model which maximizes the within sample R squared adjusted. In technical terms, the use of a 'hold out' sample protects us from the problem of 'pre-test bias'.

▶ It may be a test of the stability of the model. If it has systematic forecast errors then the model may suffer from shifting parameters (assuming it is not due to omitted variables). The Chow test given above is another way to do this.

▶ It may be of commercial usefulness. Take the example of a manufacturer engaged in quality control. They could estimate a model to predict the rate of producing faulty goods as a function of variables describing characteristics of the workers and the work situation. The expected fault rate could be projected from the success of the estimated equation in predicting the hold out sample.

MEASURING FORECAST ACCURACY

A set of forecasts is never going to be 100 per cent accurate. Therefore, anyone employed to make forecasts would like to find some way of judging the accuracy of a model. We now review some basic forecast statistics. When you get to Chapter 7, a new technique using dummy variables will be added to this collection. All methods of forecast appraisal start with the forecast errors. The simplest thing to do with these would be to add them to get the sum of forecast errors. If this were zero, then the forecast would be 100 per cent accurate. So, other things being equal, the larger the sum of forecast errors is, the worse the predictive power of the model would be. The size of this statistic will be influenced by the units of measurement and by the number of observations. Therefore, it would seem these need to be adjusted for in order to get a more useful evaluation statistic.

The first adjustment to the sum of forecast errors which suggests itself is to make sure that positive and negative errors do not cancel each other out. This leads us to our first statistic.

Forecast statistic 1: MAD [mean absolute deviation]
If we use the following formula:

$$\sum_i |fe_i|/j \tag{5.15}$$

where fe is the forecast error residual and j is the number of observations in the prediction sample, then we will get the MAD (Mean Absolute Deviation). That is, take the absolute prediction errors, add them up and divide by the size of the forecast sample.

This faces the problem of being dependent on the units of measurement and thus it is not easy to make judgements about forecast accuracy from looking at it.

Forecast statistic 2: MAPE [mean absolute percentage error]
One way of overcoming the units of measurement problem is to compute the MAPE:

$$\sum_{i+j} |100.(\hat{Y}_{i+j} - Y_{i+j})/Y_{i+j}|/j \tag{5.16}$$

which is formed by computing the absolute percentage errors and then averaging them over the j prediction periods.

The alternative means of avoiding positive and negative errors cancelling out is squaring, which leads us to the next two statistics.

Forecast statistic 3: Out of sample R squared

The use of squared forecast errors leads to the possibility of using an R squared for the forecast period.

The formula becomes

$$R^2 = 1 - \left[\sum \hat{f}^2 e_{i+j} / \sum y^2{}_{i+j} \right] \tag{5.17}$$

In this case, the sum of squared errors would be divided by the sum of squared deviations of Y in the out of sample (prediction) period. The interpretation of this R squared is that it is, when multiplied by 100, the percentage variation in the predicted variable 'explained' by the model parameters estimated in the within sample period.

Forecast statistic 4: Root mean squared error (RMSE)

The RMSE is Equation (5.18):

$$\sqrt{\left(\sum f^2 e_{i+j} \right) / j} \tag{5.18}$$

If we take the average of the squared prediction errors and then take the square root of this, then we have the RMSE. If the forecast is perfect then this statistic, like the first two above, will be zero. As the forecast is improved, *ceteris paribus*, the RMSE will tend towards zero. This is another symmetric statistic in that it weights equal-sized positive and negative deviations equally. However, it gives more weight to larger forecast errors. So, if our aim in developing a forecasting model was to minimize this statistic this would be consistent with a loss function (see Section 2.6) in which the costs of a prediction error increase at the rate of the square of the error.

Forecast statistic 5: Theil's U statistic

Named after Henri Theil, this is development of the mean squared error as follows:

$$U = \sqrt{MSE / \left(\sum A_i^2 / n \right)} \tag{5.19}$$

where MSE is the mean standard error, n is the sample size and A is the actual change in the dependent variable between the last two time periods. If the predictions are 100 per cent accurate then this statistic is equal to zero. If U is equal to 1 then this means that we have a forecast that is no better than a simple prediction of no change from the last period. If U is greater than 1 then the model is even worse at prediction than a simple 'no change' forecast. Obviously, what we hope for is a U statistic between 0 and 1, ideally the closer to 0 the better. This statistic is not valid if the model suffers from autocorrelation (tests for which are examined in Section 9.7 of Chapter 9).

Finally, we should mention a statistic obtained by using the within and without samples combined when you actually run the regression:

Forecast statistic 6: 'T' tests on individual forecast errors using dummies
This will be explained in Chapter 7 (Section 7.7).

The usual approach to forecast evaluation treats errors symmetrically. That is, the cost of an over-prediction error is treated as the same as that of an equivalent size under-prediction. A good forecast is judged in the same light as we treated the OLS estimators in Chapter 3. That is, unbiasedness and minimum variance are the criteria for the best forecast. There might be some circumstances where we do not want to treat errors symmetrically; for example, if you open a restaurant and are trying to forecast the required size and pricing structure, then the cost of having an empty seat may not be identical to the cost of turning away an excess demand customer. If you were dealing with such a problem then the forecast evaluation statistic would have to be adjusted in a manner appropriate to deal with the asymmetric loss function.

Forecasting is a large and complicated subject in its own right and this section has only been a gentle introduction to it. Nevertheless, a thorough background in the CLRM model provides a good jumping off point for you to progress into the forecasting area.

5.7 REVIEW STUDIES

The review studies in this chapter involve some methods which we have not covered yet, but this should not be an obstacle to finding these studies useful. The studies reviewed here share a common perspective and address the same problem despite the seeming disparity of their research topics – that is, one (Landes) looks at the skyjacking (i.e. hijacking aircraft) phenomenon and the other (McCormick and Tollison) looks at the behaviour of basketball players. Neither of these papers is a specialist study in the field of terrorism or sport psychology. Rather, the authors have seized upon these activities as suitable sources of data for testing the economic model of crime which is a straightforward application of standard utility-maximizing models in risky situations. The dominant theme in the early work on this subject, inspired by the paper by Becker (1968), was that increased punishment deters crime by substitution effects which lead the criminal to retire from crime or to switch time to leisure or non-crime activities. This was implied in the discussion of the regression shown in Table 5.1.

A major problem in the econometric work, which followed Becker, was non-random error in the form of correlated measurement error shared by the dependent variable and one of the independent variables. In other words, the same violation of the classical assumption discussed in Section 5.4, point (viii). In this particular case we have the problem of bias in the coefficient of the punishment variables. That is, the number of crimes counted in official statistics is not the true figure as there are more crimes which go unrecorded. If the rate of crime recording is correlated with the volume of police officers, then there will be correlated errors between these two variables and any punishment variables which may be a function of the volume of police officers – such as the clearance rate variable in Table 5.1. This variable has the further serious problem that the bottom line of the formula for clearance rates is the same as the top line of the formula for crime rates. This may create a serious negative bias in the clearance rate coefficient, which could lead us to wrongly reject the null hypothesis.

Economists are unlikely to get access to genuinely 'experimental' data on crime (or indeed most other areas), so one way round this problem is to make a clever choice. The articles considered here use data which is deliberately chosen to control for some of the problems in the crime data of the FBI and comparable organizations around the world. Both studies are time series in nature, although there is a slight difference in that Landes uses quarterly data while McCormick and Tollison use data on a time series of sport contests which are not equally spaced in the same way. Both studies are linear and use a 'count' variable on the left-hand side, which means it is not strictly correct to use an OLS model. Landes uses forecasting to work out the effect of changes in his focus variables over time, while McCormick and Tollison do not. They rely simply on the regression coefficient for the number of referees variable.

The Basic Facts

Authors: William M. Landes

Title: An Economic Study of US Aircraft Hijacking, 1961–1976

Where Published: *Journal of Law and Economics*, **21**(2), 1978, 1–32.

Reason for Study: To account for the dramatic decline in US aircraft hijackings after 1972, with particular reference to the risk and size of punishment.

Conclusion Reached: That the risks faced by hijackers are a statistically significant deterrent of aircraft hijacking. The forecasting equation is used to come to the conclusion that extra prevention measures (mandatory screening and increased post-attempt apprehension risk) saved the USA from between 47 and 67 additional hijackings in the 1973–76 period.

How Did They Do It?

Data: Quarterly observations from the USA 1961–76

Sample Size: 59–60 in Table 3. 140 in Table 4.

Technique: OLS but some results use the Cochrane–Orcutt (GLS) technique. You should concentrate mainly on the OLS equation in levels in Table 3.

Dependent Variable: Number of hijackings (Table 3) and time between hijackings (Table 4).

Focus Variables: Probability of apprehension, conditional probability of imprisonment, proportion of offenders killed, and average length of prison sentence.

Control Variables: Time trend (see Section 7.8 in Chapter 7), number of foreign hijackings, per capita consumption expenditure, unemployment rates, population, number of flights.

Presentation

How Results Are Listed: Table of coefficients with absolute 't' ratios in brackets underneath. The constant term is also given in this manner.

Goodness of Fit: R squared.

Tests: Default 't' tests as explained above. Durbin–Watson test. No 'F' tests.

Diagnosis/Stability: No explicit diagnosis/stability testing but the author does use a number of approaches to estimation and checks whether his main conclusion might be explained by a rival hypothesis (the 'fad effect').

Anomalous Results: There are a number of control variables (population, number of flights and consumption expenditure) which are not significant in the hijack numbers equation (Table 3) but are consistently significant in the Time between hijackings results (Table 4).

Student Reflection

Things to Look Out For: There are quite a lot of adjustments to the individual variables in this model in terms of use of lags (see Chapter 7) and moving averages.

Problems in Replication: It might be quite hard to get hold of the air flight-related data. The other statistics all come from standard sources of macroeconomic statistics but the flight data require access to airline industry publications.

The Basic Facts

Authors: Robert E. McCormick and Robert D. Tollison
Title: Crime on the Court
Where Published: *Journal of Political Economy,* **92**(3), 1984, 223–235.
Reason for Study: To test the economic theory of crime in the form of the hypothesis that more referees in a ball game means fewer fouls by the players.
Conclusion Reached: 'We find a large reduction, 34 per cent, in the number of fouls committed during a basketball game when the number of referees increases from two to three' (p. 223).

How Did They Do It?

Data: Games played in Atlantic Coast Conference basketball tournaments 1954–83, but data is missing for 1955 and 1962. Data is divided into separate winner and loser samples for estimation.
Sample Size: 201 in total games.
Technique: OLS but also SUR (see Chapter 13) and logit (described as logistic regression – see Chapter 8). You should concentrate on the OLS results.
Dependent Variable: Number of fouls.
Focus Variables: The variable *OFFICIAL* measuring the number of referees which is either 2 or 3. It is 2 up to the end of 1978.
Control Variables: See p. 227: measure of experience differential between teams, total score in match, year of tournament, difference in coaching experience between teams, attendance at the game, experience of the referees, dummy variables (see Chapter 8) to control for rule changes, measures of other team's accuracy.

Presentation

How Results Are Listed: Four columns – parameter estimate, standard error, 't' ratio, Prob value.
Goodness of Fit: R squared in a bracket above the results.
Tests: Default 't' tests. 'F' statistic given in brackets above the results. Two-tailed Prob value.
Diagnosis/Stability: They make some attempt to look at the influence of 'false arrests' which would be a source of measurement error (see Table 2). Footnote 8 on p. 229 reports that they tried several other control variables which did not alter their main conclusions.
Anomalous Results: Attendance at the game is not significant for winners or losers. The experience variables are not significant in the loser's fouling equation.

Student Reflection

Things to Look Out For: None.
Problems in Replication: You might be able to find cases for other sports (in various countries) in which there have been referee or rule changes, but if these have not taken place during your sample then it will not be possible to use sport as a 'laboratory' for the testing of hypotheses about the economics of crime.

These studies are extremely typical of what appears in the mainstream American economics journal. They start with a very clear message about the focus variables that will be the subject of the paper, and produce results that quite strongly support the main hypotheses about the focus variables. The discussion of the control variables is fairly brief. In both studies, the control variables are loosely specified as measures of the expected costs and benefits of the rule-breaking choice (fouling at basketball or hijacking a plane). Not too much concern is shown if some of the control variables are not significant. The question that remains is the extent to which the supportive results for the focus variables are dependent on the specific set of controls, definitions etc. used in the papers. Or to put it more crudely, might the authors be guilty of data mining? There is a slight degree of exploration of this in these papers but it is not very comprehensive.

We should not, of course, jump to the conclusion that there has been any data mining taking place. To answer this would require a thorough replication in which we can draw on the data as originally defined, but also possibly additional definitions and variables which might be relevant but are not mentioned in the original studies. It is certainly not possible to do a direct replication by checking the reported estimates using the authors' own data, as in 1978 and 1984 and as is still true today, economics journals do not, generally speaking, require the authors to provide in print (or deposit the file in an archive) the data used in their papers.

5.8 CONCLUSION

This chapter has extended the multiple linear regression model first encountered at the end of Chapter 3. The main purpose has been to improve your ability to interpret regression coefficients and to test hypotheses about them. Estimates of equations for the burglary rate and the motor vehicle death rate, in the USA, were used to illustrate the use of elasticities and 'F' tests to provide more information about our results. Another pair of articles from economics journals were used to show how the knowledge you have gained so far can help you understand a research paper. These two studies (on the hijacking of aircraft in the USA and the extent of fouling in basketball games) did involve some methods and concepts that have not been covered, but you can understand these studies to a high degree by concentrating on the features shown in our panels of review studies in Chapter 3. They are, again, simple multiple linear regressions. These studies are included to extend the skills developed in looking at the Chapter 3 review studies. You may find it profitable to go back to Chapter 3 and re-examine the review studies to see if you now feel more comfortable in working out what these papers were trying to do and the conclusions they came to. In this chapter we began the process of extending the usefulness of multiple regression by showing how it can be used for forecasting as well as for hypothesis testing. It is, fortunately, possible to make the CLRM model even more useful, in a number of ways, without having to learn any new statistical techniques or ideas. This is done in Chapters 6 and 7, which take us much further into the heart of the subject.

DOS AND DON'TS

Do

✓ Provide accurate information on how your data is defined and constructed.

✓ Make sure you understand why there are three different forms of the 'F' test in Section 5.3.

✓ Try to implement all reasonable hypothesis tests on your coefficients as the default tests from the package may not be that informative.

✓ Consider the use of some form of evaluation of the stability of your model whether it be the use of one set of data to predict performance in another set or the 'Chow' F test.

✓ Try to find the time to understand the pair of studies reviewed in the panel in Section 5.7 (or a similar pair which may have been given to you). If you can grasp the use of econometrics in these papers then you have made good progress and can expect to continue to do so.

Don't

✗ Forget that the size of coefficients in a regression is dependent on the units of observation.

✗ Fall into the trap of relying on either the point estimate or the level of statistical significance to tell a story. You need to use both to make sense of your results.

✗ Forget that reports of 'the elasticity' in a linear regression model are usually calculations at the means of the data. You will get a different elasticity at other points on the fitted line.

✗ Get over-excited at finding large values of R squared, as this is not necessarily a sign of the success of your model.

✗ Forget that the 'F test for the equation' is equivalent to a test of the null that R squared is zero.

EXERCISES

5.1 Looking at Table 5.1, work out the impact on the burglary rate of a rise of 5 percentage points in the unemployment rate and a fall of 5 percentage points in the percentage of the population classified as black. Now have a look at the 't' values on the coefficients for *UR* and *PCBLK* and comment on the accuracy of the calculations you have just made.

5.2 Go back to Tables 3.1 and 3.2 in Chapter 3 and Table 4.4 in Chapter 4. For each of these regressions calculate the R squared adjusted and the 'F' for the equation (note: this has already been given in Table 4.4 but you might like to check it).

5.3 Using Table 5.2, Equation 1, calculate the impact of a 10 mile per hour increase in average driving speed on the number of drivers killed per 100 000 registered drivers.

5.4 Do you think that forcing people to use R squared adjusted is a way of preventing 'data mining'? Give reasons for your conclusion.

5.5 State whether the following statements are true, false or indeterminate:
(i) The R^2 of a linear equation will be equal to the R^2 for its 'out of sample' forecasts.
(ii) A good forecast should have the same properties as a good estimator, that is, they should be BLUE.
(iii) An equation which has a high R^2 adjusted will be good for making out of sample predictions.

(iv) Attempting to minimize the value of RMSE for the out of sample predictions should be the aim of every good forecaster.

REFERENCES

Becker, G.S. (1968) Crime and punishment: An economic approach. *Journal of Political Economy,* **76**(1), 169–217.

Gujarati, D.N. (1988) *Basic Econometrics,* 2nd edn, McGraw-Hill, New York.

Hebden, J. (1981) *Statistics for Economists,* Philip Allan, Oxford.

Landes, W.M. (1978) An economic study of US Aircraft Hijacking, 1961–1976. *Journal of Law and Economics,* **21**(2), 1–32.

Lave, C. (1985) Speeding, coordination, and the 55 mph limit. *American Economic Review,* **75**(5), 1159–1164.

McCormick, R.E. and Tollison, R.D. (1984) Crime on the court. *Journal of Political Economy,* **92**(3), 223–235.

Theip, H. (1978) *Introduction to Econometrics,* Prentice-Hall, Englewood Cliffs, NJ.

WEBLINK

http://www.paritech.com/education/technical/indicators/trend/r-squared.asp

A basic explanation of R squared for stock market forecasters (the definition is not entirely correct).

Making Regression Analysis More Useful, I: Transformations

LEARNING OBJECTIVES

▪ Be able to estimate non-linear equations using OLS by the use of variable transformations
▪ Correctly interpret coefficients in non-linear equations including the construction of elasticities
▪ Know what a spline function is and why it might be used in preference to a polynomial function
▪ Be able to estimate an equation with lagged dependent variables and interpret the coefficients

CHAPTER SUMMARY

6.1 INTRODUCTION

So far we have covered the use of basic regression to a level where you can understand the results presented by researchers, to some extent, and you can also apply models to your own data. We still have quite a long way to go before we have a wide enough range of skills to get a fuller general understanding of most of the empirical articles published in academic journals. In this chapter, we begin this journey by showing how the CLRM (classical linear regression model) can be extended.

This chapter looks at simple techniques that involve very little in the way of learning new or difficult skills. The main requirements of this chapter are to refresh your knowledge of the elementary mathematical ideas of logarithms, powers (squared, cubed etc.) and reciprocals (i.e. dividing a number into the number one) and to be able to use these to create new variables on a computer package. Of course, being able to do this is no guarantee that the user will correctly interpret and test the results they have produced. Even experienced practitioners sometimes lapse into errors on such matters. In attempting to avoid such errors, the main thing to remember is that the principles learned in the previous chapters still apply. If you find yourself confused in this or subsequent chapters, it may be worth refreshing your memory with a selective re-read of Chapters 3 and 5 (Sections 5.1–5.3).

Knowledge of elementary calculus is useful in understanding this chapter, although it does not involve any solution of mathematical formulae, in order to understand the key concepts. The main topic of this chapter is the use of transformations of the original data and variables, before we run a regression, as a means of producing models that are different from the basic linear regression we developed in Chapters 3–5.

6.2 NON-LINEARITY AS A PROBLEM

There is one very serious limitation of what we have learned to this point. It has been assumed that all relationships between a dependent variable and its presumed causes (independent variables) are strictly linear. That is, if plotted against each other on a graph they would fall on a straight line. We know this is very unlikely to be true for two good reasons:

(i) Economic theory (and many theories in other social sciences for that matter) suggests that many relationships should follow curved or non-linear patterns: for example, the U-shaped average cost curve of the firm, the Cobb–Douglas production function, the Engel curve for the relationship between demand and income, the backward-bending supply curve for labour, among others in economics. Outside of economics, we find such suggestions as that the relationship between racist attitudes and the percentage of the 'minority' group in the population is one which might be of a roughly J-shaped form when the measure of racist attitude is plotted against minority population share. Indeed, it is most improbable that a reasonable utility function for individual consumers would yield a straight-line demand curve.

(ii) Even if the 'true' relationship was linear, errors in the data available may result in an estimated relationship which is better described as non-linear.

6.3 MAKING INTERACTION TERMS

One important limitation of a strict linear relationship is that it forces on the estimated model the property of a constant marginal response for each variable which is independent of the level of all the other variables in the model. Perhaps an agricultural example of how limiting this is will be useful. Let us assume a farmer is growing soy beans and a student has been hired to analyse the production function. Let us assume there is no water supply available so that water inputs are exogenous, that is, the farmer is totally dependent on rainfall.

From the data available, this student produces the following specification for the equation. The data is annual with the variables being the annual amounts of rain, soybeans and fertilizer. The subscript i represents the year of the observation.

$$\text{Tons of Soy Beans}_i = b_0 + b_1 \text{ Inches of Rain}_i + b_2 \text{ Tons of Fertilizer}_i + u_i \qquad (6.1)$$

where u is a classical disturbance term. The coefficient for b_1 will be the estimated change in tons of soy beans attributed to each inch of rain and for b_2 is the estimated change in tons of soy beans attributed to each ton of fertilizer added. Therefore, these parameters (b_1 and b_2) are then constant marginal productivities of rain and of fertilizer because:

$$\delta \text{ Tons of Soy Beans}_i / \delta \text{ Inches of Rain}_i = b_1 \qquad (6.2)$$

$$\delta \text{ Tons of Soy Beans}_i / \delta \text{ Tons of Fertilizer}_i = b_2 \qquad (6.3)$$

The regression coefficients will be estimates of the marginal productivities. These do not change when the levels of the variables change. This (linear) production function has the property of being non-interactive as there is no interaction between the independent variables rain and fertilizer. This might seem like an implausible restriction, as the marginal productivity of fertilizer would be expected to be different under very dry and very wet conditions. To allow for this, one approach is to introduce an interaction term. An interaction term is one where two or more variables are multiplied together. In Equation (6.1), there were only two independent variables, so the only possible interaction term is created by multiplying rain by fertilizer to give us the new variable, which we might call *RainFert* when we save it to our computer data file. We add this to Equation (6.1) to get Equation (6.4):

$$\text{Tons of Soy Beans}_i = b_0 + b_1 \text{ Inches of Rain}_i + b_2 \text{ Tons of Fertilizer}_i$$
$$+ b_3 (\text{ Tons of Fertilizer} \times \text{ Inches of Rain}) + u_i \qquad (6.4)$$

When we estimate this equation, the estimated marginal productivities of rain and fertilizer are no longer b_1 and b_2 respectively. They will in fact be as follows:

$$\delta \text{ Tons of Soy Beans}_i / \delta \text{ Inches of Rain}_i = \hat{b}_1 + \hat{b}_3 \text{ Fertilizer} \qquad (6.5)$$

$$\delta \text{ Tons of Soy Beans}_i / \delta \text{ Tons of Fertilizer}_i = \hat{b}_2 + \hat{b}_3 \text{ Inches of Rain} \qquad (6.6)$$

These are again the first derivatives of output with respect to each of the independent variables separately. We now have a situation where the impact of rain and fertilizer on output depends on the level of the other variable. Note that the marginal impact of fertilizer does not change with the level of fertilizer. The same restriction applies to rain. This model cannot allow for diminishing or increasing marginal productivities of the factor inputs when the amount of the factors is changed. These relationships are still linear in terms of the relationship between output and an input with the quantity of the other factor held constant.

Since the relationships between the dependent and independent variables have been changed by the new formulation we need to think about what this implies for the calculation of elasticities. In Chapter 6, we saw that the elasticity from a linear model is conventionally reported as the regression coefficient multiplied by the ratio of the means of X/Y. If we continue with this approach then we should calculate the elasticity of output with respect to rain as:

$$\hat{b}_1 + \hat{b}_3 \overline{Fert} \times \overline{Inches\ of\ Rain}/\overline{Tons\ of\ Soy\ Beans} \qquad (6.7)$$

and fertilizer as:

$$[b_1 + b_3 \overline{Rain}] \times \overline{Inches\ of\ Fertilizer}/\overline{Tons\ of\ Soy\ Beans} \qquad (6.8)$$

where the bar above the variables as usual stands for the mean of the series. This regression goes through the means of rain, of fertilizer and of the interaction term.

We have only dealt with a very simple case with one interaction term. But, what if we are using a large sample survey which gives us the luxury of many degrees of freedom so that we can have literally dozens of independent variables as shown in some of the papers chosen for the example studies in this book? Even with four variables we have potentially nine interaction terms: if the variables are called A, B, C, D, then we have six first order interaction terms (where two variables are interacted) – AC, AD, BC, BD, CD, AB – and four second order interaction terms (where three variables are interacted) – ABC, ABD, BCD, ACD.

When we have large numbers of variables, there are an intolerably large number of interaction hypotheses, which might be tested. Few economists will ever enter all the possible interaction terms into a model. They tend to add few (if any) interaction terms where there is some strong prior theory, or some other reason, for their inclusion and thus are adopting a maintained hypothesis that most (or all) of the possible interaction terms have zero coefficients.

We can find another justification for omitting interaction terms, which leads us into the rest of this chapter. That is, if we transform the dependent variable (in the vast majority of cases this will be into logarithms) of a regression equation then this will force the relationships between the right-hand side variables to be interactive. Despite this, some journal articles can be found which go ahead and add extra interaction terms (usually first order) for a few of the relationships in the model when the dependent variable is already in logs.

6.4 WHAT IF WE WRONGLY CHOOSE A LINEAR MODEL?

In the previous five chapters, we have worked with strictly linear and hence non-interactive models. We are now contemplating the possibility that this is a specification error. You will recall that errors in the specification of the equation are dealt with through the treatment of the disturbance term in the CLRM. Bearing this in mind, it is best to view a linear regression equation as an approximation to the 'true' equation, which may be linear, monotonically non-linear or even non-monotonically non-linear. This implies that we might expect to detect some signs of non-linearity in the pattern of residuals, which are the estimated disturbance terms. This can form the basis of a test for non-linearity.

Here is an artificially constructed example to show what happens when you try to apply a linear model to a non-linear relationship. I constructed a set of artificial data, which follows a perfectly symmetrical, inverted U-shape as found in many microeconomics textbooks when describing the average cost curve. The data are given in Table 6.1.

Table 6.1 Artificially generated data for an imaginary U-shaped average cost curve

OBS.	AC	QT
1	180.9323	1.0000
2	171.2863	2.0000
3	150.1682	3.0000
4	139.7034	4.0000
5	128.1395	5.0000
6	115.8462	6.0000
7	101.3434	7.0000
8	107.8648	8.0000
9	103.4468	9.0000
10	107.9388	10.0000
11	99.1340	11.0000
12	101.7364	12.0000
13	110.1180	13.0000
14	113.6928	14.0000
15	130.4022	15.0000
16	143.1388	16.0000
17	155.4132	17.0000
18	165.6523	18.0000
19	177.1343	19.0000
20	197.3877	20.0000

Note: AC is the 'imaginary' average cost and QT the imaginary output.

The data were obtained by simply writing down a quadratic formula to represent a U-shaped average cost curve:

$$(AC/Q) = b_0 + b_1 Q + b_2 Q^2 + u \tag{6.9}$$

where u is the classical disturbance term and subscripts have been omitted.

I then chose some output values (in fact just the numbers from 1 to 20) to feed into this, assigned some arbitrary values for the parameters and then added a set of random numbers, generated by a computer package, corresponding to the hypothetical disturbance term. If we adopt the strictly linear hypothesis then we estimate the model just by running a regression of AC on Q. This gives the results shown in Table 6.2.

Table 6.2 OLS estimates of the imaginary average cost curve data given in Table 6.1

```
Dependent variable is AC
20 observations used for estimation from 1 to 20
Regressor              Coefficient       Standard Error    T-Ratio[Prob]
INT                    125.3266          14.5666           8.6037[.000]
QT                     .92356            1.2160            .75950[.457]
R-Squared              .031052
F-statistic F(1, 18)   .57685[.457]
```

In this particular case, I have simply reproduced the first part of the output from an early version of the Microfit package rather than transferring the data into the kind of table you would use in a written report. This output uses the more technically correct term 'regressor' instead of the more easily understood phrase 'independent variables'.

The value of 'prob' given in brackets is what we called the critical significance level in Chapter 3. It is based on the further assumption that you want two-tailed (two-sided) hypothesis tests. This is the default assumption of computer packages, which give values for 'prob' in the final column of the output. This can be used to do the hypothesis testing instead of looking up the 't' values in a table. The value in the 'prob' column is the figure at which we would just switch from accepting the null to rejecting the null. Hence, we compare the figure in this column with the selected significance level. If it falls below this selected level then we reject the null. If a variable is statistically significant at a high level on the default test then you will find that the figure given in this column appears to be zero but this is due to rounding down of a very small number. In the case of the intercept shown here, prob goes to three digits, which means the appearance of what looks like zero is telling us that the significance level is 0.01 per cent.

The absence of a statistically significant relationship between the two variables is shown in the extremely low 't' ratio on the X variable (QT), as the 't' ratio is much too small to reject the null on any reasonable significance level we might choose. Consulting the prob value says we need to go to a 45.7 per cent significance level to reject the null on a two-tailed test. This implies a flat, horizontal average cost curve as shown in Figure 6.1. This diagram also shows the pattern of the 'true' relationship that we know is in the data because it was artificially forced to be there.

This indicates that one might expect a particular pattern of residuals: that is, as X increases from zero we get a string of residuals that are positive followed by a string of negative then back to positive again. I have suggested the use of visual inspection of residuals. This will be taken up again in Chapter 9, where I go on from such descriptive diagnosis of residuals to formal diagnostic tests, which are based on testing hypotheses about the residuals themselves.

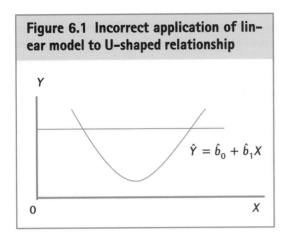

Figure 6.1 Incorrect application of linear model to U-shaped relationship

$\hat{Y} = \hat{b}_0 + \hat{b}_1 X$

The example dealt with above was a case of forcing a linear relationship on one which should be U-shaped. The latter is a non-monotonic functional form; so called because the rate of change of Y with respect to X has both negative and positive values at different levels of X. In the case of a monotonically non-linear equation, non-linearity is reflected in the intercept term.

For example, suppose we are modelling an 'adoption' scenario, such as the spread of Internet facilities, and the dependent variable is the percentage of households having this. Strictly speaking, such a situation is not suitable for the CLRM model as it has a bounded dependent variable (see Chapter 8 on logit models). This situation is often thought to follow a sigmoid curve as shown in Figure 6.2, where there is a slow response to initial changes in the dependent variables followed by a stronger response which gets weaker as we approach saturation levels. The use of a linear model to approximate this may lead to a prediction that there is some level of the causal variables at which we get the nonsensical conclusion that over 100 per cent of

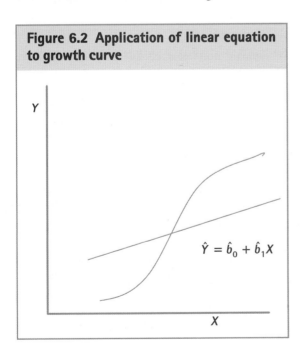

Figure 6.2 Application of linear equation to growth curve

$\hat{Y} = \hat{b}_0 + \hat{b}_1 X$

households have an Internet connection. It may also produce the other nonsensical outcome – that the model predicts a negative rate of household usage at some levels of the independent variables. This can show up in a negative estimate of the intercept. If the data is fairly closely scattered around the central part of the graph in Figure 6.2 (i.e. it does not tend to go into the top and bottom 'tails'), then a linear function may give a plausible and reliable set of estimates assuming there are no other specification errors like omitted variables.

We could form an idea of the specification error from inspecting the residuals. As we see in Figure 6.2, the pattern of residuals are all of one sign and then the other as we move across the graph. Using real data, the residuals are not going to come out in quite such a clear way as they did here or as they do in a regression performed on the artificial data reported in Table 6.1. This suggests that a hypothesis test needs to be used to provide a test for non-linearity. Some packages do have this built in as an option or a default; for example, Shazam and Microfit. One test, which is easily programmed into a linear model's results, is the 'Ramsey test', which we look at in Chapter 9.

In practice, economists do not tend to start with a linear model and then test its residuals for non-linearity to see whether a non-linear model is needed. Rather, the common practice is to simply choose some non-linear forms. In some circumstances, such as where a particular non-linear functional form is popular in the literature, it is quite usual for researchers not to report any linear estimates at all. For example, the studies in the review panels in this chapter and in Chapter 8 do not report any linear estimates. The hypothesis of linearity, which has been the basis of our previous chapters, is *not* a maintained hypothesis of economic models. Rather, it is the default choice given by using the OLS method *if* you have not manipulated the data prior to estimation. These manipulations of data are the subject of the next section.

6.5 HOW DO WE ESTIMATE NON–LINEAR EQUATIONS USING OLS?

The answer to the question, 'How do we estimate non-linear equations?', is much more straightforward than the question of how we choose the right functional form. We might use non-linear techniques estimation techniques but those are outside the remit of this book. Fortunately, OLS can easily be used to estimate a wide range of non-linear equations once we resort to the tactic of transformations of the data in our original linear model. Any model estimated by OLS is linear in the parameters attached to the variable specified in the equation. Variables can be specified in many different ways.

Often a researcher starts estimation with data in percentages, per capita rates or rates of change so they are already working with transformations rather than the 'original' or raw data. Even so, the model will be specified as linear in the parameters. Since we are still going to use OLS, we can only estimate equations that are linear in the parameters. The non-linearity of the relationship is caused by the use of transformations on the variables from a specified equation.

There are many standard mathematical transformations we can use. All of these have the effect of making the ratio between any two items in a data series different from what it was in the original data. Rather than go through a list of all of these at this stage, I shall concentrate on three major forms of transformation to generate non-linearity that dominate the daily work of applied econometricians. These transformations are used as means of estimating non-linear functional forms.

POPULAR TRANSFORMATION NUMBER 1: POWERS – SQUARES, CUBES ETC.

We can introduce non-linearity by adding powers of variables to an equation. That is, we can compute X squared, X cubed, X to the power 4 and so on and add them to the equation. The use of these terms not only introduces non-linearity but it also creates potential non-monotonicity in the equation. We have already encountered this in dealing with the incorrect linear estimation of a U-shaped curve earlier in this chapter. Returning to the example data given there: we should now add the term QT^2 to the equation estimated in Table 6.2. This requires us to create a new variable by using the transformations menu on a computer package to either explicitly square the variable or simply multiply it by itself. In our example data, QT squared has been called $QTSQ$. You should give your squared term a name that cannot be confused with other variables.

Thus, we estimate Equation (6.9) above to get:

Table 6.3 OLS estimates of the imaginary average cost function from the data in Table 6.1

Dependent variable is AC
20 observations used for estimation from 1 to 20

Regressor	Coefficient	Standard Error	T-Ratio[Prob]
INT	201.9149	3.2816	61.5300[.000]
QT	−19.9641	.71970	−27.7396[.000]
QTSQ	.99465	.033289	29.8789[.000]
R-Squared	.98189		
F-statistic	F(2, 17)		460.9527[.000]

Again, this is taken directly from the output of a version of Microfit rather than rearranged. You could check, using the data given in Table 6.1, to see if your own results come within a close distance of those shown. What do we see if we compare these results with those of Table 6.2? We now have (in absolute terms) extremely large 't' ratios suggesting that both QT and $QTSQ$ are statistically significant determinants of AC. The other main things to notice are:

▶ The size of the coefficients, in absolute terms, are very different between QT and $QTSQ$.
▶ The coefficients on QT and $QTSQ$ are of the opposite sign to each other.
▶ The R squared is now much larger than it was before.

The last of these is not very surprising, as it follows from the large rise in the 't' ratios that we should see a substantial increase in R squared. The other two changes are very important, as will be shown in the subsequent discussion. The presence of oppositely signed coefficients means that this relationship will have a turning point. In a quadratic equation, there can only be one turning point as the maximum number of turning points will be one less than the highest order of power transformation included (assuming of course that the lower order terms are all included as well).

If we omitted QT from the equation, there would be no turning points, simply a non-linear relationship between AC and QT reflected in the coefficient on $QTSQ$. The inclusion of squared terms in a quadratic does not guarantee either a U-shaped or inverted U-shaped relationship. The rules of interpretation are given in Table 6.4.

Table 6.4 Interpretation of coefficient patterns in a quadratic of the form $Y_i = b_0 + b_1 X_i + b_2 X_i^2 + u_i$		
Sign of coefficient on:		Shape of relationship
X	X^2	
$+$	$+$	Upward sloping non-linear
$-$	$-$	Downward sloping non-linear
$-$	$+$	U-shaped
$+$	$-$	Inverted U-shape

This type of relationship can have a maximum value, at the top, in an inverted U-shape, and a minimum value, at the bottom, if it is U-shaped. We use the coefficients to calculate where this point is. Given that our regression has produced a negative coefficient on the variable and a positive coefficient on its square this will be a minimum. We need to find the first derivative of AC with respect to output and set this equal to zero in order to find the turning point. That is:

$$\delta AC/\delta Q = b_1 + 2b_2 Q = 0 \qquad (6.10)$$

which can be rearranged to give:

$$Q = \frac{1}{2}(b_1/b_2)(-1) \qquad (6.11)$$

In the present case, this gives us an estimated output of 10.035741 for minimum average cost.

This popular method is used for other relationships as well as average cost curves. You can apply it to any variable where you suspect, or have a theory, that there may be a relationship that is non-monotonic. However, one needs to be a little cautious in being too dependent on the use of the quadratic form to introduce non-monotonicity for a number of reasons:

▶ The strong restriction of perfect symmetry is imposed by this method. That is, the estimated curve is identical in shape either side of the minimum or maximum point. This will be a mis-specification if the more appropriate relationship is one where the shape is more of a 'J' than a U-shape. A possible approach to such an alternative is 'piecewise linear regression' (see the discussion on spline functions in Chapter 7 at Section 7.8). Quite a lot of journal articles which use a quadratic term for a focus variable fail to consider this problem: for example, later papers in the literature reviewed in Chapter 3 have added a quadratic function for the 'lawyerification' variable without mentioning this restriction.

▶ Although you may produce a U-shaped or inverted U-shaped relationship it is always possible that the estimated curve goes through some non-real regions (such as negative output).

▶ Outliers (see Chapter 9, Section 9.2) raise problems for any type of OLS estimation. In the case of a quadratic equation, strong outliers will tend to pull the location of the minimum or maximum point a long way from where it would otherwise be. In some cases, the outlier(s) might make a relationship seem to have a turning point when it is otherwise non-monotonic.

The elasticity in the quadratic equation will vary as the value of the right-hand side variable changes. The formula is:

$$(b_1 + 2b_2 Q) \times (Q/AC) \tag{6.12}$$

which we could evaluate at the means of Q and AC as with the linear equation elasticities in Chapter 5 and the interactive elasticity in Equation (6.4) above. The fitted equation will go through the means of output, average cost and average cost squared.

For ease of understanding, the model above only has one explanatory variable, which was used to create the quadratic. Normally, you will have a regression with several variables, some of which you may decide to turn into quadratics (or higher order polynomials) and others of which you may prefer to keep linear or possibly use a different transformation, such as those we are about to look at. An average cost function is expected to be a quadratic because it is a deflated version of a total cost function, i.e. we have divided through by output. If we wanted to estimate the total cost function directly, we would use the corresponding higher order polynomial:

$$TC = b_0 + b_1 Q_i + b_2 Q_i^2 + b_3 Q_3^3 + u \tag{6.13}$$

Please bear in mind the artificial data for average costs above was a very simple example. In practice, it might not be so easy to arrive at the notion that a non-linear model is to be preferred just by running a linear regression and then having a look at its residuals. Recalling the discussion in Chapter 1, you should be basing your ideas about the choice of functional form on some prior theory. In the absence of any explicit notions about the shape of the relationships between the variables, we are forced to use a specification search. This can be done based on fitting alternative functional forms and comparing them based on goodness of fit. This is discussed in Section 6.6.

POPULAR TRANSFORMATION NUMBER 2: USE A LOGARITHM OF THE DEPENDENT VARIABLE

The correct name for this is a 'power function' but it is popularly known as a semi-log transformation. This name is also sometimes used for the case where the dependent variable is still linear but one of the independent variables has been logged (see Section 6.7 below).

You will see detailed examples of studies that use this function as illustrations of the concept of dummy variables in the next chapter. It is also used for one of the equations estimated by Zarnowitz (1999) in the review study of business cycles at the end of this chapter, although he also uses a variety of transformations on the variables on the right-hand side of his equation. Here we introduce the function and show how it leads to a difference in the treatment of the intercept and the coefficients. As far as estimation goes this is a very simple case to deal with. We simply take the natural logarithm of the dependent variable and use this, instead of the original variable, in the regression. Many papers do not use any explicit notation or name adjustment in their variables to show that a logarithm has been taken, i.e. they may just use, for example, the term GDP in their tables with a note elsewhere in the text that it is, in fact, the logarithm of GDP that has been used.

No other changes are made to the model, so the degrees of freedom stay the same. This process implies that we are using a particular underlying form of the model, which, for the two variable cases, looks like this:

$$Y = e^{[b_0 + b_1 X_1 + u]} \tag{6.14}$$

The distinct feature here is that the linear regression equation appears as the power to which the base of natural logarithms (the number e) is raised. As it stands, this cannot be estimated by OLS. To do so we take logarithms of both sides of Equation (6.14) giving us

$$\log_e Y = [b_0 + b_1 X_1 + u]\log_e e \tag{6.15}$$

The term outside brackets in the right-hand side drops out because the log of any number to its base is simply 1. We now have a model suitable for OLS estimation as it is both linear and has a classical disturbance term. The shape of relationship expected from estimating Equation (6.15) is shown in Figure 6.3.

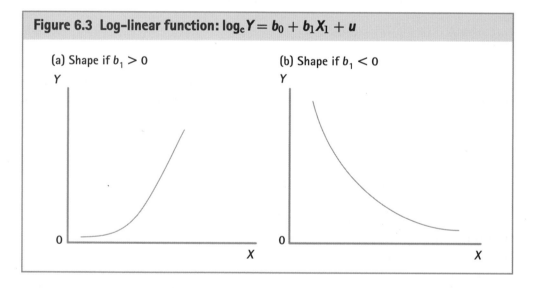

Figure 6.3 Log–linear function: $\log_e Y = b_0 + b_1 X_1 + u$

(a) Shape if $b_1 > 0$

(b) Shape if $b_1 < 0$

The shape in Figure 6.3a will come about if the estimate of $b_1 > 0$ and the shape in Figure 6.3b will come about if $b_1 < 0$.

The coefficients can no longer represent a constant impact on Y, as an equal absolute change in logarithms does not transfer back to constant changes. The coefficient is the impact of one unit change in X on the logarithm of Y. As a logarithm is approximately equal to the percentage change in a variable, the elasticity of Y with respect to X becomes the coefficient on X multiplied by X. The fitted equation will go through the mean of X and the geometric mean of Y (that is the anti-log of the arithmetic mean of the logarithm of Y). As with a linear model this elasticity will vary as X changes. We can again evaluate at the means, which requires you just to multiply the estimated b by the mean of X.

The estimate of the intercept is biased in this case. When there are two or more variables in the equation then they are interactive. These points will be illustrated more explicitly when you get to the review studies on earnings at the end of Chapter 7.

POPULAR TRANSFORMATION NUMBER 3: TAKE LOGARITHMS OF BOTH SIDES

The quadratic equation did not require us to modify the way in which the disturbance term enters the model. It was simply added to the equation. In the semi-log case the disturbance enters in the usual way but the whole equation has been raised to the power of e. In the functional form we look at next, we have to allow the disturbance term to enter multiplicatively rather than additively.

This case is an extremely popular one, often known as a double-log or log-linear transformation. The 'double' part meaning that all variables that can be transformed to logarithms have been so transformed – that is, we have transformed both sides of the equation (we cannot transform a dummy variable (see Chapter 7) in this way nor can we take logarithms of a negative number). The use of the term 'log-linear' refers to the fact that the model is linear in the parameters of its log transformed function. The double-log transformation comes about in the case of a multiplicative functional form such as the following case of the Cobb–Douglas production function:

$$Q = b_0 K^{b_1} L^{b_2} S^{b_3} e^u \tag{6.16}$$

The u term is assumed to follow the classical assumptions listed in Chapter 3. Q is a measure of output, L is the quantity of labour inputs, K is the stock of capital inputs and S is a measure of other knowledge-based inputs such as scientific research, which may shift the production function.

When we take logarithms of both sides, we get an estimating equation of the form:

$$\log Q = \log b_0 + b_1 \log K + b_2 \log L + b_3 \log S + u_i \tag{6.17}$$

The u term enters the estimating equation in a linear form because the log of a number to its base is 1.

The parameters of this equation will be the values of the elasticities for each variable. This, of course, means we have a constant elasticity function. We can now test hypotheses about elasticity directly from the equation using the 't' test. The default computer package 't' test will provide a test of whether or not the elasticity is significantly different from zero, or whether it is greater than zero or less than zero if we apply a one-tailed test. If we want to test whether the relationship is elastic or inelastic then we need to use the one-tailed hypothesis based on the null:

$$H_0: \quad b \geqslant 1$$
$$H_1: \quad b < 1 \text{ (inelastic) or the other alternate which is } b > 1 \text{ (elastic) with } H_0: b_1 \leqslant 1 \tag{6.18}$$

which must be tested at a one-tailed critical value.

The easiest way to do this is first check the sign of the coefficient. If it is already on the 'wrong' side then there is no need to go ahead with the test. If it is on the 'right' side, then you take the absolute difference between the null value (1 in this case) and the estimated value and divide that by the standard error. You then compare this with the 't' table value for the relevant significance level. If a published article does not report the standard error, then you will have to calculate it by dividing the 't' ratio in the coefficient to get the standard error. You may sometimes find authors commenting on the default 't' and the elasticity or inelasticity of the point estimate without testing whether it is above or below 1. This is incorrect. You should do the appropriate 't' test if you are going to make these kinds of comments. To give a numerical example of this, look at Table 6.5 in Section 6.6. The price elasticity of demand for cigarettes in this case is 0.423. Dividing the coefficient by the 't' ratio gives the standard error as 0.09814. The difference between the coefficient and 1 is 0.577 so the 't' statistic is 5.88 (rounded), which is quite large and well above the critical value at high (i.e. numerically low as a percentage) levels of significance, so we should conclude that the evidence strongly suggests that demand is price inelastic.

The double-log function also has the useful property that we can test hypotheses about returns to scale using the 'F' test. If there are constant returns to scale, then the coefficients in the regression will sum to 1, which will form the null hypothesis that can be imposed as a restriction on the regression.

The intercept term in this type of equation may cause a little confusion to the first time user. Its estimated value (i.e. the so-called 'regression constant') is the logarithm of the b_0 parameter shown in Equation (6.9) above. Therefore, we would need to take the anti-logarithm of the estimate of the intercept if we want to know the estimate of the b_0 term. The regression intercept can therefore be negative even though the b_0 term is positive. This will occur if the value of b_0 is smaller than the base of the logarithm. The size of this term is affected by the units of measurement. The other coefficients are not. The estimate of b_0 is subject to bias.

The possible shapes of a bivariate double-log relationship are shown in Figure 6.4.

Figure 6.4a and 6.4b show relationships that will arise if the estimate of the slope coefficient (b_1) is less than 0, while 6.4c and 6.4d show the situation if the estimated b_1 is greater than 0. Figure 6.4a and 6.4c relate to the situation where the point estimate (i.e. elasticity) is greater than 1 in absolute value, while 6.4b and 6.4d show the situation where the point estimate (i.e. elasticity) is less that 1 in absolute value.

We may want to know what the rate of change of Y with respect to X is rather than the elasticity – that is, the slope of the line in the above diagrams. This is a parameter, which varies as X changes, and it is influenced by the level of the other variables in the equation, thus demonstrating the interactive nature of the model. For the Cobb–Douglas equation of (6.9) the marginal rates of change will, as always, be the first derivatives of Q with respect to K, L and S respectively. These will be

$$\delta Q/\delta L = b_2 b_0 K^{b_1} L^{b_2-1} S^{b_3} \tag{6.19}$$

$$\delta Q/\delta K = b_1 b_0 K^{b_1-1} L^{b_2} S^{b_3} \tag{6.20}$$

$$\delta Q/\delta S = b_3 b_0 K^{b_1} L^{b_2} S^{b_3-1} \tag{6.21}$$

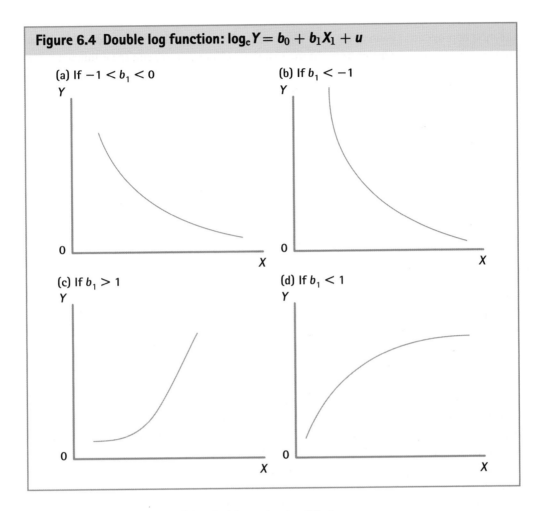

Figure 6.4 Double log function: $\log_e Y = b_0 + b_1 X_1 + u$

(a) If $-1 < b_1 < 0$

(b) If $b_1 < -1$

(c) If $b_1 > 1$

(d) If $b_1 < 1$

If we divide both sides through by Q, this can be simplified to :

$$MPK = b_1(Q/K) \tag{6.22}$$

$$MPL = b_2(Q/L) \tag{6.23}$$

$$MPS = b_3(Q/S) \tag{6.24}$$

The rate of change cannot be evaluated without fixing some values of the three variables to substitute into these formulae. If you wish to work at the mean values, then you should use the geometric mean (i.e. the anti-logarithm of the mean of the logarithms) as the regression in this case is through the mean of the logs because the data has been transformed.

The double-log form is extremely popular in research by economists as it provides immediate access to elasticities and hypothesis tests about them. It is an easy to understand alternative to the linear functional form. This does not mean that it is necessarily the best functional form in every situation. It is desirable that one experiments with other functional forms despite the tendency in many areas of research to almost automatically assume that one functional form is the most appropriate. Granted, the semi-log form's dominance in the area of earnings function (see the review studies in the next chapter) is justified based on the original human capital model put forward by Mincer (1958), but in many other cases there is no obvious *a priori* reason for choosing one functional form over another.

6.6 CHOICE OF FUNCTIONAL FORM AND A WORD ON R SQUARED

So far we have concentrated on the matters of how to perform non-linear regression and how to interpret the results. The problem remains of how we decide which functional form to choose in the first place. There are three approaches to this:

(i)   If we have a theoretical model, which makes very strict predictions about the functional form, then we should use that as our maintained hypothesis.

(ii) Experiment with several different functional forms and choose based on a goodness of fit statistic.

(iii) Experiment with different functional forms and choose on the basis of the plausibility of the coefficients in terms of their signs, magnitudes and statistical significance. In order not to be accused of data mining (or even outright dishonesty) you should make a point of providing some reference to the less plausible results of functional forms you may be rejecting.

As an illustration of how results differ between the linear model and the two popular log transformation models given in Section 6.5, we use the data from Tansel's article which was examined in Chapter 3 and Chapter 5 to show what happens when we use these instead of the linear model. Table 6.5 shows the linear results already shown in Table 3.1, column 4 so that you do not need to flick back to that chapter in order to compare the results. The semi-log is shown in column 3 and the double-log in column 2 of these results.

Table 6.5 Linear, double–log and semi–log estimates of the demand function for cigarettes in Turkey, 1960–1988

Dependent variable: Tobacco consumption per adult (*CCA*)

Equation:	Linear	Double-log	Semi-log
Constant	1.67	−4.28	0.53
	(10.84)	(2.76)	(7.9)
GNP	0.336E-3	0.66	0.153E-3
	(3.8)	(4.04)	(3.99)
RPC	−0.423	−0.49	−0.185
	(4.31)	(4.74)	(4.32)
TER	0.3995	0.21	0.0066
	(0.12)	(0.23)	(0.04)
R^2	0.645	0.717	0.659
N	29	0.29	0.29

Absolute t-ratios in brackets

The estimating equations after transformation (where necessary) are:

Linear: $$CCA = b_0 + b_1\,GNP + b_2\,RPC + b_3\,TER + u \qquad (6.25)$$

Double-log: $$\ln(CCA) = \ln b_{a0} + b_{a1}\ln GNP + b_{a2}\ln RPC + b_{a3}\ln TER + u \qquad (6.26)$$

Semi-log: $$\ln(CCA) = b_{b0} + b_{b1}\,GNP + b_{b2}\,RPC + b_{b3}\,TER + u \qquad (6.27)$$

where ln stands for natural logarithm and u is the classical disturbance term. I have added additional subscripts to the parameters in Equations (6.26) and (6.27) to highlight the fact that these are different parameters being estimated from those attached to variables with the same name in other equations.

So, what difference does it make? Not surprisingly, all the 't' ratios, coefficients, standard errors and R squareds are quite different. We cannot discuss this further just by looking at the numbers. The coefficients now have different meanings and so there is no point in commenting on whether those in one row are much bigger/smaller than their counterparts in another row. Likewise, the R squareds are not comparable when they are measured in different units for the dependent variable so we cannot readily compare equation (1) with equation (2) or equation (3) in terms of goodness of fit. Comparing (2) and (3), we find that R squared is higher in the double-log case. While good fits are desirable in econometrics, our main interest is in the meaning of the results, in particular their plausibility. All three of these equations produce the same signs for the coefficients on the corresponding variables and there are no conflicts between the equations in terms of statistical significance. That is, the education variable is not significant in any of the three equations, while the other two variables are always significant and of the expected sign. So, in terms of the broad results there is no real problem as to which functional form we would choose. This is not always going to happen as the degree of agreement between functional forms is going to depend on the properties of the data you are working with.

You could try to use R squared as a selection criterion by converting the non-linear dependent variable results to a comparable basis with the linear equation. That is, use the model to generate predictions, then anti-log the predictions and calculate the residuals from comparing these with the raw data for CCA. This method suffers from some bias. The more correct approach is to use likelihood-ratio tests. Statistical techniques exist for the purposes of making a systematic search over a range of different variables until you find the optimal one in terms of goodness of fit. These Box–Cox methods may sound like a good idea but you will not find them being employed very often in the typical article that uses regression analysis.

Before we leave the example results in Table 6.5, I ought to comment on the magnitudes of the relationships in the different functional forms. The best way to focus on the relationships for the three different functional forms is to compute the elasticity measures, at the appropriate means, as some kind of summary of the average strength of mean estimated impact. These calculations are reported in Table 6.6 for income and price. The formula used to compute elasticity is shown at the head of the table.

It is noticeable that the 'mean' income elasticities from each functional form are very similar. For price, there is a fairly large difference between the double-log and the other two but all of these are still firmly in the inelastic region. You can see clearly from comparing Table 6.5 and

Table 6.6 Income and price elasticities from Table 6.5

	Functional form		
	Linear	Double–log	Semi–log
Formula	$\hat{b}(\bar{X}/\bar{Y})$	$\hat{b}$	$\hat{b}\bar{X}$
GNP	0.626	0.66	0.629
RPC	−0.392	−0.49	−0.379

Table 6.6 that the very small coefficients for income, in the semi-log and linear case, actually yield quite large elasticities.

6.7 SOME OTHER TRANSFORMATIONS FOR NON–LINEARITY

You have now familiarized yourself with the idea that a regression can be extended by transforming the variables prior to running the regression. This is linear estimation of non-linear equations. The three main methods of doing this were dealt with above. These three methods account for the vast majority of transformations to be found in research studies by economists. There are some other methods, which need to be mentioned. The additional two that should seem obvious are the use of a square root term and the use of a reciprocal – that is, 1 divided by the original number. Again, these merely alter the ratios of the items in the original data series.

TAKE THE LOG OF A RIGHT–HAND SIDE VARIABLE

We could use the 'other' semi-log transformation. That is, take the natural logarithm of a right-hand side variable. In this case, the interpretation of the coefficient will be the impact of a one percentage change in the X variable on Y in the units in which it is measured. The elasticity then becomes simply

$$\hat{b}(1/Y) \tag{6.28}$$

which can again be calculated at the mean of Y to produce a summary statistic of the magnitude of the relationship that is independent of the units of measurement. The coefficient is interpreted as being roughly the impact of a one per cent change in X on Y in the units in which Y is measured. The regression will go through the mean of Y and the geometric mean of X (due to the log transformation of X).

TAKING THE RECIPROCAL

The reciprocal method sometimes leads to errors through people failing to remember quite how drastically they have altered the properties of the original variable. Let us take the case of the demand for money which (along with the Phillips curve relationship between unemployment and inflation) is the usual textbook example of the case where one might use a reciprocal transformation on one of the independent variables. In this case, the chosen variable is the rate of interest.

$$M = b_0 + b_1(1/r) + b_2Y + u \qquad\qquad (6.29)$$

The argument for taking the inverse of the rate of interest is that this will force the demand for money to have a 'floor' and thus produce an estimating equation which includes the features predicted by Keynes' hypothesis of the precautionary demand for money.

The shape of the relationship between M and r (holding Y constant) implied by this is shown in Figure 6.5.

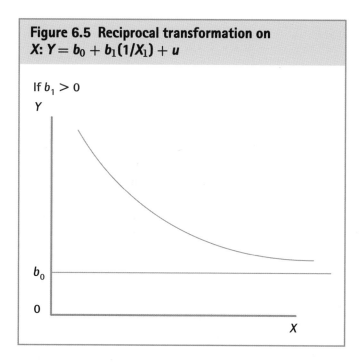

Figure 6.5 Reciprocal transformation on X: $Y = b_0 + b_1(1/X_1) + u$

If $b_1 > 0$

In Figure 6.5 the floor level is shown by the line drawn at the estimated value of b_0 and the line slopes downwards to this floor assuming that b_1 is positive. The rate at which this line declines will be determined by the size of b_1.

A little thought should convince anyone that, if the normal prediction of a negative interest rate is supported then the expected value for b_1 is the opposite, that is, the alternate hypothesis is $b_1 < 0$. The simple explanation is that $(1/r)$ must go in the opposite direction to r. The proof of the matter is found in the first derivative of M with respect to r being $-rb_1^{-2}$. This derivative must be multiplied by the ratio of the means of r/M to get the elasticity formula. In this case, the regression will go through the mean of Y and M but will go through the harmonic mean of r (that is, the mean of the reciprocals converted back to the original units).

This example is a 'mixed' equation with non-linearity in one variable but the Y variable is still treated as having a linear relationship with the others. There will be no interactivity here as the impact of either of the independent variables on the dependent variable is not a function of the level of the other variable.

Why does this equation have a 'floor' for money demand as in the Keynesian hypothesis and how is the estimated value of the floor obtained from the regression equation? Simply because as r tends towards infinity then $(1/r)$ must tend towards zero and zero times anything is zero: so the influence of the b_1 parameter drops out. This means the floor is the regression intercept plus the additional money holdings due to the level of real income.

If we used the reciprocal in a case where the coefficient in the regression turns out to be negative rather than positive (as it should be in the case just discussed), then the intercept plus the shift in it due to other variables is a 'ceiling' above which the dependent variable cannot rise. There must be an upper limit in such an equation.

Figure 6.6 shows this kind of relationship. The 'ceiling' is given by the intercept value and the rate at which the line approaches (but never touches) this ceiling is determined by the magnitude of the slope coefficient.

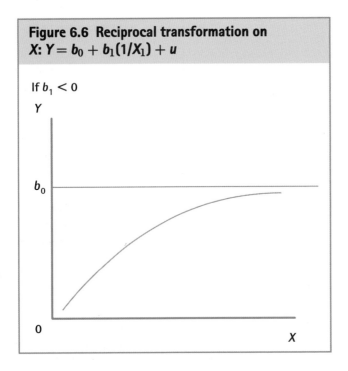

Figure 6.6 Reciprocal transformation on X: $Y = b_0 + b_1(1/X_1) + u$

If $b_1 < 0$

This might appear to be a useful approach to handling situations where there is a natural barrier such as the 100 per cent in adoption situations. But, of course, the regression technique does not guarantee that the model will not produce an estimate outside the 'natural' range. That is, the model could end up predicting a ceiling of, for example, 120 per cent or it might go through an unreal negative zone of below 0 per cent adoption rates. The correct techniques to deal with such problems are revealed in Chapter 8.

It is not that common to see a reciprocal transformation on the dependent variable. If one is performed then the equation will be non-linear with all the coefficients oppositely signed to the direction of the relationship with the X variables. The equation will also be interactive as the marginal impact of any given X on Y will depend on the levels of the other X's. The coefficients will show the impact of a one unit change in an independent variable on the dependent variable in reciprocal units. The regression will go through the harmonic mean of the Y variable and the means of the other variables.

TAKING THE SQUARE ROOT

Taking the square root has the same kind of effect as taking the logarithm of a variable as it reduces the size of the ratio between a smaller value of a variable and a larger one. It thus gives less weight to extreme observations. A square root dependent variable will force the right-hand side variable to be interactive. As we have already implied above, few economists are likely to use the square root transformation as the logarithmic transformation is much more popular.

6.8 LAG AND LEAD TRANSFORMATIONS TO PRODUCE DYNAMIC MODELS

Another useful transformation is the use of the lag (or lead) operator. The full importance of this will not be revealed until Chapter 14, but it is useful to mention it here as the logistics of estimation are the same as in the other cases discussed in this chapter. That is, you create a new variable with a simple command applied to one of your existing variables. Thus far, every equation you have seen in this book has the feature that each of the variables in the equation has the same subscript. This is because the simplest model is one where all decisions depend on the current values of the relevant variables. However, undergraduate micro- and macroeconomics introduce models that are not like this, such as the cobweb model and the accelerator theory of investment.

A very easy case to understand is the simple 'myopic' habit model for a good that might be addictive or habit forming such as the cigarette smoking case which we used for illustration in sections of Chapters 3, 5 and this chapter. In that particular case, we can transform the dependent variable by lagging it one period. The estimating equation then becomes:

$$Q_i = b_0 + b_1 GNP_i + b_2 RPC_i + b_3 TER_i + b_4 Q_{i-1} + u_i \qquad (6.30)$$

The coefficient on b_4 will indicate the strength of the habit. A hypothesis of habit formation leads to the alternate hypothesis (H_1) being $b_4 > 0$. It is also expected that b_4 will be less than 1. If b_4 is not statistically significant, then we conclude there is no habit formation and therefore a static model seems appropriate. This model will have different short- and long-run impacts of the variables. The short-run impacts are given directly by the parameters and the long-run impacts require you to divide these by $1 - b_4$.

Obviously, the larger is b_4, the greater is the difference between short-run and long-run impacts. You can calculate a long-run elasticity using the conventional formulae given above.

This model will involve the loss of a degree of freedom from the addition of an extra variable and may also involve the loss of a degree of freedom from deleting the first observation of your sample when running the regression. If you do not do this then you will have included a zero for the first value of the lagged variable, which is invalid. It may be possible to overcome this problem by finding the additional data for this observation.

As a simple illustration of this method, let us look at the Belgian consumption function estimated in Chapter 3. Table 6.7 reproduces the simple linear consumption function, from Chapter 3, in the first column and the second column shows the model with a lagged value of real consumption added as an independent variable.

Table 6.7 Estimates of the Belgian consumption function

Dependent variable: Independent variables	Real consumption	Real consumption
Intercept	0.717	0.402
	(1.42)	(0.98)
Real GDP	0.61	0.49
	(47.11)	(9.51)
Real Consumption Lagged One Period		0.194
		(2.23)
R squared	0.987	0.993
N	31	30

Note: Figures in parentheses are the 't' ratios for the null of a zero coefficient.

The estimating equations are

$$C_t = b_0 + b_1 GDP_t + u_t \tag{6.31}$$

$$C_t = b_0 + b_1 GDP_t + b_2 C_{t-1} + u_t \tag{6.32}$$

where I have used the t subscript to represent observations as this is quite usual when dealing with time series. The u term is the classical disturbance term.

You can readily see that the results are quite different. There is a small increase in the R squared but this is bound to increase when variables are added. The lagged consumption term is statistically significant at the 5 per cent level (and better), while the extremely large 't' ratio on Real GDP has fallen albeit to what is still a very large 't' value. The relevant degrees of freedom for these 't' tests are 29 in the first case and 27 in the second case.

In the first case, there is no difference between the short- and long-run marginal propensity to consume, which is 0.61. In the second equation, the short-run marginal propensity to consume is 0.49 and the long-run value is equal to this divided by 1 minus 0.194 giving a value of 0.61 (rounding to two decimal places), which is very similar to the value in the first equation. This is just a coincidence and there is no reason to suppose this will happen when you try different data sets, as is shown by the next application, which looks again at the cigarette smoking data that I have been using for illustration.

This time I have added a lagged dependent variable to the double-log model reported in column 2 of Table 6.6. Computer output from Microfit has been shown rather than the tidied-up table in the style of a journal article just shown in Table 6.7.

The estimating equation is:

$$\ln CCA = \ln b_0 + b_1 \ln GNP + b_2 \ln RPC + b_3 \ln TER + b_4 \ln CCA_{t-1} + u_t \tag{6.33}$$

where ln is the natural logarithm, u is the classical disturbance term and I have again used t as the observation subscript.

The lagged variable has been labelled *LCCAL1* and the sample now starts at 1961. Each of the other variables has been prefixed by 'L' to remind us that the natural logarithm of the original series has been taken.

The lag term is highly statistically significant. Not surprisingly, the R squared has risen a fair amount and the Durbin–Watson statistic is around 2, which would usually be seen as not surprising for reasons discussed in Chapter 9. The GNP variable is now quite weak in terms of statistical significance. The education variable is still insignificant but the price variable has changed quite a lot. The point estimate of the short-run price elasticity is now less than half what it was in Table 6.5. Of course, Table 6.5 did not distinguish between the short- and long-run elasticities. The long-run elasticity from Table 6.8 will be -0.22948 divided by $(1 - 0.61188)$ giving an estimate of around 0.59, which is much larger than the figure in Table 6.5 although it is still inelastic.

Table 6.8 Lagged dependent variable model estimates of the demand function for cigarettes in Turkey, 1961–1988

Ordinary Least Squares Estimation
Dependent variable is LCCA
28 observations used for estimation from 1961 to 1988

Regressor	Coefficient	Standard Error	T-Ratio[Prob]
INT	1.5764	1.4274	-1.1044[.281]
LCCAL1	.61188	.15485	3.9513[.001]
LGNP	.25122	.16722	1.5024[.147]
LRPC	-.22948	.10460	-2.1939[.039]
LTER	.014085	.075069	.18763[.853]
R-Squared	.81936	F-statistic F(4, 23)	26.0814[.000]
R-Bar-Squared	.78795	S.E. of Regression	.048605
Residual Sum of Squares	.054337	Mean of Dependent Variable	.79087
S.D. of Dependent Variable	.10555	Maximum of Log-likelihood	47.6964
DW-statistic	2.0396		

The cases just shown involved adding a one-period lag of the dependent variable as an independent variable. This is not without problems in terms of maintaining the assumptions of the CLRM, but we shall ignore these. We could use other lag terms in this model. For example, we could use lags of different periods such as $t - 2$ and $t - 3$. If we had cross-section data which is only collected every ten years then we would be forced to used t - 10. We can also use lead terms, which are the opposite of lag terms in that we use future values such as $t + 1$. In fact, the so-called rational theory of addiction, first estimated using cigarette data by Becker, Grossman and Murphy (1994), uses both a lead and a lag term for the dependent variable. This will involve the loss of an observation at the end of the sample as the last value, for the lead terms will be zero if you do not truncate the sample before running the regression.

You can, of course, use lag and lead terms of various orders on the independent variables. This provides a more general dynamic model than the restricted format of the equations estimated in Table 6.7 and Table 6.8.

This form of transformation requires some kind of time-series element to be present in the data set. If there is such an element we can also use the other transformations, differences and growth rates/percentage changes. A difference is obtained when we subtract an earlier period value for a variable from a current period value. For example, $X_t - X_{t-1}$ is the first difference of X. We can produce the second difference, the third difference and so on. You might decide to use a difference instead of the level (that is, the level is just X_t) if you have a prior theory which says that people's choices respond to the change in a variable rather than its level. If you were to use a difference in a bivariate model such as the following:

$$Y_i = b_0 + b_1(X_i - X_{i-1}) + u_i \tag{6.34}$$

this is in fact a restricted form of a model featuring lagged X as the model

$$Y_i = b_0 + b_1 X_i + b_2 X_{i-1} + u_i \tag{6.35}$$

reduces to Equation (6.16) when you impose the restriction that $b_1 = -b_2$. If you want to test such a restriction, it does not require an 'F' test as only one restriction is involved. The test could be performed by adding X_{i-1} to the first equation and doing a 't' test on this coefficient.

6.9 REVIEW STUDIES

We now look at a pair of contrasting studies to illustrate the ideas introduced in this chapter. The contrast between the two papers is the biggest that you will find in this book. One concerns the death of artists and the other the behaviour of business cycles. They do have in common an interest in investment and its rate of return. The paper by Zarnowitz (1999) looks at aggregate investment and the profit margin in the US economy, while that by Ekelund, Ressler and Watson (2000) looks at what happens to the price of a painting after the artist is dead. Buying works of art is chosen by some as a means of investment in the hope that it will outperform bonds or shares in the long run. It is thus important to know which artist to buy, and the length of time the artist has been dead may influence this because of rises and falls in the reputation or fashionability of the particular artist. Ekelund *et al.* give an economic explanation that goes beyond the simple reputation argument. They regard the artist as a monopolist who has a unique product, that is their own 'style'. Artists and dealers conspire to regulate the flow of such an output. When an artists dies, this painting firm has effectively closed down because copies by other artists of the style are regarded as inferior substitutes. This fall in output should influence prices, but there is the complication that the death may be anticipated by dealers, especially if the artist is quite old. Zarnowitz estimates his equations in order to assess the issue of whether the US economy has largely overcome the inherent problems of instability caused by the risks surrounding investment.

Both papers use only basic OLS to estimate the model. The paper on artworks uses a quadratic in the size of a painting. The usual argument is that people would pay more for a large painting, although the signs on the size of painting quadratic in this paper implies there is a peak beyond which the price starts to fall. The non-linearity of the 'artist death effect' variable is not chosen here because of a direct hypothesis about non-linearity. Rather, it is to overcome a practical problem – that is, that before death the 'years after death' is negative. This is what it says on p. 293 of the article. These are the only variable transformations. Note, that the years after death variable itself is not included so there is only a non-linear monotonic relationship with death not a quadratic. The other variables are two dummy variables which we shall avoid discussing much as they are the subject of the next chapter. The dependent variable is quite complicated in this paper as it is not simply the prices of paintings sold at auction but rather an adjusted price series.

The business cycle paper reports three estimated equations, which use a mixture of the transformations discussed in this chapter. The dependent variables are logarithms and the right-hand side variables include a mixture of lags and differences of some of the independent variables. The reasons for such a mixed equation are twofold:

(i) Lags are used to try to avoid the problem of violating the classical assumption of independence between the right-hand side variable and the u term. This is a pragmatic attempt to solve this problem and it is not guaranteed to work.

(ii) Lags (and/or differences) are used because it may be felt individuals respond to lags (or differences) rather than the level of variables.

The Basic Facts

Authors: Victor Zarnowitz

Title: Theory and History behind Business Cycles: An International Historical Perspective

Where Published: *Journal of Economic Perspectives* **13**(2), Spring 1999, 69–90.

Reason for Study: To establish whether the American economy has reached a new 'golden age' where macroeconomic instability is no longer a problem.

Conclusion Reached: That the idea of a new extremely stable 'golden age' is suspect due to the influence of growth on the profit margin and the level of real profits on investment.

How Did They Do It?

Data: Quarterly time-series US economy 1953–98.

Sample Size: 178 (according to p. 75).

Technique: OLS.

Dependent Variable: Log Profit margin, log Investment; also uses the first difference version of the second of these equations.

Focus Variables: In profit margin equation: real GDP growth; Investment equation: lagged real after-tax profits.

Control Variables:

In profit Equation: change in labour productivity, lagged price level, lagged unit labour costs in the business sector, inflation (appears to be a two-period lag), long-term interest rates, lagged measure of risk aversion

Investment Equation: lagged dependent variable (Investment), dollar exchange rate, lagged labour productivity, Standard & Poor's 500 share price index lagged, long-term interest rate lagged four periods and also its current values, risk aversion measure.

Presentation

How Results Are Listed: The results are in the text *not* in a table. The value of R squared adjusted is not given until a few sentences later.

Goodness of Fit: R squared adjusted.

Tests: Default 't' tests.

Diagnosis/Stability: Although there are no formal tests of this the author gives quite a lot of summaries of what happened to his results when he made changes to the model. He also notes a number of problems with autocorrelation.

Anomalous Results: There are no anomalous results in this paper. All coefficients have the expected sign and achieve acceptable levels of statistical significance. However, problems with the disturbance term being autocorrelated are noted (see Chapter 13 for more on this). This violation of the CLRM could cause the standard errors to be biased downwards.

Student Reflection

Things to Look Out For: The very large 't' ratio on lagged investment in the investment equation. This is not surprising given that successive quarters of investment will be highly correlated with each other. The model specification has been somewhat casual in this paper. There is no explicit theoretical model of investment or interest rate determination given.

Problems in Replication: The equation in this paper should be quite easy to replicate for the source country (USA) and a wide range of other countries as the data come mainly from standard macroeconomic sources, which are readily available in printed form in libraries. As the choice of lags and differences has been somewhat arbitrary, you might expect to experiment with these in a replication.

The Basic Facts

Authors: R.B. Ekelund Jr, Rand W. Ressler and John Keith Watson
Title: The 'Death Effect' in Art Prices: A Demand Side Explanation
Where Published: *Journal of Cultural Economics,* **24**(4), 2000, 283–300.
Reason for Study: To examine the impact of how long an artist has been dead on the price of their paintings.
Conclusion Reached: There does seem to be a death effect. This is based on a 't' ratio of 2.415 on the focus variable.

How Did They Do It?

Data: Time-series of US auction prices of the work of 21 Latin American visual artists 1977–96.
Sample Size: 630.
Technique: OLS.
Dependent Variable: Adjusted price of painting sold at auction.
Focus Variables: *YAD* which is the year of sale minus the year of death of the artist. It is squared in the estimated equation.
Control Variables: Dummies for auction house (*Auc. House*) and whether painting was signed or unsigned (*Signed*), size of painting in inches (*Area*) which is also included squared.

Presentation

How Results Are Listed: Table showing coefficients, 't' ratios and prob. value, and observation numbers. Final column reports mean of the variables.
Goodness of Fit: R squared.
Tests: Only default 't' tests are used.
Diagnosis/Stability: None.
Anomalous Results: Only the insignificance of the coefficient for signed paintings. This would be expected to be positive and significant.

Student Reflection

Things to Look Out For:

(i) Why did the authors not include a quadratic in *YAD* rather than only a squared term? They hint at this specification in the last sentence of section 4 but do not estimate it.

(ii) The issue of sample size. In terms of degrees of freedom in hypothesis testing the sample size is very large. However, as a sample of artists it is small. There may be 630 observations but they are from 21 artists from one niche of the art market.

Problems in Replication: It is not straightforward to replicate this paper, although it should not be difficult if you have the time to compile data from lists of auction prices. There are, by now, many papers by economists examining the investment performance of visual art works and other collectibles such as bottles of wine.

These two papers resemble the others we have looked at in that the emphasis is on a particular hypothesis for which broad support is found. However, these papers appear in journals aimed at a wider readership than the others we have examined. That is, they expect to have some readers whose econometric knowledge is limited. There is a substantial amount of discussion in these papers, with the statistical work only playing a small, albeit crucial, part in the structure of the papers. Both present models which seem to suggest to us that more work needs to be done to them. As with the other studies we have looked at, the main emphasis in the paper is on the signs of coefficients and the significance of their associated 't' ratios.

6.10 CONCLUSION

There has been no new statistical knowledge in this chapter yet it has been an important step forward in making the OLS regression model a useful tool for research. By now, you should be able to use the regression model to estimate a wide range of possible types of relationships between a dependent variable and a group of independent variables. You should be able to conduct hypothesis tests on the parameters of these models and interpret the value of the coefficients using elasticities where this is more helpful. Although we have shown how to overcome the severe limitation of only using linear relationships, we have not dealt with the problem of incorporating qualitative data into a model. This chapter has implicitly assumed that data are of a ratio/continuous nature measured in scalar units (see Chapter 2, Section 2.1, if you need to remind yourself about this). The conversion of qualitative data, which is categorical, into 'dummy variables' is the main subject of the next chapter. This chapter has taken us from the estimation of U-shaped average cost curves, back to the consumption function and demand functions of earlier chapters and finally to reviews of studies on the movement of art prices and the stability of the US economy. You can see that we are now equipped to cover quite a wide range of topics. The next chapter should enhance your insights into all the regressions we have looked at so far and pave the way for examination of studies that, up to now, would be difficult for us to understand.

DOS AND DON'TS

Do

✓ Make sure you give new names to the transformed versions of your source variables, preferably using names that indicate to you what they are (e.g. put an 'L' in front of a logarithm or SQ on the end of a squared term).

✓ Make sure when you report tables to indicate whether a variable is a transformation or not.

✓ Treat your transformed variables just like other variables for the purposes of calculating degrees of freedom and performing hypothesis tests.

Don't

✗ Try to compare two regressions with dependent variables in different units on the basis of their R squared statistics.

✗ Forget that transformations of variables may produce dramatic changes in the size of coefficients.

✗ Forget to adjust the interpretation of the estimate of the coefficient by taking account of the units of measurement of the dependent variable.

✗ Rely on just one functional form. You need to try different functional forms as you explore your data.

✗ Pick a functional form without giving some thought about what it implies for the relationships you are interested in: for example, a double-log form cannot produce a model in which returns to a factor (or scale) switch from being increasing to decreasing (or vice versa).

EXERCISES

6.1 Examine whether the following statements are true, false or indeterminate:
(i) Linear estimation methods cannot be used to estimate non-linear methods.
(ii) Linear estimation methods can be used to estimate all non-linear methods.
(iii) Any kind of log transformation of the variables, in a linear model, will result in non-monotonic relationships.
(iv) Any kind of log transformation of the variables, in a linear model, will result in R squared increasing.
(v) If you add a quadratic term to a model, then the relationship for that variable must be non-monotonic.

6.2 Re-estimate the equation in Table 4.4 (using the THEATRE.XLS file) with a quadratic term for income and interpret the results (you may find Table 6.4 helpful at this point).

6.3 Re-estimate the equation in Table 4.4 (using the THEATRE.XLS file) with the income term and the dependent variable in logarithms and interpret the results (you may find Table 6.6 helpful at this point) which should include elasticity calculations where appropriate.

6.4 Discuss the following statements briefly, giving explanations as to their degree of correctness:
(i) A study that only presents a linear equation is of virtually no use to the researcher or the reader.
(ii) You should run a whole variety of non-linear equations and pick the one with the biggest R squared and the best F-statistic.
(iii) A study that only presents a double-log transformed equation is fine because it gives you elasticities automatically and that is what most economists really want to see.
(iv) It would not be a good idea to try a quadratic on every variable in an equation 'just to see' if it would work without taking prior suggestions from economic theory as to which variables should be given a quadratic transformation.

REFERENCES

Becker, G.S., Grossman, M. and Murphy, K.M. (1994) A theory of rational addiction, *American Economic Review*, **94**(3), 675–700.

Ekelund, R.B. Jr, Ressler, R.W. and Watson, J.K. (2000) The 'death effect' in art prices: A demand side explanation, *Journal of Cultural Economics*, **24**(4), 283–300.

Mincer, J. (1958) Investment in human capital and personal income distribution, *Journal of Political Economy*, **66**, 281–302.

Zarnowitz, V. (1999) Theory and history behind business cycles: An international historical perspective, *Journal of Economic Perspectives*, **13**(2), 69–90.

WEBLINK

http://www.campbell.berry.edu/faculty/economics/CostCurves/CostCurves.htm
This is a basic guide to cost curves.

7

Making Regression Analysis More Useful, II: Dummies and Trends

LEARNING OBJECTIVES

■ Know what a dummy variable is and be able to construct and use one
■ Know what a trend variable is and be able to construct and use one
■ Be able to use a dummy variable for testing forecast errors
■ Know the difference between shift and slope dummies
■ Have a critical awareness of the limitations of using dummies to estimate the impact of non-measured variables like sexual and racial discrimination

CHAPTER SUMMARY

7.1 INTRODUCTION: MAKING A DUMMY

This chapter shows that the CLRM can be extended greatly with some simple amendments. The idea of the dummy variable was introduced in Chapter 2 when we made the distinction between the three broad types of data by information content. Dummy variables can be used to overcome the problem of data that is ordinal or categorical being unsuitable for a CLRM. It should be stressed at the outset that this chapter makes no fundamental alteration to the standard assumptions about the disturbance term in the CLRM.

Dummy variables and trends are sometimes referred to as artificial variables. Why is this? Let us take an example where we try to add political variables to an economic model. Say we are using a sample of data for 1960–99 and we happen to know that there was a change in the government running the country at several points in this period. Let us imagine that our model is designed to explain economic growth and it is felt that the stance of the government towards regulation of the competitiveness of markets depended on which political party was in force. Ideally, we would like to have an index, in the form of a continuous variable, showing the strength of regulatory posture of the government. It is likely that a satisfactory index of this type may be hard to come by, therefore we look for some kind of substitute. We could use a simple dummy variable that is 0 for when a political party is out of power and 1 when that political party is in power. Typically, a researcher would give the dummy variable the name of the party in power and simply add it to the other variables in their equation. This variable is artificial in the sense that it does not contain any 'real' data about the strength of government position towards regulation of markets.

The dummy variable is a tremendously useful extension. It has wide applications in terms of evaluating economic forecasts, assessing sex and race discrimination and much more. It is not without its drawbacks and has perhaps been used with too little caution by some researchers. It does not involve any difficult mathematics or obscure concepts from statistics, yet it often seems to be surprisingly puzzling for students on their first experience of it. You may find it less puzzling when you have had the 'hands on' experience of making your own dummy variables with data you are using. This could be done manually by simply making a new variable in the spreadsheet you are using and typing 0 and 1 at appropriate points in the column of cells as illustrated for an imaginary 5-year political party example in Table 7.1, where the Liberal Democratic Party is represented by a dummy called *LIBDEM* and the National Socialist Party by a dummy called *NATSOC*.

Table 7.1 Construction of political dummies from imaginary data			
Year	Party in power	Political dummies	
		LIBDEM	*NATSOC*
1993	Liberal Democrat	1	0
1994	National Socialist	0	1
1995	National Socialist	0	1
1996	National Socialist	0	1
1997	Liberal Democrat	1	1

If you are entering the data in a non menu-based program you can just enter the strings of text 1, 0, 0, 0, 1 and 0, 1, 1, 1, 0 respectively. Some programs allow for automatic creation of regularly used dummies, such as those for seasonal variation, which we will discuss later in this chapter. If you are using a menu-based program with a spreadsheet, you will simply enter the 0's and 1's in the appropriate cells. One could create them more quickly by setting the variable equal to 0 initially and then determining the 1's using an 'if' statement, if the package allows this.

If you want to practise on some of your own data (or one of the provided data sets), you could make a split sample dummy by setting the first half of your observations to zero for the new variable and the second half to one. Let us call this dummy SD and assuming you are using a simple bivariate model, then the model is:

$$Y_i = b_0 + b_1 X_i + b_2 SD_i + u_i \qquad (7.1)$$

where u is the classical disturbance term. As there is a sample size of n then SD will be 0 from observation 1 up to $n/2$ and 1 from observation $(n/2) + 1$ up to n.

This model is shown in Figure 7.1.

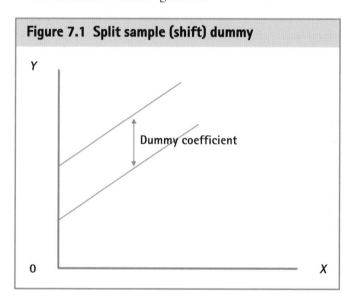

Figure 7.1 Split sample (shift) dummy

The difference between the two lines is estimated by the regression coefficient on SD that is $\hat{b}_2$. You can use the default 't' ratio on the split sample dummy coefficient to test the hypothesis that the intercept differs between the two sample periods. The coefficient can be positive or negative, although it is shown as positive in the illustrative diagram.

7.2 WHY DO WE USE DUMMIES?

There are two main reasons for using a dummy variable:

(i)   To pool differing samples which are being brought together in one bigger sample.
(ii) To 'proxy' the measurement level of some variable which is difficult to measure on a numerical ratio scale.

Case (ii) is the one in the example above, as we presumed that no index of governmental regulatory stance was available. Case (i) requires us to enter into the relationship between dummy variables and the constant term of the regression equation. This will bring us to awareness of the potential error of falling into the dummy variable trap.

In an equation without dummy variables, the constant is clearly something of an artificial variable. It is just a row of the number 1 entered into the matrix of the data. It does not appear in a spreadsheet of the researcher's originally collected data because computer packages are set up to create it by default or to accept a created intercept from a simple command. In a simple bivariate linear equation, the constant is literally the intercept as it is the predicted value of the dependent variable when the independent variable is zero. If we have more than one sample for the relationship we are exploring and we estimate these separately then we have more than one intercept, which is being estimated. The different samples could be from different populations, such as men and women or white and non-white populations. Or, they could be from different years in a time series as in the example given above where you created a political party dummy.

If we simply join all our different samples together into one file and use this one file to estimate a regression on all the data then we have what is called a 'pooled' sample. In the cases just mentioned, we would have pooled samples of men and women or of whites and non-whites. One form of pooling which researchers find useful is to pool cross-section data, such as from a group of countries, and times-series data for each country to produce a pooled cross-section time-series regression. If we do this kind of pooling but do not add any additional 'explanatory' variables to those in the equation we have specified for the relationship of interest, then we are imposing quite a strong null hypothesis. That is, we are presuming that all parameters are constant across time and space. Let us write this down fully in Equations (7.2a) and (7.2b). Say we are analysing how much unmarried/uncohabitating persons spend on clothes ($EXPCLO$) as a function solely of their disposable income (Y) and the data comes from a survey by a market research bureau:

$$EXPCLO_m = b_{0m} + b_{1m} Y_m + u_m \qquad (7.2a)$$

$$EXPCLO_f = b_{0f} + b_{1f} Y_f + u_f \qquad (7.2b)$$

where the f subscript refers to females and the m to males. As we are assuming the survey takes place at a point in time where all individuals face the same prices, we can regard nominal expenditure and income as equivalent to real expenditure and income. The f and m subscripts are used here to show that the parameters may differ between men and women as well as the values of the variables.

Now if we join the two samples, and estimate just one equation on the combined function, the following restrictions are being imposed:

$$b_{0m} = b_{0f} \qquad (7.3a)$$

$$b_{1m} = b_{1f} \qquad (7.3b)$$

I will skip over the question of the u terms differing between the two sub-populations of our combined sample (for instance, you may be wondering what happens if the variance of u for males is not equal to that for females) as that question will be picked up in Chapter 11 on heteroscedasticity. The examples that I have given so far in this chapter are all based on a maintained hypothesis that Equation (7.3a) may not hold but that (7.3b) does hold. The accommodation for Equation (7.3a) being potentially invalid is done through the dummy variable being introduced to allow the intercept term to shift. For this reason, it has often been called a 'shift dummy' while dummies used to allow for the possible invalidity of (7.2b) are called slope dummies. Slope dummies will be discussed near the end of this chapter.

Therefore, the shift dummy shifts the intercept between the sub-samples. It follows then that its coefficient must represent the numerical gap between the intercepts of the sub-samples. If we pool the samples and thus combine (7.2a) and (7.2b), using the restrictions just suggested we get the set up shown in Equation (7.4).

$$EXPCLO = b_0 + b_1(Y) + b_2\,FEMALE + u \qquad (7.4)$$

where *FEMALE* is a dummy which is 0 when the observation is for a man and 1 when the observation is for a woman.

This could be represented in Figure 7.1, which we looked at earlier, with the difference between the two lines being estimated by the coefficient on the female dummy.

In this configuration, b_0 will be the estimate of the intercept of male spending and its default 't' ratio will give us a test of whether this intercept is different from zero. The coefficient for b_2 will give us the estimate of the difference between male and female intercepts. If we expect that females will spend more on clothes then that is in effect a pre-test hypothesis of the form:

$$H_0: b_2 \leqslant 0 \qquad H_1: b_2 > 0 \qquad (7.5)$$

This would lead us to expect, in Figure 7.1, that the male line is the higher of the two shown on the diagram.

Note that this is one-tailed and should be tested accordingly rather than through any default 't'-ratio significance level, which may be given by a computer package. Getting the estimated female intercept is simply a matter of adding b_0 and b_2. Note, however, that this approach does not automatically provide the standard error for any 't' tests on the value of the female intercept $(b_0 + b_2)$.

You will recall that in the first example of this chapter we made shift dummies for both the political parties in the sample. Likewise, in this case we could make a *MALE* dummy which will be the mirror image of the *FEMALE* dummy. If we had included this *instead* of the *FEMALE* dummy then our hypothesis about the dummy coefficient would be:

$$H_0: b_2 \geqslant 0 \qquad H_1: b_2 < 0 \qquad (7.6)$$

and the intercept of the pooled regression would now become the female intercept with $(b_0 + b_2)$ becoming the estimated male intercept.

DUMMY VARIABLE TRAP

What if we had included *both* a male and female dummy as well as an intercept in the example given above? This, strictly speaking, cannot be done and we should find that when we attempt to run the regression that our computer package refuses to compute any estimates. This particular situation is known as the 'dummy variable trap'. The sum of the two dummies is always equal to the value of the intercept variable (1) and thus we have variables that are linear combinations of each other. In effect, we are trying to squeeze the same information out twice from one equation.

The solution to the problem, as has been implied throughout this chapter, is to drop one of the dummies. It does not matter, in technical terms, which one we drop as the choice makes no difference to the overall results. There is an alternate solution which is equally valid – that is, to drop the intercept term and perform a regression 'through the origin' with both dummies included. In effect, this is not really a regression through the origin as the two dummies represent an intercept term broken up into two parts.

This approach is hardly ever chosen in the case of elementary multiple regression. From a statistical perspective it is no better or worse than the 'drop a dummy' approach but it is less useful. For example, unlike the standard approach, it would fail to automatically test the hypothesis of a difference between the intercepts of the two groups in the dummy via the default 't' ratio. In most cases, this test is likely to be the main reason that you have incorporated dummies in the model.

EXAMPLE OF DUMMY USE

It might be useful if we look at some actual estimates using two category dummies before we look at seasonal dummies and then move on to shift dummies. The following is a very simple example of the use of shift dummy variables in a linear OLS regression. It is taken from a study of popular music by Cameron and Collins (1997) where all the right-hand side variables are 0–1 dummies. Note that the classical assumptions are not strictly valid here as the dependent variable is discrete with a limited range of values 1, 2, 3, 4 or 5. The estimated equation is:

$$ST\hat{A}RS = \underset{(24.8)}{3.5} - \underset{(0.76)}{0.2\,FLUSH6} - \underset{(2.46)}{0.6\,HIER} - \underset{(1.87)}{0.5\,LOSSMEM} \tag{7.7}$$

$$n = 86 \qquad R^2 = 0.12$$

(absolute 't' ratios in parentheses)

where STARS = album rating (1 to 5) from the 'Rolling Stone' Album Guide; FLUSH6 = a dummy = 0 for the first 5 albums by a band and 1 thereafter; HIER = 1 for hierarchical governance structure, that is, if the band is dictated to by a leader rather than being democratic; LOSSMEM = 1 where a significant contributor to the band, such as the originator of a distinctive approach to the guitar or keyboard, has left.

This can be regarded as a kind of production function where the measure of output is a proxy for value added in composition and playing. The independent variables are categorical measures of factors that might influence value added. The sample is from the albums of 'progressive' rock bands from the period 1967–75. For a democratic band in one of its first five albums where a significant contributor has not left the average rating is 3.5. The huge 't' of 24.8 is of no great meaning as it is for the pointless null of STARS equal zero. It is large merely because the variance of STARS is small. The other coefficients are merely estimates of the average deviation from 3.5 caused by presence of the characteristic. For example, the sixth (or later) album by a dictatorial band which has lost a significant contributor will have an expected value of $3.5 - 0.2 - 0.6 - 0.5$ which equals 2.2.

The 't' ratios on the dummies indicate whether the differences in the means between the categories and the reference group (democratic, no loss of significant contributor, first five albums) plus the category are significant. Degrees of freedom are 82. It appears that the albums after number 5 are not worse than the first 5 at the 5 per cent significance level. Conversely, on a one-tailed test, dictatorship and loss of important contributor are significant detractors from album quality at the 5 per cent level.

You will notice that this equation has three dummies on the right-hand side. The dummy variable trap has been avoided by excluding the three mirror image dummies (for first five albums, no loss of significant member, democratic organization) from the equation.

7.3 ARE DUMMIES ALWAYS 0–1 VARIABLES?

You may like to look back at the construction of the focus variable, *OFFICIAL*, in the econometric model of basketball fouling, by McCormick and Tollison (1984), used as the review study in Chapter 6. This only took the values of 2 and 3, where it was 2 up to a certain point in time and 3 thereafter. This is, in effect, a dummy variable to show the shift in the intercept between the two times. It will give exactly the same results as would a dummy replacing 2 with 0 and 3 with 1. This will be true so long as we have a linear equation. If the equation has a transformed dependent variable, such as in the earnings function studies reviewed at the end of this chapter, then using 2 and 3 would give a different answer from using 0 and 1. The convention is to use 0 and 1 rather than any other number. It seems logical to use 1 as the value when the event in the name of the dummy occurs, as the dummy is an intercept shift term. One advantage of using 0–1 is that the descriptive statistics on the dummy will show the percentage in the category labelled as 1 once we multiply by 100. You could use a different value such as making one dummy a 0–1 and another 0–2.5, or indeed any other number to represent the fact that the second impact might be present. This is a case of imposing some outside information on the data. In the case where a variable has more than two possible outcomes, you need to create additional dummies that are 0–1 rather than adjusting the value of the existing one (assuming you have no information to make the data anything stronger than categorical). An obvious case is where number of children appears on the right-hand side of the equation. This is often used as an influence on spending on discretionary goods like alcohol and cigarettes. Here we would create a five child dummy, a four child dummy and so on, taking care to avoid the dummy variable trap.

7.4 WHERE DO I GET MY DUMMIES FROM? THE SEASONS ARE AN OBVIOUS ANSWER

The example given above shows situations where the researcher is making an independent judgement about which pieces of information to represent as a dummy variable. How do researchers decide which dummies to create? Often there is no clear answer to this as it is down to their own judgement, for reasons we shall explore shortly.

The most common circumstance where there is a clear expectation that dummies should be used is in the case of time-series data, or where a 'fixed effects' model is being used to pool cross-section and time-series data. Take the case of a simple macroeconomic example – the consumption function. The most elementary Keynesian textbook case would be simply to regress aggregate consumption on aggregate national income with the slope coefficient being the marginal propensity to consume. If the data is annual, then the marginal propensity to consume is an estimate of the average during the years of the sample data. But what if the data is quarterly? There seem good reasons to suppose that consumption habits might not be the same in each quarter of the year due to so-called 'seasonal' factors. If we do not include variables to allow for this (which of course will involve losing degrees of freedom and estimation of extra parameters) then we are maintaining a null hypothesis of no seasonality.

In the simple consumption function on quarterly data, if we want a 'fixed effects model' (that is the case where the slope parameters do not vary) then we add *three* dummy variables even though we have four seasons. This must be done to avoid falling into the 'dummy variable trap', which we explained earlier.

Which one do we drop? It does not matter so long as you remember which one it was. Naming the variables accurately (D_1, D_2, D_3, D_4, for example) will ensure this. So, the general rule to avoid a dummy variable trap is for each dummy category to have one less dummy than the number of events. For seasons, there are four events so we add three dummies. One possible form of the estimating equation is thus:

$$C = b_0 + b_1 Y + b_2 D_2 + b_3 D_3 + b_4 D_4 + u \qquad (7.8)$$

where I have dropped the first quarter dummy (which would be D_1).

This model is shown in Figure 7.2.

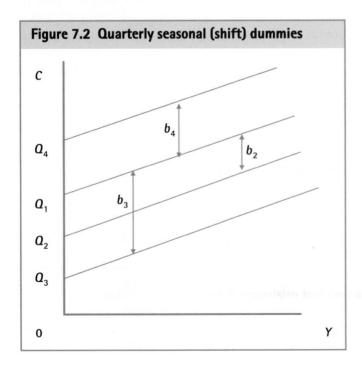

Figure 7.2 Quarterly seasonal (shift) dummies

In this diagram, there are four lines – one each for the consumption function of each quarter. This diagram shows Q_4 being higher than Q_1 which is above Q_2 which is above Q_3.

What we have done here is pool the four separate equations:

$$C = b_0 + b_1 Y + u \tag{7.9a}$$

$$C = b_2 + b_3 Y + u \tag{7.9b}$$

$$C = b_4 + b_5 Y + u \tag{7.9c}$$

$$C = b_6 + b_7 Y + u \tag{7.9d}$$

using the restriction:

$$b_1 = b_3 = b_5 = b_7 \tag{7.10}$$

As before, we can use the coefficients and standard errors for the dummies to form hypothesis tests. Each of these is with respect to the intercept. If we want to test, say, whether the Q_2 intercept is different from the Q_4 intercept, it is not possible to do so using the default 't' ratios that will be provided when we estimate Equation (7.8).

At this point, we have two options:

(i) Calculate the 't' test for this difference from the point estimates and the standard errors of the parameters b_2 and b_4.

(ii) Simply rebase the intercept by altering the dummy variables chosen. If we drop D_2 and replace it with D_1, then the coefficient on the dummy for D_4 will be the difference between D_2 and its default 't' test will test the hypothesis that the Q_2 and Q_4 intercepts differ. This could be done the other way round, that is, drop D_4 and replace it with D_1.

In the modern world of high-speed, low-cost computing, method (ii) will tend to be by far the easiest. Admittedly, testing hypotheses about seasonal differences is probably not a major interest of most economic/social science researchers. One is more likely to be occupied with the exercise of rebasing just described, when other types of dummies are being used, such as in the review studies which follow later in this chapter.

If we are not particularly interested in testing hypotheses about seasonal patterns, then our reason for including them would be to avoid specification error. That is, to eliminate biases in the estimation of the parameters in which we are primarily interested. We can view seasonal dummies in terms of either of the notions outlined earlier in this chapter. They may be a proxy standing in for a number of unmeasured time-related elements that may or may not be capable of ratio level measurement.

REASONS FOR SEASONAL VARIATION

The following are examples of such time-related elements:

▲**Festivities**: Religious or other sources of celebration may involve sudden shifts in consumption for particular foods or other goods such as fireworks and thus the demand functions for such goods would exhibit seasonal patterns. Christmas has a profound effect on the demand function for such products as Brussel sprouts and turkeys, but also on books and compact discs due to the heavy usage of these items as presents. For example, a study of UK sales of vinyl records in 1975–88 (Burke, 1994) shows an estimated increase in sales of around 78–85 per cent in the final quarter of the year due to the Christmas effect.

▲**Variations in opportunity**: Under the accepted calendar used in most of the world, February is a much shorter month, making the first quarter have fewer days on which to consume or to work or indeed to go on strike or be absent from work. Consumption opportunities are in some cases, such as cinema releases of films, affected by the strategic behaviour of firms who deliberately bunch the more desirable products in certain parts of the year. Such 'quality' variations will cause a jump in total demand in the market.

▲**Temperature**: Some quarters of the year are much colder or hotter in some climates thus leading one to predict higher or lower consumption in a given quarter for fuel and related products but also for things like ice cream or beer.

▲**Legal/administrative factors**: The desire to evade taxes might lead to bunching of certain choices, such as marriage, or the need to spend an allocated budget before the end of the accounting period might lead to a sudden unexplained upsurge in certain types of spending.

▲**Social/psychological factors**: Short-range seasonality has been observed at the level of shifts in variables due to the influence of the day of the week; probably the two most famous cases concern Monday. As the first day of the working week, it has been cited as a cause of lost productivity due to workers feeling discontent at returning from a weekend break (this is the so-called 'Blue Monday'). It is also noted in the stock market, along with Friday, as a day when prices deviate to a notable extent from other days of the week.

There are other means of removing seasonality but economists invariably use the dummy variable approach.

Ideally, we should take account of the above factors first, through adjustments or additional continuous variables, before we resort to dummies. That is, we could standardize for the number of consumption or production days in a quarter, or we could include the temperature if weather is a factor.

Someone may pool data in circumstances where there is an underlying **proxy** interpretation. The use of a male–female dummy is an example of this. We might consider that a 'sex' dummy is a proxy for an underlying ratio variable that indexes a person's position on a scale of masculinity or femininity. In the absence of an explicit measurement of such a scale, we can only use the two-value measure of whether the person is described as a man or a woman in the database. One could point out that, in cases of labour market discrimination, this might not be adequate if being homosexual, bisexual or transvestite is a characteristic used in labour market recruitment and promotion.

7.5 THE SLOPE DUMMY

We now turn to consider the so-called **slope dummy** using the simple Keynesian consumption function for illustrative purposes. In terms of construction on our computer packages, the slope dummy is an interaction term as introduced in Chapter 6. That is, we would simply multiply income (Y) by each of the included slope dummies to create three new variables as shown in Equation (7.11). We also include the three shift dummies that were used in the previous section.

$$C = b_0 + b_1 Y + b_2 D_2 + b_3 D_3 + b_4 D_4 + b_5(D_2.Y) + b_6(D_3.Y) + b_7(D_4.Y) + u \qquad \text{(7.11)}$$

This equation is the result of pooling the following four equations:

$$C = b_0 + b_1 Y + u \qquad \text{(7.12a)}$$

$$C = b_2 + b_3 Y + u \qquad \text{(7.12b)}$$

$$C = b_4 + b_5 Y + u \qquad \text{(7.12c)}$$

$$C = b_6 + b_7 Y + u \qquad \text{(7.12d)}$$

which is just the set of equations in (7.9) again, but this time we do not impose the restriction in (7.10).

This model is represented in Figure 7.3, which shows four equations all with different slopes and intercepts.

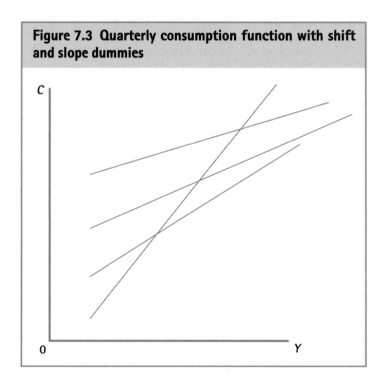

Figure 7.3 Quarterly consumption function with shift and slope dummies

The interpretation of the new coefficients in Equation (7.11) is straightforward: b_5 will be an estimate of the difference between the slope in the first quarter and the second quarter. If we add the value of b_1 to the value of b_5 then we get the estimate of the marginal propensity to consume in quarter 2. Similar reasoning applies to the other slope dummies.

This is a general model in the sense that it allows both the intercept and the marginal propensity to consume to be different in every quarter. It reduces to the fixed effects model, which is the model discussed in the sections above, when the following restriction is imposed:

$$b_5 = b_6 = b_7 = 0 \tag{7, 13}$$

We could go on to test jointly all of the dummy variables by imposing and testing the restriction:

$$H_0: \quad b_2 = b_3 = b_4 = b_5 = b_6 = b_7 = 0 \tag{7.14}$$

against its alternative. We could, of course, also maintain the hypothesis that the slope coefficients are unequal but the intercepts are the same, that is, we run a regression with only the slope dummies in and the intercept (plus Υ), thus testing:

$$H_0: \quad b_2 = b_4 = b_6 = 0 \tag{7.15}$$

However, this particular hypothesis is one that you are not that likely to see being tested by economists.

The nulls in Equations (7.13)–(7.15) would be tested using the 'F' ratio as explained in Chapter 6, Section 6.3, where the unrestricted sum of squared residuals comes from the estimation of Equation (7.8). The 'F' test for the restriction shown in Equation (7.14) is in fact equivalent to the so-called 'Chow' test for structural stability. In estimating Equation (7.8), we have, in effect, estimated separate equations for each sample. The slope and shift parameters for each season can be reconstructed from the values given in the computer output.

Many journal articles do not go beyond a fixed effects model and hence neglect to consider whether restriction (7.13) should be imposed on Equation (7.11). A variety of reasons could account for this, the main ones being as follows:

(i)   The fixed effects model is simpler to understand and report.
(ii) The fixed effects model might be preferred on pragmatic grounds, as the 'larger' a model gets in terms of the number of independent variables, then the greater is the loss of degrees of freedom if we include slope dummies for every variable.

7.6 REVIEW STUDIES

Having learnt how to use dummy variables and carry out non-linear regressions we are now in a good position to examine some major research on the determinants of earnings. So far, in order to keep a clear focus on the development of the dummy variable concept we have kept to examples involving linear equations. In such cases the coefficient on a dummy has a very simple interpretation. It is the estimated mean difference between the predicted value of the dependent variable, for the two groups represented in the dummy, all other things being equal. This value is constant. If a function is non-linear due to transformation of the dependent variable, into logarithms for example, then this simple explanation no longer holds.

Two review studies from the same issue (December 1994) of the world's leading economic journal, the *American Economic Review*, are chosen. Ashenfelter and Kreuger's focus is on the frequently asked question of estimating returns to years of education. Hamermesh and Biddle focus on the more unusual question of the influence of one's physical appearance on earnings. The huge pay of supermodels is so obvious that this may seem like a pointless research topic. Nevertheless, there is still considerable scope for debate about whether appearance can raise or lower pay in more mundane labour markets. The theoretical propositions concerning this can be read in the original article by Hamermesh and Biddle. Both papers are premised on the same theoretical notion, namely the concept of an 'earnings function', which was developed by Jacob Mincer in 1958. This related an individual's earnings to their stocks of human capital formed by formal education (or schooling) and other experiences in the workplace. Since Mincer's paper, thousands of earning functions have been estimated, by classical regression methods, using data from countries all over the world. Mincer's paper justified the use of a function in which the logarithm of earnings appeared as the dependent variable. The right-hand side variables may be linear, although many authors experiment with a quadratic in age or work experience. The usual hypotheses are that the schooling variables will have positive coefficients while any such quadratic terms will have two positive coefficients, or more strongly a positive coefficient on the linear term followed by a negative coefficient on the squared term. This pattern is based on the notion that at a certain level of age or experience diminishing returns set in. Hopefully you will recall from earlier chapters that these hypotheses should be tested by using the coefficients and estimated standard errors to construct a one-tailed 't' test (or, where there is doubt, on the direction of the relationship of a two-tailed 't' test):

$$W = e^{(b_0 + b_1 X_1 + b_2 DUM + u)} \tag{7.16}$$

which after transformation of both sides by logarithms becomes

$$\log(W) = b_0 + b_1 X_1 + b_2 DUM + u \tag{7.17}$$

If we multiply $\hat{b}_2$ by 100 then we get an estimate of the percentage difference in the predicted value of wage rates, *ceteris paribus*, between the two groups represented in the dummy. This will be a constant percentage shift, which naturally means that the absolute difference between the predicted wage for the two groups is not a constant but will depend on the values of the other variable in the equation.

Apart from the inclusion of the dummy variable, this is simply a repetition of what was shown in Chapter 6. You will recall from Chapter 6 that this convenient method of formulating an estimating equation does bring in a problem which is absent from simple linear models. That is, the intercept term as represented in the b_0 term will now be subject to bias when it is estimated. It should be clear from this chapter that a shift dummy is part of the intercept term for the category which has been set to 1 when the dummy variable was defined. As such, it is subject to the same strictures of being biased.

Both of the review papers use roughly the same techniques and types of data. The impact of appearance on pay is a more unusual question for two reasons: first, the shortage of data with measures of appearance and, second, the economic theory of microeconomics and labour market textbooks does not tend to mention this variable. The sources of data are in contrast between the studies. Both use cross-section data sets, which are large enough for the degrees of freedom to be approaching infinity for the purposes of hypothesis testing on individual parameter restrictions. In such a case, there is no real need to look up 't' tables, as the relevant critical values will be about 1.645 (10 per cent two-tailed and 5 per cent one-tailed) and 1.96 (5 per cent two-tailed and 2.5 per cent one-tailed). You should note the huge difference between the number of variables used in the papers. Full recognition of this requires scrutiny of the footnotes to Hamermesh and Biddle's tables. There is a good reason for the difference. One study controls for many of the factors beyond the focus group of variables by a careful construction of the sample. The other is forced to use a sample conducted by others prior to the study. Hence, the large number of control variables is inserted in an attempt to produce unbiased estimates of the coefficients on the focus variables. The situation of using a sample of (in a sense) 'second-hand' data, which requires heavy use of experimentation with control variables, is the more common one in econometric research.

The Basic Facts

Authors: Orley Ashenfelter and Alan Kreuger

Title: Estimates of the Economic Return to Schooling from a New Sample of Twins

Where Published: *American Economic Review*, **84**(5), December 1994, 1158–1173.

Reason for Study: To explore the problem of biases in estimates of returns to schooling arising from unmeasured ability differences.

Conclusion Reached: Using a sample of twins to control for ability factors produces higher estimates of rates of return to schooling – 12–16 per cent per year – than found previously.

How Did They Do It?

Data: Special questionnaire administered at the Twinsburg Festival (USA) in August 1991. Identical and non-identical twins were included but most of the analysis is on identical twins.

Sample Size: 147–298.

Technique: OLS/GLS (GLS is covered later in this book in Chapter 15).

Dependent Variable: Natural logarithm of hourly earnings.

Focus Variables: Own and twin's years of education.

Control Variables: Age, age squared, years of job tenure, years of mother's and father's education. Dummies for trade union coverage, gender, white, married.

Presentation

How Results Are Listed: Results for all the independent variables are reported but not for the intercept.

Goodness of Fit: R squared.

Tests: Standard errors are shown but 't' tests are not shown explicitly.

Diagnosis/Stability: Basically two sets of results are shown: one has a larger number of control variables than the other, permitting some assessment of the stability of the focus variable coefficients.

Anomalous Results: Easily the most notable is the large and statistically significant *negative* coefficient on the White dummy variable. Pages 1166–1167 try to explain this.

Student Reflection

Things to Look Out For:

(i)   Remember that dummies in a log equation when multiplied by 100 are (biased) estimates of the percentage difference in hourly earnings between the groups represented in the dummy. This is important in the discussion on male–female differences, e.g. a coefficient of −0.1 is a 10 per cent fall in earnings *ceteris paribus*. However, as female earnings tend to be much less than male, the absolute fall would typically be less for women than for men.

(ii)   The age squared coefficient has been divided by 100 to reduce the number of noughts after the decimal point.

(iii)   As the intercept is not reported, it is not possible for the reader to work out a predicted earnings value for a set of individual values for the variables.

Problems in Replication: This is a very special data set and it would be hard to construct a similar one without considerable effort and cost.

The Basic Facts

Authors: Daniel S. Hamermesh and Jeff E. Biddle

Title: Beauty and the Labor Market

Where Published: *American Economic Review*, **84**(5), December 1994, 1174—1194.

Reason for Study: To examine the impact of 'looks' on earnings. The authors' hypothesis is that attractiveness leads to higher pay.

Conclusion Reached: The 'plainness' penalty is 5–10 per cent, slightly larger than the beauty premium. Effects for men are at least as great as for women.

How Did They Do It?

Data: Two Canadian surveys and one American survey provided measures of attractiveness judged by interviewers, plus height and weight measures. Only those aged 18–64 working more than 20 hours a week and earning more than $1 are included.

Sample Size: In regression ranges from 282—887.

Technique: OLS.

Dependent Variable: Natural logarithm of hourly earnings.

Focus Variables: Six dummies for being tall, short, overweight, obese, and having above or below average looks.

Other Variables: Numerous measures of human capital and labour market conditions.

Results and Presentation

How Results Are Listed: Coefficients shown only for the focus variables – intercept not reported.

Goodness of Fit: R squared adjusted.

Tests: Standard errors are shown but 't' tests not shown explicitly. 'F' test for the block of focus variables.

Diagnosis/Stability: The authors present results with and without height dummies in Table 4. The use of three different samples provides some guidance on coefficient stability. For example, above average looks for women is not statistically significant at any reasonable level in two of the samples (Table 3 and 5), but is in two of three regressions for the other sample, at the 5 per cent level.

Anomalous Results: Some of the 'looks' dummies have the wrong signs but are statistically insignificant.

Student Reflection

Things to Look Out For:

(i) Remember that dummies in a log equation when multiplied by 100 are (biased) estimates of the percentage difference in hourly earnings between the groups represented in the dummy. This is important in the discussion on male–female differences, e.g. a coefficient of −0.1 is a 10 per cent fall in earnings *ceteris paribus*. However, as female earnings tend to be much less than male, the absolute fall would typically be less for women than for men.

(ii) Many of the individual coefficients on the focus variables are not statistically significant.

(iii) As the intercept and control variables are not reported, it is not possible for the reader to work out a predicted earnings value for a set of individual values for the variables.

Problems in Replication: This type of data is not easy to come by. It is also hard to be sure that quantitative measurement of physical attractiveness will be reliable in any survey. You may also face the problem that a survey that does have appearance measures may lack detail on other variables; for example, it may not have actual earnings.

The review panels provide guidance on how to read and interpret these studies. If one was attempting to replicate them, assuming the original surveys were provided, then a computer program would be used to generate 0–1 dummies from the original codings. One would also transform the earnings term into a logarithmic version saved to the file under a new name and used as the dependent variable. For the functional form used here, interpretation and testing of coefficients is quite straightforward although there are some differences from standard classical linear regression. Remember that the estimation technique is *still* a classical linear regression model but the data have been transformed in order to force a prescribed non-linear relationship on to the data. Because of the assumptions about how the disturbance (u) term enters this functional form, there is no alteration to the interpretation of coefficients for variables entered in continuous terms. The study of beauty and earnings does not report any of these. The study of twins and returns to schooling has several, all of which are measured in years. For example, in Table 3(i) own education has a coefficient of 0.084 implying that each additional year of schooling adds 8.4, *ceteris paribus*, to hourly earnings. In the same equation age has a coefficient of 0.088 and age squared a coefficient of 0.00087. How do we interpret this? One must first assume a given age, as the effect will not be the same at all ages. Say someone is 35, then the difference in earnings from progressing to 36 will be 0.088 minus 0.00087 multiplied by 71 (36 squared minus 35 squared) giving a gain of 0.02623. What is this 0.026263 of? Since our regression has a natural logarithm on the left-hand side, this must be a rise of 0.02623 in the logarithm of earnings. This is a meaningless answer, so we would like to convert it back to actual money amounts. We must not make the mistake of anti-logging this amount to get the money amount as this would not be the correct answer.

Unlike the case of a purely linear equation, something needs to be assumed about the person's other characteristics; for example, in the present case are they or are they not male and white and how much education do they have? We could add the relevant impacts of these and consider anti-logging the new estimated difference between being 35 and 36 to get the relevant money amount. Unfortunately, this is not possible with the reported results in this study as the intercept, which needs to be included in these calculations, is not reported.

The conclusion we just reached is not a major problem here as the main focus on such studies is on estimates of rates of return and percentage differences. The rate of return on a year of education is simply 100X the coefficient. Percentage differences are 100X the coefficient on a dummy variable, although strictly speaking this is a biased estimate. Hypothesis testing is carried out in exactly the same way, as in the linear cases of earlier chapters, using 't' and 'F' tests. Going back to Hamermesh and Biddle's study, let us look at the results for tall men and tall women in Table 3. Presumably tall men should earn more, therefore the 't' ratio of 0.6 should be subjected to a one-tail 't' test. It is not immediately obvious whether tall women should earn more or less, which suggests the use of a two-tail 't' test for the 't' ratio of 0.912 (0.104/0.114). As the degrees of freedom are effectively infinity due to the large samples then the critical values are 1.96 for the two-tailed case and 1.645 for the one-tailed case. The estimated 't' ratios fall well below these critical values and thus would be deemed to be statistically insignificant.

Comparing these two studies shows the flexibility of the basic regression model. The same theoretical underpinning is used with the same functional form. Yet, the focus variables in the two studies are entirely different and the variation in the construction of the sample data means that the models have different specifications in terms of the list of independent variables. If you read the original articles carefully, you will notice that the authors' main interest is in the magnitude and statistical significance of the coefficients, with relatively little concern being shown about the size of the goodness of fit statistic.

Finally, we may note that some anomalous results do appear here, showing that the major economics journals do not just promote the 'data mining' of entirely confirmatory results.

7.7 ANOTHER USE FOR DUMMIES: FORECAST EVALUATIONS

In Chapter 5 we briefly described the use of OLS regression equations to predict or forecast the 'out of sample' values of their dependent variables. One problem we encountered was the development of forecasting test statistics. It so happens that dummy variables provide an additional type of test. The most easily understood case is the time-series model where we wish to hold back some data from the end in order to test the validity of the model by looking at its forecasting power. Let us assume that we have 40 years of annual data and we are holding back the last 10 years. Following the approach of Chapter 5, we would restrict our sample for estimation to observations 1–30 and then generate predictions of observations 31–40, which would give us forecast errors to input into the calculation of forecast evaluation statistics.

The dummy variable approach is very different in terms of its mechanics. We do not restrict the sample. Instead, we run the regression on all 40 observations. However, we must include a number of year dummies, which is exactly equal to the number of forecast periods. Let us suppose the last 10 years of the sample are 1991–99. We would then create a dummy for each year, which is equal to 1 only in the year after which it is named and is zero in all other years. This forces the last 10 years of data to be excluded from the computer algorithm that is calculating the coefficient estimates. The value of each year dummy will be an estimate of the forecast error for that year. The standard error of the coefficients will be the estimated standard error of the forecast error. The default 't' test will be a test of whether the forecast error for a particular year is significantly different from zero.

An example of the use of this technique is shown in Table 7.2, which again uses the data

Table 7.2 Use of dummy variables for estimation and evaluation of forecasts, cigarette smoking in Turkey 1960–1988			
Regressor	Coefficient	Standard Error	T-Ratio[Prob]
INT	1.4142	.10911	12.9613[.000]
GNP	.4166E-3	.5812E-4	7.1682[.000]
RPC	−.43198	.11587	3.7281[.001]
TER	.34421	1.7318	0.19876[.844]
D84	−.40804	.083367	−4.8945[.000]
D85	−.30136	.095011	−3.1718[.005]
D86	−.57940	.084984	−6.8178[.000]
D87	−.36282	.10305	−3.5208[.002]
D88	−.034994	.19303	−0.18128[.858]

Joint test of zero restrictions on the coefficients of additional variables:
F Statistic $F(5, 20) = 16.5722[.000]$

for the smoking demand equation that was used in Chapters 3, 5 and 6. The estimating equation is:

$$CCA = b_0 + b_1 GNP + b_2 RPC + b_3 TER + b_4 D84 + b_5 D85 + b_6 D86 + b_7 D87$$
$$+ b_8 D88 + u \tag{7.18}$$

where $D84 = 0$ except for 1984, $D85 = 0$ except for 1985 and so on.

I have reproduced a computer table from a version of Microfit rather than rearranging it into a journal article type table. This shows the critical significance values as the Prob in brackets after the 't' ratio, meaning there is no need to look up 't' tables so long as you are only interested in the null hypothesis of the coefficients being equal to 0.

This is the same linear formulation as estimated in Chapter 5, but the dummies for 1984–88 mean that the parameters for the rest of the model are equivalent to estimating the model using only the 1960–83 data. The table shows computer output with critical significance levels for the individual coefficients and also for the 'F' test on the addition of the five dummies. Each year dummy except 1988 is statistically significant and negative, indicating that the model is systematically under predicting outside of the 1960–83 sample period. The 'F' statistic on adding these five dummies is highly significant, which also suggests a weak forecasting perform-ance of the 1960–83 equation over the 1984–88 period.

This is only an illustration of the technique. The results shown do not tell us how well the model estimated in Chapter 3 would predict, as that would require collecting more data to add to the end of the sample. You should note that the parameter estimates and significance tests differ between Table 3.1 and Table 7.2 for the simple reason that the former is a longer sample of the same data than the latter.

7.8 TIME TRENDS

The time pattern of data causes great complexities for statistical analysis to the extent where a whole new body of econometrics has grown up in the last 15 years or so to deal with this. The problems caused by data having a historical component are explored in Chapter 14. For the moment, we deal only with the very simple approach of adding a time trend to an OLS regression model. We can relate the addition of a trend to the properties of the intercept. Let us say we are investigating a situation where we have good prior reason to suppose that a function is shifting, over time, due to factors other than those we are able to capture in the model we have specified. This could be represented as a repeated movement of the intercept. This suggests that we could include a dummy for each shift of the intercept. However, this would mean that we would totally run out of degrees of freedom and hence be unable to estimate the equation at all. A compromise to overcome this is to assume the shift is the same in each year. This implies a restriction that each year dummy would have exactly the same coefficient. For a linear equation, this involves simply adding a new 'artificial' variable (which we might call T) to the equation. The series for the T variable must have the property of increasing by the same constant amount each period. This is therefore a linear trend.

This gives us the model:

$$Y_t = b_0 + b_1 X_t + b_2 T_t + u_t \tag{7.19}$$

assuming a simple bivariate linear model with a classical disturbance term.

We can let T be the sequence 1, 2, 3 ... up to the value of N into the data spreadsheet or via a batch entry. This will mean that the coefficient on T is an estimate of the amount by which the function is shifting in each period. It can of course be positive or negative depending on whether the function is shifting upwards or downwards. The default 't' test indicates whether or not there is a significant trend, but if you have a prior hypothesis that a trend should be in one particular direction then you need to conduct a one-tailed test. You could use any series which rises by a constant amount. In the early days of econometric packages, researchers sometimes used the variable showing which year the observation was or just the last two digits if the data only spanned one century. This will give exactly the same results for a linear equation as using 1, 2, 3 ... N in the T variable. If a series which incremented by 100 was used then the coefficient would need to be multiplied by 100 to get the annual change. If you skip forward to Table 9.4 in Chapter 9, you can see a simple example of a linear time trend using data on the sales of zip fasteners.

The coefficient is the annual change in the dependent variable holding constant the influence of the other variables. It is not the rate of growth of the dependent variable. This can be obtained using the following particular non-linear formulation of the time trend:

$$Y_t = e^{b_0 + b_1 T_t + u_t} \tag{7.20}$$

which transforms to

$$\log_e Y_t = b_0 + b_1 T_t + u_t \tag{7.21}$$

where b_1 will be the compound growth rate of Y. This is not an econometric model as such, it is purely an alternative means of calculating compound growth rates. If we add some independent variables, it becomes an econometric model in which we might choose to experiment by transforming the T term itself by adding T squared or replacing T with $1/T$ and so on. As an aside, we should just note that non-linear trend models will not be invariant to the choice of index units for the T variable. The estimated coefficients will change, in such cases, if we were to switch from using 1, 2, 3 ... N to using, say, 1965–99 if that was the span of a set of annual data.

There have been two main reasons why time trends have been added to OLS regression equations:

(i)   To act as a proxy for some unmeasured variable, which might be thought to have a trend component such as productivity growth. This does not seem a very convincing idea as the coefficient on T will reflect unmeasured trend influences in variables other than the one it is being taken to reflect. This observation leads on to:

(ii) To control for 'common trends' in a group of variables which may be producing a 'spurious' relationship in the sense of there being a misleadingly high R squared and apparently statistically significant relationships between variables that would vanish if the common trend was taken out. Thus the inclusion of T will result in a relationship where the other coefficients represent the degree of association between deviations of the variables from trend rather than absolute levels. This type of approach was quite common in economics journals in the 1960s and 1970s.

The simple approach of adding a time trend to an OLS equation estimated on time-series data to take account of the presence of a common trend in the data is now not used. Instead, the more sophisticated methods of Chapter 14 are employed, but the development of these requires knowledge of the time trend variable concept so you may like to revisit this section when you begin that chapter.

7.9 ANOTHER USE FOR DUMMIES: SPLINE FUNCTIONS TO PRODUCE NON–LINEARITY

In Chapter 6 we looked at the use of quadratics to approximate such things as the U-shaped average cost function found in microeconomics textbooks. As noted there, the quadratic function is limited in that it imposes symmetry on the non-monotonic pattern. We can overcome this using spline functions. To understand this idea, you need to begin by noting that one possible approach to non-linearity is to allow a function to be disjointed in that it could be divided into several different linear (there is no reason why they should not be non-linear) segments which are not identical, as shown in Figure 7.4.

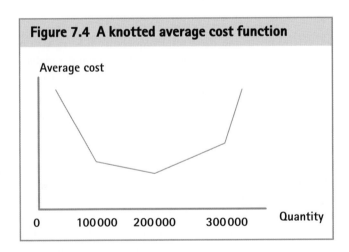

Figure 7.4 A knotted average cost function

Average cost

| 0 | 100 000 | 200 000 | 300 000 | Quantity |

Figure 7.4 shows an average cost function that is not symmetrical. Up to 100 000 units of output it has increasing returns. From 100 000 to 200 000 units it still has increasing returns, while at 200 000 units it begins to have decreasing returns. We could estimate the function shown in this graph by dividing the sample at the points where the separate functions join, and running four separate regressions. The levels of output, 100 000, 200 000 and 300 000, are called **knots**. In the spline function approach, we create dummies to represent the segments. So, here there can be three such dummies: D_1 will be 1 up to 100 000 units and zero above this; D_2 will be 1 between 100 000 and 200 000 units but zero elsewhere; and D_3 will be 1 at 200 000–300 000 units and above but zero elsewhere and so on. Due to the dummy variable

trap, we only need to use three of these, so let us assume that D_1 is dropped. This makes the estimating equation for the spline function approach to the average cost function:

$$Q = b_0 + b_1 Q + b_2 D_2 (Q - 100\,000) + b_3 D_3 (Q - 200\,000) + b_4 D_4 (Q - 300\,000) + u$$

(7.22)

An 'F' test on the null:

$$H_0: \quad b_2 = b_3 \quad b_3 = \varnothing$$

(7.23)

can be used to test the hypothesis that returns to scale do not vary along the range of output, that is, they are always determined by b_1 if the null holds. The individual 't' tests on the b_2 and b_3 will establish whether there are significant differences over these ranges. As with the case of slope dummies this involves the use of dummy variables in an interaction term.

There is a disadvantage to this method in that we have to make a prior decision as to where to locate the knots. It is very unlikely, however, that we would often have clear prior knowledge of where to make such splits in the sample. This means that we would need to explore the data by shifting the knots, making sure that we do not present the results of this in such a way that we might be found guilty of data mining.

7.10 CONCLUSION

This chapter completes the range of extensions to the basic single-equation OLS regression model. Its main objective was to introduce and clarify the use of binary $(0-1)$ dummy variables on the right-hand side of a regression equation. The next chapter goes on to consider the situation where the left-hand side (the 'independent' variable) is a dummy. Research papers are full of examples of dummy variables being used, particularly in cases where individual survey data, of households or firms, is being used. Some topic areas are heavily dependent on the use of dummy variables. For example, the growing field of Sports Economics features studies of attendance at many sports around the world, which invariably use dummies to look at such things as the effect of 'star players' and the knowledge that the same match will be broadcast on television. The simple shift dummy approach is often used in discrimination studies. That is, simple shift dummies for race/ethnicity (as in the Hamermesh and Biddle study above) and/or sex/gender are included. This is of course a highly restrictive approach as it ignores the possibility of differences in the other parameters, which would require the use of slope dummies or separate sample estimation (as is done in Hamermesh and Biddle for men and women). We also looked at the use of time trends in this chapter. The most important thing to remember about both of these is that they are in a sense 'artificial' variables and as such will run the risk of picking up specification errors from omitted variables. That is, there is a subtle danger from the linguistic habit of calling something a *SEX* dummy, of forgetting that it is not measuring sex as such and may just reflect things associated with sex.

DOS AND DON'TS

Do

✔ Make sure your dummy variables are correctly labelled with a sensible name.

✔ Make sure any newly created dummy variables are saved to your updated data file on exiting your computer package so that you are spared the effort of creating them again.

✔ Treat your dummy or trend variables just like other variables for the purposes of calculating degrees of freedom and performing hypothesis tests.

✔ State clearly in any report, or article, you write what the 'reference group' represented by the intercept is, particularly if you feel the need to, or are forced to, shorten your results table by not including all the coefficients in your report.

Don't

✘ Fall into the dummy variable trap. You must omit one dummy from each set of possible dummies if your equation already contains an intercept.

✘ Forget to adjust the interpretation of the estimate of the coefficient by taking account of the units of measurement of the dependent variable.

✘ Forget that if the dependent variable is in logarithms then all dummy variable coefficients are biased. The full explanation and attempted correction of this is given in a note by Halvorsen and Palmquist (1980).

✘ Forget that the dummy variable coefficient may represent the effect of omitted variables, which are associated with the dummy categories. This has proved an important source of assistance when so-called 'forensic economists' have been called to US courts as expert witnesses in court cases deliberating on sex and race discrimination and compensation claims on other matters.

✘ Read too much into estimates on the coefficients of a time trend or dummy. It is always better if accurate measures of the underlying variables which are being proxied can be obtained and used instead.

EXERCISES

As this chapter concludes the introductory part of the book, we have two sets of questions here. The first are on the topics in this chapter, and are in the same style as those in the other chapters. These are then followed by Study Questions which are directly concerned with a one-page article, which is reproduced for your convenience. There are more sets of one-page articles and associated questions suitable for this stage of learning. These can be found on the book website.

7.1 (i) Explain which dummies you would construct for the following situation: You are studying the impact of the presence of children on household expenditure on alcohol. You know how many children there are and whether they are under 5 years old or under 16 years old and there is a large range of other variables such as age of respondent, education, income etc.

(ii) Explain how you would interpret the coefficients on the dummies which you have just selected.

7.2 Check your answer to 7.1 and see whether you have avoided the dummy variable trap. If you are convinced that you have, explain why this is the case.

7.3 Still with question 7.1, let us imagine you have been told to make a dummy for children's age effects (we now assume we have full data on this) where the value is 1 up to age 5 and decreases in steps of 0.1. Explain how you would interpret the results on this dummy.

7.4 Using the THEATRE.XLS data set, re-estimate the equation shown in Table 4.4 using
(i) a simple shift dummy for *LEEDS*;
(ii) a slope dummy for *LEEDS* for each of the five independent variables.
  Explain the differences between these two sets of results.

7.5 Give a brief discussion of the following statements:
(i)   OLS equations will never be much use for forecasting because it is unreasonable to assume that the future will be like the past.
(ii) OLS equations will never be much use for forecasting because it is very difficult to get data on the future values of the independent variables so these have to be forecasted, which only makes things worse.
(iii) Although the above are true, you can still use OLS very successfully for evaluation of a model by holding back some data to do forecasts.
(iv) The dummy variable technique is the best way to do forecast evaluation of a model.

7.6. Using the data from the file ZIPS.XLS, estimate the following models and interpret your results:
(i) $ZIPSOLD_t = b_0 + b_1 T_t + u_i$
(ii) $\mathrm{Log}_e(ZIPSOLD_t) = b_0 + b_1 T_t + u_i$
  You can compare the answer for (i) with the results in Table 9.4 in Chapter 9.

STUDY QUESTIONS

Read the following article and answer the questions that follow.

Anthology
Savings and Loan Failure Rate Impact of the FDICIA of 1991
Christina L. Cebula, Richard J. Cebula, and Richard Austin
Georgia Institute of Technology

Not since the years of the Great Depression have the regulatory authorities closed so many Savings and Loans (S&Ls) as they did during the 1980s and early 1990s. From 1942 through 1979, few S&Ls failed due to insolvency. However, beginning with 1980 and 1981, the number of S&L failures rose sharply, reaching 205 in 1988, 315 in 1990, and 232 in 1991. Congress passed the Federal Deposit Insurance Corporation Improvement Act (FDICIA) 1991. This legislation authorized the Federal Deposit Insurance Corporation (FDIC), for the first time in its history, to charge higher deposit insurance premiums to S&Ls posing greater risk to the Savings Association Insurance Fund. The FDICIA added a requirement for 'prompt corrective action' when an insured S&L's capital falls below prescribed levels. The FDICIA included other provisions as well, such as new real estate lending guidelines and restrictions on the use of brokered deposits [FDIC, 1992 Annual Report, pp. 22–3]. Simultaneously, interest rates dropped sharply in the early 1990s, "…leading to strengthened earnings and a significant decline in the number of problem institutions" [FDIC, 1992 Annual Report, pp. 22–3]. Meanwhile, S&L failures in 1992 fell to 69, followed by 39 in 1993, and 11 in 1994.

This note examines empirically whether the recent decline in S&L failures may be due solely to the recent sharp interest rate decline or to both lower interest rates and to the FDICIA provision as well as other factors. This note represents this legislation with a dummy variable ($DUMMY = 1$) for each of the years of the study period during which FDICIA provisions were implemented ($DUMMY = 0$ otherwise). The following OLS estimate using annual data for the 1965–94 period was generated:

$$SLF_t = -2.74 - 1.42\,DUMMY_t + 0.068\,FDIC_{t-2} - 1.33\,CAR_{t-2}$$
$$\;\;(-7.99)\qquad\quad(+7.65)\qquad\qquad(-3.23)$$

$$-\,0.65(MORT - COST)_{t-1},\quad R^2 = 0.85,\quad DW = 1.76,\quad F = 36.7$$
$$(-2.55)$$

where terms in parentheses are t-values; SLF_t = S&L failure rate (percent of S&Ls in year t that were closed or forced to merge with another institution); $DUMMY$ = a binary variable indicating those years when the FDICIA was being implemented; $FDIC_{t-2}$ = ceiling level of federal deposit insurance per account in year $t-2$ in 1987 dollars; CAR_{t-2} = the average S&L capital-to-asset ratio in year $t-2$ as a percent; and $(MORT - COST)_{t-1}$ = the average 30-year mortgage rate minus the average cost of funds at S&Ls, year $_{t-1}$, as a percent.

These preliminary results indicate that S&L failures over the 1965–94 period were an increasing function of federal deposit insurance coverage ceilings and a decreasing function of the capital-to-asset ratio and the excess of the mortgage rate over the cost of funds. In addition, after accounting for these factors, it appears that the FDICIA may have helped to reduce the S&L failure rate.

You have been provided with a one-page article by Cebula *et al.* in *Atlantic Economic Journal*, September 1996.

Please answer the following questions briefly.

1. What assumptions do the authors make about the *u* term in order to arrive at the conclusions in the final paragraph?

2. What functional form is used?

3. Is any justification given for this choice?

4. What statistic is missing for the intercept term?

5. What would you say are the main hypotheses being tested here?

6. What is the correct d.f. for the 't' tests?

7. Give a precise verbal explanation of the meaning of the coefficient on the *DUMMY* variable.

8. Does the negative intercept imply that the model is invalid on the grounds that negative business failures cannot occur?

9. Explain how you would calculate the elasticity for failure percentage with respect to the capital/asset ratio.

10. Interpret the R squared statistic.

11. Explain how you would calculate the forecasted percentage of failures in 1993.

12. The 'F' shown is the 'F for the equation'. Give the degrees of freedom for this test.

13. Is the 'F' ratio significant at the 5 per cent level?

14. Why do the authors conclude, in the final paragraph, that all four independent variables are statistically significant?

15. Test the hypothesis, at the 5 per cent level, that the (negative) impact of the FDICIA exceeds 1 percentage point.

16. Outline a method for testing the hypothesis that all of the coefficients differ between the periods 1965–78 and 1979–94.

17. If the logarithm of *SLF* had been used what would the interpretation of the coefficient on *DUMMY* become?

REFERENCES

Ashenfelter, O. and Kreuger, A. (1994) Estimates of the economic return to schooling from a new sample of twins, *American Economic Review*, **84**(5), December, 1158–1173.

Burke, A. (1994) The demand for vinyl LPs 1975–1988, *Journal of Cultural Economics*, **18**(1), 41–64.

Cameron, S. and Collins, A. (1997) Transactions costs and partnerships: The case of rock bands, *Journal of Economic Behavior and Organization*, **32**(2), 171–184.

Halvorsen, R. and Palmquist, R. (1980) The interpretation of dummy variables in semilogarithmic equations, *American Economic Review*, **70**(3), 474–475.

Hamermesh, D.S. and Biddle, J.E. (1994). Beauty and the labor market, *American Economic Review*, **84**(5), 1174–1194.

Mincer, J. (1958) Investment in human capital and personal income distribution, *Journal of Political Economy*, **66**, 281–302.

WEBLINK

http://www.paritech.com/education/technical/indicators/trend/

A wide range of ideas on how to analyse trends from financial analysis.

Predicting and Explaining Discrete Events: Logit and Probit Models

LEARNING OBJECTIVES

■ Be aware of the types of situations in which a limited dependent variable may be used

■ Understand the limitations of OLS applied to models with limited dependent variables

■ Be able to interpret the coefficients of the linear probability model, the logit model and the probit model

■ Be aware of the goodness of fit measures used for logit and probit models and their limitations

■ Be able to critically assess articles which use logit and probit models, especially with respect to the interpretation of coefficients

CHAPTER SUMMARY

8.1 INTRODUCTION

This chapter deals with the analysis of data where the dependent variable is categorical (in the simplest case a 0–1 dummy variable) rather than continuous. The use of these methods has grown enormously in the last 25 years to the point where they are now extremely common in many areas of economics.

Some microeconomic topic areas would be:

▶ modelling choice of trip mode in transport economics;
▶ attendance at cultural events;
▶ purchase of insurance.

Some macroeconomic topic areas are:

▶ whether or not an international lending organization has decided to reschedule debt payments from developing countries;
▶ whether a nation has passed new laws to prevent smuggling;
▶ whether a country has introduced wage control policies to curb inflation.

The next section develops the interpretation of this type of model using the technique of OLS as a background for introducing the more difficult (maximum likelihood) techniques of probit and logit models.

In the previous chapters we have steered clear of performing an OLS regression with anything other than scalar dependent variables, although the first example given in Chapter 5 did use a limited dependent variable (i.e. it could only range from 1 to 5). This is because the presence of limited interval data (counts) and categorical data, for the dependent variable, whether ordered or unordered violates the assumptions of the CLRM. In many situations, one may also wish to model the joint decisions of whether or not to participate in an activity and how much time, effort or resources to put into it. For example, any individual would have a probability at a point in time of purchasing a new car, CD player, exercise bike, or whatever, which is jointly determined with how much money they will spend when they do make a purchase. This is obviously a more complicated problem and is one which some research papers avoid in favour of looking only at the probability issue.

Sections 8.2–8.6 deal with the simplest possible situation where there are only two possible outcomes, or where the raw data have been regrouped into only two categories. Section 8.7 deals with the more complicated situation of three or more outcomes.

8.2 PREDICTING PROBABILITIES USING OLS

To get started, let us move straight into an example that should not be taken too seriously, because I use a very simple model and have arbitrarily split a continuous variable into 'high' and 'low'. The results are shown in Table 8.1. The correct name for this is a **linear probability model**. This equation seeks to predict which individuals will have had six or more sexual partners in their lifetime so far. The variables included may be taken to represent opportunity (for example, university education brings one into contact with a wide range of possible partners) and possibly assets that an individual may possess which increase their desirability as partners. The definition of the variables is given in Table 8.1.

Table 8.1 OLS estimates of a model to predict having had six or more sexual partners

Dependent variable (*NSP*) = 1 if had six or more sexual partners; 0 otherwise

Independent variables	Coefficients/(standard errors)
Constant	0.0885
	(3.05)
Female (*FD*)	−0.0911
(= 1 if female)	(14.98)
AGE	0.0076
	(4.78)
AGE squared	−0.000135
	(6.55)
Male height dummy (*MHD*)	−0.0393
(= 1 if < 66 inches tall)	(6.44)
Education dummies:	
OL	0.00194
(= 1 if had 'O' levels which are UK school leaving age	(0.28)
level qualifications)	
AL	0.0204
(= 1 if had 'A' levels which are typically taken at age	(2.74)
18 in the UK)	
D	0.0434
(= 1 if had university degree)	(4.23)
R^2	0.048
N	13206

Notes: *OL*, *AL* and *D* are 'exclusive' dummies as the dummy represents the highest level, i.e. no one will have a value of 1 for more than one of these dummies.
Absolute 't' ratios in parentheses.
Source: National Survey of Sexual Attitudes and Lifestyles conducted in the UK in 1990/91.

The construction of the set of variables shows the use of ideas from the previous chapters: apart from the age variable all the items are dummies (see Chapter 7) and the age variable is entered as a quadratic (see Chapter 6, Section 6.5). The data is taken from a CD-ROM provided by the ESRC Data Archive at the University of Essex, UK, containing the full results from the National Survey of Sexual Attitudes and Lifestyle conducted in the UK in 1990/1991. The estimating equation is:

$$NSP = b_0 + b_1 FD + b_2 AGE + b_3 AGE^2 + b_4 MHD + b_5 OL + b_6 AL + b_7 D + u \qquad (8.1)$$

where the subscripts have been omitted and the *u* term is the same classical disturbance term that we have assumed in earlier chapters using OLS estimation. The sample was restricted prior to estimation by excluding those who had never had sexual partners, or declined to answer, or gave a vague answer. The definitions of the variables are given in Table 8.1.

Splitting the number of partners, at six, to create a binary dependent variable is not necessarily the best way to model this type of behaviour. We would also expect to see a much larger collection of independent variables using a large sample survey. I have deliberately chosen a small number of variables so that it is easier to study the example. A more satisfactory model may be produced with a larger set of independent variables. To produce this regression, I had to exclude a number of people who chose not to answer the question or did not answer it fully. This may well produce a systematic bias in the parameter estimates if the characteristics of the non-respondents differ from those of the respondents.

Note that the dependent variable has been coded as 0 for less than six and 1 for six or more. It could have been coded the other way round without making any difference to the statistical significance of the findings. The coefficients would have to be interpreted differently. The R squared would also be different. Finally, it should be noted that a proper theoretical foundation for the estimates has not been developed. It is not clear what the relationship between demand and supply of partners is and I have omitted to relate the number of partners to any kind of utility function.

WHAT DO THE COEFFICIENTS MEAN?

In the case of a linear probability model, the coefficients are the **marginal probabilities,** which are constant. The case of AGE is slightly different as it has been made into a quadratic. The effects of AGE will be given by:

$$\delta NSP / \delta AGE = b_2 + 2b_3 AGE \tag{8.2}$$

which will obviously be rising in AGE if b_3 is greater than 0 and falling in AGE if b_3 is less than 0.

The results can be used to generate predictions of the probability of the event occurring. For the dummies, the coefficient is just the difference between the likelihood of having more or less sexual partners for the two groups holding the impact of the other variables constant; for example, the impact of being a smaller man is to reduce the chance of being in the 'more partners' group by 3.93 percentage points, other things being equal. Likewise, the chance of women being in the more partners group is 9.11 per cent points less than the chance of men being in this group.

As this is survey data, you should bear in mind that these estimates may reflect the impact of the variables on people's tendency to report the 'true' value. The education variables show a clear gradient, in that more education shows a higher addition to the likelihood of being in the more sexual partners group. The 'A' level coefficient is slightly above that for 'O' levels, with the degree level of education being much larger than these. The result for degrees implies an increase of 4.34 percentage points in the chance of being in the more sexual partners group. The age quadratic shows an inverted U-shaped pattern. That is, younger people are *more likely* to report having had more sexual partners up to some age where a decline in probability sets in. The turning point occurs at just over 28 years old (this was worked out using the formula given in the last chapter).

So far we have looked at two of the three S's – sign and size. So we need to move on to hypothesis tests to assess statistical significance. The 't' ratios shown in Table 8.1 indicate that the coefficients, except that for 'O' levels, are highly significant.

The current set of results shows a positive intercept; however, there are some negative predictions for the dependent variable. The most negative prediction that was found in these results was -0.06406. The negative prediction simply reflects the fact that a linear relationship may go outside the 0–1 interval. There were no cases for this sample where the predicted value went above 1.

PROBLEMS WITH THIS MODEL

Unrealistic specification of variables

An obvious problem with this model is that it does not seem a very realistic way to model probabilities in the vast majority of cases, particularly when continuous right-hand side variables are an important part of the model. For example, in a purchase decision model, it seems very unlikely that each additional unit of income makes the same marginal change to the probability of purchase. Admittedly, we can try to overcome this by using transformations on these variables, as has been done above with the age variable entering as a quadratic. We can also alter the 'constant impact' restriction by using interaction terms as introduced in Section 6.3 of Chapter 6.

Unrealistic predictions

The OLS model was not designed to model the problems of binary choice or classification. Look at Figure 8.2 below for an illustration of this. Given that the dependent variable has only two possible values (coded as 0 and 1) the regression line is forced to steer the best fitting course between these. This may give 'impossible' or 'unrealistic' results. As mentioned above, Table 8.1 generates a negative likelihood of having more than six partners for some persons.

The impossible results are negative predictions and predictions that are more likely than being absolutely certain – a predicted probability of greater than 1 in this case. Figures 8.1 and 8.2 suppose a different example than that of the data used in Table 8.1. Let us imagine we are modelling student choice over whether or not to buy a textbook for a course in microeconomic theory. To simplify matters we assume that buying two or more books is not an issue as none of the students is ever going to buy two textbooks. Let us also assume that the model contains only one independent variable, that is, the size of the student's grant. We further assume that apart from income all students have identical tastes and are identical in all other respects.

Figure 8.1 shows the relationship for individual students, while Figure 8.2 shows the relationship for the whole sample of students. Figure 8.1 represents four students who just cross the margin into buying a book at the levels of income Y_1^*, Y_2^*, Y_3^*, Y_4^* respectively. The students are labelled in increasing order of income. Each student has therefore a 'ratchet' shaped function in which the dependent variable is 0 until we reach the levels of income shown, then it suddenly becomes 1 but stays at 1 forever afterwards. Aggregating the data produces the situation shown in Figure 8.2 where we now assume there are more than four students.

In Figure 8.2, you can see that students with no textbook lie on the X-axis, which is where the value of their grant is shown. The students with a textbook all lie on the line where 1 is situated on the graph. This could quite readily produce the result that students with low or no

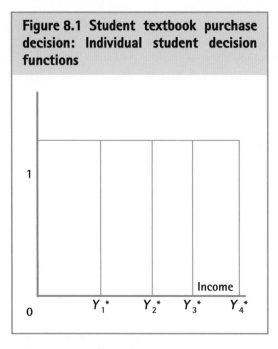

Figure 8.1 Student textbook purchase decision: Individual student decision functions

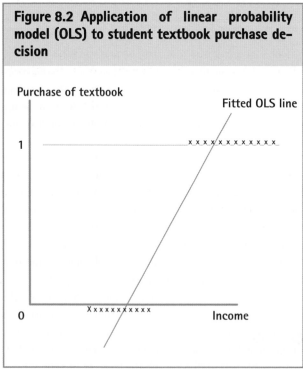

Figure 8.2 Application of linear probability model (OLS) to student textbook purchase decision

grants will buy negative textbooks, which is impossible, or that some will be more than likely to buy a textbook, which is equally impossible.

When this kind of problem arises in aggregate data we can get round it to an extent by a non-linear transformation of the dependent variable. This is not an option in the present case as there are only two values of the dependent variable (which are not 'real' measurements, but arbitrary codings of categories). Even if we took codings of 5 and 6 (to pick arbitrary numbers), so we could actually log them, this would not solve the problem, as we would just be rescaling the unit interval of the dependent variable.

Violation of classical assumptions

Because of the extremely limited nature of the dependent variable (it can only take two values) there will inevitably be a heteroscedastic error term in this kind of model. The general problem of heteroscedasticity will be dealt with in Chapters 9 and 11. One can perform a WLS (weighted least squares) estimate to 'correct' for the heteroscedasticity, but this is not particularly worthwhile as it makes more sense to go on to the probit and logit models in the rest of this chapter. This should not be taken to imply that heteroscedasticity cannot arise in those models, although we do not deal with this possibility in this chapter.

The R squared is meaningless

Using an OLS routine on a computer package will give an R squared. Table 8.1 shows this to be 0.048, but this cannot really be treated in the normal way because the dependent variable only varies between two states. You could in fact change the value of the R squared simply by reversing the coding of the dependent variable. It would not make sense to say that one coding was a better model than the other as the same variation (i.e. the distribution of outcomes between two categories) is being explained by the same set of independent variables.

Recall that the reason we use an R squared is because it is a 'goodness of fit' statistic which we use to get some indication of how well the specified relationship with the independent variables 'explains' the variation in the dependent variable. It is still true that adding variables will increase the R squared, but as explained in Chapter 6 we should not, in any case, be using this as a criterion for the inclusion or exclusion of variables.

How do we go about deciding on a goodness of fit measure in a case involving prediction of probabilities rather than predicting the values of continuous variables? Some kind of Chi-square test seems to suggest itself. To do this, we produce a contingency table by rounding the predicted values. That is, you forecast the dependent variable in the same way as explained in Section 6.6. If this is less than 0.5 we round it to 0 and if it is greater than 0.5 we round it to 1. The maximum prediction in this sample was 0.23887, which already indicates that the contingency table is going to look extremely skewed. For the record, Table 8.2 shows the contingency table.

Table 8.2 Contingency table for rounded predictions from Table 8.1

		Actual 0	Predicted 1
Predicted	0	11696	1510
	1	0	0

To perform a Chi-squared test, we need some figures to use to compute deviations between these outcomes and those under an alternative hypothesis that the model did not have any statistically significant ability to predict whether people do or do not have more than six partners. The alternate hypothesis requires us to use proportions taken from the original sample data prior to estimation, that is, the proportions based on assuming a 'naïve' model.

We seem to have found a way round the problem of not having a meaningful goodness of fit statistic but what is this result actually telling us? Our results from Table 8.1 have produced a distribution of predictions which is as polarized as can be imagined. The model is able to predict 100 per cent of the zero coded dependent variable (i.e. fewer sexual partners) accurately but 0 per cent of the other outcome. This is a dramatic illustration of the fact that you should not just report the overall percentage of cases correctly classified (as is occasionally done in articles using bivariate dependent variables). The issue of goodness of fit statistics is revisited after we have looked at the technically more correct modelling approach of probit and logit models.

8.3 SHOULD WE USE OLS TO EXPLAIN PROBABILITIES? THE ALTERNATIVES

The answer to this question is: probably not. The linear probability model has the advantage of being easy to use and interpret but most academic journals nowadays are unlikely to publish an article that mainly seeks to present a model based on this approach. When computer programs were less powerful and computing time was relatively expensive, OLS might have been more acceptable but the rapid technological advance and cost falls in computing have led to an increased emphasis on the use of more sophisticated models. One reason for this is that the use of a linear probability model may lead to incorrect inferences. In the worst possible case, Type I or Type II errors (wrongly reject or accept null hypotheses) may be committed more often than with the 'correct' model, to which I now turn.

How different the results of different techniques applied to modelling categorical variables will be depends on the data set being used. The more skewed the dependent variable is (i.e. the further from a 50–50 split it is), the more problematic using the wrong technique will tend to be and the more different the results of using different models will be. This will be dramatically illustrated when we get to Table 8.4. It is probably worth pointing out at this stage that economists are not in the habit of trying to produce balanced or matched data across the categories to be predicted. That is, probabilistic modelling tends to be done on samples that have already been compiled for some other reason. Thus we might end up modelling a 0–1 dependent variable that is very heavily concentrated in one of the two outcomes. Some situations will tend to produce heavily skewed predictions by their very nature. For example, relatively few athletes win gold medals at major tournaments and most finance companies have a fairly small number of people who fail to meet their debt repayments in total.

DISCRIMINANT ANALYSIS

Discriminant analysis is still used quite frequently in some social sciences and is available on packages like SPSS. It seldom appears in economics research, although it is very closely related to the techniques (logit and probit) we are about to discuss although the calculations are not done in the same way. Most economists do not now use discriminant analysis as they prefer to use logit or probit. Given that it is little used in economics, I provide only a brief outline of its main features.

The model underlying a discriminant analysis is quite similar to a linear probability model as the function is assumed to be linear and it is estimated using regression methods. The procedure differs mainly in its underlying motive and the way the results are presented. The basic idea is to estimate a discriminant function such as (ignoring error terms):

$$D = d_1 Z_1 + d_2 Z_2 \dots + d_j Z_j \qquad (8.3)$$

where D represents a discriminant function 'score' formed from weighting coefficients (the d's) and the Z's are the X explanatory variables in standard deviation units. The d's will be forced to lie within the unit interval (i.e. between -1 and $+1$) because of the standardization of the explanatory variables. The package output will provide figures for, among other things, the group centroids and the canonical correlation. The canonical correlation is the 'goodness of fit' statistic which is interpreted in a similar manner to the R squared, although we may also have a goodness of fit statistic of the Chi-square type presented earlier (and later) in this chapter.

The results for the individual variables are similar to the beta coefficients that can be calculated from OLS regression. Being in standardized units they can be viewed in terms of their importance judged by size; that is, a figure near 1 means a variable has a major estimated influence on classification into either of the two groups.

The underlying idea is that we can use the differences between the two groups we are looking at to try to predict or 'discriminate' between the sample observations in the sense that we can classify the likely class membership of an observation chosen at random. The membership is based on a score from the function. This could, for example, be used by a finance company to assign applicants into the 'likely to repay' or 'likely to default' case.

The algorithms used in assigning a score to the likelihood of an observation being in one of the classification groups seek to maximize some statistical measure of 'distance' between the groups. It is based on a very restrictive assumption about the variance-covariance matrix of the two groups (that is, that they are equal) which makes it a less general model than logit or probit.

Although the underlying philosophy of discriminant analysis is one of classifying observations it is possible to apply a choice interpretation to the results. If we were to estimate the equivalent model of Table 8.1 using discriminant analysis, we could regard the exercise as one in which we are trying to find weights (coefficients) for the selected variables which maximize the success of the model in correctly attributing each person to the group in which they have declared themselves (i.e. 'more than six' or 'six or less' partners). This kind of view can be taken as largely a forecasting exercise in which there is no particular theoretical model of how people came to be in either of the two groups. The alternative is to model the membership of each group as a choice process. This interpretation could be applied to the discriminant function results, but we now go on to look at it in the context of logit and probit models.

LOGIT AND PROBIT MODELS

With modern low-cost, high-speed computing it has become easy to estimate these two models even on very large samples of individual survey data. If you skip to Section 8.6, you can see that one of our review studies estimates a probit equation on over 4000 individuals and it is not uncommon to see much larger samples than this being used as, for example, when we revisit the results just given in Table 8.1 in Table 8.3 using the same 13 206 individuals. The names of the models refer to the underlying probability distributions that lie behind their estimation. The term 'logit' (you will also find the term 'logistic regression' being used) comes from the use of a logistic distribution for the **cumulative distribution.** The name 'probit' comes from its use in the biometric literature where the assumption of a normal probability distribution for the u term was reduced to 'probit' rather than 'normit'.

Different assumptions about the distribution can give us entirely new models with different names but these two are generally sufficient for everyday research use. The logit follows the sigmoid curve shown in Figure 8.2. This has strong properties of the following type:

▶ It has a point of inflection at the probability of 0.5.
▶ It is symmetrical around this point.

The precise shape of the symmetrical relationship, around the 0.5 likelihood, will be determined by the properties of the data as shown in the estimated parameters we obtain from the routine on our package. For the probit, similar properties are obtained with the main exception being in the thickness of the tails and a higher density at the central point. There is no way of knowing whether a probit (or any alternative distribution assumption which we are not looking at here) is 'better' for the data we are analysing than the logit. Given the low-cost/ high-speed computing environment we now live in, it is perfectly feasible to estimate your model using both approaches and compare the results. In practice, many data sets will tend to give fairly similar conclusions. The published journal articles, which deal with simple bivariate dependent variable modelling, tend to give only one of these two and not both, as you shall see in the studies reviewed in Section 8.6.

In terms of understanding these functions it is useful to grasp two essential features that differ from the basic OLS regression model (as used in the linear probability model in the last section).

We are using a cumulative distribution

The specification and estimation of the model depends on whether we are using a cumulative logistic (logit) or cumulative (normal) probit model. The equation is estimated using maximum likelihood methods, which does not necessarily have to involve the use of OLS but many packages will use OLS to get starting values for the parameters. The cumulative distribution is shown in Figure 8.3, which would be derived from aggregating the set of individual 'step' or 'ratchet' functions in Figure 8.1. As we increase the level of income then the percentage of students purchasing a textbook rises and we could use this percentage figure as the left-hand side variable in Equation (8.5) *if* the data consisted of a series of groups in which the percentage purchasing could be observed.

Some data does come in this aggregated form; for example, if we only had figures on the percentage of married women working full-time by country and/or age group we could use this as the dependent variable. In such circumstances, modifications of OLS (log transformations, heteroscedastic 'corrections') can be used to derive appropriate estimators. We could of course do this with individual data by forming it into groups and this was done in the days when computing resources were scarce and computation was slow. In the current climate, one would

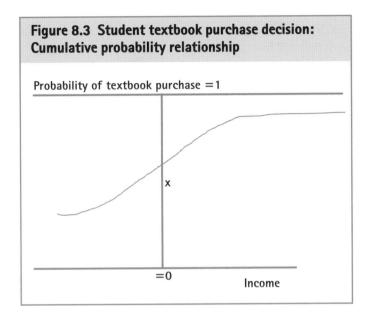

Figure 8.3 Student textbook purchase decision: Cumulative probability relationship

Probability of textbook purchase = 1

x

= 0

Income

never find economists suggesting that we should use grouped instead of individual data to model the cumulative distribution. Instead, logit and probit models are estimated by maximum likelihood methods on the individual observations.

It follows that we are not then going to be estimating directly the relationship between our explanatory variables but will instead use the following functions where P_i is the probability of the variable taking the value coded 1, that is a person reporting six or more sexual partners in our example. *exp* is exponential, that is, the base of the natural logarithm, and s is a standardized normal variable, that is, it has mean zero and variance of 1.

Probit: $\quad P_i = (1/\sqrt{2\pi}) \int_{-\infty}^{z_i} \exp - s^2 dS$ (8.4)

Logit: $\quad P_i = 1/[1 + \{\exp^{-z}\}]$ (8.5)

The term z represents the 'explanatory' part of the equation, that is, it is the right-hand side of Equation (8.1) above.

We are not now predicting the expected likelihood of the event (coded as 1)

In the case of the logit model we are predicting the log odds ratio: for our present problem we can define the log odds ratio as:

$\log [p(V)/(1 - p(V)]$ (8.6)

where V is the occurrence of an event – in this case having had more than six sexual partners. In the microeconomics textbook example in Figure 8.1, V would be the purchase of a textbook. The term shown in Equation (8.1) is what the coefficients from a set of logit or probit estimates are predicting. Thus, in the case of the example used in this chapter, we can represent the estimated model in the following form, although the specification used by the computer package to arrive at the coefficients is different from this.

$$\log\left[p(V)/(1 - p(V)\right] = b_0 + b_1\,FD + b_2\,AGE + b_3\,AGE^2 + b_4\,MHD + b_5\,OL$$
$$+ b_6\,AL + b_7\,D \tag{8.7}$$

where V is the probability of a person reporting as having had more than six partners.

The coefficients of the logit equation are thus the effects of a one-unit change in the independent variables on the log odds ratio.

8.4 THE RATIONALE FOR LOGIT AND PROBIT MODELS

The use of a logit or probit can be justified as simply an approximation to some 'true' but unknown probability distribution which is generating the observed outcomes. In other words, any distribution which can produce roughly the kind of shape shown in Figure 8.1 will do and the logit and probit happen to satisfy this requirement. This is a purely statistical solution.

We can also provide an economic explanation in terms of the estimating equation being an approximation to a **random utility model**. Suppose an individual is choosing whether or not to migrate to a different region or country. Each of these states is likely to have a different utility level. In a world of perfect certainty the individual will choose the situation that yields the highest utility, all other things being equal. It is sometimes argued that we can compute the difference between the two states as a measure of utility which will vary as the values of variables influencing the choice change.

In these models, we are dealing with the cumulative likelihood of an observation belonging to a particular group. Take the case of the textbook-buying example shown in Figure 8.1. Owning a textbook brings more utility than not owning one, other things being equal. As the student grant rises, assuming textbooks are a normal good, we would expect to find the probability of purchase to rise and the log odds ratio to rise. One way of conceptualizing this is to think of individuals as having a 'threshold function' that underlies the choice process. This can be written as Equation (8.8):

$$Z = f(G) \tag{8.8}$$

where G is grant and Z is an index of the strength of intention to buy a textbook and:

$$B = 1 \quad \text{if } Z > Z^*$$
$$B = 0 \quad \text{if } Z < Z^* \tag{8.9}$$

We regard book buying (B) as the measured impact of the unmeasurable variable (Z) which is generating it. Only when the strength of intention to buy exceeds the threshold level (Z^*) do we observe the individual buying a book. The index can continue to rise beyond this level but the observed value of the dependent variable, in the model, cannot change by definition (we are assuming no one is prepared to buy more than one textbook in order to simplify matters). The same situation applies at the other end of the distribution. That is, as G falls and the value of Z

falls below Z^* we observe a non-purchase but, by definition, further falls in G cannot lead to any declines in the dependent variable which match the declines in the Z value.

The representation of the model, in Equations (8.8) and (8.9), is equivalent to the graphical presentation in Figure 8.1 where the Υ^* (i.e. the income level at which an individual decides to buy) corresponds to the Z index, as this simple example is one with a single independent variable.

In the number of sexual partners example, which we are estimating in this chapter, the equivalent of Z, is the strength of sexual desire of the individuals in the sample. The same sort of argument would apply because we have forced the observed dependent variable to be either 0 or 1. In that example we could resort to modelling the full range of the dependent variable if we wished. There may be situations where the dependent variable is truncated and we can do nothing about it. That is, we might only be able to obtain data on categories, the extreme case being two categories.

The index function (Z) in Equation (8.5) can be regarded as linked to the level of utility the person experiences. Modern economics does not accept the notion of cardinal utility.

8.5 BASIC USE AND INTERPRETATION OF LOGIT AND PROBIT MODELS

We now show how to use probit and logit models by re-estimating the equation, estimated by OLS in Table 8.1, using probit and logit techniques. This is done in Table 8.3. These results have been obtained by using a maximum likelihood routine, which provides the appropriate standard errors for the coefficients.

So what do the results in Table 8.3 mean? If our major interest is in the coefficients themselves (the three S's of size, sign and significance), rather than prediction for its own sake,

Table 8.3 Logit and probit estimates of a model of having six or more sexual partners

Dependent variable $(NSP) = 1$ if had more than six sexual partners so far; $= 0$ otherwise

Estimation method	Logit	Probit
Independent variables		
Constant	−2.792	−0.088
	(0.311)	(3.048)
Female (FD)	−0.983	−0.0911
(= 1 if female)	(0.069)	(0.00608)
AGE	0.1	0.0076
	(0.018)	(0.0016)
AGE squared	−0.002	−0.000135
	(0.00024)	(0.0000207)
Male height dummy (MHD)	−0.439	−0.0393
(= 1 if < 66 inches tall)	(0.0068)	(0.0061)

Table 8.3   (continued)

Estimation method	Logit	Probit
Education dummies:		
OL	0.059	0.00194
(= 1 if had 'O' levels which are UK school leaving age level qualifications)	(0.079)	(0.00704)
AL	0.221	0.0204
(= 1 if had 'A' levels which are typically taken at age 18 in the UK)	(0.079)	(0.00745)
D	0.384	0.0434
(= 1 if had university degree)	(0.098)	(0.0103)
N	13206	13206

Note: Standard errors are in parentheses.
Source: National Survey of Sexual Attitudes and Lifestyles conducted in the UK in 1990/91. This data has been used by permission of the ESRC.

then we must be careful not to fall into the trap of interpreting the results 'as if' they came from a linear OLS, or even a logarithmic OLS regression.

WHAT THE PROBIT AND LOGIT COEFFICIENTS DO *NOT* MEAN

Before we go on it should be made clear that logit and probit coefficients are:

▲**not** the marginal impacts of the variables on the probability of the event coded 1 (in this case sex with more than six partners) and for dummy variables this means they are not the, *ceteris paribus*, differences in probability between the two groups in the dummy.
▲**not** elasticities. In fact, it is not meaningful to calculate the elasticity from this kind of technique in the way we have become accustomed to from Section 6.2. Instead of this, computer packages tend to report a 'quasi-elasticity' which we will come to shortly.
▲**not** in the same units as each other. We cannot make a direct comparison between the two sets of results in Table 8.3. This requires you to look at Table 8.4 below.

Let us follow the principle of the three S's for the results in Table 8.3. The sign of the coefficients can be treated in the same way as in the OLS model, so looking at Table 8.1 and Table 8.3 we can see the same sign results in each case. The significance can be assessed using 't' tests in the usual way so the OLS and probit and logit models can easily be compared, although some packages may present different test statistics. Both tables show agreement in the significance of the coefficients.

Things are less simple when we come to the magnitude issue. It is not possible to compare any pair of the three sets of results in Tables 8.1 and 8.3 directly, although methods have been derived of approximating one set of results from the other. One common approximation that has been suggested is that *all* the coefficients in a logit model can be rescaled according to the following formula:

$$0.625\hat{b}^{L} = \hat{b}^{p*} \tag{8.10}$$

where the L superscript stands for the logit model and the p* superscript stands for the estimates of a probit model derived by rescaling the logit model results.

A further formula has been proposed:

$$\hat{b}^{p*} = 2.5\hat{b}^{OLS} + \hat{b}_0{}^{OLS} - 1.25 \tag{8.11}$$

where the OLS superscript represents OLS estimates and the 0 subscript represents the intercept of the equation from which the coefficient is taken.

This process of scaling the coefficients to be comparable with the probit result is generally traced to suggestions by Ameniya (1981). The rules derive from the assumptions made about the variances in the logit and probit models that the logit value is 1 and the probit is pi squared divided by 3. The 0.625 adjustment is not the same as this and was arrived at by Ameniya by trial and error. It is widely used in textbooks, although if one searches hard enough on the Internet you can find slightly different scaling factors suggested. Obviously there is no hard and fast scientific scaling rule – if there was we would only need to use OLS to get the point estimates for the other two models.

Table 8.4 shows the effect of scaling the OLS and logit coefficients, from Tables 8.1 and 8.3, to probit units.

Table 8.4 Scaled coefficients for the results in Tables 8.1 and 8.3 in probit units

	Logit	Probit	OLS
Constant	−1.745	−0.088	−1.1615
Female (FD) (= 1 if female)	−0.614	−0.0911	−0.2278
AGE	0.0625	0.0076	0.019
AGE squared	−0.00125	−0.000135	−0.000338
Male height dummy (MHD) (= 1 if < 66 inches tall)	−0.274	−0.0393	−0.0983
Education dummies:			
OL (= 1 if had 'O' levels which are UK school leaving age level qualifications)	0.0369	0.00194	0.00485
AL (= 1 if had 'A' levels which are typically taken at age 18 in the UK)	0.138	0.0204	0.051
D (= 1 if had university degree)	0.24	0.0434	0.1085
N	13206	13206	13206

These results differ quite dramatically in contrast to many books, which provide examples where the scaling produces similar results, leading to claims that it does not really matter much whether you use probit or logit estimation. The evidential basis of this claim is derived usually from quite small samples (which will therefore have few 'tail' observations) which are only moderately unbalanced. The sample we are using is very unbalanced, and large, which may account for the differences. They could also be due to the effects of omitting important variables but we do not pursue this here. Nevertheless these results do suggest that one should make some experiments with using probits and logits, in contrast to the common practice in journal articles of using one or the other.

Before we leave Table 8.4, it is advisable to be clear what it is saying. It uses the scaling factors to derive the probit estimates *implied* by the OLS and logit estimates. This is just one convention for comparison in terms of size. We could have scaled in the other two directions using the same factors, that is, convert probit and logit to OLS units or OLS and probit to logit units. Only one of these conversions would be capable of direct comparison and that is the OLS one because it has constant marginal effects that are equal to the coefficients. If we were to use the scaled OLS or scaled logits in Table 8.4 to generate measures of the size of the impact of variables then we have to use the appropriate formula for marginal impacts in a probit model.

Hopefully, the above is not too confusing as the presence of several different estimates for the same relationship is something we have encountered before, in Chapter 6, when we looked at the comparison between different functional forms.

Interpreting the coefficients in Table 8.3 (and by implication Table 8.4) cannot be done directly. This should not be too surprising as we have already faced this problem with non-linear models in Chapter 6. To understand the results, recall the definition of the log odds ratio above. In the first column of Table 8.3, the figure of -0.439 for the men of lower height dummy indicates that, holding the level of other variables constant, a man of lower height would have a log odds ratio of being a person with more than six sexual partners, which is -0.439 less than that of a man of greater stature other things being equal.

Anti-logging this figure to work out the impact on the likelihood of having many sexual partners would be pointless, because we need to know what values the other variables in the models are to be set at when we do the calculation. Given that male height has been treated as a dummy in this model, we could calculate male height effects under various assumptions. Given that the male height dummy cannot apply to females we can set $FD = 0$ in any such comparison.

WORKED EXAMPLE OF THE IMPACT OF MALE HEIGHT ON NUMBER OF SEXUAL PARTNERS

Let us assume that we are dealing with a person with second level education (A level) and we will work with two age assumptions, 25 years old and 40 years old. The calculation will only be done for the logit results as follows where the predicted values of the log odds ratios are :

$$\text{25-year-old man} = -2.792 + 0.221 + 0.1(25) - 0.002(625) = -1.321 \qquad \textbf{(8.12a)}$$

$$\text{25-year-old man of lower height} = -2.792 + 0.221 + 0.1(25) - 0.002(625)$$
$$- 0.439 = -1.76 \qquad \textbf{(8.12b)}$$

40-year-old man $= -2.792 + 0.221 + 0.1(40) - 0.002(1600) = -1.771$ **(8.12c)**

40-year-old man of lower height $= -2.792 + 0.221 + 0.1(40) - 0.002(1600)$

$$-0.439 = -2.21 \qquad \textbf{(8.12d)}$$

The anti-logs of the predictions with the predicted probabilities in brackets are respectively 0.2669 (0.211), (0.147), . . .(0.145) 0.1097 (0.0989). Thus, the fall in the probability of having more than six sexual partners for the 25-year-old man, of lesser height, would be 6.4 percentage points for a man of greater height of the same age. The same comparison for a 40-year-old man brings a fall of 4.61 percentage points. This is a smaller absolute fall (or rise if one does the comparison the other way round from the 25-year-old case) but it is related to a much smaller comparison probability. We have just made two estimates of the impact of *MHD* from one coefficient in a logit equation. The linear probability model estimated by OLS in Table 8.1 produced just one figure of a 3.93 percentage point drop due to *MHD*. Precisely this same figure would be produced whether the individuals were aged 25, 40 or any other age. The figure of 3.93 percentage points is smaller than the two figures (6.4 and 4.1) just obtained from the calculations above. However, this may well be reversed at different ages.

These calculations are quite interesting but many published studies also seek to provide summary statistics derived from the coefficients. There are two of these you might use and you will find that most econometrics packages are likely to produce these for you.

MARGINAL PROBABILITY EFFECT

The marginal probability effect is the percentage point change in the probability of the event (e.g. buying the book in Figure 8.1 or having more than six partners in the data used above) consequent on a one-unit change in the independent variable in question. Where the variable is a dummy this will be an estimate of the difference in percentage points between the two groups in the dummy. This measure is used in the juvenile delinquency study reviewed in Section 8.6. To produce this summary measure we have to make some assumption about the levels of the other independent variables. As with the elasticity measures presented in Section 6.2, the convention adopted is to evaluate at the sample means of the variables. For the results in Table 8.3 this would involve using the mean age from the sample to do a similar calculation to that shown above for the point impact of *MHD*. This time we would be multiplying the O level, A level and degree coefficients by the means for these variables. It would not make sense to include the female dummy in this particular case. Where there are many dummy variables in the model, it is questionable whether this type of summary statistic is useful. An example of this difficulty and further commentary on it is given in Section 8.6 below.

For the probit model, the marginal probability effect is more complicated to work out as it depends on evaluation of the density function of the standard normal variable. It will typically be available, for example in Limdep, as an option in packages which will evaluate the function at the means of the data.

The marginal effect, of both logit and probit models, will *ceteris paribus* change more rapidly at low values of an impact variable and more slowly at high values, although they will not give the same result.

Quasi-elasticity

The quasi-elasticity is the percentage point change in the probability of the choice being made from a one-percentage change in the independent variable concerned. Again this would require some assumption to be made about the values of the variables and, again, the convention is to assume they take the mean values. The comments about dummy variables, which will be expanded in Section 8.6, therefore need to be borne in mind. Leaving this problem aside, we could use the type of calculation above to work out the quasi-elasticity. That is, set the mean values, then work out the predicted log odds ratio and work back to the predicted probability of $Y = 1$. Then re-do the calculation with a one-percentage increase in the variable of interest to obtain the change in probability of $Y = 1$. The difference in the two predictions can then be converted to a percentage change. As mentioned above, you will probably find that your package gives the calculation for you.

GOODNESS OF FIT

By now, you should be familiar with the idea of using R squared as a 'goodness of fit' measure in the OLS model of the previous chapters. That statistic summarized the success of the independent variables in accounting for the variation in the dependent variable round its mean. This concept is hard to apply in the current situation because the dependent variable can only be 0 *or* 1. It cannot take any values in between, although the predictions will have to do so. An R squared was given in Table 8.1 for the linear probability model, but it is of little meaning. Logit and probit estimation routines do not usually produce a conventional R squared, although one could use the residuals, adjusted in various ways to compute an R squared. Instead, their goodness of fit measure from the estimation tends to be based on log likelihoods. Log likelihood measures are produced in OLS package routines also but, under the classical assumptions, the log likelihood is maximized when the SSR is minimized, so there will be little reason to consult these figures.

Log likelihood measures can be used in hypothesis tests in binomial dependent variable models, which are equivalent to the 'F' tests (for parameter restrictions) in the OLS regression model. They can also be turned into a **pseudo R squared** which some packages may give you and which you will see reported in some published papers. The term 'pseudo R squared', used by econometricians, implies that the measure is not a 'proper' or 'real' R squared in some sense. It appears to have entered the literature from the discussion in Cragg and Uhler (1970). They propose the following pseudo R squared:

$$\text{pseudo } R^2 = (L_{ur}^{2/n} - L_R^{2/n})/[(1 - L_R^{2/n})L_R^{2/n}] \tag{8.13}$$

where L is the log likelihood value from the probit or logit, with the subscripts R and ur representing restricted and unrestricted equations respectively. As this is an R squared test; the unrestricted model will be the one that has only an intercept.

McFadden (1974) proposed an alternative:

$$\text{McFadden Pseudo } R^2 = 1 - (\log L_{ur}/\log L_R) \tag{8.14}$$

The above measures are based on the improvement of fit due to the use of the variables that have been specified in the model. We can look instead at the predicted probability and the actual outcome, which has to be the whole number 1 or 0. The gap between these will determine the goodness of fit.

Given the nature of the data, it is easy to think of another way of judging fit. That is, if we were forced to use the model to predict categorically whether an observation would fall in one group or the other then we could compare this with the actual distribution of dependent variable observations. This could be summarized in the percentage 'hit rate' of successes. We have already encountered this approach for the linear probability model in Section 8.2. Predictions of 0's or 1's were made in that case by rounding up predicted values of the dependent variable of more than 0.5 to 1 and those of less than 0.5 to 0. In the case of logit and probit models, the dependent variable has to be converted back to a probability from the log odds ratio, although your computer package should do this for you, given suitable commands. In case you were wondering what the equivalent of Table 8.2 was for the logit and probit results in Table 8.3, they were exactly the same, that is all the '1' values were predicted incorrectly and all of the zero values were predicted correctly.

Once we do this, the following R squared can be calculated:

$$R^2 = (\text{number of correct predictions}/\text{total number of observations}) \qquad (8.15)$$

Unlike likelihood-based measures, this will have the 'true' R squared property of being bounded by 0 and an upper limit of 1. It could of course be 1 when the model does not fit perfectly, for example if the observations were to all give a predicted $Y = 1$ of over 0.5, but nowhere near 1 in every case. In the model of sexual partner choice, which we have been estimating, the R squared will simply be equal to the proportions of 0's and 1's in the dependent variable.

Although we have just spent some time on R squared measures for these kinds of models, they are of limited usefulness. They are unlikely to be useful in choosing between models in terms of the appropriate estimation technique or the variables selected. For these purposes, it is more appropriate to use likelihood ratio tests or other criteria such as the plausibility of the model. We would not, for example, choose between the linear probability model, the logit or probit functions on the basis of comparing the R squared values.

The reason we have dwelt on the use of R squared in these models is because computer packages produce them and articles report them. The situation, you may recall, is not that different in the OLS model with a continuous dependent variable (see Section 6.5) as the R squared is not a particularly useful measurement there either.

So far, we have only dealt with the simplest case of a two-category probability model, that is, one of two possible events occurs for any given observation. The next section provides review studies that model such two-category probability models. The key elements of dealing with more complex models are dealt with in Section 8.7.

8.6 REVIEW STUDIES

The two studies in this section are on very disparate topics although both concern the possible long-run effects of adolescent behaviour. Amuedo-Dorantes and Mach (2002) look at drinking, smoking, and soft and hard drug consumption by young people, which may influence their consumption patterns and health status in later life. Charles Gray (1998) looks at the influence of specific types of education (art appreciation classes) on museum attendance in adult life. The two studies use some similar control variables and both find a statistically significant relationship for the coefficients of their focus variables. The results of both studies are potentially of great policy relevance. If the coefficients are reliable they could be used to suggest how much effect cultural education would have on the future demand for museums and how changes in family structure and punishment policy impact on young people's drug dealing and consumption.

We look first at the study of juvenile delinquency. From the viewpoint of the economic model of criminal and deviant behaviour as normally portrayed (see Sections 5.7 and 11.7), there would seem to be an anomaly as the punishment variables have significant positive coefficients indicating that punishment *increases* law-breaking behaviour rather than decreasing it. This does not seem particularly worrying to the authors, as it is not their primary focus. We could make two additional observations on this point:

(i)   There may be a non-monotonic relationship with punishment rather than the monotonic one used in the study by Amuedo-Dorantes and Mach.
(ii) The results on the punishment variables may represent 'taste' factors rather than 'price'/ opportunity cost effects, in that being punished may lead to an individual being labelled as a deviant and hence facing a change in their tastes as well as being more closely monitored by the authorities.

Although on very different topics, both papers highlight the problem of imposing theoretical economic models on survey data of individuals (as was also the case with the earnings functions studies reviewed in Section 7.6). In particular, many 'taste' variables are included that the economic model gives little guidance on as regards specification. This creates an area of considerable doubt around the stability of results as the size, sign and significance of the coefficients on the focus variables may be subject to change. I am not suggesting that the authors of these papers embarked on data mining to obtain their largely confirmatory results. This is quite common in published papers, as you can see from the representative selection summarized in the chapters of this book.

Neither of the papers gives us very clear guidance on the size of the relationships estimated, although the juvenile delinquency paper gives more evidence, in this regard, than the museum visits paper. Gray's museum visits paper does not make any attempt to comment on the size of the relationships he has estimated. Amuedo-Dorantes and Mach have converted their probit coefficients into what they call 'Probit marginal effects'. These are evaluated on the assumption that the variables are at their mean sample values. This is perhaps a reasonable approach, but we ought to give some thought to what it actually means in a model with many dummy variables (as is often the case in studies of survey data using probit and logit estimation).

To illustrate this further, let us look at a specific example from Amuedo-Dorantes and Mach's Table 2. The probit marginal effect of 'number of arrests' is 0.005 in the 'Sold hard drugs' equation, which is in the final column. The standard error is 0.002 and the presence of three asterisks indicates that it is significant at the 1 per cent level. This implies that the probability of a person with one more arrest selling hard drugs is 0.005 times greater than someone with the mean number of arrests (0.228). It seems that the evaluation is done at the full sample means for which one must look to the Appendix on p. 279. This allows us to learn that the impact of 0.005 is based on the assumptions (among others) that the person is 15.119 years old, is 0.506 per cent likely to be male, 0.246 likely to be black, 0.197 likely to be Hispanic, 0.713 likely to be living with a father figure and has a mother who is 0.245 per cent likely to have some college education. It is a little hard to make sense of this, as indeed is the concept of an increase of arrests from 0.228 to 1.228 for an individual. This highlights the difficulties of summarizing the results of probabilistic models. As suggested earlier in this chapter, the authors of this juvenile delinquency study could have resorted to evaluating impacts using different scenarios (i.e. whether someone is black/white, male/female etc.) rather than sample means.

Neither of these studies presents a quasi-elasticity measure nor do they construct any kind of scenario to evaluate the impact of a variable for a given type of person. You may readily find studies that do these things, but it is by no means uncommon to find logit and probit results being presented without much elaboration on the *economic* (as distinct from statistical) significance.

A final word on these two studies is perhaps necessary on the symbol superscripting of significance levels. Both display 10 per cent significance level rejection of the null as worthy of note. Given that these are fairly large sample surveys this might be judged quite a generous margin of error in hypothesis testing, although it should be pointed out that the authors rely on two-sided tests, meaning that, for directional hypothesis, the critical significance levels would be half those shown in the tables.

The Basic Facts

Authors: Catalina Amuedo-Dorantes and Traci Mach

Title: The Impact of Families on Juvenile Substance Abuse

Where Published: *Journal of Bioeconomics*, **4**(3) 2002, 269—282.

Reason for Study: To look at the effect of family composition (specifically the presence of a father figure) on juvenile participation in the consumption of alcohol, cigarettes, soft and hard drugs and in the sale of soft and hard drugs.

Conclusion Reached: 'The results underscore the importance of having a father figure in the household in deterring juvenile smoking, marijuana use and drug sale.'

How Did They Do It?

Data: National Longitudinal Study of Youth (NLSY) 1997.

Sample Size: 4127–4136 depending on estimate.

Technique: Bivariate probit model.

Dependent Variable: Seven 0–1 are used: three each for selling or buying drugs in general, marijuana or hard drugs and one for drinking alcohol. Cigarette and alcohol figures relate to the last month; drug figures relate to 'ever' apart from marijuana consumption, which is last month.

Focus Variables: Dummies for living with father figure, biological father, and biological mother and interaction terms made from these dummies. There are also dummies for whether a sibling is present and whether the sibling is involved in troublesome behaviour.

Control Variables: Dummies for male, black, Hispanic, plus measures of age, education, number of arrests, number of suspensions, income, plus seven variables whose results are not reported (parental education, household income, public school dummy, urban dummy, lives in metropolitan statistical area dummy, county level juvenile arrest).

Presentation

How Results Are Listed: It appears the figures in Tables 2 and 3 are not the coefficients but are 'Probit marginal effects' calculated at the mean values of the other explanatory variables.

Goodness of Fit: Chi-squared test and log likelihood ratio.

Tests: Standard significance tests on coefficients.

Diagnosis/Stability: Tables 2 and 3 show the model with and without the sibling dummies.

Anomalous Results: There are a number of insignificant coefficients. The main other result to notice are the significant positive coefficients on the punishment variables.

Student Reflection

Things To Look Out For: The evaluation of responses at the means of other variables in Tables 2 and 3 may be misleading on the impact of any given variable on some sub-groups in the sample.

Problems in Replication: This is based on a large sample survey which could be obtained on application to the providing body.

The Basic Facts

Authors: Charles M. Gray

Title: Hope for the Future? Early Exposure to the Arts and Adult Visits to Museums

Where Published: *Journal of Cultural Economics,* **22**(2–3) 1998, 87–98.

Reason for Study: To assess whether exposure to the arts in childhood and early adulthood is related to museum visits made in adulthood.

Conclusion Reached: Early exposure to the arts is related to adult consumption.

How Did They Do It?

Data: Survey of Participation in the Arts (SPA) in 1997 in the USA, conducted by a professional survey firm for the National Endowment for the Arts on a broadly representative sample of the US population.

Sample Size: 473–1469 depending on equation.

Technique: Logit described as logistic regression.

Dependent Variable: Art museum visits as a dummy variable = 1 if visited art museums in the last 12 months.

Focus Variables: Art lessons and art appreciation classes: whether had any and age at which took place (dummies for the ages: less than 12, 12–17, 18–24).

Control Variables: Gender, income level (low, moderate, high), education (high school, college, postgraduate), age, race (Black, Asian, Indian, Hispanic).

Presentation

How Results Are Listed: Logit coefficients are reported, with an 'a' superscript for being significant at 10 per cent on a two-tailed test, and 'b' superscript for being significant at 5 per cent on a two-tailed test. No other information is given. Results for museum visits and art appreciation classes, as the dependent variables are given side by side in Tables III and IV, although the columns are not headed with the name of the dependent variable.

Goodness of Fit: 2 log likelihood, per cent of cases correctly classified, plus a statistic described as 'goodness of fit', which is not explained. Given its magnitude (i.e. in hundreds and thousands), we can see that it is not a pseudo R squared of any type.

Tests: See above; only the 5 per cent and 10 per cent significance level two-tailed tests are used.

Diagnosis/Stability: None in particular.

Anomalous Results: Not particularly noticeable, although many control variables are not significant – for example, exposure to appreciation classes aged 12–17 is not significant, unlike that at ages 18–24 or less than 12.

Student Reflection

Things to Look Out For: The presentation of percentage of cases classified correctly is not very helpful as we really need to see the split between types of case correctly classified. Price was considered as a variable but was unavailable. The equations on p. 91 do not specify a disturbance term. The results are interpreted solely by looking at the 5 and 10 per cent significance levels and the signs of the coefficients. There is no calculation of the size of impact of the variables.

Problems in Replication: This is based on a national survey, which would require application to the originating organization. However, the set of variables is fairly basic and could be easily incorporated in a new survey of your own.

8.7 MORE COMPLEX PROBABILISTIC MODELS

This section does not derive or present models, which are more elaborate treatments of models involving discrete dependent variable elements. It simply indicates what some of the major models are and gives a brief guide to interpreting their results.

There are a large number of complex variations on the above type of model but they develop from two directions we can go in, to make the models used so far more complex. One is to assume that we are still dealing with a yes/no or either/or situation but that we also want to take account of the issue of how much of the activity is engaged in after a choice is made. Cigarette smoking is a good example of this. An individual faces the choice of whether or not to smoke and has a decision on how much to smoke once they have decided they will smoke. The other direction we can go in is to have more than two categories in the dependent variable. We shall discuss this case first as it follows more easily from the previous sections.

MULTINOMIAL MODELS

There are many situations where there may be more than two outcomes as the state of the variable being predicted. This may arise 'naturally' from the choices being modelled. Transport choice and television watching are a good example of this. An individual has many modes of travel, such as bus, own car, shared car, taxi, walking or cycling. Likewise, the person who has decided they want to watch some television has a finite number of types of programmes they could watch or in the extreme case of only having terrestrial non-digital television they will only have four or five channels to choose from. In other cases, the limitations of the data may impose a multinomial model on us. Studies of happiness based on surveys which ask people to rate their happiness on a scale (such as 1–5 or 1–10) are suddenly becoming quite popular in economics (see, for example, Blanchflower and Oswald (2000)). An OLS regression on such a scale could be carried out perhaps subject to a heteroscedastic correction (using WLS, as could be done with the binomial case), but if the scale is narrow (e.g. only three outcomes) a multinomial probit or logit model can be used.

The multinomial models can be split into two categories. The outcomes may be either unordered or ordered multinomial outcomes but they can also be nested or non-nested. A nested model involves a decision tree of some sort. For example, a person may be deciding whether to choose public or private transport in the first instance. In the public transport 'branch' of the tree they may then face a choice between bus, train or licensed taxi, while in the private branch they may face the choice between their own car or a shared car in a car pool. Modelling happiness clearly implies the need to use an ordered model as the categories are based on answers, which convey ranking information. The simplest case would be 1 = unhappy, 2 = neutral, 3 = happy. The answer labelled 3 is preferable to 2, which is preferable to 1.

The simplest type of model to apply is the unordered model. In such a model, we will have more than one log odds ratio to predict. In the case of a three-outcome model there will be a log odds ratio for case 3 over case 1, case 3 over case 2 and case 0 over case 1. Estimation of such models actually works, with reference to a base category. We would need to tell the package which of the three outcomes is our base category and it would then (typically) begin by estimating LPM using OLS of the models for each of the other categories against the base to use as starting values. These starting values would be used to initiate a maximization algorithm that stops when there is convergence of the parameter estimates. The computer output from a multinomial model is a set of parameter estimates equal to the number of categories in the dependent variable minus 1. This will *not* be the complete set of pairwise log odds ratio comparisons. The complete number in this case is 4 and this rises as the number of cases increases. It would be possible to use the C−1 set of results to estimate all the other pairwise coefficients. This is not particularly helpful to the reader if you present your results in this way. It is simpler to estimate your model again, with the base category changed so that the other pairwise results will emerge.

JOINT PROBABILITY – PARTICIPATION RATE MODELS

The earlier chapters of this book dealt with the continuous dependent variable case, while this one deals with the categorical case. Many situations would seem to require both. For example, whether or not to be a criminal and how many crimes to perform, whether or not to buy a car and how much to spend, whether or not a woman will return to work after a break due to childbirth and how many hours she would opt to work for and so on. Indeed, the studies reviewed in Section 8.6 could have (although they did not) gone down this route – the logit equations for drug dealing and the consumption of alcohol, drug and cigarette consumption could have delved into the issue of how much of these activities is engaged in.

The simplest approach to this would be to estimate two separate OLS equations where identical variables appear on the right-hand side. Let us assume there are just three of these: X_1, X_2 and X_3

$$Py = b_0 + b_1 X_1 + b_2 X_2 + b_3 X_3 + u \tag{8.16}$$

$$Y = z_0 + z_1 X_1 + z_2 X_2 + z_3 X_3 + v \tag{8.17}$$

where Py is the dummy variable for any of the activity Y arising, for example a student deciding to buy textbooks (or a married woman deciding to work or an individual deciding to smoke cigarettes) and Y is the level of involvement (spending, hours of work etc.) having decided to enter the activity. The u and v terms are the disturbance terms and the observation subscripts have been dropped.

Let us call this method of estimating both equations by OLS our first 'naïve strategy'. We have seen that there are problems with Equation (8.16) given the nature of the variable being predicted. So, we might progress to estimating this equation by logit or probit and present this along with OLS estimates of Equation (8.17) as the results of our research. Unfortunately, this is not usually seen as an adequate approach because of problems of selectivity bias in Equation (8.17). We can term this a joint probability-participation model. Equation (8.16) models the probability of criminality, car purchase, book buying or whatever and (8.17) the amount of participation in these things. The second 'naïve' strategy just suggested above ignores the problem of the relationship between the two decisions. If the decisions are related then this will be reflected in the covariance of the error terms [cov(u, v)] being non-zero. Estimating two equations separately by OLS and logit or probit implicitly adopts the assumption that cov(u, v) = 0.

We now look briefly at the two major basic alternatives to our naïve approaches: the Tobit and Heckit models.

TOBIT MODEL

James Tobin developed the Tobit model for the car purchasing decision in 1958. Alternative estimation strategies, to the two naïve approaches given above, require us to take into account the linkage between the two decisions. The simplest approach to this problem is to adopt the **Tobit** model which assumes that the same function (and hence the same parameters) can be applied to the two equations. This can be explained in terms of the 'underlying index' argument given above. We estimate only the index equation (8.8) *but we include the zero observations in our sample used for estimation*. This suggests that there is a problem with the normality assumption of the OLS model caused by **truncation**. The underlying index model has a truncated dependent variable, as non-zero values cannot occur, therefore part of the normal distribution of the error term is effectively 'sliced off' at this point. This results in the mean of the disturbance term being non-zero and dependent on the parameters of the model, the data and the error variance. OLS applied in this situation would be seriously misleading due to bias and other problems.

This is a situation where we have 'limit' observations, i.e. the index cannot take on negative values and thus cases where it would be negative are zero. A limit observation does not have to be zero in all cases. For example, there are numerous studies of attendance figures at sports events, where the data is censored at the 'other' end That is, stadia are limited in their capacity therefore tickets are only sold up to a certain level, meaning that there is excess demand when the stadium is full. There is then 'censoring' in the demand equation as the intensity of demand is rationed by the limits of the stadium.

The Tobit model is then one where the disturbance term is represented in such a way as to overcome these problems and maximum likelihood is used to estimate the parameters of this function. Most econometrics software will provide an automatic Tobit routine, which only requires one to specify the equation in the same way as for OLS.

There is an approximate relationship between OLS and Tobit estimates on the same set of data which can be summarized as follows (see Greene, 2000, p. 912):

▶ OLS estimates are almost always smaller than the Tobit estimates.
▶ The difference between these can be approximated by dividing the OLS estimates by the fraction of the sample that are non–limit observations.

This implies that the difference in impact estimation will shrink as the share of limit observations decreases. Having said this, it should be pointed out that some studies with a smallish fraction of limit observations may report the OLS results for the sample with and without the limit observations.

The Tobit model is relatively easy to interpret as we only have one set of parameter estimates once a suitable maximum likelihood routine has been used to apply the assumptions about the error distribution. It is also possible to decompose the results into effects on the likelihood of moving off the limit observation and the consequent response to changes in the dependent variables.

HECKIT MODELS

The Tobit approach can be found in papers in many areas of applied economics but it could be seriously misleading on some sets of data. For one thing, it is problematic to treat the two events (the 0–1 and the participation) with one underlying function. This led to the development of the Heckit model. The term 'Heckit model' has been applied to the two-step procedure we are about to outline, which is a more simple approach than a full maximum likelihood estimation strategy. The crucial step forward in moving to this model instead of a Tobit is that we allow the participation equation (8.16) to be generated by a different set of parameters from the 'index' equation (8.17). For example, if we were dealing with a decision over migrating to a new job in a different geographical location one might find that there are location specific variables which influence the decision to move (such as the quality of schools available for children) but might not have any influence on an earnings function.

The two stages in the model are:

(i)   first estimate a probit for Equation (8.16);
(ii) and then take the inverse Mill's ratio from this equation and add this to Equation (8.17), which is then estimated by OLS. Once we have estimated the OLS equation with the IMR included we can interpret the coefficients obtained in the same way we would with the OLS models of earlier chapters.

You should note that the second stage is different from the Tobit model as the zero observations are *excluded* from estimation. Those observations do, however, have an influence on the results obtained via the inclusion of the inverse Mill's ratio.

These coefficients should be preferable to OLS estimates of the 'index' equation (8.17) under normal circumstances. How much they differ in practice is going to depend on the properties of the data as revealed in the first round probit equation. If the probit equation is very poorly specified then we are not going to get much benefit from using this technique. This may simply reflect the use of inappropriate or inadequate data. For example, if we are secondary users of a government or other organization's survey, as were Amuedo-Dorates and Mach in Section 8.6, then we may find ourselves with a set of variables that are simply inadequate to model the likelihood of participation.

The two-stage Heckit procedure is not the only means of estimating such models. Most specialist packages contain more advanced maximum likelihood methods.

In our first naïve model strategy for the simultaneous decisions of whether or not to participate and how much to participate, we implicitly assumed that the same variables appeared in both. In reality this is something, which may be sometimes true and sometimes not. There can be factors which influence whether or not one is likely to purchase an item or migrate to a new job but have no influence on the expenditure, in the first instance or the salary in the second instance.

A complete discussion of the identification problem, in general, can be found in Chapter 12.

8.8 PROBLEMS IN INTERPRETING AND TESTING LOGIT AND PROBIT MODELS

By now, you will probably agree that it is harder to interpret the results of logit and probit models than it is to deal with OLS regression. Even in the simplest case of two outcomes (yes or no, buy or don't buy) this is the case. We find ourselves with coefficients that are harder to make sense of and the lack of any obviously useful goodness of fit statistic. However, if we make some further calculations, appropriate to the type of model and data which we have, it is reasonably easy to use the model to come to conclusions about the influence of the variables in the model. It is fairly easy to use the models for prediction purposes as all we need to do is convert the predicted log odds ratio back to a prediction of the likelihood that $\Upsilon = 1$.

The problems increase when we move to multinomial models of three or more outcomes and to models of the Heckit/Tobit type where there is a combination of two equations – one for probability and one for participation.

When we come to the multinomial dependent variable case, presentation of the results is a little more complicated as there is more than one set of coefficients even though we only have a single equation model. I have suggested above that the best solution to this is to estimate the equation using all possible base categories so that every set of pairwise comparisons is shown in the results. Unfortunately, this does not remove all the complexities of interpretation of the results as we still need to manipulate the results in some way to get an idea of the size of the relationship between the pairwise probabilities for the dependent variable and the independent variables. Some published studies make relatively little attempt to interpret ordered or unordered multinomial models giving, instead, just the significance results for the coefficients, sometimes in asterisk form.

The bigger problem in the multinomial case is that the interpretation of the three S's – size, significance and sign – is much more difficult. In particular the sign and size of an effect differs, depending on how one evaluates the model. Even with the simplest case of unordered non-nested three-way modelling, one can find that the two sets of coefficients may have opposite signs for some variables. That is, a variable may increase the log odds ratio for one pairwise comparison but decrease it for another pair. It would seem that the logical response to this is to perform calculations for 'scenarios' which may be of interest; that is, pick a reasonable set of values for the other variables (remember the discussion in Section 8.6 above) and simulate the impact of changes in the variable on which you are focusing. For example, if you were hired by a marketing firm to look at a large survey on people's decision to buy portable MP3 players you could simulate the impact of income changes for different age–sex groups.

When ordering and nesting exist it can become very difficult to interpret models and we do not attempt to do so here.

OMITTED VARIABLES

Omitted variables are a persistent problem in estimating any type of equation, as the previous chapters make clear. They can cause bias in estimated coefficients, dependent variable predictions and failures on diagnostic tests. The same issues apply to binomial and multinomial models. However, there is an additional problem in the binomial models (see Cramer, 1991). That is, even if the omitted variables are totally uncorrelated with the included variables, their omission will bias the coefficients of the model towards zero leading us towards errors in judging the impact of these variables.

SMALL SAMPLES IN A GROUP

When we have three or more groups, in logit and probit models, we have a choice of which to use as the base category for estimating. In principle, this does not make any difference to the overall set of results obtained (i.e. they are just presented differently) as the effects of a change in a given variable on a particular pairwise log odds ratio should be the same. However, if you use a base group with very small numbers this may cause problems of convergence in the maximization process used by computer packages.

8.9 CONCLUSION

This chapter has taken on a slightly different direction from the previous chapters in this book. Instead of modelling the movements of continuous variables like aggregate consumption, demand or supply of goods, growth rates, exports, imports and so on, we have turned to the prediction of categorical events. This is an extremely useful development and is very popular, and increasingly so, in many areas of applied economics. The fact that it can be easily linked to utility functions makes it more attractive.

In practical terms, there are a lot of similarities to the analysis of the previous chapters. The fundamental principles of the three S's (sign, significance and size) remain, but the second two of these are a little more complicated. Simply presenting a set of results as they come out of the computer with * for significance levels and whatever goodness of fit measures come from the package output is not very useful. One should pause to reflect that this, of course, is not particularly useful to the reader in the standard OLS model either. However, the categorical model is harder to produce a useful elasticity type measure for, it has no particularly meaningful goodness of fit statistic and the sign of the relationship with an independent variable may be subject to change when the levels of the other independent variables change.

The argument for the use of probit or logit models is based on theoretical statistical propositions. In practice, there may be situations where the OLS estimation (the linear probability model) is not seriously misleading in terms of the results obtained. This is less likely to be true the more skewed is the distribution of the independent variable. Unfortunately it is quite heavily skewed in a number of survey data based research such as the studies reviewed in Section 8.6 and the data used in Tables 8.1–8.4.

As with the previous seven chapters, I have avoided questioning the foundations on which the estimation process has been based. I have taken the underlying assumptions about error term distributions for granted and have not engaged in any testing of their properties. The next chapter returns to the standard OLS model and presents a series of tests of the validity of OLS estimates, which lead to the development of alternative estimators in Chapters 11, 13 and 14.

DOS AND DON'TS

Do

- Use logit or probit models if you have categorical dependent variables.
- Try to use both logit and probit models, particularly if you are using a large unbalanced sample.
- Attempt to construct meaningful measures of the size of relationships between variables; this is not always easy with categorical dependent variables.

Don't

- Get too worried about whether a probit or logit is the more appropriate.
- Convert a model with a continuous (ratio) dependent variable into categorical observations in order to estimate a logit or probit unless there is some good reason.

✘ Treat any pseudo R squared or goodness of fit measures in the way you treat the R squared in the OLS model.

✘ Report measures of variable impact as they come out of a computer package without checking what they mean and how they were computed.

✘ Just use the computer output if it is insufficiently illuminating.

EXERCISES

8.1 Explain briefly the key differences between an LPM (OLS) model, a logit and a probit.

8.2 Give at least three examples of situations, not mentioned in the text, where you might use a probability model to analyse choice.

8.3 How would you go about deciding if a logit or probit model is a 'good fit'?

8.4 Decide if the following statements are true, false or indeterminate and give reasons for your answer.

(i) The coefficients in an LPM (OLS) model are marginal probabilities.

(ii) The coefficients in a logit or probit model are elasticities.

(iii) We will always come to exactly the same conclusions if we use an LPM (OLS) model, a probit or a logit.

8.5 Using the THEATRE.XLS file create a dummy variable called *CARE* = 1 if *SENSLOSS* is 3 or 4 and = 0 if *SENSLOSS* is 0 or 1. Estimate equations using *CARE* as a dependent variable with dummies for age, being female, plus variables for the total number of cultural/entertainment events attended, total hours of TV and radio watched by:

(i) OLS;

(ii) Logit;

(iii) Probit.

8.6 Compare the results obtained from these three approaches in terms of the size and significance of the relationship of *CARE* to the independent variables using appropriate calculations.

8.7 Using the results shown in Table 8.1:

(i) Compute the expected probability of a man aged 53, who has a university degree, and is below five feet six tall having had six or more partners.

(ii) Would you expect this probability to be the same using the logit or probit versions of the model?

REFERENCES

Ameniya, T. (1981) Qualitative response models: A survey, *Journal of Economic Literature*, **19**, 481–536.

Amuedo-Dorantes, C. and Mach, T. (2002) The impact of families on juvenile substance abuse, *Journal of Bioeconomics*, **4**(3), 269–282.

Blanchflower, D.G. and Oswald, A.J. (2000) Well-being over time in Britain and the USA, NBER Working Paper No. 7487.

Cragg, J.G. and Uhler, R. (1970) The demand for automobiles. *Canadian Journal of Economics*, **3**, 386–406.

Cramer, J.S. (1991) *An introduction to the logit model*. Edward Arnold, London.

Gray, C.M. (1998) Hope for the future? Early exposure to the arts and adult visits to museums, *Journal of Cultural Economics*, **22**(2–3), 87–98.

Greene, W.H. (2000) *Econometric Analysis*, 4th edn, Prentice-Hall, Upper Saddle River, NJ.

MacFadden, D. (1974) The measurement of urban travel demand, *Journal of Public Economics*, **3**, 303–328.

WEBLINKS

http://www.indiana.edu/~statmath/stat/all/cat/index.html

Examples of logit and probit using SPSS and SAS.

http://home.planet.nl/~smits.jeroen/selbias/heckman.txt

How to do a Heckman two-step procedure to control for selection bias in SPSS.

More Tests: Diagnosing the Results of Basic Models

LEARNING OBJECTIVES

- To know why diagnostic tests are needed
- Understand how to use the main (most common) tests for outliers, normality, heteroscedasticity, functional form, stability and autocorrelation
- To be aware that any specific test may have rejected the null due to a range of possible specification errors

CHAPTER SUMMARY

9.1 INTRODUCTION

We have seen that it is not enough to estimate a model. It must be subjected to repeated tests to establish its validity and to enable us to draw conclusions. So far, the only tests we have used, on our regression equations, have been 't' and 'F' tests. These are hypothesis tests used to draw conclusions about the numerical values of the estimated coefficients. The 't' and 'F' testing is done on the assumption that all of the assumptions of the CLRM hold.

Let us just remind ourselves of the CLRM model in the following equation:

$$Y_i = b_0 + b_1 X_{1i} + b_2 X_{2i} \dots + b_j X_{ji} + u_i \tag{9.1}$$

where i is the observation subscript and there will be n observations in total. There are up to j variables subject to the limitations that we will run out of degrees of freedom as j approaches n. The equation is linear for the purposes of estimation by ordinary least squares. As we have seen in previous chapters, transformations can be used to turn equations that are non-linear into the form of Equation (9.1).

In previous chapters we have used hypothesis tests based on the classical assumptions about the disturbance term (u). The tests are thus open to doubt if it seems that these assumptions are not reliable. Therefore, we need tests for the following properties of the error term:

(i) Whether there is a breakdown of the assumption that the right-hand side variables are uncorrelated with the disturbance term. The assumption can be written as:

$$\text{cov}(X_{ij}, u_i) = 0 \tag{9.2}$$

where cov stands for covariance. This is the null hypothesis that will be tested in a diagnostic test of the assumption.

(ii) Normality.

(iii) Homoscedasticity, that is, a constant variance of the error term for each observation in the sample. Homoscedasticity can be summarized in Equation (9.3):

$$\sigma u_1{}^2 = \sigma u_2{}^2 = \sigma u_3{}^2 \dots = \sigma u_n{}^2 \tag{9.3}$$

where $\sigma_u{}^2$ is the variance of the u term and the number subscripts represent the particular error term distributions for each observation. Equation (9.3) is the null hypothesis that will be tested in a diagnostic test for heteroscedasticity.

(iv) Absence of autocorrelation. This can be represented in Equation (9.4):

$$\text{cov}(u_i u_{i-1}) = 0 \tag{9.4}$$

We may also want to do tests for:

(a) outliers;
(b) stability;
(c) functional form.

The last two of these are tests as to whether our specification is adequate, that is, is it reasonable to assume the parameters are constant over the sample? Is it reasonable to work with the functional form (i.e. linear, double-log or whatever) that we have chosen? The first of these three tests is really a special case of checking for stability as it involves exploration of the influence of individual observations in the data set on the regression coefficients.

Testing on parameters is usually performed using 't' and 'F' tests, however things are not so simple in the case of diagnostic testing. There are many different tests, which have been proposed by various authors whose names are usually attached to the test. This can be confusing as it gives one the problem of wondering which test to use and, if you decide to use several tests, working out how to deal with conflicting results. Assuming the community of econometrics users evolves in a rational way we would expect an individual test to emerge as the standard if it was UMP (universally most powerful). Unfortunately it does not seem easy to find UMP tests as the strength of any given test depends on underlying properties of the test situation. In view of this, pragmatic considerations dictate which tests will lead the field in terms of popularity.

These may be ease of interpretation and implementation. In the case of the latter, the driving factor is the presence or absence of a test as an easily obtained 'plug-in', or even a default, on the most popular computer packages. For example, not so long ago economists hardly every presented tests for normality of the disturbance term, but they are much more likely to do so now. This is because it is provided automatically in a lot of regression output.

The next seven sections (9.2–9.8) discuss the process of testing for each of the seven problems listed above. It will make things easier if we assume that each problem is potentially present in isolation; that is, we assume that the other six problems are not present at the same time. This chapter does not include a separate section, or any tests, for the possibility that we have omitted relevant variables or included irrelevant variables. As you will see, however, these possibilities can be factors that we might draw on as explanations of problems found in the next seven sections. Changing the specification of the list of variables included is also a possible solution to these problems.

9.2 TESTING FOR OUTLIERS

Outliers have been mentioned occasionally in the first part of this book. An outlier is a loose concept. It simply means any observation that is a long way from the general pattern of distribution of a variable: that is, it 'lies out' from the rest of the data. This meaning is the interpretation given in everyday life to the term 'outlier'.

We could represent this idea in the following equation for a variable X:

$$\text{if } (X_i - \bar{X}) > (X_i - \bar{X})^* \text{ then we have an outlier} \qquad (9.5)$$

where we are taking distance from the mean as the measure of deviation from the pattern of data and the * represents the idea of what we think is 'reasonable' in terms of how far away a value might be from the mean.

You should be a little cautious in making judgements about what is reasonable as a normally distributed variable can quite reasonably be expected to have some observations which are a long way from the mean. These would be expected to occur more often as the sample size is increased. As the normal distribution is symmetrical we would also expect that, with a large enough sample, there would be large deviations on both sides of the mean.

In the specific case of a regression model, outliers are observations that are a long way from the fitted line. In other words, we can regard them as abnormally large residuals. We should stress that the presence of outliers is *not* a violation of any of the classical assumptions of the error term. There is technically nothing wrong with an OLS equation that has outliers. However, economists might worry about the reliability and representativeness of results that are derived from a data set producing notable outliers.

If there are outliers, we may feel that some observations are having 'too much influence' on the results. The presence of outliers may also cause apparent violations of the classical assumptions.

Outliers could occur in any type of data. They might arise because of the very simple reason of data entry errors, so it is worthwhile to check this. For example, if you have put the decimal point in the wrong place when typing in data you could generate outliers. Some kind of graph of the relationship between the fitted line and the actual data is a useful starting point to assess the possible presence of an outlier. An outlier is going to produce an abnormally large positive or negative residual. This should mean that a graph of fitted against actual values of the dependent variable will help us see which observations might be outliers.

I now look at some measures and how to use them. The formulae for these can be found in the first website link at the end of this chapter.

SUGGESTED TESTS: I. MEASURES OF DISTANCE

How can we tell if a residual is large enough to be considered an outlier? Graphs cannot answer this question for us. We need some extension of the idea in Equation (9.5). Some kind of standardization, which takes account of the spread of the residuals, is needed.

As the mean of the residuals is zero we do not need to subtract anything from u. To allow for the fact that we might expect larger deviations from zero in a sample which has a wide spread of values we could simply construct a 'standardized residual' as in this equation:

$$\hat{u}_i/\sqrt{\hat{\sigma}_u^2} \tag{9.6}$$

where we have divided the residual by its estimated standard error.

One form of this is to compute 'studentized residuals' (where the use of the term 'studentized' derives from the Student 't' test) and do a standard 't' test on the extent of deviation from the regression line. That is, we test whether residuals are significantly different from zero. There are some slightly different ways of studentizing the residuals (depending on how the standard error of the residual is calculated), which may determine whether you use conventional 't' tables or the special tables given in Lund (1975). An example of some studentized residuals is given in Table 9.2 below.

SUGGESTED TESTS: II. MEASURES OF INFLUENTIAL OBSERVATIONS

So far in this section we have used hypothesis testing in an exploratory way – that is, to look for observations that might be considered as outliers. A more systematic approach is to try to measure the influence of the outlying observations. This requires that we compute results with observations omitted and then assess the magnitude of distance between these results and the 'original', i.e. full, sample results.

Large values of distance statistics will indicate high levels of influence of the observation in question. A measure of distance could be computed for the overall set of results or, as shown in Table 9.2, for each individual parameter in the equation. This links to the discussion of parameter stability in Section 9.5 below, in that we may be able to pinpoint individual observations in the data, which are making specific coefficients unstable. Table 9.2 shows standardized DFBETAS which are based on computing regressions with and without each observation and calculating the change in the regression coefficients.

A rough check for influence with these is to look at values greater than 2 in absolute value divided by the square root of the degrees of freedom. In this case, this means greater than 0.31.

EXAMPLE OF TESTS FOR OUTLIERS: A GROWTH EQUATION

To illustrate the use of tests for outliers we now specify and estimate a model to provide new evidence on the published research reviewed in Section 3.10. This is taken from work by Cameron and Thorpe (2004) using a large cross-section database of countries. The dependent variable is the rate of growth. *GDP1991* (per capita GDP in 1991) is included in the argument that high levels of national income at the start of the period lead to lower rates of growth. *LIFE* is life expectancy being a measure of the human and health capital stocks, which is thus expected to have a positive coefficient. The remaining variables are a quadratic term in the number of lawyers (*LEGAL500*) in the country. Given the discussion in Section 3.10 we can see that this is a controversial inclusion, which might, as is found in the first column of Table 3.10, generate an inverted U-shape.

Table 9.1 Growth equation: Dependent variable: Growth of real GDP 1990–1999

Independent variables	Coefficients	
	Including USA	Excluding USA
Constant	10.514	−8.752
	(1.349)	(1.137)
GDP1991	−1.9 E−04	1.719 E−04
	(2.017)	(1.848)
LIFE	0.194	0.173
	(1.677)	(1.522)
LEGAL500	2.538E−05	−2.967E−05
	(1.87)	(0.853)
(*LEGAL500*)^2	−2.209E−11	5.206E−10
	(1.727)	(1.641)
R^2	0.159	0.213
N	47	46

Note: Absolute 't' ratios are in parentheses.

This is a situation where outliers may well be a problem as the sample of countries is very diverse. Table 9.2 shows two forms of diagnostics: one based on the standardized residuals and the other showing the 'DFBETAS' for each individual coefficient as an indication of the influence of deleting a particular country on that observation.

Table 9.2	DFBETAS and studentized residuals from the equation in Table 9.1					
	(0)	(1)	(2)	(3)	(4)	Student-ized residual
Norway	0.00559	0.06730	−0.00727	−0.03l802	0.02948	0.74521
Australia	−0.01022	0.01121	0.00841	0.02543	−0.02659	0.18307
Sweden	0.00889	−0.01117	−0.00837	0.00977	−0.00775	0.20970
Belgium	−0.00221	−0.01237	0.00280	−0.00044	0.00171	−0.10808
USA	−0.23111	−0.20080	0.18365	4.14613	−42.64237	−1.67562
Iceland	−0.00189	0.00863	0.00164	−0.00706	0.00578	0.11805
Netherlands	0.00180	0.01684	−0.00246	−0.00160	−0.00033	0.17992
Japan	0.02019	−0.03159	−0.01648	−0.01850	0.02226	0.36536
Finland	0.00621	0.02072	−0.00617	−0.01649	0.01384	0.23651
Switzerland	−0.05472	−0.10935	0.05970	0.01041	−0.00165	−0.40017
Luxembourg	0.29822	0.46295	−0.31260	−0.10684	0.07036	1.50506
France	0.00927	−0.06387	0.01483	−0.05601	0.06089	−0.42149
Denmark	0.06967	0.10295	−0.07174	−0.02751	0.01892	0.47225
Austria	0.00160	0.00434	−0.00172	−0.00164	0.00119	0.03276
Ireland	−0.13253	−0.10812	0.14603	−0.09115	0.08793	1.66730
N. Zealand	0.00527	−0.00006	−0.00555	0.00356	−0.00296	−0.10974
Italy	0.04739	−0.09332	−0.02964	−0.29735	0.30174	−0.88855
Spain	0.28190	0.10064	−0.25967	−0.60324	0.59201	−01.22135
Israel	0.02946	0.01411	−0.02936	−0.01400	0.01405	−0.21276
Greece	0.28512	0.27182	−0.29551	−0.05170	0.03996	0.91316
Hong Kong	−0.00039	0.01752	−0.00054	−0.00429	0.00226	0.16651
Cyprus	−0.00452	−0.00437	0.00481	−0.00183	0.00194	0.02242
Singapore	−0.02559	0.03990	0.02877	−0.08032	0.07015	1.28332
South Korea	−0.08681	−0.11661	0.10026	−0.07089	0.07253	0.95514
Portugal	0.02057	0.02075	−0.02232	0.00021	−0.00057	−0.19901
Malta	−0.13406	−0.14166	0.14275	−.04407	0.04893	0.47550
Hungary	−0.00686	0.02564	0.00005	0.03247	−0.03229	0.40346
Poland	−0.06599	−0.09334	0.07331	0.00810	−0.00406	0.44407
Estonia	−0.10753	−0.04230	0.09504	0.10582	−0.09945	−0.83489
UAE	−0.20360	−0.25312	0.20554	0.09765	−0.07688	1.06119
Lithuania	0.10327	0.37733	−0.16609	0.37100	−0.37708	−2.78857
Latvia	−0.30493	−0.09121	0.26475	0.32098	−0.30403	−2.36815
Malaysia	0.00228	−0.05659	0.01229	−0.06375	0.06269	1.03572
Bulgaria	0.01909	0.22109	−0.06008	0.17042	−0.17463	−2.03682
Romania	−0.00586	0.15731	−0.02508	0.16212	−0.16532	1.30311

Table 9.2 (continued)						
	(0)	(1)	(2)	(3)	(4)	Student-ized residual
Mauritius	0.05171	−0.01813	−0.03682	−0.11030	0.10700	0.87542
Lebanon	−0.21919	−0.34558	0.25055	−0.13665	0.15016	1.14318
Thailand	0.01217	−0.01672	−0.00753	0.02415	−0.02361	0.40572
Philippines	0.02815	0.14060	−0.04492	−0.13126	0.12276	−1.15872
Sri Lanka	−0.05556	−0.10153	0.06597	−0.04029	0.04417	0.41563
Turkey	−0.01103	0.01307	0.00732	−0.01932	0.01883	0.30986
China	−0.35552	−0.36167	0.33977	1.45518	−1.40783	2.13673
Vietnam	0.06411	−0.23159	−0.01371	−0.27347	0.27922	1.70987
Indonesia	0.08813	0.00874	−0.07691	−0.05767	0.05573	0.48732
Egypt	0.04029	0.00168	−0.03439	−0.03690	0.03583	0.25727
Mongolia	0.03551	0.01619	−0.03508	0.06396	−0.06345	0.15861
Togo	−0.18179	−0.10919	0.17758	−0.05669	0.06117	−0.37984
Yemen	0.47395	0.25016	−0.45361	−0.05942	0.04569	0.90451

0 = intercept; 1 = life; 2 = GDP AT START; 3 = LEGAL 500; 4 = LEGAL500 SQ

The studentized residual figures show four values above 2 in absolute value. The figure for China is 2.13673. The three negative figures are for Bulgaria, Lithuania and Latvia. The DFBETAS show nothing particularly remarkable for these countries, with the exception of the DFBETAS for the lawyer variables in the China case. The standardized DFBETAS suggest that most country observations would not make much difference to the estimated parameters of the model (there are a clutch moderately above 0.3) except for a huge influence of the US data on these same parameter estimates.

WHAT SHOULD WE DO ABOUT OUTLIERS?

As mentioned above, it is worth checking that the outlier is not simply due to a data entry error. For example, simply transferring the decimal point a few places or accidentally entering some zeros (forgetting that lagging variables loses observations, for instance) can produce extreme outliers. There might be some other form of data error, such as splicing together a series from incompatible sources, without adjustments being made.

If we discover outliers, we should not ignore them. If we do, we ought at least to point out their presence when we write a report of our research. One solution that probably springs to mind is to simply delete the problematic observations from the sample. This is not strictly valid, although it can be justified as an 'exploratory' technique. That is, if the results are much the same in terms of significance and magnitude then the outlier is not exercising a very important influence. For the sake of completeness (and general interest) I present the equation from the first column of Table 9.2 re-estimated with the USA observation deleted in Table 9.1. You can see that it produces very different results for the (focus) variable of the lawyer impact.

If you have omitted outliers, the reduced sample will now have an entirely different set of residuals (following from the fact that it will have entirely different coefficients) from before. This means that you should really conduct *another investigation* for the presence of outliers as new ones may have appeared. In such circumstances, you might find yourself with a shrinking set of data as more and more newly discovered outliers get stripped out of the estimation sample.

The appearance of highly influential outliers is an unavoidable possibility when we use OLS estimators. OLS allows influence to be determined by the size of the individual pieces of data. The alternative is to use some kind of WLS (weighted least squares) method to diminish the influence of the outliers, if we wish to continue using all the data. If we are to drop the outlying data then the OLS method is sometimes called 'trimmed least squares estimator'. This is an *ad hoc* method. Another *ad hoc* solution would be to include dummies for the outliers, when we have no specific hypothesis on why the dummies should be in the model.

Finding outliers might lead us in a useful direction in our research. Once you have identified your outliers, you can look for information about these observations which might explain the presence of a significant outlier. If we were looking at share prices, it might turn out that there was some shock in markets in the period to which the outlier belongs. Alternatively, if there is a systematic pattern in the outliers this may alert us to the fact that we have omitted a relevant variable from the right-hand side of the equation. We can also address the presence of outliers by changing the functional form using the methods described in Chapter 6. Transformations of the data can reduce the influence of outliers by scaling down the proportionate weight of the outlying observations.

Before we leave this topic, it is worth pointing out that outliers can be a problem in both directions. That is, a 'poor' set of results (low 't' ratios, wrong signs, implausible magnitudes) could be caused by the presence of outliers, the removal of which may greatly improve the results. However, the reverse can also happen in that a set of 'good' results may be crucially dependent on the inclusion of outliers to the extent that they fall apart when the outliers are removed. Whichever is the case, you should not be presenting your results without indicating the influence that the outliers are having on your results by reporting the difference between the 'with' and 'without' results. You could proceed to use some kind of weighted regression where the outliers are weighted, but this is not a popular approach among economists. An alternative would be to use alternative estimation techniques, which are more 'robust' to influential observations than OLS (such as MLS – median least squares) which is sensitive, by its very nature, to extreme observations. Such techniques do have the disadvantage of being harder to conduct and harder to interpret and we shall not pursue them here.

9.3 TESTING FOR NORMALITY

Normality of the error term is a fundamental assumption of the CLRM. It is not necessary in order to obtain the parameter estimates. However, it has to be assumed to hold in order for the formulae used to calculate 't' and 'F' tests to be correct. If the normal assumption is violated, we run the risk of conducting our hypothesis tests at a significance level that is much different from what we think we are using. There are several general statistical tests for the null hypothesis that a variable has a normal distribution against the alternative that it has some other distribution. We can apply any of these tests to the residuals from a regression equation. The most usual test in econometric packages and articles is the Jarque–Bera test that is referred to as the J–B test in some articles. This is based on measures of the skewness and kurtosis of the residuals. The J–B test combines these two according to the formula:

$$J\text{--}B = n[(S^2/6) + \{(K-3)^2/24\}] \qquad\qquad (9.7)$$

where n is the sample size, S is skewness, and K is kurtosis. This is implemented as a Chi-squared test with 2 degrees of freedom. The critical value is thus 5.99 at the 5 per cent level.

The normal distribution has the property that it is completely defined by its mean and variance. Departures from normality mean that we need to look at other moments of the distribution. If we find skewness (sloping to the left or the right) in a distribution, then it cannot be symmetrical, therefore it cannot be normal as symmetry is a fundamental aspect of the normal distribution. Kurtosis refers to the 'humpiness' of the distribution, that is, how steep or flat it is rising to the most likely value in the distribution curve. Curves with values of K less than 3 are known as platykurtic (broad or heavy tailed) and those with figures below 3 as leptokurtic (narrow tailed). Values around 3 will be normal. A perfectly normal distribution would have a J–B value of zero, as no skewness would result in an S of zero (mean = median) and no kurtosis would result in a K of 3 making the second term in Equation (9.3) also zero.

If your package does not have the Jarque–Bera test you should be able to compute it by hand from measures of skewness and kurtosis that are likely to be provided as descriptive statistics. That is, you need to save the residuals and ask for descriptive statistics on these.

Although the Jarque–Bera test is the one most commonly found in regression output, it has certain weaknesses. Asymptotic properties are relied upon – it is 'under sized', even in a large sample, due to slow convergence on its limiting distribution. It has weak power with platykurtic distributions (see Cho and Im, 2002, who propose the Geary test as an alternative).

There are other less commonly used non-parametric tests. We could use any non-parametric test for normality in general to test normality of the residuals, such as the Shapiro–Wilks test or the Kolomogorov–Smirnov test. These tests are derived from measures of goodness of fit; that is, we test how well the estimated residuals approximate to the assumed normal distribution.

Whatever test statistic we use, we cannot know the 'true' error terms and must use regression residuals instead. This may be a source of error in our diagnostic tests. How well a test performs – that is, its **power** performance (crudely its ability to give us the correct answer) – depends on the nature of the distribution of the residuals.

EXAMPLE OF NORMALITY TESTING: THE GROWTH EQUATION AGAIN

We now revisit the growth equation of Table 9.1 and apply some basic outlier analysis in Table 9.2. Saving the residuals of the regression shown in Table 9.1 gives values for S of -0.607 and K of 0.878. This suggests that the residuals from column 1 of Table 9.1 are not normal as we have leptokurtosis as well as non-symmetry. Inserting these figures in Equation (9.4) gives J–B values of 10.857, rounding to three decimal places using a calculator, from the above S and K, which were supplied by a computer package. This is well above the 5 per cent level for the Chi-squared test and thus strongly suggests the residuals are not normal. As we have already seen in Section 9.2, this could possibly be attributed to the influence of specific outliers.

What should I do if my regression fails a normality test?

This is not the end of the world. It does not mean your OLS model is entirely useless even though all the test statistics assume a normal distribution.

OLS regression can still be reliable in the presence of some non-normality in the error term. The failure of a normality test may simply be telling us that there are data entry errors or that we need to improve the specification of the model in terms of the choice and definition of variables or the functional form. It may also indicate the presence of other problems such as heteroscedasticity. I have suggested above that you could modify the model using weighting or dummies to ensure that outliers are taken account of.

9.4 TESTING FOR STABILITY

You will recall that the classical linear regression model assumes that all the parameters are constant across the sample. This is an assumption for the purposes of simplification rather than something we would necessarily expect to be true. Despite the neglect of the problem in very many published studies, parameter inconstancy has been seen as a major issue for a long time. In 1938, John Maynard Keynes commented as follows in a review of a book, by Jan Tinbergen, on business cycles:

> The coefficients arrived at are apparently assumed to be constant for 10 years or for a longer period. Yet, surely we know they are not constant. There is no reason at all why they should not be different every year (quoted in Swamy *et al.*, 1988).

We can show this idea by changing Equation (9.1) to Equation (9.8):

$$Y_i = b_{0i} + b_{1i}X_{1i} + b_{2i}X_{2i} \ldots + b_{ji}X_{ji} + u_i \qquad (9.8)$$

where we have given every parameter in the model an observation subscript to represent the fact that the values would be different in every year as suggested by Keynes. In a cross-section we would be looking at the problem of parameters being different for every firm or household or country.

Earlier parts of the book have shown how to allow for some degree of parameter shifting in the model. Chapter 7 showed how shift and slope dummy variables can be used to do this. A fully specified dummy variable model (with both shift and slope dummies) can be used to do the equivalent 'F' test to the Chow test using two regressions instead of three. 'F' tests to look at structural stability require us to split the data at some point in order to have two sub-samples to compare. One can do this arbitrarily just by dividing the sample in half but, as implied in earlier chapters, we may have some prior idea of where the split might be, owing to theories or knowledge about the data. We might, for example, know that an important change in central bank policy was implemented in a particular year that might be suspected to have altered the parameters of the money demand function in the following time period.

It is possible to take a more systematic approach to assessing stability by estimating 'rolling' regressions. That is, we could start with a sub-sample that runs from the first observation to the first point at which we feel the sample size is large enough for reasonable inferences to be made. This will give us one set of results. If we now add the next observation, rerun the regression, and continue the process we may be able to detect whether there are points at which there is a 'break' in the model. You could of course follow such a systematic routine in other ways. The obvious one is to roll backwards rather than forwards; that is, start with the smallest feasible sample from the final set of observations in the sequence and go backwards in the sample adding one additional observation at a time. The complete approach is to simply run every possible regression that could ever be constructed by permutations of the sample observations. These may seem like very time-consuming processes but modern high-speed computing makes this kind of thing extremely easy. Some packages (for example, Microfit) are set up in such a way as to do this automatically and they may also provide graphs of the coefficients over all the samples in order to provide a guide to spotting where the breaks come.

It is also possible to construct a test from the recursive regressions which is called a CUSUM test (cumulative sum of squares). Define:

$$W_r = 1/\hat{\sigma}_{ols} \sum_{j=k+1}^{r} v_j \qquad r = k+1, k+2 \ldots, n \qquad (9.9)$$

where v are recursive residuals which are obtained on the basis of predicting the dependent variable for the sample of period j from the coefficients obtained using the sample of $j-1$. These are then one step ahead prediction errors, which are standardized by the regression standard error of the OLS model for the whole sample. The intuition behind inspection of W being useful as a diagnostic aid is that if the prediction errors are independently random they should cancel each other out roughly speaking and so W should not tend to be cumulating as we roll through the sample. The analysis is usually graphical, where we look at whether the W line moves outside of a confidence band given by using the following formula to plot lines around W:

$$W = + \text{ and } - \{0.948\sqrt{(n-k)} + 1.896(r-k)/\sqrt{(n-k)}\}$$
$$r = k+1, k+2 \ldots, n \qquad (9.10)$$

An alternative CUSUMSQ (cumulative sum of squares test) can be used in the same way. This statistic WW is given as Equation (9.11):

$$WW_r = \sum_{j=k+1}^{r} v^2 \Big/ \sum_{j=k+1}^{n} v^2 \qquad r = k+1, k+2 \ldots, n \qquad (9.11)$$

and a pair of lines:

$$WW = + \text{ or } - c_0 + (r-k)/(n-k) \qquad r = k+1, k+2 \ldots, n \qquad (9.12)$$

where c_0 is determined by the significance level chosen. Packages will tend to use a 5 per cent default in drawing the lines.

If these methods reveal obvious break points then we can modify our model by attempting to introduce variables which might account for the break. These may have to be dummies. Alternately we may divide the sample around the break points. This might lead our research into new directions as the pattern of differences across the periods could lead us to explanations that were not included in the original hypothesis.

The suggestions we have just made involve partitioning models into periods in which we would still be assuming the parameters are constant and thus subject to the criticism of the observation quoted by Keynes at the start of this section. Of course, no one really believes that parameters are constant. Rather, if they estimate a basic OLS regression they are hoping that random parameter fluctuation is dealt with by the error term. Alternatively, one can extend regression models to allow for some forms of systematic variation in coefficients; an example of this is dealt with later in Sections 11.5 and 11.6 of Chapter 11.

9.5 TESTING FOR FUNCTIONAL FORM

The idea of testing a linear function for mis-specification due to non-linearity was suggested in Chapter 6. Such a test has to be based on using the estimated residuals to look for patterns that should not be there if the functional form is correctly specified. If we knew exactly what the correct functional form should be, then there would be no need for such tests as we would simply estimate the correct functional form. Bearing in mind that we work with non-experimental data, for the most part, it is not obvious what the correct functional form should be as problems of errors in measurement and aggregation of individual relationships to aggregate data can make a different functional form (for example, logarithmic) a better fit to the data than that specified in the theoretical model (for example, linear). One response to this is to use a test known as the Ramsey Regression Specification Error Test (RESET), which is a broader test for specification error than just functional form. It is conducted by running an OLS regression for the model originally specified – let us suppose this is linear for Y on X_1 and X_2. We then take the predicted Y from this equation, add powers of this to the equation, and re-estimate it: for example, if we go to four powers we will be estimating

$$Y = b_0 + b_1 X_1 + b_2 X_2 + b_3 \hat{Y}^2 + b_4 \hat{Y}^3 + b_5 \hat{Y}^4 + \alpha \tag{9.13}$$

where the last term is an assumed classical disturbance term not to be confused with that of the original model and the subscripts have been omitted. If we now conduct the standard 'F' test on the null of zero values for the parameters of b_3, b_4 and b_5 this will indicate the possible presence of errors in the specification. The idea behind this test is that we are proxying a range of possible specification errors, although it makes most sense in terms of non-linearity. This is such a broad-ranging test that one does find it also suggested as a test for heteroscedasticity, which we now come to deal with more specifically.

9.6 TESTING FOR HETEROSCEDASTICITY

Heteroscedasticity is the violation of one of the classical assumptions; that is, homoscedasticity – meaning constant variances of the disturbance term. We would not expect estimates of the variance of the u term to be constant, even if the true variance is constant, as they will be subject to sampling error. Therefore we test homoscedasticity as a hypothesis in the usual way by choosing a level of significance at which we determine whether the observed departure from homoscedasticity could have come about by chance. There are several recommended tests for heteroscedasticity. This section gives details of five, which are named after the people who proposed them:

▶ Goldfeld–Quandt test
▶ Glejser test
▶ Parks test
▶ Breusch–Pagan test
▶ White test

Before we can do any tests we need an estimate of the error variance as the true error variance is unknown. How do we get an estimate of the error variance? If we assume that it is constant across the sample then we can use the full set of residuals to calculate the variance. Indeed, it is the square root of this (i.e. the standard error) that is used in constructing the 't' tests from individual regression coefficients. However, a constant error variance is our null hypothesis when we are doing a heteroscedasticity test. To construct calculations which enable us to test the alternate hypothesis of heteroscedasticity we have to use the residuals in one of two ways.

(i) Goldfeld–Quandt test

We can divide the sample in two and run two regressions on the two separate parts. This means we now have two estimates of the error variance and can therefore do a test of the equality of these variances. The procedure used is slightly more complicated than this explanation and is called a Goldfeld–Quandt test. This test is executed in the following way:

> Step 1: You must divide the sample into three parts – a 'top', a 'middle' and a 'bottom'.
> Step 2: Run the originally specified model on the top part and the bottom part. You do not perform any analysis of the middle part.
> Step 3: Save the residuals of the two sets of regressions.
> Step 4: Use these residuals to conduct an 'F' test for the null hypothesis that the variances from these two regressions are equal.

This is easy to understand once you know how to work out how to divide the sample into three parts. This may be a little confusing as there is no exactly precise scientific formula for the division. Instead, we have a 'rule of thumb', which is to leave out around one-third of the observations in the middle. We do not know the optimal split into three but this rule of thumb is the best we can do to get close to it. If we omit too few observations (the extreme case of this would be simply dividing the sample in half) or too many then the power of the test falls. That is, it will come up with the wrong answer more often.

To obtain our top and bottom regression samples, we have to order the data in some way. That is, all the observations (*not* just one variable) must be arranged in a sequence that is different from the order in which the data was originally entered into your package. It is not possible to create the sequence without having some hypothesis about what might be the cause of the heteroscedasticity. This means we have to nominate some variable from the model as the 'suspect' variable. The usual method is to pick something that measures the 'size' of the observations. The reason for this is explained in more detail in Chapter 11. The G–Q test can be completed by using the 'F' test in exactly the same way we have used it before – that is, comparing the 'F' ratio with the critical value from the 'F' tables.

The above test is distinct from the remaining four tests to be considered in two ways:

(a) It is the only one of the five which omits part of the sample data.

(b) It is the only one which does not involve specifying a form of the relationship between the error variance and other variables in the model.

(ii) Glejser and Parks tests

An alternative suggestion to performing the 'F' test involved in the G–Q test is to run a regression of the estimated error variances on a suspect variable or some other. If we do this then we can, in principle, use the 't' ratios on the coefficients and the 'F' test for the test regression.

We run into a slight problem here of obtaining the estimate of the error variances. In the G–Q test the division of the sample allowed us to have two sets of errors from which to compute variances. However, when we want to estimate a heteroscedasticity function, we can only use the *square of the residuals for each individual observation as an estimate of the variance of the error term for each observation*. Once we take this step, we can use these squared residuals as our dependent variable in an OLS regression on some function of the suspect variable. The simplest approach would be the following:

$$\hat{u}^2 = m_0 + m_1 SV + \varepsilon \tag{9.14}$$

where ε is a classical disturbance term, SV is the suspect variable which might be thought to be related to heteroscedasticity, and the m's are the parameters. If the null hypotheses about the m parameters were both accepted then there would be no heteroscedasticity at our chosen significance level. If the null on m_0 is rejected but the null of $m_1 = 0$ is accepted then we conclude in favour of homoscedasticity, with m_0 being the estimated constant value of the variance. Throughout this chapter we are doing hypothesis testing 'the other way round' from how it was generally done in Chapters 3 and 6–9: that is, we generally would prefer to find in favour of the null as we would prefer not to have a heteroscedastic error term.

There is no obvious reason why SV should have a linear relationship with u^2. Therefore, we could experiment by using various permutations of logarithms, powers and reciprocals (as detailed in Chapter 6) in place of the function used in Equation (9.9). If all of these come to the same conclusion then we have a straightforward decision: either we accept or reject the null of homoscedasticity. If, after experimenting with functional forms, we find evidence of heteroscedasticity then we need to think about the issues discussed in Chapter 11.

A test of the above type is sometimes proposed in books but with the *absolute u in place of u squared*. This version is called a Glejser test after Glejser (1969). If we continue to use the type of approach I have suggested, of running the auxiliary regression with squared residuals as the dependent variable, then it would usually be called a Parks test; although the original paper by Parks, a long time ago, proposed a specific form of the test which is a double-log relationship with the 'suspect' variable. As I have suggested, there is no good reason to stick with one functional form for this type of test and, in practice, it is likely to make little difference whether we use the Glejser or Parks formulation of the dependent variable.

(iii) Breusch–Pagan Test

We can develop the Glejser and Parks tests further into a Lagrange Multiplier test called a **Breusch–Pagan** test. This begins with an auxiliary regression as before but ends with a χ^2 test. As in a Parks test, we regress the squared residuals from the OLS regression on some formulation of the suspect variables and convert this into a χ^2 (Lagrange Multiplier) test by multiplying the unadjusted R squared by the sample size (N). The test is to be carried out at the number of degrees of freedom equal to the number of parameters (excluding the intercept) to be estimated in the auxiliary regression. This number will be determined by the researcher's decision on what to include. It is possible to do the test in a standard 'F' version as well as the Lagrange Multiplier version.

(iv) White test

This test specifies that all the X's are involved in the auxiliary regression. We save the residuals from the OLS equation and square them to be used as the dependent variable. It is related to the discussion in Chapter 11 (Section 11.4) as the suggestion there for 'correcting' standard errors is based on the functional form specified in the White test. This requires us to include all the possible first order interaction terms and additional squared terms for each variable. Thus, the formula for the White test (assuming Y is regressed on 3 X's) is:

$$(\hat{u})^2 = b_0 + b_1 X_1 + b_2 X_2 + b_3 X_3 + b_4 X_1 X_2 + b_5 X_1 X_3 + b_6 X_2 X_3$$
$$+ b_7 X_1^2 + b_8 X_2^2 + b_9 X^2 + \alpha \tag{9.15}$$

where the last term is the disturbance term, again not to be confused with the u on the left-hand side and the b's not to be confused with the b's in the original model. You might feel inclined to do an 'F' test on the parameters of Equation (9.11) but White's test requires the LM form (as in the Breusch–Pagan test) where we multiply the (unadjusted) R squared from Equation (9.10) by the sample size (n) and use this as a χ^2 statistic with the usual tables for such a test. The number of degrees of freedom is equal to the number of parameters in the auxiliary regression, which is 9 in this case. What is notable about this test is that, unlike other heteroscedasticity tests, it makes no specific assumption about a 'suspect' variable but instead uses a general formulation involving all the variables in the model.

In case you are getting confused the main differences between the tests are:

▶ Only the Goldfeld–Quandt test involves dropping observations and two separate estimates of the model originally specified.
▶ Only the White test avoids the process of nominating a 'suspect variable' as it treats the form of heteroscedasticity as some approximation of the whole function.

EXAMPLES OF THESE TESTS USING THE ECONOMIC GROWTH EQUATION OF TABLE 9.1

You will recall that in Section 9.2 we specified and estimated a model to provide new evidence on the published research reviewed in Section 3.10 of Chapter 3. The same data is used here to generate some heteroscedasticity tests. The chosen 'suspect' variable is the size of the population living in the countries in the sample. This is a fairly common choice in aggregate econometric studies. We shall maintain our 'one problem at a time' philosophy and assume that the outlier problem is not now on our agenda. The estimated equation is thus the same set of results as shown in Table 9.1 above and the same set of residuals will be used as were used in Section 9.2. To keep things simple, we use only linear and double-log formulations for the shape of the heteroscedasticity relationship. The Glejser and Parks tests for these four cases are shown in Table 9.3 and this is extended into the Breusch–Pagan test and finally we show a White test for comparison.

Table 9.3 Heteroscedasticity test using residuals of Table 9.1 with population as the suspect variable[a]		
	χ^2 (d.f. in brackets)	't' ratio on suspect variable
White	8.601 (8)	
Parks Linear		−0.468
Parks Log		−0.753
Glejser Linear		−0.42
Glejser Log		−0.585
Breusch–Pagan Linear		0.235 (1)
Breusch–Pagan Log		0.564 (1)

[a] The 't' ratios in the table are for the population variable. The White test should use the cross products and squares of all variables but we cannot use *LEGAL500* squared twice in the same equation. The regression package also excluded four of the cross product terms and the *LEGAL500* squared, squared again was excluded.

All of these results strongly accept the null of homoscedasticity. The test value for the White test may seem quite large but, for 8 degrees of freedom, the χ^2 critical value at the 5 per cent level is 15.5, which is well above the figure shown in the table. Given the problems noted in the footnote to Table 9.3 the White test is restricted from its usual form, and is a special case of an extended Breusch–Pagan test. One should not lose sight of what we are doing in this fog of tests. The fact that we have found no evidence of heteroscedasticity is not strong support for us having a 'good' model. We still need to look at plausibility and significance of coefficients along with the remaining problems in this chapter, which may be concealing the effect of measurement errors and omitted variables.

You will have noticed that the mechanics of performing these tests are quite similar, so one would expect to find broad agreement between them using actual data although in theory they do not have identical properties under departure from the other assumptions of the OLS model (for example, the Breusch–Pagan test is sensitive to departures from normality).

WHAT DO WE DO ABOUT HETEROSCEDASTICITY?

If the null hypotheses on a range of heteroscedasticity tests has been accepted then we do not need to worry about this aspect of our model. Assuming that we cannot readily identify an outlier or an omitted variable as the source of the problem then you will need to read Chapter 11, which gives a full discussion of the causes, consequences of heteroscedasticity and the proposed cures for it.

9.7 TESTING FOR AUTOCORRELATION

This section deals with the two main tests that are found on packages (Durbin–Watson test and LM test) plus a discussion on the use of non-parametric tests: a version of the χ^2 and a 'runs' test. All these tests are performed on the residuals of the OLS regression. For a long time, economists relied solely on the Durbin–Watson test, with some use of the Durbin 'h' test in models with a lagged dependent variable. Nowadays, the LM test is tending to take over. As ever, graphical inspection can be quite useful in giving us insights to problems with the error term. Partly as a means of formalizing the visual inspection of residuals, we present some non-parametric tests for serial correlation at the end of this section. One may also get some idea of the extent of serial correlation by looking at a correlogram. We shall return to the uses of this device in Chapter 14.

The terms autocorrelation and serial correlation are often used interchangeably, although serial correlation implies that there is a time pattern in the sequence of residuals. For the moment, we will assume that we are dealing with time-series data. In time-series data we will have serial correlation if there is some dependence between the error terms over time. Tests for serial correlation became very common in the era of mainframe econometrics, indeed they were much more common than tests for heteroscedasticity One reason for this is the availability of obvious hypotheses about the alternate to the null hypothesis. One does not need to nominate suspect variables or split points to do the standard hypothesis tests for serial correlation.

Serial correlation can be extremely complex. To simplify, let us assume we are dealing with a bivariate model in which the serial correlation is in the u term (which means it is of course a property of the Y series which the model is assuming is generated by the X series). We will further assume that all the other classical assumptions hold. Thus, we have:

$$Y_t = b_0 + b_1 X_t + u_t \tag{9.16}$$

We need an equation to represent the process that is generating the serial correlation in u_t. The key elements of serial correlation are its direction and its order. The direction is either positive or negative, i.e. u is positively or negatively connected with its past values. The order is the number of periods apart in any such connection. For example, if we have not dealt with seasonality, then in a quarterly model we might find some correlation between the error term and its four-period lagged value. The simplest treatment of the order of serial correlation is to choose a value of 1. Hence the equation for u_t in its most basic form is:

$$u_t = z_0 + \rho u_{t-1} + v_t \tag{9.17}$$

where v_t is another classical disturbance term and we expect ρ, the serial or autocorrelation parameter, to be between -1 and $+1$. The parameter should not be outside the -1 to 1 interval, as that would imply that the u term explodes over time and does not have a finite variance. The most usual expectation is that we have positive serial correlation ($\rho > 0$), although negative serial correlation may also occur ($\rho < 0$). As you shall see, the usual diagnostic tests take account of both possibilities.

Equation (9.17) is simply one alternate hypothesis and we could have others in which higher orders of autocorrelation occur. For example, in the case of seasonal data where not all seasonal or dynamic elements have been filtered out there may be fourth or twelfth. These higher orders require appropriate modifications to the tests we are about to illustrate including (for the Durbin–Watson test) the use of different tables for significance testing.

One obvious approach to testing for serial correlation is to use the residuals from the OLS regression to estimate Equation (9.12). That is, we would put the estimated u's as the dependent variable and regress this on an intercept and the lagged values of the estimated u's. The coefficient on the lagged residual will be an estimate of the serial correlation parameter ρ. A 't' test on this parameter will be a test for serial correlation, as acceptance of the null would suggest that there is no problem of serial correlation at the chosen significance level. Rejection of the null suggests there is a problem that will be greater the larger is the absolute size of the coefficient.

There are technical limitations of the test just shown which mean that other tests tend to be used instead. One of its main drawbacks is that the estimate of ρ will be biased towards zero because we are using estimated residuals from an OLS regression. Nevertheless, this regression does have a close relationship to the tests we are about to discuss.

DURBIN–WATSON TEST (ALSO TO BE SEEN AS 'D' AND 'D.W.' TEST)

For a long time, the vast majority of time-series econometric studies only ever reported one serial correlation test, which is the Durbin–Watson test. The D–W statistic is still routinely provided in econometrics packages. It may appear to be a rather strange test, at first sight, because of two properties:

▶ It ranges between 0 and 4, with values around 2 being the region where the null hypothesis of an uncorrelated error term is accepted.

▶ It does not necessarily give a yes or no answer to the hypothesis test. There are regions on either side of 2 where the answer is 'indeterminate'. That is, we could for example end up saying that, at the 5 per cent level we simply do not know whether the null is accepted or rejected. The zone of indeterminacy will change size as we alter the significance level.

The first of these properties arises from the formula for D–W being:

$$\text{D.W.} = \sum(e_t - e_{t-1})^2 / \sum e_t^2 \tag{9.18}$$

where e is the residual from the OLS equation and t is the observation subscript. This does of course involve the loss of the first observation in making the calculation. This formula is related to the serial correlation parameter ρ from Equation (9.12) above and is approximately equal to $\frac{1}{2}(2 - d)$.

EXAMPLE: PERFORMING THE DURBIN–WATSON TEST

You need to be careful looking up Durbin–Watson tables as they do not follow the rules we have been used to so far. There are two sets of numbers to be selected but these are not degrees of freedom. Instead, the row figure is the sample size (n) and the column figure is the

number of variables excluding the constant term. For the Turkish cigarette model, shown in Table 3.2, $n = 29$ and $k' = 3$ so at the 1 per cent level we work out the regions as follows:
    Lower limit 0.99 Upper limit 1.42

DW < 0.99 reject null in favour of hypothesis that $\rho > 0$

$0.99 <$ DW < 1.42 inconclusive

$1.42 <$ DW < 2.58 accept null

$2.58 <$ DW < 3.01 inconclusive

DW > 3.01 reject null in favour of hypothesis that $\rho < 0$

The result we are looking for in this case is then a D between 1.42 and 2.58. If we go to a 5 per cent level, the dl (lower limit) and du (upper limit) become 1.20 and 1.65 for the same example, so the null range is 1.65 to 2.35 which is a narrower band.

The indeterminate region shrinks as we:

▶ increase the sample size;
▶ decrease the number of explanatory variables.

If we are using a cross-section, which is ordered, and do a Durbin–Watson test, this will be a test for heteroscedasticity rather than for serial correlation.

LM TEST

The Lagrange Multiplier test proposed by Godfrey is now regarded as the single best test for serial correlation. It is similar to tests we have already seen in this chapter in that it is performed by running an auxiliary regression using the residuals from OLS, which is then converted to a Chi-squared test by multiplying the R squared from the auxiliary regression by n (sample size). The auxiliary regression in this case involves regressing e (residuals from original equation) on the variables from the model plus the lagged e's up to the level of serial correlation we are trying to test. For first order this will be just one lagged e and the test will be at one degree of freedom. If we increase the order of the test then the number of degrees of freedom increases accordingly. This test is valid even when the equation features lagged dependent variables. The test statistic assumes that the sample size is large (i.e. it relies on asymptotic properties).

NON–PARAMETRIC TESTS

If there is serial correlation we would expect to find a particular pattern in the residuals. That is, we would expect to find 'strings' of positive and negative residuals – consecutive positive and consecutive negative sequence – or if the serial correlation is negative rather than positive we would find strings of reversals – many pairs of positive followed by negative and vice versa. This would be obvious on a graph. However, it is not clear from a graph whether the pattern is extreme enough to have come about by something other than chance. We can never be solely reliant on 'eyeballing' data as hypothesis tests are always necessary.

CHI-SQUARED TEST OF RESIDUALS FOR SERIAL CORRELATION

Suppose we are testing for first order serial correlation, then we could tabulate the pairs of residuals from the OLS equation into a 2×2 contingency table of the type shown below from the estimates of an equation for zip fasteners against a time trend. We construct a contingency table of whether the pairs of successive residuals are a $--$, $-+$, $++$ or $+-$ combination. If there is a skew towards the $++$ or $--$ combination pairs or a skew towards the $+-$, then we would suspect there is serial correlation. The formal test is just a Chi-squared test at a suitable significance level for one degree of freedom.

RUNS TEST

A series of events can be classified into 'runs' – a 'run' is where the same event occurs repeatedly. A run can be two or more instances of the same event. When we 'eyeball' a graph of regression residuals over time we would regard runs of negatives or positives as indicative of the probable presence of serial correlation. It is possible to tabulate ranges of expected number of runs from a series that has no systematic pattern, at a given significance level, and thus by comparing the actual number of runs with this we can do a 'runs' test.

Example of all four tests using data on zip fasteners

We now run a regression for the quantity of zip fasteners sold annually in the USA over 1913–32. A very simple crude specification was used:

$$ZIPSOLD_t = b_0 + b_1 T_t + u_i \qquad (9.19)$$

where T is a linear time trend of the numbers 1, 2 ... 20 as suggested in Section 6.8. The estimated value of b_1 will be the estimate of how much the total number of zip fasteners sold changes with each year that passes. The results are shown in Table 9.4 and the data on zip fasteners is shown in Table 9.5. The data are taken from Friedel (1994).

Table 9.4 OLS estimates of a zip fastener equation	
Dependent variable:	**ZIPSOLD**
CONSTANT	−2.2E+09
	(7.638)
TIME	1172760
	(7.6565)
R-squared	0.76508
F-statistic F(1, 18)	58.6215
D–W statistic	0.57596

You can readily see that for this model the null of no serial correlation is rejected strongly by the D–W as 0.57596 is well below the 5 per cent lower limit of 1.20 for the indeterminate zone.

Let us look at the residuals in order to conduct the non-parametric tests. The data for the residuals are shown in Table 9.5 where the sign pattern has been constructed in the final column.

Table 9.5 Data on zips plus residuals and predicted zips from Table 9.4's equation

Year	Actual zips	Predicted zips	Fitted residual	Sign of residual
1913	180 000	−5 070 138	5 250 138	+
1914	193 611	−3 897 378	4 090 989	+
1915	196 664	−2 724 618	2 921 282	+
1916	131 327	−1 551 857	1 683 184	+
1917	24 072	−379 097	403 169	+
1918	90 056	793 663.2	−703 607.2	−
1919	66 769	1 966 423	−1 899 654	−
1920	110 500	3 139 184	−3 028 684	−
1921	342 152	4 311 944	−3 969 792	−
1922	759 187	5 484 704	−4 725 517	−
1923	2 026 572	6 657 464	−4 630 892	−
1924	4 081 282	7 830 225	−3 748 943	−
1925	5 189 837	9 002 985	−3 813 148	−
1926	8 517 167	101 757.45	−1 658 578	−
1927	11 944 899	11 348 505.30	596 393.7	+
1928	8 240 906	12 521 265.54	−4 280 360	−
1929	17 004 306	13 694 025.77	3 310 280	+
1930	20 041 122	14 866 786	5 174 336	+
1931	2 399 498	6 039 546.24	7 955 439	+
1932	18 286 271	17 212 306.47	1 073 965	+

We can construct the one-period lag contingency table from the above as Table 9.6.

Table 9.6 Contingency table for one-period residual sign patterns from Table 9.5

	Time t	
Residual:	**+**	**−**
Time $t-1$ Residual		
+	7	2
−	2	8

The expected value for each cell is 4.75, so the value of the Chi-squared is 6.46 which is greater than the 5 per cent significance level of 3.84.

It is easy to count the number of runs in the above series because it works out as:

One $(5+s)$ Two $(9-s)$ Three $(1+)$ Four $(1-)$ Five $(4+s)$

The expected number of runs (from tables which you can find in textbooks of non-parametric statistics) in a series of 20 is between 6 and 16 at the 5 per cent level. As our series of residuals has 'too few' runs with a total of five then we conclude that there may be evidence of positive serial correlation. Too many runs would have been indicative of negative serial correlation. The result from the runs test therefore agrees, in our example, with the results for the D–W tests that there is substantial evidence of positive autocorrelation in this series.

The positive serial correlation most likely reflects a number of specification problems which one can see in Tables 9.4 and 9.5. You will notice that there are some negative predictions of huge numbers of zips being sold which does not make sense. This may reflect non-linearity. There is also a noticeable collapse in sales during the Second World War, probably due to diversion of resources to other activities which would distort the normal supply–demand relationships in the industry.

Autocorrelation in cross-sections

If we are using a cross-section which is ordered and do a Durbin–Watson test then it will be a test for heteroscedasticity rather than for autocorrelation. We can only have genuine autocorrelation in cross-section data if it has a spatial dimension. One example of this would be if we were to try to model burglary rates across the regions of a city. We might find that one region is 'exporting' or 'importing' burglaries from a contiguous region. It is possible to construct tests by comparing pairs of residuals from contiguous regions to give us a test of spatial autocorrelation. A situation like the burglary example just mentioned points out the fact that omitted variables may well be responsible for a lot of spatial autocorrelation.

WHAT DO WE DO IF WE FIND AUTOCORRELATION?

As with any other diagnostic test, rejection of the null is telling us there is something wrong with our model or our data or both. It was once extremely common for economists to 'solve' the current problem using a GLS technique which estimated the serial correlation parameter and used this to arrive at improved estimates of the equation that should be used instead of OLS. Thanks to the developments discussed in Chapter 14, this is increasingly not the case. Indeed, most econometricians would now totally reject the use of the GLS procedure. Serial correlation can arise from a number of problems which may be readily solved in some cases.

(i) Omitted variables

Let us think for a moment about the equation for zip fasteners that we have just estimated. Note that the specimen data on the number of zip fasteners sold in the USA in 1913–32 cannot be taken seriously as an economic model because it only involves a time trend. The serial correlation may go away when we add variables, which may include lagged terms to represent the dynamic processes that may be responsible for the pattern in the residuals.

The u term is influenced by all factors that have been omitted from the model. If an omitted variable is serially correlated then adding this variable may increase the chances of accepting the null of uncorrelated errors. The following example taken from Cameron (1986, p. 298) is for a model of strike frequency in the British building industry in the period between the First and Second World Wars. The functional form is double-log and a static model is being used.

The estimating equation can be represented as:

$$\ln(\textit{Strike Frequency})_t = b_0 + b_1\ln(\textit{Real Wages})_t + b_2\ln(\textit{GDP})_t$$
$$+ b_3\ln(\textit{Unemployment Rates})_t + b_4\ln(\textit{TUD})_t + u_t \qquad \textbf{(9.20)}$$

where ln stands for natural logarithm, u is a classical disturbance term and the t subscript is for the years 1920–38.

The second equation in Table 9.7 is Equation (9.20), while the first is Equation (9.20) with the restriction that $b_4 = 0$ imposed on it.

In the first equation, the D–W is 0.63, which is below the lower limit of 0.97. This is appropriate to a sample of 19 with 3 independent variables. This is then a strong indication of positive serial correlation. When the trade union density variable is added, the D–W rises to 2.03, which is between the limits of 1.85 and 2.15, appropriate to a sample of 19 with 4 independent variables.

Table 9.7 Equation to explain strike rates in the British building industry, 1920–1938

Dependent Variable	Log (*Strike Frequency*)	Log (*Strike Frequency*)
Independent Variables		
Log (*Real Wages*)	−0.08	4.8
	(0.4)	(5.6)
Log (*GDP*)	−0.56	4.3
	(0.3)	(5.2)
Log (*Unemployment Rates*)	−0.51	0.16
	(1.3)	(1)
Log (*TUD*)		5.9
		(9.8)
Intercept	7.7	−37.1
	(0.8)	(6.8)
R^2 adjusted	0.21	0.9
F	2.6	41.6
D–W	0.63	2.03
N	19	19

(ii) Functional form

Look at Figure 9.1. This shows a linear equation fitted to a 'true' underlying log relationship. Let us assume that both variables are growing steadily over time. The residuals show a pattern of runs which would give a poor D–W or LM test and thus will be telling us that we have used the wrong functional form. Use of a different functional form may 'cure' the serial correlation.

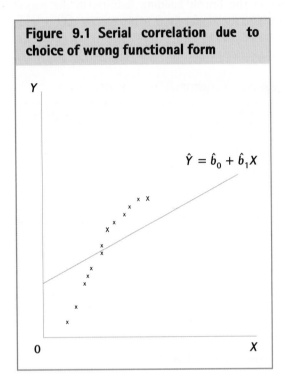

Figure 9.1 Serial correlation due to choice of wrong functional form

$$\hat{Y} = \hat{b}_0 + \hat{b}_1 X$$

(iii) Data problems

There are two sorts of data problems here: those that were in the data collected and those arising from choices made by the researcher over variable definitions. Perhaps surprisingly, problems may be caused by attempts to improve the accuracy of data by the recording agencies. Let us suppose the government decides to make an effort to improve the accuracy of data on the variable we have chosen as our dependent variable. If this is a gradual process whereby, for example, data gets closer to the true value by say 5 per cent of the gap at the start of each year, this will induce a false dynamic process in the Y variable. Definitions of rates of change may induce serial correlation in a series that was not originally serial correlated due to the form of differencing used. For example, defining rates of inflation on a 'year on year' basis rather than a continuous basis or using data already adjusted by moving average methods may induce serial correlation.

(iv) Dynamic processes

Our model may not be in approximate equilibrium at all times, but rather approaching it through some adjustment process. In a sense, this is a special case of the omitted variable problem and will be dealt with fully in Chapter 14. We have encountered simple versions of this type of model already in Chapter 6.

9.8 TESTING FOR BIAS

You will recall from Chapter 3, that the classical linear regression model assumes that the disturbance term (u) is uncorrelated (i.e. it has zero covariance) with the independent variables in the equation. This assumption facilitates the proof of the Gauss–Markov theorem that the estimates of the parameters, in the equation, are unbiased estimates of the 'true' parameters. In order to do a test for bias, we need some hypothesis about where the bias might have come from. It is not the usual practice to test for bias and then start a search for where it might have come from. There are two major sources of bias in a single equation model:

(i) Systematic measurement error. OLS regression takes account of measurement error but it relies heavily on its assumed randomness. Non-random measures will arise where one of the right-hand side variables (X's) is subject to measurement error which is correlated with that in the u term. This can happen due to calculations we might make to 'proxy' unavailable variables. The classic example is survey data which does not contain hourly wage rates. Researchers in such a situation may divide total income by hours of work to get a proxy, but if they then estimate a labour supply equation with hours as the dependent variable then the u term will be covarying with the wage rate variable by definition if there is measurement error in income – which is highly likely in a survey due to the imperfections of memory etc.

(ii) Mis-specification of the relationship between the equation and other equations which might form part of the model we are working on. We are still working with a single equation model and will do so until Chapter 12. If the equation is part of a system it can cause bias. We shall postpone discussion of testing for bias until we get to Chapter 13, as it will be much easier to understand in that context.

9.9 REVIEW STUDIES

It is not quite so easy to select review studies for this chapter as it was for earlier chapters. This is because a large percentage of published works do not provide much diagnostic information. Indeed, many studies provide none at all, while others present a few statistics of a diagnostic nature without much discussion. We might explain this situation with the argument that professional researchers have carried out diagnosis on their model and used it to perfect the final version and do not want to bore us with the intimate details. After all, if one goes to the doctor the intention is to be made better, not necessarily to see all the X-rays and tests at great length. Notwithstanding this, a case could be made that more evidence of the diagnostic efforts should appear. The effect of this would be to shed more light on the robustness of the results. As things stand, we may have grounds to worry that many results are not as substantial as the authors imply, which undermines the 'scientific' status of econometrics.

We now look at two studies concerned with broad international economics issues – one macro (on money demand in developing countries) and the other micro (on the longstanding doctrine of purchasing power parity – PPP). You should be able to understand most of the paper by Webster, having come this far in the study of this subject. The other paper, by Agenor and Kahn, does rely on some techniques we have not covered so far but you should know enough to look at the results in this paper. Both these papers look at material that is very much in the 'hard core' of economic research, namely most people agree on the basic form of the model.

The Basic Facts

Authors: Alan Webster

Title: Purchasing Power Parity as a Theory of International Arbitrage in Manufactured Goods: An Empirical View of UK/US Prices in the 1970s

Where Published: *Applied Economics*, **19**(11), November 1987, 1433—1456.

Reason for Study: To study purchasing power parity theory using data on individual industries which is more appropriate than price data aggregated to a national level.

Conclusion Reached: At a disaggregated level there is a lack of support for an arbitrage process of the type suggested by the purchasing power parity model, although there is substantial price adjustment between countries.

How Did They Do It?

Data: 35 UK industries over January 1975 to October 1980 on a monthly basis.

Sample Size: 72 in most cases.

Technique: OLS.

Dependent Variable: Price level in the UK industries.

Focus Variables: Pound–dollar exchange rate, USA prices in corresponding industries and their values lagged up to 24 periods (i.e. two years).

Control Variables: UK import tariffs and their values lagged up to 24 periods (i.e. two years).

Presentation

How Results Are Listed: Standard errors given in brackets. Asterisk system used to denote significant coefficients, although not in the full set of 35 regressions in the appendix.

Goodness of Fit: R squared and R squared adjusted (in Tables 2 and 5).

Tests: 'F' tests for joint arbitrage hypotheses.

Diagnosis/Stability: LM test for autocorrelation, Goldfeld–Quandt test, Chow test for stability, ARCH test, Jarque–Bera normality test. These test results are broadly supportive of the conclusion that the model does not suffer from problems of violation of the classical assumptions.

Anomalous Results: No real support for full purchasing power parity.

Student Reflection

Things to Look Out For: Table 2 includes R squared values in a table headed diagnostic tests – however, the R squareds are not diagnostic tests, they are goodness of fit measures.

Problems in Replication: The data are taken from published government sources so replication is not, in principle, difficult although there are likely to be difficulties with updating such a study as definitions of industry categories are prone to change.

The Basic Facts

Authors: Pierre-Richard Agenor and Moshin S. Khan

Title: Foreign Currency Deposits and the Demand for Money in Developing Countries

Where Published: *Journal of Development Economics*, **50**(1), 1996, 101–118.

Reason For Study: To estimate a rational expectations model of substitution between domestic and foreign currency deposits in the money demand function

Conclusions Reached: Rational expectations is supported in most cases although short horizons are found for countries which have had extreme macroeconomic instability. There is evidence of currency substitution.

How Did They Do It?

Data: Quarterly time series from October 1982 to March 1990 (estimation period) for ten developing countries: Bangladesh, Brazil, Ecuador, Indonesia, Malaysia, Mexico, Morocco, Nigeria, Pakistan, Philippines. All data taken from International Financial Statistics published by the International Monetary Fund.

Sample Size: 31, it seems (not explicitly stated in the results tables).

Technique: IV (see Chapter 15) on ten separate equations for each country.

Dependent Variable: Logarithm-ratio of narrow money to foreign currency accounts held abroad by residents.

Focus Variables: Lagged dependent variable; logarithm of 'world interest rate' defined as the three-month Eurodollar rate; parallel exchange rate and official exchange rates defined as end of period exchange rate between domestic and foreign currency plus lead terms up to four quarters.

Control Variables: None.

Presentation

How Results Are Listed: Standard errors are given in brackets.

Goodness of Fit: R squared adjusted, estimated standard error of the regression.

Tests: 't' tests, Wald tests of model restrictions.

Diagnosis/Stability: Jarque–Bera normality test, Engle ARCH test, LM test for serial correlation, Chow test for predicitive failure over October 1988–March 1990.

Anomalous Results: None noted.

Student Reflection

Things To Look Out For: Diagnostics reveal a few problems: non-normal residuals in Mexico, heteroscedasticity in Bangladesh, parameter instability in Morocco, Brazil, Malaysia and Mexico, no expectational effects beyond one quarter, lowish R squared in Malaysia.

Problems in Replication: This study should be quite easy to replicate as it uses data from one published source.

As mentioned, both these studies are in core areas of standard economic research topics. They present a fair number of diagnostic tests which do not show there to be too many problems and there is no mention of any attempt being made to redesign the research as a result of diagnostic tests. It should be apparent that omitted variables lurk behind many of the specification problems discussed in this chapter. Both these studies do not pay very much attention to alternate variables that might have been included. This may well be because they use models from well-established areas of economics in which there is quite a lot of agreement.

9.10 CONCLUSION

This chapter has gathered together tests for the basic assumptions of the classical linear regression model plus tests for some other problems that may arise. We have not considered every single test that there is for each of these assumptions as this would take up far too much time. We did not present a test for multicollinearity, as that is the subject of the next chapter where a suggested test is given in Section 10.5. We have also yet to consider tests for the presence of unit roots and cointegration. These will be taken up in Chapter 13 when we come to the specific problems posed by the historic properties of time-series data. We also omitted tests that deal with the hypothesis that more than one specification error has arisen. The most important of these is the family of ARCH and GARCH tests.

The material that has been covered in this chapter might leave a negative impression in the mind of the person who is new to this subject. That is, the introduction of the need for diagnostic testing seems to cast a shadow of doubt over the solid foundations of regression analysis built up in the first part of this book. That is, we now know that if these tests fail then the point estimates and significance tests from our OLS equations may be unreliable. However, we should not become pessimistic about the use of diagnostic tests that reject the null because the correct response is to look for improvements in the data and the model specification, which may resolve the difficulties that have arisen. Similar suggestions were made in many of the seven sections of this chapter, which described different problems that are a reason for diagnostic tests. The reason the same sorts of responses crop up so often is that failure (i.e. acceptance of the null) on any diagnostic test is evidence of either data problems or mis-specification of the model. If we can resolve these difficulties then we may not need to resort to the more sophisticated econometric techniques described in Chapters 11–14 of this book.

DOS AND DON'TS
Do
- Look for evidence on diagnostic tests in articles you are reading.
- Consider the use of diagnostic tests for all the seven areas mentioned above even though there may be little evidence of them being employed in work you have read.
- Check your data for entry and measurement errors as these could be responsible for good or bad results on diagnostic tests.

Don't
- Simply reproduce a set of diagnostic tests because they were on the package. Make sure you understand them and can interpret their relevance for the sort of model and data you have.

✗ Report only diagnostic tests which support your point of view while repressing the information on those which did not because this is a form of 'data mining'.

✗ Abandon a model just because of poor results on some diagnostics tests; these should be giving you hints as to how to improve your model and/or data.

✗ Forget that diagnostic tests are themselves hypothesis tests and therefore require a significance level which, of course, means you will switch from a rejection to acceptance at some 'critical' significance level.

✗ Get confused by the large number of tests we have discussed (there could have been even more). Try to remember which problem is which – for example, we can have heteroscedasticity with residuals which are still normally distributed for each observation.

✗ Assume that you have a 'good' model because it passes the tests in this chapter, because it could have other problems and it will also need to be checked to see if it gives results which are sensible in terms of sign, significance and size of coefficients.

EXERCISES

9.1 Explain clearly what the major differences are in testing for heteroscedasticity and testing for autocorrelation.

9.2 Explain why:
(i) part of the sample is omitted in the Goldfeld–Quandt test;
(ii) outliers might be considered important;
(iii) an unstable econometric equation would worry you.

9.3 Use the file for the Belgian consumption (BELGCON.XLS) function estimated in Table 3.1 (in Chapter 3) to re-estimate the equation shown there. Now:
(i) Re-estimate the equation 11 times using the samples 1–20, 1–21, 1–22 and so on.
(ii) Plot the value of the marginal propensity to consume (Y) on a diagram against time (on the X-axis) and comment on this graph.
(iii) Using this consumption function construct a CUSUM or CUSUMSQ test and comment on the results.

9.4 From the data which was used in Table 9.1 (found in the file GROWTH.XLS) estimate a linear equation to explain cross-country growth rates as a function of initial GDP, life expectancy, literacy rates, the index of economic freedom and Legal 500 divided by population.

Using appropriate methods of your choice attempt to explore the results for:
(i) stability;
(ii) mis-specification of the functional form;
(iii) outliers;
(iv) heteroscedasticity;

9.5 Use the file on cigarette smoking in Turkey (TURKCIG.XLS) to re-estimate the equation in Table 3.2 (in Chapter 3).
(i) Save the residuals from this equation and (using whatever graphical or tabular methods

you wish) comment on whether they suggest the presence of first order serial correlation.

(ii) Examine the Durbin–Watson statistic for this equation and comment on it.

REFERENCES

Agenor, Pierre-Richard and Khan, Moshin, S. (1996) Foreign currency deposits and the demand for money in developing countries, *Journal of Development Economics*, **50**(1), 101–118.

Cameron, S. (1986) Strike activity in the British building industry in the inter-war period, *Journal of Social History*, **20**(2), 291–300.

Cameron, S. and Thorpe, A. (2004) Legislating for economic sclerosis: Do lawyers have a baleful influence on economic growth, *Kyklos*, **57**(1) 45–66.

Cho, D.W. and Im, K.S. (2002) A test of normality using Geary's skewness and kurtosis statistics. Unpublished manuscript.

Friedel, R. (1994) *Zipper: An Exploration in Novelty*, Norton Publishing, London and New York.

Glejser, H. (1969) A new test for heteroscedasticity, *Journal of the American Statistical Association*, **64**, 316–323.

Lund, R.E. (1975) Tables for an approximate test for outliers in linear models, *Technometrics*, **17**(4), November, 473–476.

Swamy, P.A.V.B., Conway, R.K. and Le Blanc, M.R. (1988) The stochastic coefficients approach to econometric modelling Part I: A critique of fixed coefficients models, *Journal of Agricultural Economics Research*, **40**(2), 2–10.

Webster, A. (1987) Purchasing power parity as a theory of international arbitrage in manufactured goods: An empirical view of UK/US prices in the 1970s, *Applied Economics*, **19**(11), 1433–1456.

WEBLINK

www.faculty.sfasu.edu/f_cobledw/Regression/Lecture10/Lecture10.PDF

These lecture notes provide the complete formulae for the statistics related to outliers.

10

Multicollinearity: Serious Worry or Minor Nuisance?

LEARNING OBJECTIVES

- Be aware of the importance of the relationships between the independent variables in an OLS regression
- Have knowledge of the circumstances which are likely to give rise to problems of multicollinearity
- Understand the consequences of multicollinearity for inference in the classical linear regression model
- Be able to explore a set of data for signs of multicollinearity
- Have a critical awareness of the proposed and possible solutions for multicollinearity

CHAPTER SUMMARY

10.1 INTRODUCTION

So far, we have not said anything about the relationship between the variables appearing on the right-hand side of a single-equation model. They have been assumed, in the CLRM, to be uncorrelated with the disturbance term. Along with the other classical assumptions, this means that OLS estimates of their parameters will be BLUE. This chapter discusses multicollinearity, which is a term arising from the presence of covariance/correlation between the independent variables in our single-equation models. The precise definition of multicollinearity is given in Section 10.2. It seems unlikely that there will be absolutely no statistical relationship between the regressors in an equation. For one thing, they may share measurement errors, which could make the recorded variables correlated with each other even if there is no 'true' or causal relationship between them.

Often, theories will suggest a connection among the regressors. For example, suppose we are reviewing a study in industrial economics, which attempts to model profitability (P) as a function of industrial concentration (a proxy for the degree of monopoly) (IC) and the rate of research and development (RD) among other variables. One might well argue that research and development (R&D) will be higher in more concentrated sectors for at least two reasons: one stemming from the hypothesis that larger firms have more resources to fund such a risky activity as R&D and the other in the opposite direction that high levels of R&D may form a barrier to entry to the industry thereby raising the level of concentration.

The complete model described here could be written as:

$$P = b_0 + b_1 RD + b_2 IC + b_3 M + u \qquad (10.1)$$

$$RD = b_4 + b_5 IC + b_6 N + v \qquad (10.2)$$

where M and N are additional independent variables and u and v are classical disturbance terms. For convenience, we omit the subscripts and assume the model is linear and we also assume that $\text{cov}(u, w) = 0$.

We can substitute (10.2) into (10.1) and then get:

$$P = b_0 + b_1(b_4 + b_5 IC + b_6 N + v) + b_2 IC + b_3 M + u \qquad (10.3)$$

which shows that, although we still assume that the independent variables *are* independent of the dependent variable (P), that IC and RD are not independent of each other. The rest of this chapter deals with the problems caused by this.

The example just given suggests that perhaps the overall model needs to be made more complex to take account of these relationships. This is taken up in Chapters 12 and 13. This chapter deals only with the issue of exploring a single equation model for the presence of multicollinearity and the advisability of using various solutions to deal with it if it is found to be a problem.

10.2 WHAT IS MULTICOLLINEARITY?

It is easy to define the two polar extremes of perfect multicollinearity and the total absence of multicollinearity, but not so easy to define a level in between – what one would call a 'problem' of multicollinearity. In the case of perfect multicollinearity, each independent variable is an exact linear combination of all the other independent variables. This should result in it being impossible to estimate *any* of the parameters of the regression model, as the matrix of $X \cdot X$ will not invert, meaning that your computer package should issue a warning message of some sort. For example, in EViews, the message 'near singular matrix' will appear, and therefore no estimates will be presented if we have perfect or near-perfect multicollinearity. Some packages (for example SPSS) may decide to eliminate one or more of the variables instead and run a regression on the remaining variables while reporting a warning message that variables have been eliminated because of their collinearity. If this happens, you should not, of course, ignore it and proceed with the model that has been estimated. The whole point of this chapter is that you now need to explore why you have not been able to estimate your specified model.

The total absence of multicollinearity occurs when there is no correlation whatsoever between any combinations of the independent variables. This is referred to as orthogonality. In this situation, you will have the only case where a set of bivariate regressions of Y on each of the X's in isolation will give exactly the same set of results for the parameters as will be found in the full multiple regression. Note, however, that the R squared and standard errors of the coefficient estimates will of course change.

These two extreme cases are unlikely to occur in practice unless we have made a mistake of data or command entry (in the 'perfect multicollinearity') case, or we have used a perfectly controlled experimental design or engaged in a technique to produce orthogonalization (see Section 10.7 under 'Solutions') in the 'no multicollinearity' case. So we must return to the discussion of situations 'in between' perfect and no multicollinearity. The 'in between' case must have some degree of linear relationship between the independent variables. The question is: 'how much of a relationship is there?' When there are strong relationships between the independent variables to the extent that statistical inference (hypothesis testing) becomes difficult then we refer to there being a 'problem' of multicollinearity. The precise nature of the difficulties is addressed in the next section.

We should lay some stress on the 'multi' part of the word multicollinearity. Collinearity simply means that there is a linear relationship between variables. The 'multi' part alerts us to the fact that there may be several such relationships in a group of three or more independent variables. In the extreme case, we have pervasive or global multicollinearity in that every possible combination of variables in the set is exactly correlated with every other possible combination. However, we could have perfect, or less than perfect, 'local' multicollinearity. That is, within a group of six independent variables, for example, we could have three that are exactly related and a further group of three which have very little linear correlation with each other or the other three (individually or in any combination). That is, the problem may only be in part of the model. In general, people do not abandon research altogether because they have encountered a problem of multicollinearity. In the rest of this chapter, you will find the reasons for this.

The definition of multicollinearity is graphically illustrated in Figures 10.1 and 10.2, which are an extension of the diagrams we used to introduce the idea of covariance in Chapter 2. This time we use regular shapes (circles or ovals) to represent the variation in the data for the

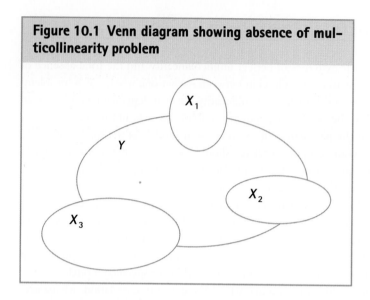

Figure 10.1 Venn diagram showing absence of mul-ticollinearity problem

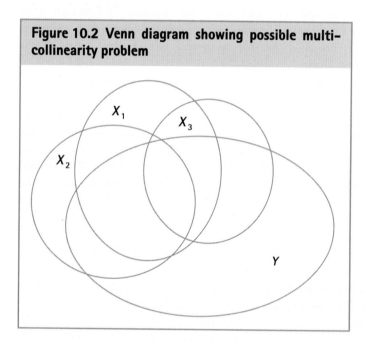

Figure 10.2 Venn diagram showing possible multi-collinearity problem

variables. We assume that we are dealing with a regression of Y on three independent variables X_1, X_2 and X_3. Figure 10.1 shows the case where there can be no multicollinearity (orthogonal or mutually uncorrelated data) as none of the shapes for the independent variables cut each other. The extent to which they overlap (cut) Y – the dependent variable – will determine the strength of any relationship found in estimating the model. Figure 10.2 shows the case where there might be a serious multicollinearity problem as there is a great deal of overlap between all the variables used.

10.3 CONSEQUENCES OF MULTICOLLINEARITY

Theoretically, there are no problematic consequences of less than perfect multicollinearity as the OLS estimators are still BLUE. As the estimators are theoretically unbiased then the prediction of Y is also unbiased. However, there are potentially serious practical consequences. In the extreme case of multicollinearity, it should be impossible to estimate an equation, and as mentioned in Section 10.2, you should be wary of computer packages that take steps to ensure you still get some results. In the less extreme cases, the BLUE properties of the estimators are still not altered but the regression model may become very limited in how useful it is for the researcher. In a bad case, it becomes very hard for the algorithm of OLS to work out how much of the variation in Y to attribute to each of the X's.

This will show itself in two major consequences.

(i) Instability

A regression equation can exhibit instability in a number of ways.

What this means is that slight changes in the method of estimation, or the data set or the specification of the variables employed, will produce quite drastic changes in the coefficients and their associated 't' ratios for the default null hypothesis. That is, removing or adding a variable or adding or deleting a small number of observations might lead to drastic swings in parameter estimates even up to the level of a switch from being highly positive to highly negative or vice versa. In extreme cases, you may find quite different results from running the same regression on different computer packages, although this seems less common now than it was in the early days of econometrics packages.

Such instability may present puzzles to those engaged in attempts to exactly replicate (see Chapter 1) earlier research, as even small changes in the measured variables might produce very different results. This could lead to incorrect suspicions about the original work, if multicollinearity was not identified as the culprit. This also suggests that research topics which show a very wide disparity in the range of estimates of the key elasticities (for example, this is the case for the demand for alcohol) might suffer from multicollinearity, although there could of course be other specification and data related explanations for this.

(ii) Over acceptance of the null hypothesis for individual regression parameters

Serious multicollinearity brings confusion into the use of the OLS regression method. The usefulness of OLS for social scientists rests heavily on its ability to separate out the influence of different variables on the dependent variable in an accurate way. If the block of independent variables are too heavily related to each other this property breaks down, meaning that the variance of the estimators becomes 'inflated' due to the inaccuracy introduced into the estimation of the standard errors. A research study, which suffers badly from multicollinearity, might lead us to the incorrect conclusion that a variable does not have significant 'explanatory power' when it does. The only way that we can know if this has happened is if we find some way of improving the research data or design to curb the multicollinearity problem.

In general, we tend to persevere with the data we have started with until we find sufficiently strong reasons to seek new data – so the next section looks at methods for finding evidence of the extent of the problem in your data set.

10.4 EXPLORING FOR MULTICOLLINEARITY

How can I know if I am likely to be a victim of serious multicollinearity in my research project? There is always likely to be some degree of collinearity in the independent variables so the issue is whether it is big enough and bad enough to be regarded as a 'multicollinearity problem'. The type of data (as discussed more fully under 'Solutions' in Section 10.7) gives us some basis for an initial idea about this. Broadly speaking, the problem is likely to be worst in a short time series.

There is a 'classic' case where we are instantly aware of the problem. This is where we get the seemingly contradictory finding of a statistically significant value of 'F for the equation' (see Chapter 5, Section 5.3, if you do not fully recall what this is) combined with acceptance of the null hypothesis (i.e. 'small' 't' ratios for *all* of the independent variables) for the individual coefficients. This may appear not to make sense, as it seems to be telling us that the variables are significant and insignificant for the same set of results. However, the results are perfectly logical, as what is happening is that we have a block or group of variables that does significantly explain the dependent variable but because it is made up of variables which share so much common variance we will find that deleting all but one of the variables (in the extreme case) will not make much difference to the overall fit as judged by the R squared.

You will recall from Section 5.3 that the 'F for the equation' is a test of the one-sided hypothesis that the R squared is greater than 0. If all the variables in our model share a high level of variation then successive deletion of variables will bring little change in the (insignificant) 't' ratios until we get down to the very last variable left. When we have pruned the model back to one variable then this *must* have a significant 't' ratio if there was a significant 'F' for the equation in the full model. It can, of course, happen that the multicollinearity is such that some variables start to have significant coefficients as we 'prune' the model back before we get to the extreme situation of only having a simple bivariate model.

To give some numerical illustration to the above using real data, we use a famous data set in Table 10.1, which is known as the 'Longley benchmarks'. A benchmark is something we use to judge accuracy or performance. These data are benchmarks for the performance of econometric packages. They relate to the USA for 1947–62 and consist of a measure of the size of the armed forces in the USA plus some economic and demographic variables.

GNP is in nominal terms. The GNP deflator is an alternative price index which includes estimates of the prices of public sector items. Let us specify a model as:

$$Y = b_0 + b_1 X_1 + b_2 X_2 + b_3 X + b_4 X_4 + u \tag{10.4}$$

where Y is total employment and the X's are armed forces, *GNP*, the *GNP deflator* and *Year* which will operate as a time trend. The time subscript has been omitted. It runs from 1947 to 1962.

The OLS estimates of this are shown in Table 10.2. You can see that the full model has only one significant variable, which is *GDP*, with the R squared being very high. The simplistic conclusion that might be drawn (ignoring multicollinearity) is that the other variables have no relationship with the dependent variable. Table 10.2 provides some alternative estimates of the model to show its stability based on deleting one year from the beginning then two years from the beginning then one year from the end and two years from the end. Further exploratory estimates are shown in Table 10.3, which repeats the first line of Table 10.2 (i.e. the full model)

Table 10.1 The Longley benchmark data

Year	GNP deflator	GNP (million $)	Armed forces	Total employment	AGR	NONAGR
1947	83.0	234 289	1 590	60 323	8 256	38 407
1948	88.5	259 426	1 456	61 122	7 960	39 241
1949	88.2	258 054	1 616	60 171	8 017	37 922
1950	89.5	284 599	1 650	61 187	7 497	39 196
1951	96.2	328 975	3 099	63 221	7 048	41 460
1952	98.1	346 999	3 594	63 639	6 792	42 216
1953	99.0	365 385	3 547	64 989	6 555	43 587
1954	100.0	363 112	3 350	63 761	6 495	42 271
1955	101.2	397 469	3 048	66 019	6 718	43 761
1956	104.6	419 180	2 857	67 857	6 572	45 131
1957	108.4	442 769	2 798	68 169	6 222	45 278
1958	110.8	444 546	2 637	66 513	5 844	43 530
1959	112.6	482 704	2 552	68 655	5 836	45 214
1960	114.2	502 601	2 514	69 564	5 723	45 850
1961	115.7	518 173	2 572	69 331	5 463	45 397
1962	116.9	554 894	2 827	70 551	5 190	46 652

Note: AGR and NONAGR stand for agricultural and non-agricultural employment.

Table 10.2 OLS estimates of a model applied to the Longley benchmark data

Dependent variable: Total employment
Independent variables:

Sample	1947–1962	1948–1962	1949–1962	1947–1961	1947–1960
Constant	1 169 088	1 156 083	1 005 747	1 459 415	1 391 872
	(1.4)	(1.32)	(0.89)	(2.043)	(2.155)
Year	−576.46	−570.46	−492.53	−721.76	−685.47
	(1.33)	(1.26)	(0.85)	(1.95)	(2.05)
GNP deflator	−19.77	0.349	−12.67	−181.23	−225.25
	(0.14)	(0.002)	(0.0073)	(1.34)	(1.81)
GNP	0.064	0.062	0.06	0.091	0.096
	(3.23)	(2.85)	(2.42)	(4.5)	(5.19)
Armed forces	−0.101	0.011	0.077	−0.075	−0.157
	(0.033)	(0.033)	(0.17)	(0.29)	(0.65)
R^2	0.974	0.969	0.965	0.98	0.983
N	16	15	14	15	14

Note: Absolute 't' ratios in parentheses.

Table 10.3 OLS estimates of a model applied to the Longley benchmark data: Successive variable deletions example

Dependent variable: Total employment
Independent variables:

Constant	1 169 088	11 579 325	56 945.04	33 189.17
	(1.4)	(1.58)	(7.64)	(15.56)
Year	−576.46	−570.66		
	(1.33)	(1.51)		
GNP	0.064	0.064	0.044	
	(3.23)	(3.45)	(3.27)	
GNP deflator	−19.77	−21.28	−85.11	315.97
	(0.14)	(0.17)	(0.69)	(15.17)
Armed forces	−0.101			
	(0.033)			
R^2	0.974	0.974	0.969	0.943
N	16	16	16	16

Note: Absolute 't' ratios in parentheses.

for ease of comparison purposes. The rest of this table shows what happens when we gradually drop selected variables from the model. Table 10.2 shows some strong fluctuations in the pattern of results. The elements common to all the results shown are a high R squared, significance of *GNP* throughout and insignificance of the *Armed forces* variable throughout. There are changes in sign and significance levels for the other variables. For the *GNP* variable, we get a larger coefficient with a bigger 't' ratio when observations from the end of period are deleted than compared with the whole sample or beginning of period. It is not immediately apparent from this set of results whether or not we have a problem with multicollinearity.

Table 10.3 estimates Equation (10.4) and estimates the following equations:

$$Y = b_0 + b_1 X_1 + b_2 X_2 + b_3 X_3 + u \tag{10.5}$$

$$Y = b_0 \qquad + b_2 X_2 + b_3 X_3 + u \tag{10.6}$$

$$Y = b_0 + \qquad\qquad b_3 X_3 + u \tag{10.7}$$

The results in Table 10.3 may perhaps give us some more clues. Purely arbitrarily, we drop one variable then another then another for the purposes of exploration. We drop the armed forces variable first, which makes very little difference to the results. This should not be too surprising when you look at the figures shown in the next two tables (Table 10.4 and Table 10.5). The next variable to be dropped is the time trend (*Year*), which causes a large increase in the significance of the intercept, a decrease in the coefficient on *GNP* and a large increase in the absolute value of the coefficient on the *GNP deflator*. There is not much change in the 't' ratios on these variables. The R squared does not fall by very much. This is what we would expect when we delete a variable which had a relatively small 't' ratio on its coefficient. So now we are left with only two explanatory variables and when we delete the one that has been statistically significant in every regression, we have run-gnp. Now we see a sudden massive increase in the 't' ratio on the *GNP deflator* to a very high level of significance and furthermore its coefficient changes sign quite dramatically. This suggests there is potentially quite a serious problem of multicollinearity which we now explore further.

LOOKING AT CORRELATIONS

Perfect multicollinearity and the 'classic' case are easy to spot but, in reality, we are more likely to have a picture which is much less clear. For example, what do we conclude if some of the coefficients are insignificant when we strongly hypothesized they should not be, or worse still we have unexpected strongly negative coefficients? Should we blame this on multicollinearity or instead conclude that the theories we have been given are wrong? The logical response is to embark on some 'exploratory data analysis', which is not to be confused with data mining (see Chapter 1).

The simplest possible type of exploration is to look at the bivariate relationships in the sets of the independent variables which can be done with the matrix of zero order (Pearsonian) correlation coefficients as shown in Table 2.2 of Chapter 2. This can provide some kind of guide to the degree of collinearity in the data. Looking back at Table 2.2, we can see some quite strong correlations. The education–GNP correlation is 0.92383 while the income–price correlation (frequently problematic in time-series demand studies) is 0.8354. Do bear in mind that the percentage of variation shared by two variables is the square of the numbers shown ($\times 100$), not the numbers themselves.

Let us return to our Longley benchmark regression model. This did not fit the 'classic case' as we had significant 't' ratios on some of the variables in the Table 10.2 regressions. The partial correlation matrix for the Longley benchmark data of Table 10.1 is shown in Table 10.4.

Table 10.4 Partial correlation matrix of independent variables (data from Table 10.1)

	Year	GNP	GNP deflator	
Year	1			
GNP	0.995	1		
GNP deflator	0.991	0.992	1	
Armed forces	0.417	0.446	0.465	1

There is a clear pattern here of high levels of correlation between the pairs of variables other than that for *Armed forces*. The partial correlation matrix is a useful tool but it has its limitations. We should note two chief ones:

(i) When we are dealing with two dummy variables, 'r' is not an appropriate measure to test for correlation, as the variables are not measured on a continuous scale. The appropriate measure of correlation should be based on a Chi-squared test with one degree of freedom on the 2×2 contingency table for the two variables. The automatic procedures on computer packages will of course compute 'r' for two dummy variables as there is no built-in check on the appropriateness of tests so it is easy to forget about the dummy variable issue when one produces a partial correlation matrix as a checking device. The appropriate 'r' in this case is in fact the square root of the Chi-squared from the contingency table divided by n the sample size. Given that it is based on categorical data, this measure (phi) does not have the same properties as 'r', for example it does not tend to 1 for a perfect fit.

(ii) Multicollinearity is not exclusively due to correlations between pairs of variables. One might fail to see a strong connection between the bivariate relationships yet there could be a strong linear relationship between a combination of three or more variables. A simple way to look at this is to compute a set of 'auxiliary' R squared rather than 'r'. We could do this, for example, by running a set of regressions where each of the independent variables is regressed in turn on all of the others to obtain an R squared which measures the percentage of variation in each variable explained by the others. It should be noted that this is a different use of regression from what we have been developing so far. There is no implication that there necessarily must be a theoretical relationship underpinning these regressions, rather they are used for descriptive purposes as part of our exploration of the properties of our data set. Table 10.5 shows the auxiliary R squared (along with VIFs, see below) from the Longley benchmarks.

Table 10.5 Auxiliary R squared and VIFs from the Longley data of Table 10.1

	Auxiliary R squareds	VIFs
Year	0.992	143.46
GNP	0.994	132.46
GNP deflator	0.989	75.67
Armed forces	0.539	1.55

You can see that the *Armed forces* term still does not seem to be particularly worrying but there is a suggestion of serious difficulty with the other three variables. The construction of an R squared from the independent variables paves the way for the Farrar–Glauber test discussed in Section 10.5 and the technique of Principal Components Analysis discussed in Section 10.7.

OTHER EXPLORATORY AVENUES
VIFs

Some computer packages will provide estimates of VIFs (variance inflation factors) as part of their collinearity diagnostics. The magnitude of the VIF gives a guide to the extent of the problem. If it is around 1 then it suggests that there is little problem as the variance has not been 'inflated'. The VIF is a meaure of how much the standard errors have been inflated when there is collinearity compared with a situation of no collinearity. The more it increases above 1, the more we have to worry. The VIF can be calculated from the R squareds just suggested for each independent variable regressed on the others. The formula for a VIF is:

$$(1 - RM^2)^{-1} \tag{10.8}$$

where RM is one of the auxiliary R squareds. If the R squared is 0 then the VIF will be 1 and the larger is the R squared, then the bigger is the VIF. It has been suggested that the rule of thumb for a VIF is 10. So a VIF of 10+ is seen as a cause for anxiety, or in other words an R squared of 0.90 or more. The average of all the VIFs for the data indicates the average inflation of the standard errors due to collinearity. It is not clear that an average VIF is a particularly useful statistic. The VIFs for the Longley data are shown in the second column of Table 10.5. Not surprisingly, given the auxiliary R squared's value we have already looked at, these show considerable grounds for alarm with the exception of the *Armed forces* variable. The other VIFs are all very much greater than the 'rule of thumb' warning value of 10.

This section has been about exploration not testing. This is the 'art' rather than the science part of econometrics. We are trying to learn about the properties of our data set so that we can produce the most insightful formulation of the core model that we began with. Nevertheless there is a strong current in econometrics of attempting to organize the whole procedure of research around testing and so we turn now to an attempt to devise tests for multicollinearity.

10.5 A PROPOSED TEST FOR MULTICOLLINEARITY

Exploration of data is time-consuming and requires a degree of judgement. It would be easier if we could find a standard hypothesis test that would come to a definite conclusion. We now look at an attempt to formally test for multicollinearity. It should be borne in mind that exploration can be useful when we come to deal with causes (Section 10.6) and solutions to the problem (Section 10.7).

Research work does not often report formal tests for multicollinearity. The more usual case is a brief verbal summary of the kind of exploration of the data described in the last section. Papers will often be sent to journals with a comment like 'multicollinearity is not a problem in this paper because none of the partial correlation coefficients was particularly large'. It is quite unusual to see discussion of VIFs in a paper by an economist, although the review study in the field of 'animal health economics', which comes in Section 10.8, does do so.

The main attempt to establish a standard test for multicollinearity like those we encountered for the CLRM assumptions in Chapter 9 was proposed by Farrar and Glauber (1967), thus giving rise to the name **Farrar–Glauber test**. This test is a logical development of the descriptive exploratory measures using r and R^2 discussed in the previous section. The test is performed as follows:

Step 1
Use the full matrix of Pearsonian correlation coefficients for the independent variables such as those shown in Table 10.3. That is, we have every figure filled in on both sides of the diagonal. From this we calculate the determinant | A | of this matrix. If there is perfect multicollinearity this determinant will be 0 as every element in the matrix will be 1. In the total absence of multicollinearity (i.e. an orthogonal data matrix), this determinant will be 1 as every element in the matrix will be 0. In practice the value will tend to be somewhere between 0 and 1. For the data of Table 10.1 the determinant is 0.0000901 which is very close to zero.

Step 2

Use a Chi-squared test to determine whether the determinant of the matrix is significantly greater than zero. The formula devised by Farrar and Glauber is:

$$\chi^2 = -\{n - 1 - 1/6(2k + 5)\}\log_e SD \tag{10.9}$$

where n is the sample size (16 in this case), k is the number of explanatory variables (4 in this case) and SD is the value of the determinant from Step 1.

This has a Chi-squared distribution with degrees of freedom of $\frac{1}{2}(k(k-1))$ which in this case is 6. The test value is approximately 119.354 while the critical value at the 5 per cent level is 12.59. This again strongly indicates the presence of multicollinearity.

Step 3

Estimate the auxiliary R squared values by regressing each of the independent variables on all of the others. Use these to perform standard 'F' tests for the hypothesis that all parameters are zero. The figures for these data are for *Year* 587.3, *GNP* 717.89, *GNP deflator* 389.6 and for *Armed forces* 5.066. All of these are strongly statistically significant indicating a problem of multicollinearity with each variable.

Step 4

Do 't' tests on the partial correlation matrix, which in this case would be Table 10.5.

IS THE FARRAR–GLAUBER TEST OF ANY USE?

Before discussing this, we need to recall why we might want to do a multicollinearity test in the first place. Remember that multicollinearity is not a violation of the classical assumptions about the disturbance term. Rather, it is a problem of the experimental design, which is likely to be present in almost all social scientific statistical work. So, what would we hope to gain from a test? Would we reject the use of an econometric model totally and try some other approach to the research question? Or perhaps, more likely, would we reject the data being used and go and look for better data?

As we are talking about a test, there is, as ever, the problem of the trade-off between Type I and Type II error which lies behind the formal definition of the 'Power' of a test. More specifically, the use of a test should worry us if it fails to find for serious multicollinearity when it should and vice versa. The reservations usually voiced about the Farrar–Glauber test fall into the latter category. That is the determinant of the partial correlation matrix may be such that we would reject a model which is, in practice, fairly stable and useful for prediction and hypothesis testing.

10.6 CAUSES OF MULTICOLLINEARITY

If we can track down the causes of multicollinearity, then we will be in a better position to come up with a solution. There are a number of factors that can give rise to multicollinearity, besides the basic one of presence of a relationship between the X variables.

(i) Entry mistake

If you mistakenly enter the same variable twice, or a variable which is a linear combination of other variables, then you will have collinearity. As was indicated in Section 10.2, this should lead your computer package to give you an error warning when it refuses to estimate the equation for you or it may simply drop one of the variables.

(ii) 'False' exact linear relationships in the source data

It is always wise to entertain doubts about the validity of one's data and these doubts are likely to multiply when things seem to be going wrong. One should never forgot that data is the result of collection by fallible humans who may even resort to concocting the data. There are stories of data for variables in government statistics in some countries being arrived at simply by taking a fraction of another variable as an estimate: for example, assuming investment in some sector is simply x per cent of that sector's output. If you had the misfortune to include the original variable and the variable derived from it, in this way, then you would be in the same situation as described above under 'Entry mistake', and should receive an error warning when you try to estimate the equation and will not be allowed to do so or one variable will be dropped and a warning given. A false non-linear relationship between two variables in a model specified as linear will not be so readily detected as the degree of correlation between the variable 'falsely' constructed will be weakened.

(iii) Inclusion of an identity relationship

Some variables may be defined in such a way that they form an identity; for example, in simple national income accounting, aggregate savings must equal income minus consumption. If we include all the components of an identity in an equation this may bring multicollinearity into a model.

(iv) Dummy variable trap

The 'dummy variable trap' was explained in Section 7.2 of Chapter 7. It should cause perfect multicollinearity and hence, as in the two causes just described, we should receive an error message from the computer, which will refuse to estimate the equation or drop one of the dummies, depending on which package you are using. This is because including an intercept and a full set of dummies (i.e. one for every group in a category) will introduce a perfect linear relationship.

(v) Too many dummies

The last mentioned situation should not occur, as you should know better than to cause the problem. However, dummies may still cause multicollinearity even when there is no dummy variable trap if there are high levels of shared occurrences between dummies. This could be caused by careless definitions of dummy variables – for example, using overlapping definitions might lead us near to a dummy variable trap.

(vi) Overspecification due to caution

In Chapters 3 and 5, we discussed the question of how many variables should be in our specified model. You will recall that social scientific theory tends to be insufficiently precise for us to be able to see exactly what the optimal list of variables in any model should be. Rather, we face problems of omitting relevant variables and including irrelevant variables because of the doubts surrounding which variables should be included as 'controls' to remove any bias in the estimation of our focus parameters. The normal suggestion in econometrics texts is that we should err on the side of caution by overspecifying rather than underspecifying a model, although we should stop short of blatant undirected 'data mining'. One problem with this is that expanding the set of variables increases the risk of serious multicollinearity arising.

(vii) Data mining

As we have just said, data mining is frowned upon. The worst symptoms of multicollinearity may be one fate which awaits the unscrupulous data miner. Data mining was discussed in Chapter 1. Let us suppose that the data miner is trying to produce a large R squared. Adding variables which have only a loose justification to be in the model may assist in this practice. These additional variables cause us to lose degrees of freedom, they may bring in shared measurement error between the variables and ultimately might lead us to accept wildly inaccurate inferences about the coefficients on the 'focus' variables.

(viii) Micronumerosity

Arthur Goldberger coined this term to describe multicollinearity as a consequence of small sample size. The smaller a sample is, all other things being equal, then the less scope there is for a set of variables to exhibit differences in their variability. The reverse does not, of course, apply. That is, a large sample is not a guarantee that we will not have multicollinearity problems as the information content of the data must also be expanded in terms of the degree of differential movement in the variables. Micronumerosity could be one of the problems in the Longley data; although we would not want to take the model that was proposed in Equation (10.1) too seriously as a 'good' specification, in the first place, as it was set up purposely to demonstrate the effects of multicollinearity.

(ix) Definition of variables

It is possible that we have set up our equation in a way which gives rise to multicollinearity. For example, if we estimate a time series of nominal macroeconomic variables rather than real ones then data may not be differentiated enough for us to produce useful and stable results. This is because the movements in all the nominal series reflect a common trend due to changes in the price index.

(x) Common trends or seasonal effects

There may also be shared variation between series if they all have a common trend. If we remove this trend using the method described in Section 7.8 then we may find that there are some meaningful relationships in the deviations of the variables from the trend. It is worth pointing out that adding a trend is a 'solution' to the problem, which is *opposite* to that sometimes suggested in that we are *adding* a variable to the model rather than removing one. The same kind of problem as common trend could occur with common seasonal effects. That is, a set of independent variables could share common seasonal movements, which mask the relationship that deviations from this have with the dependent variable. This problem could be removed when seasonal dummies are added.

10.7 SHOULD WE WORRY ABOUT MULTICOLLINEARITY OR NOT?

By this point, you should be clear on what multicollinearity is, what the likely causes are, and conscious of the fact that it is not generally considered to be worthwhile to formally test for it. However, should you be worried about it? This depends on why you are doing the regression and the availability of satisfactory 'solutions'.

ARE WE FORECASTING?

If we are using the model for forecasting then there is a standard argument as to why multicollinearity might not be a problem. We may only be interested in forecasting the dependent variable rather than testing hypotheses about the parameters of the regression equation and therefore multicollinearity does not matter. This is true, but one should not become over-excited about it, as there are limitations on the use of a forecasting equation which is seriously affected by multicollinearity because:

(i)   The pattern of multicollinearity needs to be stable over time – if it shifts between the estimation and forecast periods then the equation may become unreliable.

(ii) If we are forecasting for the purposes of formulating government policy or business strategy then we want more information from the model than just an unbiased predictor of the dependent variable.

The explanation of the argument that multicollinearity may not be a problem for forecasting is that forecasting relies on the performance of the block of variables as a combination. It does not matter how much of the forecast variation can be attributed to individual variables. However, this is of little help to formulators of government policy or makers of business decisions, who may wish to calculate the required changes to key variables such as tax rates or price changes, for example. If you were making a business forecast in which the focus was on cutting the price of a new product to help it penetrate the market, then you would want a reliable estimate of the parameter and its standard error in order to inform your judgements.

IS THE PROBLEM LOCAL?

There is one clear-cut situation where we might not want to worry too much. This is where there is only 'local multicollinearity' and this occurs only in a specific part of the model. It must occur only in the 'control' variables as it is of no help to us if the 'focus' variables are involved in the excess collinearity in the data. Let us imagine we are dealing with a case of sex discrimination and our main interest was in obtaining an accurate (unbiased) estimate of the rate of sex discrimination. This could be done using the type of earnings functions used in the review studies of Chapter 7 where we use a male/female dummy to get the percentage rate of discrimination by multiplying its coefficient by 100. As many other factors influence the rate of pay we would need to include a large range of control variables and we may well want to err on the side of overspecification of the variable set. If we do, then the problem of multicollinearity within the control variables may arise. So long as we do not wish or need to know anything about the individual contribution of these variables then all that matters is that the estimate on the focus variable (the sex dummy) is improved by including all of these variables.

SOLUTIONS

One reason not to worry is that there may be a solution to the problems that have been discovered. The best response to any econometric problem is to try to improve either the data or the model specification. Here is a list of possible solutions when you think you have a multicollinearity problem. Some of these fall into the category of data and model specification improvements, while others are technical solutions involving modifications to the estimation method.

(i) Increase the sample size

It follows from the discussion of micronumerosity in Section 10.6, that we may be able to reduce the degree of multicollinearity by extending the size of the sample. We could do this in a number of ways. One is to use more frequent data – for example, quarterly rather than annual, or we could pool cross-section and time-series data such as using 20 countries over a 15-year period instead of just one. Alternately we could just use more of the same source, for example go back and get 50 years of annual data rather than just 15. This can help us in two ways. One is purely a matter of arithmetic as, all other things being equal, bigger samples mean more degrees of freedom which means the standard errors are calculated using a larger divisor. This is going to reduce the standard error and thereby it is likely to increase the chance of finding significant 't' ratios. More importantly, increasing the size of the sample, by any of the above means, can increase the 'span' of the data; that is, there is more variability in each of the variables enabling us to identify more successfully any relationships that exist between the variables. If the span does not improve then there is little real benefit to be had from having more data. For example, if we were having problems with a set of quarterly data and we decided to triple the sample size by expanding to monthly data this may not necessarily solve the problem. Aside from the fact that some data may not be reported on a monthly basis, it might be the case that we are dealing with variables which do not exhibit meaningful month-to-month variation.

(ii) Principal Components Analysis (PCA)

This technique is mentioned quite often in statistics and econometrics textbooks, although it is not seen that frequently in research papers by economists. It is used in the article by O'Brien, Lloyd and Kaneene, which is covered in our review studies panel in Section 10.8. Principal components is a matrix manipulation technique which will turn any set of variables into a new set of variables, of the same number, which are orthogonal. Each 'component' or 'factor' is another linear equation, which is composed of all the variables which have been 'factored' with weights attached to them. These weights lie between 0 and 1 because the data are normalized to a mean of zero and a variance of 1 before the matrix manipulation. This involves subtracting the mean and dividing by the standard error. That is, we get a z-transformation:

$$X_z = (X - \bar{X})/\sigma_x \tag{10.10}$$

The set of equations will generate a factor score for each component. Let us assume that there are four variables (X_1, X_2, X_3, X_4), then a principal components analysis (PCA) of these produces the following set of results:

$$\hat{PC}1 = \hat{z}_{11}X_1, +\hat{z}_{12}X_2, +\hat{z}_{13}X_3, +\hat{z}_{14}X_4 \tag{10.11}$$

$$\hat{PC}2 = \hat{z}_{21}X_1, +\hat{z}_{22}X_2, +\hat{z}_{23}X_3, +\hat{z}_{24}X_4 \tag{10.12}$$

$$\hat{PC}3 = \hat{z}_{31}X_1, +\hat{z}_{32}X_2, +\hat{z}_{33}X_3, +\hat{z}_{34}X_4 \tag{10.13}$$

$$\hat{PC}4 = \hat{z}_{41}X_1, +\hat{z}_{42}X_2, +\hat{z}_{43}X_3, +\hat{z}_{44}X_4 \tag{10.14}$$

where the ^ denotes estimates and the z's are the loadings on each component. The subscripts have been omitted.

This transformation produces principal components that are different linear equations made up of proportions of the original variables. The number of principal components is always equal to the number of variables. The figures shown in Table 10.6 are known as factor loadings and will be in standardized units (due to the application of Equation (10.10) to all the X's) forcing them to lie between 0 and 1. Computer packages usually display the results of a PCA in order of the percentage each component contributes to the explanation of the overall variance in the original data matrix.

Those who use PCA as a proposed solution to multicollinearity sometimes then engage in the game of naming the components based on inspection of the pattern of factor loadings. They then drop some of the lower (i.e. less important in terms of explanatory power) components. The extreme case would be to include only the first component. Given that the new set of variables are orthogonal, they can be entered into a regression equation in which they will be totally free from multicollinearity. To illustrate this let us go back to the data set on Turkish cigarette smoking which was introduced in Chapter 3 (Tansel, 1993) and was used in other chapters as illustrative material. This had three independent variables for education, prices and income. If we apply principal components to these as shown in Table 10.6 we get three principal components, which are labelled PC1, PC2 and PC3.

In this particular case, the first component explains most of the variation in the set of data for the three variables. You might find that packages might stop at extracting this factor, on their default settings, as the others are too inconsequential. The factor loadings in the top half of the table do not allow us to readily label factor 1 in any obvious kind of way. Each variable has a large coefficient (well over 0.9 in every case). Let us proceed to do a regression on the first two principal components.

The estimating equation is linear with a classical disturbance term and we omit the subscripts. It is as follows:

$$CCA = b_0 + b_1 PC1 + b_2 PC2 + b_3 PC3 + u \tag{10.15}$$

This is shown in the first column of Table 10.7. The remaining equations involve placing zero restrictions on b_2 and b_3.

277

Table 10.6 Principal components of real income, relative prices and education rates

Component matrix

	Component		
	PC1	PC2	PC3
GNP	1.973	−0.117	−0.201
RPC	0.916	0.397	4.696E−02
TER	0.951	−0.263	0.160

Component	Percentage of variance	Cumulative percentage of variance explained
1	89.695	89.695
2	08.028	97.723
3	02.277	100.000

Table 10.7 OLS regression of cigarette consumption on the principal components of real income, relative prices and education rates

Dependent variable:	Per capita consumption		
Constant	2.205	2.205	2.205
	(77.465)	(69.985)	(55.593)
PC1	0.123	0.123	0.123
	(4.23)	(3.822)	(3.036)
PC2	−0.131	−0.131	
	(4.535)	(4.097)	
PC3	−0.076		
	(2.62)		
R^2	0.644	0.547	0.254
N	29	29	29

The table shows the model with all three component scores used as independent variables and then with the least important variables gradually removed. This leads to a decline in the R squared as you would expect, as we are removing 'explanatory' information. The coefficient estimates for every single parameter are the same no matter which of the three regressions on factor scores we use. This is because the components are orthogonal due to the prior process of constructing them. The 't' values change because of the loss of 'explanatory' power as we move from left to right. In each case they must decline.

Clearly, PCA 'solves' the problem in a purely mathematical sense. With one click of a mouse it abolishes all multicollinearity in a set of data. But, what use is the solution it produces? If our interest was in parameters attached to some of the original variables, then it is of very little use if these variables have been included in the data matrix which was subject to a PCA. In this particular case, it is difficult to make much sense of the results in Table 10.7 as the second two components have not 'loaded' with any noticeable pattern and in the first all the variables have loaded so heavily it cannot be seen as a composite of any pair of them.

However, there is some potential gain if the PCA has been used to handle a set of control variables. The gain will not arise from factoring the 'control' variables. This simply converts them into a set of orthogonal variables, which makes no difference to the focus variable, that was not included in the factor analysis. Where a gain might come is if we can substantially reduce the number of control variables and thereby gain degrees of freedom and eliminate 'noisy' variation that is affecting the focus parameter. For example, if we have a relatively small sample, say a cross-section of 50 or so states or counties and we want to measure some vaguely defined aspect of these, such as masculinity or political freedom, and there are up to 50 proxies that might be used, then the PCA might enable us to condense these into a small set of factors using just a few principal components.

A good example of this kind of 'data reduction' can be found in the study of crime on American university campuses by Fox and Hellman (1985). They reduced 30 variables which describe the profile of 222 universities and colleges into three components described as Quality, Urbanness and Size. This may help the precision of the results we obtain on the focus variables, although the published version of this paper presents only regressions on the three components without other variables.

This is a small shred of hope that applies to very specific situations. We should not lose sight of the fact that PCA is not some kind of 'magic' that makes the difficulties of inference with highly collinear data disappear. It is worth noting that you will find some studies which use principal components or factor analysis *without* mentioning multicollinearity at all. This is because these studies are using data reduction techniques in an attempt to measure attributes of something, such as the quality of a house or its neighbourhood, which cannot be directly represented in the data.

(iii) Factor analysis

This is a more advanced version of PCA in which we allow for a relationship between the principal components themselves. This is done through factor rotation for which there are a number of different methods, which will give different answers in terms of the factor loadings. To be more exact, the methods we are suggesting here are called 'exploratory factor analysis' in the factor analysis literature. There is, outside economics mainly, a specialist branch of 'confirmatory factor analysis', using dedicated packages such as LISREL. This involves some element of modelling in that fixed constraints are imposed on some parameters in a system of equations. It is therefore somewhat closer to the topics discussed in Chapters 12 and 13.

(iv) Ridge regression

Ridge regression has sometimes been used in applied microeconometric papers. An example is shown in the review study for cigarette smoking by Young (1983) summarized in Section 10.8, which as you will see yields spectacularly good results in terms of 't' ratios, although he does not provide any OLS results for comparison. To fully comprehend the implications of this technique, you perhaps need to refer back to the discussion in Section 3.4 of Chapter 3 on the issue of estimators being BLUE. Ridge regression estimators will *not* be BLUE as the B part of the acronym no longer applies. In order to try to obtain smaller variances on the estimated parameters, the ridge regression trades off the unbiasedness property. It involves adding a parameter (confusingly denoted by k, the same symbol we normally give to the number of parameters being estimated in econometrics) to the matrix calculation used to obtain multiple regression estimates. A k of zero is the OLS model in its usual form. The researcher chooses this parameter and there is clearly a subjective element as the results can change quite dramatically as we vary the k. In the review study shown below k is set at 0.4 simply because that was the value selected in a previous study on the topic. To illustrate the effects of ridge regression, I have estimated Equation (10.1) allowing the k value to vary up to 1 in steps of 0.05. This is depicted in Table 10.8 and Figures 10.3 and 10.4. Figure 10.4 merely graphs the second column of Table 10.8 but it strikingly illustrates the loss in R squared value as we increase the k value. Figure 10.3 shows the actual regression coefficients, while Table 10.8 shows the beta coefficients for the same results, that is, they are in standard deviation units.

Table 10.8 Ridge regression of Equation (10.1) in standardized coefficients R square and beta coefficients for different values of k

K	R squared	YEAR	GNP	GNP deflator	Armed forces
0.00000	0.97352	−0.781476	1.822464	−0.060743	−0.002010
0.05000	0.95921	0.250976	0.453688	0.243823	0.034981
0.10000	0.95702	0.278438	0.382595	0.269558	0.040955
0.15000	0.95527	0.284117	0.353691	0.275924	0.045762
0.20000	0.95338	0.284388	0.336391	0.276932	0.049807
0.25000	0.95126	0.282617	0.324020	0.275793	0.053247
0.30000	0.94890	0.279924	0.314255	0.273636	0.056188
0.35000	0.94630	0.276782	0.306070	0.270953	0.058709
0.40000	0.94349	0.273421	0.298938	0.267989	0.060872
0.45000	0.94048	0.269963	0.292558	0.264879	0.062729
0.50000	0.93730	0.266477	0.286744	0.261702	0.064322
0.55000	0.93395	0.263005	0.281376	0.258506	0.065686
0.60000	0.93046	0.259571	0.276369	0.255320	0.066852
0.65000	0.92684	0.256189	0.271662	0.252163	0.067844
0.70000	0.92311	0.252870	0.267212	0.249048	0.068683
0.75000	0.91927	0.249617	0.262984	0.245983	0.069389
0.80000	0.91534	0.246435	0.258952	0.242972	0.069977
0.85000	0.91133	0.243323	0.255093	0.240019	0.070460
9.90000	0.90724	0.240283	0.251391	0.237125	0.070851
0.95000	0.90309	0.237313	0.247831	0.234291	0.071161
1.0000	0.89888	0.234413	0.244402	0.231517	0.071397

This approach was originally developed more as a diagnostic tool than a problem-solving method. That is, the coefficient changes with the value of k as shown in Table 10.8 and Figure 10.1 may be used to indicate how stable the equation is. Table 10.8 shows very dramatic changes with the first slight increase of k to 0.05. Three coefficients change from negative to

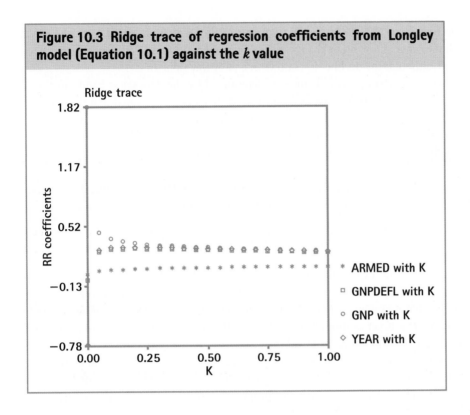

Figure 10.3 Ridge trace of regression coefficients from Longley model (Equation 10.1) against the k value

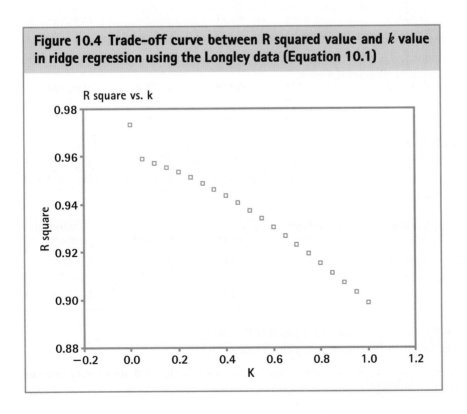

Figure 10.4 Trade-off curve between R squared value and k value in ridge regression using the Longley data (Equation 10.1)

positive while that for *GNP* falls to nearly a quarter of its OLS value. Apart from the *GNP* coefficient, all the others show slight change as k is increased to 1. The *GNP* coefficient declines as k is increased, although the decline slows down at a fairly low value of k.

How the coefficients change, as k changes, is determined by the data set at hand but the R squared value is guaranteed to decrease as k is increased. It should be stressed that this increase does not mean your model is getting 'better' in some real sense as we have now started interfering with the properties of the data set.

There are perhaps two main points to be made about the use of ridge regression:

(a)   As you can see, in the review study (by Young in Section 10.8) and Table 10.8, it can produce remarkable results in terms of getting 'good' 't' ratios by the choice of k;
    but
(b)   despite this, one seldom sees ridge regression used by economists.

Before we go on, some explanation for point (b) is called for. Difficulties arise from this method which are best summarized by observing that the process of selecting k might be seen as yet another form of data mining. Many learned papers have been written to propose methods of determining optimal k, yet as Judge *et al.* (1985, p. 915) observe, the practice of choosing k from the ridge trace is 'more of an art form' than a science. Ridge regression departs from the OLS estimators, which deliver a set of estimates to the researcher once the data and model have been set, in that it allows the researcher to vary results by choosing k. The search for k tends to be governed by ideas of what the 'correct' or 'proper' sort of results are for the model being estimated.

Given that we cannot know in advance what the 'correct' results are, for a given set of data, then 'tweaking' the k value in the search for results which confirm our prior ideas seems to be going down the path of data mining. Even if we use some predetermined algorithm, which rules out data mining, it is not clear that the set of estimates we end up with is guaranteed to be more correct than our collinear OLS ones.

(v) Use of restrictions

We have already mentioned this solution by implication under definition of variables in Section 10.6. In that case, we required variables to be real rather than nominal, which is an imposition of a prior relationship on the model. For example, take the following log linear model of demand for a product:

$$\log(QX) = b_0 + b_1 \log(Y/P) + b_2 \log(PX/P) + u \tag{10.16}$$

where QX is units of the good sold, Y is average national income, P is the retail price index and PX is the price of the good. Subscripts are omitted. This model implicitly assumes two restrictions:

▶ that the coefficient on Y is equal and opposite to that on P;
▶ that the coefficient on PX is equal and opposite to that on P.

(if PX, P and Y, are in logarithms).

This simplifies the model and is likely to reduce the presence of multicollinearity.

In the extreme case we could simply assume that a parameter took a particular value which would mean the dependent variable became $Y - b^* X$ where b^* is the assumed value and X is the variable to which it belongs. Let us assume that b_2 is equal to 0.6 (i.e. the price elasticity), then the estimating equation becomes:

$$\log(QX) - 0.6\log(PX/P) = b_0 + b_1\log(Y/P) + u \qquad \text{(10.17)}$$

(vi) Extraneous estimates

This is a development of the previous solution where we take the restriction from some prior research rather than from a hypothesis (or even an arbitrarily decided number). That is, the use of 0.6 in Equation (10.4) is justified as coming from some prior research. The term 'extraneous' is a rather unfortunate one as it implies that the estimates have no relevance to the equation being estimated. Nevertheless, this term has passed into common usage in econometrics. It would be more appropriate to refer to this method as 'external estimates'. There is one huge problem with this method. It is a good idea in theory so long as we have a reliable source of estimates for the parameter we wish to restrict. The problem is actually finding a suitable value from external information to determine the value of the restricted parameter. If the problem is one of collinearity between price and income variables in a time-series demand equation there would be no point taking the restriction value from prior studies as they cannot be regarded as reliable if the prior studies suffer equally from the problem. This means that we would have to use estimates from a different sort of data. This brings problems. It is not clear that the parameter estimate from cross-section data is appropriate for insertion into a time-series data.

In summary, the extraneous estimates solution is an idea which is appealing in principle but not of much use in practice.

(vii) Respecify the model

Changes to the functional form via variable transformations are one way of reducing the degree of multicollinearity. For example, using the lag of some variables, as alternatives to the contemporaneous variables, in a time-series model may reduce collinearity. Likewise, choosing a different transformation of variables such as reciprocals, powers, roots or logarithms may reduce the degree of multicollinearity. Respecifying the model may also involve the imposition of sets of linear restrictions as was shown in (v) above. In that case, the model was respecified as one with no 'real' effects of price changes that are matched by nominal income changes.

In the case of general dynamic models (see Chapter 14), it may be possible to reduce the size of a model by removing some lags or in the extreme case using the simple lagged dependent variable model. Remember that lags may bring multicollinearity in two ways – by reducing the size of the sample and degrees of freedom and also because lags of a variable may have very high correlations with each other.

(viii) Get some better data

The term 'better data' is not being used here simply in the sense of more accurate data. Rather, we mean data that is better in terms of being more suitable for the research topic because it has less of a problem of the variation in the independent variables being swamped by common variation. One simple approach is to use cross-section data instead of time-series data or perhaps to use pooled cross-section/time-series data or data from surveys of individual firms or households. There are, of course, limitations to this for obvious reasons. If our interest is in building macroeconomic models, it is unlikely that we will ever have useable survey data at sufficient intervals for all the key data.

10.8 REVIEW STUDIES

It is quite difficult to find model review studies for this particular chapter as most articles in economics journals do not pay that much attention to multicollinearity. It could be argued that this is because the authors may have experimented with their data and model specification prior to the presentation stage in order to eliminate any serious occurrence of the problem. It is more usual to see occasional mentions of multicollinearity in footnotes along the lines of claiming that it is not a very serious problem because a simple matrix of first order partial correlation coefficients did not reveal any particular r values. The study by O'Brien, Lloyd and Kaneene (1995), however, does contain quite an extensive discussion of multicollinearity. Although this paper appears in a journal of (veterinary) medical education the specified regression equation is open to interpretation along the lines of standard utility-maximizing approaches to demand for human capital investment. The paper models the decision to engage in activities which may augment the human capital of a veterinary practitioner. This decision will depend on income, the relative rates of return on this and rival activities and tastes. The data in the paper is derived from a postal survey of a sample of the population of vets. The independent variables have all been derived from scale questions of the type 'how much does this factor influence your decision? Answer – a lot, a little and so on'. There is a lack of other controls in this study, as the authors did not solicit information on the age, earnings etc. of the sample.

The authors of this paper seem to be quite worried about multicollinearity although they are working in a situation where it is not that likely to be a major issue. That is, they have a large sample of individuals from a specially designed survey. Any multicollinearity in such a situation is likely to have been designed in as a result of poor choice of questions and transformations of them into regressors. Such problems should usually be eliminated by an initial pilot of the study on a small sample. This paper does not mention a prior pilot study.

The second review study, by Trevor Young, is another study of cigarette demand besides the paper by Tansel we have looked at in this and several other chapters. The paper does not discuss multicollinearity as a problem. Its major focus of interest is the issue of asymmetry in addictive goods. That is, price rises might not have the same effect as equivalent compensating price falls due to the price fall promoting a higher level of addictedness in consumers. Young's study is a follow-up to an earlier one by Fujii (1980), which used ridge regression to overcome the multicollinearity problem. Multicollinearity is a serious problem in cigarette demand time-series studies particularly between prices and income, as was seen in Table 2.2 of Chapter 2 taken from Tansel's data. Young uses ridge regression and does not present any prior OLS estimates or exploration of the data in the form of VIFs, partial correlation coefficients etc. He simply assumes, following Fujii and the cumulative evidence of serious price-income collinearity in previous studies, that it is a problem warranting the use of ridge regression. Using the k value of 0.4 and asymmetric price and income variables, Young produces a set of spectacularly good 't' ratios. You might be tempted to conclude from this that ridge regression is a good thing and would then be surprised as to why it is not much more widely adopted in research methods. On this point, you should refer back to the discussion in Section 10.7.

The Basic Facts

Authors: D.J. O'Brien, J.W. Lloyd, and J.B. Kaneene

Title: A Principal Components Analysis of Factors Critical to Participation in Veterinary Lifelong Education Programs

Where Published: *Journal of Veterinary Medicine Education*, **20**(3), 1995, reproduced at: http://scholar.lib.vt.edu/ejournals/JVME/V20-3/obrien.html

Reason for Study: To look at factors influencing the decision by veterinary practitioners (i.e. animal doctors) whether or not to attend lifelong (i.e. post-qualification) education programmes.

Conclusion Reached: Administrative factors are important in determining participation in lifelong education programmes.

How Did They Do It?

Data: A questionnaire mailed to 1630 veterinarians in Michigan in January 1991.

Sample Size: 783 useable schedules were returned.

Technique: OLS; OLS on the 'top' 6 of the 8 principal components factored out of the set of questions asked.

Dependent Variable: Number of meetings, in each of 4 categories, attended in the past 24 months. That is, there are 4 separate sets of regressions.

Focus Variables: There is no real distinction between focus and control variables in this study. The answers to 8 questions from the study scaled as 1, 2, 3 answers were treated as equally important.

Control Variables: See last comment.

Presentation

How Results Are Listed: Tables give coefficients, 'p' values and * for significance levels.

Goodness of Fit: R squared.

Tests: 't' tests (although they are given as 'F' so the square root is needed to take the 't'). VIFs were calculated.

Diagnosis/Stability: None in particular.

Anomalous Results: None in particular.

Student Reflection

Things to Look Out For: Judging from this paper, the use of PCA is somewhat new in the field of 'animal health economics' and there is a slight tendency to treat it as some form of magic, which 'cures' multicollinearity. You should also note that there is not that much evidence of a severe multicollinearity problem in this paper as the VIFs range only from 1.05 to 1.28, which is fairly mild especially compared with those we saw in Table 10.5 for the Longley benchmark data. Also, the application of PCA is not strictly correct as the original r's are being calculated on data which is not continuous (all the independent variables are on a subjective 1−2−3 scale). There are no control variables as such, although the authors note in the conclusion the types of controls that could be introduced in a future study.

Problems in Replication: It is not easy to replicate this study as it is a highly specialized sample population, although you could easily conduct a similar survey on another population sample.

The Basic Facts

Author: Trevor Young

Title: The Demand for Cigarettes: Alternative Specifications of Fujii's Model

Where Published: *Applied Economics*, **15**, 1983, 203–211.

Reason for Study: To assess whether consumers respond in an asymmetric manner to price and income changes in the case of cigarettes.

Conclusion Reached: '[T]he introduction of asymmetry into the price and income variables appears to be justified' (p. 208). The price and income elasticities are quite different from the standard symmetrical model but in opposite directions for the two asymmetric specifications which are used.

How Did They Do It?

Data: USA annual time series for 1929–73.

Sample Size: 45 (it seems, as this is not explicitly stated).

Technique: Ridge regression with special transformations of the price and income variables. The *k* value in the ridge regression is 0.4 because this is a replication of Fujii's study.

Dependent Variable: Cigarettes sold per population aged over 14.

Focus Variables: *Price* and *Income* specified according to the 'ratchet' model of Wolffram and a modified version of this (these involve cumulating data separately on price rises and falls). Lagged dependent variable.

Control Variables: Advertising and health scare dummies which allow for a once and for all shift in 1953, 1963 and 1968.

Presentation

How Results Are Listed: Coefficients with default 't' test value in brackets underneath.

Goodness of Fit: R squared and R squared adjusted.

Tests: Standard 't' tests.

Diagnosis/Stability: None in particular, although the use of two different versions of the Wolffram transformation provides some evidence.

Anomalous Results: Apart from weak 't' ratios on the post-1963 shift dummy there are none as all the 't's are very high, the signs correct and the magnitudes plausible.

Student Reflection

Things to Look Out For: This is a replication so you may want to read Fujii's original article. The 't' ratios are enormous compared to what we are used to seeing in time-series studies (and indeed most econometric models), especially those on smoking, which are often quite problematic. These 'good' results can be attributed to the use of ridge regression rather than OLS. There is no presentation of results for OLS estimates in this paper.

Problems in Replication: There should be few difficulties in finding the data as it is from general government sources. Construction of the price and income asymmetry terms and the use of ridge regression requires a little more effort than is needed to do a standard OLS estimate.

10.9 CONCLUSION

Multicollinearity is a problem that everyone who estimates regression models needs to be aware of. It is an inevitable by-product of the lack of a truly experimental research design. If we were in full control of our data and research subjects, we could probably 'design out' multicollinearity by making sure that independent variables do not co-vary. Although there is some research where this may be possible, economists will continue to be heavily dependent on aggregate time-series and cross-section data, and so the problem of dealing with multicollinearity is not going to go away. There is some danger that econometric investigators will tend to build in multicollinearity either by data mining or by overspecification of the list of control variables due to caution in a doubtful situation.

Thus, multicollinearity may go unnoticed if the research simply presents a set of apparently 'good' (i.e. large R squared, high 't' ratios, correct signs) results, which are very unstable under slight variations. Discovery of the extent of the problem requires that journal editors and referees force the submitters of articles to fully investigate their data *or* that subsequent researchers replicate the earlier work in some fashion rather than merely 'data mining' some more spuriously impressive findings.

Multicollinearity does not fall into the neat format of test–decide–remedy which we can apply to most of the topics discussed in this chapter. A test for multicollinearity is not particularly useful. Rather, suspicions of multicollinearity should lead to exploration of the data. At the end of the day, the best response to a perceived problem of multicollinearity is to look for remedies in the form of more or better data rather than mechanical remedies such as principal components or the use of extraneous estimates; that is, assuming you have not realized that the problem was due to model specification errors. The only option that is usually open to us to eliminate multicollinearity, in these circumstances, is by manipulating the data into an orthogonal form by using principal components as discussed in Section 10.7 above. Although some researchers occasionally use these methods, they are not particularly helpful for the reasons given in Section 10.7.

DOS AND DON'TS

Do

- At least look at your partial correlation matrix – you may also want to check what diagnostic facilities your package provides.
- Check that your multicollinearity problem is not due to faulty data in the form of an entry error or spurious construction.
- Consider the possibility that you may have mis-specified your model.
- Consider the possibility of finding better data.

Don't

- Use ridge regression or principal components if you don't understand them just because they sound impressive and someone has claimed they solve the problem. Even if you do understand them, don't use these methods unless there is a clear benefit to using them.
- Deliberately drop some variables, without good reason, just to get good results. This is effectively data mining. It is not surprising to get a mixture of significant and insignificant results when you run a regression and by itself this neither accepts nor rejects a model.

EXERCISES

10.1 List the major factors that might give rise to a problem of multicollinearity in a regression model.

10.2 Why does it matter if you do have serious multicollinearity in your model?

10.3 Supposing you have just estimated a model and decided that it suffered from serious multicollinearity. Would you decide to abandon the equation and go and get more suitable data? If not, why not?

10.4

(i) Re-estimate the equations shown in Table 9.3 using the file LONGLEY.XLS, using a double-logarithmic specification.

(ii) Comment on the results.

(iii) Examine the partial correlation matrix of the log-transformed variables and comment on whether it suggests the presence of multicollinearity.

10.5 Use the TURKCIG.XLS file to regress the logarithm of per capita cigarette consumption on per capita income, education rates and the relative price. Explore, by suitable means, whether there is a problem of multicollinearity in this model.

REFERENCES

Farrar, D.E. and Glauber, R.R. (1967) Multicollinearity in regression analysis, *Review of Economics and Statistics*, **49**, 92–107.

Fox, J.A. and Hellman, D.A. (1985) Location and other correlates of campus crime, *Journal of Criminal Justice*, **13**, 429–444.

Fujii, T. (1980) The demand for cigarettes: Further empirical evidence and its implications for public policy, *Applied Economics*, **12**, 479–489.

Judge, G.G, Griffiths, W.E., Lutkepol, H. and Lee, T.-C. (1985) *The Theory and Practice of Econometrics*, Second Edition, Wiley Series in Probability and Mathematical Statistics.

Longley, J.W. (1967) An appraisal of least squares programs for the electronic computer from the point of view of the user, *Journal of the American Statistical Association*, **62**, 819–841.

O'Brien, D.J., Lloyd, J.W. and Kaneene, J.B. (1995) A principal components analysis of factors critical to participation in veterinary lifelong education programs, *Journal of Veterinary Medicine Education*, **20**(3), reproduced at : http://scholar.lib.vt.edu/ejournals/JVME/V20-3/obrien.html

Young, T. (1983) The demand for cigarettes: Alternative specifications of Fujii's model, *Applied Economics*, **15**, 203–211.

11

Problem Solving: Heteroscedasticity

LEARNING OBJECTIVES

- Be aware that heteroscedasticity does not alter the unbiasedness property of OLS estimators but does alter the 'best' property
- Understand the rationale for using weighted least squares or heteroscedasticity corrected standard errors
- Know the factors that may cause heteroscedasticity to be present in OLS residuals
- Be able to estimate and interpret GLS equations or those with heteroscedasticity corrected standard errors

CHAPTER SUMMARY

11.1 INTRODUCTION

Heteroscedasticity has been mentioned in earlier chapters. It was introduced in Chapter 3 when the classical assumptions, which ensure that OLS estimators are BLUE, were introduced. Heteroscedasticity is a violation of the assumption of constant variances of the error term (homoscedasticity). In Chapter 9, we encountered tests for heteroscedasticity as diagnostic tests on the regression residuals. When an equation has heteroscedasticity in its error term, then the OLS estimators will still be unbiased but they will no longer be of minimum variance. Thus the 'best' property of the BLUE-ness of OLS estimators is violated. This would not be a problem if all we wanted to do is forecast the point estimate of the dependent variable or indeed obtain point estimates of the coefficients. However, the hypothesis tests, that is the 't' and 'F' tests on the regression coefficients we previously performed will now be inaccurate due to the presence of heteroscedasticity. Generally speaking, this will mean we are *more* inclined to reject the null than we should be. This would seem to be a serious problem if econometrics is to be regarded as a scientific discipline as it suggests OLS estimates will lead to an excess of 'false positives' in research findings (this is assuming most interest focuses on trying to reject null hypotheses).

There are two 'mechanical' approaches to solving this problem. Either we correct the hypothesis testing statistics themselves or we transform the estimating equation so that it produces more reliable 't' and 'F' statistics. The second approach has been the more common one in the history of econometrics. The first approach has only surfaced relatively recently (the last 20 years or so) due to its being plugged into the SHAZAM software developed by Professor Kenneth White, giving rise to the appearance of 'heteroscedasticity corrected standard errors' (HCSE) and 't' ratios in many packages.

It has been traditional to assume that heteroscedasticity is generally a problem of cross-section data that would, of course, include sample surveys of individuals. We would therefore expect that anyone using this kind of data should consider the possibility of heteroscedasticity, do some of the tests in Section 9.6 of Chapter 9 and go on to look at the responses in Sections 11.3, 11.4 and 11.6. However, ARCH (autoregressive conditional heteroscedasticity) models have become the norm in financial econometrics where it is considered that the serial correlation problem (autoregression) is present at the same time as heteroscedasticity. These tests were involved in the panel review studies in Chapter 9, although we did not enter into a discussion of them.

11.2 CONSEQUENCES OF HETEROSCEDASTICITY

The introduction to this chapter summarized the important facts that OLS estimators are unbiased but no longer of minimum variance. Why is this the case? We need to go back to the proofs of Section 3.7, specifically Equation (3.17). In the present case, we will assume a simpler model that has no intercept that is written as:

$$y_i = b_i + u_i \text{ where variance } (u_i) = \sigma_i^2 \qquad (11.1)$$

The symbol for the variance of the disturbance is subscripted in recognition of the fact that, unlike in Chapter 3, we must now allow for the presence of differences in the variance for each disturbance term in the sample. The OLS estimator of b is:

$$\hat{b} = \sum x_i y_i / \sum x_i^2 = b + \left(\sum x_i u_i \right) / \sum x_i^2 \qquad (11.2)$$

where the summation scripts have been omitted from the sigma operator.

If we keep the assumptions that u has an expectation (mean) of zero and that its covariance with the x is zero then Equation (11.2) must give an unbiased estimator of b, as the final term on the line becomes zero because its top line is zero by definition.

Keeping the assumption that the disturbance terms are mutually independent, let us denote the term $\sum x_i^2$ as S_{xx}. We can then write the variance of the disturbance term as:

$$V(\hat{b}) = V[(x_1/S_{xx})u_1 + (x_2/S_{xx})u_2 + \ldots (x_{n1}/S_{xx})u_n] \qquad (11.3)$$

which equals

$$1/S_{xx}^2[x_1^2\sigma_1^2 + x_2^2\sigma_2^2 + \ldots x_n^2\sigma_n^2] \qquad (11.4)$$

which reduces to:

$$\sum x_i^2\sigma_i^2 / \left(\sum x_i^2 \right)^2 \qquad (11.5)$$

The correct estimator of the error variance, when we come to do hypothesis testing, should be Equation (11.5). If all the error variances were equal, then this formula would be the same as the formula normally used in OLS to estimate the error variance. Heteroscedasticity will mean that the variances are not equal and hence these two estimators cannot be equal.

The extent of bias in the estimation of the regression standard errors, using the OLS formula, could be modelled in terms of σ_i^2 being a function of x_i. If this is a positive (monotonic) relationship, then the OLS estimates of the standard errors of the coefficients will be under-estimated, that is, biased downwards, meaning that the default 't' ratios will be biased upwards. The opposite applies if the relationship is a negative (monotonic) one.

Given the retention of the unbiasedness property, the OLS estimators would still be entirely appropriate for generating forecasts of the dependent variable (assuming other factors which are sources of bias are not in operation). This does not help us much if our main interest is in hypothesis testing. Accurate hypothesis testing requires that *the formulae used to calculate the standard errors be unbiased*, as well as the point estimates of the regression parameters. If the standard errors are biased upwards then the 'true' value of each 't' ratio will be understated leading us to be more likely to accept the null than we otherwise would be. This would not seem to be a very worrying event if we have significant 't' ratios if we are trying to demonstrate the importance of a variable. If we were trying to show that a variable was not important then we would not be so worried. In this case, the results of our OLS estimates would be 'better' than they seem, as the 'true' value of the critical significance level will be lower than it appears to be. Obviously, the opposite situation is going to apply when the bias, due to heteroscedasticity, in the calculation of the OLS estimators is downwards. In that case, the 't' ratios for research with a confirmatory focus will look 'better' than they really are. Stated alternately, the true confidence intervals will be wider than the stated ones and the critical significance level will be higher than the calculated one.

So which one of these two situations is more likely? It is useful to know the answer to this question, as we would usually find the case of downward bias of the standard errors to be quite worrying. Many econometrics textbooks proceed on the (largely unstated) premise that the relationship between the error variance and the proportionality factor is *positive*. In this case the bias will be downwards and thus 't' ratios will be biased upwards. The reason for assuming this is that we would expect most 'suspect' variables to have a positive relationship with the error variance rather than a negative one. A more general model is where the dependent variable is positively related with the size of the error variance. If we have initially carried out some tests for heteroscedasticity (see Section 9.6) then (except in the case of the Goldfeld–Quandt test) we will have obtained some evidence on whether or not the 'size' relationship in the error variance is decreasing or increasing. For example, in a Parks–Glejser test of the simplest type as depicted in Equation (9.9) and reported in Table 9.3, we can look at whether the coefficient on the suspect variable is positive or negative. A positive sign would confirm the assumption, made in most econometrics textbooks, leading to OLS estimates providing 't' ratios larger than the true ones. You can see in Table 9.3 that the coefficients on the suspect variable must be negative as they have negative 't' ratios. However, remember that this particular example found that there was no evidence of heteroscedasticity for the data and assumptions used.

In the rest of this chapter we will be proceeding on the assumption that we do have heteroscedasticity in our models. Given the above discussion of the consequences of heteroscedasticity for OLS estimators, something needs to be done if we are still adhering to the notion that estimators should be BLUE. In a sense, the problem we face is only one of calculation errors due to the use of an inappropriate formula – the standard error estimates from OLS. Thus it should be easy to fix if we know the correct formula and use it instead.

There is a problem that you should bear in mind before we proceed. That is, totally accurate correction of the faults in OLS estimates would require us to know the 'true' error variances of the model. Unfortunately it is impossible for us to know this in any case involving real world data. Therefore we have to use estimates of some type and these may introduce additional sources of error into the revised estimates, which we are producing as an alternative to the OLS estimates.

11.3 SOLVING THE PROBLEM OF HETEROSCEDASTICITY, I: USE TRANSFORMED DATA TO OBTAIN WEIGHTED LEAST SQUARES (WLS) ESTIMATES

TRANSFORMING AN EQUATION TO REMOVE HETEROSCEDASTICITY

It is easier to solve a problem the more you know about it. For the moment, let us avoid the problem mentioned at the end of Section 9.2 and assume we have prior knowledge about the form of the heteroscedasticity; for example, that it is proportional to the variance of the disturbance term as follows:

$$\text{var}(\varepsilon_i) = \lambda_i^2 \sigma^2 \tag{11.6}$$

where ε_i is the disturbance term in a model of the form:

$$Y_i = b_0 + b_1 X_{1i} + b_2 X_{2i} + \varepsilon_i \qquad (11.7)$$

Y is the dependent variable, the X's are independent variables, σ^2 is the constant component of the variance and $\lambda_i{}^2$ is the proportionality factor. The last equation cannot have a constant error variance unless the proportionality factor, in the previous equation, was also constant. Assuming that it is not, we can divide through this equation by the square root of the proportionality factor to get the following equation:

$$(Y_i/\lambda_i) = b_0/\lambda_i + b_1(X_{1i}/\lambda_i) + b_2(X_{2i}/\lambda_i) + (\varepsilon_i/\lambda_i) \qquad (11.8)$$

We will have an error variance, which is constant because the variance of the final term in this equation cancels out to be σ^2.

This seems to give us a simple rule to 'get rid of' heteroscedasticity: *Divide through the whole equation, i.e. including the intercept, by the square root of the factor which is proportionate to the variance of the error term.*

This transformed equation will now have the properties that the OLS estimators were supposed to have.

Such a transformation means we are using a different estimator from OLS. These are variously described as generalized least squares (GLS) estimators or weighted least squares (WLS). The reasons for these names are quite simple. The word 'generalized' denotes that we have expanded the OLS range of assumptions into a wider more 'general' set of assumptions. The use of the word 'weight' denotes the fact that we have altered the ratios within the variables of the original model by attaching unequal weightings to each observation. Here we have weighted the whole equation, which is why it is called a weighted least squares regression. To avoid confusion, it should be pointed out that the weighting, which is going on, is not weighting by λ but by the reciprocal of this. That is, the weight is the term you multiply all the data by. So, if a statistics package asks you to state the weight for WLS estimation you should be requiring it to be *the reciprocal of the square root of the proportionality factor.*

There are other reasons for weighting and other assumptions, which might be changed in order to 'generalize' a least squares model. In the present case of heteroscedasticity, assuming that all other classical properties hold, the only weight we need to consider is the one just given.

HOW TO DO IT?

You may well have a package that has a command or option to do WLS estimation, in which case you should follow the rule just given. However, it is possible to do a GLS/WLS 'correction' to your model 'by hand' as it were, through using your computer package to create new variables that are weighted versions of the original. You may wish to do this in any case, in order to improve your understanding of the WLS 'solution' to the heteroscedasticity problem. You simply apply transformations as explained in Chapter 6. Give a new name to each of the variables, which have been weighted by $(1/\sqrt{\lambda})$. For the intercept, this means we use the reciprocal of the square root of the factor and this means that we must estimate an equation that does not have an intercept *unless* it so happens that one of the variables in the original specification is exactly the same as the proportionality factor.

The exclusion of an intercept can be done by not including an intercept in your equation, or if you have a package, which automatically includes an intercept, you will have to instruct the program to drop the intercept. These instructions might lead to some confusion so it is worth pointing out that it is only the estimating equation that does not have an intercept. The specified equation *does* have an intercept but when it is transformed it gives an estimating equation with no intercept. The intercept of the specified equation is given by the parameter b_0 in Equation (11.8), which is attached to the weight. One would generally expect that if you were using a package that provides options for WLS that the output would include an intercept, which is the intercept of the original model.

In practice, you *will not usually know the form which heteroscedasticity takes.* Therefore you will not know the weighting factor needed to perform the transformations above to get a GLS regression. This requires us to make some assumption about the form of the relationship between the error variance and variables, which could be used as the weight. But where do we look for our possible weight variables? The method employed is to use some relationship from the set of independent variables as we did in the specification tests for heteroscedasticity explained in Section 9.6. The most basic way of doing this is to assume a proportionate relationship between one of these and the error variance. You should *not* be using a variable which does not appear in the model as the weight, as this implies that this variable should be part of the model, therefore you would have appeared to have mis-specified the set of variables and need to amend this.

Assuming that we are going to use a single variable to determine the weight we still face two problems:

(i) What is the relationship between the variable and the error variance?
(ii) Which variable do we pick?

As far as question (i) goes, you should refer back to Section 9.6 on tests for heteroscedasticity. If you have performed a Goldfeld–Quandt test this will not give you any clues as to the nature of the relationship. Tests based on auxiliary regressions on the residuals, such as the Glejser and Parks tests will potentially give us this information. That is, experimentation with different functional forms for the relationship between the estimate error variance and the suspect variable may suggest which is correct. We could of course try several of the forms chosen as the basis for the weights and if the results of this are similar then there is little to worry about.

As far as question (ii) goes, we should ideally rely on prior knowledge, on which subject we will return to in Section 11.5. Most economists proceed on the assumption that heteroscedasticity is something to do with differing size or scale of the observation units and hence they select a size-related variable from the group of independent variables. In a cross-section we have many observations of different sizes. Here are some examples with specimen topics of inquiry.

▶ In a sample of firms where we might want to study the determination of profit rates (*PR*). The sample may contain large firms and small firms who might well have different error variances. The heteroscedasticity might then be assumed proportional to the turnover (*TR*) of the firm as a measure of size.

Our model would then be something like:

$$PR_i = b_0 + b_1 TR_i + b_2 X_i + u_i \qquad (11.9)$$

assuming a linear functional form and that X is another independent variable. The heteroscedasticity would possibly take the form:

$$var(u_i) = \sigma_u{}^2 TR^2 \qquad (11.10)$$

where $\sigma_u{}^2$ is the constant component of the error variance. You should bear in mind we have just adopted one of the popular assumptions people would make. If we follow the methods given above then we would use the function (11.11) to estimate the equation to give us correct standard errors:

$$PR_i/TR_i = b_0/TR_i + b_1 + b_2 X_i/TR_i + u_i/TR_i \qquad (11.11)$$

This equation has an intercept but its value is that for the slope parameter on turnover (the measure of firm size), while the value of the intercept from Equation (11.9) is now on the reciprocal of turnover.

▶ In a sample of households used to study expenditure on pet food (PX), we would have households with large incomes (Y) and households with low incomes who might well have different error variances. In a pioneering study by Prais and Houthakker (1955) it was discovered that error variance from family budget data increased with household income.

This time let us assume the model is:

$$PX_i = b_0 + b_1 RP_i + b_2 Y_i + u_i \qquad (11.12)$$

where RP is the relative price of pet food (an index of pet food prices divided by an index of general retail prices), and that heteroscedasticity is a linear function of the variable, which 'causes' it, i.e.

$$var(u_i) = \sigma_u{}^2 Y \qquad (11.13)$$

Following the methods given above we end up with the following estimating equation after dividing by the square root of Y:

$$PX_i/\sqrt{Y_i} = b_0/\sqrt{Y_i} + b_1 RP_i/\sqrt{Y_i} + b_2\sqrt{Y_i} + u_i/\sqrt{Y_i} \qquad (11.14)$$

Unlike the previous estimating example (see Equation 11.11) this time we have no intercept at all in the estimating equation. If we are using a package which includes an intercept by default then this would require us to find the command that allows us to remove it. We will then have an incorrect formula for R squared and the residuals will not sum to zero. Although we have no intercept, the value of the intercept from the specified equation (11.12) is attached to the variable which is the reciprocal of the square root of income.

▶ In a cross-section of different nations to study the share of public expenditure (PEX) in GNP we may have a great variation in the wealth of the nations. This could cause error variances to differ from measurement error. That is, the larger nations may have much more accurate measurement of 'true' GNP than the smaller ones due to better data collection methods.

Let us assume that this time we have a double-log model:

$$\ln(PEX/GNP)_i = \ln b_0 + b_1 \ln X_i + b_2 \ln GNP_i + u_i \tag{11.15}$$

with a logarithmic heteroscedasticity relationship as in:

$$var(u_i) = \sigma_u^2 \ln GNP \tag{11.16}$$

Using the same method again the appropriate WLS/GLS method is:

$$\ln(PEX/GNP)_i/\sqrt{\ln GNP_i} = \ln b_0/\sqrt{\ln GNP_i} + b_1 \ln X_i/\sqrt{\ln GNP_i} + b_2\sqrt{\ln GNP_i} + u_i \tag{11.17}$$

To make the above more intelligible, we now give an example using the model of growth rates used in Sections 9.2 and 9.6 to conduct tests for outliers and tests for heteroscedasticity. To keep this simple we adopt the strategy of many economists of using the square root of the suspect variable as the weighting factor. This strategy is also deployed in the paper by Ehrlich on the supply of crime which is examined in the review studies panels in Section 11.7.

To save you having to look back to Section 9.2, in Table 11.1 we reproduce the OLS results shown there and present the WLS results, which use the reciprocal of the square root of population as the weight.

Table 11.1 OLS and WLS/GLS estimates of an equation for growth rates

Dependent variable: Growth of real GDP 1990–1999		
	OLS	WLS
Independent variables		
Constant	10.514	−20.379
	(1.349)	(2.285)
GDP1991	−1.9 E−04	−1.469E−04
	(2.017)	(1.797)
LIFE	0.194	0.321
	(1.677)	(2.53)
LEGAL500	2.538E−05	8.757E−06
	(1.87)	(0.355)
(LEGAL500)^2	−2.209E−11	−7.429E−12
	(1.727)	(0.308)
R^2	0.159	0.131
N	47	47

Notes: Absolute 't' ratios are in parentheses. The weight in the WLS regression is the reciprocal of the square root of population.

There are fairly obvious differences between these two sets of estimates: the R squared has fallen; coefficient values have fallen for all the variables except the life expectancy variable, which has substantially increased; 't' ratios have risen fairly dramatically for the constant term and the life expectancy variable. The most striking result is that the quadratic term in the 'number of lawyers' variable (*LEGAL500*) has lost the statistical significance it had in the OLS results shown in the first column. This is quite a mixture of results and is an illustration of the fact that *we cannot predict in advance what will happen when we do WLS/GLS corrections of an OLS model*. The point estimates will not be exactly the same as they were in the OLS case. Some may rise and some may fall. We are also unable to know in advance what will happen to the 't' ratios. Some may rise and some may fall. The precise changes are due to the properties of the sample data. One should always bear in mind that part of these properties may be the other problems with the model highlighted in Chapters 9 and 10.

So, if we did have heteroscedasticity, and we leave aside the asymptotic properties problem, then the preference should be for the second set, that is, the WLS estimates. However, you will recall from Section 10.6 that for this set of data we found in favour of the null hypothesis of homoscedasticity when we conducted tests. Therefore, we should not use WLS estimates, but should stick to our OLS estimates. That is, assuming we could not improve on those in some other way. You will recall from Section 9.2 that outlier problems were found with this set of data and that trimming the most conspicuous outlier (the USA) resulted in quite different OLS estimates. A simple Glejser–Parks type test on the residuals of the reduced sample from the second equation in Table 9.1, using population as the suspect variable, gave a 't' of 0.718 using linear population and −1.262 using the log of population as the suspect variable. Given these results we do not pursue the matter of using WLS on the restricted sample (omitting the USA).

Thus, in this case we prefer the OLS estimates, as it seems there was no grounds for doing the WLS estimates in the first place. However, if we are in the situation where there is evidence of heteroscedasticity we should prefer the WLS estimates for the purposes of hypothesis testing, but the OLS estimates should be used for making inferences such as the calculation of elasticities and forecasts of the dependent variable.

There may of course be some other form of the heteroscedasticity function that we might find from prior knowledge, or exploratory analysis of the OLS residuals, that would result in WLS estimators, which are an improvement over the OLS estimates in terms of the standard errors obtained. Remember that the expected value of the parameters themselves is the same whichever the form of heteroscedastic 'correction' we use as the estimators remain unbiased. The actual values will differ as we have just seen in Table 11.1.

IMPROVING ON A SIMPLE GLS ESTIMATOR

We have looked at a very simple GLS estimator solution to the heteroscedasticity problem. We simply assumed a specific relationship for Equation (11.6), which was very restrictive in that we nominated population as the proportionality factor. Slightly more complicated alternatives are available. We could estimate more specific relationships between the error variance and 'suspect' variables in the process of conducting some of the tests in Section 9.6 and use the weights derived from these tests instead of an assumed weight factor. These are essentially 'two-step' or 'two-stage' procedures. Step 1 is the estimation of the heteroscedasticity relation and Step 2 is the substitution of this in the form of the weight into the WLS estimating equation. It is possible that we might be able to improve further on the WLS estimators by a process of iteration where we compute a successive sequence of estimates of the parameters using the residuals from each 'new' set of estimates to improve the next estimators. This is essentially an iterative least squares method. For many years, before the revolution in time-series econometrics described in Chapter 14, this method was extremely popular in dealing with the problem of serial correlation in the form of the Cochrane–Orcutt iterative technique. Yet it was surprisingly seldom seen in the case of heteroscedasticity which has, effectively, the same consequences for OLS estimates.

In an iterative WLS method, the first step is to estimate the heteroscedasticity function using the OLS residuals in the way that we have done in the tests in Section 9.6. Having done so, we obtain the first set of WLS estimates of the regression parameters. If we now substitute these new parameters into the originally specified model this will give us a new set of residuals, which can be used to derive new WLS estimates of the model. The process can be continued for hundreds of iterations if one really wished to do so. The usual practice in econometrics is to continue the iterations until we achieve convergence in the sense that the results are not changing by very much after each iteration (in this case the result we would look at in terms of convergence would be the estimated error variance). Such methods presume that we are iterating towards an optimum but it is possible that the optimum may be merely local rather than global.

11.4 SOLVING THE PROBLEM OF HETEROSCEDASTICITY, II: USE CORRECTED STANDARD ERRORS

As mentioned above, many statistics packages now provide an option to generate 'heteroscedasticity corrected standard errors' (HCSE) in place of the OLS standard errors and this will lead to 'corrected' 't' ratios appearing in the output in place of the OLS based 't' ratios. These arise from a proposal in an article by Halbert White (1980). It is not uncommon to see articles in journals which report only the 'White' standard errors and not the OLS standard errors. Indeed, some academic papers will report only the White standard errors, sometimes with little mention of heteroscedasticity testing having been performed.

The White approach to getting HCSE, and their associate 't' ratios, is in a sense completely opposite to the WLS approach. It involves using the regression residuals of the OLS model to derive a new set of standard errors and 't' ratios. It is important to note that it does *not* lead to a new set of estimates for the regression parameters which as we saw, in Table 11.1, can produce different results when we compare OLS with WLS. This difference arises because the White approach relies on the unbiasedness property of OLS estimators, in the presence of heteroscedasticity. It uses the residuals from the OLS regression to estimate the standard errors.

The HCSE will be an improvement on the OLS standard errors but they will still be biased with the bias becoming vanishingly small as the sample size becomes infinite. Thus, there is the same asymptotic property problem as we have with the WLS solution. There are adjustments to the estimated standard errors that have been proposed to reduce the small sample bias but they cannot eliminate it. This is a largely theoretical issue if we are not in a position to increase the size of the sample. There is a practical problem of interpretation when we come to look at the HCSE results presented by a researcher. That is, we cannot be sure that any two computer packages have used the same method to obtain 'White' residuals.

11.5 CAUSES OF HETEROSCEDASTICITY

Let us start this section with an unusual question. Do we really need to know the causes of heteroscedasticity? Or to be more precise, do we need to know the general range of causes or the causes in our specific case? If you are going to use the White standard errors of Section 11.4 then it would seem that you don't really need to know the causes as you simply hit the right button on the computer and you automatically get 'correct' standard errors. This is certainly the way some people approach the question, but we will arrive at the conclusion that you would be better off knowing what the causes of heteroscedasticity are.

First, it will be helpful to go through a list of causes including those we have already encountered. Before we do so, there is a subtle distinction to be made between a 'genuine' cause of heteroscedasticity and an untested problem of some other type which might show up in a heteroscedasticity test. The following list includes both types of item.

(i) Grouped data

Grouped data is data where the original information has been condensed in some way. The usual case is where we have a range of values rather than the original data. For example, published tables of household expenditure from government surveys might show the number of people who fell into the category of, for example, 0–10, 10–20, 20–30, 30–40 etc. dollars per month spent on cinema attendance. These days, a serious researcher would usually be able to get the source data which lies behind these kinds of tables, so would not face this problem. They may still face the problem if they are given survey data in which some of the responses are grouped. For example, to improve response rates, surveys may ask for ranges on variables like age or income. Grouped data introduces heteroscedasticity if the numbers in the groups are unequal, as variance will change as the size of group is increased. This will imply that, *ceteris paribus*, the standard errors are biased downwards from the true standard errors.

If you do have to deal with a situation where data is grouped (for example, say you are regressing mean household expenditure of a group on the mid-point of ranges of household income data) it does have the advantage that you should automatically be able to arrive at the correct answer provided you know the number of respondents in each group. For the situation just given, the appropriate weight is the square root of the sample size within each income grouping. This kind of solution is premised on the assumption that the underlying model that would be applied to ungrouped data, if it were available, does not suffer from heteroscedasticity. If one made an assumption about any such heteroscedasticity in the ungrouped version of the data, which has been grouped, then this would need to be incorporated in the weight being used.

(ii) Aggregation

Many of the examples given to illustrate the subject of heteroscedasticity come from cross-sections of individual data where the 'size' factor is at work. Unfortunately, the aggregation of data may also bring heteroscedasticity problems. This has already been suggested in case (i) above for grouped data, which is not quite aggregation but it does involve loss of information. Aggregation occurs at its most extreme in the single country time-series regression, such as a per capita demand function (like the Tansel (1993) data we have used in many previous chapters), where we use average figure, per time period, to represent the spending of millions of

301

people and other single average figures to represent other factors such as prices and disposable incomes. This case is, in fact, probably the one where heteroscedasticity is least likely to occur. The reason for this is that the aggregation is taking place over a similar number of observations in each year. This is not likely to be the case in an example such as an equation to study industry differences in profit rates. The number of firms in the chemical industry may be very different from the number of firms in the rubber industry. The problem we face, of variance increasing, *ceteris paribus* with the numbers in the sample used to obtain the mean for an observation, is the same as in the grouped data case, although we do here have the actual mean of the data rather than being forced to use its mid-point in a regression equation.

(iii) Size

This case, and examples of it, was discussed in Section 11.3. Most economists typically assume size is the cause when they have no clear prior knowledge of what might be causing heteroscedasticity. Section 9.6 made it clear that the size assumption is called upon to develop tests for heteroscedasticity. The size cause is based on the assumption that the mean of some variable in the equation may be related to the error variance. This could be 'genuine' in the sense that such a relationship truly exists or it could be an artifact of measurement errors or specification error in choosing the functional form, as was implied in Chapter 9.

(iv) Outliers

We dealt with testing for outliers in Section 9.2. Estimated error variances may be unlikely to be judged equal if some observations generate very large absolute values of the OLS residual. When we square these we will get a very large estimated variance compared with the non-outlying error terms. This will not, by itself, necessarily result in the rejection of the null on a hypothesis test unless the outliers are sufficiently correlated with the suspect variable used in the test. The question to be addressed is whether the outliers are in some sense 'distorting' the heteroscedasticity test.

(v) Limited dependent variables: Binary case

Chapter 8 dealt with the linear probability model where the dependent variable was a dummy variable. In this case, heteroscedasticity is inevitable and it could be addressed using a weighted least squares correction approach. However, this will not be the most efficient way of estimating these kinds of models and we should use the maximum-likelihood methods illustrated in Chapter 8.

(vi) Count models

The problem of counts is different from the probability model problem and the standard regression model using continuous data. Broadly speaking, it is somewhere in between these two. If you look back to Section 7.2 you will see an example of a regression on 'count data' where the variable could only range from 1 to 5. Sports examples probably provide a good example of this kind of problem, for example the number of goals scored in a soccer season by a player, or the number of home runs in a baseball season, or the number of world titles won by a tennis player. These variables are limited in the sense that they have some kind of upper limit and they could also have the problem of zero observations appearing. They are also not continuous data in that they have an integer dimension – you cannot have 1.3 of a home run or win 2.5 ranking tennis tournaments. This property would of course disappear if we were using averages across units of observation that have counts. In the more everyday economic sphere, the number of strikes is a good example of a count observation.

The count model where the dependent variable is limited within a narrow range of integer values will impose heteroscedasticity on the disturbance term and thus make OLS estimates of greater than the minimum variance estimator that could be obtained.

The original recognition that counts would follow a distribution different from the normal distribution occurred in the analysis of the number of soldiers being kicked by horses. This non-symmetrical distribution is called a Poisson distribution and is one of the major statistical distributions we did not consider in Chapter 2. A full treatment of this subject, with details of appropriate estimators for Poisson models, can be found in Cameron and Trivedi (1998). Count models could follow other forms of distribution from the Poisson, which require different estimators.

(vii) Pooled samples

Chapter 8 introduced the method of estimating a pooled sample using dummy variables to allow the intercept to shift between the samples. This approach is called a 'fixed effects' model. It assumes that the error variances across the different samples are equal. This may not be true. For example, in earnings functions of the type reviewed in Chapter 8, it may well be the case that the variance of earnings between whites and non-whites and men and women are not equal. This would mean that there are distinct 'partitions' within the sample where *it might* be reasonable to assume that there is homoscedasticity within the individual samples but different variances across the samples. This would make developing a WLS estimator fairly straightforward as we could derive the weights from the OLS residuals of the individual sample regressions. Things are less straightforward if there is within sub-sample heteroscedasticity which we may need to model and allow for different parameters in each sub-sample heteroscedasticity function.

(viii) Random coefficients

A core assumption of the CLRM model is that the parameters of the regression equation are stable over the whole sample. Tests for this assumption have been considered at various points in Chapters 5 and 9; so far, we have not looked at any models that might incorporate the possibility of shifting parameters. The only suggestion made so far is to divide the model into separate samples for estimation, or to use dummy variables in the way we have just been discussing for pooled samples. An alternate possibility suggested by Hildreth and Houck (1968) – the proposed estimators to deal with this have come to be known as Hildreth–Houck–Swamy estimators – is a random **coefficient model**, which leads to a regression equation with a heteroscedastic error term. These models are applied to pooled data sets such as panel data.

RANDOM COEFFICIENTS MODEL

This model can be written as follows (Equation 11.18) where there are two sets of subscripts to represent the two sources of data that have been pooled. The i subscript represents cross-section variation and the t subscript, the time-series variation. The i subscript runs up to the Nth observation and the t subscript runs up to the Tth observation.

$$y_{it} = b_i x_{it} + u_{it} \tag{11.18}$$

Each coefficient is treated as a random variable in contradiction to the assumption introduced in Chapter 3. For the purposes of simplification, we are assuming there is no intercept term. The random coefficients regression model allows for both the intercept and all the other parameters to be constant. A more restricted model is the variance components model in which the intercepts are fixed and the slope parameters are allowed to vary.

We assume that b_i is generated by the following relationship:

$$b_i = b + v_i \tag{11.19}$$

with the u and v terms being classical disturbances, i.e. with zero mean and constant variance although they will not have the same variance as each other.

The parameters therefore consist of a constant component and a random component. Substituting (11.19) into (11.18) gives us:

$$y_{it} = b x_{it} + (u_{it} + v_i x_{it}) = b x_{it} + {}_t w_{it} \tag{11.20}$$

which gives rise to the following covariance relationship for the disturbance term of (11.20) (w is defined below in Equation (11.23):

$$
\begin{aligned}
\text{Cov}(w_{it}, \, w_i) &= \sigma_i^2 + \delta^2 x_{it} && \text{if } t = s \\
&= \delta^2 x_{it} x_{is} && \text{if } t \, ! \, j \\
\text{Cov}(w_{it}, \, w_{js}) &= 0 && \text{if } i \, ! \, j
\end{aligned}
\tag{11.21}
$$

It can be shown that the GLS estimator of the slope coefficient is a weighted average of the OLS estimators from the set of cross-section regressions, that is:

$$\hat{b}_{gls} = \sum w_i \hat{b}_i \tag{11.22}$$

where

$$w_i = \frac{1/(\delta^2 + v_i)}{\sum\limits_{i=1}^{n}[1/(\delta^2 + v_i)]} \tag{11.23}$$

where v_i is the variance of the estimate of b_i.

Thus the use of an OLS model means we have heteroscedasticity due to a specification error of treating parameters as constant when there is heterogeneity across the sample. Solving this problem requires the use of a GLS estimator which, in this case, means we need values for σ_i^2 and δ^2 because these are not known to us. One way of doing this is to estimate *separate equations* for the N cross-section units and use the residuals from these equations to estimate σ_i^2. The estimate of δ^2 can be formed from the variances of the b estimates across the separate equations just estimated. These values can then be substituted into Equations (11.22) and (11.23) above to obtain a GLS estimator, which is a weighted average of a set of OLS estimators. The procedure will be more complicated in a model which has a full set of parameters on the right-hand side of Equation (11.18) but the underlying principle is the same. You can see an example of this technique in the review study by Guy (2000), summarized below in Section 11.7, which uses a panel of 99 firms over 17 years.

Now we return to the question which began Section 11.5: Do we need to know the causes? The answer should really be: it is much better if we do know the causes for the following reasons:

▶ Knowing the causes may lead to more efficient GLS estimates than using 'mechanical' correction techniques. That is, we can get closer to the 'true' pattern of heteroscedasticity than we would using arbitrarily chosen weights or White standard errors.

▶ Knowing the causes may lead to an improved specification of the model as a whole which ultimately gives us more insights into the behaviour we are trying to explain than the *ad hoc/* mechanical approach. Suitable respecification of the model may give us an error term which is homoscedastic, meaning that we do not need to resort to White standard errors or WLS methods.

11.6 SHOULD I CORRECT FOR HETEROSCEDASTICITY?

Before you correct for heteroscedasticity, you should test for it using the methods explained in Section 10.6. If it does not appear to be present after a substantial exploration of the residuals of your OLS model, then it does not make sense to proceed to WLS/GLS estimates as you may be introducing new sources of error into your model. If heteroscedasticity tests reject the null of homoscedasticity, then given the violation of BLUE as far as the b part goes it would seem that you should proceed to some corrections. The gains are inevitable if you have a large enough sample size given the asymptotic properties of the proof in Section 11.2. If the sample size is small then it is not guaranteed that the correction will be an improvement. As was indicated in Section 11.5, you should not correct for heteroscedasticity if you can remedy the situation with an improved model specification or better data.

There were eight causes of heteroscedasticity given in Section 11.5. Some of them could be remedied, at least in part, by simple changes in the model. Others, such as case (v), (vi) and (viii), require the use of specific modifications that take account of the fact that we are dealing with a situation that does not fit the standard OLS approach. The techniques for case (v) have already been given in Chapter 9 due to the current popularity of research using limited dependent variables. Another possibility is to use the Hildreth–Houck–Swamy (HHS) estimator for random coefficient regression This estimator is given in a number of econometric packages such as STAT and LIMDEP. An example that uses the HHS estimator is covered in the second panel review study in Section 11.7.

11.7 REVIEW STUDIES

This section presents two studies on very different topics – criminal activity and the remuneration of chief executive officers (CEOs) of corporations. We have touched on related topics in other review study panels. The two studies reviewed here are very different in terms of their approach, although the difference here is nothing to do with the nature of the topics being researched. The study of crime by Issac Ehrlich, published in 1973, uses the simple approach of assuming a given pattern of heteroscedasticity and applying the corresponding WLS/GLS estimators. The study of CEO pay by Fred Guy, published in 2000, applies the random coefficients regression model of the Hildreth–Houck–Swamy approach. The Ehrlich paper uses cross-sections at three points in time – 1940, 1950 and 1960 – separately, that is Ehrlich does not pool these three different years in his estimation process. In contrast, the paper by Guy uses a pooled cross-section time series of 99 firms over 1982–99.

The underlying theories being tested in both papers are fairly standard microeconomics. It is a straightforward application of the marginal productivity theory of payment that high-level decision-makers in firms might receive greater rewards when the firm is more successful. Ehrlich's study of crime is premised on supply of labour considerations. Crime rate changes are due to two factors: movements into and out of the 'occupation' of being a criminal (this is the participation decision) and changes in the rate of offending by those who are currently in the occupation. The title of Ehrlich's article implies that he is only dealing with the participation effect although the data he uses do not allow the two effects to be separated.

Both these studies take place in areas where there is cause to be concerned about the accuracy and validity of data. Neither author gives too much attention to this issue as they rely on two common strategies among economists, when faced with less than perfect data. That is, apply some techniques to the data that are more advanced than OLS and, ultimately, rely on the discovery of 'good' results in terms of the coefficients and 't' ratios to justify the exercise that has been undertaken.

The Basic Facts

Authors: Isaac Ehrlich

Title: Participation in Illegitimate Activities: A Theoretical and Empirical Investigation

Where Published: *Journal of Political Economy*, **81**, 1973, 521–564. It is reprinted in various books on the economics of crime, and in *Essays in the Economics of Crime and Punishment*, edited by G.S. Becker and W.M. Landes, National Bureau of Economic Research, New York, 1974 (although this is a slightly longer version). This summary is based on the latter version.

Reason for Study: To test the economic theory of crime (Becker, 1968) that the supply of offences is negatively related to the risk of capture and punishment and the size of punishment. Additional interest focuses on the relative magnitude of elasticities of crime with respect to the amount of punishment and the probability of being punished.

Conclusion Reached: There is broad support for the economic model of crime (as was found in the studies in Section 5.7) on the basis of the 't' ratios for the focus variables. Deterrence elasticities are not generally smaller for crimes of violence than they are for property crimes ('contrary to popular opinion' as Ehrlich puts it). The results for property crime are said to indicate that the perpetrators are risk averse, on grounds of the different size of the elasticities for punishment size and probability.

How Did They Do It?

Data: Cross-section from 1940, 1950, 1960 for seven crime categories at the state level for the USA.

Sample Size: 21 separate regression samples of 36–47 observations.

Technique: WLS (Tables 2 and 3) with the weight being $1/\sqrt{N}$ where N is the symbol Ehrlich uses for population; also 2SLS and SUR (see Chapter 13). Table 6 presents some alternate models concerning age and crime in which OLS estimates (described in the table as OLS unweighted) and WLS estimates are reported.

Dependent Variable: Log Crime rate divided by population.

Focus Variables: Log of probability of apprehension by imprisonment and punishment (P) and log of average length of time served in prison (T).

Control Variables: All in logarithms: W = median family income; X = percentage of families below $\frac{1}{2}$ median income (i.e in the lower quartile of income distribution); NW = percentage of non-whites in the population. Other variables are introduced as instruments for the 2SLS estimates (see Chapter 13).

Presentation

How Results Are Listed: Coefficient values.

Goodness of Fit: Adjusted R^2.

Tests: 't' tests not fully reported for the $b = 0$ and also for the difference between the coefficients on the two focus variables.

Diagnosis/Stability: Some investigation of heteroscedasticity in the OLS versions of the model is described in footnote 39. This appears to have consisted of a regression of the absolute residuals on population size (the Parks test of Section 9.6).

Anomalous Results: Some equations have the order of punishment and probability the 'wrong way round' implying that individuals are risk preferers contrary to the model put forward by Becker (1968), which assumes risk aversion. However, it should be noted that there are economic models of crime in which these results are consistent with risk aversion.

Student Reflection

Things to Look Out For: The tables are titled in a slightly misleading fashion as OLS (weighted) regression rather than WLS. The presentation of 't' tests is a little unusual – a superscripted symbol A is attached to results where the coefficient is *not* twice its standard error. As indicated in Chapter 6, the log-linear specification gives elasticities. Almost all the coefficients on the focus variables (P and T) are significant, all are of the correct sign (negative), all are less than 1 in absolute value.

Problems in Replication: In principle this study should be easy to replicate as it is based entirely on aggregate published data and a replication of the data collection has already been published in Vandaele (1978). In fact the book chapter by Vandaele corrects some data entry errors, which were made in the original study by Ehrlich.

The Basic Facts

Authors: Fred Guy

Title: CEO Pay, Shareholder Returns and Accounting Profitability

Where Published: *International Journal of the Economics of Business*, 7(3), 2000, 263–274.

Reason for Study: To test whether there are relationships between CEO pay, shareholder returns and accounting returns in the company.

Conclusion Reached: CEO pay is related to company profitability but not to shareholder returns.

How Did They Do It?

Data: 99 British companies over the period 1972–89.

Sample Size: $99 \times 17 = 1683$.

Technique: Hildreth–Houck–Swamy random coefficients regression (RCR).

Dependent Variable: CEO pay.

Focus Variables: ROCE and SRET; both of these are also entered as one-period lags.

Control Variables: Log of Sales.

Presentation

How Results Are Listed: Coefficients with absolute standard errors in brackets.

Goodness of Fit: There is no R^2 statistic presented here as it is not meaningful in this context.

Tests: 't' tests are not given explicitly but significance is indicated by an asterisk system where ** is significant at the 1 per cent level and * is significant at the 5 per cent level.

Diagnosis/Stability: Section 5.2 of the paper looks at what would have happened if time-wise heterogeneity had been ignored. The result is that the response of CEO pay to profits would have been higher and that to shareholder returns would have been smaller.

Anomalous Results: Shareholder return terms are insignificant.

Student Reflection

Things to Look Out For: There is some degree of selectivity in the sample of 99 firms in that they tend to be large and the author has also chosen firms that stay in business (which includes not being taken over) for the whole 18-year period. It is not explained exactly how the list of 99 firms was arrived at.

Problems in Replication: An exact replication is not difficult although it may be time consuming. Replication is facilitated by the author having listed the names of all the firms used in Appendix 1.

11.8 CONCLUSION

In this chapter you have learned techniques to deal with the problem of heteroscedasticity, tests for which were described in Section 9.6. In theory these techniques are an improvement over OLS if heteroscedasticity is present in the error term of the model and we do not have to deal with any other problems that may be present. However, the superiority of 'heteroscedasticity corrected' WLS estimates is based on mathematical proofs which show that the WLS estimators are asymptotically more efficient when the correction is based on some form of estimation. In reality, we are almost certainly going to have to use estimates of the heteroscedasticity relationship. If our samples are not large then we cannot rely on the asymptotic properties of GLS/WLS. It is probably wise to report OLS results for your models as well as WLS ones. If there is no major contradiction between these then there is little to worry about. However, you should not assume that any *individual* set of WLS estimates is necessarily best (that is, of minimum variance). Once we depart from the classical assumptions it is not clear how we can arrive at best estimators unless we know exactly the nature of the departure from the classical assumptions. In practice, dealing with heteroscedasticity involves using estimates of the unknown heteroscedasticity pattern, which has two consequences:

(i)   There may be a better pattern than the one we have assumed/estimated, that produces more efficient estimates.
(ii) We may have introduced a new source of error into the model when we produce our estimates of the pattern of heteroscedasticity. This is not going to be made known to us by the tests of the equation.

You should be careful in interpreting your GLS/WLS heteroscedasticity corrected estimates. The following factors need to be borne in mind. Some of these points have been made already but it is worth repeating them.

▶ R squareds from GLS estimates cannot be compared with their OLS equivalents in any meaningful way.
▶ Although the OLS estimates are theoretically unbiased as are the WLS, the two sets of results may not give identical coefficients due to sampling fluctuations.
▶ The GLS estimating equation may not have an intercept but the specified model, on which it is based, does have one.
▶ If the GLS estimating equation does still have an intercept term, its coefficient is *not* the intercept value for the original estimating equation.
▶ You might expect from the theoretical argument that all the 't' ratios will fall when you move from an OLS to a GLS estimate. This is not necessarily the case; some may fall and some may rise as this depends on the properties of the sample. Remember that the sample data may contain problems other than heteroscedasticity.

Ultimately, heteroscedasticity correction methods are measures of 'last resort' when you cannot find other ways to remove heteroscedasticity from the error term. These methods remove the bias (found in OLS estimates when heteroscedasticity is present) from the estimates of the variance of the error term and hence from the estimated standard errors and 't' ratios.

309

Any individual correction does not necessarily minimize the variance of the estimtors even though it removes the bias because there may always be a better estimator than the one we have tried. If the sample size is small, we have the additional problem that we cannot be sure that the bias, in the error variance estimation, has been removed.

DOS AND DON'TS

Do

✓ Remember to look at some heteroscedasticity tests on your OLS model rather than moving straight to a WLS 'correction' for heteroscedasticity.

✓ Look at all other possible avenues of dealing with rejection of the null on heteroscedasticity tests such as changes of functional form, variable definitions and specification before you resort to a 'correction' for heteroscedasticity.

Don't

✗ Use an arbitrary *ad hoc* form of adjustment for heteroscedasticity, such as using the inverse square root of population as the weight, when there may be better corrections available from either knowledge of the probable cause of the problem or from exploration of the OLS residuals.

✗ Make foolish comparisons between the OLS and WLS results in terms of the R squared.

✗ Forget that, for a given set of data and model specification in terms of variables and functional form, there is a unique set of parameter estimates and standard errors/'t' ratios in the case of OLS, *but* in a GLS estimation there are several different possible sets of results depending on the approach taken by a researcher and/or the default assumptions in the computer package they are using.

✗ Assume that your model is perfect just because you have used a technique to 'correct' its heteroscedasticity problem. It may be possible to improve the model using specification changes instead.

EXERCISES

11.1 **Explain why there are two different approaches to 'correcting' for heteroscedasticity.**

11.2 **Using the data set provided (in the THEATRE.XLS file) estimate the equation in Exercise 4.2 (Chapter 4) if you have not already done so.**
(i) Explain why you might suspect this equation of suffering from heteroscedasticity.
(ii) If this equation did have heteroscedastic errors, how would this alter the conclusions you would draw from the results?

11.3 **Re-estimate the equation in Exercise 11.2 using the *GROSSINC* variable as the proportionality factor in the heteroscedasticity relationship (i.e the weight will be the reciprocal of the square root of *GROSSINC*). Comment on the difference between these two sets of results.**

11.4 **Are the following remarks true, false or indeterminate? Explain your choice of answer:**
(i) The R squared should not be used to decide between an OLS and a GLS estimator.
(ii) The R squared adjusted should be used to decide between an OLS and a GLS estimator.

(iii) If there is heteroscedasticity in the error of the OLS equation you have just estimated, then it is not possible to improve on the GLS estimator proposed in Exercise 11.3.

(iv) You can choose between the OLS and WLS equations by picking the one which has the largest value of 'F for the equation'.

(v) If you were to run a regression using the logarithm of the dependent variable for an OLS equation with heteroscedastic residuals, then there would be no need to perform a GLS transformation or use heteroscedasticity corrected standard errors.

11.5 **Explain how you would decide whether the OLS or WLS/GLS estimates are the ones you would choose to base your conclusions on.**

11.6 **Obtain heteroscedasticity corrected standard errors for the equation estimated in your answer to Exercise 11.2. Compare the conclusions you reach from this method with those you derived from the WLS 'correction'.**

REFERENCES

Becker, G.S. (1968) Crime and punishment: An economic approach, *Journal of Political Economy*, **76**(1), 169–217.

Cameron, A.C. and Trivedi, P.K. (1998) *Regression Analysis of Count Data*, Econometric Society Monographs, Cambridge University Press, Cambridge.

Ehrlich, I. (1973) Participation in illegitimate activities: A theoretical and empirical investigation, *Journal of Political Economy*, **81**, 521–564. The version used is in *Essays in the Economics of Crime and Punishment*, edited by G.S. Becker and W.M. Landes, National Bureau of Economic Research, New York, 1974.

Guy, F. (2000) CEO pay, shareholder returns and accounting profitability, *International Journal of the Economics of Business*, **7**(3), 263–274.

Hildreth, C. and Houck, J.P. (1968) Some estimates for a linear model with random coefficients, *Journal of the American Statistical Association*, **63**, 584–595.

Prais, S.J. and Houthakker, H.S. (1955) *The Analysis of Family Budgets*, Cambridge University Press, New York.

Vandaele, W. (1978) Participation in illegitimate activities, I: Ehrlich revisited, in A. Blumstein and J. Cohen, *Deterrence and Incapacitation: Estimating the Effects of Criminal Sanctions on Crime Rates*, National Academy of Sciences, Washington.

White, H. (1980) A heteroscedasticity consistent covariance estimator and a direct test of heteroscedasticity, *Econometrica*, **48**, 817–838.

12

Multiple Equation Models: Specification and the Identification Problem

LEARNING OBJECTIVES

- Know what is meant by identification of a structural equation
- Know the difference between over identified, under identified and just identified equations
- Understand the difference between a reduced form and a structural equation
- Have a critical awareness of how one arrives at an identified model
- Be aware that you should not be attempting to estimate an unidentified equation
- Be able to explain what use can be made of the reduced forms of a model

CHAPTER SUMMARY

12.1 INTRODUCTION

In this chapter we move on to models that are more complex than considered so far. We now allow for the fact that a model may contain more than one equation. When there is more than one equation, we face a new problem which is the subject of this chapter. That problem is known as the **identification problem**.

Unlike most of the other chapters in this book, there are no review studies or data-based examples. These will, instead, be given when we come to the next chapter, which deals with estimation methods for simultaneous systems. This chapter deals only with identification in linear models.

Identification is a problem of specification, but the use of a system of equations brings issues of estimation in that we would generally find that our OLS estimators no longer have all of the BLUE properties. The next chapter deals with the estimation problems that arise when we have a system of equations, in particular the violation of the classical assumption that $(\text{cov}\, x, u) = 0$.

The identification problem was first brought to the attention of economists in an article by the agricultural economist E.J. Working, which was published in 1927 and is still worth reading today. Using simple supply and demand diagrams (which we shall repeat later in this chapter), Working was able to show that statistical estimates which were claimed to be of the parameters of demand functions may not be so after all. This difficulty is not specific to supply and demand models of markets and can be found in all areas of economics such as the IS-LM model, the Phillips curve and it is particularly problematic in the study of the economics of crime (a topic covered in the review study in Section 11.7 by Ehrlich) as shown in Exercise 12.3 below.

The basic concept of identification should be quite simple to grasp, although some effort may be required to master the mathematical rules for identification. Failure to achieve identification will restrict the scope of the inferences that you could derive from a model. However, it does not mean that your models will be totally useless for purposes of hypothesis testing, government policy formulation or business consultancy. This is because the reduced form equation of an unidentified model may still prove to be applicable for these purposes.

As this subject can be quite confusing, the chapter ends with a question and answer section to review the problems that have come up in the chapter.

12.2 DO WE NEED MORE THAN ONE EQUATION IN OUR MODEL?

The approach of the previous chapters can be the target of one very serious criticism. That is, one equation is not enough to adequately describe the complexity of the relationships we are trying to model. Economics is founded on a set of models, which involve more than one equation. In microeconomics, we have supply and demand models while in macroeconomics we find simple IS-LM models. Beyond this, we find macroeconometric models with dozens of equations in them. This is really just an applied version of the general equilibrium model of microeconomic theory, which can contain any number of equations.

A model with just one equation has the attractive feature of simplicity. It implies that there is only one set of causal relationships between the left-hand side variable and the right-hand side variables. Thus, it ignores the following possibilities:

▶ Relationships between variables may flow in both directions. Some of what we have been calling the 'independent' variables may be dependent on the left-hand side variable that we have been calling the 'dependent' variable. If this is the case then these variables can no longer be truly independent and there will be problems with OLS estimates of their parameters (as the covariance of the variable with the error term will not be zero).

▶ There may be relationships between the right-hand side variables themselves – this was covered to some extent in Chapter 10 on multicollinearity but a full exploration requires that we write out new equations to describe these relationships.

Let us go back to the lipstick example of Chapter 3, as originally shown in Equation (3.2), but we now add an income variable to make it Equation (12.1):

$$\text{Quantity of Lipstick Demanded} = b_0 + b_1(\text{Price of Lipstick}) + b_2(\text{Income}) + u \qquad (12.1)$$

where the subscripts have been dropped for convenience.

Using OLS to draw inferences about the parameters of this model assumes that quantity *depends on price and not the other way round,* as the CLRM supposes that the left-hand side variable is dependent and the right-hand side variable is independent. Price is therefore treated as an exogenous variable.

There are two obvious reasons why one equation may not suffice to describe adequately the lipstick market.

(i) Utility maximization

We know from basic microeconomics that a demand relationship, such as that for lipstick, is derived from the assumption that individuals are maximizing their utility by equating the marginal utility of lipstick divided by its price to the marginal utilities of other goods divided by their prices. Identification of the model does rely on the assumption of utility maximization as we assume that each point on the demand curve represents a point of utility maximization with deviations being random errors.

However, it follows that spending on lipstick is co-determined with spending on other goods, as there is a complex of income and substitution effects caused by the change in the price of any good on all other goods. A simple single-equation model usually deals with this by including a measure of the price of 'all other goods', usually the retail price index/consumer price index on the right-hand side of the equation. The common practice of dividing this into the price of the good demanded is a restriction on the properties of the utility function.

This kind of reason for needing more than one equation is not restricted to demand equations. It can obviously apply equally to supply equations including the supply of labour, and in the case of the crime example shown in the review study by Ehrlich in Section 11.7 on the supply of crime. Ehrlich's study used the SUR (seemingly unrelated regression) technique, which we cover in Chapter 13. This allows for non-zero covariances between different equations in the system.

We shall now leave aside this issue to concentrate on models where the presence of more than one equation is due to the presence of different sectors in the model (e.g. firms and households) rather than different choices open to a decision maker.

(ii) Supply and demand

If we regress the quantity of lipstick sold on prices and income and choose to tell people that this is the market demand curve, how can we justify ignoring the influence of supply? One thing that you will notice when you look at research estimating supply or demand functions for any commodity, or labour for that matter, is that statistics do not allow us to observe separate amounts offered for sale and desired by consumers at a point in time. Thus, we do not actually have information on supply and demand in the vast majority of cases. All we have is one set of prices and quantities for each observation and nothing to tell us whether these are the quantities demanded or supplied. This problem is dealt with, in most cases, by invoking an assumption of market equilibrium, which therefore implies that the observed price and quantity lies on *both* the supply function and the demand function because it is at a point of intersection between them. Unless otherwise stated we will hold to this assumption in this, and the next, chapter.

There is no reason why we cannot have a model that has dozens of equations. Modern low-cost, high-speed computing means that time and money should not be constraints on estimating large models. Large econometric models are mainly to be found in the area of macroeconometric modelling with a focus on forecasting for the purposes of policy formulation by the government.

Having said all this, we could still argue that the use of a single-equation model in a piece of research is justified, as we are only interested in that equation and not the rest of the system. For example, if a firm has hired me to forecast demand for its products why should I bother to model its supply behaviour? There are two problems with this response. The first, dealt with in the following chapter (Chapter 13) is that choosing to ignore the properties of a system of equations may cause problems with the validity of our estimators. In particular, certain assumptions of the CLRM may be violated. The second problem, which we deal with in this chapter, is the issue of identification. If my demand function is not identified then I will be making conceptual errors in drawing inferences about the results as well as errors in hypothesis testing.

12.3 HANDLING SYSTEMS OF EQUATIONS

It is not difficult to write down a system of equations instead of a single equation. For example, let us begin with our lipstick market, and add a supply equation (12.2) to the demand equation (12.1) as follows:

$$\textit{Supply of Lipstick} = b_3 + b_4(\textit{Price of Lipstick}) + v \tag{12.2}$$

where v is another classical disturbance term. It will therefore have the same mean of u, which is zero, but there is no necessity for its variance to be identical to that of u.

This is a very simple system, as we have not added any new variables to the model: remember that the quantity measure on the left-hand side of Equation (12.2) will be taken from exactly the same figures as the quantity measure on the left-hand side of Equation (12.1). The same considerations apply to the price figures; that is, exactly the same data would be used to attempt to obtain b_4 as would be used in the attempt to obtain b_1.

In such a model, we also need to specify how the two equations are connected with each other; this can be put in the form of a third equation such as:

$$Q^s = Q^d \tag{12.3}$$

where Q^s is the supply of lipstick and Q^d is the demand for lipstick. This assumes that the market is in equilibrium, this being a common assumption in econometric models as we have already said.

The model we now have is a simple simultaneous equation system in which price and quantity are jointly determined rather than one of them 'causing' the other to happen without any feedback.

WHAT CHANGES DO WE NOW HAVE?

▶ We now have an additional disturbance term for each equation, which is assumed to have the same classical properties as in the first part of this book. For ease of understanding, we are continuing with the 'one thing at a time' approach and thus ignore problems of heteroscedasticity etc.

▶ Because we have an additional disturbance term for each new equation, we need to specify the relationship between the disturbance terms. The simplest assumption to make is to assume $\text{Cov}(u, v) = 0$ in order to try to preserve the efficiency properties of the OLS estimation approach.

▶ We now have additional parameters for some variables; for example, in the above system there are two parameters on price: one for supply and one for demand. There is still only one parameter for income as it does not appear in the supply function.

▶ We need to learn some new terminology. The parameters in the lipstick market model written above are known as **structural parameters**. This term is applied to any parameter on a variable in a structural equation.

▶ There is another type of equation which emerges from such a system that we have not yet seen. This equation is called a **reduced form**. Its parameters will be the **reduced form parameters.**

▶ It follows from the above that one could estimate more equations than just the structural equations shown in the model. That is, we could also estimate the reduced form. How many more additional equations, in the shape of reduced forms, there are depends on properties of the model which we are about to explore. The number of reduced form equations will be equal to the number of endogenous variables which, in this case, is two – price and quantity.

The reduced form equations are derived by solving the model in terms of its exogenous variables. The number of reduced form equations will therefore be equal to the number of endogenous variables. In the simple supply and demand model for lipstick there will be two reduced forms: one for price and one for quantity. These are going to be of the form:

$$Q = z_0 + z_1 Y + \Psi \tag{12.4}$$

$$P = z_2 + z_3 Y + \xi \tag{12.5}$$

where Ψ and ξ are the (classical) disturbance terms of the reduced form equations.

The Q terms no longer have a superscript as they are now regarded as the equilibrium values, not the quantities offered or desired at a set of prices.

We know from the start of this chapter that there is an identification problem that may arise in this system of equations. The problem is that two equations may be too similar to each other, in terms of the variables they contain, in order for us to tell them apart. This does not apply to the reduced form. Both reduced forms look identical in terms of what appears on the right-hand side and this is true even in a more complex model with large numbers of equations and large numbers of endogenous variables. Although they are identical in format, the value of z_0 is not the same as z_3 and the value of z_1 is not the same as the value of z_4. One set of solutions for these variables – obtained by substituting Equations (12.1) and (12.2) into Equation (12.3), rearranging and then substituting the equilibrium value of Q into Equation (12.3) – is:

$$z_0 = b_3 + b_4[(b_0 - b_3)/(b_4 - b_1)] \qquad (12.6)$$

$$z_1 = b_4 b_2 Y/(b_4 - b_1) \qquad (12.7)$$

$$z_2 = (b_0 - b_3)/(b_4 - b_1) \qquad (12.8)$$

$$z_3 = b_2/(b_4 - b_1) \qquad (12.9)$$

The disturbance terms of the two equations will differ as they are composites of the disturbance terms in the structural equation. From the above solution they are:

$$\Psi = b_4[(u - v)/(b_4 - b_1)] + v \qquad (12.10)$$

$$\xi = (u - v)/(b_4 - b_1) \qquad (12.11)$$

Therefore, our lipstick market model now has four equations, which we could possibly estimate. The two reduced forms can be estimated, no matter what the structure of the model is, but the other two equations require identification. We may discover circumstances where the structural equations cannot be estimated, meaning that we can only explore the model using the reduced forms.

Before we go on to spell out fully the nature of the identification problem, it might be helpful to look at a model, which is not a simultaneous equations system, and then comment on the general format of systems of equations.

A Recursive Model

Take the following example to model the spending by a child:

$$\text{Parents' income} = f(\text{wage rates, disturbance term}) \qquad (12.12)$$

$$\text{Child's expenditure} = f(\text{prices of goods, parents' income, disturbance term}) \qquad (12.13)$$

This is a recursive system where the linkage between the equations is a two-stage process.

The equations here are linked in a non-symmetrical way. That is, the outcome of one is a constraint on the other. There is no feedback from the spending of children to the income of *parents*. If there was, we would have a simultaneous equations model rather than a **recursive** model, which is the name given to the system above. Again, we would need to make some assumptions about the covariance of the error terms in the two equations.

The simplest assumption to make would be that the covariance is zero. In this model parents' income is a **predetermined** (i.e. exogenous) variable, thus Equation (12.13) contains only predetermined/exogenous variables even though it is part of a system of equations.

These simple examples have only two equations in the structural model and thus there can only be a limited range of interdependency between the parts of the model. Only four things can happen in the examples we have discussed in this chapter:

(i) The first equation is recursive on the second.
(ii) The second equation is recursive on the first.
(iii) The two equations are simultaneously determined.
(iv) The two equations do not have any feedback to each other.

We cannot have any two of the above four possibilities arising at the same time in a two-equation system. However, a large system of equations can contain different segments within it. If we had a 63-equation macro model designed to explain such things as money demand, aggregate investment, aggregate consumption, aggregate imports, aggregate employment and so on, then we may find some sets of equations which have no simultaneous or recursive linkage along with some others which are simultaneous and some which are recursive. Finally, we should point out that a system may also contain identities, for example $C + S = Y$ in the simple macro model.

Now that we have covered the basic idea of systems of equations in a general way, it is time to move on to consider why the 'identification problem' may trouble us in a system of equations.

12.4 IDENTIFICATION: THE ORDER CONDITION

To the person unfamiliar with econometrics, identification, like multicollinearity, might seem to be a serious threat which runs the risk of undermining the whole of the discipline. Until now, we have been happy to assume that any equation we estimate is what we say it is, but the need for identification suggests that we may in fact have in some sense estimated the 'wrong' equation. Worse still, it seems to say that no matter how hard we try we might never be able to excavate the 'correct' equation from the set of data that we are using.

So, what is the 'identification problem'? In simple terms, it is the problem of whether or not we can be sure that the equation we have estimated is, in fact, what we think it is. If we fail to identify the single equation, out of a system, then the failure is because we cannot distinguish it from some combination of itself plus fractions of the other equation in the system.

The formal definition is, taking the case of the lipstick demand equation:

> The demand equation is not identified if we can not distinguish the demand equation from the following equation where $\lambda > 0$
>
> $$b_0 + b_1(Price\ of\ Lipstick)_i + b_2(Income) + u + \lambda[b_3 + b_4(Price\ of\ Lipstick) + v] \quad \textbf{(12.14)}$$

Equation (12.8) is the demand function plus a fraction of the supply function. It can be written as:

$$\{b_0 + b_3\} + \{b_1 + b_4\}(\textit{Price of Lipstick}) + b_2(\textit{Income}) + \{u + \lambda v\} \tag{12.15}$$

The problem with a regression of quantity on prices and income is that we do not seem to be able to show that we have estimated the 'right' equation. The computer package, when fed the information that quantity is the dependent variable and price and income are the independent variables, will provide us with the slope coefficients for the two variables on the right-hand side. But, it has no way of knowing whether it has just provided you with $\{b_1 + \lambda.b_4\}$ instead of b_1.

It is important to stress that identification is an entirely separate matter from estimation techniques and should be addressed *before* you move on to consider the choice of estimation technique. If an equation turns out to be 'unidentified', which is the same thing as 'under identified', then you should *not* under any circumstances be attempting to estimate it.

Although they are not the only ways of ensuring identification, in practice there are two sets of rules for identification which are usually used. Their names are derived from matrix algebra as a system of equations is essentially a relationship between a matrix of coefficients, and vectors of variables. These rules revolve around the matter of whether or not a variable appears in an equation. The rules are:

▶ **Order condition.** The order condition involves counting the number of variables that do not appear in an equation but are included in other equations in the system.
▶ **Rank condition.** The rank condition involves the formation of a matrix to represent the structure of the model and the examination of whether this matrix has suitable properties of its determinants in order for us to establish identification.

In the remainder of this section, we give diagrammatic illustrations of the order condition using similar cases to those originally employed by E.J. Working. The mathematical form of the order condition is stated in Section 12.5.

DIAGRAMMATIC ILLUSTRATIONS

We now look at four different diagrams to illustrate the identification problem. When we do this, we are assuming that the data collected and used is generated by the models we have decided to adopt and therefore any specification errors in these models are captured in the disturbance terms.

(i) Supply identified but demand not identified: Figure 12.1

Figure 12.1 shows the lipstick model where demand depends on prices and incomes. For illustration, we have three demand curves for three different levels of income (D_1, D_2, D_3) assuming that lipstick is a normal good. As income is not included in the supply function we find that the S curve does not shift its position when the D curves shift. There are thus four schedules on Figure 12.1 with three different equilibrium positions shown for price and quantity ($P1$, $Q1$; $P1$, $Q2$; $P3$, $Q3$).

Both the S and D schedules will be shifting randomly about the diagram due to the error terms so, although the model is based on equilibrium, the model is not assumed to be in

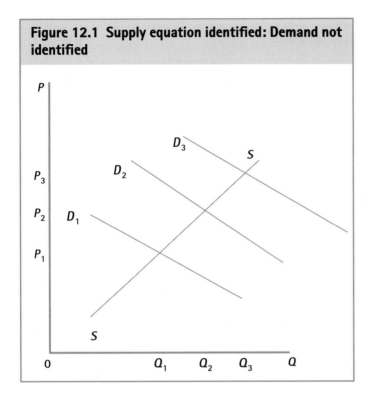

Figure 12.1 Supply equation identified: Demand not identified

equilibrium at all times. The equilibrium points all lie on the same schedule for the price–quantity supply relationship but they are on different schedules for the price–quantity demand relationship. Thus it seems that the supply relationship can be identified because the movements in the demand schedule trace out a path representing the supply schedule. Conversely, the demand schedule cannot be identified because the price–quantity relationship for demand cannot be observed, therefore any regression of quantity on price, plus the income variable, cannot possibly be an estimate of b_1.

(ii) Neither equation identified: reduced form which is of no use – Figure 12.2
If we now assume that $b_2 = 0$ then income drops out of the demand equation. What difference does this make? Well, we are now unable to estimate either equation, as both contain exactly the same variables. In fact, apart from the random fluctuations of u and v, we should find that price and quantity will not deviate from their equilibrium levels. This situation is shown in Figure 12.2. We should point out that, since we now have a model with no exogenous variables at all, that we will get a reduced form which consists only of regressing P or Q on an intercept term which is a composite of the parameters in the model. There is clearly no point in estimating such an equation.

(iii) Demand identified but supply function not identified: Figure 12.3
If we keep the assumption that $b_2 = 0$ and add a new variable to the supply equation such as a measure of the cost of production (X), then we can represent this in Figure 12.3 where three levels of X are shown leading to shifts in the supply function. The three equilibrium points in our new model will trace out a demand curve meaning that we can now identify the demand

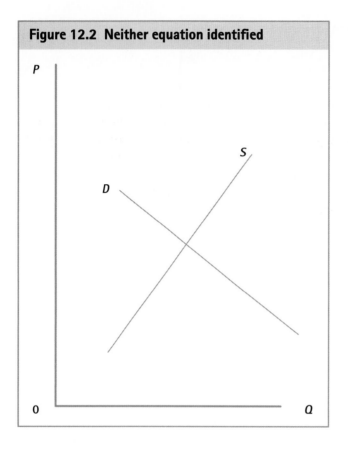

Figure 12.2 Neither equation identified

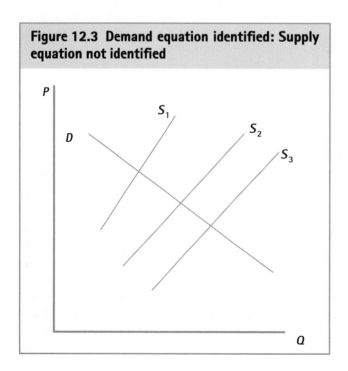

Figure 12.3 Demand equation identified: Supply equation not identified

function and therefore, in principle, obtain an estimate of b_1. However, we cannot obtain an estimate of b_3 as the set of equilibrium points does not trace out a supply curve.

(iv) Both equations identified: Figure 12.4

So far, we have had situations where one function was identified but the other was not and a situation where neither was identified because only price appeared on the right-hand side of the model. What if we now allow for exogenous variables that are different in both equations? Let us reintroduce income, by assuming that $b_2 \neq 0$ and keeping the assumption that we have a cost variable in the supply function. This situation is shown for three sets of income level and three levels of costs in Figure 12.4. This shows a total set of nine equilibrium points. In theory, this model allows for the identification of both functions.

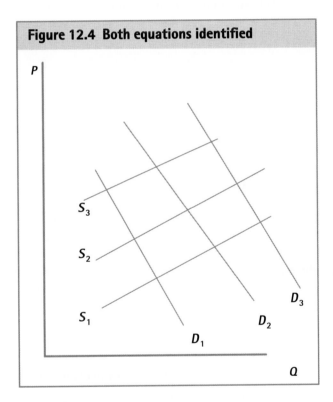

Figure 12.4 Both equations identified

All that we need is to be able to separate the two equations. Remember that we will be working with only one set of values for quantity at any point in time and, therefore, we do not, unfortunately, have the option of dividing the sample up into separate parts, some of which are on the supply function and some of which are on the demand function. Thus, in this example we would estimate both the equations because they are identified using all the data in both cases. This would give us the structural equation parameters of the whole model. Unfortunately, OLS estimates of this will be biased, as we shall see later.

In the above four cases, we could always opt to estimate the reduced forms of the model, although in case (ii) this would be pointless since there are no variables on the right-hand side of the equation. This problem would not have arisen if there was at least one exogenous variable appearing in one of the equations. Hence, we would almost always still be able to use the reduced forms to make inferences about relationships in the model, even if part or all of it is unidentified, because economists will almost always have exogenous variables in a multiple equation model.

Zero restrictions

These diagrammatic examples are an illustration of the order condition where identification is based on the absence or presence of a variable in an equation. This can be more correctly expressed in terms of **zero restrictions** on the parameters of some variables. The reason we achieved identification of the whole model in Figure 12.4, is that income does not appear in the supply equation – which is equivalent to it having a parameter of zero in that equation – and costs of production do not appear in the demand equation – which is equivalent to it having a parameter of zero in that equation.

THE ORDER CONDITIONS FOR IDENTIFICATION

This process of counting can be summed up in a rule that is the Order Condition:

if $k - M = g - 1$: the equation is just identified

if $k - M < g - 1$: the equation is under identified

if $k - M > g - 1$: the equation is over identified

where $M =$ the total number of variables in the *equation* – both endogenous and exogenous; $g =$ the number of endogenous variables in the *whole model*; $k =$ the number of variables (both endogenous and exogenous) in the *whole model*.

In our lipstick model, g will be 2. Therefore, $k - M$ will have to be equal to, or less than, 1 for an equation to be identified. You should note that the term 'under identified' means not identified; that is, you do not have enough restrictions to be able to recover the structural parameters. The term 'identified' is used to cover both 'just' identified and 'over' identified. Both terms mean that you are able to establish the structural parameters of an equation. The difference between the two terms is that just identified means you have just enough restrictions in the model to identify an equation while over identified means you have more restrictions than you need.

With the rule, written as above, we find for our original lipstick model of Equations (12.1) and (12.2) that the following hold:

Demand $g = 2$ $k - M = 0$ Result: under identified

Supply $g = 2$ $k - M = 1$ Result: just identified.

This agrees with the conclusion we came to looking at the diagram in Figure 12.1. For Figure 12.2 the value of $k - M$ is 0 and so identification is not possible. For Figure 12.3 we have:

Demand $g = 2$ $k - M = 1$ Result: just identified.

Supply $\quad g = 24k - M = 0 \quad$ Result: under identified

For Figure 12.4 (so long as a different variable is 'shifting' each schedule) we have:

Demand $\quad g = 2 \quad k - M = 1 \quad$ Result: just identified

Supply $\quad\quad g = 2 \quad k - M = 1 \quad$ Result: just identified.

So, as we would expect, these rules give the same results as we arrived at from our earlier inspection of the diagrams.

ALTERNATIVE FORMS OF IDENTIFICATION

In the case of the lipstick model, identification was achieved using continuous (ratio) variables. The exogenous variables, which permit us to identify a structural equation, do not have to be of this type. The identifying restrictions may be achieved using dummy variables or lagged values of the exogenous variables. For example, if the commodity in question in our supply and demand example exhibited seasonality in production or consumption (but not both) then seasonal dummies in a quarterly model could be used to enable identification. Likewise, in the example we have used we could achieve identification even if both functions contained the same determinants, if there was a dynamic relationship on one side of the market and the same dynamic relationship was not operating on the other side of the model. A standard textbook case is the cobweb model where there is a lagged relationship in supply but consumers are assumed to be in instantaneous equilibrium (apart from the effect of random errors).

We have just brought up the use of dummies and lagged terms in the context of a simple two-equation model. In a bigger model, we would of course have to follow the order condition counting rule to check whether the inclusion of such variables facilitates identification. We now consider four additional ways in which identification could be achieved.

(i) Covariance restrictions

It should be clear by now that identification is mainly about finding differences in the sources of movement/variation between the structural equations of a model. So far, we have dealt with the obvious case of the differences between equations being due to the fact that some variables appear in one equation, but not in another and therefore face a zero parameter restriction.

Even assuming constant parameters, the variables in a regression are not the only sources of movement as we do also have the behaviour of the error terms to look at. Let us think back to the hopeless case of Figure 12.2 where both equations were identical, containing only the endogenous variable, price, on the right-hand side. The only observable movement, in the data, for such a model has to be attributed to the uncorrelated random disturbances of the error terms in the supply and demand functions. However, what if we knew that one of these equations had a very small variance in its error term while the other had, by comparison, a very large variance.

This is shown in Figure 12.5 where the dotted lines enclose the range of fluctuation in the demand schedule and the two solid lines enclose the range of fluctuation in the supply function. If we took just the extreme case where supply simply oscillated between just these two solid lines (S_{max} and S_{min}), then this looks very similar to the case of using a dummy variable shift in S

325

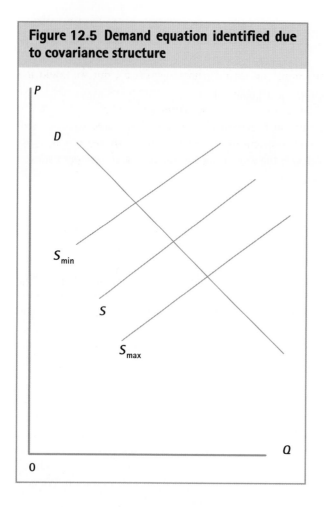

Figure 12.5 Demand equation identified due to covariance structure

to enable identification of the demand function. For the less extreme case, where the supply function fluctuates between the bands shown, we would still seem to have identification. So, a covariance restriction could be a means of achieving identification. This is of limited usefulness in practice and one seldom sees articles that try to use this method of identifying equations.

(ii) Parameter restrictions

The order condition has been introduced as the main means of identifying the structural equations in a model with several simultaneous equations (remember that the diagrammatic illustrations were a depiction of the order condition). This is the use of a specific restriction – that some parameters are zero in some equations. One might think that we could use other restrictions to identify a model (for example, that $b_2 = 1$ or $b_3 + b_4 = 1$) and this is indeed the case. For example, if we knew that the parameter on Y in Equation (12.1) was 5 then (as we saw in our discussion of multicollinearity) we could simply run a regression with $5Y$ taken over to the other side so the equation becomes:

$$Q - 5Y = b_0 + b_1 P + u \tag{12.16}$$

This equation will be identified so long as an exogenous variable appears in the supply equation, even if that variable is Y or, as we have already indicated above, even if it is Q_{t-1} or P_{t-1}.

In this case, we used equality restrictions (i.e. that a parameter was 5), but we could use inequality constraints (i.e. that the sum of two parameters is less than one) in some cases. However, such models could not be estimated using OLS or modifications of it.

The comments made in Chapter 10 on the use of extraneous estimates to deal with multicollinearity apply here. That is, such restrictions may be hard to justify apart from some well-known ones from economic models such as constant returns to scale in production and homogeneity of degree zero in utility functions.

(iii) Disequilibrium models

So far, we have assumed that our models contain a stable, unique equilibrium from which deviations are only found due to random errors and (in a dynamic model) short-run temporary departures from equilibrium. Due to this assumption we have been required to treat the quantity data, in a supply and demand model, as being both the quantity demanded and the quantity supplied.

Although equilibrium is a pervasive concept in economics, there are situations where we may have more-or-less permanent disequilibria, such as where prices are 'administered' (such as in the case of minimum wage laws or rental controls) rather than freely determined by the market. In such circumstances, Equation (12.3) no longer applies and the relevant factor is which side of the market are we on, i.e. excess supply or excess demand.

Take the specific example shown in Figure 12.6 of the labour market for a public sector employment such as police or prison officers or state hospital workers. The disequilibrium assumed here is that wage settlements are consistently too low and therefore create excess demand. We assume that this excess demand cannot be eliminated by taxpayers independently supplementing the wage rates, therefore we will find that the data points must lie around the lower portion (i.e. below the equilibrium wage rate and employment levels) of the supply curve. Thus it seems that the supply curve is identified although, if it is non-linear, we would seem to face problems of inference about its total shape.

If the opposite situation occurred and the wage settlements were consistently too high then the data points would be regarded as falling around the demand curve and we would be in a situation of excess supply. This would again be censored in that we would not be able to observe the lower part of the supply curve.

(iv) Monopoly and monopsony

Supply and demand models are premised on there being large numbers of competing consumers and providers in the market. If we had pure monopoly in our lipstick model then the supply curve would no longer exist, as the sole firm would set either price or quantity in such a way as to satisfy its own objectives. If it was a revenue-maximizing firm or a profit-maximizing firm with negligible marginal costs and sufficiently low fixed costs then, for a linear demand curve, we should find it locating at half-way along the demand curve; that is, where output supplied is half the figure that the equation says would be demanded at zero price and the price elasticity of demand is minus 1.

In such a case as the above, it would appear that the demand equation cannot be identified unless something shifts the positions chosen by the monopolist, as all we will be observing is

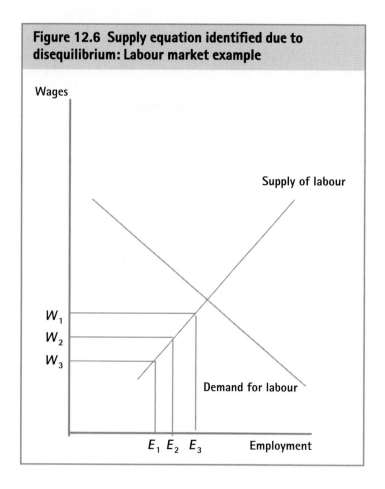

Figure 12.6 Supply equation identified due to disequilibrium: Labour market example

random error. One thing which could provide identification is exogenous tax-setting behaviour by regulators. If they chose a number of different rates of per-unit taxation then this would push the firm up the top half of the demand curve. This, as would any other factor shifting marginal costs, allows the demand curve to be identified although, as with the disequilibrium cases, the schedule would be 'censored' because we only observe part of it, causing us particular problems if the relationship is non-linear.

One can apply the above argument in reverse. That is, if there is a pure monopsony, then we could identify the supply curve due to the fact that the monopsonist will be picking a point on the supply curve in order to maximize its objectives.

In a model that combines monopoly and monopsony, we have bilateral monopoly in which the equilibrium is indeterminate between maximum and minimum points. To achieve identification in such a model would require the specification of bargaining equations.

We have just described four types of cases, outside the standard market equilibrium model, where identification might be achieved. You should bear in mind that we have said nothing about estimation in such cases and it will not necessarily be the case that OLS estimates, for these cases, will be BLUE. We now come to a fifth case.

(v) Non-linearity

Throughout this chapter, we adhere strictly to the assumption of totally linear models which are much easier to deal with than non-linear models. However, it is possible, in principle, to achieve identification when a variable enters into one equation in a different way than it enters into other equations. An obvious case would be where one equation features the variable entered in a linear fashion, while it enters another equation in the model as a quadratic. This does bring additional complications as the rules for identification will not be the same as those we have learnt.

12.5 RULES FOR IDENTIFICATION CONTINUED: ORDER CONDITIONS IN A LARGER MODEL

We now come to a statement of the order conditions. This will be done in the context of a slightly more complex model than the lipstick supply and demand model used so far. We will now use a basic old-fashioned macro model, which has a few, plausible, additional variables added to it. This model is written down in Equations (12.17–12.20), which is a set of four equations. There are three structural equations, which therefore have error terms plus an equilibrium condition. The money supply is fixed.

$$C = b_0 + b_1 Y + u \tag{12.17}$$

$$I = b_2 + b_3 R + b_4 BC + v \tag{12.18}$$

$$Md = b_5 + b_6 Y + b_7 R + w \tag{12.19}$$

$$C + I = Y \tag{12.20}$$

$$Md = \overline{M}s \tag{12.21}$$

where C is consumption; Y is national income; I is investment; R is the rate of interest; BC is business confidence in the economy; and Md is demand for money, $\overline{M}s$ is the (fixed) supply of money.

ORDER CONDITIONS FOR THIS MODEL

There are four endogenous variables in this model (consumption, income, investment and interest rates) and two exogenous variables (money stock and the level of business confidence). So, let us look at the three structural equations in terms of their identification state using the rule given above.

Recall that if these two numbers are equal then we have a 'just identified equation', which can, in principle, then be estimated. If the left-hand side number is less than the right-hand side then the equation is 'over identified'. Again, it is possible to estimate the equation. Both these states are states where we have identification. In the final case where the left-hand side is less than the right-hand side then we have 'under identification', which means that it is not possible to recover the value of the structural parameters from the system and therefore the equation should not be identified.

329

For this model the relationship turns out as below, given that $g = 4$ and $k = 6$:

Consumption Function:	$4(k - 2) > 3(g - 1)$	Identified
Investment Function:	$3(k - 3) = 3(g - 1)$	Identified
Money Demand Function:	$3(k - 3) = 3(g - 1)$	Identified

Therefore, the conclusion from this is that all three functions are identified, with the consumption function being the only one that is over identified. This means that you can proceed to estimate these functions given the assumptions of your model. There is no guarantee that the assumptions of your model are correct. Therefore, one may well go on to produce OLS estimates of structural equations, which are meaningless jumbles of the structural parameters in a 'true' model.

12.6 SOME IMPORTANT QUESTIONS

In Section 12.5 we looked at the formal mathematical rules about identifying structural equations. These rules do not cover every issue that we would encounter in practice. We now deal with these issues in a question and answer format.

(i) Has the data got anything to do with it?
Yes. The rank and order conditions only deal with the formal theoretical model that you are proposing to use. When you come to the stage of actually estimating your model then the properties of the data may help or hinder the process of identification. This was implied in the discussion of covariance restrictions, namely, if it so happened in the real world data we were using that one function had much more random variation than the other then we might be able to identify a model. This reflects the fact that the presence of the identification problem highlights the difficulties of working with non-experimental data. If we had complete, 'laboratory style' control over our data then the identification problem should not arise as we could hold constant all the factors that might cause identification problems.

(ii) Can we simply adjust the restrictions in order to achieve identification?
The answer to this question should be 'no', as tinkering with the properties of a model purely in order to achieve identification of its equations would seem to be an offence in the same category as data mining. If it was actually done as part of a process of reacting to experiments with the specification of the exogenous variables in the model, then it would be data mining.

Given this, one needs to ask: What is to stop people from simply writing down a model, which they claim is identified, that depends heavily on arbitrary exclusions of variables from equations? The extent of this depends on the solidity of the body of theory that underlies a particular piece of research and the nature of the data that is being used. If we are using data in which a large range of variation could be attributed to variables that are loosely defined in theory, then there is scope for differences in opinion about whether a variable belongs in the model or not.

For example, the core micro theory of demand might be seen as solid in the sense that price and income would be guaranteed to be in the model and likewise a model of the consumption function would be guaranteed to have an income variable. If we now expand these models into more psychological areas (as was done in the model used in Section 12.5), the model becomes less solid and there is room for one researcher's model to differ from another's in terms of which exogenous variables appear in which equation. In these circumstances, it may become a matter of opinion (or 'faith') as to whether an equation is identified. The extreme case of this, as will be seen in the discussion of instrumental variables in Chapter 13, is where identification is taken for granted and an *ad hoc* treatment of endogeneity is assumed for the purposes of estimation.

(iii) If some equations in the model are not (under) identified can we interpret the identified (just or over) structural equations without any difficulty?

Yes, we can. The only problem that will exist is with the need to use an appropriate estimation technique to deal with problems of simultaneity bias. This is covered in Chapter 13.

(iv) Does it make any difference to the last answer if the identified equations are just or over identified?

No – the only difference this makes is that the structural equations in a just identified model can be estimated via ILS (indirect least squares), which only requires the OLS estimates of the reduced form. This is a simple process but it is now somewhat irrelevant as economists will use IV/2SLS methods, as explained in the next chapter, rather than OLS.

(v) How do we interpret the reduced form?

The coefficients in a reduced form show the impact of a one-unit change in the exogenous variables on the equilibrium values of the endogenous variables in the model. They will be made up of a combination of the parameters from the structural equation.

(vi) Does it make any difference to the last answer if some (or indeed all) the equations are not identified?

No, it does not. This interpretation holds even if none of the equations are identified.

(vii) Is a model in which most (or even all) of the equations are not identified of no use to us whatsoever?

No, this is not the case, as the answer to the previous question implies. We can still make some use of a partly unidentified model, or even a wholly unidentified model, provided it contains at least one exogenous variable. How useful the model will be depends on what your major research focus is. Obviously if your concern is with the sign, size and significance of particular structural parameters, for example, the interest elasticity of the demand for money or the export elasticity with respect to the exchange rate, then your model is of little use if the equations containing these parameters are not identified. However, if our research is concerned with the impact of changes in an exogenous variable on the equilibrium values of the endogenous variables then the reduced form is extremely important and may be more relevant than the structural equations. Take the model in Section 12.5. If we wanted to know the impact of an increase in business confidence on equilibrium national income then we would look at the coefficient on *BC* in the reduced form. We can still do this even if all of the structural equations are not identified.

(viii) Can we do tests for identification?

The answer to this is yes, and no to some extent, and we need to consider a supplementary question as to what the precise usefulness of such tests is.

We have found that the usual first step in checking identification is based on restrictions on the value of certain parameters, usually that they are zero. As this is a straightforward application of the null hypothesis, it would seem that we should quite easily be able to perform tests for identification.

You might think that the standard 'F' and 't' tests could be used to check for identification. That is, we could estimate the equations in the lipstick model, and the macro model used above in the usual way, by OLS (or any GLS technique) and test whether the relevant coefficients are zero. An obvious problem with this is that identification relies on simultaneous restrictions, for example that a coefficient is zero in one equation and not in another one. However, there is a more serious conceptual problem, which is that, in order to generate estimates of the parameters we have to have identification in the first place. It follows that, as we cannot legitimately estimate unidentified equations, we will find it impossible to make a comparison of them with the identified equations.

There are indeed tests, which have been proposed for the **over identifying restrictions,** beginning with the likelihood-ratio test of Anderson and Rubin (1950). Most of these tests culminate in the use of a Chi-squared statistic derived from comparing different estimators.

Quite a large proportion of econometric studies do not attempt to perform these types of tests. For example, the two review studies in our next chapter do not attempt to test for identification. It is more common to find tests for exogeneity (as can be seen in one of the review studies in Chapter 13) and causality in the typical piece of applied econometrics.

(ix) Are the order conditions sufficient for identification?

No. The order conditions can be satisfied and yet the model may still not be identified. There are additional conditions called the rank conditions which require the use of matrix algebra to form determinants from a particular way of presenting the structure of the model. The order conditions are therefore necessary but not sufficient conditions for identification.

12.7 CONCLUSION

This chapter has dealt exclusively with a problem of the specification of a model – that is, the identification of its structural equations. We have said nothing about how you should go about estimating a just or over identified model. These problems are taken up in the next chapter.

You should by now be aware that we should *not* be trying to estimate structural equations, which are not (i.e. under) identified. The structure of the model simply does not allow one to recover these parameters from a set of regressions regardless of the technique employed.

Identification is definitely a problem in econometrics but it is one which it is sometimes possible to avoid or overcome depending on the nature of the data one is working with. It is a problem that researchers often choose to ignore altogether or they deal with it in a way that may not be entirely convincing. That is, they may take it into account by writing down a structural equation model in which the focus variables of the research are embedded. However, the structure of a model may simply represent a set of assumptions about the inter-relationships between the variables, which need not be correct. All of these points should become clearer by the time you have finished the next chapter.

DOS AND DON'TS

Do

✓ Consider whether your equations are identified by trying to write down a model in which the equation belongs.

✓ Make sure you look at other people's work to see what grounds they have given for believing that an equation is identified.

Don't

✗ Just rely on counting rules to be convinced that an equation can be considered to be identified.

✗ Try to estimate equations which you know to be unidentified.

EXERCISES

12.1 Are the following statements about identification true, false or indeterminate:

(i)   Every equation in a 69-equation macro econometric model is bound to be identified.

(ii) The covariance relationship between the error terms of a two-equation (equilibrium) are irrelevant to the process of establishing whether or not a structural equation is identified.

(iii) Dummy variables are not included when you are using counting rules to check a structural equation for identification.

(iv) If you are only using the reduced form equations, you do not need to worry about identification.

(v)   You never have to worry about identification if you have 'good' data.

12.2 You should now examine the equations reported earlier in this book in the tables and review studies and try to think of how you would set up a model to examine whether these equations are identified.

Good cases to look at are in Chapters 3, 5, 6, 7, 10 and 11.

12.3 Here is a three-equation model to explain the supply of crime and the response to it in terms of public spending:

$$CS = b + b\,AR + b\,PS + AGEM + MINC + UR + u$$

$$AR = b + b\,CS + b\,POLEX + b\,TRAV + DENS + v$$

$$POLEX = b/b\,MINC + b\,CS + b\,PWR + b\,POLEX_{t-1} + w$$

Where CS is crime supply (crimes per capita); AR is arrest rate (number of arrests / number of crimes); POLEX is spending on police forces; MINC is median income; PS is length of prison sentence; UR is unemployment rates; AGEM is percentage of population males aged 15–24; TRAV is distance police; DENS is population density (number of people per acre); *PWR* is police wage rates. *MINC, UR, AGEM, TRAV, DENS* and *PWR* are treated as exogenous variables. There are no specific equilibrium conditions in this model.

Answer the following questions with respect to the above model:

(i)   Check the identification state of each of the three structural equations using the order conditions.

(ii) Write down the three reduced form equations for the endogenous variables.

(iii) Explain whether you can possibly do each of the following, and if you can, then explain how you would do it:

    (a) Establish the effect of a rise in police wage rates on crime supply.

    (b) Establish the effect of a rise in police wage rates on arrest rates.

    (c) Establish the effect of a rise in police wage rates on police expenditure.

    (d) Establish the effect of a rise in crime rates on arrest rates.

    (e) Establish the effect of a rise in arrest rates on crime rates.

    (f) Establish the effect of a rise in arrest rates on crime rates.

    (g) Establish the effect of a fall in the length of prison sentences on police expenditure.

    (h) Establish the effect of a fall in the length of prison sentences on arrest rates.

REFERENCES

Anderson, T.W. and Rubin, H. (1950) The asymptotic properties of estimators of estimates of the parameters of a single equation in a complete system of stochastic equations, *Annals of Mathematical Statistics*, **31**, 570–582.

Working, E.J. (1927) What do statistical 'demand curves' show? *Quarterly Journal of Economics*, reprinted in G.J. Stigler and K.E. Boulding, *Readings in Price Theory*, George Allen and Unwin, London, 1953.

13

Multiple Equation Models: Methods of Estimation

LEARNING OBJECTIVES

- Understand why OLS might not usually be the preferred choice of estimation technique in a multiple equation model
- Be able to estimate and interpret equations using IV (instrumental variables)/2SLS (two-stage least squares regression)
- Know the difference between IV and 2SLS
- Be aware of the possible dangers of using systems methods of equations
- Be able to understand and use seemingly unrelated regression

CHAPTER SUMMARY

13.1 INTRODUCTION: IDENTIFICATION AGAIN

The previous chapter gave the case for using multiple equation models arising from jointness in choice (such as consumer demand for different goods or firms' demands for capital and labour) and from simultaneity. This chapter addresses the question: how should we go about estimating the parameter values of the individual equations within such multiple equations?

We could use OLS, but we shall discover serious problems with this leading to the suggestion that we should prefer more advanced techniques. The most basic modifications are another form of GLS (generalized least squares), but that term has been reserved for methods which attempt to deal with heteroscedasticity and serial correlation. The simplest way of dealing with a system of equations that are linked by common choices is the SUR (seemingly unrelated regression) method.

The most common methods for dealing with the simultaneity found in the IS-LM, supply and demand or the police and crime model (of the last chapter exercises) are referred to as two-stage least squares (2SLS or TSLS), instrumental variables (IV) and three-stage least squares (3SLS).

Given the last chapter, we proceed on the assumption that you are dealing with equations that are identified. If you are not completely familiar with the issue of identification of a structural equation then you need to read the previous chapter. Provided that an individual equation within a multiple equation model is identified it is legitimate to go ahead and estimate it. If an equation is not identified you should *not* attempt to estimate it by any means. However, there will be nothing to physically stop you from trying if you have not fully specified your model. This can occur if you are using IV estimation. If you are using 2SLS on an equation which is not identified, then the typical computer package will not allow estimation of the equation.

The next section deals with the use of OLS to estimate multiple equation models. The rest of the chapter deals with the use of the other techniques and potential problems in their interpretation.

13.2 USING OLS TO ESTIMATE A MULTIPLE EQUATION MODEL: THE BIAS PROBLEM

The simplest way to approach a multiple equation model is to estimate each equation separately. This could be done by ordinary least squares. We assume that the problems of specification error such as heteroscedasticity, serial correlation and non-normality of the error term are absent.

Let us recall the first version of the lipstick model of Chapter 3 that was reformulated in Chapter 12 as follows:

$$Quantity\ of\ Lipstick\ Demanded = b_0 + b_1(Price\ of\ Lipstick) + b_2(Income) + u \qquad (13.1)$$

$$Supply\ of\ Lipstick = b_3 + b_4(Price\ of\ Lipstick) + v \qquad (13.2)$$

We showed, in Chapter 12, that the supply equation in this version of the model is identified. So, we could go ahead and estimate this by OLS. The demand equation is not identified and therefore we should not attempt to estimate it. The reduced forms for price and quantity can be estimated by OLS without any problems provided the usual classical assumptions hold. Following the principles we have learned, there are two main questions that should worry us once we have done this:

▶ Will the estimates be unbiased? Suppose our work is intended to provide us with measures of the price elasticity of supply response. Can we be confident that it is not systematically over- or under-estimated?
▶ Will hypothesis testing be influenced by other problems that will lead the estimates not to be of minimum variance; in other words, will the OLS estimates be efficient?

I now give an intuitive explanation of the reason why least squares estimates are not satisfactory in the simultaneous equation case. Let us suppose there is a small shock to the error term (v) of the supply equation. This is transmitted to the equilibrium value of prices. This will create a negative relationship between price and quantity over and above any 'genuine' relationship that there may be. Therefore there is a downward bias in the coefficient. This point is repeated below, in connection with measurement error, in Section 13.4. The bias will not vanish as the sample size is increased and the OLS estimate is therefore inconsistent.

We have seen that OLS is a flexible technique capable of being modified to accommodate breakdowns in the assumptions of the classical regression model. So, it is no surprise that we can modify the least squares regression approach to generate estimators which, under suitable assumptions, are superior to OLS in their statistical properties. The next two sections deal with the simplest and most obvious way of doing this. We then go on to explore how the results from using these modified estimators – known as two-stage least squares (abbreviated as 2SLS or TSLS) and instrumental variables (abbreviated as IV) – are to be interpreted. Following this, we look at some additional techniques.

The simplest approaches, IV or 2SLS, are still single-equation estimation methods, rather than systems methods of estimation that would simultaneously determine all the parameter estimates in the system.

13.3 2SLS: MODIFIED OLS

The OLS estimators can easily be modified to give us 2SLS estimates but there are limitations to the usefulness of this improvement in practice. We assume in this section that we are dealing with a fully and correctly specified model, that is, we know how many equations there are, exactly which variables belong in each equation and exactly which variables are the endogenous and exogenous variables.

Let us begin the explanation of 2SLS estimators by explaining where the name comes from. This is perhaps not a very good name; it could be confusing as we do have other estimators which are derived in two stages. To further add to the confusion, it is the case that the two-stage least square estimator to deal with the bias arising from simultaneity does *not* require two stages of estimation. In practice, computer packages use only one stage in generating their 2SLS estimates.

The name seems to come from the way in which the estimator was originally explained and justified. The steps are:

(i) The 'first stage' involves an OLS regression of the endogenous variables on the set of exogenous variables to get predicted values of the endogenous variables. In the example we are currently studying the relevant predicted variables is for price. The stage one equation is therefore (using P for Price and Y for Income):

$$\hat{P} = \hat{m}_0 + \hat{m}_1 Y \tag{13.3}$$

This is the estimated equation, hence it is shown with ^ on top of the parameters and P so we do not need to represent the disturbance term as its predicted value is already in predicted P. Equation (12.3) is the reduced form for price and contains only Y, on the right-hand side, as Y is the only exogenous variable in our model.

(ii) In the second stage, we estimate the structural equation, in which we are interested, using the predicted value from the first stage in place of the actual value of P.

So for the lipstick model, we would regress price on income then save the predicted prices from this regression and run a regression of quantity on the predicted price series.

Hence the estimated equation is:

$$\hat{Q} = \hat{b}_3 + \hat{b}_4 \hat{P} \tag{13.4}$$

which is the two-stage least squares estimate of the supply equation in (13.2) which is why the same parameter names have been used. You should recall that we have only estimated the supply equation and *not* the demand equation because the demand equation is not identified.

The coefficient on the predicted price series in this regression is then expected to be an unbiased estimate of the price responsiveness of supply. Unless the variables are in logarithms, this is not an elasticity, so if we wanted an elasticity we would have to adjust the coefficient. The 2SLS estimate we have just described will still have the property of passing through the means of data series, as the predicted value of a series, from a regression, will have the same mean as the original series.

WHY DOES THE 2SLS METHOD REMOVE BIAS?

The method can be interpreted in terms of using the results from one regression as an independent variable in another regression. Why does this work? Taking the model above, the problem we faced was that $\mathrm{cov}(P, u) \neq 0$ in the (identified) supply equation.

One approach to the problem is to try to find a way of breaking down the variation in the right-hand side endogenous variable into two components so that we can generate a 'replacement' measure of P that has a zero covariance with the error term in the supply equation. The replacement measure of P must then have two properties:

(i) It must be genuinely correlated with P which, in a well-specified model, should be the case for the predicted P from the reduced form.

(ii) It must be uncorrelated with the u term in the equation originally specified.

A failure on point (ii) would mean that we still have bias in the estimates of the supply response to price. If we fail on point (ii), but still have a smaller degree of covariance between v_t and the variable representing P in the lipstick supply equation, then bias will be less than in OLS (asymptotically) even though it still exists. All other things being equal we would prefer to use the less biased of two biased estimators if it proved impossible to find better ones.

A failure on point (i) (the reduced form for price would have an R squared of zero) means that our results will be effectively meaningless and therefore the use of 2SLS is a waste of time. This possibility would be ruled out by the assumption we have made that the model is well specified. This may not be true in practice, which is a factor we shall return to at various points in this chapter.

If the reduced form for price was a perfect fit (its R squared would be 1) then the 2SLS method would not work as we would be replacing prices with a series which is exactly the same as itself.

Even assuming that we have a perfectly specified model, we are still at the mercy of the data to some extent in eliminating least squares bias by using 2SLS, specifically a small sample size may give us a problem as the superiority over OLS estimators is only asymptotically justified.

As mentioned above the model does not literally have to be estimated in two stages. Any regression package will allow you to do this with one command which will be similar to the OLS command apart from the need to specify with some kind of 'switch' which variables are to be used in the first round. If it is a menu driven package, in Windows OS style, then you would simply have to paste an additional list of variables. The results from a package will arrive in the same format as those for OLS, that is, there will be regression coefficients, standard errors, 't' ratios and so on. We will postpone full discussion of this until Section 13.5 where we give some examples of results using data that we have already explored in earlier chapters. The next section seeks first to clarify the precise difference between 2SLS and IV.

13.4 THE RELATIONSHIP BETWEEN 2SLS AND IV

Not all the articles you read will use 2SLS (or more advanced techniques surveyed later in this chapter). Some will use instrumental variables (IV) instead. Clearly we need to know what the exact difference is between these and whether it is important.

It will be helpful if we begin by clarifying the use of the term 'instrumental variables'. Instrumental variables refer to the use of variables designated as 'instruments'. A variable becomes an instrument when someone chooses to use it as an instrument. This choice should be made according to certain principles. In regression models, an instrument is a variable used to generate a variable that is substituted for another one. If we simply use the model as written down and estimate it by OLS then each variable is its own instrument.

For the problem of simultaneity bias, in an equation which is part of a system, an instrument is an exogenous variable, which you use as an independent variable in generating the 'replacement' for the endogenous variables on the right-hand side of the equation.

The method of instrumental variables has applications beyond the problem we are currently dealing with. It is a general estimation method leading to the use of such terms as GIVE (generalized instrumental variable estimation) for the first of David Hendry's packages dedicated to the analysis of time series. An IV estimator can be derived for a range of specification errors such as measurement error (see below) and serial correlation of a lagged dependent variable with the error term. IV is then a technique for dealing with 'errors in variables', that is, $\text{cov}\,(X_t,\,u_t) \neq 0$ arising from any source.

In the 2SLS example we have just been discussing, the list of instruments was automatically given to us once we had specified our model, as we must use *all* the exogenous variables in the model. In research where the authors deal with endogeneity bias you may find a seemingly arbitrary list of instruments. Often in time-series studies, several lagged values of the exogenous variables are used as instruments. This has the virtue of convenience as one already has these variables in the data set. We give an example of this in Table 13.1 in the next section, which re-examines the Turkish cigarette data used in earlier chapters of the book.

The justification for picking a list of instruments without setting down a full model to tell us the exact list, that is, all the endogenous variables in the model, is that we may not know the full model but we are aware that 'out there' in the data there may be some endogeneity and we can improve the estimates by coping with it. This gives theoretically unbiased estimators, although ones of less efficiency than full 2SLS.

We may find that it is impossible to compute 2SLS estimates if the model is such that the number of exogenous variables is so large compared with the sample size that it is not possible to use them all. It is often suggested that in these circumstances the method of principal components (discussed in Chapter 10 as a 'cure' for multicollinearity) be used to extract a feasible number of instrumental variables from the set of candidates available. However, there is no very obvious principle one can use to determine what number of principal components to use in place of the instruments from which they were derived. If one uses, for example, the first six principal components extracted from a matrix of 40 variables then the six instruments we use contain some variation from each of the 40 variables, but a certain amount of variation within the 40 variables has been discarded. It should be added that the problem of having 'too many' instruments is not one that comes up often in practice, as the opposite situation is much more usual.

The relationship between IV and 2SLS can be summarized as follows:

▶ A 2SLS estimator is automatically an IV estimator but not the other way round.

▶ The 2SLS estimator is a special case of the IV where the choice of instruments is absolutely fixed once you have specified your model. That is, all the exogenous variables in the model will be the instruments.

▶ For a given model specification, and data set, there will only be *one* possible set of 2SLS estimators.

▶ For a given single equation model to be estimated by IV, there will be several different IV estimators depending on how many combinations of instrument you try (see Table 13.1 as an example of this).

▶ In the case of the fully specified model using 2SLS, it will be physically impossible to estimate an unidentified equation. You should find that your computer package will warn you if you try to do this and will not give you any results. This is because the package will check the list of independent variables and the list of instruments to see if you do have identification. Bear in mind that you should include the intercept in the instrument list (assuming you are not using a package which included an intercept by default in the equation and the instruments).

▶ In the IV estimation approach, you may have estimated an equation which would have been considered to be unidentified if a fully specified model had been written down. You have no way of knowing this unless you write down a fully specified model.

On a computer package, there is no real difference between these two approaches, as you simply need to tell the program which variables are the instruments. The only difference is the way you choose the instruments.

MEASUREMENT ERROR LEADING TO ERROR IN VARIABLES: ANOTHER CASE FOR THE USE OF IV

Before we leave the distinction between IV and 2SLS, we need to discuss how some measurement error brings about 'accidental endogeneity' as opposed to the 'designed endogeneity' of the cases discussed so far, where the problem of bias arises from the structure of the model which is being adopted as the best approximation to the truth that is feasible in the circumstances.

Measurement error, as such, is not the problem, as you should be aware by now that OLS does not require accurate measurement in order to obtain unbiased estimates. The problem comes from systematic relationships of measurement error across variables. The most obvious example is where the dependent variable is divided by a variable, measured with error, which also appears in some form in the list of independent variables. The presence of this variable on the left-hand side of the equation is not a problem as measurement error there is accommodated by the u (disturbance term) in the equation. However, the appearance of this variable on the right-hand side of the equation means that it can no longer be true that $\text{cov}(X, u) = 0$.

Technically this is the same problem that we have been dealing with throughout this chapter. It is appropriately dealt with under IV estimation, as we would not normally be able to fully specify equations to explain measurement error. Some common examples of where this problem arises are:

▶ Per capita deflation. Say we divide the dependent variable, such as quantity demanded, by population and also divide independent variables, such as income, by population. If the population series has substantial error then this means that there is an upwards bias in the coefficient for income as a shift in the per capita demand series, due to an error in the population series, occurs at the same time as a shift in the same direction for the per capita income series.

▶ Labour supply. Household surveys make it difficult to obtain measures of the hourly wage rate so researchers often resort to dividing annual income by reported weekly hours of work times the number of weeks worked. This is not a perfect measure and the divisor of the wage rate proxy (hours of work) is the dependent variable as well. This causes downward bias in the coefficient for the wage responsiveness of hours worked and so, in the extreme case, it could generate a spuriously significant negative relationship when there is no relationship or even a negative relationship.

Similar considerations apply to estimating a cost function in average cost form where we regress average costs (total costs divided by output) on output.

▶ Crime models such as that of Ehrlich (see Chapter 11) where the crime supply function typically features the supply of crime as the dependent variable, which is Crime divided by Population, and on the right-hand side we find a proxy for the risk of being caught and punished – such as the arrest rate, which is the number of arrests divided by the number of crimes. This introduces a downward bias into the estimate of the supply response to the risk variable. In an extreme situation, where the bias is severe, in such models the elasticity may tend towards minus 1 (as the models are typically in log form) when there is no relationship at all.

IV estimation can be used to attempt to curb these problems. The success of this depends on the ease with which we can find suitable instruments in the data set. In the case of the crime models of Ehrlich that we just discussed, the matter is complicated a little by the fact that we are also using IV to control for endogeneity as well as measurement error.

HISTORY OF IV

Before we go on, you may be interested to know that the IV method was invented around 1928 but, as yet, no one is entirely sure who deserves the credit (see Stock and Trebbi, 2003). This treatment was given in Appendix B of a treatise on the effects of Tariffs on Animal and Vegetable Oils which also provided, apparently, the first solution of the identification problem, although there have been claims for earlier non-English language work. In this work the method of path coefficients was proposed rather than the use of the actual terminology of 'instrumental variables'; the difference between path analysis and 2SLS/IV is given below. It was not until around the Second World War that a group of workers began to take seriously the problems of identification and estimation in simultaneous equations that had been identified by researchers on agricultural markets. The methods of IV and 2SLS had finally arrived when the Cowles foundation monograph edited by Hood and Koopmans was published in 1953. It would, however, be another 20 years or so before such methods would become very widely used.

13.5 INTERPRETATION OF THE RESULTS OF 2SLS/IV ESTIMATES: SOME EXAMPLES

By now, you should have a thorough knowledge of how to interpret the results of OLS and GLS estimates. This should make it relatively easy to understand how to use the results of two-stage least squares and instrumental variables estimation.

The coefficients of the structural equations can be treated in the same way as OLS estimates, as they are simply the same equation with an attempt having been made to purge the coefficient on the endogenous variables of the bias from which they suffer. If the equation is not in log-linear form we can use the coefficients to calculate elasticities in the manner described in Chapter 6, if we so wish. Likewise the standard errors of the coefficients can be used in the same way as before to construct 't' tests on the relevant hypotheses; that is, so long as the correct formulae have been used to obtain the standard errors. Any computer package that you use which has a built-in 2SLS/IV command should be using the correct standard errors for these estimation techniques. The R squared is more of a problem as we shall see in Table 13.1. I shall postpone discussion of the problem of interpreting goodness of fit in systems of equations until after we look at Table 13.1.

We do face some new questions when it comes to obtaining the coefficients for the reduced forms. There are two ways to calculate the reduced forms. One is to directly estimate the reduced forms from a set of OLS regressions of all the endogenous variables on all the exogenous variables. These estimates have the BLUE properties we have been taught to look for.

This applies even if parts, or all, of the model are under identified. Where all of the structural equations are identified we can arrive at another way of estimating the reduced form coefficients – that is, by substituting the structural parameters estimated by 2SLS into the reduced form equation.

On a practical level, this method has the disadvantage that we do not automatically get the standard errors for these derived reduced form coefficients.

EXAMPLE I: IV ESTIMATES OF THE CIGARETTE DEMAND EQUATION

We now look at some examples of the differences between OLS and IV/2SLS estimates in data sets (TURKCIG.XLS and THEATRE.XLS) which have been used in earlier chapters. We shall approach the cigarette demand model in terms of using IV and use the theatre demand data to develop 2SLS estimates on the basis of a fully specified model. We are therefore assuming that these equations can be justified as being identified. The cigarette demand results are in Table 13.1 and the theatre results are in Table 13.2.

Table 13.1 OLS and IV estimates of the cigarette demand equation using Turkish data for 1960–89

Dependent variable	CCA	CCA	CCA
Technique:	OLS	IV	IV
Constant	1.655	0.25	1.70
	(13.47)	(0.019)	(11.08)
RPC	−0.42	8.02	−0.39
	(4.39)	(0.11)	(1.02)
GNP	0.0003	−0.00035	0.00032
	(6.57)	(0.104)	(1.92)
R^2	0.644	−112.89	0.5998
D.W.	0.91	0.79	0.86
List of instruments:	n.a.	Constant, GNP, GNP(−1)	Constant, GNP, GNP(−1), GNP(−2)

Note: Absolute 't' ratios in parentheses.

Our cigarette demand equation is assumed to be

$$CCA = b_0 + b_1 RPC + b_2 GNP + u \tag{13.5}$$

where, as before, CCA is packs of cigarettes per population over 15, RPC is the price of cigarettes divided by the retail price index and GNP is per capita. We omit the education variable used earlier. The observation subscripts have been omitted from the written down version of the model.

Price might be endogenous from the supply side, which may come from producers, or from the taxation activities of government. For example, if the government was strongly influenced by health considerations then it might increase the tax rate when consumption rises.

As we assume that the precise nature of the supply influence is not known, we do not write down a second equation and therefore choose some instrumental variables. In this particular case, we use two different sets, that is, the second equation in Table 13.1 uses as instruments the constant term, GNP and one lag of GNP, while the third uses the same list with one more lag on GNP. You should make sure to include the constant term in the list of instruments when you are completing the IV/2SLS regression command in a computer package. The first equation in Table 13.1 is the OLS estimate included for comparison. The samples are not identical because the use of the lag variables means a decrease of one in the first IV equation and a further decrease by one in the second IV equation.

These results were produced by an older version of Microfit using a single command, which requires the instruments to be listed after the equation has been listed.

The first column of Table 13.1 shows the OLS estimates of the equation, while the remaining columns show a set of results using different selections of variables for the instrumental variables. Not surprisingly the results are not identical. In fact, there are some remarkable differences. The OLS estimates look quite convincing as far as the sign and significance go. However, the statistically significant findings of a positive income coefficient and negative relative price coefficient are almost completely wiped out when we use IV estimation. Only one of the four coefficients is now significant and even this (GNP in the IV estimate in column 3) has a much smaller 't' ratio than before.

Quite the strangest result (and easily the strangest in this whole book) is the value of R squared in the second column, where far from being between 0 and 1 it is -112.89, although the addition of the second lag term, in the instrument list, removes this apparent anomaly since it gives a sensible looking figure for R squared.

We should certainly *not* jump to the conclusion that one will be using R squared to decide which of these equations is the more suitable. Even if the R squareds looked sensible (i.e. between 0 and 1), the whole basis of generating the residuals has been changed due to the substitution of a predicted value of a variable for its original value.

You should have noticed that these equations appear to be suffering from other specification errors because there is a fairly low Durbin–Watson value for all three equations. The D–W test will not, strictly speaking, be valid when we leave the conditions of the simple CLRM single-equation model. However, it is reasonable to assume that when it is extremely low there is a problem.

EXAMPLE 2: 2SLS ESTIMATES OF (PERCEIVED) THEATRE PRICE EQUATIONS

Rather than pursue the matter of full 2SLS estimation on the cigarette data, we go back to the theatre data that was introduced in Chapter 4. Let us focus on willingness to pay (WTP) as a function of, among other things, what people think is the normal price ($NORMP$). The WTP function is (omitting observation) subscripts specified as:

$$WTP = b_0 + b_1\,NORMP + b_2\,Leeds + b_3\,Grossinc + b_4\,Female + b_5\,Age + b_6\,Loyalty$$
$$+\ b_7\,Sensloss + u \tag{13.6}$$

$$NORMP = b_8 + b_9\,WTP + b_{10}\,Leeds + b_{11}\,Totgoout + b_{12}\,Aware + b_{13}\,Rsnprice + v$$
$$\tag{13.7}$$

The two endogenous (i.e. dependent) variables are measures of perceived price decisions. *WTP* is the amount (in £0.50 units) that people are prepared to pay for a ticket if they could pay what they liked. The function thus reflects the usual demand elements for any good, such as income, but it could reflect other things such as:

▶ Opportunism, where an individual would like to pay below the normal price;
▶ implied 'option value' where the individual would pay above the normal price in order to help support the maintenance of the local public good represented by the existence of the theatre.

The normal price used is not the actual price of a ticket, but the price that the respondents think is the normal price. As both *WTP* and *NORMP* may reflect judgements about what local theatre is worth there is a case for using a simultaneous model.

The system in Equations (13.6–13.7) does not specify any kind of adjustment process, to equilibrium, between the two equations. It will be identified on the basis of the order conditions. There are two endogenous variables and nine exogenous variables and each equation has a constant term, which also must be used as an instrument. Three of the exogenous variables do not appear in the *WTP* equation while five do not appear in the *NORMP* equation. There are then a total of 14 parameters (including both intercepts) to be estimated in the structural equations and 20 parameters (including both intercepts) to be estimated from the reduced forms.

The data set used here was described in Chapter 4, with a full list of variables and definitions in Table 4.1. Some of the variables here are exactly as their equivalents in Table 4.1, but others have been constructed from those variables. *Leeds* is a dummy to represent the pooling of two samples via a shift in the intercept term. *Grossinc* is gross income of the decision-making unit taken at the mid-point of a range. The parameter b_3 is expected to be greater than 0 on the grounds that more income means a greater willingness to pay for goods in general and local public goods in particular. *Female* is a dummy which is 1 for women. *Age* is taken as the mid-point of a range. *Loyalty* and *Sensloss* are indices (i.e. scales of subjective ratings) of how much people feel attached to the local public theatre over and above the services it offers as a normal consumer good. Given this, we have the expectations $b_7 > 0$ and $b_7 > 0$.

The variables *Totgoout* and *Aware* are proxies for how much information people are likely to have on the normal price of a ticket. Hence, we have the expectation that $b_{11} > 0$ and $b_{12} > 0$. The *Aware* variable is from a scale of how aware the person has been of the programme offered at the local public theatre. *Totgoout* is constructed by adding up all the different arts and entertainment events that the person had attended in the last 12 months. The *Rsnprice* variable is the figure that people gave as what they think is a reasonable price for an evening out in general. Our expectation is that $b_{13} > 0$, as this perceived price is likely to 'anchor' people's ideas about what the normal price is for any event on which they are not fully informed.

The results of estimating this model are shown in Table 13.2. These were obtained using SPSS. Six equations were estimated: each structural equation was estimated by OLS and 2SLS to provide comparison of the results and both reduced forms are also shown in the table. You will find that many studies do not report the reduced forms in such a situation and that some will also omit to report the OLS results.

Not surprisingly the results differ. We still stick to the principle of the three S's – sign, significance and size – when we come to interpret our findings. Our primary interest is in the structural parameters b_1 and b_9. These show quite dramatic changes when we move from OLS

Table 13.2 Estimates of willingness to pay and perceived normal price equations: OLS and 2SLS estimates

Dependent variable	WTP	WTP	WTP	NORMP	NORMP	NORMP
Type of equation:	Structural	Reduced form	Reduced form	Structural	Structural	Structural
Technique	OLS	2SLS	OLS	OLS	2SLS	OLS
Intercept	7.263	7.512	0.126	5.336	5.394	7.103
	(1.99)	(2.58)	(0.02)	(2.47)	(4.07)	(3.82)
Leeds	5.669	3.141	0.57	3.63	2.65	3.855
	(3.65)	(2.03)	(0.26)	(3.75)	(3.72)	(3.34)
Grossinc	0.0168	0.017	0.0173	−0.000463		
(×1000)	(2.16)	(2.24)	(2.08)	(0.17)		
Sensloss	1.167	0.708	1.006	0.00946		
	(1.26)	(0.2)	(1.02)	(0.17)		
Totgoout	−0.08			−0.0049	−0.00253	−0.006
	(1.37)			(0.13)	(0.1)	(0.21)
Aware	0.0035			−0.159	−0.107	−0.216
	(0.004)			(0.27)	(0.26)	(0.45)
Female	−2.358	−3.038	−3.609	1.403		
	(1.58)	(2.09)	(2.19)	(1.52)		
Age	−0.0537	−0.0589	−0.087	0.0125		
	(1.13)	(1.32)	(1.69)	(0.44)		
Rsnprice	−0.505		0.361	0.261	0.371	
	(3.42)			(4.02)	(3.82)	(3.49)
Loyalty	−0.622	0.111	−0.101	−0.612		
	(0.651)	(0.81)	(0.101)	(1.04)		
WTP					0.102	−0.141
					(2.94)	(0.86)
NORMP	0.615	1.44				
	(4.3)	(2.94)				
R^2	0.151	0.151	0.125	0.151	0.219	0.159
N	193	184	180	180	186	180

to 2SLS estimation. Both are positive and statistically significant in the OLS results, although the point estimates show the effect of normal price on willingness to pay to be more than six times greater than the effect in the other direction. Once we move to 2SLS the coefficient of willingness to pay price on normal price becomes negative and insignificant. On the other hand, the effect of the normal price on willingness to pay more than doubles although its 't' ratio decreases (to 2.94), but it is still a 'strong' result.

The coefficients on the exogenous variables in the structural equations do not tend to change very dramatically in the switch from OLS to 2SLS estimation. The variables to proxy awareness, level of attachment to the local public good and the measure of age are not significant in any of the equations. Reasonable price perceptions and gross income have the expected positive coefficients, which are statistically significant. The *Female* dummy has a statistically significant negative effect on willingness to pay. The *Leeds* dummy has a statistically significant positive relationship with willingness to pay price; however, this completely collapses when we move from OLS to 2SLS.

It is of interest to look at the reduced forms. These show, for example, that net effect of gross income on *WTP* is estimated to be 0.0168 per £1000. If we accepted the present structural model as being an acceptable representation of the system determining *WTP* and *NORMP*, then the reduced form relationship is the appropriate one to look at if we wish to know the impact of income on the amount people are willing to pay.

However, you will recall that we can derive a different estimate of this by substituting the structural equations parameters into the reduced form. In the present case, we would need to divide by $(1 - b_9)$.

Some observations on the model estimated in Table 13.2

▶ No explicit justification was given for the set of restrictions used to identify each equation.
▶ No experiments were made with the functional form.
▶ No rescaling of the arbitrary index scale answers was made; for example, we could have collapsed them into dummies.
▶ The model could have become a recursive model if either b_1 or b_9 were restricted to be zero. Identification in this case would depend on the covariance of the error terms. If both coefficients were zero this would become simply a set of two separate equations assuming we do not have covariance $(u, v) \neq 0$. In the latter case we would be required to use the SUR method discussed below.

We have now looked at one example where IV estimation was used, and another where 2SLS was used. There was no presentation of a reduced form in the IV case, as we could not, strictly speaking, know what it is without writing down the full model. However, given the choice of instruments we could generate a 'pseudo-reduced form' by regressing cigarette (relative) prices and per capita packets smoked on the complete list of instruments (which would include the intercept and per capita income).

The motivation in both empirical examples has to deal with bias induced by the presence of an endogenous variable. Both the examples featured only one endogenous variable on the right-hand side of the equation. However, we would use the same techniques if there were more than one endogenous variable on the right-hand side of an equation. That is, we would use the set of instruments to generate a 'replacement' predicted value for the right-hand side endogenous variable.

Recap: How do I know when to use OLS, IV or 2SLS?

When IV/2SLS first became widely used in applied econometrics there was a tendency to rush to use these and assume they were automatically better than OLS. We should exercise some caution in doing this, as there is the problem of small samples undermining the reliance on asymptotic properties. There are also issues of specification and instrument availability.

We come finally to the question of whether in fact we should regard variables as endogenous. Economic theory may suggest that the concentration ratio is endogenous in an equation to explain inter-industry profit rates (see the review study in Section 13.7) or that price is endogenous in the demand equation, but this does not mean that this is true. In other words, assumptions about endogeneity or exogeneity are yet more hypotheses grafted on to our model. In all of the discussion so far, I have kept endogeneity or exogeneity of particular variables as maintained hypotheses. As they are still hypotheses, however, they are therefore open for testing of some type. We now come to the proposal of using exogeneity tests.

13.6 EXOGENEITY TESTING

The issues discussed in this chapter so far involve correcting specification error in OLS regression modelling – that is, bias in parameter estimation induced by the presence of endogenous variables on the right-hand side of an equation.

As I have just suggested, endogeneity is an assumption that might be tested. It is not uncommon to find such tests in academic articles these days, usually the Hausman test, also known as the Hausman–Wu test. There are several such tests and I give here a very simple version. To do such a test requires us to find some instrumental variables before we can test the hypothesis that a variable is endogenous. It will not be possible to do such a test without selecting instrumental variables, as the method is based on the idea of comparing the OLS estimates with a set of IV estimates.

Let us assume, for the moment, that there is no difficulty in finding these and they can be called Z_1 and Z_2 and that X_3, in the model, can be used as an instrument because it is not endogenous. X_1 and X_2 in the model are assumed to be possibly endogenous so the specified equation is:

$$Y = b_0 + b_1 X_1 + b_2 X_2 + b_3 X_3 + u \tag{13.8}$$

omitting subscripts.

The steps of the test are:

Step 1: Regress the possibly endogenous variables X_1 and X_2 on the selected instruments X_3, Z_1 and Z_2 which gives predicted values for X_1 and X_2. This is, of course, exactly the same as the notional 'first step' in IV/2SLS estimation.

Step 2: Save the residuals from the Step 1 regressions (let us call these η and ξ respectively).

Step 3: Run an expanded regression in which the residuals are added as variables to the right-hand side:

$$Y = m_0 + m_1 X_1 + m_2 X_2 + m_3 X_3 + m_4 \eta + m_5 \zeta + u \tag{13.9}$$

in which we simply add the residuals, from the second step, and use OLS.

Step 4: Perform an 'F' test on the joint restriction of the additional parameters being zero. We may have only one candidate for exogeneity, in which case the 't' test would be sufficient.

If this 'F' test accepts the null, then we have exogeneity. In this case, then, the estimates will be unbiased. As ever, a specification test is still a hypothesis test and is therefore subject to possible errors like any other test. As with the general use of instrumental variables, there is scope for getting very different sets of results when different selections of instruments are used. This simply highlights the problem that the tests are sensitive to specification errors.

The review study by Gisser in the next section provides an example where exogeneity tests were used in the research.

13.7 REVIEW STUDIES

We now come to two review studies which use IV/2SLS methods and are on topics of continual interest and policy relevance: the behaviour of exports in response to price incentives in a transitional economy and the relationship between advertising and competitiveness in a leading developed economy.

The IMF working paper by Cerra and Saxena (2002) looks at export performance during a period when varying levels of government restrictions were in force, in this case for China. Earlier work had found 'perverse' supply responses, which were attributed to the influence of export value quotas; that is, if export prices fell, then exporters had to increase volume in order to meet quotas. This is clearly a source of potential welfare loss in the economy as a whole. Over time, the restrictiveness of trade regimes in China has been relaxed, which might lead us to expect a transition to more conventional, i.e. positive, relationships between the supply of exports and the (exchange rate adjusted) price at which they are sold abroad. This is what the authors seek to investigate by running a series of quarterly models for different time periods to see if the estimated parameter on the focus variables is shifting over time as restrictions are relaxed. They use the following model:

$$\log X_{it}{}^s = b_0 + b_1 \log P_{it} + b_2 \log E_{it} + b_3 \log P^{dom} + b_4 \log C + b_5 \log Y^{dom} + u \quad \textbf{(13.10)}$$

$$\log X_{it}{}^d = b_6 + b_7 \log P_{it} + b_8 \log P_{it}{}^w + b_9 \log Y^w + v \quad \textbf{(13.11)}$$

The first equation is the supply equation, and the second is the demand equation. There is no explicit discussion of the equilibrium process, or properties, of the model so we may assume that it is a standard equilibrium model where movements in exchange rates tend to bring supply and demand for Chinese exports into equilibrium.

I have slightly altered the notation to be consistent with the rest of this book. The t and i subscripts represent the time period (quarter) and the industry being used, as this is a panel (pooled cross-section time-series) data set. The superscripts are not mathematical operators and represent domestic values (dom) and world values (w), supply (s) and demand (d). The model is in logarithms, implying multiplicative functional forms, with the parameters being constant elasticities.

The variables are as follows: X is the volume of the good; P is the export price of the good in dollars; E is the exchange rate; C is domestic credit; Y is demand for Chinese exports; and P^w is world price in dollars.

The major focus of this paper is then on the b_2 parameter in the above equation, where the expectation is of a significant negative value if the producers are behaving as we would expect if they were rational and free from perverse restraint factors. If this is less than 1 in absolute value then we have an inelastic supply of exports. Two-stage least squares is used in this study because of endogeneity bias, under OLS. The reduced forms are of no interest here because the focus variable will drop out of them and thus estimation, or derivation, of the reduced forms, would shed no light on supply responsiveness to price factors. Identification is simply assumed in this model as there is no attempt to justify why certain variables should appear in one equation and not in the other.

A large portion of the paper is actually taken up with the methods used to construct the index numbers and there is relatively little discussion of the specification of the model.

We turn now to the paper by Gisser (1991), which looks at some classic issues which emerge from criticisms of the SCP (structure–conduct–performance) in industrial economics. These revolve around the simultaneity of relationships between profits (a measure of performance), industrial concentration and advertising, which is a measure of conduct. This is represented in three equations (labelled 6, 7 and 8) in the original text. Here are those equations (with an apparent typo corrected) as they appeared in the original text:

$$Ad/S = b_0 + b_1 C + b_2 (Prof/S) + b_3 Hetro + u \qquad (13.12)$$

$$C = b_4 + b_5 Ad/S + b_6 Ener/S + v \qquad (13.13)$$

$$Prof/S = b_7 + b_8 C + b_9 Ad/S + b_{10} Gro + w \qquad (13.14)$$

The disturbance terms were not written down or specified in the original paper but I have added three classical disturbance terms u, v and w. I have rewritten the parameters in the convention we have been using, i.e. to number consecutively from subscript 0 for the first intercept and use the letter 'b' in each case.

The variables are as follows: Ad/S is the advertising/sales ratio; C is the concentration ratio; $Prof/S$ is the profit to sales ratio; $Hetro$ is a dummy which is 1 for 'heterogenous' industries; $Ener/S$ is the energy expenditure to sales ratio; and Gro is industry growth rates 1972—77.

We have here a model of three structural equations with ten parameters to be estimated. There are three reduced forms, although these are not dealt with in the paper because its primary focus is on structural parameters on endogenous variables. There are three exogenous variables in the system ($Hetro$, Gro and $Ener/S$) available to be used as instruments (along with the constant term) in estimating the three structural equations.

Identification is simply assumed in this study, as there is no attempt to justify why certain variables appear in one equation and not in the others.

The Basic Facts

Authors: Micha Gisser

Title: Advertising, Concentration and Profitability in Manufacturing

Where Published: *Economic Inquiry*, **39**(1), January 1991, 148—165.

Reason for Study: To test a theory that there is an inverted U relationship between concentration and advertising for oligopolistic industries facing relatively less elastic demand curves.

Conclusion Reached: The effect of advertising on profitability is positive and significant and greater for industries producing homogenous goods.

How Did They Do It?

Data: Industry level data for the USA in 1977.

Sample Size: 445 industries in the USA, although the sample for estimation is smaller due to some missing data and a number of sub-sample regressions are performed later in the paper.

Technique: OLS and 2SLS regressions.

Dependent Variable: Industrial concentration, profitability, advertising.

Focus Variables: Advertising, profits and concentration – these are the exogenous variables. Concentration is a ratio, with there being two different measures of the concentration ratio used alternately. Advertising and Profits are treated as rates from dividing them by sales figures.

Control Variables: The exogenous variables – dummy for heterogeneity of the product mix in the industry (*Hetro*), energy expenditure (*Ener*), growth rates in the industry (*Gro*) from 1972–77.

Presentation

How Results Are Listed: Coefficients with 't' ratios in brackets underneath.

Goodness of Fit: R squared.

Tests: F for the equation.

Diagnosis/Stability: The endogeneity issue is addressed by comparing OLS and 2SLS results and also by conducting Hausman–Wu tests. This leads to the dropping of the equation to model concentration from the original three structural equations.

Anomalous Results: None.

Student Reflection

Things to Look Out For: This paper does not mention the identification issue at all. It is simply assumed that the equation written down (which just happens to have the right number of exclusion restrictions to identify the structural equations) is the correct representation of the structure of the model.

Problems in Replication: In theory it should be quite easy to collect this kind of data in a wide range of different countries, although it would be unlikely that the level of aggregation in published statistics would be such as to allow you such a large sample size as in the USA.

The Basic Facts

Authors: Valerie Cerra and Sweta Chaman Saxena

Title: An Empirical Analysis of China's Export Behavior

Where Published: International Monetary Fund Working Paper, WP/02/200, published November 2002.

Reason for Study: To examine the responsiveness of Chinese exports to economic factors during the period of liberalization of the trade regime.

Conclusion Reached: There is some evidence for an increasing supply responsiveness to price incentives in the aggregate equations; however, the results by commodity group often show 'perverse', i.e. negative, effects of price incentives on the supply of exports. The results for aggregate supply seem to be 'better' in terms of conforming to the usual expectations of economic models.

How Did They Do It?

Data: Panel (pooled cross-section time series) quarterly series for China, 1985 fourth quarter to 2001 first quarter.

Sample Size: Varies because the estimation was done over a number of sub-periods rather than the whole sample.

Technique: 2SLS (weighted).

Dependent Variable: Logarithms of export volume (for supply and demand).

Focus Variables: Export price of goods in US$, exchange rate per US$.

Control Variables: Supply – consumer price index, domestic credit and industrial production. Demand – world price of good, world demand for Chinese exports.

Presentation

How Results Are Listed: Coefficients with absolute standard errors in brackets underneath.

Goodness of Fit: No goodness of fit statistic.

Tests: Asterisk system *= 10 per cent, ** 5 per cent and *** 1 per cent two-tailed.

Diagnosis/Stability: The work explicitly set out to estimate over many different sub-periods and thus automatically contains an *ad hoc* analysis of parameter instability. There is an explicit test for a structural break in Table 7 using a shift dummy for 1994.

Anomalous Results: The perverse supply responses.

Student Reflection

Things to Look Out For: There is one slightly misleading passage in this paper which seems to imply that the 2SLS technique actually provides identification of a model, rather than being dependent on identification as a prerequisite before one proceeds to estimation. You might also like to think about whether the aggregate results should be preferred to disaggregate ones just because they conform better to expectations.

Problems in Replication: It should not be that difficult to obtain these data as the sources given are national government statistics. The more difficult part is constructing the index numbers but the authors explain very carefully how they did this in the first pages. One should be able to conduct similar studies for other countries easily using published sources. It might also be worthwhile trying different index number methods in any replication.

We have just looked at two studies that use simple methods (2SLS) of dealing with some estimation problems that trouble OLS when an equation is part of a system. Before we move on to look at some other methods, let us summarize some of the features these studies had in common and the extent to which they share these with other research in general.

- Panel data was used by Cerra and Saxena – this is quite common nowadays.
- Identification was simply assumed – this is not unusual.
- The reduced forms were not reported. This is because the authors were only interested in the structural parameters.
- There were no tests of over identifying restrictions – again this is very common.
- Little attention was paid to goodness of fit. This is not something to worry about as, by now, you should have realized that the statistical fit of an equation is not that important in the appraisal of econometric models.
- Exogeneity tests were used in one of the papers. These tests are quite common.

13.8 OTHER TYPES OF SYSTEMS MODEL: SUR ESTIMATION AND PATH MODELS

We began both this and the last chapter by talking about how systems of equations are generated by different types of linkage between the equations. The case dealt with in the previous sections was where the covariance between the error term and a right-hand side variable was not zero, due to a link between it and the dependent variable caused either by measurement error or a causal link. IV and 2SLS were proposed as solutions to this problem. There are other forms of linkage between equations that give rise to other techniques. We now look at SUR and briefly at 'path models'.

SEEMINGLY UNRELATED REGRESSION

As explained in Section 13.1, equations may be linked because they represent the outcome of a common choice process. For example, if we had data on a set of firms then we might expect there to be cross-equation correlation between the factor demand equations (demand for labour and demand for capital). We can approach the cross-equation linkage in the error terms using SUR (seemingly unrelated regression). The SUR method has an unfortunate name as the term 'seemingly unrelated regression' is applied to situations where we would expect there to be some relationship between the regressions.

The review study by Ehrlich, in Section 11.7, provides an example of SUR estimation because it treated a group of crime supply equations as a set of seemingly unrelated regressions. In such a case the argument is, say, we write down three aggregate crime functions for robbery, burglary and theft. We could estimate these by OLS or 2SLS (to deal with endogeneity in the probability of punishment parameter. This is what Ehrlich does, although he also uses WLS/GLS because of suspected heteroscedasticity. This combination of estimation methods ignores the possible presence of non-zero covariances between the three error terms.

If these covariances are not zero, then we should be able to improve our estimators by taking account of them. This is not done to deal with bias because the non-zero error covariance does not cause bias in the parameter estimates. Rather, it causes a loss of efficiency, i.e. the estimators are not 'best', as there are estimators with lower variance in the shape of SUR estimators. So it would seem the first step when considering SUR is to look at the correlations between the residuals, which can be easily done by saving the residuals of the OLS regressions and computing the correlations.

The following method of SUR estimation was proposed by Arnold Zellner in (1962). As usual, a specialist econometric package will usually provide this with little more effort required than typing in the equations you are using. It may help to explain the steps by which this can be done. Zellner's original estimator was a two-step estimators, although this can be iterated. We should stress that this method assumes that the model does *not* suffer from specification error within the individual equations. In this respect it is unlike IV/2SLS. OLS estimate of the model should still then produce unbiased estimates with the gain of using SUR coming, as with 'corrections' for heteroscedasticity, in removing bias from the estimates of the variances/ standard errors of the coefficients.

Referring back to Ehrlich's crime, and ignoring the 2SLS and WLS steps, the steps would be:

Step 1: Fit all the OLS regressions and save the sets of residuals as new variables.

Step 2: Perform new OLS regressions, which are the same as the equations estimated in step 1, except for the fact that we would now add the fitted residuals from the other equations to each equation. For example, the new OLS regression for burglary would now contain the residuals from the step 1 equations for the other crimes, as independent variables, in addition to those specified in the model.

We can stop at this stage, although we may proceed to an iterative process which, if convergent, will approximate a maximum likelihood estimator, which is asymptotically optimal. In small samples it may be optimal to stop at step 2.

If we go beyond step 2, the iterations do *not* use the residuals from the step 2 regressions. Instead, we have to compute a new set of residuals by substituting the equation parameters obtained in step 2 into the original model and thus generating different predictions. We add this set of residuals in the next round. We then go through this whole process again – that is, another set of residuals is computed on the basis of the latest revised parameter estimates for adding to the next OLS regression.

If the system of equations were to contain exactly the same set of variables on the right-hand side in each equation then the correlation between the residuals of each equation will be zero (for example, in a household demand system). In such a case the SUR approach should give the same coefficient estimates as OLS but they will be superior asymptotically in terms of the B property of the BLUE criteria for an estimator.

As is usually the case with regression analysis, we would, in practice, have no clear expectations about how the SUR and OLS estimates will differ in a model with a system of equations that do not all contain the same independent variables.

It should be borne in mind that we have assumed there is no specification error within the individual equations. If there is, then we have the possibility that the zero error covariance across any pair of equations may be due to shared measurement error in the data or possibly due to common omitted variables. If there is a risk of this then it is desirable that these problems be explored before going on to use SUR estimation, as otherwise the improvement gained may be largely an illusion.

PATH MODELS

Economists do not often use the term 'path model'. As explained above, it was proposed in the 1920s when IV methods were first being developed. It is more commonly found in sociology and psychology. The estimation of path models actually involves similar techniques to those used above (OLS, 2SLS /IV or some form of dealing with cross-equation correlation), so the only purpose of this section is to prevent confusion about the possible existence of another approach to multiple equation modelling.

The 'path' in the title simply refers to a direction of causation – for example, in basic supply and demand economics there is a 'path' from prices to quantity demanded. Where the term 'path models' has been used, there has been one major difference from the presentation in structural equation regression models – that is, the coefficients are presented as beta coefficients rather than regression coefficients. This means they can be compared by size, at least in rank order terms, and they are standardized to lie in the range −1 to 1. A minor difference is that the presentation of path models is often done using diagrams, using lines with arrows to show the paths between variables with the beta coefficients written on the lines showing the direction of the relationship.

The 'path' in a 'path' model refers to the direction of causality in the model. Take the case of the theatre price perception model above. If we impose the restriction that $b_9 = 0$, then we have in effect what was termed a 'recursive' model before. In this version the variables that appear in the second equation influence *WTP* by going on a 'path' to influence the value of *NORMP*, which then has a 'path' of influence to *WTP*. This means that, if one of these variables appears in both equations its total impact has to be worked out by adding its direct effect to the indirect effect through the path. The only variable to which this applies in our model is the *Leeds* dummy. The total effect of *Leeds* on *WTP* in the recursive model just proposed would be $b_2 + (b_1 \cdot b_{10})$ assuming that the *b*'s are now in beta coefficient form.

Path models are also sometimes known as 'causal models' in the social science literature. All such methods are basically regression methods because regression methods, as used in econometrics, are inherently causal. That is, we suppose that the variable on the left-hand side of the regression is being 'caused' in some sense by the variable on the right-hand side. If we do not do this then we are simply performing a data description which explores the statistical communality between variables by putting one arbitrarily on the left-hand side. If we do this for all variables then we would be performing the analysis that was suggested for multicollinearity in Chapter 10.

13.9 MORE ADVANCED METHODS, I: 3SLS

So far, we have encountered two types of improvements over OLS estimation when dealing with single-equation estimation of the components of a system – 2SLS and SUR. We now come to 3SLS, which is roughly speaking a combination of these two methods. The name is derived from the fact that, if we were performing this estimation method from scratch we would first estimate 2SLS and then proceed to another stage. This final stage takes account of cross-equation correlation. As ever, you should not actually need more than one stage to do 3SLS as it is provided in most computer packages designed for statistical analysis.

In principle we should be able to apply 3SLS to any identified equation in a simultaneous equations system, however large or small it is. The method would seem to be an improvement over 2SLS, but it is not automatically guaranteed that it will be better in terms of reliability in hypothesis testing. This is because of the usual problems of sample size and specification error. 2SLS/3SLS methods rely on asymptotic properties. Further, the 3SLS method is sensitive to specification error in the model. In particular, the linking of the equations via the covariances in the error terms will spread error from a poorly specified equation to one that is correctly specified.

13.10 MORE ADVANCED METHODS, II: FIML AND GMM

FIML (FULL INFORMATION MAXIMUM LIKELIHOOD)

The term FIML is used in contrast to LIML (limited information maximum likelihood models). The FIML approach to a system of equations is a complete systems method rather than a 'one equation at a time' approach like 2SLS. That is, a likelihood function is formulated from all the equations in the model. However, it shares the 2SLS assumptions of no specification error in the model, classical disturbances and zero covariances between the equations.

GENERALIZED METHOD OF MOMENTS

Since the paper by Hansen (1982), economists have increasingly used the GMM method of estimation. This framework is a general one – that is, one can arrive at other methods of estimating systems of equations by imposing restrictions on the GMM model. It is possible to include OLS, 2SLS, exogeneity tests and tests of over identifying restrictions as methods of moments problems. It is also easier to handle non-linearity within such a framework.

There are two main difficulties with this method. It relies heavily on asymptotic properties and thus needs fairly large samples. It is also computationally more demanding than all the methods we have considered so far and may require some additional programming on packages which do not include it as routine.

GMM, although more general than the methods we have been dealing with, is a special case of ML estimation. There are two reasons why GMM may be preferred to ML: first, it may be easier to compute and, second, we may be in a situation where not enough is known about the data generating process to attempt a FIML estimate, but enough is known to specify moment conditions for the purposes of GMM estimation.

13.11 CAN WE TEST FOR IDENTIFICATION?

So far, we have assumed that the equations we are dealing with are identified and therefore there is no conceptual problem in going ahead and estimating them by regression methods so long as we can preserve the classical properties. Identification is then an untested assumption in very many economic models. Indeed, in those pieces of research where the focus is solely on a single equation it is even an unstated, as well as untested, assumption.

It would seem then that we ought to test for identification as we might be making a big mistake in drawing conclusions from a model that we have mistakenly assumed to be identified. Why might this come about? The worst possible case, the nightmare scenario, is that every single variable on the right-hand side of every equation in a model is endogenous. In this case the model has no exogenous variables and identification would seem to be impossible. All that we need for this to happen in a regression model is that there is feedback from the 'dependent variable' to the so-called 'independent' variables. In such a situation, the claim is that the non-experimental nature of real world data makes the correct estimation of the structural elements of econometric models impossible. All that is left in such a situation is the use of the reduced forms, although in the worst-case scenario we have just described, the reduced forms would also be useless as all they would consist of is a regression of the endogenous variables on an intercept.

Such views were put forward in a controversial paper by Liu (1960), who argued that probably none of the equations in econometric models are ever identified. Although econometricians are resistant to acceptance of this view, they are unable to reject it through empirical testing. Tests of over identification can be carried out, as was discussed in Chapter 12, and tests for endogeneity/exogeneity as explained above, but identification itself is a state that has to be assumed *before* we can go ahead and estimate anything. Therefore, identification is not tested in economic models. As the review studies should have made clear, economists tend to assume a model structure that looks plausible, which is identified, and simply take the restrictions required to achieve identification as an act of faith.

13.12 A RECAP: FOUR PROBLEMS

In order to make for a clearer learning experience this chapter began by largely ignoring problems with methods devised for dealing with estimation in systems of equations. However, several problems have gradually emerged and it may be helpful if we now summarize the main problems that we face.

Problem 1: Asymptotic properties
The superiority of 2SLS and 3SLS methods to OLS depends on asymptotic properties. It is not clear whether 2SLS and 3SLS are more appropriate methods than OLS when there is only a fairly small sample available.

Problem 2: Specification of instruments
To use IV/2SLS/3SLS methods we need to have some instruments. In some circumstances we may simply not be able to obtain a suitable collection of instruments. Quite often, researchers simply use a number of lag terms of the variables in the model as instruments without exploring too deeply whether this is appropriate. It may be useful to ponder Exercise 13.2 (iv) below.

Problem 3: Identification might be impossible
Up until the last chapter of this book we implicitly assumed that equations were identified because we treated them as if they did not come from a larger multi-equation system. Now we are regarding all single-equation estimates as potentially part of a multiple-equation system.

Problem 4: Transmission of specification error
The ability to improve on OLS with simultaneous equations estimation methods requires not only that the previous three problems be absent (or negligible) but also that specification error

in parts of the model do not undermine the BLUE properties. It will again be useful to ponder the question asked below in Exercise 13.2 (iv) in recognizing this problem.

13.13 CONCLUSION

In this chapter, we have finally moved away from relying on estimates of a single equation to describe the whole of an economic model. We could still simply estimate all the parameters in all the equations of a multiple-equation system by OLS. Unfortunately, this runs into the problem that, when there are endogenous right-hand side variables, the unbiased-ness assumption of the classical linear regression model breaks down. That is, the covariance between the right-hand side variables and the error term is no longer zero. In a sense they can no longer be called 'independent variables' as they are part of a system in which there is feedback from the left-hand side variable to the right-hand side variables.

As we have seen, methods are available which attempt to remove endogeneity bias. In choosing such methods we would also wish them to satisfy the B (i.e. minimum variance) part of the BLUE criteria as well as the U part.

The simplest of these methods is the IV/2SLS approach, which simply requires us to add a list of instrumental variables to a regression command. This method is asymptotically efficient.

In an ideal world where we had large samples, perfectly specified models and well-behaved data, the IV/2SLS and more sophisticated 'systems' methods would be guaranteed to be better than OLS. On the other hand, if we had full experimental control of data generation there would be no need for any of these methods. That is, if the researcher could control the variables in an economic model the way a biologist or physicist could, then we would not have these problems because the simultaneity could be 'designed' out of the data collection process. Although there is a growing amount of experimental economics (notably in game theory) it is unlikely that the main subject areas of applied econometrics can be dealt with in this way.

DOS AND DON'TS

Do

✓ Think about the specification of the rest of your model if you have simply written down a single equation which contains the relationship that is the focus of your article.

✓ Adopt a critical attitude towards the case for identification and the choice of instruments when you are reading a piece of work by someone else.

Don't

✗ Simply assume that 2SLS is better than OLS and that 3SLS has to be better than 2SLS.

✗ Try to compare different estimation techniques for an equation, in a system of equations, using the R squared, as this is not relevant.

EXERCISES

13.1 **You have been asked to read a time–series study of aggregate investment in manufacturing in which the author used IV rather than 2SLS methods. The estimating equation is a regression of investment in real terms on GDP, real rates of interest, inflationary expectations and investment lagged one period.**

(i)   How do you think this choice of approach would be justified?

(ii)   Why might an OLS approach be deemed unsuitable?

(iii)   Would you expect to see much attention paid to the conventional R squared measure in such a study?

(iv)   Suppose a critic of the paper says: 'not using 2SLS is bad enough but this paper is marred by the failure to consider the use of 3SLS'; how would you reply?

13.2   What would you do in the following situations:

(i)   You need to estimate an equation by 2SLS but the package you are using only lists a command for IV estimation.

(ii)   Your package does not provide an R squared when IV, 2SLS or 3SLS estimates are given.

(iii)   You have been asked to work out the impact of income tax cuts (which are assumed to be exogenous) on the level of investment in the above model (Exercise 13.1) but it has been discovered that none of the equations in the structural model are identified.

(iv)   You plan to use 2SLS to estimate an equation and you have already estimated the reduced forms. You discover that these are extremely poor at explaining the endogenous variables (i.e. low R squared and low 't' ratios).

13.3   Re-estimate the IV equations shown in Table 13.1 using a double-logarithmic version of the model.

13.4   Using the results in Table 13.2 work out the reduced form coefficients for *Grossinc*, *Female* and *Age*, using the 2SLS estimates, for the 'normal price'. Compare these figures with the direct reduced form coefficients shown in the fourth equation of Table 13.2.

13.5   Re-estimate the structural equations in Table 13.2 using heteroscedasticity corrected least squares estimation (this should be automatically available on most packages designed specifically for econometrics).

REFERENCES

Cerra, V. and Saxena, C.S. (2002) An empirical analysis of China's export behavior, International Monetary Fund Working Paper WP/02/200, published November. Downloadable from http://ideas.repec.org/p/imf/imfwpa/02200./html.

Gisser, M. (1991) Advertising, concentration and profitability in manufacturing, *Economic Inquiry*, **39**(1), January, 148–165.

Hansen, L.P. (1982) Large sample results for generalized methods of moments estimators, *Econometrics*, **50**, 1029–1054.

Hood, W.C. and Koopmans, T.C. (1953) *Studies in Econometric Method*, Cowles Foundation Monograph 14, Yale University Press, New Haven and London.

Liu, T.C. (1960) Underidentification, structural estimation and forecasting, *Econometrica*, **28**, 855–865.

Stock, J.H. and Trebbi, F. (2003) Retrospectives: Who invented instrumental variables regression?, *Journal of Economic Perspectives*, **17**(3), 177–194.

Zellner, A. (1962) An efficient method of estimating seemingly unrelated regression and tests for aggregation bias, *Journal of the American Statistical Association*, June, 348–368.

14

Problem Solving: Time Series

LEARNING OBJECTIVES

▇ To know what a 'spurious regression' is
▇ Be able to do unit root and cointegration tests and know why they are necessary
▇ Be able to formulate an E–G two-step model and interpret its results
▇ Be aware of the limitations of the usual pre-tests in economic analysis of time-series

CHAPTER SUMMARY

14.1 INTRODUCTION

This chapter deals with tests and methods specific to the use of time-series data. In the next section we review our knowledge about time-series data from the previous chapters. We then look at the problem that an OLS regression equation may be 'spurious' in the sense that apparently 'good' and meaningful results may be obtained from data that are totally unrelated to each other. The rest of the chapter is mainly devoted to looking at tests we can use to help us avoid this pitfall and methods of proceeding if we can establish that our specified relationship is not spurious. We begin with the simplest possible set of circumstances and then discuss some complications.

Our example regressions and review studies are based on annual data, which means problems of seasonality are excluded. Finally, the chapter considers how the economic analysis of time series relates to the 'time-series analysis' developed independently of the body of econometric techniques and methodology.

14.2 WHAT WE ALREADY KNOW ABOUT TIME SERIES

The term 'time series' is applied to specific techniques that can be used to analyse time-series data, thus we find references to 'time-series econometrics' and 'time-series analysis'. These imply something more advanced than OLS regression applied to time-series data. Before we consider the more advanced treatments, it will be helpful to review what we already know about the analysis of time-series data.

We have encountered time-series data many times in the previous chapters of this book. Several issues that arise in time series, which would be absent in cross-section data, have therefore already been seen in this book. These are:

▶ Seasonality (see Section 7.4)
▶ The problem of separating 'common trend' in a series of data (see Section 7.8)
▶ Serial correlation (see Section 9.7)
▶ Lagged variables (see Section 6.8)

We used dummy variables to deal with the presence of seasonal components in a data series. The problem of common trend was dealt with by including a trend term in the OLS regression equation, which is just a set of increasing numbers (the simplest case being 1, 2, 3, 4 ... n). This additional variable is assumed to remove the common trend in a set of variables, thus leaving us with coefficients that reflect the degree of covariance of the deviations of the variables around the trend. Thus, we might get drastically different results when we add a time trend to an OLS regression, in that the coefficients and 't' ratios may change dramatically. The same applies for dummy variables.

The problem of autocorrelation between the error (u) terms of the model across the sample, which was examined in Section 9.7, can arise in cross-section data, but it is a problem that must always be considered in a set of time-series data. A number of tests for autocorrelation were presented in Section 9.7 which can tell us something about the properties of the data we are examining.

We did not present any techniques for 'correcting' or 'adjusting' for the impact that autocorrelation has on the B (best) property of the BLUE requirement of OLS estimators. There is a reason for this. Before the revolution in time-series econometrics, which is covered in the next section, the usual approach to serial-correlation was to use a GLS procedure, most usually the Cochrane–Orcutt technique to 'correct' for the presence of serial correlation in the error term of a static equation. A researcher was expected to examine the Durbin–Watson statistic and if it did not accept the null hypothesis of $\rho = 0$ sufficiently convincingly (i.e. if the D–W was a long way from 2) then they would apply GLS techniques. Such techniques are still available on many econometrics packages but they are now discouraged in serious econometrics to the point where they are not even mentioned in works on the analysis of time series. This is because they imply a very implausible 'common factor' restriction which should be tested.

The modern approach to time series in economics consists of two things:

(i) Starting from a general dynamic model and working down to a more specific model via restrictions on the lag structures. This is the 'general to specific' methodology.

(ii) **Pre-testing** to ensure that we do not encounter the problem of spurious regression, which is dealt with in the next section.

14.3 THE PROBLEM OF SPURIOUS REGRESSION

In 1974, Granger and Newbold published an article in the *Journal of Econometrics* which seemed to rock the foundations of existing econometric research on time-series data. In this paper, it was shown that the use of OLS on what is called **non-stationary data** can give us a set of results with a high R squared and statistically significant 't' ratio *even when there is no relationship whatsoever between the data series used in the regression equation*. Most economists at the time would have regarded any regression, based on accepted theoretical models, with these results as 'good' provided the signs on the coefficients were correct and the magnitudes were plausible.

The experiments reported by Granger and Newbold, and later replicated by others, suggested that much econometric research might be arriving at completely incorrect conclusions, as there could be an in-built tendency to serious over-rejection of the null hypotheses of zero-valued parameters. The regressions estimated, in these circumstances, were termed 'spurious regressions' because they were regressions without any foundation or meaning.

We have yet to explain how this problem of spurious regression can come about. It arises when we have a set of data in which there is no relationship between the variables but the variables suffer from being **non-stationary**. The use of OLS regression, to test hypotheses, supposes that data are stationary. If a series of data is not stationary then it must have some property which tends to drift upwards or downwards as the series unfolds over time. The presence of these properties means that the distribution of the 't' statistic does not follow that which we normally assume for it and therefore it is inappropriate.

There are three ways in which data can be stationary or non-stationary.

(i) Mean stationary

A series (say T_X), which is mean stationary, fluctuates around its mean level, over time, without showing any tendency to drift away from it. We could say that it has a tendency to **revert** to its mean value as time passes, despite temporary deviations from it. This suggests that a graph of the series may give evidence of non-stationary if there is clear movement upwards or downwards.

(ii) Variance stationary

A series, which is variance stationary, fluctuates around its variance, over time, without showing any tendency to drift away from this given level.

(iii) Covariance stationary

The covariance referred to here is that between values of the series and those at other time periods ($\text{cov}(Y_t, Y_{t-1})$). A series, which is covariance stationary, will fluctuate around a given covariance, over time, without showing any tendency to drift away from this given level.

Given the definitions above, we should be able to test the individual data series for stationarity *before* we use them in a regression. Having done so we should be in a position to avoid making the mistake of a spurious regression. These tests are presented in the next section.

Exploration of the properties of time-series data cannot take place in a vacuum. We need to make some assumptions about the way the values of a variable may be evolving over time. It is now common to refer to the equation in which these assumptions are embodied as a data generating process or **DGP**. The work by Granger and Newbold involved generating two artificial sets of data by using a **DGP** for each, which followed a simple first order autoregressive process of the following type:

$$Y_t = Y_{t-1} + u_t \tag{14.1}$$

where u_t is a classical disturbance term. It therefore has a zero mean and constant (but unknown) variance.

We do not include a constant term at the moment. If we removed Y_{t-1} and replaced it with a constant term then the series would be stationary, with the mean value being the constant term. Such a process is what we have been assuming to operate up until now. You will note that the disturbance term is assumed to be stationary due to the assumptions made. This DGP has a history in the sense that every value of Y is connected to all the Y's in the past.

There is no parameter attached to the lagged Y variable in Equation (14.1) appearing on the right-hand side. This implies that it is equal to one. If this is the case then the above is a simple **random-walk** process in which the series Y is said to have a **unit root**.

In Equation (14.1) the variance of u_t is not constant, it will become larger as time passes, and in fact it will tend towards infinity. The concept of a mean for Y is problematic as the expected time for Y to return to any given value (say, for example, it began as being equal to 10) is infinite because the parameter on Y_{t-1} is equal to 1.

The series for Y are non-stationary but, if they follow the simple random walk process in Equation (14.1), we can take the first difference of Y_t:

$$\Delta Y_t = Y_t - Y_{t-1} \tag{14.2}$$

This series will be stationary as it is equal to the classical disturbance term. Therefore it has a mean of zero and a constant variance (bearing in mind we assume that the u term is assumed to be free from autocorrelation). Thus the first difference of a random walk is stationary.

The facility to turn a non-stationary variable into a stationary variable by differencing is important in all forms of time-series analysis. If we can make a series stationary by differencing it once, it is referred to as '*integrated of order one*' and this is written as the series being I(1). If it requires more differencing, then it is regarded as being integrated to the order of which it has been differenced and is thus written as a series which is I(2), I(3) and so on if those are the required differencing factors. Although we are ignoring seasonality at present, one might reasonably expect to find quarterly series which are I(4). A series, which is stationary, has the property of being I(0), as it does not require any differencing. As the DGP will differ from series to series we might well find that within our dataset some series are of different orders of integration from each other.

Granger and Newbold (1974) generated two sets of random-walk variables to represent the Y and X terms in a simple regression model They created these figures by using a random number generator to provide values of u subject to the requirement that it has classical properties of zero mean and constant variance. In this case both variables will be I(1) because they follow this DGP, which was devised by the researchers.

They then took one variable as the dependent and one as the independent variable and ran the regression of the dependent variable on the independent variable and a constant. They did this with a large number of artificially generated samples and discovered that around 74 per cent of the time the null hypothesis of a zero slope coefficient was rejected at the 5 per cent level.

This far exceeds what should have occurred according to the models we have been studying so far. One would have some errors, but anything that is well outside the range of 5 per cent is very worrying and the figure found by Granger and Newbold is very far outside of this range. Thus we are being 'fooled' by an artifact of the data into thinking there is a relationship between the two variables when there is not.

From this we learn that:

▷ We need to be more careful in terms of representing the DGP in our model building.
▷ We need to test the data *before* we rush into estimating a relationship to see if it is suitable for model building.
▷ We need to check that the model is not spurious.

These issues are dealt with in the next sections of this chapter, beginning with the second of the above points, that is 'pre-testing'.

14.4 AVOIDING SPURIOUS REGRESSION: PRE-TESTING – UNIT ROOTS AND OTHER TESTS

We are now about to engage in 'pre-testing' which is a different form of hypothesis testing from the two types we have so far used. In the first part of the book we tested hypotheses about a fitted model, which was assumed to be correctly specified. In Chapter 10, we moved on to diagnostic tests, which questioned the validity of the assumptions on which hypothesis testing of the model was based. The tests we are about to look at are, in contrast, carried out *before* the model is estimated in order to best arrive at its specification and estimation.

Tests for the stationarity of variables are known as unit root tests because they involve checking for statistically significant differences of the parameter on Y_{t-1} from 1 in Equation (14.1).

Unit root tests are carried out on individual variables in isolation; that is, we do not take into account any relationship there may be between the variable being tested and any other variables selected to be in the model. Testing for the relationship between the variables, in the model, is examined in Section 14.5 on cointegration.

Assuming we are dealing with the variable Y_t, it would seem we could carry out our pre-testing for unit roots by estimating Equation (14.1) by OLS. The way in which unit root tests are now usually done is slightly different from this for several reasons:

▶ Inconvenience: it is a slight nuisance to have to test a null of 1 versus an alternate of less than 1 compared with testing against a null of zero, so the DGP is reformulated to facilitate this.

▶ Invalid 't' tests: we are not able to use conventional 't' tests because they are not valid if the data are non-stationary

▶ Serial correlation will influence the tests and we may need to deal with it.

▶ Deterministic trends may be present (that is, of the type modelled in Chapter 7).

▶ An intercept may be included in the testing equation.

When we take these things into account the most general formulation of the equation used for testing is of the following form:

$$Y_t - Y_{t-1} = b_0 + (b_1 - 1)Y_{t-1} + b_2 T + augmentation\ terms + u_t \qquad (14.3)$$

which is arrived at by subtracting lagged Y from both sides of the equation. T is the time trend, b_0 is an intercept term and the final set of terms are the augmentation terms included to 'clean up' any serial correlation which may exist in the series. These are a number of lags of the dependent variable (the first difference of the variable). We shall ignore for the moment the question of how many of these you should use, and will simply choose to use two in the results we are about to produce for cinema attendance and population in Australia. There is nothing wrong with using the original form of the random-walk process to do the test, but the above version is what everyone now uses.

If $b_1 = 1$, then the data will be non-stationary. Due to the problem with the use of the Student 't' tables we have used so far, we have to use the Dickey–Fuller tables, which have higher critical values than the Student 't' tables. If the augmentation terms are dropped from Equation (14.3) this test is known as the Dickey–Fuller (DF) test, otherwise it is known as the augmented Dickey–Fuller (ADF).

The remaining specification issues in doing ADF tests are whether or not there should be an intercept and/or a trend term. If we include an intercept in the differenced series (Equation 14.3) this is equivalent to having a deterministic trend in the DGP for Y. If a trend is included in the equation, we are allowing for the possibility that the change in Y is increasing or decreasing (depending on the sign of b_2) by a constant amount.

One can, of course, do tests on various combinations of the terms that we have now added to the simple differenced version of the original random-walk process shown in Equation (14.3). Most software now automatically offers you the chance to test the combinations of restrictions that are possible.

We now give an example of unit root tests, with the ADF, using data for the Australian cinema industry, shown in Table 14.1. This is a short series of only 27 years and the table does not contain enough variables for us to develop a full-scale model of demand.

Table 14.1 Australian cinema admissions			
Year	Adm.	Pop.	Adm/Pop
1976	28.9	14.0	2.1
1977	24.1	14.2	1.7
1978	34.1	14.4	2.4
1979	33.6	14.5	2.3
1980	38.6	14.7	2.6
1981	38.7	14.9	2.6
1982	42.0	15.2	2.8
1983	37.1	15.4	2.4
1984	28.9	15.6	1.9
1985	29.7	15.8	1.9
1986	35.5	16.0	2.2
1987	30.8	16.3	1.9
1988	37.4	16.5	2.3
1989	39.0	16.8	2.3
1990	43.0	17.1	2.5
1991	46.9	17.3	2.7
1992	47.2	17.5	2.7
1993	55.6	17.7	3.1
1994	68.1	17.8	3.8
1995	69.9	18.0	3.9
1996	74.0	18.3	4.1
1997	76.0	18.5	4.1
1998	80.0	18.7	4.3
1999	88.0	18.9	4.6
2000	82.0	19.2	4.3
2001	92.5	19.5	4.7
2002	92.5	19.8	4.7

The growth of cinema admissions in Australia is a problem for the balance of trade because the composition of films exhibited is predominantly American, thus rendering this sector of the economy largely one of import demand.

At first glance, these figures seem to be non-stationary as there is clear evidence of a trend in the number of tickets sold. There is also something of a trend in population; however, this does not seem to match the trend in admissions as the per capita admissions series also shows a trend.

The trend in admissions is clearly visible in Figure 14.1. Figure 14.2 shows that it is possible to turn the series into something that looks much more likely to be stationary by first

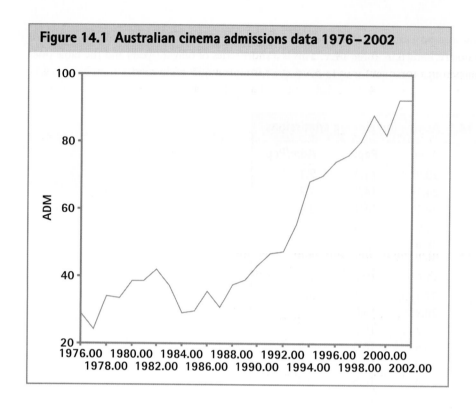

Figure 14.1 Australian cinema admissions data 1976–2002

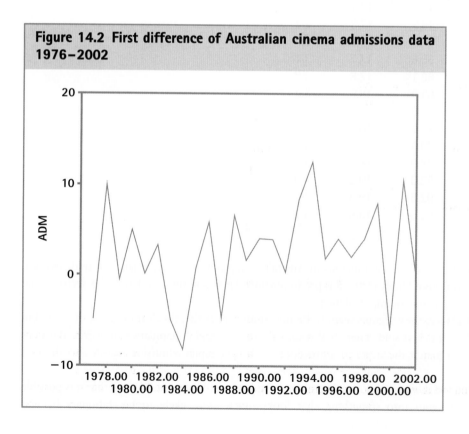

Figure 14.2 First difference of Australian cinema admissions data 1976–2002

differencing the series. In contrast to Figure 14.1, the series of admissions first differenced, shown in Figure 14.2, has no distinct sign of a trend.

We now perform some unit root tests on the admissions and population data in Table 14.1. These are shown in Table 14.2. In this table we have adopted the following specifications for the unit root tests:

$$\Delta Adm_t = b_0 + b_1 Adm_{t-1} + b_2 T_t + b_3 \Delta Adm_{t-1} + b_4 \Delta Adm_{t-2} + \delta t \qquad (14.4)$$

$$\Delta Pop_t = b_5 + b_6 Pop_{t-1} + b_7 T_t + b_8 \Delta Pop_{t-1} + b_9 \Delta Pop_{t-2} + \varepsilon_t \qquad (14.5)$$

where δ and ε are classical disturbance terms.

Table 14.2 ADF tests for unit root tests on Australian population and cinema admissions

Variable:	Adm	Pop
Constant	1.149	8.063
	(0.408)	(2.953)
T	0.646	0.134
	(1.921)	(2.944)
Adm_{t-1}	−0.169	
	(−1.392)	
Pop_{t-1}		−0.596
		(-2.891)
DADM(-1)	-0.089744	
	(-0.40258)	
DADM(-2)	0.14365	
	(0.67573)	
DPOP (-1)		0.40321
		(1.9123)
DPOP (-2)		0.20778
		(0.93825)
R squared	0.224	0.391
DW statistic	2.15	1.87
N	24	24

A few points need to be made about the 't' tests for b_1 and b_6:

▶ The sign will be negative and the 't' ratio will thus be negative.
▶ Be aware that if you do conduct the estimation of the above equations using OLS, rather than simply clicking on a pre-programmed option in a package (which offers unit root tests), then you might be provided with the wrong critical significance levels as the package has no way of knowing what you are doing. Therefore it will be giving you significance levels based on Student 't' values *not* the correct ADF values. Hence you should ignore probability/critical

369

significance levels if you do use standard OLS and instead use the 't' value provided by your package in comparison with the tabulated Dickey–Fuller values. These tables can be quite cumbersome as the values have to be recalculated each time there is a change in the specification of Equation (14.2); that is, the critical values differ when the intercept is removed or the trend is removed.

The addition of a time trend increases the absolute value of the critical 't' values substantially so that they are even further above the Student 't' ratio values. Specialist time-series packages will generally provide you with the critical values but you need to check that they are giving you the right one.

The results of doing the ADF tests set down above, on the Australian data in Table 14.1, are shown in Table 14.2.

There are several things to note in these results, although our primary focus is on the 't' test for the lagged variable in each equation, as this will indicate whether or not there is a unit root.

▶ There is evidence of a significant time trend in the equations suggesting that the rate of change of the variables is drifting upwards, as would be suspected from looking at Figure 14.1.
▶ Both equations seem to be free of serial correlation judged by the values of the Durbin–Watson statistic (this is confirmed by other tests which I have not reported).
▶ The 'nuisance terms' to control for serial correlation do not seem to be statistically significant for the most part. This does not necessarily mean we should drop them.

There is no guarantee that the formulations just used were the best means of testing for the presence of unit roots. Exploration of this is left to the reader in the end of chapter exercises. Let us turn to the main issue, which is the size of the 't' ratios on Adm_{t-1} and Pop_{t-1} in Table 14.2. There are only 17 degrees of freedom as we have lost observations at the start and used up degrees of freedom due to adding so many variables to the basic random walk model. There is no need to find out the ADF critical values for the admissions case as the value of -1.392 is much too small to reject the null even using Student 't' tables, which have to have smaller critical values than DF tables. The value for the Population series is -2.891, which would be statistically significant at fairly high levels on conventional 't' ratios. However, it is not significant on ADF test values and thus on the basis of these results neither series is stationary.

We conclude that the data series are not I(0). If we now difference the series once and do the tests again and reject the hypothesis of a unit root then we would conclude that the series was I(1). If we cannot do so, then we can carry on differencing the data until we find the order of integration. Many annual economic time series will not require us to go above I(1) and few would require us to go beyond I(2). If the series were quarterly or monthly we would expect to find fourth or twelfth orders of integration within the data.

SOME ALTERNATIVES TO THE UNIT ROOT TEST

Visual inspection

Simply looking at the data is not a statistical test but it can often give us a reasonable indication as to whether a variable is stationary. As mentioned above, Figure 14.1 suggests non-stationarity.

Correlogram

This is a more formal visual inspection method and derives from traditional time-series analysis, which is discussed later in this chapter. It involves plotting the **autocorrelation coefficient** over time. The autocorrelation coefficient (ρ_k) is calculated computing the covariance between a variable and its kth lagged value and dividing this value by the variance of the series.

This will lie between 0 and 1. This diagram is to be inspected in terms of how rapidly the autocorrelation function declines as we increase the lag length. If the series 'damps', i.e. rapidly declines without subsequent 'spiking', then the series is stationary. If there are regular spikes this may be indicative of some kind of seasonality, for example day of the week effects in commodity trading.

We can also inspect the correlogram of the differenced series to get further information about it. For example, if the first differenced series has an autocorrelation function which damps rapidly then it would seem to be stationary. If there are regular spikes then we should choose a difference equal to the spike order for this process.

The correlogram for Australian cinema admissions is shown in Figure 14.3. It seems to damp fairly quickly without later spiking and thus does not seem very suggestive of non-stationarity. The correlogram for the first difference series is shown in Figure 14.4. This damps quickly and has some weak spiking later on suggestive of the use of a first-difference to achieve stationary data.

Perron test

The Perron test seems to be the main alternative to Dickey–Fuller type tests used by researchers. It is proposed to deal with the presence of structural breaks in time series. For example, a major natural disaster would cause a huge 'blip' in many production series. These breaks can be modelled using 'step' or 'pulse' dummies where the step dummy refers to a permanent shift and the pulse dummy refers to a temporary shift that only applies at the time of the intervention.

The important feature of such structural changes for the Dickey–Fuller type of tests is that there will be a bias towards acceptance of the null of a unit root when a variable is stationary. We could explain this by saying that a sequence of two I(0) series for a variable with different means may be mistaken for an I(1) series when we treat it as all one series with the same mean.

For the additive outlier type of shift we have just described, it is *not* satisfactory to simply add a dummy to an equation such as (14.3). Rather the test requires us to:

(i) Estimate an equation with a pulse or step dummy of the form:

$$Y_t = b_0 + b_1 S_t + u_t \tag{14.6}$$

Figure 14.4 Correlogram of first difference Australian admissions data

Lag	Auto-Corr.	Stand. Err.
1	-.221	.185
2	.171	.182
3	.065	.178
4	.020	.174
5	.073	.170
6	-.108	.166
7	-.044	.162
8	.244	.157
9	-.300	.153
10	-.072	.148
11	-.100	.144
12	-.127	.139
13	.144	.134
14	-.190	.128
15	.018	.123
16	.098	.117

Figure 14.3 Correlogram of Australian admissions data

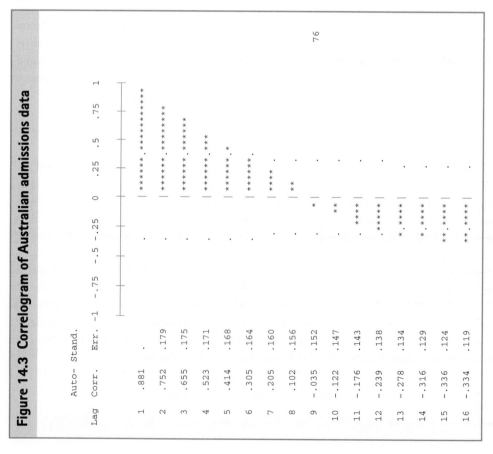

Lag	Auto-Corr.	Stand. Err.
1	.881	.
2	.752	.179
3	.655	.175
4	.523	.171
5	.414	.168
6	.305	.164
7	.205	.160
8	.102	.156
9	-.035	.152
10	-.122	.147
11	-.176	.143
12	-.239	.138
13	-.278	.134
14	-.316	.129
15	-.336	.124
16	-.334	.119

76

where u is a classical disturbance term and S is the step, or pulse, dummy; then save the residuals.

(ii) We then test these residuals for stationarity using an equation of the form (14.3) where the residuals take the place of Y but we include S in this equation also.

(iii) The tests for a unit root use tables which are similar to Dickey–Fuller tables but an extra parameter λ, the fraction of observations before the break point, is involved in using the tables.

The Perron test does of course suffer from the problem that we need some prior knowledge of where the structural break occurs. It is quite common to see both ADF and Perron tests being applied to a set of data and also sometimes correlograms. This is only likely to cause problems when the methods do not agree, which is going to depend on the properties of the individual data set.

WHAT NEXT?

This section has only dealt with individual variables, so in the next we will look at the nature of the time-series relationship between variables. We need to know how to proceed from unit root testing to the specification of a model. If all the variables in our model are stationary then we could estimate an OLS model without problems. That is, if all the variables are I(0) we can estimate an OLS regression without fear of spurious results, leading us to incorrect conclusions on the relevant hypothesis tests – that is, provided the other standard problems of econometrics, dealt with earlier in this book, are not present. As has been indicated, this happy circumstance – all variables being I(0) – will seldom arise as the great bulk of time series are not stationary.

It would be a mistake to imagine that statisticians did not know about the risks of spurious inference before the Granger and Newbold paper gained widespread acceptance. It was often suggested that a simple time trend be included to remove spurious trended relations or alternately that we use some mechanical means of detrending the individual series prior to estimation.

Another popular approach was to run the regression in differences rather than levels, i.e. replace Y with ΔY and each X variable with ΔX. This will inevitably have the effect of massively reducing the huge R squareds (something which at least creates the suspicion of a spurious regression especially in comparison with the Durbin–Watson value) often found in regressions involving trending time series. Given what has been said above, a regression in first differences would be a regression on stationary variables if all the original series were I(1), which still requires pre-testing of the data. Likewise, the use of a deterministic time trend to 'correct' for non-stationarity is a highly restrictive assumption, which might not apply.

The problem with such methods is that they are *ad hoc* and may only apply to special cases, which the data may not support. Perhaps the most important thing to know at this stage is that the presence of unit roots in the individual variables does not necessarily mean that we will have a spurious regression. In fact, if the variables are I(1), then we can potentially continue to build a model provided that the two series cointegrate as discussed in the next section. Testing for cointegration is a second stage of pre-testing. Only when this stage has been passed should we move on to model-building.

A rule of thumb has been suggested by Granger and Newbold (1974) that an equation is spurious if the following holds:

$$R^2 > D\text{-}W$$

This is not a hard and fast rule so we still do need to go on and do the formal testing.

14.5 COINTEGRATION: DEFINITION AND TESTING

We now move to the second stage of pre-testing. This takes the set of variables we have specified in the model and explores the nature of the relationship between them. In particular, it attempts to discover if there are **cointegrating vectors** within the set of variables. If there are, then it can be said to have cointegration. The term 'cointegration' is a development from the use of the term 'integration' to describe the stationarity properties of individual series. As the individual series are said to be integrated of order 0 if they are stationary, order 1 if they need to be differenced once to be stationary and so on, then the cointegration relationship is of order 0, 1, 2 or whatever order of differencing is required to make the residual from the **cointegrating regression** stationary.

The easiest case to deal with, in explaining cointegration, is a simple model with only two variables in it, such as the example of the Australian cinema data which we have been using in this chapter so far. This is what we have been calling a model with a dependent variable and one independent variable. As there are only two variables, there can only be one cointegrating vector, as each variable does not have any other variables with which to be cointegrated. An applied example of this very simple case is found in the study of the 'Gibson paradox', which is used as a review study in Section 14.6. For the purposes of illustration we will look at whether population and cinema attendances in the Australian data in Table 14.1 are cointegrated, with the test results being shown in Table 14.3.

For the two-variable case we can therefore write down the following simple demand model as:

$$Adm_t = b_0 + b_1 POP_t + b_2 T_t + u_t \tag{14.7}$$

This specification of the relationship involves both a constant term and a deterministic time trend (T), although we could of course place restrictions on the coefficients of these two terms. In Table 14.3, the first regression has the restriction $b_2 = 0$ and hence has no time trend term, unlike the second regression.

TESTING FOR COINTEGRATION, I: THE CRDW (COINTEGRATING REGRESSION DURBIN–WATSON TEST)

Tests for cointegration are derived from the residuals of this OLS equation and a number of these tests are presented at the foot of Table 14.3. In fact, one suggestion that has been made is that we can simply use the Durbin–Watson value from the OLS estimate of Equation (14.6). In this context, it requires a new set of critical values for testing the null that it is zero, and is now known as the CRDW – cointegrating regression Durbin-Watson test. It was proposed by

Table 14.3 Cointegration tests For Australian population and cinema attendance

Dependent variable:	Original regression	
	Att	Att
Intercept	−140.78	36.25
	(−8.07)	(0.11)
Population	11.48	−1.49
	(11.09)	(0.06)
T		2.89
		(0.53)
R^2	0.831	0.833
DW	0.346	0.33
Unit root test for residuals:		
DF	−1.654	−1.64
ADF(1)	−1.371	−1.03
ADF(2)	−1.556	−1.477

Note: The bottom three figures are the values of the 't' tests for a unit root in the residuals using, respectively, 0, 1 and 2 augmentation terms in the test regression.

Bhargava and Sargan (1983). There are limitations of this test in that it depends on strong assumptions about the DGP.

Looking at Table 14.3, we can, in fact, see that the D–W values are extremely low and well below the R squared, suggesting a high likelihood of the regression being spurious.

TESTING FOR COINTEGRATION, II: AUGMENTED ENGLE–GRANGER TESTS

The most popular method of looking at cointegration of a set of time series is to *use the same kinds of tests on the residuals that we used on the individual data series for the variables* – that is, we use Dickey–Fuller or augmented Dickey–Fuller tests on the residuals. Many computer packages will do this for you, and those that are specially designed for time-series data certainly will. If they do not, you can simply save the residuals from your regressions and use these to estimate an equation of the same form as (14.3) with the fitted residuals replacing Y.

We should pause to consider whether the equation to perform the augmented Engle–Granger (AEG) test is exactly like Equation (14.3). In fact, it is not, as we have a choice as to where the intercept and trend terms go in the two-stage process of estimating an OLS regression and then using its residuals to conduct a cointegration test. If the original OLS equation included an intercept and trend (as do the ones we reported in Table 10.3) then we do not include these again in the test equation performed on the residuals.

Six such tests are shown at the foot of Table 14.3; three for each version of the model. The first of each set is done without 'nuisance' terms and the next two are augmented tests with one and two nuisance terms (lagged differences of the residuals) respectively.

These tests show that the residuals do not seem to be I(0) and hence they can be said to have a unit root. Therefore the series of population and cinema do not appear to be cointegrated.

There have been many other tests for cointegration published in econometrics journals, but the AEG test continues to be the one that is most widely available in econometrics packages and the most widely used.

ECONOMIC INTERPRETATION OF COINTEGRATION

So far in this section all we have done is learn how to do cointegration tests without knowing precisely why we were doing them. It is convenient to distinguish between the **statistical property** of cointegration and the **theoretical interpretation** that economists are inclined to give to a finding of statistical evidence of cointegration. What we have just done in Table 14.3 is test the statistical property of cointegration – that is, we have tested whether the behaviour of data series over time corresponds to a specific null hypothesis.

Economic theory suggests that a finding of cointegration indicates that there *may* be a long-run equilibrium relationship in the collection of time-series variables. Taking this proposition the other way round, we would usually come to the conclusion that, if the combination of variables does not contain a cointegrating vector, then we have been unable to find any support for the presence of a long-run equilibrium relationship. This would seem to pose serious problems for our model-building strategy.

A failure to find cointegration does not necessarily mean that there is no long-run equilibrium relationship between two or more series, as there could be errors in the specification of the hypothesis test. There may, for example, be artifacts in the data that could be removed in order to discover an equilibrium relationship.

A bivariate regression, such as that just used, is highly likely to be mis-specified because there would normally be more than just one determinant of the dependent variable specified in the relevant economic model. Once we adopt a model with more variables, this opens up the issue of how many cointegration vectors are in the model. The simplest and strongest assumption to make is the one made in the next section – that is, that the set of right-hand variables form a cointegration vector with the left-hand side variable.

At this point, we need to go on to show how the results of the cointegration analysis feed into the specification of a model. We shall abandon the Australian cinema analysis at this point. Curiously there is no detailed econometric analysis of Australian cinema attendances that I am aware of but, interestingly, a UK analysis of time series for cinema demand by Macmillan and Smith (2001) also finds problems of obtaining integration of the individual series and cointegration of the group of series. In contrast, a Spanish study of cinema attendance by Fernandez Blanco and Banos Pino (1997) does find cointegration in a model of demand.

14.6 FORMULATING A TIME-SERIES ECONOMETRICS MODEL: ENGLE–GRANGER TWO-STEP MODEL

The modern economic approach to time series, which has grown up in the wake of Granger's work, tries to separate out explicitly the long-run equilibrium relationships in a model from its short-run movements towards equilibrium. Before we specify the model, we should have pre-tested the individual series of data to see if they are I(0) and if they are not we should have tested the residuals for cointegration.

Let us suppose that we are dealing with a set of data where the individual variables are all I(1) and there is also cointegration, i.e. the residuals of the equation are I(0). Let us further assume that there is only one cointegrating vector and remember that we are ignoring such issues as seasonality and structural shifts in the parameters.

Given all this, we have the simplest possible situation in which we could find ourselves – other than giving up because of widespread problems in the pre-testing or going on to use a simple static model because the pre-testing discovered that there were unit roots in any of the data.

We have just discussed two forms of pre-testing that are needed before we go on to formulate a suitable model to apply to time-series data. We are assuming that the individual series are I(1) and therefore we cannot use a simple static OLS model to estimate the relationship. However, in the E–G two-step model we do make use of this equation but the interpretation of it is changed and it acquires a new name. The static OLS model estimating equation is now seen as the **cointegrating equation**. It can be treated as the long-run equilibrium relationship that is inherent in the model, but we now need to develop a model that links the short-run behaviour of the model to the long-run.

The simplest approach is to assume that we are dealing with an underlying model that contains a lagged dependent variable and a single lag on each of the independent variables. This is referred to as an ARDL (autoregressive distributed lag) model of order one. In principle we could have written down such a model by the end of Chapter 6 as we already knew enough by then to interpret such an equation. It has a short-run impact for each parameter that will be smaller than the long-run impact.

Given the above we will assume the underlying model is:

$$Y_t = b_0 + b_1 Y_{t-1} + b_2 X_t + b_3 X_{t-1} + u_t \tag{14.8}$$

which is a simple first order ARDL model with no trend. The u term is assumed to be a classical disturbance term. The short-run impact of X on Y is given by b_2 and the long-run impact is given by $[(b_2 + b_3)/(1 - b_1)]$.

If we were to estimate this model directly by OLS, the discussion in the preceding sections suggest that we should first check whether the individual series are stationary and whether X and Y cointegrate. If X and Y do not cointegrate, then we should not be proceeding with this model. If X and Y were individually I(0) we could set $b_1 = b_3 = 0$. If they are not I(1) then we would need to explore further before we go on.

There is no particular reason not to estimate Equation (14.8) directly but the fashion that has developed in econometrics is to use the following approach instead, after the necessary pre-testing. This type of model is known as an ECM (error correction model or mechanism). There are many forms that this can take but the basic idea is that an equation, which cointegrates, can be used to form an appropriate representation of the way in which it moves from short-run to long-run equilibrium. In the simple approach we are about to use, the ECM consists of running an equation in differences (which may be lagged to various lengths) with an added variable consisting of the lagged residual from an OLS equation in levels.

SUMMARY OF HOW TO PERFORM THE ENGLE–GRANGER TWO-STEP ESTIMATOR

Step 1: Estimate the long-run solution of the model and save the residuals.
   That is, we estimate:

$$Y_t = z_0 + z_1 X_t + u_t \tag{14.9}$$

which is the long-run solution of Equation (14.7).

Step 2: Use the residuals from step one in a specification which represents the short-run ECM (error correction model).
   The model we are trying to estimate is the error correction model

$$\Delta Y_t = v_0 + v_1 \Delta X_{t-1} - v_2[Y_{t-1} - \hat{z}_0 - \hat{z}_1 X_{t-1}] + \varepsilon \tag{14.10}$$

where ε is another classical disturbance term. A regression, which is just in differences, i.e. $v_2 = 0$, would give us the short-run relationship between the non-stationary variables which are I (0) but would not provide any long-run relationship. The link between the short and long run is provided by the final term in brackets which represents 'error correction'. So, the estimate of v_2 will be a measure of the speed of adjustment of the model towards long-run equilibrium. The value of v_2 should be between 0 and 1.
   The expression in square brackets is unknown, and hence we use the first stage residuals in its place.

This method has the appeal of being simple to use and understand. It only requires the user to be able to do two OLS regressions, presuming they have already performed the pre-tests for unit roots and cointegration. It is developed on the basis of the proof of **superconsistency** of the OLS estimators of the long-run parameters.

We should be careful, however, in the use we make of the first stage equation. The fact that we can use it to obtain unbiased parameter estimates when the variables cointegrate does *not* mean that we can use it to perform hypothesis tests, as the standard errors will not be valid. In other words, hypothesis tests on the long-run estimates should be worked out from the second stage of the estimation process.

To illustrate the method we present some results that have not been motivated by any particular economic theoretical model. The data are taken from the website of the Office of National Statistics in the UK (**www.ons.gov.uk**), where you can find more data relevant to the improvement of this work if you wish to continue. The data is shown in Table 14.4.

Let us propose a simple relationship of the form:

$$NVR_t = b_0 + b_1 RPI_t + b_2 GDP_t + b_3 RPI_{t-1} + b_4 GDP_{t-1} + b_5 NVR_{t-1} + u_t \tag{14.11}$$

If we set $b_3 = b_4 = b_5 = 0$, this becomes the cointegrating regression, which is shown in the first column of Table 14.5. The residual from this is saved and then lagged and appears as the last item in the second column where the Engle–Granger two-step estimates are given. The second equation is thus the error correction model.

Table 14.4 New car registrations, retail price index and per capita income in the UK, 1987–2002			
Year	RPI	GDP	New vehicle registrations (NVR) in 000s
1987	101.9	7 387	2 016.3
1988	106.9	8 229	2 210.4
1989	115.2	9 010	2 304.7
1990	126.1	9 737	2 005.0
1991	133.5	10 204	1 600.3
1992	138.5	10 612	1 599.1
1993	140.7	11 137	1 776.5
1994	144.1	11 789	1 906.3
1995	149.1	12 414	13 149.0
1996	152.7	13 149	2 018.4
1997	157.5	13 942	2 157.0
1998	162.9	14 741	2 261.6
1999	165.4	15 455	2 241.7
2000	170.3	16 211	2 337.3
2001	173.3	16 839	2 577.5
2002	176.2	17 614	2 682.0

Note: GDP is in market prices, being gross domestic product per capita.
RPI is the retail price index.

The relatively high Durbin–Watson statistic in Equation (1) suggests that the residuals from the equation may cointegrate. An AEG test on these residuals produced (using one nuisance/augmentation term) a value of −5.21 which exceeds (in absolute terms) the critical value of −4.41, but you should try the end of chapter exercise to look at this further.

Now you have before you a simple example of the E–G estimates you should be able to see if they make sense. Remember that you should *not* be commenting on the 't' ratios in the first equation as they are not strictly valid. So we look at Equation (2) and we see that the coefficient on the lagged residual term does not seem very satisfactory, as it is more than 1 in absolute value. Admittedly, given the value of its 't' ratio it would seem to be not significantly different from 1. This suggests that 100 per cent of the gap between the current position for vehicle registrations and long-run equilibrium is made up in each period. Or, to put it another way, the model does not seem to have an error correction representation with these data. Further exploration of this is left to Exercise 14.6.

If we now simply dropped the lagged residual term we would be running a regression in differences. This is the correct approach when *we have an equation with non-stationary data that do not cointegrate.*

Table 14.5 Engle–Granger two-step estimates of a model for new vehicle registrations		
Equation	(1)	(2)
Dependent variable:	NVR	ΔNVRCARS
INT	4092.4	−214.67
	(13.9655)	(1.77)
RPI	−49.3759	
	(9.8249)	
GDP	0.41528	
	(11.2372)	
ΔRPI		−0.66
		(4.02)
ΔGDP		−37.6
		(3.96)
Residual from Equation 1		−1.08
Lagged one period		(4.11)
R squared	0.92575	0.845
F statistic F(2, 13)	81.0385	19.942
DW statistic	1.6810	2.018

Note: Absolute 't' ratios are in parentheses.

There is a three-step extension of the above model proposed by Engle and Yoo (1991). It retains the assumption of a unique cointegration vector and seeks to improve the properties of the first-stage estimates. The third stage is an OLS regression of the residuals from the second stage on the estimated speed of adjustment parameter from the second stage multiplied by X_{t-1}. The resulting parameter is added to the b value from the first stage and these are worked through the model with adjusted standard errors to get a new set of estimates. The purpose of this is to correct finite sample bias in the first step estimates.

HOW THINGS HAVE CHANGED

Before this chapter we were happy to use OLS to test hypotheses about the parameters of a time-series equation, if the Durbin–Watson (or alternative) test was satisfactory. Now we know that two stages of pre-testing are required before we build a model and even after these we would normally find that a static OLS model is not satisfactory. We now look at the Durbin–Watson test in a different light. So, if we go back to studies conducted before the arrival of testing for unit roots and cointegration, then low Durbin–Watson values may worry us because they may now provide us with some support for an absence of cointegration. They may suggest that the equation is not just subject to biased standard errors but, even worse, they may be spurious.

14.7 REVIEW STUDIES

The two studies we now look at concern themselves with some very old propositions about economic relationships. Both deal with propositions named after the people who first proposed them. One concerns a so-called 'law' in the form of Wagner's Law, proposed in 1887, while the other concerns a paradox, termed by J.M. Keynes in 1925 (see Corbak and Oulliaris, 1989) the 'Gibson Paradox', which is therefore an observation that an empirical 'law' of economics seems to be refuted by the facts.

Wagner's Law concerns the relationship between public spending and levels of real national income while the Gibson Paradox is the allegedly illogical positive relationhsip between price levels and interest rates.

Both papers use unit root tests and cointegration to test for the presence of equilibrium relationships in the data, which would support or refute the propositions being tested. Both use annual time series; the Wagner's Law study by Demirbas (1999) uses Turkish data while the study of the Gibson Paradox by Corbae and Oulliaris (1989) uses UK and USA data. These papers do not go on to build models of the relationship between short-run and long-run equilibria using the Engle–Granger two-step method (or indeed the more complicated methods outlined in Section 14.9). Demirbas supplements his analysis by performing Granger causality tests to establish whether public expenditure is causing national income, being caused by it, or both.

The Basic Facts

Authors: Dean Corbae and Sam Oulliaris
Title: A Random Walk Through the Gibson Paradox
Where Published: *Journal of Applied Econometrics*, 1989, **4**, 295–304.
Reason For Study: To re-examine the relationship between interest rates and inflation, which is known as the Gibson Paradox.
Conclusion Reached: 'The high correlation between nominal interest rates and the price level is simply a statistical anomaly and should not be used as grounds for acceptance or rejection of the Gibson paradox.' This is based on the absence of cointegration.

How Did They Do It?

Data: Separate annual data sets for UK 1920–1982 and the USA 1920–1996.
Sample Size: Varies depending on equation.
Technique: DF/ADF tests via OLS.
Dependent Variable: Short- and long-term interest rates.
Focus Variables: Natural log of prices.
Control Variables: There are none in this case.

Presentation

How Results Are Listed: DF and ADF tests.
Goodness of Fit: R^2.
Tests: Augmented Dickey–Fuller tests, D.W., F for the equation.
Diagnosis/Stability: None.
Anomalous Results: See conclusion.

Student Reflection

Things To Look Out For: The authors do not go on to develop a properly specified model and thus cannot really come to a conclusion about the Gibson Paradox. A more detailed model may find cointegration.
Problems in Replication: In principle it should be easy to replicate this study using national statistics for the UK or the USA or other countries.

The Basic Facts

Authors: Safar Demirbas

Title: Cointegration Testing, Causality Analysis and Wagner's Law: The Case of Turkey.

Where Published: University of Leicester, Department of Economics, Working Paper May 1999, presented at conference. You can download this study from the IDEAS website: www.repec.org

Reason for Study: To determine whether the long-run relationship between aggregate public expenditure and aggregate national income (known as Wagner's Law) is supported by the presence of cointegration between income and public expenditure.

Conclusion Reached: There is no empirical support for Wagner's Law in the data used in this paper as the regression of expenditure on income is deemed to be spurious. All data series are integrated of order 1 – they are stationary after first differencing. Six versions of Wagner's Law are estimated and five of these do not show cointegration. Further, there is no evidence of causality between public expenditure and GNP in the data.

How Did They Do It?

Data: Annual Turkish data for 1950–1990.

Sample Size: 41.

Technique: ADF tests for unit roots.

Dependent Variable: Logarithm of Public Expenditure.

Focus Variables: Logarithm of GNP.

Control Variables: None.

Presentation

How Results Are Listed: Coefficients.

Goodness of Fit: R^2.

Tests: Dickey–Fuller tests, augmented Dickey–Fuller tests, CRDW test.

Diagnosis/Stability: Different versions of the test are tried, i.e. with or without intercept and trend.

Anomalous Results: See conclusion.

Student Reflection

Things to Look Out For: As with the other review study on the Gibson Paradox, this paper should be treated with some caution as an explicit model of public expenditure is not developed. Complete models may lead to different conclusions.

Problems in Replication: This study is not, in principle, difficult to replicate as the data used should be easily available for Turkey and a wide range of other countries.

14.8 SOME RESERVATIONS ON THE ABOVE METHODS

So far we have steered clear of problems in the use of unit root tests, cointegration tests and the E–G two-step model. Not surprisingly there are problems. The major ones are listed below. Underlying many of these points is the inherently difficult nature of time-series data. This is reflected in two main issues. One is that we often have quite a small number of observations, meaning that with the use of lag variables we have serious problems with degrees of freedom. The second main problem is that we are dealing with historical data in which there may be unpredictable structural changes. These make forecasting difficult and even when modelling retrospectively they may be hard to account for.

LIMITATIONS OF UNIT ROOT/COINTEGRATION TESTS

Any test is liable to Type I and Type II errors and specification errors. Tests for cointegration and unit roots are, as ever, subject to the problem that we can never know what the true DGP is and can only make assumptions about what may be useful.

Further, the tests are based on autoregressive (AR) processes when there may be moving average (MA) processes at work. This may not be a problem as some simple MA processes can be represented as AR processes but the presence of 'mixed' – that is, combinations of AR and MA processes – may lead to errors of inference.

NUMBER OF COINTEGRATION VECTORS

One problem we may have is that the 'true' relationship in the data set consists of more than one cointegrating vector while the E–G method assumes that there is only one cointegrating vector. Even with exogeneity and hence only one equation in the model we can still have more than one cointegration vector. The maximum number of independent cointegration vectors will be $m - 1$ where m is the number of variables in the model. Ignoring the other cointegration vectors may involve loss of efficiency due to not using all the information in the system effectively. This is similar to the problem of OLS versus systems methods of estimation.

Addressing this limitation requires use of the reduced rank regression methods applied to a VAR (vector autoregression) system in Section 14.11. Ultimately, then, we look to further tests incorporated in computer packages to help us deal with this problem.

COMPLICATIONS IN THE ORDER OF INTEGRATION

The simplest state of the world would be where all our series are I(0) as then we could apply the OLS model of our first eight chapters without fear of serious error, provided there were none of the other specification problems. Given the absence of stationary data, the next most easily dealt with case is where all variables are I(1). Differing orders of integration between series should also not be a serious problem. Things are more problematic if a series has different orders of integration within it. The common cause of this is seasonality (which of course need not be common, in pattern, to all the series used in a model), which can sometimes be dealt with by seasonal differencing. If this is not satisfactory we look to further tests incorporated in computer packages to help us deal with this problem.

ENDOGENEITY

The simple ECM in the Engel–Granger two-step model not only assumed that there was only one cointegration vector, it also assumed that the direction of the relationship ran only from the group of variables designated as independent to the variable chosen as dependent. Tests for exogeneity are incorporated in the Johansen method discussed below at Section 14.11, although we first take a simpler look at this question using bivariate Granger causality tests in the next section.

14.9 GRANGER CAUSALITY

Before moving on to review the most complete approaches to time-series modelling in the next two sections, we briefly look at the method of Granger causality testing which was used by Demirbas in one of the studies in the review panels above.

This test adopts the premise, found in Box–Jenkins time-series analysis (see next section), that a variable can potentially be 'explained' by using its own past values without any use of other variables which might be thought to 'cause' its movements. Let us focus on a case of just two variables, Y_1 and Y_2. We have here four possible outcomes:

Y_1 causes Y_2 and Y_2 causes Y_1

Y_1 causes Y_2 and Y_2 does not cause Y_1

Y_1 does not cause Y_2 and Y_2 does cause Y_1

Y_1 does not cause Y_2 and Y_2 does not cause Y_1

We may say that a variable 'Granger causes' another variable if appropriate results are obtained. For example, in studying inflation the tests will lead to a conclusion on whether 'money growth causes inflation' and/or inflation causes money growth.

The use of the term 'Granger causality' involves exploring which of the four outcomes is correct by running an OLS regression of a series on its own past values but also past values of the other variable. If an 'F' test on the past values of the other variable are statistically significant then it is said to 'Granger cause' the other variable.

Here is another example from cigarette smoking using an unusual sample in that it contains measures of the nicotine content in the cigarettes. The data are taken from Simonich (1991) and the nicotine content is measured in laboratory testing of the cigarettes. The causality arguments are that lower nicotine content would lead to lower consumption due to lesser addiction but there is the converse possibility that weaker cigarettes lead to more cigarettes being purchased. The 'puff rate' may also change – that is, a smoker can get more nicotine out of a given cigarette from changes in the way it is consumed. These are arguments that 'nicotine causes smoking'. The opposite argument is that ' smoking causes nicotine'.

The equations being estimated in Table 14.6 are:

$$CIGPC_t = b_0 + b_1 CIGPC_{t-1} + b_2 CIGPC_{t-2} + b_3 CIGPC_{t-3}$$
$$+ b_4 CIGPC_{t-4} + b_5 NIC_{t-1} + b_6 NIC_{t-2} + b_7 NIC_{t-3}$$
$$+ b_8 NIC_{t-4} + b_9 SG64_t + u_t \qquad (14.12)$$

Table 14.6 Cigarette and nicotine equations: Granger causality tests, USA data 1959Q3–1989Q4

Dependent variable	CIGPC	NIC
INT	170.05	−0.037
	(1.55)	(0.48)
$CIGPC(-1)$	0.367	0.00012
	(3.83)	(1.75)
$CIGPC(-2)$	0.099	−0.00012
	(0.96)	(1.61)
$CIGPC(-3)$	0.167	0.0001
	(1.62)	(1.39)
$CIGPC(-4)$	0.294	0.000041
	(3.024)	(0.6)
$NIC(-1)$	−297.241	1.145
	(1.91)	(10.45)
$NIC(-2)$	263.376	−0.006
	(1.12)	(0.36)
$NIC(-3)$	−34.777	−0.22
	(0.145)	(1.35)
$NIC(-4)$	22.217	0.07
	(0.79)	(0.62)
SG64	−142.78	−0.04
	(3.95)	(1.58)
R squared	0.577	0.987
F(9, 84)	12.7398	688.14
DW statistic	1.7842	1.92
Chi-sq(4) AR(4)	7.8095	2.09
Chi-sq(1) Reset	0.0171	0.005
Chi-sq(2) Normality	1.1446	4.08
Chi-sq(1) Heteroscedast.	1.2737	0.05

Note: *CIGPC* is per capita cigarette consumption in the adult population; *NIC* is the average nictoine content in a cigarette; *SG64* is a health scare dummy which is 1 for 1964 quarters.

$$NIC_t = b_{10} + b_{11} CIGPC_{t-1} + b_{12} CIGPC_{t-2} + b_{13} CIGPC_{t-3}$$
$$+ b_{14} CIGPC_{t-4} + b_{15} NIC_{t-1} + b_{16} NIC_{t-2} + b_{17} NIC_{t-3}$$
$$+ b_{18} NIC_{t-4} + b_{19} SG64_t + v_t \tag{14.13}$$

where *CIGPC* is per capita (adult) consumption, *NIC* is the nicotine content and *SG64* is a dummy for the impact of the health scare caused by the Surgeon General's Report. The *u* and *v* are classical disturbance terms.

The $F_{(4,84)}$ test is 2.72 for the 'nicotine causes smoking hypothesis' which is significant at the 3.5 per cent level, while that for the 'smoking causes nicotine' hypothesis is 1.196 which is significant at the 32 per cent level. There seems to be unidirectional causation running from nicotine to cigarettes. Only the first of the four *NIC* terms is individually significant. Given that it is negative there is support for the idea that lower nicotine cigarettes are consumed in greater numbers. Although these data do not take account of the 'puff rate' it is extremely unlikely that the puff rate would ever be positively correlated with the laboratory measured nicotine yield.

We should note that the usual kind of problems apply here as in any statistical test, most notably that different results may be obtained with different lengths of lag and that the causality may be illusory due to such things as shared measurement error, other specification problems or even the fact that one variable is caused by a different variable which just happens to be correlated with one we have chosen to test.

14.10 TIME–SERIES ANALYSIS AS OPPOSED TO (STRUCTURAL) ECONOMIC ANALYSIS OF TIME SERIES

Long before testing for unit roots and cointegration, and estimating models by Engle–Granger two-step and Johansen–Juselius methods became fashionable among economists, there was an approach known as time-series analysis. This was seen as 'measurement without theory', since its primary purpose was to derive accurate forecasts by modelling the behaviour of series as statistical processes without references to any causal relationships that might be assumed to exist between the variables. This type of work is known as ARIMA (autoregressive integrated moving average) modelling and is usually thought to have begun with work by Box and Jenkins (1982). Estimates of these models are often described as being an application of Box–Jenkins methods. They have been available on computer packages for a long time and caused some embarrassment to economists because its users could perform more accurate forecasting than the structural model based approaches dominant in econometrics.

These models are distinguished from structural economic models (i.e. those in which an equation tries to 'explain' the dependent variable) in a number of ways:

▶ It was proposed that you could use past values of a series to forecast itself without any need for a theoretical model to explain its behaviour. A major motivation for this was to produce efficient forecasts.
▶ Whereas structural economic models have used a restrictive form of DGP – specifically one which focuses on autoregression as in Equation (14.1) – Box–Jenkins models entertain a wider range of processes. Indeed economists have often restricted themselves solely to first order autoregression in their model building.

▶ As there is no theoretical model to guide the building and refinement of the statistical model, there needs to be some sort of criteria or guidelines on how to proceed.

The first of these points should be sufficiently explained in the previous section on Granger causality. The second point can be illustrated in an equation such as the following:

$$Y_t = \mu + \gamma_1 Y_{t-1} + \gamma Y_{t-2} + \ldots + \gamma Y_{t-p} + \varepsilon_t \tag{14.14}$$

which is an autoregressive moving average model of order (p, q), where p is the number of autoregressive terms and q is the number of moving average terms.

The Box–Jenkins methodology required the user to difference the series a number of times in order to achieve stationarity. As we can refer to the number of differences needed as d, we can then talk about an AR (I) MA process of (p, d, q).

There are three broad steps involved in ARIMA modelling:

(i) Identification/model selection

The values of p, d and q must be determined. This is done using the correlogram of the autocorrelation function (ACF) or the corresponding figure for the partial autocorrelation function (PACF) in which the autocorrelation of period k is calculated holding constant the effects of other periods. If a series is not I(0), then, through differencing we should arrive at a series which is I(0). We would determine this from the correlogram.

Once this has been done we look in more detail at the correlogram to determine what type of ARMA process best describes the DGP. This could be one which is solely AR – that is, q will be zero – or one which is solely MA – that is, p will be zero or a mixture of both.

The mixture of both does not need to have the same length of lag on p and q. The way in which one decides on the process to be used is through looking at the combinations of patterns in the ACF and PACF looking for exponential decays, sine waves and significant spikes. For example, the pure MA process has significant spikes at intervals that we would decide are the q value and it should show an exponential decline in its PACF.

It will probably strike you that this does not sound like a very precise process as there does not seem to be a set of rules for identification that can be followed by everyone. Instead the individual has to scrutinize a set of graphs and make a decision, which requires personal skill in decision making. Thus there seems to be an element of 'art' rather than science in ARIMA modelling. Nevertheless, there is no need for an individual to keep secret (except, of course, if it is of commercial value) the (p, d, q) values which they used or the ACF/PACF on which they were based. Therefore someone else could readily propose a different model to test the sensitivity of the results to the choices made.

(ii) Estimation

Under certain circumstances, these models can be estimated by OLS but non-linear least squares methods may be required. There should be no need for you to seek out specific methods of estimation on a computer package as most packages will contain Box–Jenkins procedures usually in a menu which is listed as **Time Series**. Once you tell the package the appropriate values of p and q that you have arrived at from the previous stage, then it should go ahead and estimate the model for you. Given that you are simply telling the computer what to do, there is no reason why you cannot go ahead and estimate an entirely inappropriate model, which is a poor representation of the 'true' underlying DGP which we can never know.

(iii) Diagnostic checking

This simply involves looking at the residuals of the fitted model. If these are not satisfactory, then we go back and change the ARIMA model in the hope of obtaining a better set of results. This process goes on until we achieve a satisfactory set of residuals.

PROBLEMS WITH BOX–JENKINS METHODS

Traditional Box–Jenkins style modelling worried economists because it seemed to be a form of 'measurement without theory' and as such would seem to threaten the importance of economics in the formulation of econometrics. It is important to preclude that it does not rule out the addition of a set of 'explanatory' variables that would be proposed in a structural econometric model. When this is done we refer to the process as ARMAX modelling and this is, again, readily available in the menus of most major software packages. For example, in Limdep the menu command is ARMAX. You should be aware that using an ARMAX command may result in a warning message as there is nothing to stop you specifying values in the (p, d, q) set which cannot or should not be used.

The worry about Box–Jenkins is that, in the extreme case, it might even be seen as legitimating data mining as we simply explore the data and fit a model that the data dictates. This is not quite the same as what we have claimed earlier because the 'traditional' data mining allegation is that someone has acted 'as if' the model estimated is a validation of a theoretical model they claim to be testing.

In such models, forecasts may have been accurate because fairly stable relationships existed in the data. If the forecasts start to worsen then the method says we would respecify the ARMA/ARMAX using the three steps outlined above until we get a better model which we would maintain until further forecasting problems present themselves.

14.11 MORE SOPHISTICATED APPROACHES TO COINTEGRATION TESTING AND SYSTEM MODELLING

In this section we will assume that problems with unit root tests have been handled and that we are concerned solely with how best to establish and model the cointegration relationships that can be found in a set of data.

The two-step method, given above, limited itself to the specification of one cointegration vector between the dependent variable and the independent variables. If it was discovered that the model had more cointegration vectors then the single equation two-stage use of OLS would be inappropriate.

A more sophisticated model would allow for the presence of endogeneity and multiple cointegration vectors. It would do this within the context of simultaneous estimation of the parameters in the model.

The Johansen method of reduced rank regression has been widely adopted to address these issues. This follows the proposals by Sims to model sets of time-series variables using a VAR which is unrestricted subject to the limitation of sample size/model size and hence degrees of freedom.

Sims' VAR involves a set of equations of the form which we previously saw in the Granger causality test for a set of variables which covers the whole model – that is, every variable enters into every other variable.

Each equation is a reduced form where it is regressed on lagged values of itself and lagged values of the other variables in the system. This representation is closely linked to the Granger causality tests we looked at above and has obvious sympathy with the Box–Jenkins way of looking at the evolution of DGPs. It would seem that, with a few adjustments, we can fit all the matters discussed earlier in this chapter into this kind of framework.

This is the approach taken in the Juselius method of reduced rank regression. I cannot go into the technical details of how this is done in a work of this kind. The approach uses maximum likelihood estimation to estimate a VAR, which provides tests for the number of cointegrating vectors. These tests come in the form of comparing hypothesis tests of 0 against 1 or more, 1 against 2 or more and so on.

If there are no cointegrating vectors then we cannot sensibly go on to formulate a model with the existing set of variables and data. If there is one then we will obtain a single equation model from the cointegrating vector, which we would hope is the relationship that we are seeking to investigate. However, we cannot guarantee this is the case, as the data and technique may generate different cointegrating vectors from the ones we are effectively looking for. If there are two or more cointegrating vectors then we have to interpret these as parts of a system of structural equations.

We can still influence the outcome of these results by specification of the overall set of variables and the length of lag and so it is possible to get conflicting results. Tests are used to determine the length of lag that should be used but there are still arguments that there is an element of subjectivity in arriving at a 'final' or preferred specification of a dynamic model.

14.12 CONCLUSION

This chapter has looked at problems of estimation that are specific to time-series data. Due to developments in the econometrics journals, and their incorporation in computer packages, we now find widespread use of tests for unit roots and cointegration. Additionally we also find frequent applications of error correction models (ECM) in many areas of research. A finding of cointegration implies that the set of data can be represented by an ECM. ECMs will contain within them long-run equilibrium solutions.

However, it would be a mistake to suppose that a finding of cointegration necessarily validates economic theory as the belief that it shows long-run equilibrium to exist is an interpretation given to a statistical finding. There are intrinsic problems with time-series data that technical developments in estimation methods do not change. These problems are mainly related to each other:

▶ Sample size
▶ Stability
▶ Aggregation of relationships

Perhaps the most important point highlighted by this chapter, is the degree to which you have to make individual choices of a judgemental nature in building a model once we move out of the most basic level of econometrics. In the first part of this book, once you had decided on your data set and the specification of the list of variables in your model there were relatively few decisions to be made. The introduction of diagnostic testing increased the number of decisions one might have to make – for example, what might be done about possible multicollinearity. When we move to dealing with issues of the DGP in a time series and endogeneity, the number of choices that have to be made greatly multiplies. We can use statistical tests to guide us in making such decisions but ultimately it seems to be the case that personal elements enter into econometric modelling. That is, we cannot guarantee that two people presented with the same data set and asked to answer the same broad question would come up with the same answer.

DOS AND DON'TS

Do

✔ Perform unit root tests and cointegration tests before estimating a time-series model.

✔ Remember that the small sample sizes in many time series limit the power of these tests.

Don't

✘ Confuse the interpretation of the first round regression of the Engle–Granger two-step process with the static model of the earlier chapters where stationarity of all series was assumed.

✘ Forget that there are many different ways of setting up unit root and cointegration tests in terms of the inclusion of constant, trend or augmentation (nuisance) terms.

✘ Forget about the standard econometric problems, which have been highlighted in other chapters, that have been motivated by a finding of cointegration.

EXERCISES

14.1 Give brief answers to the following:

(i) Why do economists now deem it necessary to perform unit root tests on each series before estimating a time-series model?

(ii) What is the meaning of a failure to find cointegration after using an appropriate test?

(iii) What is the interpretation of the adjustment parameter in the Engle–Granger two-step estimation process?

(iv) Is it necessarily the case that time-series studies published before the advent of cointegration and unit root testing are now of no use as pieces of research?

14.2 The following OLS model is regarded as the long-run equation for the demand for motor vehicles:

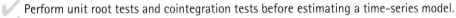

$$\log\left(QMV/POP\right) = \underset{(0.18)}{0.36} + \underset{(0.6)}{0.18\log\left(Y/POP\right)} - \underset{(0.56)}{0.33\log\left(P/Px\right)}$$

$$R^2 = 0.97 \quad D.W. = 1.93$$

where *QMV* is quantity sold; *POP* is population; *Y* is GDP; *P* is price of motor vehicles; *Px* is price of other goods. Standard errors are in parentheses.

(i)   On the basis of this information give a rough idea of whether the model seems to suggest the existence of cointegration.

(ii)   Discuss further your answer to (i) in terms of the economic interpretation of the equilibrium properties of this model.

(iii)   Make some suggestions as to how a valid short-run model might be developed, making sure to include a discussion of the necessary pre-testing of the three regression variables.

(iv)   If the pre-testing in part (iii) indicates that the variables are non-stationary, can the standard errors of the results given above be used to test hypotheses about the long-run parameters.

14.3 **Using the data provided in Table 14.1 (or the same data in the file AUSCIN.XLS) repeat the unit root tests provided in Table 14.2 for the *Admit* and *Pop* variables:**

(i)   With the trend and lagged difference terms omitted.

(ii)   With the trend term omitted and just the first lagged difference term included.

(iii)   With the lagged difference terms omitted but the trend term included.

(iv)   Comment on the differences between the results for these three alternatives and the results in Table 14.2.

14.4 **(i) Repeat the original results of Table 14.1 and the questions asked in the previous exercise with the cinema attendance and population now in natural logarithms.**

(ii)   Comment on the difference between these new results and the previous ones.

14.5 **Using the same data try to establish whether the population and attendance series are I(1) or I(2).**

14.6 **Using the data from Table 14.4 and any further data you may wish to collect, consider making the following additions or alterations to the exploration of the model.**

(i)   Use logarithms instead of linear series.

(ii)   Conduct unit root tests on the three individual series.

(ii)   Reformulate the model in terms of variables included (e.g. prices of cars, use of real income etc., time trend).

(iv)   Re-examine the evidence for cointegration of the residuals in the cointegrating regression given any changes you have made above and using different numbers of nuisance/augmentation terms in the testing process.

14.7 **Comment on the following statement: 'The equations in Table 14.5 are obviously very good as they have high R^2 and strong 't' ratios.'**

REFERENCES

Banerjee, A., Dolado, J.J., Galbraith, J.W. and Hendry, D.F. (1993) *Co-integration, Error Correction and the Econometric Analysis of Non-stationary Data: Advanced Texts in Econometrics*, Oxford University Press, Oxford.

Bhargava, A. and Sargan, J.D. (1983) Testing residuals from least squares regression for being generated by the least squares random walk, *Econometrica*, **51**, 153–174.

Corbae, D. and Oulliaris, S. (1989) A random walk through the Gibson Paradox, *Journal of Applied Econometrics*, **4**, 295–304.

Demirbas, S. (1999) Cointegration testing, causality analysis and Wagner's Law: The case of Turkey, University of Leicester, Department of Economics, Working Paper, May 1999, presented at conference. You can download this study from the IDEAS website: www.repec.org

Engle, R.F. and Granger, C.W.J. (1987) Cointegration and error correction: Representation, estimation and testing, *Econometrica*, **55**, 251–276.

Engle, R.F. and Yoo, B.S. (1991) Cointegrated economic time-series: an overview with new results, in R.F. Engle and C.W.J. Granger (eds.), Long-run Economic Relationships, Oxford University Press, Oxford, 237–266.

Fernandez Blanco, V. and Banos Pino, J.F. (1997) Cinema demand in Spain: A cointegration analysis, *Journal of Cultural Economics*, **21**(1), 57–75.

Granger, C.W.J. and Newbold, P. (1974) Spurious regressions in econometrics, *Journal of Econometrics*, **2**, 111–120.

MacMillan, P. and Smith, I. (2001) Explaining post-war cinema attendance in Great Britain, *Journal of Cultural Economics*, **25**(2), 91–108.

Simonich, W. (1991) *Government Anti-smoking Policies*, Long Highlights, New York.

15

Conclusion

LEARNING OBJECTIVES

- Recapitulate the topics dealt with in the previous chapters and appraise their significance in the overall framework of econometrics
- Be aware of the linkage between the topics dealt with in different chapters of the book
- Increase your recognition of the importance of the nature of the data set in generating econometric problems and the solutions to them

CHAPTER SUMMARY

15.1 INTRODUCTION: TIME TO REVIEW THE SUBJECT FIELD OF ECONOMETRICS – DATA AND TECHNIQUE

This is the final chapter of this book. It does not contain any data or examples as it is assumed that we are not now learning new things but instead reviewing the level of knowledge that has been achieved. This section provides an overview of the subject while the following sections take each chapter in turn and review their contents. These sections also indicate which topics might now be gone into in more depth and what extensions might be made. There is some degree of repetition of earlier material in this chapter. This is deliberate as this chapter is intended primarily for the reader who is going through the book in its actual sequence (or an alternative route map) so that a chance is provided to see how firmly the material already read has lodged in the mind.

You have now completed a journey into the world of econometrics and more generally the application of statistics to the explanation and prediction of human behaviour. The surface manifestation of this journey is the ability to switch on a computer and estimate an equation, or set of equations, using data that you have been given or data that you have collected yourself. Hopefully you can now explain your equations to others and defend them against criticisms. Likewise, you should be able to critically appraise the equations which have been estimated by other people.

Beneath the surface of econometrics there is a rigorous and coherent body of thought which supports the arguments made. This is essentially a book about how to 'do' econometrics in the sense of collecting data, analysing it and coming to some sort of conclusion. There is a large and growing literature on purely theoretical econometrics which has very little connection to any real world data sets although it may take its inspiration from problems thrown up by real world data.

It would seem obvious to anyone beginning the study of econometrics that data is very important, but it is easy to lose sight of this once you are struggling to come to terms with the many pieces of terminology, concepts and techniques which have to be mastered. The body of econometric techniques is based on assumptions, some of which go mainly untested. It might be said that, in econometrics, the quality of the data is important. However, it is not essential for econometrics that data is 'good' in the sense that it is entirely accurate. What is really important is that it does not contain systematic patterns of error (the obvious one being where the errors of a right-hand side variable in a single equation model are correlated with the dependent variable) which interfere with the BLUE properties of the estimators.

Throughout the latter half of the book we have been looking at methods to deal with such problems. Nevertheless, it would be better if we did not have to do so and could obtain data which is more appropriate for the research. Our econometric research is meant to be 'scientific' in the sense that we are conducting an experiment in which models are being tested in an experiment. If our data were experimental then we could 'design' out problems that arise with the use of non-experimental data such as that available as a by-product of the work of government agencies. Unfortunately, given that data is not usually like this we may be left with problems of identification and multicollinearity that no amount of technical sophistication can remove.

Given that our data is never exactly as we would wish, and our models are likewise subject to lack of perfection, it follows that there is something of an 'art' component to econometrics as well as a 'science' component. By this distinction between art and science we mean the following:

THE COMPONENTS OF ECONOMETRICS

▲**Scientific component:** following the rules that you have been taught in the academic study of the subject, which everyone will agree on if the field of econometrics is in a stable state.

▲**Art component:** using elements of personal hunch or judgement to come up with conclusions which someone else, following the same set of scientific rules, might not have come up with.

Neither the art component nor the science component are supposed to be infected by aspects of data mining. One could take the cynical view that data mining is an inevitable feature of human nature and thus the vast bulk of hypothesis tests in applied econometric research are, strictly speaking, invalid. Such serious concerns about data mining could lead to the abandonment of the classical approach for a Bayesian approach, which is discussed below (see Section 15.2).

If we stay in the classical model, and overlook the risk of omnipresent data mining, then the main problem we encounter is: where the basic equation is allowed to be more complex, then two things tend to happen:

(i) The test statistics become unreliable as they do not follow the assumed distribution functions.

(ii) The results for the OLS, or modified estimators, if they can be shown to be valid, will only hold asymptotically, leaving us with the problem of relying on Monte Carlo studies in small samples.

The main technical development (other than a Bayesian approach), in terms of moving beyond the classical OLS model estimators, is to use Maximum Likelihood (ML) estimators. If all of the classical assumptions can be assumed to hold, then the OLS estimators are *exactly equivalent to the ML estimators*. In situations where the classical assumptions do not hold then it is possible to derive ML estimators which have superior properties to the OLS estimators. Because this book is based on the classical approach, we have generally presented modified OLS estimators to deal with specification problems, rather than the 'full' ML estimators. For example, the chapter on simultaneous equations gave some tables of examples of results for IV/ 2SLS (i.e. modified least squares) but did not show any FIML (estimates). However, the chapter on logits and probits did give results from the ML estimation methods, which did use OLS estimates as starting points for the computer algorithm.

If you wished to progress further into the specialist study of econometrics then it would be necessary to become fully familiar with ML methods, as they would be needed in order to develop your own estimators in situations that do not fit the ready-made solutions that we have been dealing with. I now move on to remind you of the main points of each chapter and point out some directions in which you could go in further study of the topics in them.

15.2 CHAPTER 1 REVISITED: METHODOLOGY – BAYESIAN ECONOMETRICS

Chapter 1 provided a very brief tour of the main points of methodological debate in econometrics. The discussion of testing and falsification was rooted in the 'classical' approach to statistics whereby we formulate a hypothesis and then test it, under certain assumptions, with the result that we accept or reject the hypothesis at some level of significance. Although this approach dominates the various 'etrics' (econometrics, sociometrics, psychometrics, cliometrics), there is an alternative approach which has fervent devotees within the academic discipline of pure statistics. It also has some notable supporters, in econometrics, the chief one being Edward Leamer. This alternative is the Bayesian approach.

The term 'Bayesian' stems from the fact that this approach was first proposed by the Reverend Thomas Bayes. Bayesian econometrics is simply application of the general principles of Bayesian statistics to econometrics. There are two key points of difference between Bayesian and classical statistics:

▶ The Bayesian approach explicitly incorporates non-sample information in the form of 'priors'.
▶ The Bayesian approach explicitly allows for the presence of uncertainty about hypotheses and parameters.

The Bayesian approach focuses not on the point estimate of the parameter but instead on the *posterior density function.* You will be aware that there is a density function in the classical regression model also but this is assumed to follow a pre-determined normal distribution, which *all* researchers will accept as the maintained hypothesis. In the Bayesian case, the researcher formulates a *prior* distribution which is combined with the data, using Bayes' theorem to give us the posterior distribution. A good example of this can be found in papers by Leamer (1983) and McManus (1985) on the subject of capital punishment, which deal with a number of different priors about what variables should, or should not, be in the equation. Clearly, the classical approach also takes account of such possibilities but it does so by simply adding or dropping variables without taking into account prior beliefs in formulating significance levels and hypothesis tests.

It follows that the Bayesian approach may give different results to the classical approach and is also more difficult to compute. The latter point is becoming much less important due to the progress in computing power and software. Let us return to the first point: the Bayesian approach will always be controversial to a degree as it may involve simply rejecting certain hypotheses outright from the beginning. That is, if a school of thought has a prior that certain variables categorically *do not* belong in a model then there is little point of them discussing their work with opposing schools of thought except on matters of the range of outcome values over parameters of mutual interest. The Bayesian approach then seems to throw out the idea of a fight between different beliefs to find a winner. This might be thought to be a good thing as classical statistics are full of difficulties if we try to use them in this way. Essentially Bayesians might argue that they are making the whole process more transparent and honest.

A Bayesian approach can be, and has been, applied to all the subsequent topics in this book. There are certainly pockets of Bayesian thought and teaching in econometrics but it is fair to say that the day-to-day practice of econometrics is still dominated by the classical approach taken in this book. This is perhaps hard to explain as, in many ways, a Bayesian approach (as Leamer has consistently argued) seems a better way to incorporate much of what really takes place in econometric work into a coherent framework.

15.3 CHAPTER 2 REVISITED: THE SIGNIFICANCE OF SIGNIFICANCE TESTING

The most important idea introduced in Chapter 2 was the notion of hypothesis testing under classical assumptions. You will notice that the idea of hypothesis testing was greatly extended in later chapters. The hypothesis testing in Chapter 2 was only concerned with the values of the regression parameters. We later encountered two other uses of hypothesis testing: one which comes *before* hypothesis testing of a model in the form of 'pre-testing' and one which comes afterwards in the form of diagnostic testing. So, the modern approach of structural economic time-series analysis starts with pre-tests, then tests the model and then conducts diagnostic tests.

We cannot have classical hypothesis tests without deciding on a significance level. Throughout the book, you will have noticed that the studies reviewed, and the examples given, used significance levels that were, to a degree, arbitrary – that is, there was no particular rationale for using 5 per cent and 10 per cent levels other than that a convention had grown up that people use them. Thus, the rest of the book has completely ignored the discussion of the loss function that was given in Chapter 2 because this is what most economists do. You will recall that a loss function would attribute costs to errors in hypothesis testing and seek to choose a significance level that minimizes these costs of making mistakes.

If we were to take account of the loss function it would have to incorporate pre-tests and diagnostic tests also. It would not make sense to ignore the information about statistical significance that is contained in these when a model is formulated.

The full incorporation of a loss function into the econometric model is meant to be a part of the Bayesian approach outlined in Section 15.2 and this might be considered another argument in its favour. However, it has to be said that Bayesian studies do not always take account of the loss function.

15.4 CHAPTER 3 REVISITED: THE BASIC REGRESSION EQUATION – ARE SINGLE EQUATION MODELS OF ANY USE?

Chapter 3 takes us to the heart of applied econometrics. In it we tested and interpreted coefficients, which was further developed throughout the book. We began with the single equation model, in which there is a variable on the left-hand side that we called the 'dependent' variable, and one or more on the right-hand side that we termed the 'independent' variables. By now you should see that these terms are not really accurate (having looked at systems of equations) and the more correct terms are really to call these the 'regressand' for the left-hand side variable and the 'regressors' for the right-hand side variable.

Having reached this stage you should adopt a critical and cautious approach when you see a single-equation model or decide to use one yourself. You might ask the following questions based on Chapters 12 and 13:

(i) Is it a reduced form equation?

(ii) Are there some special circumstances which mean that this model is entirely appropriate as a structural model even though it contains only one equation?

(iii) If the answer to (ii) is no, what are the likely endogenous variables on the right-hand side of the equation and what would be suitable equations to model these – or failing this, what might be suitable instruments for an IV estimate?

(iv) If the answer to (ii) is no, is it more appropriate to regard the equation that has been estimated as a 'data description' rather than a structural model? That is, we may have arbitrarily selected a variable to be on the left-hand side of an equation rather than choosing it on the basis of prior theory. In such a situation, we are merely interested in the coefficients and 't' tests as indicating the strength of association.

STOCHASTIC REGRESSORS

The later chapters in this book dealt with what happens when assumptions about the CLRM break down. This begins with the process of testing then moves (usually) to the construction of modified estimators. There is another assumption, which might not be tested for, and in some cases could not be tested for. This is the assumption of non-stochastic regressors (or independent variables in the terminology we have used).

It is important to be clear here that we are talking about stochastic regressors which do not co-vary with the *u* term, as that problem is dealt with when we come to the properties of simultaneous equations models.

A constant problem with economics is that the data tends to be non-experimental and therefore the variables on the right-hand side of a regression equation are not controlled by the researcher. To remind you of the difference, an agricultural research station could deliberately vary seed type, fertilizer and so on, to see what happens. Economists are rarely in the position of asking governments to set the tax rate, or any other variable, for their benefit. In such circumstances, the independent variables are stochastic as each variable contains a random term of its own to add to the disturbance term, which is 'added on' to the model. Proofs have been established of the effect of this situation. The conclusion is that OLS estimates are only asymptotically valid. Thus the 't' and 'F' values and critical significance levels will be 'over optimistic' in a finite sample. This means that the hypothesis testing which goes on, for example, of an export supply equation using 44 observations and 6 variables is less reliable than we think it is. And this loss of accuracy is before we get down to the problems of bias due to data mining and the presence of other econometric specification errors (even if corrected for).

MORE ADVANCED METHODS THAN OLS

We should now stress the limitations of the approach taken in Chapter 3. The limitations stem from the reliance on ordinary least squares regression (OLS) as the central method in modelling a set of equations. The advantage of using OLS as the starting point and organizing principle in the study of econometrics is that it is easy to understand and flexible. It does provide a jumping off point to other techniques with some simple modifications. However, it does have its limitations when the classical assumptions are violated.

There are two directions for a more advanced approach to modelling equations under such circumstances. One, maximum likelihood (as mentioned above), deals with model specification problems in a more sophisticated way while the other, **non-parametric regression**, reduces the amount of assumptions that are made when a model is being estimated. We have encountered, at various points, the use of non-parametric statistics for testing single hypotheses (such as the association between two categorical variables) and in doing diagnostic tests (for example on the serial correlation pattern in a set of residuals). The important difference between a non-parametric test and a parametric test is that we do not make distributional assumptions. In particular, the variables do not have to be normally distributed in order for us to conduct a non-parametric test. The same applies to non-parametric regressions which are, however, more difficult to estimate. There are also estimators known as **semi-parametric,** which make some distributional assumptions, but fewer than those of the classical least squares approach.

15.5 CHAPTER 4 REVISITED: MEASUREMENT

The primary purpose of this chapter was to highlight some simple, practical issues involved in the organization and analysis of data. You do not need to be a genius to thoroughly check the sources, meanings and constructions of a data set but you would be rather stupid not to put some effort into doing so.

Apart from the notion of a proxy variable, this chapter did not introduce any additional econometric concepts. The use of a proxy variable seems to allow us to get more out of a data set than we might have expected. That is, it allows us to model something we cannot measure by using other sources of information to which it might be related. We could do this using just one variable to represent the unmeasured variables or we could use a number of variables for each unobserved variable. This kind of thinking can be extended using the methods of principal components and factor analysis which were introduced when we came, later, to the topic of multicollinearity. That is, a number of variables can be combined to make a single proxy using the weights that arise from a factor analysis.

The dangers of the use of proxy variables is that we may tend to forget that we have not really measured the thing we claim to measure. Indeed, we could make this into a deeper criticism of econometrics in that all variables tend to be proxies because many economic concepts are not measurable or statistics are used which are not suitable measures. You could argue that this does not really matter if there is a stable relationship between the variable and its proxy but we have no way of knowing this. Even so, the proxy variable is another example of a stochastic regressor and thus introduces the problem of reliance on asymptotic properties again.

The use of a proxy is another avenue for data mining to creep in. Take the case where we try several different proxies and decide to persevere with the one that 'works best'. This seems close to data mining. Further to this, matters of opinion or judgement enter decisions on the adequacy of a proxy. If one person says that something is a good proxy for risk and uncertainty and someone else says it is not, then it is difficult to resolve this objectively.

15.6 CHAPTER 5 REVISITED: GOODNESS OF FIT AND MODEL SELECTION TESTS

This chapter contains much of the basics of a good grasp of the core of using econometrics.

GOODNESS OF FIT

Chapter 3 presents only one way of measuring goodness of fit, which is the use of the R squared. You should be well aware that, as this is not a test, it cannot be used as a criterion for model selection. That is, we cannot decide between functional forms or which set of variables to include in the equation we are using. We could look at the latter issue using the 'F' statistic in the way that is described in Chapter 6. This involves using the 'explained' sum of squared residuals (ESS) subject to an adjustment dependent on the size of sample (n) and the number of variables (k) in the model. There are a number of other statistics that have been proposed as model selection criteria, which also use the values of n, k and ESS. With the exception of the Akaike Information Criterion (AIC):

$$AIC = (ESS/n) \exp^{(2k/T)} \tag{15.1}$$

Few of these are reported in computer packages or in articles.

Although people like to comment on the highness or lowness of R squared, you should by now be aware that it is of limited usefulness as it does not really tell us anything important. We might be said to be focusing on the fact that it is meaningfully greater than zero when we say it is 'high' and we might be impressed by the fact that it has gone up when we compare different models. If we are doing these things then the relevant approach is to use some kind of specification test such as the 'F' test to compare models.

NESTED AND NON-NESTED TESTS

'F' tests are only applicable in the case of 'nested models' and will, like 't' tests, be invalid under most specification errors in the classical model. Even when we use modified least squares estimators we will be forced to rely on asymptotic properties when using 'F' tests.

All of the examples of 'F' tests in this book used 'nested models', which are models where you can move to one model from the other by the simple process of imposing restrictions on some of the parameters. This amounts to simply dropping variables from the larger model when we use the simplest case of zero restrictions. However, a non-nested model presents more problems. This type of test situation arises when we have models which each contain variables that do not occur in the other model. We deal with this problem by developing test statistics, which use the notion of there being an 'artificial' regression which encompasses these two models. The usual tests employed are the Cox test and the Davidson–Mackinnon 'J' test which is a linearized version of the Cox test.

I shall avoid going into the mechanics of how these tests are done and simply comment on the methodological aspects. There are in fact two tests rather than one in these cases because the hypothesis is set in such a way that each model has the opportunity to be the 'true' model to be tested against the other one. In such a contest between model specifications we can have inconclusive results where it is not possible to decide on one model being superior as the two tests may not agree. While these kinds of tests are appealing, there are many questions over their robustness, which means it would be naive that they could ever successfully make the decisions for us in some kind of statistical 'boxing match' between Monetarists and Keynesians for example.

FORECASTING

This chapter only gave the bare rudiments of model-based forecasting methods. All we did was use estimated coefficients to predict out-of-sample values and then presented some forecast evaluation statistics.

Later chapters have added to the sophistication of the methods used for forecasting. We could use Box–Jenkins methods or structural economic analysis of time series. In the case of simultaneous equation models, where we want to forecast from the equilibrium values of the endogenous variables we have the choice of using directly estimated reduced form predictions or constructing forecasts indirectly from the parameters of the structural equations.

15.7 CHAPTER 6 REVISITED: SIMPLE DYNAMIC MODELS AND NON–LINEARITY

In Chapter 6, the model was extended into two areas: non-linearity and dynamics. This was done in a very simple way – by transforming one or more variables in the set of those appearing in our specified models. For the non-linear case, the logic behind this approach was that we could use *linear estimation methods to estimate non-linear specifications*. For the dynamic model, we were imposing a particular lag structure on the model. This point was taken up further in Chapter 13.

SIMPLE DYNAMIC MODELS

We may use simple dynamic models because of the problem of our lack of knowledge about the complexity of the lag structure for any economic model. While economic theory suggests a wide range of agreement about the relevant explanatory variables in a number of models, it does not give us very clear guidance on how models move towards equilibrium over time. This makes it hard to decide on the treatment of the lagged variables we use to represent adjustment.

A model in which we have unrestricted lags tends to use up degrees of freedom and can give quite unreliable results due to multicollinearity.

Quite the simplest model we can have is the one shown in Table 7.7 (for the Belgian consumption function) where only one lagged variable is used. The development of this model was not explained but it can be arrived at in several different ways:

▶ The Koyck model
▶ The partial adjustment model
▶ The adaptive expectations model

The Koyck model is simply the proposal that all variables follow a geometrically declining pattern. The partial adjustment model assumes that the dependent variable is moving towards some notional equilibrium. Examples of this are the purchases of industrial equipment, houses and the sizes of families. The adaptive expectations model assumes that there is an expected value of a variable, on the right-hand side of the model, such as interest rates in a savings function. An expectational variable cannot be observed directly so we can follow an assumption that its change per period is related to the 'error' in expectations. Manipulation of this relationship gives the lagged dependent variable estimating equation.

These three methods of deriving a simple lagged dependent variable model look exactly the same when we use a computer package to estimate them. Obviously the interpretation of the coefficient on the lagged dependent variable is different. Apart from this the error terms also differ in their properties. Only the partial adjustment model does not suffer from inherent serial correlation. The other models ideally need to be estimated by some kind of IV method.

This means that if our model is supposed to be a partial adjustment model and there are no other specification errors it does not suffer from serial correlation, yet if it is a Koyck model or adaptive expectation model it does so. There is a philosophical peculiarity to this situation. That is, each model looks exactly the same yet they have different meanings and different properties.

These models do have the limitation of only allowing declining lag structures and they are restrictive in other ways such as imposing the same rate of decay. They are best regarded as models to be used for convenience when we have relatively small data sets, which do not permit enough degrees of freedom for elaborate dynamic modelling.

ALMON LAG

These models are still discussed in many textbooks but have tended to be replaced in practice by the general-to-specific modelling approach. They reflect the way in which econometrics developed, until recent times, as a specific-to-general approach. Almon lags are just one example of a general procedure of imposing restrictions on a finite lag distributed lag structure as opposed to the infinite lags just discussed above. Almon lags can allow for lag responses, which increase and then decrease. The Almon technique works by using a polynomial to approximate the lag structure and thereby reducing the number of parameters that have to be estimated.

The Almon lag structure requires the researcher to make decisions about its shape. It is (as are the infinite lag models discussed above) a form of imposing prior restrictions on a model in order to simplify the process of estimation.

NON-LINEAR MODELS: CHOICE OF FUNCTIONAL FORM

Chapter 7 simply presented some linearizations of non-linear models but did not go into the matter of model selection. One way of doing this is, obviously, to choose some specific functional forms and choose between them on the basis of a specification test. The easiest case of this is where we use a simple quadratic because we can then just do a 't' test on the hypothesis that the parameter on the squared term is zero. In more complicated cases, some form of likelihood ratio test could be used to choose between two models.

However, once we leave behind the simple situation of choosing between a linear version of our specified equation and a non-linear version, the question arises of which non-linear version is the best or optimal choice. The form in which I have just stated the problem automatically implies the use of some kind of search process where a computer algorithm adjusts some parameter and arrives at the form, which has the best goodness of fit. There is such a technique, called the Box–Cox method, which can be found on some computer packages.

This consists of estimating, for example, the following functional form when we are searching over a Y transformation:

$$(Y^k - 1)/k = b_0 + b_1 X_1 + u \tag{15.2}$$

As k tends towards 1 this becomes effectively the linear model and as it approaches 0 it is the form with a log dependent variable. Similar transformations can be applied to the X values.

If you think that Box–Cox sounds like a good idea you may be wondering why it was not included in the main body of the book and why it is not a compulsory requirement of all applied econometricians to subject their model to such a search method. The answer to this takes us back to the fundamental issues of econometric methodology. If we use a search process to determine the functional form then we are allowing 'fit' to decide the model and we may end up preferring models which are difficult to interpret and have results which are against our expectations.

In a way this is the opposite of data mining as we are not forcing much structure at all on to the data but instead letting it tell us what the shape of the function is once we have decided the list of variables that go in the model. It should be apparent that the optimal search result would be different if we changed some other aspects of the model. That is, say we add a new variable and re-run the Box–Cox estimation then we will end up with a different functional form.

In practice, applied econometricians tend to do *ad hoc* specification searches over a limited set of combinations of model specification, meaning that you are unlikely to see Box–Cox methods used that often in the typical journal article.

One reason why you are not that likely to see specification searches over functional form is that economists have distinct preferences for certain functional forms. The functional forms in Chapter 6 are particularly restrictive in the case of cost functions. For example, if we use a log-linear model then factor shares must be constant and there can only be increasing, decreasing or constant returns to scale throughout the range. We cannot have a combination of these taking place. Given this problem, the translog cost function has been proposed as a flexible function to be used rather than the simple quadratic type of cost function, which is again very restrictive.

An alternative approach to a search method is to use a functional form, which is sufficiently flexible to incorporate several different forms within it. This type of method has been particularly popular in the case of cost functions. The translog (transcendental logarithmic) cost function has been proposed as a flexible function to be used rather than the simple quadratic type of cost function, which is again very restrictive.

The translog cost function is as follows for a two-factor – capital (K) and labour (L) – model of production (Q) (omitting subscripts):

$$\log Q = \log b_0 + b_1 \log K + b_2 \log L + b_3 \log K.\log L + b_4 (\log K)^2 + b_5 (\log L)^2 + u \qquad \textbf{(15.3)}$$

This has a number of useful properties and has enjoyed a certain degree of popularity in a number of areas of applied econometrics.

As you can see that this includes an interaction term and squared terms, you would not be surprised that, in practice, this can suffer from severe problems of multicollinearity when you try to estimate it.

METHODS OF ESTIMATION

Chapter 6 dealt only with linear methods of estimating models that could be transformed into a linear form. The logical alternative is to use non-linear estimation methods to estimate the non-linear models. Even the most general statistical packages which are not designed specifically for econometrics (such as SPSS) contain non-linear estimation routines.

Direct non-linear estimation would have to be used if we were using a functional form that had mathematical properties such that it could not be transformed. This would require us to write out the functional form explicitly in the appropriate menu window in the software. Non-linear least squares methods use a search method to minimize the sum of squared residuals, as they would not be able to do this directly. The main problem with non-linear estimation techniques is that they may not converge to a unique optimum value.

15.8 CHAPTER 7 REVISITED: ARE ARTIFICIAL VARIABLES SAFE TO PLAY WITH?

Chapter 7 introduced us to the use of trend and dummy variables, which are (like proxy variables) concepts that seem to offer us the chance to do more with our models than might have seemed possible.

There is not an 'advanced' analysis of dummy variables on to which you might move other than, of course, the ML analysis of categorical dependent variable models. The main extension that can be made, which we did not show in the examples in the chapter, would be to have dummies of non-constant weighting or the step/impulse dummies introduced later when we moved to time-series analysis. The point is that dummies do not have to be simply on/off in alignment with the 'event' the impact of which is being measured. Take the following examples:

▶ You are trying to measure the impact of a major event such as 'September the 11th' on share prices.
▶ You are trying to measure the impact of a major public health warning on consumption: such as the heavy publicity given, in early 2004, to the alleged toxicity of farmed salmon.

You could simply model these by allowing for a dummy to take the value of 1 in the period in which the 'shock' takes place. In the case of shares this would usually be a day, and for consumption it would most likely be a quarter. This implies a particular model for the transmission of the shock; that is, that the impact is totally spent in the first observation in the data series. An alternative specification is to let the shock last for a length of time by keeping the dummy set equal to 1 for several periods. But how many do we choose? There is no obvious answer, as we have no clear theory as to people's adaptation to such impulses.

The same problem of end point for the impact of the process still arises if we use a 'decay' dummy (one which fades away) or an 'attack' dummy (one which increases) or some combination of the two. These kinds of dummies would allow the impact to be varying over time.

There are two main problems with dummies:

(i) Their *ad hoc* nature. A specification search over dummy formulation (e.g. experimenting with simple on–off dummies, different lengths of on or off, different patterns of attack etc.) may lead to a model specification which has simply been mined out of the data. We are again back to this familiar problem, which might lead us to again argue for a more Bayesian approach in terms of explicit specification of priors about the dummy variables.

(ii) Bias. A dummy variable is really a special (limited) type of proxy variable. The practice of using simple 0–1 shift dummies for measures of race and sex in log wage equations, to take a familiar example, will give a biased estimate of the percentage of 'discrimination' attributed to the dummy *even if* the model was correctly specified. If there are specification errors in a model in terms of omitted variables then these will be reflected in the size of the coefficient on the dummy. This is a very obvious point. If you simply regressed the log of earnings on a sex dummy the resulting coefficient ($\times 100$) would be an estimate of the gross percentage differential. You would expect this to diminish as you add measures of training, education, union membership and so on, so that you would be getting closer to a 'true' measure, but errors in the measurement of the included variables and omitted variables will cause systematic deviations of the estimate from the 'true' value.

The above passage largely repeats observations made in the dummy variables chapter: it emphasizes the fact that a dummy does *not* measure the impact of some variable correctly. All it really is is a means of attributing a part of the regression residual variation to differences in the composition of the sample.

The arguments made above also apply to the use of trend variables.

15.9 CHAPTER 8 REVISITED: LIMITED DEPENDENT VARIABLE MODELS

The development of models for categorical or 'qualitative' models has been the most rapid area of expansion in econometrics along with time-series modelling in the modern era of high-speed computing. Chapter 8 dealt extensively with the simple and very obvious case of a $0-1$ variable and gave some background for the more complex models. We saw an example in which rescaling the coefficients actually gave quite different results for OLS, probit and logit estimates. This was due to the degree of imbalance in the sample caused by (as is usually the case) using non-experimental data. It is fairly rare for economists to strive to balance the data or structure the responses in any way for the purposes of altering the estimators. The usual approach (as seen in the panel review studies) is to simply include all the data that can be obtained without making any adjustments.

These days academic journals would tend to require the usage of logit or probit for a simple single-equation binary or multiple choice model. If the equation is to be combined with a continuous response element (for example, the 'whether or not to work/how many hours to work') model then the Tobit model is unduly restrictive and one should use Heckit type models.

There are numerous extensions of categorical models in terms of simultaneity, censorship, sample selection, heteroscedasticity and so on, which can be found in the advanced econometrics textbooks and specialist texts.

15.10 CHAPTER 9 REVISITED: THE RELIABILITY OF DIAGNOSTIC TESTS

TESTS

Diagnostic tests are an essential part of econometric work. The simple single equation modelling explored in the first part of this book relies on the classical assumptions if we are to do any hypothesis testing. Chapter 9 presented a number of tests for different assumptions, which we normally make when using single equation OLS models.

The true importance of diagnostic testing is not simply finding out whether or not we are suffering from problem X and trying to 'cure' it but rather any failure on a test is a sign of mis-specification. In other words, we may have a faulty model although we could simply have faulty, or inappropriate, data.

We can think of the tests in Chapter 9 as 'second round' tests that are providing information on the reliability of the first round tests. But this would seem to raise another question, which is: can we trust the results of the second round tests? As these are themselves hypothesis tests, then we need to think about the significance levels that are chosen for them and any problems of bias etc. that there might be in the diagnostic tests. This factor could be incorporated in the loss function.

OBTAINING RESIDUALS

The major weakness of diagnostic tests conducted using the OLS residuals, from an estimated model, is that these may deviate in important ways from the 'true' value of the unobservable disturbance terms. There is a built-in problem of bias here in the estimation of the residuals because we are using OLS estimates to get the residuals in a situation where OLS is only appropriate if the tests did not need to be done. Because of this problem, there has been a long-standing specialist econometrics literature on the idea of using differently constructed residuals to conduct diagnostic tests.

These kinds of residuals are LUS or BLUS, that is, best, linear and possess a scalar covariance matrix. There are methods to calculate LUS residuals by first partitioning the observations. We can also use 'recursive residuals' as these will have the LUS property. These methods are largely confined to the specialist econometrics literature as the vast majority of applied econometrics is carried on using the unsatisfactory, but easy to obtain, OLS residuals to perform hypothesis tests.

15.11 CHAPTER 10 REVISITED: MULTICOLLINEARITY

We saw that multicollinearity arises when there are linear relationships between the variables on the right-hand side of a regression equation. It seems to be a serious threat to the testing and use of econometric models despite the fact that it does not violate any of the classical assumptions about the disturbance term.

If multicollinearity is so bad that a model becomes unusable then we should really blame the situation on bad model building and bad data collection. So it follows that multicollinearity is not an area in which there has been technical progress in solving the problem nor is there likely to be. Ridge regression type methods can be refined but they do not solve the problem in anything other than a mechanical method.

It is probably safe to say that compared with the other topics being reviewed in this chapter, there is not much you can further learn about multicollinearity that will be of much use. The lesson to be learned is to check for it and better still put some effort into gathering data and setting up a model that will not be multicollinear. You may feel that given such a simple message, we have been wasting time going through some of the material in the multicollinearity chapter. However, it is necessary to be aware of the discussions on 'cures' and tests for multicollinearity as it may give you useful insights into the nature of the CLRM in general.

15.12 CHAPTER 11 REVISITED: HETEROSCEDASTICITY

This chapter looked at dealing with the violation of the assumption of homoscedasticity. We have already introduced the idea of using (B)LUS residuals rather than the regression residuals in this final summary chapter.

Heteroscedasticity causes the 't' and 'F' statistics to be incorrect leading (usually) to us being too ready to reject the null. We saw two ways of dealing with this – the use of modified (GLS/WLS) estimators to produce 'correct' standard errors and the correction of the standard errors themselves by White's method. The improvement in estimators via these methods relies on asymptotic properties.

There are obviously a large number of heteroscedastic 'corrections' that we could apply to any OLS equation unless we have some explicit reason to use a particular formulation such as knowledge about the nature of the data. The alternative to the 'trial and error' method is to use a fairly flexible general formulation (which is the idea behind the 'White standard errors').

In day-to-day practice, most econometrics is carried out along a simple *ad hoc* strategy of the following type:

▶ Ignore heteroscedasticity unless the data, model or tests give you a reason to suspect its presence. If it does seem to be present then
▶ Simply report the White standard errors (or 't' ratios) in the hope that this provides a reasonably adequate hypothesis test.

The main development of the treatment of heteroscedasticity into a more advanced topic is in the case of ARCH (autoregressive conditional heteroscedasticity) and GARCH (generalized autoregressive conditional heteroscedasticity) models, which are used mainly in financial time-series analysis. Many econometric packages contain routines for these, particularly those specializing in time series.

15.13 CHAPTER 12 REVISITED: IDENTIFICATION

We have taken the unusual step of giving identification a whole chapter to itself. Econometrics textbooks usually include a section on identification within a chapter on simultaneous equation methods. This section tends to come after the estimation issues surrounding multiple equation models have been outlined. There are a number of reasons for taking the approach used here:

▶ As other books make clear, identification is logically prior to the estimation of the equations so it makes sense to know exactly what it is and how to check it before becoming accustomed to the estimation techniques.
▶ Identification is a philosophically important issue, which deserves to be highlighted.

From a methodological point of view, identification (along with the general difficulty of correct measurement of variables) is perhaps the major weak spot of econometric modelling. The fundamental difficulty of establishing that a model is identified cannot be 'solved' by the fantastic advances in testing and computer software implementation that have taken place in recent decades. Identification requires a degree of 'faith' by the researcher in the assumptions that have been made and it is this which makes it a philosophical rather than merely technical issue.

15.14 CHAPTER 13 REVISITED: SYSTEMS OF EQUATIONS

Assuming that we can accept that an equation is capable of being identified, it is essential to know about systems estimation for the simple reason that it will, in theory, provide 'better' estimates. These methods fall into two broad categories:

▶ Single equation methods
▶ Full systems methods

We tend to expect that the latter are better than the former because it would seem logical that the more information you use in formulating estimators then the more satisfactory they should be. Given that we have adhered to the notion of BLUEness as the criteria for estimators, the usual gain from more complex estimators is in terms of the E (efficiency) part.

However, it is important to remember the perpetual problem of econometrics, which is of course the data itself. Data on variables may not only be of poor quality it may be non-existent, i.e. there is no information to generate a measure for a particular concept or the proxies may be so weakly linked to the original variable as to be questionable. In these circumstances, more sophisticated methods face the problem of transmission of specification error across the model. That is, better techniques will not necessarily give better results when the models cannot be specified adequately.

We also face the persistent problem, when we go beyond simple OLS, that the justification for improved estimator properties is asymptotic.

The general view, in applied econometrics, is that an IV/2SLS estimate would generally be superior to an OLS estimate in terms of its properties and should therefore be given more weight in coming to conclusions. We also face the problems of identification already discussed above. As has been stressed in the chapter itself, you can produce an IV estimate, which may look plausible, but is, in fact, conceptually meaningless because the equation is not identified – but this has not been brought to light because a full model has not been specified.

15.15 CHAPTER 14 REVISITED: TIME-SERIES ANALYSIS

Of all the topics in this book, the analysis of time series is the one in which there has been most development in the last 20 years or so. The arrival of cointegration and unit root tests led to a series of papers testing for stationarity of individual data series and the residuals from OLS single equation models. The papers I chose for the review studies are examples of this early literature.

The next stage of development from this type of treatment of time series was the arrival of the Engel–Granger two-step model, which is still popular in many areas of applied economics. You should not be confused by the way this model is presented into overlooking the fact that it is a simple ARDL model of the type which could be specified simply by using lagged variables. The E–G two-step model is simply an alternative method of estimating such a model from direct OLS.

Structural time-series econometrics has produced a growing complexity of modelling ideas. As in all areas of econometrics, when these have full user-friendly implementation in software packages the newer, more 'difficult' methods will trickle down into everyday use by the average applied econometrician.

There is a continual flow of work by specialist econometricians on the further refinement of unit root testing, cointegration testing and the estimation of models. It is probably fair to say that the main developments in this field have been made as far as practical use of econometrics goes. The main problem we still face in time-series analysis is the obvious, but serious one, of data limitations.

15.16 FINAL WORDS: WHAT USE IS ECONOMETRICS?

As indicated in Chapter 1, despite the widespread use of econometrics there are some people within the economics profession who would consider econometrics to be of no use whatsoever. There are others who hold a variety of less extreme views which might include some of these propositions:

► Econometrics is useful to a degree but, like weapons, can be dangerous in the wrong hands.
► Econometrics is useful to a degree but it leads to a waste of resources due to a narrow focus on testing propositions – often with weak data. Thus econometrics may hold back the growth of useful ideas as it only focuses on ideas that can be tested.
► Econometrics is useful and can promote the growth of scientific knowledge in economics.

The third argument was well debated in the clinometric literature arising from the expansion of econometrics into economic history. The key point made was that the use of econometrics forced people to put their ideas into a clear and concise format where ideas could be rejected and reformulated and thus debate could move on. This would not happen in any systematic way if there was no test-based use of data.

The basis of most negative views of econometrics lies in these points:

(i) Data mining is bound to occur and so any results are just a fiction produced by an econometrician setting out to make sure they get certain results in order to be published in a journal or receive consultancy fees or funds.

(ii) The most important equations cannot possibly be stable as there are so many reasons for change in the underlying behaviour that the parameters cannot possibly be constant. In this view, then, even the most fantastically sophisticated and hard-to-understand econometric model is really only a 'snapshot' data description of what is going on in a particular set of data.

Econometrics is, then, the logical extension of the 'scientific' or 'positivist' orientation that has dominated the thinking of economics. Economists have striven to generate models that deliver hypotheses that are supposed to be free from prejudice or opinion. Things can never be perfect nor can we expect progress in accumulating supported hypotheses to be quick. Normative elements may always creep into modelling, for example if a person believes that some activity is 'bad' for moral reason they may be subconsciously led into trying to support this. The hope of econometricians is that open debate particularly with explicit methodologies of modelling and substantial replication can clarify the stability of particular findings and the reasons why they were obtained. As I have been stressing in this chapter, the logical alternative is for a bigger infusion of Bayesian ideas into the everyday uses of econometrics.

EXERCISES

15.1 List the major differences between econometrics and statistics as academic disciplines.

15.2 Explain the difference between an 'economically significant' and a 'statistically significant' finding.

15.3 Can we conduct research without falling into 'data mining'? Discuss.

15.4 Read Chapter 1 of this book again and consider whether it makes more sense to you now than it did before.

FURTHER READING

Leamer, E. (1983) Let's take the con out of econometrics, *American Economic Review*, **73**, 31–43.
McManus, W. (1985) Estimates of the deterrent effect of capital punishment, *Journal of Political Economy*, **93**, 417–425.

Hopefully you will have read some of the articles that were summarized in the highlighted panels of previous chapters and a sample of others in your particular topic areas of interest. The additional techniques and approaches mentioned in this chapter can be found in advanced textbooks of econometrics such as:

Greene, W.H. (2000) *Econometric Analyis*, 4th edn, Prentice-Hall, Upper Saddle River, NJ.
Judge, G.G., Griffiths, W.E., Hill, R.C., Lütkepohl, H. and Lee, T.C. (1985) *The Theory and Practice of Econometrics*, 2nd edn, Wiley, New York.

Appendix 1

BLANK TEMPLATE FOR REVIEW STUDIES

The Basic Facts

Authors:
Title:
Where Published:
Reason for Study:
Conclusion Reached:

How Did They Do It?

Data:
Sample Size:
Technique:
Dependent Variable:
Focus Variables:
Control Variables:

Presentation

How Results Are Listed:
Goodness of Fit:
Tests:
Diagnosis/Stability:
Anomalous Results:

Student Reflection

Things to Look Out For:
Problems in Replication:

Appendix 2: Data sets

The following list gives file names of Excel files which can be downloaded from the website for the book. A brief description is given. Fuller details can be found on the website.

AUSCIN.XLS
Short time series of Australian cinema and population statistics.
BELGCONS.XLS
Short time series of Belgian aggregate consumption and expenditure data.
GROWTH.XLS
Cross-section data for a number of countries on economic growth and variables thought to be related to it.
LONGLEY.XLS
Short time series for the USA which has been used to demonstrate multicollinearity problems and check the accuracy of software.
NEWCARS.XLS
Short time series for the UK which features new car registrations and some other relevant data.
THEATRE.XLS
Individual level interview study conducted in the UK in July/August 2003 on people's attitudes to attendance at local theatre and their general arts/entertainment consumption.
TURKCIG.XLS
Short time series on cigarette consumption, and some other relevant data, for Turkey.
USADAT.XLS
Cross-section (from 1980) of data for all states in the USA on a range of social and economic data including crime rates.
ZIPS.XLS
Short time series on the sales of zip fasteners.

Aside from the data sets given above, users of SPSS should also find that their copy of the package has a large number of specimen data sets located in the program folder. This is also true of most dedicated econometric packages.

Appendix 3: The notion of causality

Econometrics now contains frequent uses of the word 'causality'. Even when the word is not being used, any study is based on some ideas about the causality which is present in the model and data being analysed. Time-series analysis, particularly Granger causality tests, have made the word more prominent.

However, there have always been ideas about causality in basic econometrics and statistics teaching. The remark 'correlation does not imply causality' has frequently been impressed upon the beginning student of statistics. This is usually in the context of partial correlation coefficients. The idea is that if we find, say, an r of 0.9 between two variables this is purely a statistical association which cannot be used to show that either 'X causes Y' or conversely that 'Y causes X'. The relationship could be due to correlated measurement errors. It could be 'spurious' in the sense discussed in Chapter 14. It may also be spurious in the sense that some other (omitted) variable is responsible for the observed correlation.

Econometrics books do not tend to extend the 'correlation does not imply causation' into an equivalent remark that 'regression does not imply causation'. Rather, they express caution about the meaning of statistical associations in regression by putting the word 'explains' in quotation marks as in a statement like 'the independent variables "explain" 63 per cent of the dependent variable'. The use of quotation marks is done to imply that we do not literally mean that the right-hand side variables are explaining the left-hand side variable as we have no way of knowing that this is true. All we can know is that we have found a statistical relationship between series of data for some variables. A statistical relationship does not necessarily demonstrate a 'real' relationship when we are dealing with non-experimental data or data which has poor experimental controls.

The situation is more complicated when we come to the multiple equation models such as the IV/2SLS and path models of Chapter 13 and to the problem of multiple cointegration vectors in Chapter 14. Now the notion of causality has to be expanded as it can go in numerous directions. In a model of many variables there can be causal relationships in both directions and between any combination of variables. In the extreme case, where we do not exclude any of the possible causal relationships, we would have a model where none of the structural equations are identified. Identification of equations is therefore achieved by deliberately ruling out certain causal relationships. This is based on assumptions made prior to testing the model. Identification is thus achieved by maintained hypotheses.

Outside of econometrics, there has been a long debate on the notion of causality among philosophers. What we are talking about is the relationship between **cause** and **effect**. The classic example of this in economics would be the debate about money supply and the rate of inflation. If we observe, other things being equal, that higher money supply growth means higher inflation rates then we have to ask: which is the cause and which is the effect or do we have a situation where each is causing the other? This is what the Granger causality tests in Section 14.9 of Chapter 14 seek to establish.

Such tests require that time be involved because the only way we would seem to be able to separate cause and effect is by finding a cause and looking to see if it is followed by the expected effect at a later date. This is much easier to do in the case of a 'natural' experiment. For example, we might give different amounts of drugs to laboratory rats to see how much it takes to make them go blind. The crucial issue is the time lag – that is, how long after the cause does it take before the effect arises. This is more of a problem in the non-experimental context where other factors may be operating in variable and unpredictable ways in between the time of the cause happening and the effect being observed.

As the pattern of causes and effects are spread over time we face the difficulty of working out which is which. It is obvious, in a laboratory, that rats do not 'cause' drugs. Likewise Christmas cards, birthday cards or cards celebrating religious festivals do not cause the events they celebrate even though they happen before them, using a calendar year as the time frame.

These circumstances allow us to come to a clear conclusion about the direction of causality. That is, we have unicausal relationships where X causes Y but not the other way round. We come to clear conclusions because we have prior knowledge. In the laboratory experiment, the prior knowledge is that the experimenter has control of the situation and has therefore excluded the reverse causal relationship. In the celebration cards situation, we know from our knowledge of the institutions of society what the causal relationship is.

In most economics research, we can only make limited reliance on these factors in dealing with the focus variables we have selected. Hence, we fall back on the approaches given above. Either we simply make assumptions about the direction of causality or we do Granger causality tests or tests for the number of cointegration vectors.

Appendix 4: Statistical tables

The following tables provide critical values for a number of well-known statistical distributions.

Critical values for the normal distribution

Area under the Normal Curve from 0 to X

X	0.00	0.01	0.02	0.03	0.04	0.05	0.06	0.07	0.08	0.09
0.0	0.00000	0.00399	0.00798	0.01197	0.01595	0.01994	0.02392	0.02790	0.03188	0.03586
0.1	0.03983	0.04380	0.04776	0.05172	0.05567	0.05962	0.06356	0.06749	0.07142	0.07535
0.2	0.07926	0.08317	0.08706	0.09095	0.09483	0.09871	0.10257	0.10642	0.11026	0.11409
0.3	0.11791	0.12172	0.12552	0.12930	0.13307	0.13683	0.14058	0.14431	0.14803	0.15173
0.4	0.15542	0.15910	0.16276	0.16640	0.17003	0.17364	0.17724	0.18082	0.18439	0.18793
0.5	0.19146	0.19497	0.19847	0.20194	0.20540	0.20884	0.21226	0.21566	0.21904	0.22240
0.6	0.22575	0.22907	0.23237	0.23565	0.23891	0.24215	0.24537	0.24857	0.25175	0.25490
0.7	0.25804	0.26115	0.26424	0.26730	0.27035	0.27337	0.27637	0.27935	0.28230	0.28524
0.8	0.28814	0.29103	0.29389	0.29673	0.29955	0.30234	0.30511	0.30785	0.31057	0.31327
0.9	0.31594	0.31859	0.32121	0.32381	0.32639	0.32894	0.33147	0.33398	0.33646	0.33891
1.0	0.34134	0.34375	0.34614	0.34849	0.35083	0.35314	0.35543	0.35769	0.35993	0.0.36214
1.1	0.36433	0.36650	0.36864	0.37076	0.37286	0.35314	0.37698	0.37900	0.38100	0.38298
1.2	0.38493	0.38686	0.38877	0.39065	0.39251	0.39435	0.39617	0.39796	0.39973	0.40147
1.3	0.40320	0.40490	0.40658	0.40824	0.40988	0.41149	0.41308	0.41466	0.41621	0.41774
1.4	0.41924	0.42073	0.42220	0.42364	0.42507	0.42647	0.42785	0.42922	0.43056	0.43189
1.5	0.43319	0.43448	0.43574	0.43699	0.43822	0.43943	0.44062	0.44179	0.44295	0.44408
1.6	0.44520	0.44630	0.44738	0.44845	0.44950	0.45053	0.45154	0.45254	0.45352	0.45449
1.7	0.45543	0.45637	0.45728	0.45818	0.45907	0.45994	0.46080	0.46164	0.46246	0.46327
1.8	0.46407	0.46485	0.46562	0.46638	0.46712	0.46784	0.46856	0.46926	0.46995	0.47062
1.9	0.47128	0.47193	0.47257	0.47320	0.47381	0.47441	0.47500	0.47558	0.47615	0.47670
2.0	0.47725	0.47778	0.47831	0.47882	0.47932	0.47982	0.48030	0.48077	0.48124	0.48169
2.1	0.48214	0.48257	0.48300	0.48341	0.48382	0.48422	0.48461	0.48500	0.48537	0.48574
2.2	0.48610	0.48645	0.48679	0.48713	0.48745	0.48778	0.48809	0.48840	0.48870	0.48899
2.3	0.48928	0.48956	0.48983	0.49010	0.49036	0.49061	0.49086	0.49111	0.49134	0.49158

2.4	0.49180	0.49202	0.49224	0.49245	0.49266	0.49286	0.49305	0.49324	0.49343	0.49361
2.5	0.49379	0.49396	0.49413	0.49430	0.49446	0.49461	0.49477	0.49492	0.49506	0.49520
2.6	0.49534	0.49547	0.49560	0.49573	0.49585	0.49598	0.49609	0.49621	0.49632	0.49643
2.7	0.49653	0.49664	0.49674	0.49683	0.49693	0.49702	0.49711	0.49720	0.49728	0.49736
2.8	0.49744	0.49752	0.49760	0.49767	0.49774	0.49781	0.49788	0.49795	0.49801	0.49807
2.9	0.49813	0.49819	0.49825	0.49831	0.49836	0.49841	0.49846	0.49851	0.49856	0.49861
3.0	0.49865	0.49869	0.49874	0.49878	0.49882	0.49886	0.49889	0.49893	0.49896	0.49900
3.1	0.49903	0.49906	0.49910	0.49913	0.49916	0.49918	0.49921	0.49924	0.49926	0.49929
3.2	0.49931	0.49934	0.49936	0.49938	0.49940	0.49942	0.49944	0.49946	0.49948	0.49950
3.3	0.49952	0.49953	0.49955	0.49957	0.49958	0.49960	0.49961	0.49962	0.49964	0.49965
3.4	0.49966	0.49968	0.49969	0.49970	0.49971	0.49972	0.49973	0.49974	0.49975	0.49976
3.5	0.49977	0.49978	0.49978	0.49979	0.49980	0.49981	0.49981	0.49982	0.49983	0.49983
3.6	0.49984	0.49985	0.49985	0.49986	0.49986	0.49987	0.49987	0.49988	0.49988	0.49989
3.7	0.49989	0.49990	0.49990	0.49990	0.49991	0.49991	0.49992	0.49992	0.49992	0.49992
3.8	0.49993	0.49993	0.49993	0.49994	0.49994	0.49994	0.49994	0.49995	0.49995	0.49995
3.9	0.49995	0.49995	0.49996	0.49996	0.49996	0.49996	0.49996	0.49996	0.49997	0.49997
4.0	0.49997	0.49997	0.49997	0.49997	0.49997	0.49997	0.49998	0.49998	0.49998	0.49998

Upper critical values of Chi-square distribution with degrees of freedom

Probability of exceeding the critical value

d.f.	0.10	0.05	0.025	0.01	0.001
1	2.706	3.841	5.024	6.635	10.828
2	4.605	5.991	7.378	9.210	13.816
3	6.251	7.815	9.348	11.345	16.266
4	7.779	9.488	11.143	13.277	18.467
5	9.236	11.070	12.833	15.086	20.515
6	10.645	12.592	14.449	16.812	22.458
7	12.017	14.067	16.013	18.475	24.322
8	13.362	15.507	17.535	20.090	26.125
9	14.684	16.919	19.023	21.666	27.877
10	15.987	18.307	20.483	23.209	29.588
11	17.275	19.675	21.920	24.725	31.264
12	18.549	21.026	23.337	26.217	32.910
13	19.812	22.362	24.736	27.688	34.528
14	21.064	23.685	26.119	29.141	36.123
15	22.307	24.996	27.488	30.578	37.697
16	23.542	26.296	28.845	32.000	39.252
17	24.769	27.587	30.191	33.409	40.790
18	25.989	28.869	31.526	34.805	42.312
19	27.204	30.144	32.852	36.191	43.820
20	28.412	31.410	34.170	37.566	45.315
21	29.615	32.671	35.479	38.932	46.797
22	30.813	33.924	36.781	40.289	48.268
23	32.007	35.172	38.076	41.638	49.728
24	33.196	36.415	39.364	42.980	51.179
25	34.382	37.652	40.646	44.314	52.620
26	35.563	38.885	41.923	45.642	54.052
27	36.741	40.113	43.195	46.963	55.476
28	37.916	41.337	44.461	48.278	56.892
29	39.087	42.557	45.722	49.588	58.301
30	40.256	43.773	46.979	50.892	59.703

UPPER CRITICAL VALUES OF THE F DISTRIBUTION

The following tables for values from 5 to 100 are included:

One sided, 5% significance level, = 1–10
One sided, 10% significance level, = 1–10
One sided, 1% significance level, = 1–10

	Upper critical values of the F distribution for numerator degrees of freedom and denominator degrees of freedom, 5% significance level								
	1	2	3	4	5	6	7	8	9	10
5	6.608	5.786	5.409	5.192	5.050	4.950	4.876	4.818	4.772	4.735
6	5.987	5.143	4.757	4.534	4.387	4.284	4.207	4.147	4.099	4.060
7	5.591	4.737	4.347	4.120	3.972	3.866	3.787	3.726	3.677	3.637
8	5.318	4.459	4.066	3.838	3.687	3.581	3.500	3.438	3.388	3.347
9	5.117	4.256	3.863	3.633	3.482	3.374	3.293	3.230	3.179	3.137
10	4.965	4.103	3.708	3.478	3.326	3.217	3.135	3.072	3.020	2.978
11	4.844	3.982	3.587	3.357	3.204	3.095	3.012	2.948	2.896	2.854
12	4.747	3.885	3.490	3.259	3.106	2.996	2.913	2.849	2.796	2.753
13	4.667	3.806	3.411	3.179	3.025	2.915	2.832	2.767	2.714	2.671
14	4.600	3.739	3.344	3.112	2.958	2.848	2.764	2.699	2.646	2.602
15	4.543	3.682	3.287	3.056	2.901	2.790	2.707	2.641	2.588	2.544
16	4.494	3.634	3.239	3.007	2.852	2.741	2.657	2.591	2.538	2.494
17	4.451	3.592	3.197	2.965	2.810	2.699	2.614	2.548	2.494	2.450
18	4.414	3.555	3.160	2.928	2.773	2.661	2.577	2.510	2.456	2.412
19	4.381	3.522	3.127	2.895	2.740	2.628	2.544	2.477	2.423	2.378
20	4.351	3.493	3.098	2.866	2.711	2.599	2.514	2.447	2.393	2.348
21	4.325	3.467	3.072	2.840	2.685	2.573	2.488	2.420	2.366	2.321
22	4.301	3.443	3.049	2.817	2.661	2.549	2.464	2.397	2.342	2.297
23	4.279	3.422	3.028	2.796	2.640	2.528	2.442	2.375	2.320	2.275
24	4.260	3.403	3.009	2.776	2.621	2.508	2.423	2.355	2.300	2.255
25	4.242	3.385	2.991	2.759	2.603	2.490	2.405	2.337	2.282	2.236
26	4.225	3.369	2.975	2.743	2.587	2.474	2.388	2.321	2.265	2.220
27	4.210	3.354	2.960	2.728	2.572	2.459	2.373	2.305	2.250	2.204
28	4.196	3.340	2.947	2.714	2.558	2.445	2.359	2.291	2.236	2.190
29	4.183	3.328	2.934	2.701	2.545	2.432	2.346	2.278	2.223	2.177
30	4.171	3.316	2.922	2.690	2.534	2.421	2.334	2.266	2.211	2.165
31	4.160	3.305	2.911	2.679	2.523	2.409	2.323	2.255	2.199	2.153
32	4.149	3.295	2.901	2.668	2.512	2.399	2.313	2.244	2.189	2.142
33	4.139	3.285	2.892	2.659	2.503	2.389	2.303	2.235	2.179	2.133
34	4.130	3.276	2.883	2.650	2.494	2.380	2.294	2.225	2.170	2.123
35	4.121	3.267	2.874	2.641	2.485	2.372	2.285	2.217	2.161	2.114
36	4.113	3.259	2.866	2.634	2.477	2.364	2.277	2.209	2.153	2.106
37	4.105	3.252	2.859	2.626	2.470	2.356	2.270	2.201	2.145	2.098
38	4.098	3.245	2.852	2.619	2.463	2.349	2.262	2.194	2.138	2.091
39	4.091	3.238	2.845	2.612	2.456	2.342	2.255	2.187	2.131	2.084

	1	2	3	4	5	6	7	8	9	10

Upper critical values of the F distribution for numerator degrees of freedom and denominator degrees of freedom, 5% significance level (continued)

	1	2	3	4	5	6	7	8	9	10
40	4.085	3.232	2.839	2.606	2.449	2.336	2.249	2.180	2.124	2.077
41	4.079	3.226	2.833	2.600	2.443	2.330	2.243	2.174	2.118	2.071
42	4.073	3.220	2.827	2.594	2.438	2.324	2.237	2.168	2.112	2.065
43	4.067	3.214	2.822	2.589	2.432	2.318	2.232	2.163	2.106	2.059
44	4.062	3.209	2.816	2.584	2.427	2.313	2.226	2.157	2.101	2.054
45	4.057	3.204	2.812	2.579	2.422	2.308	2.221	2.152	2.096	2.049
46	4.052	3.200	2.807	2.574	2.417	2.304	2.216	2.147	2.091	2.044
47	4.047	3.195	2.802	2.570	2.413	2.299	2.212	2.143	2.086	2.039
48	4.043	3.191	2.798	2.565	2.409	2.295	2.207	2.138	2.082	2.035
49	4.038	3.187	2.794	2.561	2.404	2.290	2.203	2.134	2.077	2.030
50	4.034	3.183	2.790	2.557	2.400	2.286	2.199	2.130	2.073	2.026
51	4.030	3.179	2.786	2.553	2.397	2.283	2.195	2.126	2.069	2.022
52	4.027	3.175	2.783	2.550	2.393	2.279	2.192	2.122	2.066	2.018
53	4.023	3.172	2.779	2.546	2.389	2.275	2.188	2.119	2.062	2.015
54	4.020	3.168	2.776	2.543	2.386	2.272	2.185	2.115	2.059	2.011
55	4.016	3.165	2.773	2.540	2.383	2.269	2.181	2.112	2.055	2.008
56	4.013	3.162	2.769	2.537	2.380	2.266	2.178	2.109	2.052	2.005
57	4.010	3.159	2.766	2.534	2.377	2.263	2.175	2.106	2.049	2.001
58	4.007	3.156	2.764	2.531	2.374	2.260	2.172	2.103	2.046	1.998
59	4.004	3.153	2.761	2.528	2.371	2.257	2.169	2.100	2.043	1.995
60	4.001	3.150	2.758	2.525	2.368	2.254	2.167	2.097	2.040	1.993
61	3.998	3.148	2.755	2.523	2.366	2.251	2.164	2.094	2.037	1.990
62	3.996	3.145	2.753	2.520	2.363	2.249	2.161	2.092	2.035	1.987
63	3.993	3.143	2.751	2.518	2.361	2.246	2.159	2.089	2.032	1.985
64	3.991	3.140	2.748	2.515	2.358	2.244	2.156	2.087	2.030	1.982
65	3.989	3.138	2.746	2.513	2.356	2.242	2.154	2.084	2.027	1.980
66	3.986	3.136	2.744	2.511	2.354	2.239	2.152	2.082	2.025	1.977
67	3.984	3.134	2.742	2.509	2.352	2.237	2.150	2.080	2.023	1.975
68	3.982	3.132	2.740	2.507	2.350	2.235	2.148	2.078	2.021	1.973
69	3.980	3.130	2.737	2.505	2.348	2.233	2.145	2.076	2.019	1.971
70	3.978	3.128	2.736	2.503	2.346	2.231	2.143	2.074	2.017	1.969
71	3.976	3.126	2.734	2.501	2.344	2.229	2.142	2.072	2.015	1.967
72	3.974	3.124	2.732	2.499	2.342	2.227	2.140	2.070	2.013	1.965
73	3.972	3.122	2.730	2.497	2.340	2.226	2.138	2.068	2.011	1.963
74	3.970	3.120	2.728	2.495	2.338	2.224	2.136	2.066	2.009	1.961
75	3.968	3.119	2.727	2.494	2.337	2.222	2.134	2.064	2.007	1.959
76	3.967	3.117	2.725	2.492	2.335	2.220	2.133	2.063	2.006	1.958
77	3.965	3.115	2.723	2.490	2.333	2.219	2.131	2.061	2.004	1.956
78	3.963	3.114	2.722	2.489	2.332	2.217	2.129	2.059	2.002	1.954
79	3.962	3.112	2.720	2.487	2.330	2.216	2.128	2.058	2.001	1.953
80	3.960	3.111	2.719	2.486	2.329	2.214	2.126	2.056	1.999	1.951
81	3.959	3.109	2.717	2.484	2.327	2.213	2.125	2.055	1.998	1.950

	1	2	3	4	5	6	7	8	9	10
	Upper critical values of the F distribution for numerator degrees of freedom and denominator degrees of freedom, 5% significance level (continued)									
82	3.957	3.108	2.716	2.483	2.326	2.211	2.123	2.053	1.996	1.948
83	3.956	3.107	2.715	2.482	2.324	2.210	2.122	2.052	1.995	1.947
84	3.955	3.105	2.713	2.480	2.323	2.209	2.121	2.051	1.993	1.945
85	3.953	3.104	2.712	2.479	2.322	2.207	2.119	2.049	1.992	1.944
86	3.952	3.103	2.711	2.478	2.321	2.206	2.118	2.048	1.991	1.943
87	3.951	3.101	2.709	2.476	2.319	2.205	2.117	2.047	1.989	1.941
88	3.949	3.100	2.708	2.475	2.318	2.203	2.115	2.045	1.988	1.940
89	3.948	3.099	2.707	2.474	2.317	2.202	2.114	2.044	1.987	1.939
90	3.947	3.098	2.706	2.473	2.316	2.201	2.113	2.043	1.986	1.938
91	3.946	3.097	2.705	2.472	2.315	2.200	2.112	2.042	1.984	1.936
92	3.945	3.095	2.704	2.471	2.313	2.199	2.111	2.041	1.983	1.935
93	3.943	3.094	2.703	2.470	2.312	2.198	2.110	2.040	1.982	1.934
94	3.942	3.093	2.701	2.469	2.311	2.197	2.109	2.038	1.981	1.933
95	3.941	3.092	2.700	2.467	2.310	2.196	2.108	2.037	1.980	1.932
96	3.940	3.091	2.699	2.466	2.309	2.195	2.106	2.036	1.979	1.931
97	3.939	3.090	2.698	2.465	2.308	2.194	2.105	2.035	1.978	1.930
98	3.938	3.089	2.697	2.465	2.307	2.193	2.104	2.034	1.977	1.929
99	3.937	3.088	2.696	2.464	2.306	2.192	2.103	2.033	1.976	1.928
100	3.936	3.087	2.696	2.463	2.305	2.191	2.103	2.032	1.975	1.927

Upper critical values of the F distribution for numerator degrees of freedom and denominator degrees of freedom, 10% significance level

	1	2	3	4	5	6	7	8	9	10
5	4.060	3.780	3.619	3.520	3.453	3.405	3.368	3.339	3.316	3.297
6	3.776	3.463	3.289	3.181	3.108	3.055	3.014	2.983	2.958	2.937
7	3.589	3.257	3.074	2.961	2.883	2.827	2.785	2.752	2.725	2.703
8	3.458	3.113	2.924	2.806	2.726	2.668	2.624	2.589	2.561	2.538
9	3.360	3.006	2.813	2.693	2.611	2.551	2.505	2.469	2.440	2.416
10	3.285	2.924	2.728	2.605	2.522	2.461	2.414	2.377	2.347	2.323
11	3.225	2.860	2.660	2.536	2.451	2.389	2.342	2.304	2.274	2.248
12	3.177	2.807	2.606	2.480	2.394	2.331	2.283	2.245	2.214	2.188
13	3.136	2.763	2.560	2.434	2.347	2.283	2.234	2.195	2.164	2.138
14	3.102	2.726	2.522	2.395	2.307	2.243	2.193	2.154	2.122	2.095
15	3.073	2.695	2.490	2.361	2.273	2.208	2.158	2.119	2.086	2.059
16	3.048	2.668	2.462	2.333	2.244	2.178	2.128	2.088	2.055	2.028
17	3.026	2.645	2.437	2.308	2.218	2.152	2.102	2.061	2.028	2.001
18	3.007	2.624	2.416	2.286	2.196	2.130	2.079	2.038	2.005	1.977
19	2.990	2.606	2.397	2.266	2.176	2.109	2.058	2.017	1.984	1.956
20	2.975	2.589	2.380	2.249	2.158	2.091	2.040	1.999	1.965	1.937
21	2.961	2.575	2.365	2.233	2.142	2.075	2.023	1.982	1.948	1.920
22	2.949	2.561	2.351	2.219	2.128	2.060	2.008	1.967	1.933	1.904
23	2.937	2.549	2.339	2.207	2.115	2.047	1.995	1.953	1.919	1.890
24	2.927	2.538	2.327	2.195	2.103	2.035	1.983	1.941	1.906	1.877
25	2.918	2.528	2.317	2.184	2.092	2.024	1.971	1.929	1.895	1.866
26	2.909	2.519	2.307	2.174	2.082	2.014	1.961	1.919	1.884	1.855
27	2.901	2.511	2.299	2.165	2.073	2.005	1.952	1.909	1.874	1.845
28	2.894	2.503	2.291	2.157	2.064	1.996	1.943	1.900	1.865	1.836
29	2.887	2.495	2.283	2.149	2.057	1.988	1.935	1.892	1.857	1.827
30	2.881	2.489	2.276	2.142	2.049	1.980	1.927	1.884	1.849	1.819
31	2.875	2.482	2.270	2.136	2.042	1.973	1.920	1.877	1.842	1.812
32	2.869	2.477	2.263	2.129	2.036	1.967	1.913	1.870	1.835	1.805
33	2.864	2.471	2.258	2.123	2.030	1.961	1.907	1.864	1.828	1.799
34	2.859	2.466	2.252	2.118	2.024	1.955	1.901	1.858	1.822	1.793
35	2.855	2.461	2.247	2.113	2.019	1.950	1.896	1.852	1.817	1.787
36	2.850	2.456	2.243	2.108	2.014	1.945	1.891	1.847	1.811	1.781
37	2.846	2.452	2.238	2.103	2.009	1.940	1.886	1.842	1.806	1.776
38	2.842	2.448	2.234	2.099	2.005	1.935	1.881	1.838	1.802	1.772
39	2.839	2.444	2.230	2.095	2.001	1.931	1.877	1.833	1.797	1.767
40	2.835	2.440	2.226	2.091	1.997	1.927	1.873	1.829	1.793	1.763
41	2.832	2.437	2.222	2.087	1.993	1.923	1.869	1.825	1.789	1.759
42	2.829	2.434	2.219	2.084	1.989	1.919	1.865	1.821	1.785	1.755
43	2.826	2.430	2.216	2.080	1.986	1.916	1.861	1.817	1.781	1.751
44	2.823	2.427	2.213	2.077	1.983	1.913	1.858	1.814	1.778	1.747
45	2.820	2.425	2.210	2.074	1.980	1.909	1.855	1.811	1.774	1.744
46	2.818	2.422	2.207	2.071	1.977	1.906	1.852	1.808	1.771	1.741

Upper critical values of the F distribution for numerator degrees of freedom and denominator degrees of freedom, 10% significance level (continued)

	1	2	3	4	5	6	7	8	9	10
47	2.815	2.419	2.204	2.068	1.974	1.903	1.849	1.805	1.768	1.738
48	2.813	2.417	2.202	2.066	1.971	1.901	1.846	1.802	1.765	1.735
49	2.811	2.414	2.199	2.063	1.968	1.898	1.843	1.799	1.763	1.732
50	2.809	2.412	2.197	2.061	1.966	1.895	1.840	1.796	1.760	1.729
51	2.807	2.410	2.194	2.058	1.964	1.893	1.838	1.794	1.757	1.727
52	2.805	2.408	2.192	2.056	1.961	1.891	1.836	1.791	1.755	1.724
53	2.803	2.406	2.190	2.054	1.959	1.888	1.833	1.789	1.752	1.722
54	2.801	2.404	2.188	2.052	1.957	1.886	1.831	1.787	1.750	1.719
55	2.799	2.402	2.186	2.050	1.955	1.884	1.829	1.785	1.748	1.717
56	2.797	2.400	2.184	2.048	1.953	1.882	1.827	1.782	1.746	1.715
57	2.796	2.398	2.182	2.046	1.951	1.880	1.825	1.780	1.744	1.713
58	2.794	2.396	2.181	2.044	1.949	1.878	1.823	1.779	1.742	1.711
59	2.793	2.395	2.179	2.043	1.947	1.876	1.821	1.777	1.740	1.709
60	2.791	2.393	2.177	2.041	1.946	1.875	1.819	1.775	1.738	1.707
61	2.790	2.392	2.176	2.039	1.944	1.873	1.818	1.773	1.736	1.705
62	2.788	2.390	2.174	2.038	1.942	1.871	1.816	1.771	1.735	1.703
63	2.787	2.389	2.173	2.036	1.941	1.870	1.814	1.770	1.733	1.702
64	2.786	2.387	2.171	2.035	1.939	1.868	1.813	1.768	1.731	1.700
65	2.784	2.386	2.170	2.033	1.938	1.867	1.811	1.767	1.730	1.699
66	2.783	2.385	2.169	2.032	1.937	1.865	1.810	1.765	1.728	1.697
67	2.782	2.384	2.167	2.031	1.935	1.864	1.808	1.764	1.727	1.696
68	2.781	2.382	2.166	2.029	1.934	1.863	1.807	1.762	1.725	1.694
69	2.780	2.381	2.165	2.028	1.933	1.861	1.806	1.761	1.724	1.693
70	2.779	2.380	2.164	2.027	1.931	1.860	1.804	1.760	1.723	1.691
71	2.778	2.379	2.163	2.026	1.930	1.859	1.803	1.758	1.721	1.690
72	2.777	2.378	2.161	2.025	1.929	1.858	1.802	1.757	1.720	1.689
73	2.776	2.377	2.160	2.024	1.928	1.856	1.801	1.756	1.719	1.687
74	2.775	2.376	2.159	2.022	1.927	1.855	1.800	1.755	1.718	1.686
75	2.774	2.375	2.158	2.021	1.926	1.854	1.798	1.754	1.716	1.685
76	2.773	2.374	2.157	2.020	1.925	1.853	1.797	1.752	1.715	1.684
77	2.772	2.373	2.156	2.019	1.924	1.852	1.796	1.751	1.714	1.683
78	2.771	2.372	2.155	2.018	1.923	1.851	1.795	1.750	1.713	1.682
79	2.770	2.371	2.154	2.017	1.922	1.850	1.794	1.749	1.712	1.681
80	2.769	2.370	2.154	2.016	1.921	1.849	1.793	1.748	1.711	1.680
81	2.769	2.369	2.153	2.016	1.920	1.848	1.792	1.747	1.710	1.679
82	2.768	2.368	2.152	2.015	1.919	1.847	1.791	1.746	1.709	1.678
83	2.767	2.368	2.151	2.014	1.918	1.846	1.790	1.745	1.708	1.677
84	2.766	2.367	2.150	2.013	1.917	1.845	1.790	1.744	1.707	1.676
85	2.765	2.366	2.149	2.012	1.916	1.845	1.789	1.744	1.706	1.675
86	2.765	2.365	2.149	2.011	1.915	1.844	1.788	1.743	1.705	1.674
87	2.764	2.365	2.148	2.011	1.915	1.843	1.787	1.742	1.705	1.673
88	2.763	2.364	2.147	2.010	1.914	1.842	1.786	1.741	1.704	1.672

	Upper critical values of the F distribution for numerator degrees of freedom and denominator degrees of freedom, 10% significance level (continued)									
	1	**2**	**3**	**4**	**5**	**6**	**7**	**8**	**9**	**10**
89	2.763	2.363	2.146	2.009	1.913	1.841	1.785	1.740	1.703	1.671
90	2.762	2.363	2.146	2.008	1.912	1.841	1.785	1.739	1.702	1.670
91	2.761	2.362	2.145	2.008	1.912	1.840	1.784	1.739	1.701	1.670
92	2.761	2.361	2.144	2.007	1.911	1.839	1.783	1.738	1.701	1.669
93	2.760	2.361	2.144	2.006	1.910	1.838	1.782	1.737	1.700	1.668
94	2.760	2.360	2.143	2.006	1.910	1.838	1.782	1.736	1.699	1.667
95	2.759	2.359	2.142	2.005	1.909	1.837	1.781	1.736	1.698	1.667
96	2.759	2.359	2.142	2.004	1.908	1.836	1.780	1.735	1.698	1.666
97	2.758	2.358	2.141	2.004	1.908	1.836	1.780	1.734	1.697	1.665
98	2.757	2.358	2.141	2.003	1.907	1.835	1.779	1.734	1.696	1.665
99	2.757	2.357	2.140	2.003	1.906	1.835	1.778	1.733	1.696	1.664
100	2.756	2.356	2.139	2.002	1.906	1.834	1.778	1.732	1.695	1.663

Upper critical values of the F distribution for numerator degrees of freedom and denominator degrees of freedom, 1% significance level

	1	2	3	4	5	6	7	8	9	10
5	16.258	13.274	12.060	11.392	10.967	10.672	10.456	10.289	10.158	10.051
6	13.745	10.925	9.780	9.148	8.746	8.466	8.260	8.102	7.976	7.874
7	12.246	9.547	8.451	7.847	7.460	7.191	6.993	6.840	6.719	6.620
8	11.259	8.649	7.591	7.006	6.632	6.371	6.178	6.029	5.911	5.814
9	10.561	8.022	6.992	6.422	6.057	5.802	5.613	5.467	5.351	5.257
10	10.044	7.559	6.552	5.994	5.636	5.386	5.200	5.057	4.942	4.849
11	9.646	7.206	6.217	5.668	5.316	5.069	4.886	4.744	4.632	4.539
12	9.330	6.927	5.953	5.412	5.064	4.821	4.640	4.499	4.388	4.296
13	9.074	6.701	5.739	5.205	4.862	4.620	4.441	4.302	4.191	4.100
14	8.862	6.515	5.564	5.035	4.695	4.456	4.278	4.140	4.030	3.939
15	8.683	6.359	5.417	4.893	4.556	4.318	4.142	4.004	3.895	3.805
16	8.531	6.226	5.292	4.773	4.437	4.202	4.026	3.890	3.780	3.691
17	8.400	6.112	5.185	4.669	4.336	4.102	3.927	3.791	3.682	3.593
18	8.285	6.013	5.092	4.579	4.248	4.015	3.841	3.705	3.597	3.508
19	8.185	5.926	5.010	4.500	4.171	3.939	3.765	3.631	3.523	3.434
20	8.096	5.849	4.938	4.431	4.103	3.871	3.699	3.564	3.457	3.368
21	8.017	5.780	4.874	4.369	4.042	3.812	3.640	3.506	3.398	3.310
22	7.945	5.719	4.817	4.313	3.988	3.758	3.587	3.453	3.346	3.258
23	7.881	5.664	4.765	4.264	3.939	3.710	3.539	3.406	3.299	3.211
24	7.823	5.614	4.718	4.218	3.895	3.667	3.496	3.363	3.256	3.168
25	7.770	5.568	4.675	4.177	3.855	3.627	3.457	3.324	3.217	3.129
26	7.721	5.526	4.637	4.140	3.818	3.591	3.421	3.288	3.182	3.094
27	7.677	5.488	4.601	4.106	3.785	3.558	3.388	3.256	3.149	3.062
28	7.636	5.453	4.568	4.074	3.754	3.528	3.358	3.226	3.120	3.032
29	7.598	5.420	4.538	4.045	3.725	3.499	3.330	3.198	3.092	3.005
30	7.562	5.390	4.510	4.018	3.699	3.473	3.305	3.173	3.067	2.979
31	7.530	5.362	4.484	3.993	3.675	3.449	3.281	3.149	3.043	2.955
32	7.499	5.336	4.459	3.969	3.652	3.427	3.258	3.127	3.021	2.934
33	7.471	5.312	4.437	3.948	3.630	3.406	3.238	3.106	3.000	2.913
34	7.444	5.289	4.416	3.927	3.611	3.386	3.218	3.087	2.981	2.894
35	7.419	5.268	4.396	3.908	3.592	3.368	3.200	3.069	2.963	2.876
36	7.396	5.248	4.377	3.890	3.574	3.351	3.183	3.052	2.946	2.859
37	7.373	5.229	4.360	3.873	3.558	3.334	3.167	3.036	2.930	2.843
38	7.353	5.211	4.343	3.858	3.542	3.319	3.152	3.021	2.915	2.828
39	7.333	5.194	4.327	3.843	3.528	3.305	3.137	3.006	2.901	2.814
40	7.314	5.179	4.313	3.828	3.514	3.291	3.124	2.993	2.888	2.801
41	7.296	5.163	4.299	3.815	3.501	3.278	3.111	2.980	2.875	2.788
42	7.280	5.149	4.285	3.802	3.488	3.266	3.099	2.968	2.863	2.776
43	7.264	5.136	4.273	3.790	3.476	3.254	3.087	2.957	2.851	2.764
44	7.248	5.123	4.261	3.778	3.465	3.243	3.076	2.946	2.840	2.754
45	7.234	5.110	4.249	3.767	3.454	3.232	3.066	2.935	2.830	2.743
46	7.220	5.099	4.238	3.757	3.444	3.222	3.056	2.925	2.820	2.733

	1	2	3	4	5	6	7	8	9	10
Upper critical values of the F distribution for numerator degrees of freedom and denominator degrees of freedom, 1% significance level (continued)										
47	7.207	5.087	4.228	3.747	3.434	3.213	3.046	2.916	2.811	2.724
48	7.194	5.077	4.218	3.737	3.425	3.204	3.037	2.907	2.802	2.715
49	7.182	5.066	4.208	3.728	3.416	3.195	3.028	2.898	2.793	2.706
50	7.171	5.057	4.199	3.720	3.408	3.186	3.020	2.890	2.785	2.698
51	7.159	5.047	4.191	3.711	3.400	3.178	3.012	2.882	2.777	2.690
52	7.149	5.038	4.182	3.703	3.392	3.171	3.005	2.874	2.769	2.683
53	7.139	5.030	4.174	3.695	3.384	3.163	2.997	2.867	2.762	2.675
54	7.129	5.021	4.167	3.688	3.377	3.156	2.990	2.860	2.755	2.668
55	7.119	5.013	4.159	3.681	3.370	3.149	2.983	2.853	2.748	2.662
56	7.110	5.006	4.152	3.674	3.363	3.143	2.977	2.847	2.742	2.655
57	7.102	4.998	4.145	3.667	3.357	3.136	2.971	2.841	2.736	2.649
58	7.093	4.991	4.138	3.661	3.351	3.130	2.965	2.835	2.730	2.643
59	7.085	4.984	4.132	3.655	3.345	3.124	2.959	2.829	2.724	2.637
60	7.077	4.977	4.126	3.649	3.339	3.119	2.953	2.823	2.718	2.632
61	7.070	4.971	4.120	3.643	3.333	3.113	2.948	2.818	2.713	2.626
62	7.062	4.965	4.114	3.638	3.328	3.108	2.942	2.813	2.708	2.621
63	7.055	4.959	4.109	3.632	3.323	3.103	2.937	2.808	2.703	2.616
64	7.048	4.953	4.103	3.627	3.318	3.098	2.932	2.803	2.698	2.611
65	7.042	4.947	4.098	3.622	3.313	3.093	2.928	2.798	2.693	2.607
66	7.035	4.942	4.093	3.618	3.308	3.088	2.923	2.793	2.689	2.602
67	7.029	4.937	4.088	3.613	3.304	3.084	2.919	2.789	2.684	2.598
68	7.023	4.932	4.083	3.608	3.299	3.080	2.914	2.785	2.680	2.593
69	7.017	4.927	4.079	3.604	3.295	3.075	2.910	2.781	2.676	2.589
70	7.011	4.922	4.074	3.600	3.291	3.071	2.906	2.777	2.672	2.585
71	7.006	4.917	4.070	3.596	3.287	3.067	2.902	2.773	2.668	2.581
72	7.001	4.913	4.066	3.591	3.283	3.063	2.898	2.769	2.664	2.578
73	6.995	4.908	4.062	3.588	3.279	3.060	2.895	2.765	2.660	2.574
74	6.990	4.904	4.058	3.584	3.275	3.056	2.891	2.762	2.657	2.570
75	6.985	4.900	4.054	3.580	3.272	3.052	2.887	2.758	2.653	2.567
76	6.981	4.896	4.050	3.577	3.268	3.049	2.884	2.755	2.650	2.563
77	6.976	4.892	4.047	3.573	3.265	3.046	2.881	2.751	2.647	2.560
78	6.971	4.888	4.043	3.570	3.261	3.042	2.877	2.748	2.644	2.557
79	6.967	4.884	4.040	3.566	3.258	3.039	2.874	2.745	2.640	2.554
80	6.963	4.881	4.036	3.563	3.255	3.036	2.871	2.742	2.637	2.551
81	6.958	4.877	4.033	3.560	3.252	3.033	2.868	2.739	2.634	2.548
82	6.954	4.874	4.030	3.557	3.249	3.030	2.865	2.736	2.632	2.545
83	6.950	4.870	4.027	3.554	3.246	3.027	2.863	2.733	2.629	2.542
84	6.947	4.867	4.024	3.551	3.243	3.025	2.860	2.731	2.626	2.539
85	6.943	4.864	4.021	3.548	3.240	3.022	2.857	2.728	2.623	2.537
86	6.939	4.861	4.018	3.545	3.238	3.019	2.854	2.725	2.621	2.534
87	6.935	4.858	4.015	3.543	3.235	3.017	2.852	2.723	2.618	2.532
88	6.932	4.855	4.012	3.540	3.233	3.014	2.849	2.720	2.616	2.529

Upper critical values of the F distribution for numerator degrees of freedom and denominator degrees of freedom, 1% significance level (continued)

	1	2	3	4	5	6	7	8	9	10
89	6.928	4.852	4.010	3.538	3.230	3.012	2.847	2.718	2.613	2.527
90	6.925	4.849	4.007	3.535	3.228	3.009	2.845	2.715	2.611	2.524
91	6.922	4.846	4.004	3.533	3.225	3.007	2.842	2.713	2.609	2.522
92	6.919	4.844	4.002	3.530	3.223	3.004	2.840	2.711	2.606	2.520
93	6.915	4.841	3.999	3.528	3.221	3.002	2.838	2.709	2.604	2.518
94	6.912	4.838	3.997	3.525	3.218	3.000	2.835	2.706	2.602	2.515
95	6.909	4.836	3.995	3.523	3.216	2.998	2.833	2.704	2.600	2.513
96	6.906	4.833	3.992	3.521	3.214	2.996	2.831	2.702	2.598	2.511
97	6.904	4.831	3.990	3.519	3.212	2.994	2.829	2.700	2.596	2.509
98	6.901	4.829	3.988	3.517	3.210	2.992	2.827	2.698	2.594	2.507
99	6.898	4.826	3.986	3.515	3.208	2.990	2.825	2.696	2.592	2.505
100	6.895	4.824	3.984	3.513	3.206	2.988	2.823	2.694	2.590	2.503

Upper critical values of the Student 't' distribution

Probability of exceeding the critical value

d.f.	0.10	0.05	0.025	0.01	0.005	0.001
1.	3.078	6.314	12.706	31.821	63.657	318.313
2.	1.886	2.920	4.303	6.965	9.925	22.327
3.	1.638	2.353	3.182	4.541	5.841	10.215
4.	1.533	2.132	2.776	3.747	4.604	7.173
5.	1.476	2.015	2.571	3.365	4.032	5.893
6.	1.440	1.943	2.447	3.143	3.707	5.208
7.	1.415	1.895	2.365	2.998	3.499	4.782
8.	1.397	1.860	2.306	2.896	3.355	4.499
9.	1.383	1.833	2.262	2.821	3.250	4.296
10.	1.372	1.812	2.228	2.764	3.169	4.143
11.	1.363	1.796	2.201	2.718	3.106	4.024
12.	1.356	1.782	2.179	2.681	3.055	3.929
13.	1.350	1.771	2.160	2.650	3.012	3.852
14.	1.345	1.761	2.145	2.624	2.977	3.787
15.	1.341	1.753	2.131	2.602	2.947	3.733
16.	1.337	1.746	2.120	2.583	2.921	3.686
17.	1.333	1.740	2.110	2.567	2.898	3.646
18.	1.330	1.734	2.101	2.552	2.878	3.610
19.	1.328	1.729	2.093	2.539	2.861	3.579
20.	1.325	1.725	2.086	2.528	2.845	3.552
21.	1.323	1.721	2.080	2.518	2.831	3.527
22.	1.321	1.717	2.074	2.508	2.819	3.505
23.	1.319	1.714	2.069	2.500	2.807	3.485
24.	1.318	1.711	2.064	2.492	2.797	3.467
25.	1.316	1.708	2.060	2.485	2.787	3.450
26.	1.315	1.706	2.056	2.479	2.779	3.435
27.	1.314	1.703	2.052	2.473	2.771	3.421
28.	1.313	1.701	2.048	2.467	2.763	3.408
29.	1.311	1.699	2.045	2.462	2.756	3.396
30.	1.310	1.697	2.042	2.457	2.750	3.385
31.	1.309	1.696	2.040	2.453	2.744	3.375
32.	1.309	1.694	2.037	2.449	2.738	3.365
33.	1.308	1.692	2.035	2.445	2.733	3.356
34.	1.307	1.691	2.032	2.441	2.728	3.348
35.	1.306	1.690	2.030	2.438	2.724	3.340
36.	1.306	1.688	2.028	2.434	2.719	3.333
37.	1.305	1.687	2.026	2.431	2.715	3.326
38.	1.304	1.686	2.024	2.429	2.712	3.319
39.	1.304	1.685	2.023	2.426	2.708	3.313
40.	1.303	1.684	2.021	2.423	2.704	3.307
41.	1.303	1.683	2.020	2.421	2.701	3.301

Upper critical values of the Student 't' distribution (continued)

Probability of exceeding the critical value

d.f.	0.10	0.05	0.025	0.01	0.005	0.001
42.	1.302	1.682	2.018	2.418	2.698	3.296
43.	1.302	1.681	2.017	2.416	2.695	3.291
44.	1.301	1.680	2.015	2.414	2.692	3.286
45.	1.301	1.679	2.014	2.412	2.690	3.281
46.	1.300	1.679	2.013	2.410	2.687	3.277
47.	1.300	1.678	2.012	2.408	2.685	3.273
48.	1.299	1.677	2.011	2.407	2.682	3.269
49.	1.299	1.677	2.010	2.405	2.680	3.265
50.	1.299	1.676	2.009	2.403	2.678	3.261
51.	1.298	1.675	2.008	2.402	2.676	3.258
52.	1.298	1.675	2.007	2.400	2.674	3.255
53.	1.298	1.674	2.006	2.399	2.672	3.251
54.	1.297	1.674	2.005	2.397	2.670	3.248
55.	1.297	1.673	2.004	2.396	2.668	3.245
56.	1.297	1.673	2.003	2.395	2.667	3.242
57.	1.297	1.672	2.002	2.394	2.665	3.239
58.	1.296	1.672	2.002	2.392	2.663	3.237
59.	1.296	1.671	2.001	2.391	2.662	3.234
60.	1.296	1.671	2.000	2.390	2.660	3.232
61.	1.296	1.670	2.000	2.389	2.659	3.229
62.	1.295	1.670	1.999	2.388	2.657	3.227
63.	1.295	1.669	1.998	2.387	2.656	3.225
64.	1.295	1.669	1.998	2.386	2.655	3.223
65.	1.295	1.669	1.997	2.385	2.654	3.220
66.	1.295	1.668	1.997	2.384	2.652	3.218
67.	1.294	1.668	1.996	2.383	2.651	3.216
68.	1.294	1.668	1.995	2.382	2.650	3.214
69.	1.294	1.667	1.995	2.382	2.649	3.213
70.	1.294	1.667	1.994	2.381	2.648	3.211
71.	1.294	1.667	1.994	2.380	2.647	3.209
72.	1.293	1.666	1.993	2.379	2.646	3.207
73.	1.293	1.666	1.993	2.379	2.645	3.206
74.	1.293	1.666	1.993	2.378	2.644	3.204
75.	1.293	1.665	1.992	2.377	2.643	3.202
76.	1.293	1.665	1.992	2.376	2.642	3.201
77.	1.293	1.665	1.991	2.376	2.641	3.199
78.	1.292	1.665	1.991	2.375	2.640	3.198
79.	1.292	1.664	1.990	2.374	2.640	3.197
80.	1.292	1.664	1.990	2.374	2.639	3.195
81.	1.292	1.664	1.990	2.373	2.638	3.194
82.	1.292	1.664	1.989	2.373	2.637	3.193

Upper critical values of the Student 't' distribution (continued)

Probability of exceeding the critical value

d.f.	0.10	0.05	0.025	0.01	0.005	0.001
83.	1.292	1.663	1.989	2.372	2.636	3.191
84.	1.292	1.663	1.989	2.372	2.636	3.190
85.	1.292	1.663	1.988	2.371	2.635	3.189
86.	1.291	1.663	1.988	2.370	2.634	3.188
87.	1.291	1.663	1.988	2.370	2.634	3.187
88.	1.291	1.662	1.987	2.369	2.633	3.185
89.	1.291	1.662	1.987	2.369	2.632	3.184
90.	1.291	1.662	1.987	2.368	2.632	3.183
91.	1.291	1.662	1.986	2.368	2.631	3.182
92.	1.291	1.662	1.986	2.368	2.630	3.181
93.	1.291	1.661	1.986	2.367	2.630	3.180
94.	1.291	1.661	1.986	2.367	2.629	3.179
95.	1.291	1.661	1.985	2.366	2.629	3.178
96.	1.290	1.661	1.985	2.366	2.628	3.177
97.	1.290	1.661	1.985	2.365	2.627	3.176
98.	1.290	1.661	1.984	2.365	2.627	3.175
99.	1.290	1.660	1.984	2.365	2.626	3.175
100.	1.290	1.660	1.984	2.364	2.626	3.174
≡	1.282	1.645	1.960	2.326	2.576	3.090

Note: This is a one-tailed table. This can always be worked out by locating the values 1.645 and 1.96 in the infinite degrees of freedom row. 1.645 is the 5% value for a one-tailed test and 1.96 is the 2.5% value as these are 'z' values for the normal distribution given that the 't' distribution becomes the normal distribution with infinite degrees of freedom. The two-tailed tests require you to double the values at the top of the table – for example, the critical value for a 10% two-tailed test is exactly the same as the critical value for a 5% one-tailed test.

Critical values for the Durbin–Watson test: 5% significance level							
n	K	dL	dU	n	K	dL	dU
6.	2.	0.61018	1.40015	14.	8.	0.28559	2.84769
7.	2.	0.69955	1.35635	14.	9.	0.20013	3.11121
7.	3.	0.46723	1.89636	14.	10.	0.12726	3.36038
8.	2.	0.76290	1.33238	15.	2.	1.07697	1.36054
8.	3.	0.55907	1.77711	15.	3.	0.94554	1.54318
8.	4.	0.36744	2.28664	15.	4.	0.81396	1.75014
9.	2.	0.82428	1.31988	15.	5.	0.68519	1.97735
9.	3.	0.62910	1.69926	15.	6.	0.56197	2.21981
9.	4.	0.45476	2.12816	15.	7.	0.44707	2.47148
9.	5.	0.29571	2.58810	15.	8.	0.34290	2.72698
10.	2.	0.87913	1.31971	15.	9.	0.25090	2.97866
10.	3.	0.69715	1.64134	15.	10.	0.17531	3.21604
10.	4.	0.52534	2.01632	15.	11.	0.11127	3.43819
10.	5.	0.37602	2.41365	16.	2.	1.10617	1.37092
10.	6.	0.24269	2.82165	16.	3.	0.98204	1.53860
11.	2.	0.92733	1.32409	16.	4.	0.85718	1.72773
11.	3.	0.75798	1.60439	16.	5.	0.73400	1.93506
11.	4.	0.59477	1.92802	16.	6.	0.61495	2.15672
11.	5.	0.44406	2.28327	16.	7.	0.50223	2.38813
11.	6.	0.31549	2.64456	16.	8.	0.39805	2.62409
11.	7.	0.20253	3.00447	16.	9.	0.30433	2.86009
12.	2.	0.97076	1.33137	16.	10.	0.22206	3.08954
12.	3.	0.81221	1.57935	16.	11.	0.15479	3.30391
12.	4.	0.65765	1.86397	16.	12.	0.09809	3.50287
12.	5.	0.51198	2.17662	17.	2.	1.13295	1.38122
12.	6.	0.37956	2.50609	17.	3.	1.01543	1.53614
12.	7.	0.26813	2.83196	17.	4.	0.89675	1.71009
12.	8.	0.17144	3.14940	17.	5.	0.77898	1.90047
13.	2.	1.00973	1.34040	17.	6.	0.66414	2.10414
13.	3.	0.86124	1.56212	17.	7.	0.55423	2.31755
13.	4.	0.71465	1.81593	17.	8.	0.45107	2.53660
13.	5.	0.57446	2.09428	17.	9.	0.35639	2.75688
13.	6.	0.44448	2.38967	17.	10.	0.27177	2.97455
13.	7.	0.32775	2.69204	17.	11.	0.19784	3.18400
13.	8.	0.23049	2.98506	17.	12.	0.13763	3.37817
13.	9.	0.14693	3.26577	17.	13.	0.08711	3.55716
14.	2.	1.04495	1.35027	18.	2.	1.15759	1.39133
14.	3.	0.90544	1.55066	18.	3.	1.04607	1.53525
14.	4.	0.76666	1.77882	18.	4.	0.93310	1.69614
14.	5.	0.63206	2.02955	18.	5.	0.82044	1.87189
14.	6.	0.50516	2.29593	18.	6.	0.70984	2.06000
14.	7.	0.38897	2.57158	18.	7.	0.60301	2.25750

Critical values for the Durbin–Watson test: 5% significance level (continued)

n	K	dL	dU	n	K	dL	dU
18.	8.	0.50158	2.46122	21.	8.	0.63710	2.28988
18.	9.	0.40702	2.66753	21.	9.	0.54645	2.46051
18.	10.	0.32076	2.87268	21.	10.	0.46055	2.63324
18.	11.	0.24405	3.07345	21.	11.	0.38035	2.80588
18.	12.	0.17732	3.26497	21.	12.	0.30669	2.97600
18.	13.	0.12315	3.44141	21.	13.	0.24033	3.14129
18.	14.	0.07786	3.60315	21.	14.	0.18198	3.29979
19.	2.	1.18037	1.40118	21.	15.	0.13166	3.44827
19.	3.	1.07430	1.53553	21.	16.	0.09111	3.58322
19.	4.	0.96659	1.68509	21.	17.	0.05747	3.70544
19.	5.	0.85876	1.84815	22.	2.	1.23949	1.42888
19.	6.	0.75231	2.02262	22.	3.	1.14713	1.54079
19.	7.	0.64870	2.20614	22.	4.	1.05292	1.66398
19.	8.	0.54938	2.39602	22.	5.	0.95783	1.79744
19.	9.	0.45571	2.58939	22.	6.	0.86285	1.93996
19.	10.	0.36889	2.78312	22.	7.	0.76898	2.09015
19.	11.	0.29008	2.97399	22.	8.	0.67719	2.24646
19.	12.	0.22029	3.15930	22.	9.	0.58843	2.40718
19.	13.	0.15979	3.33481	22.	10.	0.50363	2.57051
19.	14.	0.11082	3.49566	22.	11.	0.42363	2.73452
19.	15.	0.07001	3.64241	22.	12.	0.34926	2.89726
20.	2.	1.20149	1.41073	22.	13.	0.28119	3.05662
20.	3.	1.10040	1.53668	22.	14.	0.22003	3.21061
20.	4.	0.99755	1.67634	22.	15.	0.16642	3.35756
20.	5.	0.89425	1.82828	22.	16.	0.12028	3.49463
20.	6.	0.79179	1.99079	22.	17.	0.08315	3.61880
20.	7.	0.69146	2.16189	22.	18.	0.05242	3.73092
20.	8.	0.59454	2.33937	23.	2.	1.25665	1.43747
20.	9.	0.50220	2.52082	23.	3.	1.16815	1.54346
20.	10.	0.41559	2.70374	23.	4.	1.07778	1.65974
20.	11.	0.33571	2.88535	23.	5.	0.98639	1.78546
20.	12.	0.26349	3.06292	23.	6.	0.89488	1.91958
20.	13.	0.19978	3.23417	23.	7.	0.80410	2.06093
20.	14.	0.14472	3.39540	23.	8.	0.71493	2.20816
20.	15.	0.10024	3.54250	23.	9.	0.62821	2.35988
20.	16.	0.06327	3.67619	23.	10.	0.54478	2.51449
21.	2.	1.22115	1.41997	23.	11.	0.46541	2.67038
21.	3.	1.12461	1.53849	23.	12.	0.39083	2.82585
21.	4.	1.02624	1.66942	23.	13.	0.32172	2.97919
21.	5.	0.92719	1.81157	23.	14.	0.25866	3.12852
21.	6.	0.82856	1.96350	23.	15.	0.20216	3.27216
21.	7.	0.73149	2.12355	23.	16.	0.15274	3.40865

n	K	dL	dU	n	K	dL	dU
		Critical values for the Durbin–Watson test: 5% significance level (continued)					
23.	17.	0.11029	3.53549	26.	2.	1.30219	1.46139
23.	18.	0.07619	3.65007	26.	3.	1.22358	1.55281
23.	19.	0.04801	3.75327	26.	4.	1.14319	1.65225
24.	2.	1.27276	1.44575	26.	5.	1.06158	1.75911
24.	3.	1.18781	1.54639	26.	6.	0.97937	1.87274
24.	4.	1.10100	1.65649	26.	7.	0.89717	1.99240
24.	5.	1.01309	1.77526	26.	8.	0.81561	2.11722
24.	6.	0.92486	1.90184	26.	9.	0.73529	2.24629
24.	7.	0.83706	2.03522	26.	10.	0.65683	2.37862
24.	8.	0.75048	2.17427	26.	11.	0.58079	2.51315
24.	9.	0.66589	2.31774	26.	12.	0.50775	2.64877
24.	10.	0.58400	2.46431	26.	13.	0.43825	2.78436
24.	11.	0.50554	2.61260	26.	14.	0.37279	2.91872
24.	12.	0.43119	2.76111	26.	15.	0.31182	3.05067
24.	13.	0.36156	2.90835	26.	16.	0.25578	3.17904
24.	14.	0.29723	3.05282	26.	17.	0.20499	3.30253
24.	15.	0.23869	3.19285	26.	18.	0.15977	3.42006
24.	16.	0.18635	3.32700	26.	19.	0.12041	3.53067
24.	17.	0.14066	3.45402	26.	20.	0.08677	3.63257
24.	18.	0.10150	3.57167	26.	21.	0.05983	3.72404
24.	19.	0.07006	3.67769	27.	2.	1.31568	1.46878
24.	20.	0.04413	3.77297	27.	3.	1.23991	1.55620
25.	2.	1.28791	1.45371	27.	4.	1.16239	1.65101
25.	3.	1.20625	1.54954	27.	5.	1.08364	1.75274
25.	4.	1.12276	1.65403	27.	6.	1.00421	1.86079
25.	5.	1.03811	1.76655	27.	7.	0.92463	1.97449
25.	6.	0.95297	1.88634	27.	8.	0.84546	2.09313
25.	7.	0.86803	2.01252	27.	9.	0.76726	2.21588
25.	8.	0.78400	2.14412	27.	10.	0.69057	2.34190
25.	9.	0.70154	2.28007	27.	11.	0.61593	2.47026
25.	10.	0.62133	2.41924	27.	12.	0.54385	2.59997
25.	11.	0.54401	2.56041	27.	13.	0.47482	2.73007
25.	12.	0.47019	2.70229	27.	14.	0.40933	2.85950
25.	13.	0.40046	2.84360	27.	15.	0.34780	2.98721
25.	14.	0.33536	2.98300	27.	16.	0.29062	3.11215
25.	15.	0.27536	3.11913	27.	17.	0.23816	3.23327
25.	16.	0.22090	3.25058	27.	18.	0.19072	3.34944
25.	17.	0.17231	3.37604	27.	19.	0.14853	3.45967
25.	18.	0.12995	3.49447	27.	20.	0.11188	3.56318
25.	19.	0.09371	3.60384	27.	21.	0.08057	3.65833
25.	20.	0.06465	3.70220	28.	2.	1.32844	1.47589
25.	21.	0.04070	3.79041	28.	3.	1.25534	1.55964

Critical values for the Durbin–Watson test: 5% significance level (continued)

n	K	dL	dU	n	K	dL	dU
28.	4.	1.18051	1.65025	30.	6.	1.07060	1.83259
28.	5.	1.10444	1.74728	30.	7.	0.99815	1.93133
28.	6.	1.02762	1.85022	30.	8.	0.92564	2.03432
28.	7.	0.95052	1.95851	30.	9.	0.85351	2.14102
28.	8.	0.87366	2.07148	30.	10.	0.78217	2.25080
28.	9.	0.79754	2.18844	30.	11.	0.71202	2.36307
28.	10.	0.72265	2.30862	30.	12.	0.64345	2.47714
28.	11.	0.64947	2.43122	30.	13.	0.57685	2.59233
28.	12.	0.57848	2.55540	30.	14.	0.51259	2.70793
28.	13.	0.51013	2.68025	30.	15.	0.45105	2.82319
28.	14.	0.44486	2.80489	30.	16.	0.39255	2.93738
28.	15.	0.38308	2.92838	30.	17.	0.33740	3.04971
28.	16.	0.32517	3.04976	30.	18.	0.28590	3.15946
28.	17.	0.27146	3.16812	30.	19.	0.23830	3.26584
28.	18.	0.22228	3.28249	30.	20.	0.19485	3.36811
28.	19.	0.17787	3.39189	30.	21.	0.15572	3.46549
28.	20.	0.13843	3.49546	31.	2.	1.36298	1.49574
28.	21.	0.10421	3.59248	31.	3.	1.29685	1.57011
29.	2.	1.34054	1.48275	31.	4.	1.22915	1.65002
29.	3.	1.26992	1.56312	31.	5.	1.16021	1.73518
29.	4.	1.19762	1.64987	31.	6.	1.09040	1.82522
29.	5.	1.12407	1.74260	31.	7.	1.02008	1.91976
29.	6.	1.04971	1.84088	31.	8.	0.94962	2.01834
29.	7.	0.97499	1.94420	31.	9.	0.87940	2.12046
29.	8.	0.90036	2.05196	31.	10.	0.80979	2.22562
29.	9.	0.82626	2.16358	31.	11.	0.74115	2.33323
29.	10.	0.75316	2.27837	31.	12.	0.67387	2.44273
29.	11.	0.68148	2.39562	31.	13.	0.60828	2.55347
29.	12.	0.61166	2.51459	31.	14.	0.54474	2.66484
29.	13.	0.54413	2.63447	31.	15.	0.48358	2.77618
29.	14.	0.47929	2.75449	31.	16.	0.42513	2.88680
29.	15.	0.41753	2.87381	31.	17.	0.36966	2.99604
29.	16.	0.35918	2.99160	31.	18.	0.31748	3.10322
29.	17.	0.30461	3.10700	31.	19.	0.26882	3.20762
29.	18.	0.25409	3.21917	31.	20.	0.22392	3.30859
29.	19.	0.20790	3.32728	31.	21.	0.18298	3.40545
29.	20.	0.16625	3.43042	32.	2.	1.37340	1.50190
29.	21.	0.12931	3.52786	32.	3.	1.30932	1.57358
30.	2.	1.35204	1.48936	32.	4.	1.24371	1.65046
30.	3.	1.28373	1.56661	32.	5.	1.17688	1.73226
30.	4.	1.21380	1.64981	32.	6.	1.10916	1.81867
30.	5.	1.14262	1.73860	32.	7.	1.04088	1.90931

Critical values for the Durbin–Watson test: 5% significance level (continued)							
n	K	dL	dU	n	K	dL	dU
32.	8.	0.97239	2.00381	34.	10.	0.88506	2.16190
32.	9.	0.90401	2.10171	34.	11.	0.82091	2.25735
32.	10.	0.83609	2.20255	34.	12.	0.75755	2.35473
32.	11.	0.76897	2.30583	34.	13.	0.69527	2.45359
32.	12.	0.70299	2.41102	34.	14.	0.63433	2.55348
32.	13.	0.63847	2.51758	34.	15.	0.57503	2.65392
32.	14.	0.57573	2.62493	34.	16.	0.51760	2.75442
32.	15.	0.51510	2.73248	34.	17.	0.46231	2.85449
32.	16.	0.45685	2.83963	34.	18.	0.40939	2.95361
32.	17.	0.40129	2.94576	34.	19.	0.35907	3.05127
32.	18.	0.34866	3.05028	34.	20.	0.31155	3.14697
32.	19.	0.29923	3.15253	34.	21.	0.26704	3.24020
32.	20.	0.25319	3.25193	35.	2.	1.40194	1.51914
32.	21.	0.21078	3.34784	35.	3.	1.34332	1.58382
33.	2.	1.38335	1.50784	35.	4.	1.28330	1.65282
33.	3.	1.32119	1.57703	35.	5.	1.22214	1.72593
33.	4.	1.25756	1.65110	35.	6.	1.16007	1.80292
33.	5.	1.19272	1.72978	35.	7.	1.09735	1.88351
33.	6.	1.12698	1.81282	35.	8.	1.03424	1.96743
33.	7.	1.06065	1.89986	35.	9.	0.97099	2.05436
33.	8.	0.99402	1.99057	35.	10.	0.90788	2.14395
33.	9.	0.92743	2.08455	35.	11.	0.84516	2.23585
33.	10.	0.86115	2.18137	35.	12.	0.78311	2.32966
33.	11.	0.79554	2.28061	35.	13.	0.72197	2.42501
33.	12.	0.73086	2.38177	35.	14.	0.66200	2.52146
33.	13.	0.66745	2.48437	35.	15.	0.60346	2.61858
33.	14.	0.60559	2.58789	35.	16.	0.54659	2.71593
33.	15.	0.54558	2.69181	35.	17.	0.49162	2.81306
33.	16.	0.48769	2.79558	35.	18.	0.43878	2.90951
33.	17.	0.43219	2.89865	35.	19.	0.38829	3.00481
33.	18.	0.37933	3.00046	35.	20.	0.34034	3.09851
33.	19.	0.32935	3.10046	35.	21.	0.29513	3.19013
33.	20.	0.28246	3.19808	36.	2.	1.41065	1.52451
33.	21.	0.23887	3.29275	36.	3.	1.35365	1.58716
34.	2.	1.39285	1.51358	36.	4.	1.29530	1.65387
34.	3.	1.33251	1.58045	36.	5.	1.23583	1.72447
34.	4.	1.27074	1.65189	36.	6.	1.17545	1.79873
34.	5.	1.20779	1.72770	36.	7.	1.11441	1.87643
34.	6.	1.14393	1.80758	36.	8.	1.05294	1.95730
34.	7.	1.07944	1.89129	36.	9.	0.99128	2.04104
34.	8.	1.01462	1.97849	36.	10.	0.92967	2.12737
34.	9.	0.94973	2.06882	36.	11.	0.86836	2.21594

Critical values for the Durbin–Watson test: 5% significance level (continued)							
n	K	dL	dU	n	K	dL	dU
36.	12.	0.80759	2.30642	38.	14.	0.73886	2.43775
36.	13.	0.74759	2.39844	38.	15.	0.68284	2.52581
36.	14.	0.68861	2.49162	38.	16.	0.62799	2.61444
36.	15.	0.63089	2.58557	38.	17.	0.57448	2.70332
36.	16.	0.57463	2.67990	38.	18.	0.52253	2.79207
36.	17.	0.52008	2.77418	38.	19.	0.47229	2.88036
36.	18.	0.46745	2.86800	38.	20.	0.42396	2.96784
36.	19.	0.41692	2.96095	38.	21.	0.37769	3.05412
36.	20.	0.36871	3.05259	39.	2.	1.43473	1.53963
36.	21.	0.32299	3.14249	39.	3.	1.38210	1.59686
37.	2.	1.41900	1.52971	39.	4.	1.32827	1.65754
37.	3.	1.36354	1.59044	39.	5.	1.27338	1.72152
37.	4.	1.30678	1.65501	39.	6.	1.21761	1.78863
37.	5.	1.24891	1.72327	39.	7.	1.16116	1.85870
37.	6.	1.19014	1.79499	39.	8.	1.10419	1.93153
37.	7.	1.13071	1.86998	39.	9.	1.04692	2.00692
37.	8.	1.07081	1.94799	39.	10.	0.98953	2.08460
37.	9.	1.01066	2.02876	39.	11.	0.93220	2.16437
37.	10.	0.95051	2.11203	39.	12.	0.87514	2.24594
37.	11.	0.89057	2.19749	39.	13.	0.81853	2.32904
37.	12.	0.83105	2.28481	39.	14.	0.76257	2.41340
37.	13.	0.77219	2.37369	39.	15.	0.70743	2.49872
37.	14.	0.71421	2.46378	39.	16.	0.65333	2.58469
37.	15.	0.65734	2.55471	39.	17.	0.60044	2.67100
37.	16.	0.60177	2.64613	39.	18.	0.54891	2.75733
37.	17.	0.54771	2.73765	39.	19.	0.49896	2.84336
37.	18.	0.49537	2.82891	39.	20.	0.45072	2.92876
37.	19.	0.44494	2.91951	39.	21.	0.40437	3.01320
37.	20.	0.39661	3.00907	40.	2.	1.44214	1.54436
37.	21.	0.35054	3.09719	40.	3.	1.39083	1.59999
38.	2.	1.42702	1.53475	40.	4.	1.33835	1.65889
38.	3.	1.37301	1.59368	40.	5.	1.28484	1.72092
38.	4.	1.31774	1.65625	40.	6.	1.23047	1.78594
38.	5.	1.26140	1.72229	40.	7.	1.17541	1.85378
38.	6.	1.20418	1.79164	40.	8.	1.11983	1.92426
38.	7.	1.14627	1.86409	40.	9.	1.06391	1.99717
38.	8.	1.08787	1.93942	40.	10.	1.00782	2.07233
38.	9.	1.02919	2.01742	40.	11.	0.95174	2.14950
38.	10.	0.97045	2.09782	40.	12.	0.89585	2.22843
38.	11.	0.91183	2.18033	40.	13.	0.84035	2.30888
38.	12.	0.85356	2.26470	40.	14.	0.78539	2.39060
38.	13.	0.79583	2.35061	40.	15.	0.73115	2.47330

	Critical values for the Durbin–Watson test: 5% significance level (continued)						
n	K	dL	dU	n	K	dL	dU
40.	16.	0.67782	2.55672	42.	18.	0.62350	2.66432
40.	17.	0.62556	2.64056	42.	19.	0.57474	2.74389
40.	18.	0.57454	2.72455	42.	20.	0.52726	2.82328
40.	19.	0.52492	2.80836	42.	21.	0.48121	2.90220
40.	20.	0.47687	2.89172	43.	2.	1.46278	1.55773
40.	21.	0.43054	2.97431	43.	3.	1.41507	1.60905
41.	2.	1.44927	1.54895	43.	4.	1.36629	1.66319
41.	3.	1.39922	1.60307	43.	5.	1.31655	1.72002
41.	4.	1.34803	1.66028	43.	6.	1.26600	1.77944
41.	5.	1.29584	1.72048	43.	7.	1.21476	1.84132
41.	6.	1.24280	1.78353	43.	8.	1.16298	1.90552
41.	7.	1.18907	1.84926	43.	9.	1.11080	1.97189
41.	8.	1.13481	1.91753	43.	10.	1.05837	2.04027
41.	9.	1.08019	1.98813	43.	11.	1.00581	2.11047
41.	10.	1.02536	2.06089	43.	12.	0.95328	2.18231
41.	11.	0.97050	2.13561	43.	13.	0.90093	2.25562
41.	12.	0.91576	2.21204	43.	14.	0.84891	2.33017
41.	13.	0.86132	2.28998	43.	15.	0.79734	2.40577
41.	14.	0.80736	2.36919	43.	16.	0.74639	2.48220
41.	15.	0.75402	2.44941	43.	17.	0.69619	2.55922
41.	16.	0.70146	2.53039	43.	18.	0.64688	2.63664
41.	17.	0.64987	2.61187	43.	19.	0.59860	2.71419
41.	18.	0.59940	2.69358	43.	20.	0.55149	2.79164
41.	19.	0.55018	2.77525	43.	21.	0.50568	2.86878
41.	20.	0.50238	2.85660	44.	2.	1.46920	1.56193
41.	21.	0.45615	2.93734	44.	3.	1.42257	1.61196
42.	2.	1.45615	1.55340	44.	4.	1.37490	1.66467
42.	3.	1.40730	1.60608	44.	5.	1.32631	1.71996
42.	4.	1.35733	1.66172	44.	6.	1.27692	1.77772
42.	5.	1.30640	1.72019	44.	7.	1.22685	1.83784
42.	6.	1.25463	1.78137	44.	8.	1.17624	1.90017
42.	7.	1.20218	1.84512	44.	9.	1.12522	1.96460
42.	8.	1.14918	1.91130	44.	10.	1.07390	2.03095
42.	9.	1.09581	1.97972	44.	11.	1.02245	2.09907
42.	10.	1.04219	2.05023	44.	12.	0.97099	2.16881
42.	11.	0.98851	2.12262	44.	13.	0.91964	2.23997
42.	12.	0.93489	2.19670	44.	14.	0.86856	2.31237
42.	13.	0.88151	2.27227	44.	15.	0.81787	2.38581
42.	14.	0.82852	2.34909	44.	16.	0.76771	2.46011
42.	15.	0.77607	2.42694	44.	17.	0.71822	2.53505
42.	16.	0.72431	2.50558	44.	18.	0.66953	2.61043
42.	17.	0.67341	2.58480	44.	19.	0.62177	2.68601

	Critical values for the Durbin–Watson test: 5% significance level						
n	K	dL	dU	n	K	dL	dU
44.	20.	0.57507	2.76161	47.	2.	1.48715	1.57386
44.	21.	0.52954	2.83698	47.	3.	1.44352	1.62038
45.	2.	1.47538	1.56602	47.	4.	1.39894	1.66923
45.	3.	1.42980	1.61482	47.	5.	1.35350	1.72033
45.	4.	1.38320	1.66618	47.	6.	1.30731	1.77361
45.	5.	1.33571	1.71999	47.	7.	1.26047	1.82895
45.	6.	1.28744	1.77618	47.	8.	1.21309	1.88627
45.	7.	1.23849	1.83462	47.	9.	1.16526	1.94545
45.	8.	1.18899	1.89520	47.	10.	1.11710	2.00636
45.	9.	1.13907	1.95778	47.	11.	1.06873	2.06889
45.	10.	1.08886	2.02222	47.	12.	1.02026	2.13290
45.	11.	1.03846	2.08839	47.	13.	0.97178	2.19824
45.	12.	0.98802	2.15611	47.	14.	0.92342	2.26478
45.	13.	0.93765	2.22524	47.	15.	0.87529	2.33235
45.	14.	0.88750	2.29558	47.	16.	0.82751	2.40080
45.	15.	0.83769	2.36698	47.	17.	0.78018	2.46998
45.	16.	0.78833	2.43924	47.	18.	0.73341	2.53970
45.	17.	0.73955	2.51218	47.	19.	0.68732	2.60980
45.	18.	0.69149	2.58559	47.	20.	0.64200	2.68011
45.	19.	0.64427	2.65929	47.	21.	0.59759	2.75044
45.	20.	0.59801	2.73306	48.	2.	1.49275	1.57762
45.	21.	0.55282	2.80672	48.	3.	1.45004	1.62308
46.	2.	1.48136	1.56999	48.	4.	1.40640	1.67076
46.	3.	1.43677	1.61763	48.	5.	1.36192	1.72061
46.	4.	1.39121	1.66769	48.	6.	1.31672	1.77253
46.	5.	1.34477	1.72012	48.	7.	1.27087	1.82645
46.	6.	1.29756	1.77482	48.	8.	1.22447	1.88226
46.	7.	1.24969	1.83167	48.	9.	1.17764	1.93987
46.	8.	1.20127	1.89058	48.	10.	1.13046	1.99915
46.	9.	1.15242	1.95141	48.	11.	1.08306	2.05999
46.	10.	1.10325	2.01404	48.	12.	1.03552	2.12227
46.	11.	1.05388	2.07834	48.	13.	0.98794	2.18586
46.	12.	1.00443	2.14416	48.	14.	0.94045	2.25062
46.	13.	0.95503	2.21134	48.	15.	0.89314	2.31641
46.	14.	0.90578	2.27974	48.	16.	0.84614	2.38309
46.	15.	0.85681	2.34918	48.	17.	0.79951	2.45049
46.	16.	0.80825	2.41950	48.	18.	0.75340	2.51847
46.	17.	0.76020	2.49051	48.	19.	0.70789	2.58687
46.	18.	0.71278	2.56205	48.	20.	0.66309	2.65552
46.	19.	0.66611	2.63391	48.	21.	0.61909	2.72427
46.	20.	0.62032	2.70593	49.	2.	1.49819	1.58129
46.	21.	0.57550	2.77790	49.	3.	1.45635	1.62573

Critical values for the Durbin–Watson test: 5% significance level (continued)								
n	K	dL	dU		n	K	dL	dU
49.	4.	1.41362	1.67230		51.	6.	1.34305	1.77005
49.	5.	1.37007	1.72095		51.	7.	1.29995	1.82007
49.	6.	1.32580	1.77159		51.	8.	1.25632	1.87178
49.	7.	1.28090	1.82415		51.	9.	1.21224	1.92510
49.	8.	1.23546	1.87852		51.	10.	1.16780	1.97994
49.	9.	1.18958	1.93463		51.	11.	1.12308	2.03620
49.	10.	1.14336	1.99236		51.	12.	1.07818	2.09378
49.	11.	1.09687	2.05160		51.	13.	1.03319	2.15258
49.	12.	1.05024	2.11224		51.	14.	0.98817	2.21249
49.	13.	1.00354	2.17415		51.	15.	0.94324	2.27338
49.	14.	0.95690	2.23723		51.	16.	0.89847	2.33515
49.	15.	0.91040	2.30131		51.	17.	0.85396	2.39767
49.	16.	0.86415	2.36628		51.	18.	0.80978	2.46083
49.	17.	0.81824	2.43199		51.	19.	0.76604	2.52448
49.	18.	0.77278	2.49829		51.	20.	0.72282	2.58848
49.	19.	0.72786	2.56505		51.	21.	0.68021	2.65272
49.	20.	0.68358	2.63211		52.	2.	1.51352	1.59174
49.	21.	0.64003	2.69930		52.	3.	1.47410	1.63339
50.	2.	1.50345	1.58486		52.	4.	1.43388	1.67692
50.	3.	1.46246	1.62833		52.	5.	1.39290	1.72228
50.	4.	1.42059	1.67385		52.	6.	1.35124	1.76942
50.	5.	1.37793	1.72135		52.	7.	1.30899	1.81827
50.	6.	1.33457	1.77077		52.	8.	1.26622	1.86874
50.	7.	1.29059	1.82203		52.	9.	1.22299	1.92076
50.	8.	1.24607	1.87504		52.	10.	1.17941	1.97426
50.	9.	1.20110	1.92972		52.	11.	1.13553	2.02913
50.	10.	1.15579	1.98597		52.	12.	1.09146	2.08528
50.	11.	1.11021	2.04368		52.	13.	1.04727	2.14263
50.	12.	1.06445	2.10276		52.	14.	1.00304	2.20106
50.	13.	1.01862	2.16307		52.	15.	0.95887	2.26046
50.	14.	0.97280	2.22452		52.	16.	0.91481	2.32074
50.	15.	0.92709	2.28698		52.	17.	0.87099	2.38176
50.	16.	0.88159	2.35032		52.	18.	0.82745	2.44341
50.	17.	0.83638	2.41440		52.	19.	0.78431	2.50559
50.	18.	0.79156	2.47910		52.	20.	0.74163	2.56816
50.	19.	0.74723	2.54428		52.	21.	0.69949	2.63099
50.	20.	0.70348	2.60978		53.	2.	1.51833	1.59505
50.	21.	0.66040	2.67548		53.	3.	1.47967	1.63585
51.	2.	1.50856	1.58835		53.	4.	1.44022	1.67845
51.	3.	1.46838	1.63088		53.	5.	1.40002	1.72282
51.	4.	1.42734	1.67538		53.	6.	1.35918	1.76890
51.	5.	1.38554	1.72179		53.	7.	1.31774	1.81661

Critical values for the Durbin–Watson test: 5% significance level (continued)							
n	K	dL	dU	n	K	dL	dU
53.	8.	1.27579	1.86590	55.	10.	1.21199	1.95902
53.	9.	1.23340	1.91668	55.	11.	1.17049	2.01008
53.	10.	1.19063	1.96889	55.	12.	1.12875	2.06233
53.	11.	1.14757	2.02244	55.	13.	1.08685	2.11568
53.	12.	1.10430	2.07723	55.	14.	1.04485	2.17003
53.	13.	1.06090	2.13318	55.	15.	1.00284	2.22532
53.	14.	1.01743	2.19019	55.	16.	0.96087	2.28146
53.	15.	0.97399	2.24817	55.	17.	0.91902	2.33833
53.	16.	0.93065	2.30700	55.	18.	0.87736	2.39585
53.	17.	0.88749	2.36659	55.	19.	0.83597	2.45392
53.	18.	0.84459	2.42682	55.	20.	0.79492	2.51244
53.	19.	0.80204	2.48757	55.	21.	0.75427	2.57131
53.	20.	0.75990	2.54874	56.	2.	1.53197	1.60452
53.	21.	0.71826	2.61021	56.	3.	1.49541	1.64295
54.	2.	1.52300	1.59829	56.	4.	1.45810	1.68300
54.	3.	1.48506	1.63825	56.	5.	1.42012	1.72461
54.	4.	1.44636	1.67998	56.	6.	1.38152	1.76776
54.	5.	1.40693	1.72339	56.	7.	1.34237	1.81238
54.	6.	1.36687	1.76844	56.	8.	1.30271	1.85841
54.	7.	1.32622	1.81508	56.	9.	1.26263	1.90579
54.	8.	1.28506	1.86324	56.	10.	1.22217	1.95448
54.	9.	1.24345	1.91283	56.	11.	1.18141	2.00438
54.	10.	1.20149	1.96381	56.	12.	1.14040	2.05542
54.	11.	1.15921	2.01609	56.	13.	1.09922	2.10755
54.	12.	1.11672	2.06959	56.	14.	1.05793	2.16067
54.	13.	1.07408	2.12420	56.	15.	1.01659	2.21470
54.	14.	1.03136	2.17987	56.	16.	0.97530	2.26956
54.	15.	0.98864	2.23647	56.	17.	0.93408	2.32515
54.	16.	0.94600	2.29392	56.	18.	0.89304	2.38140
54.	17.	0.90349	2.35213	56.	19.	0.85222	2.43820
54.	18.	0.86122	2.41097	56.	20.	0.81170	2.49546
54.	19.	0.81925	2.47036	56.	21.	0.77155	2.55309
54.	20.	0.77766	2.53019	57.	2.	1.53628	1.60754
54.	21.	0.73651	2.59033	57.	3.	1.50036	1.64524
55.	2.	1.52755	1.60144	57.	4.	1.46372	1.68449
55.	3.	1.49031	1.64062	57.	5.	1.42642	1.72526
55.	4.	1.45232	1.68149	57.	6.	1.38852	1.76751
55.	5.	1.41362	1.72399	57.	7.	1.35008	1.81119
55.	6.	1.37431	1.76807	57.	8.	1.31114	1.85622
55.	7.	1.33442	1.81368	57.	9.	1.27177	1.90257
55.	8.	1.29403	1.86074	57.	10.	1.23203	1.95018
55.	9.	1.25319	1.90921	57.	11.	1.19198	1.99896

n	K	dL	dU	n	K	dL	dU
		Critical values for the Durbin–Watson test: 5% significance level (continued)					
57.	12.	1.15168	2.04887	59.	14.	1.09482	2.13510
57.	13.	1.11121	2.09982	59.	15.	1.05545	2.18564
57.	14.	1.07060	2.15175	59.	16.	1.01605	2.23698
57.	15.	1.02994	2.20456	59.	17.	0.97668	2.28902
57.	16.	0.98929	2.25820	59.	18.	0.93739	2.34171
57.	17.	0.94871	2.31257	59.	19.	0.89826	2.39495
57.	18.	0.90825	2.36758	59.	20.	0.85932	2.44869
57.	19.	0.86800	2.42316	59.	21.	0.82065	2.50283
57.	20.	0.82802	2.47920	60.	2.	1.54853	1.61617
57.	21.	0.78836	2.53563	60.	3.	1.51442	1.65184
58.	2.	1.54047	1.61048	60.	4.	1.47965	1.68891
58.	3.	1.50517	1.64747	60.	5.	1.44427	1.72735
58.	4.	1.46918	1.68598	60.	6.	1.40832	1.76711
58.	5.	1.43254	1.72594	60.	7.	1.37186	1.80817
58.	6.	1.39532	1.76733	60.	8.	1.33493	1.85045
58.	7.	1.35755	1.81009	60.	9.	1.29758	1.89393
58.	8.	1.31931	1.85418	60.	10.	1.25987	1.93856
58.	9.	1.28063	1.89954	60.	11.	1.22183	1.98427
58.	10.	1.24159	1.94610	60.	12.	1.18354	2.03101
58.	11.	1.20224	1.99382	60.	13.	1.14505	2.07873
58.	12.	1.16263	2.04262	60.	14.	1.10640	2.12734
58.	13.	1.12283	2.09245	60.	15.	1.06764	2.17681
58.	14.	1.08289	2.14323	60.	16.	1.02885	2.22705
58.	15.	1.04288	2.19489	60.	17.	0.99007	2.27800
58.	16.	1.00287	2.24735	60.	18.	0.95135	2.32958
58.	17.	0.96289	2.30054	60.	19.	0.91276	2.38173
58.	18.	0.92304	2.35436	60.	20.	0.87435	2.43437
58.	19.	0.88335	2.40875	60.	21.	0.83616	2.48742
58.	20.	0.84389	2.46362	61.	2.	1.55240	1.61892
58.	21.	0.80473	2.51889	61.	3.	1.51886	1.65396
59.	2.	1.54455	1.61336	61.	4.	1.48468	1.69035
59.	3.	1.50985	1.64967	61.	5.	1.44989	1.72808
59.	4.	1.47448	1.68745	61.	6.	1.41455	1.76708
59.	5.	1.43848	1.72663	61.	7.	1.37871	1.80732
59.	6.	1.40191	1.76720	61.	8.	1.34240	1.84876
59.	7.	1.36481	1.80908	61.	9.	1.30568	1.89137
59.	8.	1.32723	1.85226	61.	10.	1.26860	1.93507
59.	9.	1.28923	1.89665	61.	11.	1.23120	1.97984
59.	10.	1.25086	1.94223	61.	12.	1.19355	2.02560
59.	11.	1.21218	1.98893	61.	13.	1.15567	2.07232
59.	12.	1.17325	2.03668	61.	14.	1.11763	2.11992
59.	13.	1.13410	2.08543	61.	15.	1.07950	2.16835

Critical values for the Durbin–Watson test: 5% significance level							
n	K	dL	dU	n	K	dL	dU
61.	16.	1.04129	2.21755	63.	18.	0.99096	2.29612
61.	17.	1.00309	2.26744	63.	19.	0.95394	2.34518
61.	18.	0.96492	2.31796	63.	20.	0.91703	2.39474
61.	19.	0.92686	2.36904	63.	21.	0.88029	2.44473
61.	20.	0.88896	2.42062	64.	2.	1.56348	1.62683
61.	21.	0.85126	2.47262	64.	3.	1.53152	1.66011
62.	2.	1.55619	1.62161	64.	4.	1.49897	1.69463
62.	3.	1.52318	1.65605	64.	5.	1.46587	1.73033
62.	4.	1.48957	1.69180	64.	6.	1.43223	1.76720
62.	5.	1.45536	1.72881	64.	7.	1.39813	1.80520
62.	6.	1.42061	1.76708	64.	8.	1.36359	1.84429
62.	7.	1.38536	1.80655	64.	9.	1.32865	1.88444
62.	8.	1.34967	1.84718	64.	10.	1.29336	1.92561
62.	9.	1.31356	1.88893	64.	11.	1.25775	1.96775
62.	10.	1.27709	1.93176	64.	12.	1.22188	2.01081
62.	11.	1.24031	1.97561	64.	13.	1.18576	2.05475
62.	12.	1.20326	2.02044	64.	14.	1.14949	2.09952
62.	13.	1.16599	2.06620	64.	15.	1.11306	2.14507
62.	14.	1.12856	2.11282	64.	16.	1.07655	2.19134
62.	15.	1.09100	2.16026	64.	17.	1.04000	2.23829
62.	16.	1.05338	2.20844	64.	18.	1.00345	2.28584
62.	17.	1.01573	2.25732	64.	19.	0.96694	2.33395
62.	18.	0.97812	2.30681	64.	20.	0.93053	2.38255
62.	19.	0.94058	2.35687	64.	21.	0.89425	2.43159
62.	20.	0.90319	2.40742	65.	2.	1.56699	1.62936
62.	21.	0.86597	2.45840	65.	3.	1.53553	1.66210
63.	2.	1.55987	1.62425	65.	4.	1.50349	1.69602
63.	3.	1.52741	1.65810	65.	5.	1.47092	1.73110
63.	4.	1.49433	1.69321	65.	6.	1.43782	1.76731
63.	5.	1.46068	1.72957	65.	7.	1.40426	1.80462
63.	6.	1.42650	1.76712	65.	8.	1.37027	1.84298
63.	7.	1.39183	1.80584	65.	9.	1.33589	1.88238
63.	8.	1.35672	1.84569	65.	10.	1.30115	1.92276
63.	9.	1.32121	1.88663	65.	11.	1.26611	1.96408
63.	10.	1.28534	1.92860	65.	12.	1.23080	2.00631
63.	11.	1.24915	1.97159	65.	13.	1.19525	2.04939
63.	12.	1.21269	2.01552	65.	14.	1.15952	2.09329
63.	13.	1.17602	2.06035	65.	15.	1.12364	2.13795
63.	14.	1.13917	2.10603	65.	16.	1.08767	2.18331
63.	15.	1.10219	2.15250	65.	17.	1.05165	2.22934
63.	16.	1.06512	2.19971	65.	18.	1.01560	2.27597
63.	17.	1.02803	2.24761	65.	19.	0.97960	2.32315

Critical values for the Durbin–Watson test: 5% significance level (continued)								
n	*K*	dL	dU		*n*	*K*	dL	dU
65.	20.	0.94367	2.37083		68.	2.	1.57706	1.63665
65.	21.	0.90785	2.41894		68.	3.	1.54701	1.66784
66.	2.	1.57043	1.63184		68.	4.	1.51642	1.70011
66.	3.	1.53945	1.66404		68.	5.	1.48531	1.73345
66.	4.	1.50790	1.69740		68.	6.	1.45373	1.76781
66.	5.	1.47583	1.73188		68.	7.	1.42171	1.80318
66.	6.	1.44326	1.76745		68.	8.	1.38928	1.83952
66.	7.	1.41023	1.80409		68.	9.	1.35647	1.87679
66.	8.	1.37677	1.84175		68.	10.	1.32332	1.91497
66.	9.	1.34293	1.88041		68.	11.	1.28987	1.95403
66.	10.	1.30874	1.92004		68.	12.	1.25614	1.99393
66.	11.	1.27424	1.96058		68.	13.	1.22218	2.03462
66.	12.	1.23947	2.00200		68.	14.	1.18803	2.07606
66.	13.	1.20447	2.04426		68.	15.	1.15372	2.11823
66.	14.	1.16928	2.08731		68.	16.	1.11929	2.16106
66.	15.	1.13394	2.13110		68.	17.	1.08477	2.20453
66.	16.	1.09850	2.17559		68.	18.	1.05021	2.24857
66.	17.	1.06298	2.22074		68.	19.	1.01563	2.29315
66.	18.	1.02744	2.26648		68.	20.	0.98109	2.33822
66.	19.	0.99192	2.31277		68.	21.	0.94663	2.38371
66.	20.	0.95646	2.35954		69.	2.	1.58027	1.63898
66.	21.	0.92111	2.40676		69.	3.	1.55066	1.66970
67.	2.	1.57378	1.63427		69.	4.	1.52052	1.70146
67.	3.	1.54328	1.66596		69.	5.	1.48988	1.73425
67.	4.	1.51221	1.69877		69.	6.	1.45877	1.76803
67.	5.	1.48063	1.73267		69.	7.	1.42723	1.80279
67.	6.	1.44856	1.76762		69.	8.	1.39529	1.83849
67.	7.	1.41604	1.80360		69.	9.	1.36298	1.87512
67.	8.	1.38311	1.84060		69.	10.	1.33032	1.91262
67.	9.	1.34979	1.87856		69.	11.	1.29737	1.95098
67.	10.	1.31613	1.91744		69.	12.	1.26415	1.99014
67.	11.	1.28216	1.95723		69.	13.	1.23069	2.03009
67.	12.	1.24792	1.99787		69.	14.	1.19704	2.07078
67.	13.	1.21345	2.03934		69.	15.	1.16322	2.11216
67.	14.	1.17878	2.08158		69.	16.	1.12928	2.15421
67.	15.	1.14396	2.12453		69.	17.	1.09524	2.19688
67.	16.	1.10903	2.16819		69.	18.	1.06115	2.24012
67.	17.	1.07401	2.21248		69.	19.	1.02704	2.28388
67.	18.	1.03897	2.25735		69.	20.	0.99295	2.32813
67.	19.	1.00394	2.30277		69.	21.	0.95892	2.37281
67.	20.	0.96894	2.34868		70.	2.	1.58341	1.64127
67.	21.	0.93402	2.39503		70.	3.	1.55422	1.67152

447

Critical values for the Durbin–Watson test: 5% significance level (continued)

n	K	dL	dU	n	K	dL	dU
70.	4.	1.52452	1.70278	72.	6.	1.47317	1.76881
70.	5.	1.49434	1.73505	72.	7.	1.44300	1.80187
70.	6.	1.46369	1.76827	72.	8.	1.41245	1.83581
70.	7.	1.43262	1.80245	72.	9.	1.38154	1.87059
70.	8.	1.40115	1.83754	72.	10.	1.35030	1.90618
70.	9.	1.36932	1.87353	72.	11.	1.31877	1.94256
70.	10.	1.33716	1.91037	72.	12.	1.28698	1.97970
70.	11.	1.30469	1.94805	72.	13.	1.25495	2.01756
70.	12.	1.27196	1.98652	72.	14.	1.22272	2.05611
70.	13.	1.23899	2.02574	72.	15.	1.19031	2.09532
70.	14.	1.20582	2.06569	72.	16.	1.15776	2.13516
70.	15.	1.17249	2.10634	72.	17.	1.12510	2.17558
70.	16.	1.13902	2.14762	72.	18.	1.09237	2.21655
70.	17.	1.10544	2.18951	72.	19.	1.05959	2.25803
70.	18.	1.07182	2.23197	72.	20.	1.02680	2.29997
70.	19.	1.03816	2.27495	72.	21.	0.99403	2.34236
70.	20.	1.00451	2.31840	73.	2.	1.59243	1.64788
70.	21.	0.97091	2.36230	73.	3.	1.56446	1.67681
71.	2.	1.58648	1.64352	73.	4.	1.53599	1.70667
71.	3.	1.55771	1.67331	73.	5.	1.50709	1.73745
71.	4.	1.52844	1.70409	73.	6.	1.47775	1.76911
71.	5.	1.49868	1.73584	73.	7.	1.44801	1.80164
71.	6.	1.46849	1.76854	73.	8.	1.41789	1.83502
71.	7.	1.43787	1.80214	73.	9.	1.38743	1.86923
71.	8.	1.40686	1.83664	73.	10.	1.35663	1.90422
71.	9.	1.37551	1.87202	73.	11.	1.32556	1.93999
71.	10.	1.34381	1.90823	73.	12.	1.29421	1.97649
71.	11.	1.31182	1.94524	73.	13.	1.26262	2.01370
71.	12.	1.27957	1.98304	73.	14.	1.23084	2.05159
71.	13.	1.24707	2.02157	73.	15.	1.19889	2.09013
71.	14.	1.21437	2.06081	73.	16.	1.16678	2.12927
71.	15.	1.18150	2.10073	73.	17.	1.13456	2.16899
71.	16.	1.14851	2.14128	73.	18.	1.10226	2.20925
71.	17.	1.11539	2.18242	73.	19.	1.06991	2.25001
71.	18.	1.08222	2.22412	73.	20.	1.03753	2.29124
71.	19.	1.04900	2.26634	73.	21.	1.00517	2.33290
71.	20.	1.01579	2.30903	74.	2.	1.59530	1.65001
71.	21.	0.98261	2.35215	74.	3.	1.56772	1.67852
72.	2.	1.58949	1.64571	74.	4.	1.53966	1.70793
72.	3.	1.56112	1.67507	74.	5.	1.51115	1.73825
72.	4.	1.53226	1.70539	74.	6.	1.48222	1.76943
72.	5.	1.50293	1.73664	74.	7.	1.45289	1.80144

Critical values for the Durbin–Watson test: 5% significance level (continued)							
n	K	dL	dU	n	K	dL	dU
74.	8.	1.42321	1.83429	76.	10.	1.37473	1.89886
74.	9.	1.39316	1.86793	76.	11.	1.34493	1.93288
74.	10.	1.36281	1.90235	76.	12.	1.31488	1.96761
74.	11.	1.33217	1.93752	76.	13.	1.28458	2.00299
74.	12.	1.30127	1.97341	76.	14.	1.25408	2.03900
74.	13.	1.27013	2.01000	76.	15.	1.22340	2.07563
74.	14.	1.23878	2.04724	76.	16.	1.19257	2.11283
74.	15.	1.20725	2.08511	76.	17.	1.16161	2.15057
74.	16.	1.17559	2.12359	76.	18.	1.13056	2.18883
74.	17.	1.14379	2.16263	76.	19.	1.09942	2.22757
74.	18.	1.11192	2.20220	76.	20.	1.06825	2.26676
74.	19.	1.07998	2.24227	76.	21.	1.03706	2.30638
74.	20.	1.04801	2.28280	77.	2.	1.60361	1.65614
74.	21.	1.01605	2.32375	77.	3.	1.57710	1.68348
75.	2.	1.59813	1.65209	77.	4.	1.55015	1.71166
75.	3.	1.57091	1.68020	77.	5.	1.52279	1.74065
75.	4.	1.54323	1.70920	77.	6.	1.49503	1.77044
75.	5.	1.51511	1.73904	77.	7.	1.46690	1.80102
75.	6.	1.48659	1.76975	77.	8.	1.43842	1.83235
75.	7.	1.45767	1.80127	77.	9.	1.40961	1.86443
75.	8.	1.42840	1.83360	77.	10.	1.38048	1.89722
75.	9.	1.39877	1.86670	77.	11.	1.35108	1.93071
75.	10.	1.36884	1.90057	77.	12.	1.32143	1.96487
75.	11.	1.33863	1.93516	77.	13.	1.29155	1.99969
75.	12.	1.30815	1.97046	77.	14.	1.26146	2.03511
75.	13.	1.27744	2.00643	77.	15.	1.23119	2.07113
75.	14.	1.24652	2.04304	77.	16.	1.20076	2.10772
75.	15.	1.21542	2.08028	77.	17.	1.17020	2.14485
75.	16.	1.18418	2.11811	77.	18.	1.13954	2.18248
75.	17.	1.15281	2.15649	77.	19.	1.10881	2.22059
75.	18.	1.12135	2.19540	77.	20.	1.07801	2.25914
75.	19.	1.08982	2.23480	77.	21.	1.04721	2.29811
75.	20.	1.05825	2.27465	78.	2.	1.60626	1.65812
75.	21.	1.02668	2.31492	78.	3.	1.58010	1.68509
76.	2.	1.60090	1.65413	78.	4.	1.55351	1.71287
76.	3.	1.57404	1.68185	78.	5.	1.52651	1.74145
76.	4.	1.54673	1.71043	78.	6.	1.49912	1.77081
76.	5.	1.51900	1.73985	78.	7.	1.47136	1.80093
76.	6.	1.49086	1.77009	78.	8.	1.44325	1.83178
76.	7.	1.46233	1.80113	78.	9.	1.41483	1.86337
76.	8.	1.43346	1.83295	78.	10.	1.38610	1.89565
76.	9.	1.40425	1.86553	78.	11.	1.35711	1.92862

Critical values for the Durbin–Watson test: 5% significance level								
n	K	dL	dU	n	K	dL	dU
78.	12.	1.32785	1.96224	80.	14.	1.28259	2.02423
78.	13.	1.29836	1.99650	80.	15.	1.25348	2.05857
78.	14.	1.26867	2.03136	80.	16.	1.22422	2.09343
78.	15.	1.23879	2.06680	80.	17.	1.19481	2.12881
78.	16.	1.20876	2.10279	80.	18.	1.16529	2.16467
78.	17.	1.17860	2.13932	80.	19.	1.13568	2.20099
78.	18.	1.14832	2.17634	80.	20.	1.10600	2.23772
78.	19.	1.11797	2.21384	80.	21.	1.07628	2.27487
78.	20.	1.08756	2.25177				
78.	21.	1.05712	2.29011				
79.	2.	1.60887	1.66006				
79.	3.	1.58304	1.68667				
79.	4.	1.55679	1.71407				
79.	5.	1.53015	1.74225				
79.	6.	1.50312	1.77118				
79.	7.	1.47572	1.80086				
79.	8.	1.44800	1.83126				
79.	9.	1.41994	1.86237				
79.	10.	1.39160	1.89416				
79.	11.	1.36299	1.92661				
79.	12.	1.33411	1.95970				
79.	13.	1.30501	1.99342				
79.	14.	1.27571	2.02773				
79.	15.	1.24622	2.06261				
79.	16.	1.21658	2.09804				
79.	17.	1.18679	2.13398				
79.	18.	1.15690	2.17041				
79.	19.	1.12693	2.20730				
79.	20.	1.09689	2.24464				
79.	21.	1.06680	2.28237				
80.	2.	1.61143	1.66197				
80.	3.	1.58592	1.68823				
80.	4.	1.56001	1.71526				
80.	5.	1.53370	1.74304				
80.	6.	1.50703	1.77156				
80.	7.	1.47999	1.80081				
80.	8.	1.45262	1.83077				
80.	9.	1.42495	1.86142				
80.	10.	1.39698	1.89272				
80.	11.	1.36873	1.92469				
80.	12.	1.34024	1.95727				
80.	13.	1.31151	1.99046				

$n = 6$ to 80, $K = 2$ to 21 ($K \leqslant T-4$)
K includes intercept
Source: http://www.stanford.edu/~clint/bench/dw05a.htm

Appendix 5: Probability

The set of all possible outcomes of a random event is the **sample space**. For example, if there is just one **event** – tossing a coin – and this only takes place once then the sample space has just two elements: H (Head) or T (Tail). If the coin is tossed twice the sample space expands to the following possibilities:

| HH | TT | HT | TH |

If there is no relationship between events in the sample space they are said to be mutually exclusive (or independent). In the one-coin toss case we cannot have H and T only H or T, so these must be independent events. In the two-toss case, we can also say that each (of the four) events in the sample space is independent.

The definition of **probability** is:

> The number of times an event will occur in repeated trials of the same experiment. This is expressed as a fraction of the number of trials.

This is the 'objective' probability as opposed to the 'subjective' probability, which is how often someone thinks an event will occur. Classical statistics only uses the concept of objective probability in testing hypotheses. When we handle data, we assume that there is an objective probability even though we do not know it. For example, we are unlikely to know the probability that women, chosen from a series of samples of women, will be over 66 inches tall.

Probability has these properties, where P_i is the probability of an event X_i happening:

(i) Any individual $P_i(X_i)$ lies between zero and one.
(ii) The sum of the $P_i(X_i)$ is one: that is, the events exhaust the sample space.
(iii) The probabilities of independent events can be summed: for example, if heights are measured only in inches then

$$P(66\text{-}70) = P(66) + P(67) + P(68) + P(69) + P(70)$$

This will not be true if the events are not independent. In this case, we must have independence because a normal person would not have two different heights at the same time.

The toin-coss example features **discrete** variables. These can only take on certain numerical values. You cannot have half a head or half a tail. The measurement of heights in the above example is **continuous,** in principle, as we can calibrate each observation to whatever fraction is appropriate. In economics we have many important continuous variables such as income, wage inflation, unemployment rates, exchange rates and so on.

The probability density function (PDF) of a continuous random variable should have a number of properties. We define $f(x)dx$ as the probability attached to a small change in the interval of a continuous variable; for example, the probability that household weekly spending on food lies between 80 dollars and 80 dollars and 10 cents. It follows that

$$\int_{-\infty}^{\infty} f(x)dx = 1$$

as an infinite expansion of the size of interval must exhaust the whole probability distribution. We also have

$$\int_{a}^{b} f(x)dx = P(a \leqslant x \leqslant b)$$

where a is the lower end of the interval for the value of x and b is the upper end of this interval.

The PDF of a continuous variable has the property that the probability of an individual numerical value occurring is effectively zero. For this reason, we must conduct hypothesis tests over a range of values. Thus we do *not* test the hypothesis that the marginal propensity to consume is one, for example; rather, we test a hypothesis about a range on either or both sides of 1. That is, that it is either more than 1, less than 1 or just 'different from 1'.

Single variable distributions, by themselves, are of little use to economists. In econometrics, we are concerned with **joint probability density** functions, which will usually be multivariate in regression analysis. That is, we might have, for example, a joint distribution of variables such as quantity, prices, prices of other goods and income if we are studying a demand function.

A single-equation regression model specifies that one of the variables is dependent (belongs on the left-hand side of the equation) while the others are independent (belong on the right-hand side). This means we have **conditional probability density functions (CPDF)** because quantity would be conditional on price, other prices and income. The CDPF will show the probability that Y takes on particular values given that X has taken on particular values.

The joint PDF of two continuous variables is:

$$\int_{-\infty}^{\infty} \int_{-\infty}^{\infty} f(x, y)\,dx\,dy = 1$$

and we also have:

$$\int_{c}^{d} \int_{a}^{b} f(x, y)dx = P(a \leqslant x \leqslant b, c \leqslant x \leqslant d)$$

As before (a, b) is the interval for the change of x and we now add (c, d) for the interval for the change in y.

The two variables will be statistically independent if the product of the **marginal probability density functions** are equal to the joint PDF.

The marginal PDFs (MPDF) are:

$$f(x) = \int_{-\infty}^{\infty} f(x,\ y) d y \qquad \text{MPDF for } x$$

$$f(y) = \int_{-\infty}^{\infty} f(x,\ y) dx \qquad \text{MPDF for } y$$

DESCRIPTION OF THE PDF IN TERMS OF ITS MOMENTS

PDFs can be described in terms of their **moments**. The first moment is the **mean**, the second is the **variance**, the third is the **skewness** and the fourth is **kurtosis**. These four moments can be said to describe a PDF and therefore are used to distinguish one PDF from another. For the use of a joint PDF we may also use the **covariance**.

All of these measures depend on the concept of **expected value** or, if you prefer, the expectation of a variable. The expected value of a continuous random variable is:

$$E(X) = \int_{-\infty}^{\infty} x f(x) dx$$

Expected values (EV) have certain properties:

(i) The EV of a constant is a constant: $E(c) = c$ where c is the constant.
(ii) If c and d are constants: $E(cX + d) = cE(X) + d$.
(iii) $E(XY) = E(X)E(Y)$ for two independent (mutually exclusive) random variables – if the variables are not independent then this is not true and the covariance of X and Y will have to be taken into account.
(iv) If X is a random variable with PDF $f(x)$ and if $g(X)$ is a function of X:

$$E[g(x)] = \int_{-\infty}^{\infty} g(X) f(x)$$

$$E[g(x)] = \int_{-\infty}^{\infty} x^2 f(X) dx$$

The **variance** of a random variable X is the square of the expectation of the difference between X and its expectation (which will be the mean):

$$Var(X) = \sigma_x^2 = E(X - E(X))^2$$

For a CPDF this is:

$$\int_{-\infty}^{\infty} (X - E(X))^2 f(X) dx$$

which for the purposes of calculation is: $E(X)^2 - [E(X)]^2$.

Properties of the variance

The variance of a constant is zero. The variance of the sum of two independent random variables is the sum of their individual variances:

$$\text{Var}(X + Y) = \text{var}(X) + \text{var}(Y)$$

The following also applies (where a and b are constants):

$$\text{Var}(X - Y) = \text{Var}(X) + \text{Var}(Y)$$

$$\text{Var}(aX + bY) = a^2\text{Var}(X) + b^2\text{Var}(Y)$$

The covariance of X and Y is:

$$\text{Cov}(X, Y) = E[XY] = E(XY) - E(X)E(Y)$$

which is zero for statistically independent variables.

Conditional expectation and conditional variance

If $f(y, x)$ is the joint PDF of two random variables X and Y, the conditional expectation of Y given X is:

$$E(Y|X = x) = \int_{-\infty}^{\infty} yf(y|X = x)\mathrm{d}y$$

if X and Y are continuous variables. Y is a random variable 'conditioned' by X but specific values of X (x) are treated as constants.

The conditional variance in the same case (continuous variables) is:

$$\text{Var}(Y|X = x) = \int_{-\infty}^{\infty} [Y - E(Y|X = x)]^2 f(y|X = x)\mathrm{d}y$$

Skewness

The third moment of a distribution represents the extent to which the distribution is not symmetrical in that it slopes to the right or to the left. It is defined as:

$$E(\boldsymbol{x})^3$$

where $\boldsymbol{x}$ is the expected deviation of x from its mean.

Kurtosis

The fourth moment of a distribution (kurtosis) is defined as:

$$E(\boldsymbol{x})^4$$

The fourth moment of a distribution represents the extent to which the distribution has a 'high' or 'low' peak relative to the rest of the spread of the events. This is sometimes described as its 'humpiness'.

In Section 9.3 of Chapter 9 you will find the skewness and kurtosis used to test whether or not a distribution is normal.

INFERENCE

The idea of probability and PDFs is used to make inferences from sample data. That is, we perform calculations on the data and infer certain things about the behaviour of the variables on the basis of assumptions about the probability distributions generating the data.

Inference begins with derivation of an **estimator**. For example, we have the value of 0.61 for the marginal propensity to consume, in Belgium, from Table 3.1 of this book. The estimator, in that case, is the OLS formulae, which are produced by using an algorithm, which maximizes the fit as measured by the R squared (so long as there is a constant in the regression equation). The value of 0.61 is the **estimate**.

This estimate (0.61) is treated as the mean of the PDF for the regression slope. The estimate is treated as a random variable, which is a function of the sample data. 0.61 is the **point estimate** because it is a single value rather than a range of values. This is the central tendency of the distribution of the estimator and will be the most likely value to emerge from the distribution of the estimator. As we assume a normal distribution the PDF of the regression estimate will be symmetrical. Inferences are used from the properties of the normal distribution in terms of its mean and variance to test hypotheses about the range in which the point estimate lies with respect to the null hypothesis.

As explained in the text the estimator is examined in terms of whether it has BLUE (best linear unbiased estimator) properties. **Unbiasedness** occurs if we have:

$$E(\hat{b}) = b$$

where b is a parameter if we are dealing with a regression. Bias is equal to the difference between these two magnitudes. The absence of bias relies on the assumption of repeated sampling to 'average out' any unusually large or small estimates, which arise from a given sample.

Best estimators are those with the smallest variance. In econometrics we usually require that this property occurs in conjunction with unbiasedness. If we have estimators that are both best and unbiased, these are called **efficient estimators**. This is a purely statistical definition and must not be confused with other uses of the word 'efficiency' in economics and elsewhere.

The properties of estimators may depend on the size of sample. Samples are not likely to be infinite and therefore we deal with finite sample properties. As the finite sample is increased, estimators may gradually approach the position where they satisfy one of the above properties. In such cases, they will be described as **asymptotically** efficient or asymptotically unbiased. Thus, the asymptotic properties refer to 'large' samples but we would not generally know what 'large' is in terms of real numbers. Small sample bias is inevitable in some cases. For example, the estimated variance of a random variable (such as height of women) in a sample would have the expectation:

$$E(V) = \sigma^2(1 - 1/n)$$

which is biased with the bias decreasing to a negligible fraction as n approaches infinity.

In some cases, estimation formulae are reworked to include a 'correction' for bias. Such corrections may remove the amount of bias but will not eliminate it altogether in a finite sample.

When dealing with asymptotic properties the concept of a **plim** is used. This refers to the probability that will be approached at the limit, i.e. as n approaches infinity. An estimator that is unbiased in a small sample would therefore also be unbiased in a large sample . However, given that we are using samples and not populations we cannot have estimators which are **consistent** except in large samples. The consistency property is that the estimator is approaching the true value of the item being estimated, rather than simply approaching the mean which is required by the property of asymptotic unbiasedness.

An estimator could be BLUE but still lacking in the consistency property. In such a case it would be termed an **inconsistent estimator**. If an estimator is to be consistent then, roughly speaking, its bias and variance should both tend to zero in the probability limit.

Econometricians would prefer to have estimators which are BLUE and consistent in small samples because economic data frequently involves small samples. Often this is not possible and they then work with estimators which have asymptotically desirable properties, i.e. they are asymptotically BLUE and consistent. In this situation, one might feel the need to defend the use of estimators, which are asymptotically justified, on small samples. That is, we could find that an asymptotically BLUE and consistent estimator has very poor properties in small samples. The defence against this point tends to involve a branch of econometrics based on **Monte Carlo** studies. The key feature of a Monte Carlo study is that it does not involve the use of any real data. The researcher generates the data themselves according to some set of criteria. They might impose conditions on the data that it satisfies certain requirements, e.g. the artificially created disturbance term might have a zero mean but a non-constant variance. Given that the researcher has generated the data, they will know exactly what the true values of all the relevant parameters are and they can therefore assess the extent to which the estimators being tested are deficient in small samples. The study of 'spurious regression' by Granger and Newbold discussed in Section 14.3 of Chapter 14 is an example of a Monte Carlo study, although it was not focusing on the small-sample properties issue.

Statistical inference is carried out, in practice, using either significance tests or confidence intervals. We may also use the same information packaged in the form of prob (or 'critical significance') values on some computer packages. As explained in the text, inference takes the form of hypothesis testing. This requires us to pick a significance level, formulate a null and then work out the appropriate test statistic values in terms of degrees of freedom and whether they are one-tailed or two-tailed.

Econometricians tend to favour three things:

(i) Use of 't' tests rather than confidence intervals for individual parameters.
(ii) Minimizing the risk of Type I error at the expense of Type II error.

(iii) Use of agreed conventions about suitable significance levels (5 per cent being the most popular) rather than the loss function shown in Equation 2.7 of Chapter 2.

If our estimators are efficient and consistent then we could rely on our hypothesis tests and the inferences we draw from them as being accurate. The failure of estimators to have these properties results from breakdowns of the classical assumptions of the regression model which may be due to data problems or errors in model specification.

Appendix 6: Matrix derivation of the OLS estimating equation

Note: This Appendix relates to Section 3.9 of Chapter 3.

It is much easier to represent a multivariate regression if we use matrix algebra. Writing down the model in matrix notation requires much less space and it facilitates solution of the model to provide parameter estimates via the 'normal equations'. Letting k be the number of variables we can see our regression as solving the following set of simultaneous equations if we write out the model in full:

$$Y_1 = b_0 + b_1 X_{11} + b_2 X_{21} + b_3 X_{31} + \ldots + b_k X_{k1} + \hat{u}_1$$
$$Y_2 = b_0 + b_1 X_{12} + b_2 X_{22} + b_3 X_{32} + \ldots + b_k X_{k2} + \hat{u}_2$$
$$\ldots$$
$$Y_n = b_0 + b_1 X_{1n} + b_2 X_{2n} + b_3 X_{3n} + \ldots + b_k X_{kn} + \hat{u}_n$$

(A6.1)

This is a set of n equations with $k + 1$ unknown parameters (the parameters on the X variables for which we have collected data and the intercept). The size of n depends on how much data we have collected.

In fully written-out matrix form this becomes

$$
\begin{bmatrix} Y_1 \\ Y_2 \\ Y_n \end{bmatrix} =
\begin{bmatrix} 1 & X_{11} & X_{21} \ldots X_{k1} \\ 1 & X_{12} & X_{22} \ldots X_{k2} \\ 1 & X_{1n} & X_{2n} \ldots X_{kn} \end{bmatrix}
\begin{bmatrix} \hat{b}_0 \\ \hat{b}_1 \\ \hat{b}_k \end{bmatrix} +
\begin{bmatrix} \hat{u}_1 \\ \hat{u}_2 \\ \hat{u}_3 \end{bmatrix}
$$

(A6.2)

We now have the Y observations as a vector (this could for example be the set of data on demand for a product) and we have the X observations as a matrix (this could for example be the set of data for prices, incomes and so on with the inclusion of the row of 1's to accommodate the constant (intercept) term. The set of regression parameters becomes a vector as does the set of disturbance terms. The length of the vectors and the matrix for the independent variables (with the row of 1's added) will be equal to the number of valid observations in the data set.

Using bold typeface to represent matrices and vectors we can then write (A6.2) as:

$$Y = X.\hat{b} + \hat{u} \tag{A6.3}$$

where: Y is the vector of independent variable data; X is the matrix of independent variable data; b is the vector of regression parameters; and u is the vector of disturbance terms. The classical assumptions are assumed to hold for the u term.

In matrix form, we can write the sum of squared residuals (using e to represent estimated u) as:

$$e'e = (Y - X.\hat{b}).(Y - X.\hat{b})$$
$$= y'y - 2\hat{b}'X'y + b'X'Xb \tag{A6.4}$$

The objective of OLS is to minimize Equation (A6.4) by differentiating it and setting it equal to zero. This produces a set of simultaneous equations that are the normal equations which are, in matrix notation:

$$(X'.X)\hat{b} = X'y \tag{A6.5}$$

which after rearrangement becomes:

$$\hat{b}' = (X'X)^{-1}.X'Y \tag{A6.6}$$

The data for all of Equation (A6.6) are known with the exception of those in the b vector. Thus a computer package will solve the problem of finding regression coefficients by first inverting the matrix of the cross-products of the independent variables. The package will multiply by the matrix formed as the product of the independent variables and the dependent variable.

This shows that the unknowns (i.e. the regression parameters) can be obtained from the data. This holds so long as the matrices are well behaved. If the cross-product matrix for the independent variables could not be inverted then it will be impossible to obtain any regression parameters. This is what will happen when there is extreme multicollinearity. If this happens you should normally get a warning message from your package about singularity of the matrix.

Index